Spain

"When it comes to information on regional history, what to see and do, and shopping, these guides are exhaustive."

—*USAir Magazine*

"Usable, sophisticated restaurant coverage, with an emphasis on good value."

—Andy Birsh, *Gourmet Magazine* columnist

"Valuable because of their comprehensiveness."

—*Minneapolis Star-Tribune*

"Fodor's always delivers high quality...thoughtfully presented...thorough."

—*Houston Post*

"An excellent choice for those who want everything under one cover."

—*Washington Post*

Fodor's Travel Publications, Inc.
New York • Toronto • London • Sydney • Auckland
http://www.fodors.com/

Fodor's Spain

Editor: Jason Oliver Nixon

Contributors: Rob Andrews, Robert Blake, Hilary Bunce, Philip Eade, Anita Guerrini, Nancy Hennessey, Deborah Luhrman, Conrad Paulus, Linda K. Schmidt, Mary Ellen Schultz, M. T. Schwartzman, George Semler, Dinah Spritzer

Creative Director: Fabrizio La Rocca

Cartographer: David Lindroth

Cover Photograph: Joe Viesti/Viesti Associates

Text Design: Between the Covers

Copyright

Special Sales

CONTENTS

Maps

ON THE ROAD WITH FODOR'S

WE'RE ALWAYS THRILLED to get letters from readers, especially one like this:

It took us an hour to decide what book to buy and we now know we picked the best one. Your book was wonderful, easy to follow, very accurate, and good on pointing out eating places, informal as well as formal. When we saw other people using your book, we would look at each other and smile.

Our editors and writers are deeply committed to making every Fodor's guide "the best one"—not only accurate but always charming, brimming with sound recommendations and solid ideas, right on the mark in describing restaurants and hotels, and full of fascinating facts that make you view what you've traveled to see in a rich new light.

About Our Writers

Our success in achieving our goals—and in helping to make your trip the best of all possible vacations—is a credit to the hard work of our extraordinary writers and editors.

Born and educated in the United States, writer, journalist, and translator **George Semler** has lived in Spain for the last 25 years. Druing that time he has published works on Spain, Catalonia, the Pyrenees, France, North Africa, and the Mediterranean area for the *International Herald Tribune,* the *Los Angeles Times, Forbes,* and *Saveur* among other publications. When not hiking, skiing, playing hockey, or fly-fishing in the streams of the Pyrenees, being accosted by Moroccan belly dancers or hosting Fodor's editors in his hometown of Barcelona, Semler finds time to work on Fodor's guides, write poetry and work on a magnum opus about the Pyrenees. He is also the author of books on Madrid and Barcelona.

New York–based writer and translator **Mary Ellen Schultz** has been exploring Spain since her first visit there as a child. A believer in reincarnation, Mary Ellen has traced her ancestors back to the 15th-century Sephardim who escaped the Spanish Inquisition, and feels she knew Miguel Cervantes way back when. The niece of a flamenco dancer, Mary Ellen yearns to run away to Seville with a gypsy troupe and learn to break hearts with her castanets. Or else get to act in an Almodóvar film.

Californian journalist **Deborah Luhrman** has visited many corners of the globe as a travel writer and in her current job as the press attaché for the Madrid-based World Tourism Organization—a job where she helps other journalists write about tourism and assists tourism ministries in dealing with the media. For the past eight years she has called Spain home and still thinks it is a great place to live. Among other destinations, last year she had adventures in Egypt, China, Atlanta, and Berlin. She has worked on the Spain guide since 1989; this year she updated the Madrid and Canary Islands chapters.

Spanglophile editor **Jason Oliver Nixon** grew up in Tampa, Florida where he inflicted his rudimentary high school Spanish on the Cuban inhabitants of Ybor City. Later, as a Spanish literature major at Colby College, Jason traveled to Salamanca, Spain to study the works of Unamuno, Cervantes, and Becquer. He now lives in New York City and, when not furiously editing away at Fodor's, he spends his evenings reviewing restaurants for the downtown rag, *Paper.* He hopes to one day move to Arcos de la Frontera where, with his trusty laptop computer, he will crank out screenplays and plod about in his garden.

New This Year

This year we've reformatted our guides to make them easier to use. Each chapter of *Fodor's Spain '97* begins with brand-new recommended itineraries to help you decide what to see in the time you have; a section called When to Tour points out the optimal time of day, day of the week, and season for your journey. You may also notice our fresh graphics, new in 1997. More readable and more helpful than ever? We think so—and we hope you do, too.

Also check out Fodor's Web site (http://www.fodors.com/), where you'll find travel information on major destinations around the world and an ever-changing array of travel-savvy interactive features.

How to Use This Book

Organization

Up front is the **Gold Guide.** Its first section, **Important Contacts A to Z,** gives addresses and telephone numbers of organizations and companies that offer destination-related services and detailed information and publications. **Smart Travel Tips A to Z,** the Gold Guide's second section, gives specific information on how to accomplish what you need to in Spain as well as tips on savvy traveling. Both sections are in alphabetical order by topic.

Chapters in *Fodor's Spain '97* are arranged either by city (Madrid and Barcelona) or by grouping together several provinces into a distince entity, i.e. Around Madrid or The Costa del Sol. Each city chapter begins with an Exploring section, which is subdivided by neighborhood; each subsection recommends a walking or driving tour and lists sights in alphabetical order. Each regional chapter is divided by geographical area; within each area, towns are covered in logical geographical order, and attractive stretches of road and minor points of interest between them are indicated by the designation *En Route*. Throughout, Off the Beaten Path sights appear after the places from which they are most easily accessible. And within town sections, all restaurants and lodgings are grouped together.

To help you decide what to visit in the time you have, all chapters begin with recommended itineraries; you can mix and match those from several chapters to create a complete vacation. The A to Z section that ends all chapters covers getting there, getting around, and helpful contacts and resources.

Icons and Symbols

★	Our special recommendations
✕	Restaurant
☆	Lodging establishment
✕☆	Lodging establishment whose restaurant warrants a detour
☺	Rubber duckie (good for kids)
☞	Sends you to another section of the guide for more information
✉	Address
☎	Telephone number
☉	Opening and closing times
⌖	Admission prices (those we give apply only to adults; substantially reduced fees are almost always available for children, students, and senior citizens)

Numbers in white and black circles—②and **❷**, for example—that appear on the maps, in the margins, and within the tours correspond to one another.

Dining and Lodging

The restaurants and lodgings we list are the cream of the crop in each price range. Price charts appear in the Pleasures and Pastimes section that follows each chapter introduction.

Hotel Facilities

We always list the facilities that are available—but we don't specify whether they cost extra: When pricing accommodations, always ask what's included.

Restaurant Reservations and Dress Codes

Reservations are always a good idea; we note only when they're essential or when they are not accepted. Book as far ahead as you can, and reconfirm when you get to town. Unless otherwise noted, the restaurants listed are open daily for lunch and dinner. We mention dress only when men are required to wear a jacket or a jacket and tie.

Credit Cards

The following abbreviations are used: **AE,** American Express; **DC,** Diners Club; **MC,** MasterCard; and **V,** Visa.

Don't Forget to Write

You can use this book in the confidence that all prices and opening times are based on information supplied to us at press time; Fodor's cannot accept responsibility for any errors. Time inevitably brings changes, so always confirm information when it matters—especially if you're making a detour to visit a specific place. In addition, when making reservations be sure to mention if you have a disability or are traveling with children, if you prefer a private bath or a certain type of bed, or if you have specific dietary needs or any other concerns.

Were the restaurants we recommended as described? Did our hotel picks exceed your expectations? Did you find a museum we recommended a waste of time? If you have complaints, we'll look into them and revise our entries when the facts warrant it. If you've discovered a special place that we haven't included, we'll pass the information along to our correspondents and have them check it out. So send your feedback, positive *and* negative, to the Spain Editor at 201 East 50th Street, New York, New York 10022—and have a wonderful trip!

Karen Cure
Editorial Director

Spain

Autonomous Regions and Provinces

Bay of Biscay

La Coruña
LA CORUÑA
Santiago de
Compostela
Pontevedra
PONTEVEDRA

LUGO
Lugo

GALICIA

Orense
ORENSE

Oviedo
Gijón
ASTURIAS

León
LEON

Santander
CANTABRIA

VIZCAYA
Bilbao

BURGOS
Burgos
PALENCIA
Palencia

LA

PORTUGAL

ZAMORA

Zamora

Salamanca
SALAMANCA

CASTILLA Y LEON

Valladolid
VALLADOLID

Duero

SEGOVIA
Segovia

AVILA
Avila

Guadalajara
MADRID
MADRID

CACERES
Cáceres
Trujillo

Tajo

EXTREMADURA

Mérida

Badajoz
BADAJOZ

Guadiana

Toledo
TOLEDO
Aranjuez

CASTILLA - LA MAN

CIUDAD REAL

Ciudad
Real

Alcázar

Valdepeñas

CORDOBA

Córdoba

HUELVA

Guadalquivir

SEVILLA

Huelva
Seville

Jerez

Cádiz
CADIZ

COSTA DE LA LUZ

ATLANTIC
OCEAN

Jaén

JAEN

ANDALUCIA

Antequera

MALAGA

Granada
GRANADA

Málaga

COSTA DEL SOL

Gibraltar

PAIS VASCO
(EUSKADI)
San
Sebastián
GUIPUZCOA
Victoria
ALAVA
TREVIÑO
Logroño
RIOJA
Soria
SORIA
GUADALAJARA
CUENCA
Cuenca
MANCHA
Albacete
ALBACETE
MURCIA
Murcia
Lorca
Almería
COSTA DE
ALMERIA
ALMERIA

FRANCE

ANDORRA
Pamplona
NAVARRA
HUESCA
Huesca
LERIDA
GERONA
CATALUNYA
(CATALONIA)
Gerona
Zaragoza
Lérida
BARCELONA
COSTA
BRAVA
ARAGON
Barcelona
ZARAGOZA
TARRAGONA
Tarragona
TERUEL
Tortosa
COSTA
DORADA
Balearic
Sea
Teruel
CASTELLON
Menorca →
Castellón
de la Plana
COSTA DEL AZAHAR
Valencia
Palma
Requena
Mallorca
VALENCIA
Ibiza
BALEARIC
ISLANDS
Játiva
Eivissa
ALICANTE
Formentera
Alicante
COSTA BLANCA

Menorca
Ciudadela
Mahón

Cartagena

Mediterranean
Sea

COSTA
CALIDA

Almería

N

KEY
—·—·— Regions
— — — Provinces
⊙ Provincial
capitals

0   50 miles
0   75 km

ALGERIA

Ebro
Tajo
Júcar
Segura

IMPORTANT CONTACTS A TO Z

An Alphabetical Listing of Publications, Organizations, and Companies that Will Help You Before, During, and After Your Trip

No single travel resource can give you every detail about every topic that might interest or concern you at the various stages of your journey—when you're planning your trip, while you're on the road, and after you get back home. The following organizations, books, and brochures will supplement the information in Fodor's *Spain '97*. For related information, including both basic tips on visiting Spain and background information on many of the topics below, study the second section of the gold pages, Smart Travel Tips A to Z.

A

AIR TRAVEL

All transatlantic flights arriving in Spain from the United States and Canada pass through Madrid's **Barajas** airport (☎ 91/305–8343). The country's other major gateway is Barcelona's **El Prat de Llobregat** (☎ 93/478–5000). Flying time is 7 hours from New York and 14½ hours from Los Angeles.

CARRIERS

The six airlines that fly nonstop from North America are **AeroMexico** (☎ 800/237–6639), **American Airlines** (☎ 800/433–7300), **Continental** (☎ 800/231–0856), **Delta** (☎ 800/221–1212), **Iberia** (☎ 800/772–4642), and **TWA** (☎ 800/892–4141).

Carriers from the U.S. that fly into **Madrid** include AeroMexico, American, Continental, Delta, Iberia, and TWA. If you prefer to fly into **Barcelona,** call Delta, Iberia, and TWA.

For flights from New York to the Canary Islands, *see* Chapter 15.

Three of the best known charters for flights to Spain are **Air Europa** (contact **Spanish Heritage** ☎ 718/244–6017, 718/544–2752, or 800/221–2580), **Oasis International** (through **Club Vacations** ☎ 615/373–7904 or 800/234–1700) and **Toto Tours International** ☎ 718/237–2312 or 800/676–7843).

FROM THE U.K.➤ Contact **British Airways** (☎ 0171/897–4000) or **Iberia** (☎ 0171/437–5622).

COMPLAINTS

To register complaints about charter and scheduled airlines, contact the U.S. Department of Transportation's **Aviation Consumer Protection Division** (✉ C-75, Washington, DC 20590, ☎ 202/366–2220). Complaints about lost baggage or ticketing problems and safety concerns may also be logged with the **Federal Aviation Administration (FAA) Consumer Hotline** (☎ 800/322–7873).

CONSOLIDATORS

For services that will help you find the lowest airfares, *see* Discounts, *below.*

DISCOUNT PASSES

If you buy a round-trip transatlantic ticket on **Iberia** (☎ 800/772–4642), you might want to purchase a Visit Spain pass, good for four domestic flights during your trip. It must be purchased before you arrive in Spain, all flights must be booked in advance, and the cost is $300, or $350 if you want to include flights to the Canary Islands (prices are $50 less if you travel during the low season, between 10/1–6/15).

On certain days of the week, Iberia also offers minifares, which can save you 40% on domestic flights. Tickets must be purchased in advance, and you must stay over Saturday night. ☞ Discounts, *below.*

PUBLICATIONS

For general information about charter carriers, ask for the Department of Transportation's free brochure **"Plane Talk: Public Charter Flights"** (✉ Aviation Consumer Protection Division, C-75, Washington, DC

20590, ☎ 202/366–2220). The Department of Transportation also publishes a 58-page booklet, **"Fly Rights,"** available from the Consumer Information Center (✉ Supt. of Documents, Dept. 133B, Pueblo, CO 81009; $1.75).

For other tips and hints, consult the Consumers Union's monthly **"Consumer Reports Travel Letter"** (✉ Box 53629, Boulder, CO 80322, ☎ 800/234–1970; $39 1st year) and the newsletter **"Travel Smart"** (✉ 40 Beechdale Rd., Dobbs Ferry, NY 10522, ☎ 800/327–3633; $37 per year).

Some worthwhile publications on the subject are *The Official Frequent Flyer Guidebook,* by Randy Petersen (✉ Airpress, 4715-C Town Center Dr., Colorado Springs, CO 80916, ☎ 719/597–8899 or 800/487–8893; $14.99 plus $3 shipping); *Airfare Secrets Exposed,* by Sharon Tyler and Matthew Wunder (✉ Studio 4 Productions, Box 280400, Northridge, CA 91328, ☎ 818/700–2522 or 800/408–7369; $16.95 plus $2.50 shipping); *202 Tips Even the Best Business Travelers May Not Know,* by Christopher McGinnis (✉ Irwin Professional Publishing, 1333 Burr Ridge Pkway., Burr Ridge, IL 60521, ☎ 800/634–3966; $11 plus $3.25 shipping); and *Travel Rights,* by Charles Leocha (✉ World Leisure Corporation, 177 Paris St., Boston, MA 02128, ☎ 800/444–2524;

$7.95 plus $3.95 shipping).

For information on how to avoid jet lag, there are two publications: *Jet Lag, A Pocket Guide to Modern Treatment* (✉ MedEd Publishers, 1421 W. 3rd Ave., Columbus, OH 43212, ☎ 800/875–8489; $5.95) and *How to Beat Jet Lag* (✉ Henry Holt, 115 W. 18th St., New York, NY 10011, ☎ 800/288-2131; $14.95).

Travelers who experience motion sickness or ear problems in flight should get the brochures **"Ears, Altitude, and Airplane Travel"** and **"What You Can Do for Dizziness & Motion Sickness"** from the American Academy of Otolaryngology (✉ 1 Prince St., Alexandria, VA 22314, ☎ 703/836–4444, FAX 703/683–5100, TTY 703/519–1585).

WITHIN SPAIN

Iberia (☎ 91/329–4353) and its sister carrier, **Aviaco** (☎ 91/559–5682) are the main airlines offering domestic service. Two independent airlines, **Air Europa** (☎ 91/559–1500 and 305–8159) and **Spanair** (☎ 91/393–6740), offer a number of domestic routes at lower prices.

B
BETTER BUSINESS
BUREAU

For local contacts in the hometown of a tour operator you may be considering, consult the **Council of Better Business Bureaus** (✉ 4200 Wilson Blvd., Suite 800,

Arlington, VA 22203, ☎ 703/276–0100, FAX 703/525–8277).

BUS TRAVEL

For reservations and information on service from the United Kingdom, contact **Eurolines/National Express** (☎ 0171/730–0202).

C
CAR RENTAL

The major car-rental companies represented in Spain are **Avis** (☎ 800/331–1084; in Canada, 800/879–2847), **Budget** (☎ 800/527–0700; in the U.K., 0800/181181), **Dollar** (☎ 800/800–4000; in the U.K., 0990/565656, where it is known as Eurodollar), **Hertz** (☎ 800/654–3001; in Canada, 800/263–0600; in the U.K., 0345/555888), and **National InterRent** (sometimes known as Europcar InterRent outside North America; ☎ 800/227–3876; in the U.K., 01345/222–525). Rates in Spain begin at $65 a day and $151 a week for an economy car with unlimited mileage. This does not include tax on car rentals, which is 16%.

The leading car-rental firm in Spain is **ATESA** (✉ Infante Mercedes 90, Madrid, ☎ 91/571–1931; ✉ Plaza Carmen Benítez 7, Seville, ☎ 95/441–9712).

RENTAL WHOLESALERS

Contact **Auto Europe** (☎ 207/828–2525 or 800/223–5555), **Europe by Car** (☎ 800/223–1516; in CA, 800/252–9401), or the **Kemwel Group** (☎ 914/835–

5555 or 800/678–0678).

CHILDREN & TRAVEL

FLYING

Look into **"Flying with Baby"** (✉ Third Street Press, Box 261250, Littleton, CO 80163, ☎ 303/595–5959; $4.95 includes shipping), cowritten by a flight attendant. **"Kids and Teens in Flight,"** free from the U.S. Department of Transportation's Aviation Consumer Protection Division (✉ C-75, Washington, DC 20590, ☎ 202/366–2220), offers tips on children flying alone. Every two years the February issue of *Family Travel Times* (☞ Know-How, *below*) details children's services on three dozen airlines. **"Flying Alone, Handy Advice for Kids Traveling Solo"** is available free from the American Automobile Association (AAA) (✉ send stamped, self-addressed, legal-size envelope: Flying Alone, Mail Stop 800, 1000 AAA Dr., Heathrow, FL 32746).

GAMES

Milton Bradley has games to help keep little (and not so little) children from fidgeting while in planes, trains, and automobiles. Try packing the Travel Battleship sea-battle game ($7); Travel Connect Four, a vertical strategy game ($8); the Travel Yahtzee dice game ($6), the Travel Trouble dice and board game ($7), and the Travel Guess Who mystery game ($8).

Parker Brothers has travel versions of Clue!, Sorry, and Monopoly.

KNOW-HOW

Family Travel Times, published quarterly by Travel with Your Children (✉ TWYCH, 40 5th Ave., New York, NY 10011, ☎ 212/477–5524; $40 per year), covers destinations, types of vacations, and modes of travel.

The *Family Travel Guides* catalog (✉ Carousel Press, Box 6061, Albany, CA 94706, ☎ 510/527–5849; $1 postage) lists about 200 books and articles on traveling with children. Also check *Take Your Baby and Go! A Guide for Traveling with Babies, Toddlers and Young Children,* by Sheri Andrews, Judy Bordeaux, and Vivian Vasquez (✉ Bear Creek Publications, 2507 Minor Ave. E, Seattle, WA 98102, ☎ 206/322–7604 or 800/326–6566; $5.95 plus $1.50 shipping).

LODGING

The **Novotel** hotel chain (☎ 800/221–4542) allows up to two children to stay free in their parents' room.

THE CHANNEL TUNNEL

For information, contact **Le Shuttle** (in the U.S., ☎ 800/388–3876; in the U.K., 0990/353535), which transports cars, or **Eurostar** (in the U.S., ☎ 800/942–4866; in the U.K., 0345/881–881), the high-speed train service between London (Waterloo) and

Paris (Gare du Nord). Eurostar tickets are available in the U.K. through **InterCity Europe,** the international wing of BritRail (✉ Victoria Station, London, ☎ 0171/834–2345 or 0171/828–0892 for credit-card bookings), and in the United States through **Rail Europe** (☎ 800/942–4866) and **BritRail Travel** (☎ 800/677–8585).

CUSTOMS

IN THE U.S.

The **U.S. Customs Service** (✉ Box 7407, Washington, DC 20044, ☎ 202/927–6724) can answer questions on duty-free limits and publishes a helpful brochure, "Know Before You Go." For information on registering foreign-made articles, call 202/927–0540.

COMPLAINTS➤ Note the inspector's badge number and write to the commissioner's office (✉ 1301 Constitution Ave. NW, Washington, DC 20229).

CANADIANS

Contact **Revenue Canada** (✉ 2265 St. Laurent Blvd. S, Ottawa, Ontario K1G 4K3, ☎ 613/993–0534) for a copy of the free brochure **"I Declare/Je Déclare"** and for details on duty-free limits. For recorded information (within Canada only), call 800/461–9999.

U.K. CITIZENS

HM Customs and Excise (✉ Dorset House, Stamford St., London SE1 9NG, ☎ 0171/202–4227) can answer questions about U.K.

customs regulations and publishes a free pamphlet, **"A Guide for Travellers,"** detailing standard procedures and import rules.

D

DISABILITIES & ACCESSIBILITY

COMPLAINTS

To register complaints under the provisions of the Americans with Disabilities Act, contact the U.S. Department of Justice's **Disability Rights Section** (✉ Box 66738, Washington, DC 20035, ☎ 202/514–0301 or 800/514–0301, FAX 202/307–1198, TTY 202/514–0383 or 800/514–0383). For airline-related problems, contact the U.S. Department of Transportation's **Aviation Consumer Protection Division** (☞ Air Travel, *above*). For complaints about surface transportation, contact the Department of Transportation's **Civil Rights Office** (☎ 202/366–4648).

ORGANIZATIONS

TRAVELERS WITH HEARING IMPAIRMENTS➤ The **American Academy of Otolaryngology** (✉ 1 Prince St., Alexandria, VA 22314, ☎ 703/836–4444, FAX 703/683–5100, TTY 703/519–1585) publishes a brochure, "Travel Tips for Hearing Impaired People."

TRAVELERS WITH MOBILITY PROBLEMS➤ Contact the **Information Center for Individuals with Disabilities** (✉ Box 256, Boston, MA 02117, ☎ 617/450–9888; in MA, 800/462–5015; TTY 617/424–6855); **Mobil-**

ity International USA (✉ Box 10767, Eugene, OR 97440, ☎ and TTY 503/343–1284, FAX 503/343–6812), the U.S. branch of a Belgium-based organization (☞ *below*) with affiliates in 30 countries; **Moss-Rehab Hospital Travel Information Service** (☎ 215/456–9600, TTY 215/456–9602), a telephone information resource for travelers with physical disabilities; the **Society for the Advancement of Travel for the Handicapped** (✉ 347 5th Ave., Suite 610, New York, NY 10016, ☎ 212/447–7284, FAX 212/725–8253; membership $45); and **Travelin' Talk** (✉ Box 3534, Clarksville, TN 37043, ☎ 615/552–6670, FAX 615/552–1182) which provides local contacts worldwide for travelers with disabilities.

TRAVELERS WITH VISION IMPAIRMENTS➤ Contact the **American Council of the Blind** (✉ 1155 15th St. NW, Suite 720, Washington, DC 20005, ☎ 202/467–5081, FAX 202/467–5085) for a list of travelers' resources or the **American Foundation for the Blind** (✉ 11 Penn Plaza, Suite 300, New York, NY 10001, ☎ 212/502–7600 or 800/232–5463, TTY 212/502–7662), which provides general advice and publishes "Access to Art" ($19.95), a directory of museums that accommodate travelers with vision impairments.

IN THE U.K.

Contact the **Royal Association for Disabil-**

ity and Rehabilitation (✉ RADAR, 12 City Forum, 250 City Rd., London EC1V 8AF, ☎ 0171/250–3222) or **Mobility International** (✉ rue de Manchester 25, B-1080 Brussels, Belgium, ☎ 00–322–410–6297, FAX 00–322–410–6874), an international travel-information clearinghouse for people with disabilities.

PUBLICATIONS

Several publications for travelers with disabilities are available from the **Consumer Information Center** (✉ Box 100, Pueblo, CO 81009, ☎ 719/948–3334). Call or write for its free catalog of current titles. The Society for the Advancement of Travel for the Handicapped (☞ Organizations, *above*) publishes the quarterly magazine **"Access to Travel"** ($13 for 1-year subscription).

The 500-page **Travelin' Talk Directory** (✉ Box 3534, Clarksville, TN 37043, ☎ 615/552–6670, FAX 615/552–1182; $35) lists people and organizations who help travelers with disabilities. For travel agents worldwide, consult the **Directory of Travel Agencies for the Disabled** (✉ Twin Peaks Press, Box 129, Vancouver, WA 98666, ☎ 360/694–2462 or 800/637–2256, FAX 360/696–3210; $19.95 plus $3 shipping).

TRAVEL AGENCIES & TOUR OPERATORS

The Americans with Disabilities Act requires

that all travel firms serve the needs of all travelers. That said, you should note that some agencies and operators specialize in making travel arrangements for individuals and groups with disabilities, among them **Access Adventures** (⌧ 206 Chestnut Ridge Rd., Rochester, NY 14624, ☎ 716/889–9096), run by a former physical-rehab counselor.

TRAVELERS WITH MOBIL-ITY PROBLEMS➤ Contact **Flying Wheels Travel** (⌧ 143 W. Bridge St., Box 382, Owatonna, MN 55060, ☎ 507/451–5005 or 800/535–6790), a travel agency specializing in European cruises and tours; **Hinsdale Travel Service** (⌧ 201 E. Ogden Ave., Suite 100, Hinsdale, IL 60521, ☎ 708/325–1335 or 800/303–5521), a travel agency that benefits from the advice of wheelchair traveler Janice Perkins; and **Wheelchair Journeys** (⌧ 16979 Redmond Way, Redmond, WA 98052, ☎ 206/885–2210 or 800/313–4751), which can handle arrangements worldwide.

TRAVELERS WITH DEVEL-OPMENTAL DISABILITIES➤ Contact the nonprofit **New Directions** (⌧ 5276 Hollister Ave., Suite 207, Santa Barbara, CA 93111, ☎ 805/967–2841).

TRAVEL GEAR

The **Magellan's** catalog (☎ 800/962–4943, FAX 805/568–5406), includes a range of products designed for travelers with disabilities.

AIRFARES

For the lowest airfares to Spain, call 800/FLY–4–LESS.

CLUBS

Contact **Entertainment Travel Editions** (⌧ Box 1068, Trumbull, CT 06611, ☎ 800/445–4137; $28–$53, depending on destination), **Great American Traveler** (⌧ Box 27965, Salt Lake City, UT 84127, ☎ 800/548–2812; $49.95 per year), **Moment's Notice Discount Travel Club** (⌧ 163 Amsterdam Ave., Suite 137, New York, NY 10023, ☎ 212/486–0500; $25 per year, single or family), **Privilege Card** (⌧ 3391 Peachtree Rd. NE, Suite 110, Atlanta, GA 30326, ☎ 404/262–0222 or 800/236–9732; $74.95 per year), **Travelers Advantage** (⌧ CUC Travel Service, 49 Music Sq. W, Nashville, TN 37203, ☎ 800/548–1116 or 800/648–4037; $49 per year, single or family), or **Worldwide Discount Travel Club** (⌧ 1674 Meridian Ave., Miami Beach, FL 33139, ☎ 305/534–2082; $50 per year for family, $40 single).

HOTEL ROOMS

For hotel room rates guaranteed in U.S. dollars, call **Steigenberger Reservation Service** (☎ 800/223–5652).

PASSES

☞ Air Travel, *above*, and Train Travel, *below*.

STUDENTS

Members of Hostelling International–American Youth Hostels (☞ Students, *below*) are eligible for discounts on car rentals, admissions to attractions, and other selected travel expenses.

PUBLICATIONS

Consult *The Frugal Globetrotter*, by Bruce Northam (⌧ Fulcrum Publishing, 350 Indiana St., Suite 350, Golden, CO 80401, ☎ 800/992–2908; $15.95). For publications that tell how to find the lowest prices on plane tickets, *see* Air Travel, *above*.

Also see Fodor's **Affordable Europe** (available in bookstores, or ☎ 800/533–6478; $18.50).

AUTO CLUBS

The large car-rental companies, Hertz and Avis, have 24-hour breakdown service. If you are a member of an automobile club (AAA, CAA, or AA), you can get help from the Spanish auto club **RACE** (⌧ José Abascal 10, Madrid, ☎ 91/447–3200; emergency assistance, 91/593–3333).

To become a member of the AAA, call 800/564–6222. In the United Kingdom, contact the Automobile Association (AA) or the Royal Automobile Club (RAC).

FERRIES FROM THE U.K.

For reservations and information: **Brittany Ferries** (☎ 0752/221–321), **Hover-Speed** (☎ 0171/554–7061), **P&O European Ferries** (☎ 0181/575–8555), **Sealink** (☎ 0223/47047), **SNCF** (for

Motorail, ☎ 0171/
409–3518).

G

GAY & LESBIAN
TRAVEL

ORGANIZATIONS

The **International Gay
Travel Association** (✉
Box 4974, Key West,
FL 33041, ☎ 800/448–
8550, FAX 305/296–
6633), a consortium of
more than 1,000 travel
companies, can supply
names of gay-friendly
travel agents, tour
operators, and accom-
modations.

Information about gay
culture, nightlife, and
medical and legal assis-
tance is available in
Madrid (✉ **Gai Inform,**
C. Carretas 12, 3-2a,
28012 Madrid, ☎ 91/
523–0070) and in
Barcelona (✉ **Teléfono
Rosa,** C. Carolinas 13,
08012 Barcelona,
☎ 93/234–7070).

PUBLICATIONS

The premier interna-
tional travel magazine
for gays and lesbians is
the 16-page monthly
"Out & About" (☎ 212/
645–6922 or 800/929–
2268, FAX 800/929–
2215; $49 for 10 issues
and quarterly calen-
dar), which covers
gay-friendly resorts,
hotels, cruise lines,
and airlines.

TOUR OPERATORS

Cruises and resort
vacations for gays are
handled by **R.S.V.P.
Travel Productions**
(✉ 2800 University
Ave. SE, Minneapolis,
MN 55414, ☎ 612/
379–4697 or 800/328–
7787). **Toto Tours** (✉
1326 W. Albion St.,
Suite 3W, Chicago, IL
60626, ☎ 312/274–

8686 or 800/565–
1241) offers group
tours to worldwide
destinations.

TRAVEL AGENCIES

The largest agencies
serving gay travelers
are **Advance Travel** (✉
10700 Northwest Fwy.,
Suite 160, Houston, TX
77092, ☎ 713/682–
2002 or 800/695–
0880), **Islanders/
Kennedy Travel** (✉ 183
W. 10th St., New York,
NY 10014, ☎ 212/
242–3222 or 800/988–
1181), **Now Voyager**
(✉ 4406 18th St., San
Francisco, CA 94114,
☎ 415/626–1169 or
800/255–6951), and
Yellowbrick Road (✉
1500 W. Balmoral Ave.,
Chicago, IL 60640,
☎ 312/561–1800
or 800/642–2488).
Skylink Women's Travel
(✉ 3577 Moorland
Ave., Santa Rosa, CA
95407, ☎ 707/588–
9961 or 800/225–
5759) serves lesbian
travelers.

H

HEALTH ISSUES

FINDING A
DOCTOR

For its members, the
**International Association
for Medical Assistance
to Travellers** (IAMAT,
membership free; ✉ 417
Center St., Lewiston,
NY 14092, ☎ 716/
754–4883; ✉ 40 Regal
Rd., Guelph, Ontario
N1K 1B5, ☎ 519/836–
0102; ✉ 1287 St. Clair
Ave., Toronto, Ontario
M6E 1B8, ☎ 416/652–
0137; ✉ 57 Voirets,
1212 Grand-Lancy,
Geneva, Switzerland, no
phone) publishes a
worldwide directory of
English-speaking physi-
cians meeting IAMAT
standards.

MEDICAL
ASSISTANCE
COMPANIES

The following compa-
nies are concerned
primarily with emer-
gency medical assis-
tance, although they
may provide some
insurance as part of
their coverage. For a list
of full-service travel
insurance companies,
see Insurance, *below.*

Contact **International
SOS Assistance** (✉
Box 11568, Philadel-
phia, PA 19116, ☎
215/244–1500 or 800/
523–8930; ✉ Box 466,
Pl. Bonaventure, Mont-
réal, Québec H5A 1C1,
☎ 514/874–7674 or
800/363–0263; ✉ 7
Old Lodge Pl., St. Mar-
garets, Twickenham
TW1 1RQ, England,
☎ 0181/744–0033),
**Medex Assistance Corpo-
ration** (✉ Box 10623,
Baltimore, MD 21285,
☎ 410/453–6300 or
800/573–2029), **Trav-
eler's Emergency Net-
work** (✉ 3100 Tower
Blvd., Suite 3100A,
Durham, NC 27702,
☎ 919/490–6065 or
800/275–4836, FAX 919/
493–8262), **TravMed**
(✉ Box 5375, Balti-
more, MD 24094,
☎ 800/732–5309),
or **Worldwide Assis-
tance Services** (✉ 1133
15th St. NW, Suite 400,
Washington, DC 20005,
☎ 202/331–1609
or 800/821–2828,
FAX 202/828–5896).

I

INSURANCE

IN CANADA

Contact **Mutual of
Omaha** (✉ Travel
Division, 500 University
Ave., Toronto, Ontario
M5G 1V8, ☎ 800/268–
8825 or 416/598–4321).

IN THE U.S.

Travel insurance covering baggage, health, and trip cancellation or interruptions is available from **Access America** (✉ Box 90315, Richmond, VA 23286, ☎ 804/285–3300 or 800/284–8300), **Carefree Travel Insurance** (✉ Box 9366, 100 Garden City Plaza, Garden City, NY 11530, ☎ 516/294–0220 or 800/323–3149), **Near Travel Services** (✉ Box 1339, Calumet City, IL 60409, ☎ 708/868–6700 or 800/654–6700), **Tele-Trip** (✉ Mutual of Omaha Plaza, Box 31716, Omaha, NE 68131, ☎ 800/228–9792), **Travel Guard International** (✉ 1145 Clark St., Stevens Point, WI 54481, ☎ 715/345–0505 or 800/826–1300), **Travel Insured International** (✉ Box 280568, East Hartford, CT 06128, ☎ 203/528–7663 or 800/243–3174), and **Wallach & Company** (✉ 107 W. Federal St., Box 480, Middleburg, VA 22117, ☎ 703/687–3166 or 800/237–6615).

IN THE U.K.

The **Association of British Insurers** (✉ 51 Gresham St., London EC2V 7HQ, ☎ 0171/600–3333) gives advice by phone and publishes the free pamphlet **"Holiday Insurance,"** which sets out typical policy provisions and costs.

L

LODGING

The new **Estancias de España** (✉ Menéndez Pidal 31-bajo izq., 28036 Madrid, ☎ 91/345–4141, FAX 91/345–5174) is an association of 20 independently owned hotels located in restored palaces, monasteries, mills, and post houses, generally in rural Spain; a free directory is available.

For information on hotel consolidators, *see* Discounts, *above.*

APARTMENT & VILLA RENTAL

Among the companies to contact are **At Home Abroad** (✉ 405 E. 56th St., Suite 6H, New York, NY 10022, ☎ 212/421–9165, FAX 212/752–1591), **Europa-Let** (✉ 92 N. Main St., Ashland, OR 97520, ☎ 541/482–5806 or 800/462–4486, FAX 541/482–0660), **Hometours International** (✉ Box 11503, Knoxville, TN 37939, ☎ 615/588–8722 or 800/367–4668), **Interhome** (✉ 124 Little Falls Rd., Fairfield, NJ 07004, ☎ 201/882–6864, FAX 201/808–1742), **Property Rentals International** (✉ 1008 Mansfield Crossing Rd., Richmond, VA 23236, ☎ 804/378–6054 or 800/220–3332, FAX 804/379–2073), **Rental Directories International** (✉ 2044 Rittenhouse Sq., Philadelphia, PA 19103, ☎ 215/985–4001, FAX 215/985–0323), **Rent-a-Home International** (✉ 7200 34th Ave. NW, Seattle, WA 98117, ☎ 206/789–9377 or 800/488–7368, FAX 206/789–9379), **Vacation Home Rentals Worldwide** (✉ 235 Kensington Ave., Norwood, NJ 07648, ☎ 201/767–9393 or 800/633–3284, FAX 201/767–5510), or **Villas International** (✉ 605 Market St., Suite 510, San Francisco, CA 94105, ☎ 415/281–0910 or 800/221–2260, FAX 415/281–0919). Members of the travel club **Hideaways International** (✉ 767 Islington St., Portsmouth, NH 03801, ☎ 603/430–4433 or 800/843–4433, FAX 603/430–4444; $99 per year) receive two annual guides plus quarterly newsletters and arrange rentals among themselves.

HOME EXCHANGE

Some of the principal clearinghouses are **HomeLink International/Vacation Exchange Club** (✉ Box 650, Key West, FL 33041, ☎ 305/294–1448 or 800/638–3841, FAX 305/294–1148; $70 per year), which sends members three annual directories, with a listing in one, plus updates; and **Intervac International** (✉ Box 590504, San Francisco, CA 94159, ☎ 415/435–3497, FAX 415/435–7440; $65 per year), which publishes four annual directories.

PARADORS

Contact the central reservations office: **Paradores de España** (✉ Central de Reservas, Requena 3, Madrid 28013, ☎ 91/559–0069, FAX 91/559–3233); or in the United States, **Marketing Ahead** (✉ 433 5th Ave., New York, NY 10016, ☎ 212/686–9213 or 800/223–1356); and in the United Kingdom, **Keytel International** (✉ 402 Edgeware Rd., London W2 1ED, ☎ 0171/402–8182).

M

MAIL

You can pick up mail at **American Express:** Call ☎ 800/528–4800 for a list of foreign American Express offices.

MONEY MATTERS

ATMS

For specific foreign **Cirrus** locations, call ☎ 800/424–7787; for foreign **Plus** locations, consult the Plus directory at your local bank.

CURRENCY EXCHANGE

If your bank doesn't exchange currency, contact **Thomas Cook Currency Services** (☎ 800/287–7362 for locations). **Ruesch International** (☎ 800/424–2923 for locations) can also provide you with foreign banknotes before you leave home and publishes a number of useful brochures, including a "Foreign Currency Guide" and "Foreign Exchange Tips."

WIRING FUNDS

Funds can be wired via **MoneyGram℠** (for locations and information in the U.S. and Canada, ☎ 800/926–9400) or **Western Union** (for agent locations or to send money using MasterCard or Visa, ☎ 800/325–6000; in Canada, 800/321–2923; in the U.K., 0800/833833; or visit the Western Union office at the nearest major post office).

P

PACKING

For strategies on packing light, get a copy of **The Packing Book,** by Judith Gilford (✉ Ten Speed Press, Box 7123, Berkeley, CA 94707, ☎ 510/559–1600 or 800/841–2665, FAX 510/524–4588; $7.95).

PASSPORTS & VISAS

IN THE U.S.

For fees, documentation requirements, and other information, call the State Department's **Office of Passport Services** information line (☎ 202/647–0518).

CANADIANS

For fees, documentation requirements, and other information, call the Ministry of Foreign Affairs and International Trade's **Passport Office** (☎ 819/994–3500 or 800/567–6868).

U.K. CITIZENS

For fees, documentation requirements, and to request an emergency passport, call the **London Passport Office** (☎ 0990/210–410).

PHOTO HELP

The **Kodak Information Center** (☎ 800/242–2424) answers consumer questions about film and photography. The **Kodak Guide to Shooting Great Travel Pictures** (available in bookstores; or contact Fodor's Travel Publications, ☎ 800/533–6478; $16.50) explains how to take expert travel photographs.

S

SAFETY

"Trouble-Free Travel," from the AAA, is a booklet of tips for protecting yourself and your belongings when away from home. Send a stamped, self-addressed, legal-size envelope to Flying Alone (✉ Mail Stop 75, 1000 AAA Dr., Heathrow, FL 32746).

SENIOR CITIZENS

EDUCATIONAL TRAVEL

The nonprofit **Elderhostel** (✉ 75 Federal St., 3rd Floor, Boston, MA 02110, ☎ 617/426–7788), for people 60 and older, has offered inexpensive study programs since 1975. Courses cover everything from marine science to Greek mythology and cowboy poetry. Costs for two- to three-week international trips—including room, board, and transportation from the United States—range from $1,800 to $4,500.

For people 50 and over and their children and grandchildren, **Interhostel** (✉ University of New Hampshire, 6 Garrison Ave., Durham, NH 03824, ☎ 603/862–1147 or 800/733–9753) runs 10-day summer programs that feature lectures, field trips, and sightseeing. Most last two weeks and cost $2,125–$3,100, including airfare.

ORGANIZATIONS

Contact the **American Association of Retired Persons** (✉ AARP, 601 E St. NW, Washington, DC 20049, ☎ 202/434–2277; annual dues $8 per person or couple). Its Purchase Privilege Program secures discounts for members on lodging, car rentals, and sightseeing, and the AARP Motoring Plan (☎ 800/334–3300) furnishes domestic trip-routing information and emergency road-service aid for an annual fee of $39.95 ($59.95 for a premium version). Senior citizen travelers can also join the AAA for emergency road service and other travel benefits (☞ Driving, *above, and* Discounts & Deals *in* Smart Travel Tips A to Z).

Additional sources for discounts on lodgings, car rentals, and other travel expenses, as well as helpful magazines and newsletters, are the **National Council of Senior Citizens** (⊠ 1331 F St. NW, Washington, DC 20004, ☎ 202/347–8800; annual membership $12) and Sears's **Mature Outlook** (⊠ Box 10448, Des Moines, IA 50306, ☎ 800/336–6330; annual membership $9.95).

PUBLICATIONS

The 50+ Traveler's Guidebook: Where to Go, Where to Stay, What to Do, by Anita Williams and Merrimac Dillon (⊠ St. Martin's Press, 175 5th Ave., New York, NY 10010, ☎ 212/674–5151 or 800/288–2131; $13.95), offers many useful tips. **"The Mature Traveler"** (⊠ Box 50400, Reno, NV 89513, ☎ 702/786–7419; $29.95), a monthly newsletter, covers all sorts of travel deals.

SIGHTSEEING

Bus tours are a popular way to see large cities and the surrounding sights. Among the largest operators, most with tours in English, are **Julià Tours** (⊠ Gran Vía 68, Madrid, ☎ 91/571–5300), **Pullmantur** (⊠ Plaza de Oriente 8, Madrid, ☎ 91/541–1805), and **Marsans** (⊠ Gran Vía 59, Madrid, ☎ 91/547–7300). In most cases you can book bus tours through your hotel.

Guided bicycling tours are offered by **Bicibus** (⊠ Puerta del Sol 14, 2nd Floor, Madrid, ☎ 91/522–4501).

SPORTS

For water sports, the tourist office (☞ Visitor Information, *below*) publishes a map listing facilities at hundreds of marinas; for further information contact the **Federación Española de Vela** (⊠ Spanish Sailing Federation, Luís de Salazar 12, 28002, Madrid, ☎ 91/519–5008), the **Federación de Actividades Subacuáticas** (⊠ Spanish Underwater Activities Federation, Santaló 15, 08021 Barcelona, ☎ 93/200–6769), and the **Federación Española de Esquí Nautico** (⊠ Spanish Waterskiing Federation, Sabiano Aran 30, 08028 Barcelona, ☎ 93/330–8903). Scattered around the Iberian coast are some 250 mooring points for pleasure craft; in many places are companies specializing in sea charters. For information on parking your own or chartering, contact the **Federación Española de Motonautica** (⊠ Spanish Motorboat Federation, Avda. de América 33, 4-B, 28002 Madrid, ☎ 91/415–3769.

For fishing permits and information, contact **ICONA** (⊠ Instituto Nacional para la Conservación de la Naturaleza, Madrid, ☎ 91/347–6000) and the **Federación Española de Pesca** (⊠ Navas de Tolosa 3, 28013 Madrid, ☎ 91/532–8353).

The **Real Federación Española de Golf** (⊠ Capitán Haya 9, 28020 Madrid, ☎ 91/555–2757) can answer all your golf-related questions.

Hikers should contact the tourist office or the **Federación Española de Montañismo** (⊠ Alberto Aguilera 3, 28015 Madrid, ☎ 91/445–1382).

A ski map is provided by the tourist office, or you can contact the **Federación Española de Deportes de Invierno** (⊠ Infanta María Teresa 14, 28016 Madrid, ☎ 91/344–0944) and **ATUDEM (Asociación Turística de Estaciones de Esquí y Montaña** (Tourism and Ski-run Information Line, ☎ 91/359–1557).

Pilots can contact **Federación Nacional de Deporte Aéreo** (⊠ Spanish Flying Federation, Ferraz 16, 28008 Madrid, ☎ 91/547–5922) for information on aerodromes.

Contact the **Federación Española de Polo** (⊠ Spanish Polo Federation, Comandante Zorita 13, 28020 Madrid, ☎ 91/533–7569), or the **Federación Hípica Española** (⊠ Spanish Horseracing Federation, Monte Esquinza 8, 28010 Madrid, ☎ 91/319–0233) for information relating to these sports.

Racquet swingers should contact the **Real Federación Española de**

Tenis (✉ Spanish Tennis Federation, Diagonal 618, 01028 Barcelona, ☎ 93/201–0844 for a list of the approximately 1,100 tennis clubs registered in the country.

If your idea of working out involves sipping cups of and soaking in mineral spring waters, contact **La Asociación Nacional de Estaciones Termales** (✉ National Health Spa Association, Rodrígues San Pedro 56-3, 28015 Madrid, tel. 91/549–0300) for a list of health resorts and thermal spas.

STUDENTS

GROUPS

The major tour operators specializing in student travel are **Contiki Holidays** (✉ 300 Plaza Alicante, Suite 900, Garden Grove, CA 92640, ☎ 714/740–0808 or 800/466–0610) and **AESU Travel** (✉ 2 Hamill Rd., Suite 248, Baltimore, MD 21210-1807, ☎ 410/323–4416 or 800/638–7640).

HOSTELING

In the United States, contact **Hostelling International–American Youth Hostels** (✉ 733 15th St. NW, Suite 840, Washington, DC 20005, ☎ 202/783–6161 or 800/444–6111 for reservations at selected hostels, ℻ 202/783–6171); in Canada, **Hostelling International–Canada** (✉ 205 Catherine St., Suite 400, Ottawa, Ontario K2P 1C3, ☎ 613/237–7884); and in the United Kingdom, the **Youth Hostel Association of England and Wales** (✉ Trevelyan House, 8 St. Stephen's Hill, St. Albans, Hertfordshire AL1 2DY, ☎ 01727/855215 or 01727/845047). Membership (in the U.S., $25; in Canada, C$26.75; in the U.K., £9.30) gives you access to 5,000 hostels in 77 countries that charge $5–$30 per person per night.

I.D. CARDS

To be eligible for discounts on transportation and admissions, get either the **International Student Identity Card,** if you're a bona fide student, or the **GO 25: International Youth Travel Card,** if you're not a student but under age 26. Each includes basic travel-accident and illness coverage, plus a toll-free travel hot line. In the United States, either card costs $18; apply through the Council on International Educational Exchange (☞ *below*). In Canada, cards are available for $15 each ($16 by mail) from Travel Cuts (☞ *below*), and in the United Kingdom for £5 each at student unions and student travel companies.

ORGANIZATIONS

A major contact is the **Council on International Educational Exchange** (✉ mail orders only: CIEE, 205 E. 42nd St., 16th Floor, New York, NY 10017, ☎ 212/661–1450, info@ciee.org), with walk-in locations in Boston (✉ 729 Boylston St., 02116, ☎ 617/266–1926), Miami (✉ 9100 S. Dadeland Blvd., 33156, ☎ 305/670–9261), Los Angeles (✉ 10904 Lindbrook Dr., 90024, ☎ 310/208–3551), 43 other college towns in the U.S., and in the United Kingdom (✉ 28A Poland St., London W1V 3DB, ☎ 0171/437–7767). Twice per year, it publishes *Student Travels* magazine. The CIEE's Council Travel Service is the exclusive U.S. agent for several student discount cards.

The **Educational Travel Centre** (✉ 438 N. Frances St., Madison, WI 53703, ☎ 608/256–5551 or 800/747–5551, ℻ 608/256–2042) offers rail passes and low-cost airline tickets, mostly for flights that depart from Chicago.

In Canada, also contact **Travel Cuts** (✉ 187 College St., Toronto, Ontario M5T 1P7, ☎ 416/979–2406 or 800/667–2887).

PUBLICATIONS

Check out the *Berkeley Guide to Europe* (available in bookstores; or contact Fodor's Travel Publications, ☎ 800/533–6478; $18.95).

T

TELEPHONE

MATTERS

The country code for Spain is 34. Area codes normally begin with a 9 and are different for each province. If you're dialing from outside the country, drop the 9. For local access numbers abroad, contact **AT&T** USA Direct (☎ 800/874–4000), **MCI** Call USA (☎ 800/444–4444), or **Sprint** Express (☎ 800/793–1153).

In Madrid the **main telephone office** is at ✉

THE GOLD GUIDE / IMPORTANT CONTACTS

THE GOLD GUIDE / IMPORTANT CONTACTS

Gran Vía 28. There is another at the main post office and a third at ✉ Paseo Recoletos 43, just off Plaza Colón. In Barcelona calls can be placed from the office at ✉ Carrer de Fontanella 4, off Plaça de Catalunya.

TOUR OPERATORS

Among the companies that sell tours and packages to Spain, the following are nationally known, have a proven reputation, and offer plenty of options.

GROUP TOURS

SUPER-DELUXE➤ **Abercrombie & Kent** (✉ 1520 Kensington Rd., Oak Brook, IL 60521-2141, ☎ 708/954-2944 or 800/323-7308, ᶠᵃˣ 708/954-3324) and **Travcoa** (✉ Box 2630, 2350 S.E. Bristol St., Newport Beach, CA 92660, ☎ 714/476-2800 or 800/992-2003, ᶠᵃˣ 714/476-2538).

DELUXE➤ **Globus** (✉ 5301 S. Federal Circle, Littleton, CO 80123-2980, ☎ 303/797-2800 or 800/221-0090, ᶠᵃˣ 303/795-0962), **Maupintour** (✉ Box 807, 1515 St. Andrews Dr., Lawrence, KS 66047, ☎ 913/843-1211 or 800/255-4266, ᶠᵃˣ 913/843-8351), and **Tauck Tours** (✉ Box 5027, 276 Post Rd. W, Westport, CT 06881, ☎ 203/226-6911 or 800/468-2825, ᶠᵃˣ 203/221-6828).

FIRST-CLASS➤ **Abreu Tours** (✉ 25 W. 45th St., #1309, New York, NY 10036-4902, ☎ 212/869-1840 or 800/223-1580, ᶠᵃˣ 212/354-1840), **Brendan Tours** (✉ 15137 Califa St., Van Nuys, CA 91411,

☎ 818/785-9696 or 800/421-8446, ᶠᵃˣ 818/902-9876), **Caravan Tours** (✉ 401 N. Michigan Ave., Chicago, IL 60611, ☎ 312/321-9800 or 800/227-2826), **Collette Tours** (✉ 162 Middle St., Pawtucket, RI 02860, ☎ 401/728-3805 or 800/832-4656, ᶠᵃˣ 401/728-1380), **Insight International Tours** (✉ 745 Atlantic Ave., #720, Boston, MA 02111, ☎ 617/482-2000 or 800/582-8380, ᶠᵃˣ 617/482-2884 or 800/622-5015), **Odysseys Adventures** (✉ Box 305, 537 Chestnut St., Cedarhurst, NY 11516-2223, ☎ 516/569-2812 or 800/344-0013, ᶠᵃˣ 516/569-2998), **Trafalgar Tours** (✉ 11 E. 26th St., New York, NY 10010, ☎ 212/689-8977 or 800/854-0103, ᶠᵃˣ 800/457-6644), and **Viajes Corte Inglés** (✉ 500 5th Ave., #1044, New York, NY 10110, ☎ 212/944-9400 or 800/333-2469).

PACKAGES

Just about every airline that flies to Spain sells packages that include round-trip airfare and hotel accommodations. Among U.S. carriers, contact **American Airlines Fly AAway Vacations** (☎ 800/321-2121), **Delta Dream Vacations** (☎ 800/872-7786), and **United Vacations** (☎ 800/328-6877). Other leading packagers include: **DER Tours** (✉ 11933 Wilshire Blvd., Los Angeles, CA 90025, ☎ 310/479-4140 or 800/782-2424), **4th Dimension Tours** (✉ 7101 S.W. 99th Ave., #105, Miami, FL 33173, ☎ 305/279-

0014 or 800/877-1525, ᶠᵃˣ 305/273-9777), **Jet Vacations** (✉ 1775 Broadway, New York, NY 10019, ☎ 212/474-8740 or 800/538-2762), **Spain Tours and Beyond** (✉ 261 W. 70th St., New York, NY 10023, ☎ 212/595-2400, ᶠᵃˣ 212/580-8935), and **VE Tours** (☎ 305/477-5161 or 800/222-8383). **Funjet Vacations** based in Milwaukee, Wisconsin, and **Gogo Tours**, based in Ramsey, New Jersey, sell packages only through travel agents.

FROM THE U.K.

Contact **Mundi Color** (✉ 276 Vauxhall Bridge Rd., London SW1V 1BE, ☎ 0171/828-6021), **Page & Moy Ltd.** (✉ 136-140 London Rd., Leicester LE2 1EN, ☎ 0116/250-7676), and **Magic of Spain** (✉ 227 Shepherds Bush Rd., London W6 7AS, ☎ 0181/741-4440).

THEME TRIPS

ARCHAEOLOGY➤ **Archeological Tours** (✉ 271 Madison Ave., New York NY 10016, ☎ 212/986-3054, ᶠᵃˣ 212/370-1561) has trips to Madrid and Barcelona. **Earthwatch** (✉ Box 403, 680 Mount Auburn St., Watertown, MA 02272, ☎ 617/926-8200 or 800/776-0188, ᶠᵃˣ 617/926-8532) recruits volunteers to serve in its Earth-Corps as short-term assistants to scientists on research expeditions, including some that explore ancient archaeological sites.

ART AND ARCHITECTURE➤ Contact **Esplanade Tours** (✉ 581

Boylston St., Boston, MA 02116, ☎ 617/266–7465 or 800/426–5492, FAX 617/262–9829) and **4th Dimension Tours** (✉ 7101 S.W. 99th Ave., #105, Miami, FL 33173, ☎ 305/279–0014 or 800/877–1525, FAX 305/273–9777).

BICYCLING➤ **Camino Tours** (✉ 1101 Post Oak Blvd., #9535, Houston, TX 77056, ☎ 713/622–4010 or 800/938–9311) is dedicated exclusively to bicycle tours in Spain. Other bike tours are available from **Back-roads** (✉ 1516 5th St., Berkeley, CA 94710-1740, ☎ 510/577–1555 or 800/462–2848, FAX 510/527–1444), **Butter-field & Robinson** (✉ 70 Bond St., Toronto, Ontario, Canada M5B 1X3, ☎ 416/864–1354 or 800/678–1147, FAX 416/864–0541), **Euro-Bike Tours** (✉ Box 990, De Kalb, IL 60115, ☎ 800/321–6060, FAX 815/758–8851), **RMF Biking and Walking in Europe** (✉ 1342 Birch-cliff Dr., Oakville, Ontario, Canada L6M 2A4, ☎ 905/825–4177, FAX 905/825–0796), and **Uniquely Europe** (✉ 2819 1st Ave., #280, Seattle, WA 98121-1113, ☎ 206/441–8682 or 800/426–3615, FAX 206/441–8862).

FOOD AND WINE➤ **Odysseys Adventures** (☞ Group Tours, *above*) organizes wine-tasting tours coupled with meals in fine restaurants around the country.

GARDENS➤ **Cooper-smith's England** (✉ Box 900, Inverness, CA 94937, ☎ 415/669–

1914, FAX 510/339–7135) explores the gardens, art, and archi-tecture of Madrid and Anadalucía.

GOLF➤ For packages to the famous courses of Costa del Sol, try **Golf International** (✉ 275 Madison Ave., New York, NY 10016, ☎ 212/986–9176 or 800/833–1389, FAX 212/986–3720), **ITC Golf Tours** (✉ 4134 Atlantic Ave., #205, Long Beach, CA 90807, ☎ 310/595–6905 or 800/257–4981) and **Odysseys Adven-tures** (☞ Group Tours, *above*).

HIKING AND WALKING➤ **Abercrombie & Kent** (☞ Group Tours *above*), **Adventure Center** (✉ 1311 63rd St., #200, Emeryville, CA 94608, ☎ 510/654–1879 or 800/227–8747, FAX 510/654–4200), **Country Walkers** (✉ Box 180, Waterbury, VT 05676-0180, ☎ 802/244–1387 or 800/464–9255, FAX 802/244–5661), **Himalayan Travel** (✉ 112 Prospect St., Stam-ford, CT 06901, ☎ 203/359–3711 or 800/225–2380, FAX 203/359–3669), **Mountain Travel-Sobek** (✉ 6420 Fairmount Ave., El Cerrito, CA 94530, ☎ 510/527–8100 or 800/227–2384, FAX 510/525–7710), and **Wilderness Travel** (✉ 801 Allston Way, Berke-ley, CA 94710, ☎ 510/548–0420 or 800/368–2794, FAX 510/548–0347) have a large selection of hiking trips in Spain.

HISTORY➤ Contact **Herodot Travel** (✉ 7 S. Knoll Rd., Mill Valley, CA 94941, ☎ FAX 415/

381–4031) for a trip into Spanish history.

HORSEBACK RIDING➤ **FITS Equestrian** (✉ 685 Lateen Rd., Solvang, CA 93463, ☎ 805/688–9494 or 800/666–3487, FAX 805/688–2943) has year-round departures and tours for every level of rider.

JEWISH HERITAGE➤ **Abreu Tours** (☞ Group Tours, *above*), **Kesher Tours** (✉ 370 Lexington Ave., New York, NY 10017, ☎ 212/949–9580), and **Odysseys Adventures** (☞ Group Tours, *above*) visit synagogues and historic Jewish sites throughout Spain.

LEARNING➤ Contact **Smithsonian Study Tours and Seminars** (✉ 1100 Jefferson Dr. SW, Room 3045, MRC 702, Wash-ington, DC 20560, ☎ 202/357–4700, FAX 202/633–9250).

MOTORCYCLING➤ **Edelweiss Bike Travel** (✉ Armonk Travel, 146 Bedford Rd., Armonk, NY 10504, ☎ 914/273–8880 or 800/255–7451, FAX 914/273–4438) has 15 years experience in touring by motorcycle.

SPAS➤ Contact **Spa-Finders** (✉ 91 5th Ave., #301, New York, NY 10003-3039, ☎ 212/924–6800 or 800/255–7727).

YACHT CHARTERS➤ **Huntley Yacht Vacations** (✉ 210 Preston Rd., Wernersville, PA 19565, ☎ 610/678–2628 or 800/322-9224, FAX 610//670–1767), **Lynn Jachney Charters** (✉ Box 302 Marblehead, MA 01945, 617/639–0787 or 800/223–

2050, FAX 617/639–0216), **The Moorings** (⊠ 19345 U.S. Hwy. 19 N, 4th floor, Clearwater, FL 34624-3193, ☎ 813/530–5424 or 800/535–7289, FAX 813/530–9474), **Ocean Voyages** (⊠ 1709 Bridgeway, Sausalito, CA 94965, ☎ 415/332–4681, FAX 415/332–7460).

ORGANIZATIONS

The **National Tour Association** (⊠ NTA, 546 E. Main St., Lexington, KY 40508, ☎ 606/226–4444 or 800/755–8687) and the **United States Tour Operators Association** (⊠ USTOA, 211 E. 51st St., Suite 12B, New York, NY 10022, ☎ 212/750–7371) can provide lists of members and information on booking tours.

PUBLICATIONS

Contact the USTOA (☞ Organizations, *above*) for its **"Smart Traveler's Planning Kit."** Pamphlets in the kit include the "Worldwide Tour and Vacation Package Finder," "How to Select a Tour or Vacation Package," and information on the organization's consumer protection plan. Also get copy of the Better Business Bureau's **"Tips on Travel Packages"** (⊠ Publication 24-195, 4200 Wilson Blvd., Arlington, VA 22203; $2).

TRAIN TRAVEL

LUXURY TRAIN

The luxurious turn-of-the-century *Al Andalus Express* makes five-day trips in Andalucía for sightseeing in Córdoba, Granada, and Seville; The cost is about

$2,600 per person. Contact **Marketing Ahead** (⊠ 433 5th Ave., New York, NY 10016, ☎ 212/686–9213 or 800/223–1356) or **DER Tours** (⊠ Box 1606, Des Plaines, IL 60017, ☎ 800/782–2424, FAX 800/282–7474).

DISCOUNT PASSES

Spain Flexipasses, Eurail, and EuroPasses are available through travel agents and **Rail Europe** (⊠ 226-230 Westchester Ave., White Plains, NY 10604, ☎ 914/682–5172 or 800/438–7245; ⊠ 2087 Dundas E., Suite 105, Mississauga, Ontario L4X 1M2, ☎ 416/602–4195, **DER Tours** (⊠ Box 1606, Des Plaines, IL 60017, ☎ 800/782–2424, FAX 800/282–7474), or **CIT Tours Corp.** (⊠ 342 Madison Ave., Suite 207, New York, NY 10173, ☎ 212/697–2100 or 800/248–8687 or 800/248–7245 in western U.S.).

FROM THE U.K.

Contact **British Rail Travel Centers** (☎ 0171/834–2345). Excellent deals for those under 26 can be found at **Eurotrain** (⊠ 52 Grosvenor Gardens, London SW1W OAG, ☎ 0171/730–3402) and **Transalpino** (⊠ 71–75 Buckingham Palace Rd., London SW1W ORE, ☎ 0171/834–9656).

TRAVEL GEAR

For travel apparel, appliances, personal-care items, and other travel necessities, get a free catalog from **Magellan's** (☎ 800/962–4943, FAX 805/568–5406), **Orvis Travel** (☎ 800/541–

3541, FAX 703/343–7053), or **TravelSmith** (☎ 800/950–1600, FAX 415/455–0554).

ELECTRICAL CONVERTERS

Send a self-addressed, stamped envelope to the **Franzus Company** (⊠ Customer Service, Dept. B50, Murtha Industrial Park, Box 142, Beacon Falls, CT 06403, ☎ 203/723–6664) for a copy of the free brochure "Foreign Electricity Is No Deep, Dark Secret."

TRAVEL AGENCIES

For names of reputable agencies in your area, contact the **American Society of Travel Agents** (⊠ ASTA, 1101 King St., Suite 200, Alexandria, VA 22314, ☎ 703/739–2782), the **Association of Canadian Travel Agents** (⊠ Suite 201, 1729 Bank St., Ottawa, Ontario K1V 7Z5, ☎ 613/521–0474, FAX 613/521–0805) or the **Association of British Travel Agents** (⊠ 55-57 Newman St., London W1P 4AH, ☎ 0171/637–2444, FAX 0171/637–0713).

U

U.S.

GOVERNMENT

TRAVEL BRIEFINGS

The U.S. Department of State's American Citizens Services office (⊠ Room 4811, Washington, DC 20520; enclose SASE) issues **Consular Information Sheets** on all foreign countries. These cover issues such as crime, security, political climate, and health risks as well as listing embassy locations, entry requirements, currency regulations, and providing other useful information. For the latest information, stop in at any U.S. passport office, consulate, or embassy; call the interactive hot line (☎ 202/647–5225, FAX 202/647–3000); or, with your PC's modem, tap into the department's computer bulletin board (☎ 202/647–9225).

V
VISITOR INFORMATION

Contact the **Spanish National Tourist Office** (✉ 666 5th Ave., 35th fl., New York, NY 10103, ☎ 212/265–8822, FAX 212/265–8864; ✉ Water Tower Pl., Suite 915, 845 N. Michigan Ave., Chicago, IL 60611, ☎ 312/642–1992, FAX 312/642–9817; ✉ 1221 Brickell Ave., Miami, FL 33131, ☎ 305/358–1992, FAX

305/358–8223; ✉ 8383 Wilshire Blvd., Suite 960, Beverly Hills, CA 90211, ☎ 213/658–7188, FAX 213/658–1061; ✉ 102 Bloor St. W, Suite 1450, Toronto, Ontario M5S 1M8, ☎ 416/961–3131, FAX 416/961–1992; ✉ 57–58 St. James's St., London SW1A 1LD, ☎ 0171/499–0901, FAX 0171/629–4257).

IN SPAIN

Information on hotels, transportation, museum hours, and the like is dispensed by friendly multi-lingual operators on the **Tourist Information Line** (☎ 901–300–600) daily 10–2.

IN THE U.K.

Spanish National Tourist Office has an **information line** (✉ 57–58 St. James's St., London SW1A 1LD, ☎ 0891/669–920, FAX 0171/629–4257). Calls

cost 49p per minute peak rate or 39p per minute cheap rate.

W
WEATHER

For current conditions and forecasts, plus the local time and helpful travel tips, call the **Weather Channel Connection** (☎ 900/932–8437; 95¢ per minute) from a Touch-Tone phone.

The *International Traveler's Weather Guide* (✉ Weather Press, Box 660606, Sacramento, CA 95866, ☎ 916/974–0201 or 800/972–0201; $10.95 includes shipping), written by two meteorologists, provides month-by-month information on temperature, humidity, and precipitation in more than 175 cities worldwide.

SMART TRAVEL TIPS A TO Z

Basic Information on Traveling in Spain and Savvy Tips to Make Your Trip a Breeze

The more you travel, the more you know about how to make trips run like clockwork. To help make your travels hassle-free, Fodor's editors have rounded up dozens of tips from our contributors and from travel experts all over the world, as well as basic information on visiting Spain. For names of organizations to contact and publications that can give you more information, *see* Important Contacts A to Z.

A
AIR TRAVEL

If time is an issue, **always look for nonstop flights,** which require no change of plane. If possible, **avoid connecting flights,** which stop at least once and can involve a change of plane, even though the flight number remains the same; if the first leg is late, the second waits.

For better service, **fly smaller or regional carriers,** which often have higher passenger satisfaction ratings. Sometimes they have such in-flight amenities as leather seats or greater legroom and they often have better food.

CUTTING COSTS

The Sunday travel section of most newspapers is a good place to look for deals.

MAJOR AIRLINES➤ The least-expensive airfares from the major airlines are priced for round-trip travel and are subject to restrictions. Usually, you must **book in advance and buy the ticket within 24 hours** to get cheaper fares, and you may have to **stay over a Saturday night.** The lowest fare is subject to availability, and only a small percentage of the plane's total seats is sold at that price. It's smart to **call a number of airlines, and when you are quoted a good price, book it on the spot**—the same fare may not be available on the same flight the next day. Airlines generally allow you to change your return date for a $25 to $50 fee. If you don't use your ticket, you can apply the cost toward the purchase of a new ticket, again for a small charge. However, most low-fare tickets are nonrefundable. To get the lowest airfare, **check different routings.** If your destination has more than one gateway, **compare prices to different airports.**

FROM THE U.K.➤ To save money on flights, **look into an APEX or Super-Pex ticket.** APEX tickets must be booked in advance and have certain restrictions. Super-PEX tickets can be purchased right at the airport.

CONSOLIDATORS➤ Consolidators buy tickets for scheduled flights at reduced rates from the airlines, then sell them at prices below the lowest available from the airlines directly—usually without advance restrictions. Sometimes you can even get your money back if you need to return the ticket. Carefully read the fine print detailing penalties for changes and cancellations. If you doubt the reliability of a consolidator, **confirm your reservation with the airline.**

CHARTER FLIGHTS➤ Charters usually have the lowest fares and most restrictions. Departures are infrequent and seldom on time, and you can lose all or most of your money if you cancel. (The closer to departure you cancel, the more you lose, although sometimes you can pay only a small fee if you supply a substitute passenger.) The flight may be canceled for any reason up to 10 days before departure (after that, only if it is physically impossible to operate). The charterer may also revise the itinerary or increase the price after you have bought the ticket, but only if the new arrangement constitutes a "major change" do you have the right to a refund. Before buying a charter ticket, **read the fine print** regarding the company's refund policies. Money for charter flights is usually paid into a bank escrow account, the name of which should be on the contract, and if you don't pay by credit card, **make your check payable to the carrier's escrow account** (unless you're dealing with a travel agent, in which case his or her check should be made payable to the escrow account). The U.S. Department of Transportation's Aviation Consumer Protection Division has jurisdiction over charters.

Charter operators may offer flights alone or with ground arrangements that constitute a charter package. Normally, you must book charters through a travel agent.

ALOFT

AIRLINE FOOD➤ If you hate airline food, **ask for special meals when booking.** These can be vegetarian, low-cholesterol, or kosher, for example; commonly prepared to order in smaller quantities than standard fare, they can be tastier.

JET LAG➤ To avoid this syndrome, which occurs when travel disrupts your body's natural cycles, try to maintain a normal routine. At night, **get some sleep.** By day, move about the cabin to **stretch your legs, eat light meals, and drink water—not alcohol.**

SMOKING➤ Smoking is banned on all flights of less than six hours' duration within the United States and on all Canadian flights; the ban also applies to domestic segments of international flights aboard U.S. and foreign carriers. Delta has banned smoking system-wide. On U.S. carriers flying to Spain and other destinations abroad, a seat in a no-smoking section must be provided for every passenger who requests one, and the section must be enlarged to accommodate such passengers as long as they have complied with the airline's deadline for check-in and seat assignment. If smoking bothers you, request a seat far from the smoking section.

Foreign airlines are exempt from these rules but do provide no-smoking sections; some countries have banned smoking on all domestic flights, and others may not allow smoking on some flights. Talks continue on the feasibility of broadening no-smoking policies.

B

BEACHES

Although Spain has more than 2,000 miles of coastline, **it's hard to find an unspoiled Spanish beach.** Sewage and industrial wastes have made swimming dangerous on beaches surrounding Barcelona, Tarragona, Valencia, Cadiz, Bilbao, Aviles, and La Coruña. High-rise development casts an unpleasant shadow over popular resorts on the Costa del Sol and Costa Blanca.

Try beaches in the provinces of Almería, Murcia, Huelva, and the Rías Bajas of Galicia for cleaner water and smaller crowds.

BUS TRAVEL

An array of private companies operate Spain's buses, providing service that ranges from knee-crunching basic to luxurious. Some buses have televisions and free drinks. Fares are lower than for rail travel. If you want to reach a town not served by train, you can be sure a bus will go there. Spanish towns don't usually have a central bus depot, so ask at the tourist office where to pick up a bus to your destination.

BUSINESS HOURS

Banks are generally open weekdays 8:30 to 2, Saturdays 8:30 to 1, but in the summer most banks close at 1 PM weekdays and do not open on Saturday. Money exchanges at airports and train stations stay open later. Traveler's checks can also be cashed at the El Corte Inglés department stores until 9 PM.

Most museums are open from 9:30 to 2 and from 4 to 7, and are closed one day a week, usually Monday, but opening hours vary widely, so check before you set off. A few big museums, such as the Prado, the Reina Sofía Museum in Madrid, and the Picasso Museum in Barcelona, do not close at midday.

Almost all **shops close at midday** for at least three hours, except for the big department store chain El Corte Inglés. Generally store hours are from 10 to 1:30 and 5 to 8. Shops are closed all day Sunday, and in Madrid and several other places they are also closed Saturday afternoon.

C
CAMERAS, CAMCORDERS, & COMPUTERS

LAPTOPS

Before you depart, **check your portable computer's battery;** at security you may be asked to turn on the computer to prove that it is what it appears to be. At the airport, you may prefer to **request a manual inspection,** although security X-rays do not harm hard-disk or floppy-disk storage. Also, **register your foreign-made laptop with U.S. Customs.** If your laptop is U.S.-made, call the consulate of the country you'll be visiting to find out whether it should be registered with local customs upon arrival. You may want to **find out about repair facilities at your destination** in case of problems.

PHOTOGRAPHY

If your camera is new or if you haven't used it for a while, **shoot and develop a few rolls of film** before you leave. Always **store film in a cool, dry place**—never in your car's glove compartment or on the shelf under the rear window.

Select the right film for your purpose—**use print film if you plan to frame or display your pictures,** but **use slide film if you hope to publish your shots.** Also, **consider black-and-white film** for different and dramatic images. For best results, **use a custom lab** for

processing; use a one-hour lab only if time is a factor.

The chances of your film growing cloudy increase with each pass through an X-ray machine. To protect against this, carry it in a clear plastic bag and **ask for hand inspection at security.** Such requests are virtually always honored at U.S. airports, and are usually accommodated abroad. Don't depend on a lead-lined bag to protect film in checked luggage—the airline may increase the radiation to see what's inside.

Keep a skylight or haze filter on your camera at all times to protect the expensive (and delicate) lens glass from scratches. Better yet, **use an 81B warming filter,** which—unlike skylight or haze filters—really works in overcast conditions and will pump up those sunrises and sunsets.

VIDEO

Before your trip, **test your camcorder, invest in a skylight filter to protect the lens, and charge the batteries.** (Airport security personnel may ask you to turn on the camcorder to prove that it's what it appears to be.) The batteries of most newer camcorders can be recharged with a universal or worldwide AC adapter-charger (or multivoltage converter), whether the voltage is 110 or 220. All that's needed is the appropriate plug.

Videotape is not damaged by X-rays, but it

may be harmed by the magnetic field of a walk-through metal detector, so **ask that videotapes be hand-checked.** Prerecorded videotape sold in Spain is based on the PAL standard, which will not play back in the United States. Blank tapes bought in Spain can be used for camcorder taping, but they are pricey. Some U.S. audiovisual shops convert foreign tapes to U.S. standards; contact an electronics dealer to find the nearest.

CAMPING

Camping in Spain is not a wilderness experience. There are more than 500 campgrounds, and many of them have excellent facilities, including hot showers, restaurants, swimming pools, tennis courts, and even discotheques. But in summer, especially in August, **the best campgrounds are filled with Spanish families who move in with their entire household:** pets, grandparents, even the kitchen sink and stove! A government guide listing all Spanish campgrounds can be obtained from the tourist office or purchased at the main post office in Madrid.

CAR RENTAL

CUTTING COSTS

To get the best deal, **book through a travel agent who is willing to shop around.** Ask your agent to **look for fly-drive packages,** which also save you money, and **ask if local taxes are included** in the rental or fly-drive price. These can be as high as

20% in some destinations. Don't forget to find out about required deposits, cancellation penalties, drop-off charges, and the cost of any required insurance coverage.

Also **ask your travel agent about a company's customer-service record.** How has it responded to late plane arrivals and vehicle mishaps? Are there often lines at the rental counter, and—if you're traveling during a holiday period—does a confirmed reservation guarantee you a car?

Always **find out what equipment is standard** at your destination before specifying what you want; automatic transmission and air-conditioning are usually optional—and very expensive.

Be sure to **look into wholesalers**—companies that do not own their own fleets but rent in bulk from those that do and often offer better rates than traditional car-rental operations. Prices are best during off-peak periods; rentals booked through wholesalers must be paid for before you leave the United States.

INSURANCE

When driving a rented car, you are generally responsible for any damage to or loss of the rental vehicle. Before you rent, **see what coverage you already have** under the terms of your personal auto insurance policy and credit cards.

If you do not have auto insurance or an umbrella insurance policy

that covers damage to third parties, purchasing CDW or LDW is highly recommended.

Collision policies that car-rental companies sell for European rentals typically do not cover stolen vehicles. Before you buy additional coverage for theft, find out if your credit card or personal auto insurance will cover the loss.

LICENSE REQUIREMENTS

In Spain your own driver's license is acceptable. An International Driver's Permit is a good idea; it's available from the American or Canadian automobile associations, or, in the United Kingdom, from the AA or RAC.

SURCHARGES

Before you pick up a car in one city and leave it in another, **ask about drop-off charges or one-way service fees,** which can be substantial. Note, too, that some rental agencies charge extra if you return the car before the time specified on your contract. To avoid a hefty refueling fee, **fill the tank just before you turn in the car**—but be aware that gas stations near the rental outlet may overcharge.

THE CHANNEL TUNNEL

The "Chunnel" is the fastest way to cross the English Channel short of flying—35 minutes from Folkestone to Calais, 60 minutes from motorway to motorway, or 3 hours from Waterloo, London, to Paris's Gare du Nord. It

consists of two large 50-kilometer- (31-mile-) long train tunnels, and a smaller service tunnel running between them.

CHILDREN & TRAVEL

Spaniards love children, and bringing them along on your trip should not be a problem. You will see children accompanying their parents everywhere, including bars and restaurants. Shopkeepers will shower your child with *caramelos* (sweets), and even the coldest waiters tend to be friendlier when you have a youngster with you. But although you will not be shunted into a remote corner when you bring children into a Spanish restaurant, **you won't find high chairs or special kids' menus.** Children are expected to eat what their parents do, and it is perfectly acceptable to ask for an extra plate and share your food. Museum admissions and bus and metro rides are generally free for children up to age five. Be prepared for late bedtimes. Especially in summer, it is surprisingly common to see under-fives playing cheerfully outdoors until midnight. Disposable diapers (*pañales*), formula (*papillas*), and bottled baby foods are readily available at supermarkets and pharmacies.

When traveling with children, **plan ahead** and **involve your youngsters** as you outline your trip. When packing, **include a supply of things to keep them busy** en route (☞ Children & Travel *in* Important Contacts A to Z). On sightseeing days, try to **schedule activities of special interest to your children,** like a trip to a zoo or a playground. If you **plan your itinerary around seasonal festivals,** you'll never lack for things to do. In addition, **check local newspapers for special events** mounted by public libraries, museums, and parks.

BABY-SITTING

For recommended local sitters, **check with your hotel desk.**

DRIVING

If you are renting a car, don't forget to **arrange for a car seat when you reserve.** Sometimes they're free.

FLYING

Always **ask about discounted children's fares.** On international flights, infants under 2 not occupying a seat generally travel free or for 10% of the accompanying adult's fare; the fare for children ages 2–11 is usually half to two-thirds of the adult fare. On domestic flights, children under 2 not occupying a seat travel free, and older children are charged at the lowest applicable adult rate.

BAGGAGE➤ In general, the adult baggage allowance applies to children paying half or more of the adult fare. If you are traveling with an infant, **ask about carry-on allowances** before departure. In general, for infants charged 10% of the adult fare you are allowed one carry-on bag and a collapsible stroller; you may be limited to less if the flight is full.

SAFETY SEATS➤ According to the FAA, it's a good idea to **use safety seats aloft** for children weighing less than 40 pounds. Airline policies vary. U.S. carriers allow FAA-approved models but usually require that you buy a ticket, even if your child would otherwise ride free, since the seats must be strapped into regular seats. Foreign carriers may not allow infant seats, may charge a child rather than an infant fare for their use, or may require you to hold your baby during takeoff and landing—defeating the seat's purpose.

FACILITIES➤ When making your reservation, **request for children's meals or freestanding bassinets** if you need them; the latter are available only to those seated at the bulkhead, where there's enough legroom. If you don't need a bassinet, **think twice before requesting bulkhead seats**—the only storage space for in-flight necessities is in inconveniently distant overhead bins.

LODGING

Most hotels allow children under a certain age to stay in their parents' room at no extra charge; others charge them as extra adults. Be sure to **ask about the cutoff age.**

CUSTOMS & DUTIES

IN SPAIN

From countries that are not part of the EU, visitors age 15 and over are permitted to bring into Spain up to 200 cigarettes or 50 cigars, up to 1 liter of alcohol over 22 proof, and up to 2 liters of wine. Dogs and cats are admitted, providing they have up-to-date vaccination records from their home country.

IN THE U.S.

You may bring home $400 worth of foreign goods duty-free if you've been out of the country for at least 48 hours and haven't already used the $400 allowance, or any part of it, in the past 30 days.

Travelers 21 or older may bring back 1 liter of alcohol duty-free, provided the beverage laws of the state through which they reenter the United States allow it. In addition, regardless of their age, they are allowed 100 non-Cuban cigars and 200 cigarettes. Antiques and works of art more than 100 years old are duty-free.

Duty-free, travelers may mail packages valued at up to $200 to themselves and up to $100 to others, with a limit of one parcel per addressee per day (and no alcohol or tobacco products or perfume valued at more than $5); on the outside, the package should be labeled as being either for personal use or an unsolicited gift, and a list of its contents and their retail value should be attached. Mailed items do not affect your duty-free allowance on your return.

IN CANADA

If you've been out of Canada for at least seven days, you may bring in C$500 worth of goods duty-free. If you've been away for fewer than seven days but for more than 48 hours, the duty-free allowance drops to C$200; if your trip lasts between 24 and 48 hours, the allowance is C$50. You cannot pool allowances with family members. Goods claimed under the C$500 exemption may follow you by mail; those claimed under the lesser exemptions must accompany you.

Alcohol and tobacco products may be included in the seven-day and 48-hour exemptions but not in the 24-hour exemption. If you meet the age requirements of the province or territory through which you reenter Canada, you may bring in, duty-free, 1.14 liters (40 imperial ounces) of wine or liquor *or* 24 12-ounce cans or bottles of beer or ale. If you are 16 or older, you may bring in, duty-free, 200 cigarettes, 50 cigars or cigarillos, and 400 tobacco sticks or 400 grams of manufactured tobacco. Alcohol and tobacco must accompany you on your return.

An unlimited number of gifts with a value of up to C$60 each may be mailed to Canada duty-free. These do not affect your duty-free allowance on your return. Label the package "Unsolicited Gift—Value Under $60." Alcohol and tobacco are excluded.

IN THE U.K.

If your journey was wholly within European Union (EU) countries, you no longer need to pass through customs when you return to the United Kingdom. If you plan to bring back large quantities of alcohol or tobacco, check in advance on EU limits.

D

DISABILITIES & ACCESSIBILITY

Unfortunately, Spain has done little to make traveling easy for visitors with disabilities; however, **most public buildings constructed within the past five years are accessible.** Only the Prado and newer museums, such as the Reina Sofía and the Thyssen-Bornemisza museum in Madrid, have entrances or elevators that are accessible for people who use wheelchairs. Most of the churches, castles, and monasteries on a tourist's itinerary involve quite a bit of walking and climbing uneven terrain.

When discussing accessibility with an operator or reservationist, **ask hard questions.** Are there any stairs, inside *or* out? Are there grab bars next to the toilet *and* in the shower/tub? How wide is the doorway to the room? To the bathroom? For the most extensive facilities, meeting the latest legal specifications, **opt for newer accommodations,** which more often have been designed with access in mind. Older properties or ships must usually be retrofitted and may offer more

limited facilities as a result. Be sure to **discuss your needs before booking.**

DISCOUNTS & DEALS

You shouldn't have to pay for a discount. In fact, you may already be eligible for all kinds of savings. Here are some time-honored strategies for getting the best deal.

LOOK IN YOUR WALLET

When you **use your credit card to make travel purchases,** you may get free travel-accident insurance, collision damage insurance, medical or legal assistance, depending on the card and bank that issued it. Visa and MasterCard provide one or more of these services, so **get a copy of your card's travel benefits.** If you are a member of the AAA or an oil-company-sponsored road-assistance plan, always **ask hotel or car-rental reservationists for auto-club discounts.** Some clubs offer additional discounts on tours, cruises, or admission to attractions. And don't forget that auto-club membership entitles you to free maps and trip-planning services.

SENIORS CITIZENS & STUDENTS

As a senior-citizen traveler, you may be eligible for special rates, but you should mention your senior-citizen status up front. If you're a student or under 26 you can also get discounts, especially if you have an official ID card (☞ Senior-

Citizen Discounts *and* Students on the Road, *below*).

DIAL FOR DOLLARS

To save money, **look into "1-800" discount reservations services,** which often have lower rates. These services use their buying power to get a better price on hotels, airline tickets, and sometimes even car rentals. When booking a room, always **call the hotel's local toll-free number** (if one is available) rather than the central reservations number—you'll often get a better price. Ask the reservationist about special packages or corporate rates, which are usually available even if you're not traveling on business.

JOIN A CLUB?

Discount clubs can be a legitimate source of savings, but you must use the participating hotels and visit the participating attractions in order to realize any benefits. Remember, too, that you have to pay a fee to join, so **determine if you'll save enough to warrant your membership fee.** Before booking with a club, **make sure the hotel or other supplier isn't offering a better deal.**

GET A GUARANTEE

When shopping for the best deal on hotels and car rentals, **look for guaranteed exchange rates,** which protect you against a falling dollar. With your rate locked in, you won't pay more even if the price goes up in the local currency.

DRIVING

Driving is the best way to see rural areas and get off the beaten track. Roads are classified as follows: A for *autopista* (toll road or *peaje*); N for *nacional* (main roads that are either divided highways or two lanes); and C for *comarcal* (local roads that crisscross the countryside).

Spain's highway system now includes some 6,000 km (3,600 mi) of superhighways. Still, you'll find some stretches of major national highways that are two lanes wide, where traffic often backs up behind heavy trucks. Autopista tolls are steep.

Most Spanish **cities have notoriously long morning and evening rush hours** that can try any driver's patience. Traffic jams (*atascos*) are especially bad in and surrounding Barcelona and Madrid, where the morning rush hour can last until noon. Evening rush hour runs from 7 PM to 9 PM.

Driving is on the right, and **horns are banned in cities,** but that doesn't keep Spaniards from blasting away. Children under 10 may not ride in the front seats, and seat belts are compulsory everywhere. Speed limits are 60 km per hour (37 mph) in cities, 100 km per hour (62 mph) on N roads, 120 km per hour (74 mph) on the autopista, and 90 km per hour (56 mph) unless otherwise signposted on other roads.

Gas stations are plentiful. Prices, decontrolled in 1993, were 112 ptas. a liter for *normal* (regular; 92 octane) and 117 ptas. a liter for *super* (97 octane) at press time. Many small-town service stations do not sell unleaded gas. Credit cards are frequently accepted, especially along main routes.

G

GAY & LESBIAN TRAVEL

Since the end of Franco's dictatorship, the situation for gays and lesbians has improved dramatically: The paragraph in the Spanish civil code that made homosexuality a crime was repealed in 1978. However, violence against gays does exist.

During the summer, the beaches of the Balearics (especially Ibiza), the Costa del Sol (Torremolinos and Benidorm), and the Costa Brava (Sitges and Lloret del Mar) are gay and lesbian hot spots; Playa del Inglés and Maspaloma in the Canary Islands are popular in winter.

H

HEALTH CONCERNS

Two problems frequently encountered during Spanish summers are sunburn and sunstroke. On hot, sunny days, even people who are not normally bothered by strong sun should cover themselves with a long-sleeve shirt, a hat, and long pants or a beach wrap. These are essential for a day at the beach but are also advisable for a long day of touring. Carry some sunblock lotion for nose, ears, and other sensitive areas, such as eyelids or ankles. Be sure to drink enough liquids. Above all, limit your sun time for the first few days until you become accustomed to the heat.

Spain has recently had the highest number of AIDS cases in Europe. Those applying for work permits will be asked for proof of HIV-negative status.

HOLIDAYS

National holidays include: January 1, January 6 (Epiphany), March 19 (St. Joseph), April 5 (Good Friday), April 8 (Easter Monday), May 1 (May Day), August 15 (Assumption), October 12 (National Day), November 1 (All Saints Day), December 6 (Constitution), December 8 (Immaculate Conception), December 25, and December 26 (Boxing Day).

In addition, each city and town has its own holidays honoring political events and patron saints. Madrid holidays include May 2 (Madrid Day), May 15 (San Isidro), and November 9 (Almudena). Barcelona celebrates April 23 (Sant Jordi), September 11 (Catalunya Day), and September 24 (Merced). Valencia's community day is October 9.

If a public holiday falls on a Tuesday or Thursday, **many businesses also close on the nearest Monday or Friday**

for a long weekend called a *puente* (bridge).

I
INSURANCE

Travel insurance can protect your monetary investment, replace your luggage and its contents, or provide for medical coverage should you fall ill during your trip. Most tour operators, travel agents, and insurance agents sell specialized health-and-accident, flight, trip-cancellation, and luggage insurance as well as comprehensive policies with some or all of these coverages. Comprehensive policies may also reimburse you for delays due to weather—an important consideration if you're traveling during the winter months. Some health-insurance policies do not cover preexisting conditions, but waivers may be available in specific cases. Coverage is sold by the companies listed in Important Contacts A to Z; these companies act as the policy's administrators. The actual insurance is usually underwritten by a well-known name, such as The Travelers or Continental Insurance.

Before you make any purchase, **review your existing health and homeowner's policies** to find out whether they cover expenses incurred while traveling.

BAGGAGE

Airline liability for baggage is limited to $1,250 per person on domestic flights. On international flights, it amounts to $9.07 per

pound or $20 per kilogram for checked baggage (roughly $640 per 70-pound bag) and $400 per passenger for unchecked baggage. Insurance for losses exceeding the terms of your airline ticket can be bought directly from the airline at check-in for about $10 per $1,000 of coverage; note that it excludes a rather extensive list of items, shown on your airline ticket.

COMPREHENSIVE

Comprehensive insurance policies include all the coverages described above plus some that may not be available in more specific policies. If you have purchased an expensive vacation, especially one that involves travel abroad, comprehensive insurance is a must; **look for policies that include trip delay insurance,** which will protect you in the event that weather problems cause you to miss your flight, tour, or cruise. A few insurers will also sell you a waiver for preexisting medical conditions. Some of the companies that offer both these features are Access America, Carefree Travel, Travel Insured International, and TravelGuard (☞ Insurance *in* Important Contacts A to Z).

FLIGHT

You should **think twice before buying flight insurance.** Often purchased as a last-minute impulse at the airport, it pays a lump sum when a plane crashes, either to a beneficiary if the insured dies or sometimes to a surviving passenger who loses his or her eyesight or a limb. Supplementing the airlines' coverage described in the limits-of-liability paragraphs on your ticket, it's expensive and basically unnecessary. Charging an airline ticket to a major credit card often automatically provides you with coverage that may also extend to travel by bus, train, and ship.

HEALTH

Medicare generally does not cover health care costs outside the United States; nor do many privately issued policies. If your own health insurance policy does not cover you outside the United States, **consider buying supplemental medical coverage.** It can reimburse you for $1,000–$150,000 worth of medical and/or dental expenses incurred as a result of an accident or illness during a trip. These policies also may include a personal-accident, or death-and-dismemberment, provision, which pays a lump sum ranging from $15,000 to $500,000 to your beneficiaries if you die or to you if you lose one or more limbs or your eyesight, and a medical-assistance provision, which may either reimburse you for the cost of referrals, evacuation, or repatriation and other services, or automatically enroll you as a member of a particular medical-assistance company. (☞ Health Issues *in* Important Contacts A to Z.)

U.K. TRAVELERS

You can buy an annual travel insurance policy valid for most vacations during the year in which it's purchased. If you are pregnant or have a preexisting medical condition make sure you're covered before buying such a policy.

TRIP

Without insurance, you will lose all or most of your money if you cancel your trip regardless of the reason. Especially if your airline ticket, cruise, or package tour is nonrefundable and cannot be changed, it's essential that you **buy trip-cancellation-and-interruption insurance.** When considering how much coverage you need, look for a policy that will cover the cost of your trip plus the nondiscounted price of a one-way airline ticket should you need to return home early. Read the fine print carefully, especially sections that define "family member" and "preexisting medical conditions." Also **consider default or bankruptcy insurance,** which protects you against a supplier's failure to deliver. Be aware, however, that if you buy such a policy from a travel agency, tour operator, airline, or cruise line, it may not cover default by the firm in question.

L

LANGUAGE

Although Spaniards exported their language to all Central and South America, you may be surprised to find that **Spanish is not the principal language of many regions of Spain.** The Basques speak Euskera; in Catalunya (Catalonia), you'll hear Catalan; in Galicia, Gallego; and in Valencia, Valeniciano. While almost everyone in these regions also speaks and understands Spanish, local radio and television stations broadcast in these languages and road signs are either printed or spray-painted over with the preferred regional language. Spanish is referred to as Castellano, or Castilian.

Roughly half the people you come in contact with will speak some English. But they may speak the British variety, so don't be surprised if you are told to queue (line up) or take the lift (elevator) to the loo (toilet). All your attempts at Spanish are genuinely appreciated, and Spaniards will not make fun of your mistakes. Try to use at least the following basic phrases: *por favor* (please), *gracias* (thank you), *buenos días* (hello—until 2 PM), *buenas tardes* (good afternoon—until 8 PM), *buenas noches* (hello—after dark), *adiós* (good-bye), *encantado/encantada* (pleased to meet you), *sí* (yes), *no* (no), *los servicios* (the toilets), *la cuenta* (bill/check), *habla inglés?* (do you speak English?), *no comprendo* (I don't understand). Many guided tours offered at museums and historic sites are in Spanish; ask about the language that will be spoken before signing up.

LODGING

The government has spent decades buying up old castles and historic buildings and converting them into outstanding lodgings for its parador hotel chain. The rest of Spain's hotels tend to be newish high-rises, although there is a growing trend toward the restoration of historic buildings. By law, prices must be posted at the reception desk and should indicate whether tax is included. Breakfast is not usually included in the price of a room.

APARTMENT & VILLA RENTAL

If you want a home base that's roomy enough for a family and comes with cooking facilities, **consider taking a furnished rental.** This can also save you money, but not always—some rentals are luxury properties (economical only when your party is large). Home-exchange directories list rentals—often second homes owned by prospective house swappers—and some services search for a house or apartment for you (even a castle if that's your fancy) and handle the paperwork. Some send an illustrated catalog; others send photographs only of specific properties, sometimes at a charge; up-front registration fees may apply.

HOME EXCHANGE

If you would like to find a house, an apartment, or some other type of vacation property to exchange for your own while on holiday, **be-come a member of a home-exchange organization,** which will send you its updated listings of available exchanges for a year, and will include your own listing in at least one of them. Arrangements for the actual exchange are made by the two parties involved, not by the organization.

HOTELS

Hotels are rated by the government with one to five stars. While quality is a factor, the **ratings also indicate how many facilities the hotel offers.** You may find a three-star hotel just as good as a four-star hotel, but lacking a swimming pool, for example.

The major private hotel groups in Spain include the upscale Melia chain and the moderately priced Tryp and Sol chains. Dozens of reasonably priced beachside high-rises along the coast cater to package tours.

High-season rates prevail not only in summer, but also during Easter week and local fiesta periods.

PARADORS

There are about 100 paradors in Spain: Some are in castles on a hill with sweeping views; others are in historic monasteries or convents filled with art treasures; still others are in modern buildings on Spain's choicest beachfront property. Prices are reasonable, considering that most paradors are four- and five-star hotels. Paradors are immaculate and tastefully furnished, often with antiques or repro-ductions. All have restaurants that serve some regional special-ties. You can stop for a meal or a drink without spending the night. Breakfast, however, is an expensive buffet, and you'll do better to go down the street for a cup of coffee and a roll.

Because paradors are extremely popular with foreigners and Spaniards alike, **make reservations well in advance.**

M
MAIL

Airmail letters to the United States and Canada cost 87 ptas. up to 15 grams. Letters to the United Kingdom and other EU countries cost 62 ptas. up to 20 grams. Letters within Spain are 30 ptas. Postcards are charged the same rate as letters. Letters and postcards mailed within the same city are 17 ptas. Stamps can be bought at post offices and government-run tobacco shops.

RECEIVING MAIL

Because mail delivery in Spain can often be slow and unreliable, it is best to have your mail sent to American Express. An alternative is to have mail held at a Spanish post office; have it addressed to **Lista de Correos** (general deliv-ery) in a town you will be visiting. Postal addresses should in-clude the name of the province in parentheses, e.g., Marbella (Málaga).

MEDICAL ASSISTANCE

No one plans to get sick while traveling, but it

happens, so **consider signing up with a medical assistance company.** These outfits provide referrals, emergency evacuation or repatriation, 24-hour telephone hot lines for medical consultation, cash for emergencies, and other personal and legal assistance. They also dispatch medical personnel and arrange for the relay of medical records.

MONEY & EXPENSES

The peseta (pta.) is Spain's currency unit. Bills are 10,000, 5,000, 2,000, and 1,000 ptas. Coins are 500, 200, 100, 50, 25, 10, 5, and 1 pta. Be careful not to mix up the 100- and 500-pta. coins—they are the same color and almost the same size. There are two types of 25-pta. coins, large silver ones and small bronze ones with a hole in the center. Five-pta. coins are always called *duros,* but watch out for the new microsize 1- and 5-pta coins. At press time (spring 1996) the currency markets of Europe were highly unstable, with exchange rates of 121 ptas. to the U.S. dollar, 89 ptas. per Canadian dollar, and 186 ptas. to the pound sterling.

ATMS

CASH ADVANCES➤ Cirrus, Plus, and many other networks that connect automated teller machines operate internationally. Chances are that you can **use your bank card, MasterCard, or Visa at ATMs to** withdraw money from an account or get a cash

advance. Before leaving home, **check on frequency limits** for withdrawals and cash advances. Also **ask whether your card's PIN must be reprogrammed** for use in Spain. Four-digit numbers are commonly used overseas. Note that Discover is accepted mostly in the United States.

TRANSACTION FEES➤ On credit-card cash advances you are charged interest from the day you receive the money, whether from a teller or an ATM. Although fees charged for ATM transactions may be higher abroad than at home, Cirrus and Plus exchange rates are excellent, because they are based on wholesale rates offered only by major banks.

COSTS

Coffee in a bar: 125 ptas. (standing), 150 ptas. (seated). Beer in a bar: 125 ptas. (standing), 150 ptas. (seated). Small glass of wine in a bar: 100 ptas. Soft drink: 150–200 ptas. a bottle. Ham-and-cheese sandwich: 300–450 ptas. One-mile taxi ride: 400 ptas, but the meter keeps ticking in traffic jams. Local bus or subway ride:125–150 ptas. Movie-theater seat: 500–600 ptas. Foreign newspaper: 225 ptas.

EXCHANGING CURRENCY

For the most favorable rates, **change money at banks.** You won't do as well at exchange booths in airports or rail and bus stations, in hotels, in restaurants, or in stores, although you

may find their hours more convenient. To avoid lines at airport exchange booths, **get a small amount of the local currency before you leave home.**

TAXES

Value-added tax (or sales tax) is called IVA in Spain. It is charged on services, such as hotels and restaurants, and many categories of consumer products. When in doubt as to whether tax is included, ask, *Está incluido el IVA* (ee-vah)?

HOTEL AND RESTAURANT➤ The IVA rate (7%) is the same for all categories of restaurants and hotels, regardless of their number of forks or stars. A special tax law for the Canary Islands allows all hotels and restaurants there to charge 4% IVA. Menus will generally say at the bottom whether tax is included (*IVA incluido*) or not (*más 7% IVA*).

VAT➤ A number of **shops, particularly large stores and boutiques in holiday resorts, offer a refund of 16% IVA sales tax on purchases of more than 15,000 ptas.** You show your passport, fill out a form, and the store then mails you the refund at your home. The receipt must detail the purchase, IVA paid, be signed by vendor and customer, and be sealed.

You can also present your original receipt in the VAT office at the airport (there is an IVA booth in both the Barcelona and Madrid airports near the duty-free shops). Customs signs the original and gives it back to the tourist, who mails it to the vendor. The vendor will then mail the refund to the purchaser.

TRAVELER'S CHECKS

Whether or not to buy traveler's checks depends on where you are headed; **take cash to rural areas and small towns, traveler's checks to cities.** The most widely recognized checks are issued by American Express, Citicorp, Thomas Cook, and Visa. These are sold by major commercial banks for 1%–3% of the checks' face value—it pays to **shop around.** Both American Express and Thomas Cook issue checks that can be countersigned and used by either you or your traveling companion. So you won't be left with excess foreign currency, **buy a few checks in small denominations** to cash toward the end of your trip. Before leaving home, **contact your issuer for information on where to cash your checks** without a incurring a transaction fee. Record the numbers of all your checks, and keep this listing in a separate place, crossing off the numbers of checks you have cashed.

WIRING MONEY

For a fee of 3%–10%, depending on the amount of the transaction, you can have money sent to you from home through Money-Gram^{SM} or Western Union (☞ Money Matters *in* Important Contacts A to Z). The transferred funds and the service fee can be charged to a Master-Card or Visa account.

P

PACKING FOR SPAIN

Pack light. Although baggage carts are free and plentiful in most Spanish airports, they are rare in train and bus stations.

On the whole, **Spaniards dress up more than Americans or the British.** What you bring will depend a great deal on what time of year you visit. Summer will be hot nearly everywhere, but **don't forget a raincoat or an umbrella.** Visits in winter, fall, and spring call for warm clothing and boots.

It is sensible to wear casual, comfortable clothing and shoes when sightseeing, but **dressier outfits are required for the cities, especially at fine restaurants and nightclubs.** American tourists can be spotted easily in Spain because they are the ones wearing sneakers. If you want to blend in, wear leather shoes.

On the beach, anything goes; it is common to see females of all ages wearing only bikini bottoms, and **many of the more remote beaches allow nude sunbathing.** Bring a cover-up to wear over your bathing suit when you leave the beach.

Bring an extra pair of eyeglasses or contact lenses in your carry-on luggage, and if you have a health problem, **pack enough medication** to last the trip or have your doctor write you a prescription using the drug's generic name, because brand names vary from country to country (you'll then need a duplicate prescription from a local doctor). It's important that you **don't put prescription drugs or valuables in luggage to be checked,** for it could go astray. To avoid problems with customs officials, carry medications in the original packaging. Also, don't forget the addresses of offices that handle refunds of lost traveler's checks.

ELECTRICITY

To use your U.S.-purchased electric-powered equipment, **bring a converter and an adapter.** The electrical current in Spain is 220 volts, 50 cycles alternating current (AC); wall outlets take Continental-type plugs, with two round prongs.

If your appliances are dual-voltage, you'll need only an adapter. Hotels sometimes have 110-volt outlets for low-wattage appliances near the sink, marked FOR SHAVERS ONLY; don't use them for high-wattage appliances like blow-dryers. If your laptop computer is older, carry a converter; new laptops operate equally well on 110 and 220 volts, so you need only an adapter.

LUGGAGE

Airline baggage allowances depend on the airline, the route, and the class of your ticket; ask in advance. In general, on domestic flights and on international flights between the United States and foreign destinations, you are entitled to check two bags. A third piece may be brought on board, but it must fit easily under the seat in front of you or in the overhead compartment. In the United States, the FAA gives airlines broad latitude regarding carry-on allowances, and they tend to tailor them to different aircraft and operational conditions. Charges for excess, oversize, or overweight pieces vary.

If you are flying between two foreign destinations, note that baggage allowances may be determined not by piece but by weight—generally 88 pounds (40 kilograms) in first class, 66 pounds (30 kilograms) in business class, and 44 pounds (20 kilograms) in economy. If your flight between two cities abroad *connects* with your transatlantic or transpacific flight, the piece method still applies.

SAFEGUARDING YOUR LUGGAGE➤ Before leaving home, **itemize your bags' contents** and their worth, and label them with your name, address, and phone number. (If you use your home address, cover it so that potential thieves can't see it readily.) Inside each bag, **pack a copy of your itinerary.** At check-in, **make sure that each bag is correctly tagged** with the destination airport's three-letter code. If your bags arrive damaged—or fail to arrive at all—file a

written report with the airline before leaving the airport.

PASSPORTS & VISAS

If you don't already have one, **get a passport.** It is advisable that you **leave one photocopy of your passport's data page** with someone at home and keep another with you, separated from your passport, while traveling. If you lose your passport, promptly call the nearest embassy or consulate and the local police; having the data page information can speed replacement.

IN THE U.S.

All U.S. citizens, even infants, need only a valid passport to enter Spain for stays of up to 90 days. Application forms for both first-time and renewal passports are available at any of the 13 U.S. Passport Agency offices and at some post offices and courthouses. Passports are usually mailed within four weeks; allow five weeks or more in spring and summer.

CANADIANS

You need only a valid passport to enter Spain for stays of up to 90 days. Passport application forms are available at 28 regional passport offices, as well as post offices and travel agencies. Whether for a first or a renewal passport, you must apply in person. Children under 16 may be included on a parent's passport but must have their own to travel alone. Passports are valid for five years and are usually mailed

within two to three weeks of application.

U.K. CITIZENS

Citizens of the United Kingdom need only a valid passport to enter Spain for stays of up to 90 days. Applications for new and renewal passports are available from main post offices and at the passport offices in Belfast, Glasgow, Liverpool, London, Newport, and Peterborough. You may apply in person at all passport offices, or by mail to all except the London office. Children under 16 may travel on an accompanying parent's passport. All passports are valid for 10 years. Allow a month for processing.

S

SENIOR-CITIZEN DISCOUNTS

To qualify for age-related discounts, **mention your senior-citizen status up front** when booking hotel reservations, not when checking out, and before you're seated in restaurants, not when paying the bill. Note that discounts may be limited to certain menus, days, or hours. When renting a car, **ask about promotional car-rental discounts**—they can net even lower costs than your senior-citizen discount.

STUDENTS ON THE ROAD

To save money, **look into deals available through student-oriented travel agencies.** To qualify, you'll need to have a bona fide student ID card. Members of international student groups are also eligible (☞ Students *in* Important Contacts A to Z).

T

TELEPHONES

LONG-DISTANCE

To call other provinces from within Spain, both from pay and private phones, dial the area code first. Large cities such as Madrid (91), Barcelona (93), Bilbao (94), Sevilla (95), and Valencia (96), have a two-digit area code followed by a seven-digit local number. A massive overhaul of the telephone system aims to install this pattern throughout Spain, but less-populated regions still have a three-digit area code followed by a six-digit local number. All provincial codes begin with a 9, but you don't need to use the 9 when dialing from outside Spain.

International calls are awkward from public pay phones because of the enormous amount of coins needed, and can be expensive from hotels, which often add a surcharge. The best way to make them is to go to the local telephone office. Every town has one, and big cities have several. When the call is connected, you will be sent to a quiet cubicle, and you will be charged according to the meter. If the price is 500 ptas. or more, you can pay with Visa or Master-Card.

To make an international call yourself, dial 07 and wait for a loud tone. Then dial the country code (1 for the United States, 01 for Canada, 44 for the United Kingdom), followed by the area code and number.

The long-distance services of AT&T, MCI, and Sprint make calling home relatively convenient, but in many hotels you may find it impossible to dial the access number. The hotel operator may also refuse to make the connection. Instead, the hotel will charge you a premium rate—as much as 400% more than a calling card—for calls placed from your hotel room. To avoid such price gouging, travel with more than one company's long-distance calling card—a hotel may block Sprint but not MCI. If the hotel operator claims that you cannot use any phone card, ask to be connected to an international operator, who will help you to access your phone card. You can also dial the international operator yourself. If none of this works, try calling your phone company collect in the United States. If collect calls are also blocked, call from a pay phone in the hotel lobby. Before you go, **find out the local access codes** for your destinations.

OPERATORS AND INFORMATION

For general information in Spain, dial 003; the international information and assistance operator is at 025 (some operators do speak English).

PAY PHONES

There are three types of pay phones in Spain, all of them bright green. The most common kind has a digital readout, so you can see your money ticking away. You need at least 25 ptas. for a local call, 75 ptas. to call another province. Simply insert coins and wait for a dial tone. (At older models, you must line coins up in a groove on top of the dial and they drop down as needed.) Neither model accepts the new microsize 5- and 10-pta. coins or the small 25-pta. coins.

Newer pay phones work on special telephone credit cards, which can be purchased at any tobacco shop for 1,000 or 2,000 ptas.

TIPPING

Pride keeps Spaniards from acknowledging tips, but waiters and other service people are poorly paid, and you can be sure your contribution will be appreciated. On the other hand, if you run into some bad or surly service, don't feel obligated to leave a tip.

Restaurant checks may or may not include service, but **no more than 10% of the bill is necessary for a tip,** and if you eat tapas or sandwiches at a bar, leave less, enough to round out the bill to the nearest 100. Cocktail servers get 50–75 ptas. a drink, depending on the bar.

Taxi drivers get about 10% of the total fare, but more for long rides or extra help with luggage, although there is an official surcharge for airport runs and baggage.

Hotel porters are tipped 50–100 ptas. a bag; 50–100 ptas. also goes to someone who brings you room service. A doorman who calls a taxi for you gets 100 ptas. If you stay in a hotel for more than two nights, tip the maid about 100 ptas. per night. A concierge should be tipped for any additional help he or she gives you.

Tour guides should be tipped about 300 ptas., ushers in theaters or bullfights 25–50 ptas., barbers 100 ptas., and ladies' hairdressers at least 200 for a wash and set. Washroom attendants are tipped 10–25 ptas.

TOUR OPERATORS

A package or tour to Spain can make your vacation less expensive and more hassle-free. Firms that sell tours and packages reserve airline seats, hotel rooms, and rental cars in bulk and pass some of the savings on to you. In addition, the best operators have local representatives available to help you at your destination.

A GOOD DEAL?

The more your package or tour includes, the better you can predict the ultimate cost of your vacation. Make sure you know exactly what is covered, and **beware of hidden costs.** Are taxes, tips, and service charges included? Transfers and baggage handling? Entertainment and excursions? These can add up.

Most packages and tours are rated deluxe, first-class superior, first

class, tourist, or budget. The key difference is usually accommodations. If the package or tour you are considering is priced lower than in your wildest dreams, **be skeptical.** Also, **make sure your travel agent knows the accommodations** and other services. Ask about the hotel's location, room size, beds, and whether it has a pool, room service, or programs for children, if you care about these. Has your agent been there in person or sent others you can contact?

BUYER BEWARE

Each year a number of consumers are stranded or lose their money when operators—even very large ones with excellent reputations— go out of business. To avoid becoming one of them, take the time to **check out the operator**—find out how long the company has been in business and ask several agents about its reputation. Next, **don't book unless the firm has a consumer-protection program.** Members of the USTOA and the NTA are required to set aside funds for the sole purpose of covering your payments and travel arrangements in case of default. Nonmember operators may instead carry insurance; look for the details in the operator's brochure— and for the name of an underwriter with a solid reputation. Note: When it comes to tour operators, **don't trust escrow accounts.** Although there are laws governing those of charter-flight operators, no

governmental body prevents tour operators from raiding the till.

Next, **contact your local Better Business Bureau and the attorney general's offices** in both your own state and the operator's; have any complaints been filed? Finally, **pay with a major credit card.** Then you can cancel payment, provided that you can document your complaint. Always **consider trip-cancellation insurance** (☞ Insurance, *above*).

Big vs. Small➤ Operators that handle several hundred thousand travelers per year can use their purchasing power to give you a good price. Their high volume may also indicate financial stability. But some small companies provide more personalized service; because they tend to specialize, they may also be more knowledgeable about a given area.

USING AN AGENT

Travel agents are excellent resources. In fact, large operators accept bookings made only through travel agents. But it's good to **collect brochures from several agencies** because some agents' suggestions may be skewed by promotional relationships with tour and package firms that reward them for volume sales. If you have a special interest, **find an agent with expertise in that area;** ASTA can provide leads in the United States. (Don't rely solely on your agent, though; agents may be unaware of small-niche operators, and some special-interest travel companies only sell direct.)

SINGLE TRAVELERS

Prices are usually quoted per person, based on two sharing a room. If traveling solo, you may be required to pay the full double-occupancy rate. Some operators eliminate this surcharge if you agree to be matched up with a roommate of the same sex, even if one is not found by departure time.

TRAIN TRAVEL

International overnight trains run from Madrid to Lisbon and Barcelona to Paris (both 11½ hours). A daytime trip is offered from Barcelona to Grenoble and Geneva (10 hours).

If you purchase a same-day round-trip ticket while in Spain, a 20% discount applies; if you purchase a different-day round-trip ticket, you will get a 10% discount.

DISCOUNT PASSES

If Spain is your only destination in Europe, **consider purchasing a Spain Flexipass.** Prices begin at $144 for three-days of second-class travel within a two-month period and $180 for first class. Passes good for more days and for longer periods are also available.

Spain is one of 17 countries in which you can **use EurailPasses,** which provide unlimited first-class rail travel, in all of the participating countries, for the duration of the pass. If you plan to rack up the miles, get a standard pass. These

are available for 15 days ($522), 21 days ($678), one month ($838), two months ($1,148), and 3 months ($1,468). If your plans call for only limited train travel, **look into a Europass,** which costs less money than a EurailPass. Unlike EurailPasses, however, you get a limited number of travel days, in a limited number of countries, during a specified time period. For example, a two month pass ($316) allows between five and fifteen days of rail travel, but costs $200 less than the least expensive EurailPass. Keep in mind, however, that the Europass is good only in France, Germany, Italy, Spain, and Switzerland, and the number of countries you can visit is further limited by the type of pass you buy. For example, the basic two-month pass allows you to visit only three of the five participating countries.

In addition to standard EurailPasses, **ask about special rail-pass plans.** Among these are the Eurail Youthpass (for those under age 26), the Eurail Saverpass (which gives a discount for two or more people traveling together), a Eurail Flexipass (which allows a certain number of travel days within a set period), the Euraildrive Pass and the Europass Drive (which combines travel by train and rental car).

Whichever pass you choose, remember that you must **purchase your pass before you leave** for Europe.

Many travelers assume that rail passes guarantee them seats on the trains they wish to ride. Not so. You need to **book seats ahead even if you are using a rail pass;** seat reservations are required on some European trains, particularly high-speed trains, and are a good idea on trains that may be crowded—particularly in summer on popular routes. You will also need a reservation if you purchase sleeping accommodations.

FROM THE U.K.

Train services to Spain are not as frequent, fast, or inexpensive as airplane travel.

To reach Spain from Britain, you have to change trains (and rail stations) in Paris. It's worth paying extra for a "TALGO" express or for the "Puerta del Sol" express to avoid having to change trains again at the Spanish border. Journey time to Paris is around six hours; to Madrid from Paris, an additional 13 hours. Allow at least two hours in Paris for changing trains.

WITHIN SPAIN

Spain's high-speed train, the AVE, travels between Madrid and Seville in less than three hours. However, the rest of the government-run railroad, RENFE, remains below par by European standards. Train travel can be tediously slow, and most long-distance runs are made at night. While overnight trains have comfortable sleeper cars, first-class fares that include a sleeping compartment are about the same as those for air travel.

For most journeys, however, trains are the most economical way to go. First- and second-class seats are reasonably priced, and you can get a bunk in a compartment with five other people for a supplement of about $25. The most comfortable train, TALGO, has a special inverted suspension system designed to give a faster and smoother ride on winding rails. Food in the dining cars and bars is overpriced and uninspired.

Most Spaniards buy train tickets in advance by standing in long lines at the station. But the overworked clerks rarely speak English, so you are better off going to a travel agency that displays the blue and yellow RENFE sign; the price is the same.

TRAVEL GEAR

Travel catalogs specialize in useful items that can **save space when packing** and make life on the road more convenient. Compact alarm clocks, travel irons, travel wallets, and personal-care kits are among the most common items you'll find. They also carry dual-voltage appliances, currency converters and foreign-language phrase books. Some catalogs even carry miniature coffeemakers and water purifiers.

W
WHEN TO GO

May and October, when the weather is generally warm and dry, are considered the best months for touring Spain. May gives you more hours of daylight for sightseeing, while October offers a chance to enjoy the harvest season, especially colorful in Spain's many wine regions.

April is good for catching a glimpse of some of Spain's most spectacular Semana Santa (Holy Week) fiestas. Weather in the southern part of the country warms up enough by April to make sightseeing comfortable.

Because Spain is the number-one destination for European tourists, **the months of June, July, August, and September tend to be crowded and more expensive,** especially along the coasts. Most people find the waters of the Mediterranean too cold for swimming the rest of the year. Beach season on the Atlantic coast is slightly shorter. August is the month when Spaniards take vacations; the annual migration to the beach causes huge traffic jams on August 1 and 31. During August big cities are delightfully relaxed and empty. Small shops and some restaurants shut down for the entire month, but museums remain open.

Summers in Spain are hot; temperatures frequently hit 100°F (38°C), and **air-conditioning is not widely used.** Try to limit your touring to the morning hours and take a siesta in the afternoon. Warm summer nights are one of the most enjoyable things about Spain.

Winters in Spain are mild and rainy along the coasts, especially in Galicia. Elsewhere winter blows bitterly cold. Snow is infrequent except in the mountains, where skiing is possible from December to March in the Pyrenees and other resorts near Granada, Madrid, and Burgos.

CLIMATE

The following are average daily maximum and minimum temperatures for major cities in Spain.

Climate in Spain

MADRID

Jan.	48F	9C	May	70F	21C	Sept.	77F	25C
	36	2		50	10		57	14
Feb.	52F	11C	June	81F	27C	Oct.	66F	19C
	36	2		59	15		50	10
Mar.	59F	15C	July	88F	31C	Nov.	55F	13C
	41	5		63	17		41	5
Apr.	64F	18C	Aug.	86F	30C	Dec.	48F	9C
	45	7		63	17		36	2

BARCELONA

Jan.	55F	13C	May	70F	21C	Sept.	77F	25C
	43	6		57	14		66	19
Feb.	57F	14C	June	77F	25C	Oct.	70F	21C
	45	7		64	18		59	15
Mar.	61F	16C	July	82F	28C	Nov.	61F	16C
	48	9		70	21		52	11
Apr.	64F	18C	Aug.	82F	28C	Dec.	55F	13C
	52	11		70	21		46	8

SEVILLE

Jan.	59F	15C	May	81F	27C	Sept.	90F	32C
	43	6		55	13		64	18
Feb.	63F	17C	June	90F	32C	Oct.	79F	26C
	45	7		63	17		57	14
Mar.	68F	20C	July	97F	36C	Nov.	68F	20C
	48	9		68	20		50	10
Apr.	75F	24C	Aug.	97F	36C	Dec.	61F	16C
	52	11		68	20		45	7

CÓRDOBA

Jan.	55F	13C	May	79F	26C	Sept.	88F	31C
	41	5		55	13		63	17
Feb.	61F	16C	June	90F	32C	Oct.	77F	25C
	43	6		63	17		55	13
Mar.	66F	19C	July	99F	37C	Nov.	66F	19C
	46	8		68	20		48	9
Apr.	73F	23C	Aug.	97F	36C	Dec.	57F	14C
	50	10		68	20		41	5

GRANADA

Jan.	54F	12C	May	73F	23C	Sept.	84F	29C
	36	2		50	10		59	15
Feb.	57F	14C	June	86F	30C	Oct.	73F	23C
	37	3		59	15		50	10
Mar.	63F	17C	July	93F	34C	Nov.	63F	17C
	41	5		63	17		43	6
Apr.	68F	20C	Aug.	91F	33C	Dec.	54F	12C
	45	7		63	17		37	3

THE GOLD GUIDE / SMART TRAVEL TIPS

1 Destination: Spain

A SECOND CHANCE AT A RENAISSANCE

THE SENSE OF EXCITEMENT in Spain today is contagious. Probably the first thing that will strike the visitor is this palpable exhilaration, a feeling that seems to electrify Spain from remote mountain villages to the ritzy avenues in Madrid and Barcelona. Naturally, there are many dark spots in the picture—beggars in the streets, continuing Basque terrorism, huge economic adjustments required by the country's 1986 entry into the European Union—and yet it's difficult not to be infected by the overall optimism. You can see its results, in the general sprucing up of recent years. You can feel it, especially in the bars and restaurants. Life is loved here, and celebrated; few peoples seem to have such a capacity for enjoyment. In many ways, the Spanish have always been like this— Richard Wright, visiting in the 1950s, called it "pagan Spain"—but for 36 years of this century, its citizens lived and labored under a repressive, ultra-conservative regime that ended only with the death of Francisco Franco in 1975. The renaissance that followed has been not just political, but also creative and economic.

Spain is surprising in many ways. In imagining its landscape, you may picture the orange, scorched plains of La Mancha, where Don Quixote tilted, or the softly rolling hills of southern Andalucía, or even the overdeveloped Mediterranean beaches. But after Switzerland, Spain is the most mountainous country in Europe. It is also one of the most geographically diverse: from the soggy northwest (wetter than Ireland) to the airless plains of the central Meseta, from the cascading trout streams of the Pyrenees to the marshes and dunes of Coto Doñana National Park on its southwest Atlantic coast. There are deep caves, lonely coves, rock canyons. There are also mountain meadows, coastal rice paddies, volcanic island peaks. The great, snowy wall of the Pyrenees has always isolated Spain, keeping the people apart from one another.

More than almost any country its size— the second largest in Europe after France—

Spain is characterized by the distinct nature of its many regions and peoples. The Galicians, of the northwest, are descended from the same Celtic tribes that colonized the British Isles. Bagpipes are a local instrument there, and kilts not unheard of; the local language, Gallego, is a mix of Spanish and Portuguese. The Basque Country, east of Galicia and abutting the northern border with France, also has its own language: Euskera, a tongue so strange that linguists are baffled as to where it began. Local pride is fierce here, where independence movements have been strong for centuries. The most famous expression of this separatist yen is the terrorist group ETA (Euskadi Ta Askatasuna), which has killed almost 900 Spaniards over the course of three decades. (The violence is extremely unlikely to affect visitors.) The Catalans, who populate northeastern Spain around Barcelona, speak the country's third regional language, Catalan, which is related to old Provençal; inhabitants of the Balearic islands and Valencia province boast their own local variants. All of these areas, and several others that are less obviously distinct, suffered terribly under Franco's virulent centralism (when regional languages were banned).

The peninsula's early peoples included Basques, Celts, Iberians, Greeks, Romans, and Visigoths. But Christians in the centuries after Christ widely intermarried with Jewish and Arabic minorities. Today, most Spaniards see themselves as purely Catholic, but in fact, almost all have Jewish and Muslim ancestors.

Spain changed from a peasant economy to a modern, capitalist one in remarkably little time. Now a lively economy reaches even provincial towns—despite an enormous official unemployment rate and recession in the early 1990s. Roads, trains, and telephones—once legendary for their poor quality—are being modernized.

Modernity has come at a price. For generations, Spain was the destination of choice for the penniless artist, the adventurer willing to forego comfort for rugged romance. That is now not true. After years of inflation, and a value-added tax imposed as a condition of entry into the European Union, Spain's cost of living compares to that of partners like France. The festivities of 1992—the Olympic Games in Barcelona and the International Exposition in Seville—further inflated hotel and restaurant prices in those cities. But the rate of price increases has slowed, and Americans can now enjoy the benefits of a relatively strong dollar.

SPAIN HAS AN extraordinary heritage of history, art, and architecture. It begins with the caves at Altamira, in which men wearing skins for warmth painted delicate animals on a rock ceiling. From hardscrabble Extremadura, Spain's poorest province, robust adventurers left to explore the New World. Some returned and built great stone palaces in the stark, scrubby landscape. Stretched across northern Spain are the Romanesque churches of the Camino de Santiago (Way of St. James), which in the Middle Ages became the most famous religious pilgrimage in Europe; the journey culminated at the soaring cathedral of Santiago de Compostela. Cave churches of the early Christians, scattered across the north, are a graphic counterpoint. Seville, the pastel-colored city of Don Juan, still clusters elegantly along the banks of the Guadalquivir. More than ten thousand castles dot the peninsula, some merely ruins, others in extraordinarily good shape. Villages of whitewashed buildings, harbors crowded with brightly painted fishing boats, and majestic towns welded to craggy mountaintops are common. Above all, the Spanish countryside remains unchanged, still washed by that subtle light that inspired Velázquez.

The story of this land, a romance-tinged tale of counts and caliphs, crusaders and kings, begins long before formally recorded history. The Basques were among the first here, huddling in the cold mountain valleys of the north. The Iberians came next, apparently crossing the Mediterranean from North Africa around 3,000 BC. The Celts arrived from the north about a thousand years later. The seafaring Phoenicians founded Gadir (now Cádiz) and several southern coastal cities. The parade continued with the Greeks, who settled parts of the east coast, and then the Carthaginians, who founded Cartagena around 225 BC—and who dubbed the country they found Spania. It was a wild, forested place, quite unlike present-day Spain.

Modern civilization really began with the Romans, who expelled the Carthaginians and turned the peninsula into three imperial provinces. The Romans didn't manage to subdue fiercely resisting natives for two centuries ending shortly before the birth of Christ, but their influence was lasting. Evidence of the Roman epoch is found today in the great ruins in Mérida, Segovia, Tarragona, and other cities, in the peninsula's legal system, and in the Latin base for its three Romance languages. In the early fifth century invading barbarians crossed the Pyrenees to attack the weakening Roman empire. The Visigoths, who adopted Christianity, became the dominant force in northern Spain by 419, establishing their kingdom at Toledo.

But they, too, were to fall before the might of invaders, this time that of the Moors, a Berber-led Arab force that crossed the Strait of Gibraltar from North Africa. The Moors swept through the country in an astonishingly short time, meeting only token resistance and beginning almost eight centuries of Muslim rule—a period that in many respects was the pinnacle of Spanish civilization. Unlike the semibarbaric Visigoths, they were extremely cultured. During their reign, Jews, Arabs, and Christians lived together in peace, although many Christians did convert to Islam. The Moors also brought with them the complex irrigation system still used around Valencia, citrus fruits, rice, cotton, sugar, palm trees, and glassmaking. Their influence is evident in modern Spanish, where most words beginning with "al" are Arabic in origin, such as albóndig (meatball), alcalde (mayor), almohada (pillow), and alcázar (fortress). To the visitor, the most spectacular evidence of Moorish culture will be found in modern-day Andalucía, the region the Moors called al-Andalus. The fairy-tale Alhambra, an ocher-color palace that crowns the southern city of Granada, is testimony to the delicacy of the Moorish aesthetic.

The Moors never managed to subdue northwestern Galicia and Asturias, and it was in the latter that a minor Christian king, Pelayo, began the long crusade that came to be known as the *Reconquista* (Reconquest). By 1085, Alfonso VI of Castile had captured Toledo, giving the Christians a firm grip on the north. During the 13th century, Valencia, Seville, and finally Córdoba—the former capital of the Muslim caliphate in Spain—fell to Christian forces, leaving only Granada in Moorish hands. It would be some two centuries more before two Catholic monarchs, Ferdinand of Aragón and Isabella of Castile, were joined in a marriage that would change the world.

THE YEAR 1492 is a watershed in Spanish history, the beginning of the nation's political golden age and the moment of some of its worst excesses of intolerance. That year, the twenty-third of Ferdinand and Isabella's marriage, Christian forces conquered Granada to unify all of current-day Spain as a single kingdom, though at the expense of Jews and Muslims who didn't embrace Christianity and were expelled from the country en masse. Christopher Columbus, under the sponsorship of Isabella, landed in the Americas, initiating the age of discoveries. But the departure of educated Muslims and Jews was a blow to the nation's economy from which it would never recover; the Inquisition, established in 1478, further hurt those who chose to stay. The lands of the New World would greatly enrich Spain at first, but massive shipments of Peruvian and Mexican gold later produced terrible inflation. The so-called Catholic Monarchs and their centralizing successors maintained the unity of Spain, but they sacrificed the spirit of free trade among nations that was beginning to bring capitalist prosperity to other European countries.

Ferdinand and Isabella were succeeded by their grandson, Carlos, who became the first Spanish Habsburg and one of the most powerful rulers in history. Under him, Cortés reached Mexico and Pizarro conquered Peru. He also inherited Austria and the Netherlands, and in 1519, three years into his reign, was elected Holy Roman Emperor (as Charles V), wasting little time in annexing Naples and Milan.

He championed the Counter-Reformation, and the Jesuit order was created to help defend Catholicism against European Protestantism. But Charles cost the nation by his penchant for waging war, particularly against the Ottomans and German Lutherans. His son, Philip II, followed in the same, expensive path. Philip defeated the Turks and ordered the building of the Escorial, a somber monastery outside Madrid. It was there he died, 10 years after losing his Armada in an attack on Protestant England.

The War of the Spanish Succession was ignited by the death, without issue, in 1700 of Charles II, the last Spanish Habsburg. Philip of Anjou was crowned Philip V, and he inaugurated the Bourbon line in Spain (a representative of which sits on the throne today). The Bourbons of that era, a Frenchified lot, copied many of the attitudes and fashions of their northern neighbors. But the infatuation ended with the 1808 installation by Napoléon of his brother, José Bonaparte. Mocked bitterly as "Pepe Botella" for his fondness for drink (*botella* means bottle), Bonaparte was widely despised, and an 1808 uprising in Madrid—chronicled harrowingly by the great painter Francisco de Goya y Lucientes (1746–1828)—began the War of Independence, known to foreigners as the Peninsular War. Britain, siding with Spain, sent the Duke of Wellington to the rescue. With the aid of Spanish guerillas, the French were finally expelled, but not before they had looted Spain's major churches and cathedrals. Most of Spain's American colonies took advantage of the war to claim their independence.

The rest of the century was not a happy one for Spain, as conservative regimes grappled with civil wars and revolts inspired by the currents of European republicanism. The final blow came with the loss of Cuba, Puerto Rico, and the Philippines in 1898, in a military disaster that ironically sparked a remarkable literary renaissance—the so-called Generation of '98, whose members included writers Miguel de Unamuno and Pío Baroja and poet Antonio Machado. In 1902 Alfonso XIII came to the throne, but rising civil strife got the better of him and ended in his self-imposed exile in 1931. A fledgling republic followed, to the delight of most Spaniards, but the

1936 election of a left-wing Popular Front government ignited bitter opposition from the right. In the end, a young general named Francisco Franco used the assassination of a monarchist leader as an excuse for a military revolt.

The Spanish Civil War (1936–39) was one of the most tragic episodes in Spanish history. More than half a million people died in the conflict. Intellectuals and leftists the world over sympathized with the elected government. The International Brigades, with many American, British, and Canadian volunteers, took part in some of the worst fighting, including the storied defense of Madrid. But Franco, backed by the Catholic Church, got far more help from Nazi Germany, whose Condor legions destroyed the Basque town of Guernica in a horror made infamous by Picasso's monumental painting, and from Fascist Italy. For three years, European governments stood quietly by as Franco's armies vanquished Barcelona, Madrid, and finally, the last capital of the Republic, Valencia.

Spain, officially neutral during World War II but sympathetic to the Axis powers, was largely shunned by the world until, in a 1953 agreement, the United States provided aid in exchange for the building of NATO bases. Gradually, the shattered economy began to pick up, especially with the boom in tourism that gathered steam in the late 1960s. But when Franco announced in 1969 that his successor would be Juan Carlos, the grandson of Alfonso XIII and a prince whose militaristic education had been strictly overseen by the aging general, the hopes of a nation longing for freedom sagged. Imagine the Spaniards' surprise when, six years later, Franco died and the young monarch revealed himself to be a closet democrat. Under his nurturing, a new constitution restoring civil liberties and freedom of expression was adopted in 1978. On February 23, 1981, the king proved his mettle again, when a disgruntled Guardia Civil colonel burst into the nation's parliament and held its members at gunpoint for some 24 hours. The coup attempt, aimed at bringing back a right-wing government, was by all accounts only routed through the heroism of the king, who personally called military commanders across the country to ensure their loyalty to the elected government.

The Socialists ruled Spain from 1982 to early 1996 when conservative José María Aznar was elected prime minister.

In the arts, there was a remarkable flowering in the first third of the 20th century that produced poet Federico García Lorca, filmmaker Luis Buñuel, and painters Pablo Picasso, Joan Miró, and Salvador Dalí. The century ended in the exile of these and other artists, producing the cultural wasteland of the Franco years. But today, the arts are blossoming. The world has come to know filmmaker Pedro Almodóvar and writer Camilo José Cela, whose first novel, *The Family of Pascual Duarte,* which subtly describes life in the Franco years, won the Nobel Prize in 1989.

Dip into the portraits of Spain (found in the last chapter of this book) before you leave home. When you get here, take the country as the Spaniards do, a little at a time. Before you know it, you may well discover, as travelers have for centuries before you, that it's almost impossible not to get caught up in the excitement of Spain.

— *Mark Potok*

French-born and American-raised journalist Mark Potok has lived in Greece, Italy, and Spain. He currently lives in Texas, where he is the Southwest correspondent for USA Today.

WHAT'S WHERE

Madrid

At the heart of Spain, Madrid has a pulsing energy that makes it Europe's liveliest capital. Madrileños are a joyful lot, famous for their ability to defy the need for sleep. Visitors with the same talent can take in the city's museum mile, with more masterpieces per meter than anywhere else in the world; regal Madrid, with stops at the royal convent and the sumptuous royal palace; and the narrow streets of medieval Madrid, which trace the city's history from its beginnings as an Arab fortress.

Around Madrid

Castile, the area around Madrid, is a vast, windswept plateau with clear skies and endless vistas. Outstanding Roman monuments and a fairy-tale castle make Segovia one of the most popular excursions from Madrid. The walled city of Ávila has relics of St. Teresa, the female patron saint of Spain; Salamanca, a university town, is a showpiece of the Spanish Renaissance. The contrast between Aranjuez, with its French-style elegance and Bourbon palace, and nearby Toledo, dramatic and austere with a rich Moorish legacy, is marked.

León, Galicia, and Asturias

León, Galicia, and Asturias, in green, rain-swept northwestern Spain, have heavy industry but also wild mountain scenery, pristine beaches, and Celtic influence. The city of Santiago de Compostela, whose cathedral houses the remains of the apostle St. James, has been attracting pilgrims for almost a millennium.

Burgos, Santander, and the Basque Country

Burgos, home of legendary hero El Cid, is a somber city in a parched region of whitewashed villages; Santander is a very Spanish beach resort in a mountainous zone; and the Basque country, with its own language, moist green hills, and rugged coastline, has a large population who live close to the land and a small population who want independence from Spain.

The Pyrenees

The Pyrenees, snowcapped mountains that seal off the Iberian Peninsula from the rest of Western Europe, are a source of legend and superstition. They have protected within their meadows and valleys the last vestiges of several ancient cultures. Thoroughly exploring any one of these valleys—its flora and fauna, its local gastronomy and architecture, its remote glacial lakes and streams, and its Romanesque art hidden in a thousand chapels and hermitages—could take a lifetime.

Barcelona

Barcelona is one of Europe's most beautiful cities: Few places can rival the medieval atmosphere of the Gothic Quarter's narrow alleys or the elegance and distinction of the Moderniste Eixample's boulevards. Artists such as Miró, Picasso, and Dalí have links to this fashionable city, which has a strong Catalan identity. Under Franco, the Catalan language and culture were suppressed; home rule was granted in 1975, and now Catalan is heard in every street.

Southern Catalunya and the Levante

In southern Catalunya and the Levante, grayish, arid mountains provide a stark backdrop for a lush coast marred by ugly developments. Inland, the rugged landscape is dotted with small fortified towns that were strategically important in medieval times. The Romans left many archaeological reminders, nowhere more so than in Tarragona; Valencia, a rich trove of art and architecture, is Spain's third-largest city.

The Southeast

The southeastern corner of Spain has a flat, fertile coastal plain that produces oranges; rice paddies that stretch miles down the coast; and mountains that give rise to the strange, almost lunar desert landscape in Almería. Most visitors come for the beaches and for the striking, white architecture that attests to long Moorish occupation.

The Balearic Islands

The strategic position of the Balearic Islands of Mallorca, Menorca, Ibiza, and Formentera—off Spain's coast, between France and Africa—has made them the object of territorial squabbles through the ages. Now the Balearics are an autonomous province, and Catalan is gradually replacing Castilian Spanish. Great overdeveloped stretches of the coastlines of Mallorca and Ibiza cater to tourists.

The Costa del Sol

Most of the stretch of Andalucían shore known as the Costa del Sol is an overdeveloped, package-tour mecca for northern European sunseekers and a retirement haven for Britons and Americans. With its luxury hotels, Marbella attracts a more glamorous crowd. In the mountains are remote villages—steeped in medieval lore and the scene of turbulent battles of the Reconquest—that belong to a world light years from the hedonistic carnival of the coast. The tiny British colony of Gibraltar provides English atmosphere.

Granada, Córdoba, and Eastern Andalucía

Two of Spain's most famous monuments, the great mosque of Córdoba and the palace of the Alhambra in Granada, are in Andalucía. Ruined fortresses dot the landscape and orange blossoms perfume its plazas. The Sierra Nevada mountain range is here as is the Guadalquivir River, which feeds Cordoban orchards and vineyards.

Seville and Western Andalucía

The flat landscape of fertile pastures, muddy marshlands, chalky vineyards, and sandy beaches in western Andalucía contrasts vividly with the mountainous provinces to the east. Flamenco, wildlife, horses, and sherry are keynotes of the region. The career of Christopher Columbus can be traced here; and the region is known all over the world for its distinctive local cuisine.

Extremadura

The name Extremadura suggests the wild, remote, and isolated character of this region. The area, which has poor soil and is scarcely industrialized, has experienced extreme poverty. Once, however, it was a hub of activity: No other place in Spain has so many Roman monuments as Mérida, and magnificent palaces constitute the glory of such towns as Cáceres and Trujillo.

The Canary Islands

The Canary Islands are Europe's winter place in the sun. The volcanic archipelago, much closer to Morocco than to Spain, is comprised of seven major islands, each with its own personality. Visitors can explore caves, mountains, banana plantations, and pine forests or bask on beaches and dance till dawn at glittering discos.

PLEASURES AND PASTIMES

Bullfighting

Bullfighting is a form of ritualized slaughter: The bull never wins, and gorings are unusual. Those who can conceive of the bull as a symbol rather than as an animal, who can remain undisturbed by the blood, and who can appreciate the drama and the fanfare will get the most out of a bullfight. To Spaniards, it's an art form and a national passion. Even one of today's most passionate and controversial pop-stars, Madonna, filmed a couple of steamy videos in Spain, featuring a wildly attractive torero (matador).

Bullfights start with a procession of banderilleros, picadors, and matadors. First, the matador waves capes to encourage the bull's charges. Then a picador, on horseback, stabs the bull's neck and shoulder area. Next, banderilleros plant darts in the bull's back. After more cape taunting, the matador kills the bull with a sword: He or she (some matadors are female) may receive the bull's ears and/or tail for a job well done. Six bulls are killed per day, by several different matadors.

Fights are normally held around 5 PM on Sundays, from April to early November. Hemingway made famous **Pamplona**'s running of the bulls and bullfighting during the Fiesta de San Fermín, in the first week of July; but nowhere is bullfighting better than at **Madrid**'s Las Ventas. Three weeks of daily fights in May mark the festival of San Isidro. **Seville** has one of Spain's leading bullrings. During the April Fair, fights take place daily with Spain's leading toreros. **Valencia** hosts the best bullfighters on July 25 and during the Fallas in March. **Ronda**'s picturesque bullring is rarely used for fights except during fairs in May and September.

Dining

Seafood and roast meats are the national specialties; foods are lightly seasoned, although garlic is considered a basic ingredient. Salads are delicious and are usually served topped with canned tuna and olives. If you feel like eating something very plain, order an *ensalada mixta* (mixed salad) and a *solomillo* (filet mignon).

Breakfast in Spain is usually coffee and a roll; in Madrid, it's chocolate (thick, hot cocoa) and *churros* (strips of fried dough). Spanish coffee is strong espresso taken straight (café *solo*) or with hot milk (café *con leche*); if you prefer weaker coffee, ask for café *américano*.

Spaniards eat paella, the delicious seafood and rice dish, exclusively at midday and preferably at a beachside restaurant or cooked over a campfire at a country picnic, but it is served to tourists at dinnertime as well.

Lunch usually consists of the first plate, which is a salad, soup, vegetable, or smoked fish or cured meat; the second plate, almost always meat or fish; and dessert, which can be ice cream, yogurt, or flan, but is more typically a piece of fresh fruit, which natives peel deftly with a knife and fork. All this is accompanied by bread (no butter) and washed down with a bottle of wine. In big cities some workers now grab a quick sandwich instead of stopping for the traditional three-course lunch.

Restaurants are required by law to offer a menú *del día* at lunch that includes all the above at a price that is 80% of what each course would cost separately. Restaurants that specialize in a menú del día post it at the door; in other establishments you must ask, and the menú del día may be only a couple of unappetizing choices designed to get you to order from the regular menu.

Supper is three courses, sometimes with lighter fare replacing the meat course. Some restaurants may offer a menú del día, but it is usually leftover lunch.

For more culinary background, *see* "Spain's Food and Wine" *in* Chapter 16.

Shopping

Clothing is expensive in Spain: World-famous Spanish **leather** jackets and shoes are beautiful, if no bargain. Madrid has the best selection of leather clothing, purses, and shoes; shoes are generally made in Alicante and the Balearic Islands. Distinctive, country-style **ceramics** can be purchased throughout the country; most are made in Talavera, Puente del Arzobispo (Toledo), and Seville.

In any **stationery** shop you'll find a wide selection of unusual pen and pencil boxes.

Other shopping in Spain will probably have something to do with **alcohol.** Each region produces its own wine, with the sherries of Jerez, the riojas of the north, and the sparkling wines of Catalunya famous around the world.

Sports

Sailing, boating, and **water sports** are popular along the Mediterranean coast and in the Balearic Islands. Mountain streams of the Pyrenees and other ranges offer excellent **fishing.** The **golf** course at El Saler, south of Valencia, is considered the best in Continental Europe. Marbella has 14 excellent courses; and the Costa Brava and Costa Blanca also have commendable courses. The Valderrama Golf Club on the Costa del Sol will host the prestigious Ryder Cup this year. **Hiking** is possible in the interior of Spain and in the numerous national parks ranges—from the marshy Doñana to the mountainous Picos de Europa. The Pyrenees and the Sierra de Gredos are also popular with hikers. Spain has excellent **skiing and winter sports** facilities. Major resorts include Baqueira-Beret, Port del Compte, Llessui, and Formigal in the Pyrenees. Skiing is excellent at Sierra Nevada, near Granada (which hosted the 24th Annual Alpine World Ski Championship in 1996), and close to Madrid at Navacerrada, Valcoto, and Valdesqui. Spain is famed for its horses: **Polo** is played at the magnificent Puerta de Hierro Country Club in Madrid and the Royal Polo Club in Barcelona. Thousands of pedal pushers turn out in early summer when the roads are closed off for Madrid's annual bicycle day. While **bicycling** is impossible in crowded cities, many coastal resorts offer bike rentals.

NEW AND NOTEWORTHY

Madrid

The construction clutter is due to come down around the Plaza de Oriente in front of Madrid's Royal Palace in 1997. A new tunnel and parking garge beneath the plaza should alleviate many of the traffic problems here, leaving the palace with an exhaust-free pedestrian zone in front, rather than the busy street that used to run between the palace and the plaza.

Bilbao

The new Guggenheim Museum designed by Frank Gehry is an important step in revitalizing Bilbao's somewhat smokestack-studded industrial image.

Galicia

If you are planning to visit Galicia, do not miss the amazing Casa del Hombre, or Domus. Open since 1995 in La Coruña, this is the first interactive museum devoted to the study of mankind. Exhibits include being able to hop on a bicycle and then watching your skeleton in action, tracking down information on any of the

60 trillion cells in your body on one video disk, and the *Giaconda Sapiens,* a reproduction of the Mona Lisa (La Gioconda) made of a composite of over 10,000 faces from 110 countries, demonstrating the incredible diversity and unity of the human race.

Barcelona

Art is always news in Barcelona, but the opening of the MACBA (Barcelona Museum of Contemporary Art), the CCCB (Barcelona Center for Contemporary Culture), the reopening of the MNAC (National Museum of Catalonian Art), and the world's best Romanesque art collection, along with the opening of the new Catalonian History Museum will make Barcelona even more exciting in 1997.

Andalucía

Al-Andalus Express, a luxurious train comprised of five exquisitely restored vintage 1920's coaches, winds its way during 6-and 7-day journeys through the dramatically beautiful southwestern region of Andalucía. This is a wonderful, 5-star alternative to driving those challenging mountain roads yourself; this way, you get to enjoy the constantly changing views of Granada, Córdoba, and Seville while being shamelessly pampered.

The Canaries

A new conference and convention center is set to open in Playa de las Américas on Tenerife at the start of 1997, bringing with it several big new hotels in a complex called Mare Nostrum. The results of a downtown beautification program can be seen in Puerto de la Cruz, where traffic through the business district has been re-routed, trees planted, and storefronts refurbished.

FODOR'S CHOICE

No two people will agree on what makes a perfect vacation, but it can be helpful to know what others think. We hope you'll have a chance to experience some of Fodor's Choices while visiting Spain. For detailed information on individual entries, see the relevant sections of this guidebook.

Castles and Palaces

★**Alarcón, Cuenca.** Crossing the narrow bridge into the walled city and castle of Alarcón—a parador with a memorable restaurant—will take you back to medieval times. Throw open the shutters of the turret's bedroom window and exclaim, "The legions are approaching!"

★**Alhambra, Granada.** One of Spain's most visited attractions, this citadel is an intricate fantasy of endless, lavishly colored and adorned patios, arches, and cupolas.

★**Castle, Sigüenza.** At the very top of the beautiful town of Sigüenza, this mighty, crenellated parador has hosted royalty over the centuries, from Ferdinand and Isabella to Juan Carlos.

★**Palacio Real, Aranjuez.** This palace, surrounded by extensive gardens and woods, reflects a French grandeur. The high point of the sumptuous interior is a room covered entirely with porcelain.

★**Palacio Real, La Granja.** The palace's gardens are the draw: Terraces, lakes, classical statuary, woods, and elaborate fountains encourage wandering. In summer, the fountains are turned on, one by one, creating an exciting spectacle.

★**Palacio Real, Madrid.** A highlight of this palace is King Carlos III's private apartments, a riot of Rococo decoration, with swirling, inlaid floors and curlicued ceiling decorations glistening in the light of a 2-ton crystal chandelier.

Churches, Monasteries, and Mosques

★**Capilla Real, Granada.** A masterpiece of the ornate Gothic style known in Spain as Isabelline, this royal chapel is the resting place of the Catholic Monarchs.

★**Cathedral, Léon.** The flying buttresses of Léon's soaring Gothic cathedral, begun in 1205, support walls that are built with more windows than stone. The ethereal feeling of the lofty interior is enhanced by a kaleidoscope of stunning colors: The cathedral contains 125 stained-glass windows and three giant rose windows.

★**Cathedral, Santiago de Compostela.** Site of pilgrimages for almost a millennium, this enormous, opulent building houses the relics of the apostle St. James, Romanesque sculpture, a gold and silver high altar, and a dazzling array of decoration and drapery.

★**Cathedral, Seville.** Seville's cathedral can be described only in superlatives: It is the biggest and highest cathedral in Spain, the largest Gothic building in the world, and the world's third-largest church. The exterior, with its rose windows and magnificent flying buttresses, is a monument to pure Gothic beauty.

★**El Escorial, Madrid.** This great, granite monastery contains the bodies of many Spanish kings. There are also priceless tapestries, paintings by Velázquez and El Greco, a lavish library with rare works, and a basilica with a Titian fresco here.

★**Mezquita, Córdoba.** Built between the 8th and 9th centuries, the Mezquita (mosque), is a breathtaking example of Spanish Muslim architecture. There are some 850 columns that create a forest of onyx, jasper, marble, and granite. There's also an endless array of red-and-white-striped horseshoe arches, and delicate mosaics and plasterwork.

★**Temple Expiatori de la Sagrada Família, Barcelona.** Unfinished at the time of Antoni Gaudí's death in 1926, this striking, surreal cathedral has been added to by other architects, who have themselves not shied away from controversy. Take an elevator to one of the spires for a magnificent view of the city.

★**Monasterio de Guadalupe, Puebla de Guadalupe.** Christopher Columbus came here before and after his voyage of discovery to pay respects to the Virgin of this wondrous, art-filled, 14th-century, Gothic and Moorish hybrid monestary, nestled in the Altamira mountains of Extremadura, land of the Conquistadors. One of the most important spiritual centers of Spain and the New World, UNESCO declared Guadalupe a World Heritage Site in 1993.

Museums

★**Archbishops's Palace, Astorga.** No expense was spared in Gaudí's fairy-tale, neo-Gothic building, which houses the Museum of the Way of St. James.

★**Museu Picasso, Barcelona.** You expect to see Juliet leaning over the courtyard balcony of this 15th-century palace housing Picasso's childhood sketches and paintings from his Blue Period. The neighborhood of ancient, cobblestone streets has many tapas bars and shops to explore.

★**National Museum of Religious Sculpture, Valladolid.** Set in a masterpiece of the Isabelline Plateresque—an ornamental style of exceptional intricacy—this museum superbly displays an impressive collection of different styles of religious sculpture, from the highly polished and decorative to the severely plain.

★**Prado, Madrid.** One of the world's greatest museums, the Prado has masterpieces by Italian and Flemish painters, but its jewels are the works of Spaniards: Goya, Velázquez, and El Greco.

Other Sights

★**Roman ruins in Mérida, Segovia, and Tarragona.** Mérida has the largest concentration of Roman monuments including a 64-arch bridge, a fortress, and a theater. The enchanting city of Segovia, near Madrid, has a nearly 3,000-foot aqueduct that dates from the 3rd century BC; and Tarragona, near Barcelona, has many classical remains, the highlight of which is an amphitheater near the sea.

★**Pasajes de San Juan.** Near San Sebastían, this charming, tiny settlement of 18th- and 19th-century buildings on a bay is famous for its fine restaurants.

★**Ronda, Malaga.** Atop a rock, Ronda has spectacular views, a dramatic ravine, an old Moorish section, and a picturesque bullring with a bullfighting museum.

★**University, Salamanca.** Founded in 1220, Salamanca's university is one of the most prestigious in Europe. The architectural highlight is the Escuelas Mayores, a building with a glorious, enameled frontispiece that is surrounded by graceful quadrangles and greens.

GREAT ITINERARIES

Essential Spain for First-Time Visitors

The best of historic and modern Spain awaits the visitor who follows this basic itinerary: Take in the sophistication of Madrid and Barcelona, the medieval luster of Toledo and Segovia, the Moorish splendor of Granada and Córdoba, and end up in romantic Seville.

DURATION➤ 14 days

GETTING AROUND➤ This tour can be followed by car (on divided highways), train, bus, or plane. A one-hour plane trip will save a day's travel time between Barcelona and Madrid. A rented car between Granada, Córdoba, and Seville will allow you to see more of the Andalusian countryside and will be faster than the train, which tends to stop in every village. For the trip home, the ultra-modern, high-speed train (AVE) can return you from Seville to Madrid in less than three hours.

THE MAIN ROUTE➤ **Day 1: Barcelona.** Stay near the center of the city. Visit the cathedral and stroll through the Gothic Quarter. Promenade along the Ramblas and duck into the Boquería market. Sample paella or seafood at an outdoor restaurant on the Barceloneta peninsula by the port. Explore the new Port Vell area.

Day 2: Barcelona. Visit the fantasylike Sagrada Familia cathedral, designed by Gaudí and still under construction. Walk by one of Gaudí's other buildings, the Casa Milà, and visit the Renaissance palace that houses the Picasso museum.

Day 3: Barcelona–Madrid. If you go by car, stop outside Barcelona at the mountaintop monastery of Montserrat.

Day 4: Madrid. Visit the Royal Palace, then stroll through old Madrid. Stop at one of the bars of the Plaza Mayor.

Day 5: Segovia. Using Madrid as your base, make a day trip to Segovia to see the Roman aqueduct, cathedral, and turreted castle. Have a big Segovian lunch of roast suckling pig or see the huge, gray monastery built by Philip II at El Escorial.

Day 6: Madrid. Stroll the leafy Paseo del Prado, visit the Prado museum, and then recover with a stop at Retiro Park.

Day 7: Toledo. Less than an hour from Madrid, Toledo is the spiritual center of Spain. It can be seen as a day trip from Madrid or for those traveling by car, as the first stop on the way to Granada. Soak up history from its cobbled alleyways, explore the cathedral, visit the synagogue, and get a glimpse of daily life in medieval Spain at El Greco's house.

Day 8: Madrid–Granada. En route, detour to the sleepy town of Consuegra in La Mancha to see the windmills of Don Quixote.

Day 9: Granada. Explore the lush Moorish palace and gardens of the Alhambra. Visit the Royal Chapel adjoining the cathedral, where Ferdinand and Isabella are buried, and dine in the hillside Arab quarter, the Albaicín.

Day 10: Granada–Córdoba. In Córdoba, once the headquarters of all the Moorish kingdoms in Spain, see the red-and-white-striped mosque with its jewel-encrusted altar.

Day 11: Córdoba–Seville. Stop in Carmona, one of the oldest villages in Spain. Then in Seville, stroll alongside the Guadalquivir River and lose yourself amid the winding streets and patios of the romantic barrio Santa Cruz.

Day 12: Seville. Visit the splendid Moorish palaces of the Alcázar, climb the Giralda, relax in the sweet-smelling, orange blossom patio by the cathedral, and hire a horse-drawn carriage to take you to the tile-encrusted Plaza de España.

Day 13: Jerez de la Frontera and Arcos de la Frontera. Visit a sherry winery in Jerez and then make your way to the white hilltop town of Arcos in time for sunset.

Day 14: Seville–Madrid. Return by highway, plane, or the AVE train.

Art and Architectural Treasures

From north to south, this unique tour avoids the big cities, while concentrating on Spain's rich architectural treasures. This route offers superb examples of every major building style since the Romans.

DURATION➤ 12 days

GETTING AROUND➤ A car is essential for following this route, which sometimes winds over steep back roads and through narrow gates into walled cities.

THE MAIN ROUTE➤ **Day 1: Oviedo.** The capital of the province of Asturias, Oviedo is home to Europe's best examples of pre-Romanesque art. Visit the primitive yet graceful, 9th-century chapels of Santa Maria del Naranco and San Miguel de Lillo on a hill overlooking the city. Don't miss the treasures of Oviedo's Gothic cathedral, which include Visigoth-style, jeweled crosses that commemorate the first Christian victory over the Moors in 718.

Day 2: Oviedo–León. Cross the Pajares pass and descend to the high plains of Castile. In León, stay at the Parador San Marcos, a sumptuous, Renaissance monastery that was once the headquarters for the Knights of St. James. Visit the basilica of San Isidro, with its primitive, medieval frescoes; spend time in the 13th-century Gothic cathedral that glitters with stained glass; and visit the arcaded Plaza Mayor with its half-timber houses.

Day 3: León–Segovia. Follow the back roads and stop at the imposing castles of Peñafiel and Coca, two of Spain's best.

Day 4: Segovia. Visit the Roman aqueduct and the turreted castle filled with furnishings from the period of Spain's Catholic Kings. From here it is possible to take excursions to the French-inspired palace of La Granja or the medieval stone village of La Pedraza.

Day 5: Segovia–Ávila–Salamanca. In Ávila, walk the ramparts of the city walls, the best preserved in Spain. A detour through Puerto del Pico pass in the Gredos Mountains allows you to walk over a still-intact Roman road, the likes of which once crisscrossed this countryside.

Day 6: Salamanca. The arcaded Plaza Mayor and the Plateresque buildings of the University make the entire city of Salamanca an architectural monument.

Day 7: Salamanca–La Alberca–Cáceres. Nestled in one of the poorest and most primitive corners of Spain, La Alberca has changed little since medieval times. Its winding streets are full of rustic, half-timber houses and squares. In Cáceres, stay in the unspoiled old town; its stone palaces and plazas served as backdrops for Ridley Scott's film on the life of Columbus.

Day 8: Cáceres–Mérida. Explore Mérida's Roman theater (24 BC), amphitheater, and archaeology museum.

Day 9: Mérida–Seville. Travel day.

Day 10: Seville. Visit the splendid Moorish palaces of the Alcázar, climb the Giralda, a 12th-century minaret, and tour the immense cathedral—the largest in Spain. Stroll under flowered Andalusian balconies in the barrio Santa Cruz and hire a horse-drawn carriage to take you to the tile-encrusted Plaza de España. Some of Spain's most modern architecture, including two soaring suspension bridges, can be found on the island of La Cartuja, site of the 1992 Expo.

Day 11: Seville–Córdoba. In Córdoba, stroll the narrow streets and look for the flowering patios typical of Andalucía. Visit the red-and-white-striped mosque with its jewel-encrusted altar, once the spiritual center of Spain's Moorish kingdoms.

Day 12: Córdoba–Granada. End your trip with a stop at the lush palaces and gardens of the Alhambra, the last Moorish outpost in Europe. Explore the old Arab quarter with its unforgettable views of the Alhambra.

Castles in Spain

The Spanish countryside is packed with castles—this tour takes you to some of the best and allows you to spend the night in medieval splendor. The route fans out from Madrid and zigzags through Spain's midsection, where castles of Castile and La Mancha once served as the front line of defense between Christian and Moslem Spain. Children will enjoy this tour and any of the days described could also stand on its own as an excursion from the capital.

DURATION➤ 7 days

GETTING AROUND➤ A car is essential for this tour, which goes through some fairly hilly, rugged territory. Rent in Madrid.

THE MAIN ROUTE➤ **Day 1: Madrid–Belmonte–Alarcón.** On the way to Belmonte stop by the Royal Palace of Aranjuez, the inspiration of Spain's romantic composers and poets. The 15th-century Belmonte castle is a powerful fortress overlooking the La Mancha plains. Crossing the narrow bridge into the walled city and castle of Alarcón will take you back to medieval times. The castle is a national parador; try to book a room in the tower.

Day 2: Alarcón–Sigüenza. The ruined castle of Jadraque is worth a stop en route to Sigüenza, where a crenellated 14th-century castle lords over the village. Sigüenza's castle is one of the most popular national paradors. Be sure to ask to see the chapel.

Day 3: Sigüenza–Manzanares El Real–Segovia. Crossing back through Madrid, head for the charming foothill village of Manzanares El Real, whose storybook-perfect square castle is one of Spain's best examples of double-walled fortification.

Day 4: Segovia. The turreted castle of Segovia, although scorned by purists because of its massive reconstruction, is one of Spain's most famous landmarks. Unlike most Spanish castles, which are empty inside, this one houses a fine collection of armor and furnishings from the period of the Catholic Kings.

Day 5: Turégano–Coca–Peñafiel. Using Segovia as a base, make an excursion through the castle-rich countryside of Castile. The 12th-century castle of Turégano contains a beautiful church, while the brick fortress of Coca shows unmistakable Moorish influence in its design. The shiplike, 14th-century castle of Peñafiel sits on a plateau with views of three valleys.

Day 6: Segovia–Ávila. While Ávila does not have a castle as such, the thick city walls turn the entire city into a fortress. Walk the ramparts and be sure to see the walls lit up at night (the best viewpoint is at Cuatro Postes below the city). You can stay in a national parador built into the walls.

Day 7: Ávila–Madrid. Return to Madrid through the Gredos mountains and over the Puerto del Pico with its Roman road. Below the pass visit the romantic castle of Mombeltran, built in the 14th century by the Duke of Albuquerque.

Camino de Santiago

Pilgrims have made the lengthy and dangerous journey to the shrine of St. James in Santiago de Compostela for over a thousand years. They have left in their wake a wealth of Romanesque buildings and art treasures. A number of books and tourist-office brochures describe the route and the attractions along the way. It is also possible to pick up the road in León and still see a good representation of its offerings.

DURATION➤ 6 days

GETTING AROUND➤ The whole trail is signposted, and it is possible to walk the entire distance, but the less energetic can make their pilgrimage by car.

THE MAIN ROUTE➤ **Day 1: Roncesvalles–Estella.** This pass in the Pyrenees was the traditional entry point for pilgrims arriving from France. Visit the chapel. In Estella, see the 12th-century palace of the dukes of Granada and the early churches.

Day 2: Estella–Burgos. Visit the church of Santiago in Logroño, the cathedral in Santo Domingo de la Calzada, the many monasteries along the way, and the arcaded square of Belorado. In Burgos, see the massive cathedral.

Day 3: Burgos–León. Explore the half-timber medieval section of León; see the cathedral, decorated with 125 stained-glass windows.

Day 4: León–Villafranca del Bierzo. Stop at the pilgrims' museum in Astorga, housed in a palace designed by Gaudí. Explore the Knights Templar castle in Ponferrada. In Villafranca, see the Church of Santiago.

Day 5: Villafranca–Santiago de Compostela. Examine primitive, round Celtic houses in O Cebreiro. In Santiago, the cathedral and Hotel of the Catholic Monarchs are masterpieces of stone carving.

Day 6: Santiago. Explore the city and the nearby town of Padrón.

FESTIVALS AND SEASONAL EVENTS

From solemn, pre-Easter processions to hilarious wine and tomato battles, Spain has a fiesta for every occasion. The best known is probably the Running of the Bulls in Pamplona, immortalized by Ernest Hemingway in *The Sun Also Rises*. The *Fallas* (end-of-winter celebrations) in Valencia and Seville's *Semana Santa* (Holy Week) and April Fair also top the list. All require hotel reservations far in advance.

WINTER

DEC.➤ **New Year's Eve** ticks away at Madrid's Puerta del Sol, where crowds gather to eat 12 grapes, one on each stroke of midnight to guarantee good fortune in the coming year.

JAN.➤ **Epiphany,** on the 6th, is a Spanish child's Christmas. Youngsters leave their shoes on the doorstep to be filled with gifts by the three wise men, or Three Kings. In towns throughout Spain the Kings arrive by camel or car in a parade the night of January 5.

FEB.➤ **Carnival** dances through Spain as a final fiesta before Lent. The most flamboyant parades take place in Santa Cruz de Tenerife, Cádiz, and Sitges (Barcelona).

SPRING

MAR.➤ Papier-mâché figures up to 30 feet tall are torched for the **Fallas,** lighting up the sky of Valencia.

APR.➤ The **April Fair** of Seville brings out the best of Andalusian hospitality. Horse parades and flouncy-skirted women make this one of Spain's most picturesque fiestas. April 9 to 15 is **Semana Santa,** Spain's most spectacular fiesta. The most famous Semana Santa processions take place in Seville, Valladolid, Toledo, Murcia, Lorca, and Cuenca.

MAY➤ The **Jerez Horse Fair** (second week of May) prances out a pageant of equestrian events, bullfighting, flamenco music, and dance. **San Isidro** (May 15) begins two weeks of the best bullfighting in Spain in honor of the patron saint of Madrid. **Romería del Rocío** (May 18–20) rolls across the dusty fields of Almonte (Huelva) and across a hip-deep river, as religious statues are carried on backs and in covered wagons.

SUMMER

JUNE➤ Beginning in midmonth, the **International Festival of Music and Dance** in Granada brings symphony orchestras, opera companies, and ballet corps from around the world to perform on the grounds of the Alhambra through mid-July. The **Classical Theater Festival** uses the beautifully preserved 1st-century BC Roman Theater in Mérida (Badajoz) to present Greek and Roman dramas in Spanish from mid-June through mid-August. **Corpus Christi** (June 25) is celebrated with processions throughout Spain, but the most magnificent are in Toledo and Sitges (Barcelona). The **Wine War** in Haro (La Rioja, on June 29) wastes thousands of gallons of delicious Rioja wine and proves that a bota bag makes a better squirt gun than a canteen.

JULY➤ Veranos de la Villa cools off Madrid's summer nights with a series of outdoor films, and concerts of everything from flamenco to rock and roll all summer long. The **Running of the Bulls** (July 6–13) through the streets of Pamplona (Navarra) unleashes wine-drinking, merrymaking, and macho bravado. The first two weeks of the month attract the country's finest flamenco guitarists and singers to the **Flamenco Guitar Festival of Córdoba.** The **Moors and Christians Festival** at the end of the month, in Valencia, finds local residents in medieval costumes re-enacting battles of long ago (a delicious meal of rice and beans here is called *Moros y Cristianos*).

Aug.➤ For four weeks in August, the **International Music and Ballet Festival** brings world-class performances to the popular beach resort of Santander. **El Misteri** of Elche (Alicante, August 11–15) is Europe's oldest, Christian, mystery play. Also in mid-month, the upper-crust resort of San Sebastián lets down its hair for **Big Week,** with parades, fireworks, sporting events, and cardboard-bull running. **Tomato Battle** (August 28) turns the entire town of Buñol (Valencia) red. The end of the month is also tinged another color, heralding the **Saffron Rose Festival** in Consuegra (near Toledo), the world's saffron capital. Participants celebrate the harvest of the world's most expensive spice with three days of music, dance, and regional folklore exhibits.

AUTUMN

Sept.➤ In late August or early September, the **International Folkloric Gala** kicks off five days of folk dance and song from around the world at the elegant bullring in Ronda (Málaga). **La Merced** is celebrated in Barcelona on September 24 with concerts, fireworks, and parades featuring people wearing giant, papier-mâché heads.

Oct.➤ On the 12th, **El Pilar** gives the children of Zaragoza a chance to dress up in regional costumes for parades and *jota* dance contests.

2 Madrid

At the heart of Spain, Madrid has a pulsing energy that makes it Europe's liveliest capital. Madrileños are a joyful lot, famous for their seeming ability to defy the need for sleep. Visitors with the same talent can take in the city's museum mile, with more masterpieces per meter than anywhere else in the world; regal Madrid, with stops at the royal convent and the sumptuous royal palace; and the narrow streets of medieval Madrid, which trace the city's history from its beginnings as an Arab fortress.

By Mark Potok
and Deborah
Luhrman

AT THE HEART OF SPAIN, Madrid's pulsing energy and openness make it Europe's most lively capital. Its people—called Madrileños—are a joyful lot, famous for their seeming ability to defy the need for sleep. Life here is lived in the crowded streets and in the noisy cafés, where endless rounds of socializing last long into the night. The publicness of Madrid's lifestyle makes it especially easy for visitors to get involved, and its allure is hard to resist.

Madrid's other chief attraction is its unsurpassed collection of paintings by some of the world's great artists, among them Goya, El Greco, Velázquez, Picasso, and Dalí. Nowhere else will you find such a concentration of masterpieces as in the three museums—the Prado, the Reina Sofía, and the Thyssen-Bornemisza—that make up Madrid's so-called golden triangle of art.

The bright blue sky, as immortalized in Velázquez's paintings, is probably the first thing you'll notice about Madrid. Despite 20th-century pollution, that same color sky is still much in evidence thanks to breezes that sweep down from the Guadarrama mountains, blowing away the urban smog.

The city's skyline has its share of soaring, modern skyscrapers, but the more typical Madrid towers of red brick crowned by gray, slate roofs and spires far outnumber them. This Hapsburg-era architecture, built in the 1500s and 1600s by Spain's Austrian kings who made Madrid capital of the realm, gives parts of town a timeless, Old World feel.

Monumental neoclassical structures, like the Prado Museum, the Royal Palace, and the Puerta de Alcalá arch, make up Madrid's other historic face. These are the sights most visited by tourists, and most were built in the 1700s during the reign of Bourbon monarch Charles III, who, inspired by the enlightened ideas of the age, also created Retiro Park, and the broad, leafy boulevard called Paseo del Prado.

Modern-day Madrid sprawls northward in block after block of dreary, high-rise, brick apartment buildings and office towers. A swelling population of 3.2 million is also moving into surrounding villages and new suburbs, creating traffic problems in and around the capital.

While these new quarters and many of Madrid's crumbling old residential neighborhoods may seem unappealing to the visitor, don't be put off by first impressions. The city's attractiveness has mostly to do with its people and the electricity they generate—whether at play in the bars and discotheques or at work in the advertising, television, and film industries headquartered here.

Situated on a plateau 2,120 feet above sea level, Madrid is the highest capital in Europe. It can also be one of the world's hottest cities in summer, and freezing cold in winter. Spring and summer are the most delightful times to visit when a balmy evening has virtually everyone in town lingering at an outdoor café, but each season has its own charms; in winter steamy café windows beckon and the famous blue skies are especially crisp and bright. That's when Madrid, as the local bumper stickers will tell you, is the next best place to heaven.

The sophistication of Madrid stands in vivid contrast to the ancient ways of the historic villages close to the capital. Less than an hour away from the downtown skyscrapers, you can find villages where farm fields are still plowed by mule. Like city dwellers the world over, Madrileños like to visit the countryside. Getaways to the dozens of Castilian hamlets nearby and excursions to Toledo, El Escorial, and Segovia are a favorite pastime of both locals and tourists.

Pleasures and Pastimes

Art Museums

Madrid's greatest attractions are its three world-class art museums, the Prado, the Reina Sofía, and the Thyssen-Bornemisza, all located within 1 km/⅗ mi of each other along the leafy Paseo del Prado, which is sometimes refered to as the "golden triangle of art." The Prado houses Spain's Old Masters, with the world's foremost collections of Goya, El Greco, and Velázquez, along with hundreds of other 17th-, 18th-, and 19th-century masterpieces. The Reina Sofía focuses on modern art, especially Dalí, Miró and Picasso, whose famous Guernía is displayed here. It also shows modern Spanish sculptors, such as Eduardo Chillida and hosts excellent temporary exhibits. The Thyssen-Bornemisza museum attempts to trace the entire history of Western art and includes good collections of impressionist and German expressionist works.

Dining

Unlike most regions of Spain, Madrid does not really have a native cuisine. But, as capital of the realm and home of the king, Madrid has attracted generations of courtiers, foreign diplomats, politicians, and tradesmen, all of whom brought their own styles of and tastes in cooking, whether from another region of Spain or from abroad.

The roast meats of Castile and the seafood dishes of the Cantabrian coast are just as at home in Madrid as they are in their native lands. Basque cooking, Spain's haute cuisine, is the specialty of Madrid's best restaurants, and seafood houses take advantage of the capital's abundant supply of fish and shellfish, trucked in nightly from the coast. Spaniards joke that Madrid is Spain's biggest seaport.

The only truly local dishes are *cocido a la Madrileño* (garbanzo-bean stew) and *callos a la Madrileño* (stewed tripe). Given half a chance, Madrileños will spend hours waxing lyrically over the mouth watering merits of both. Cocido is a delicious and hearty winter meal consisting of garbanzo beans, vegetables, potatoes, sausages, and pork. The best cocidos are slowly simmered in earthenware crocks over open fires and served as a complete meal in several courses, first the broth, which comes with angel hair pasta, then the beans and vegetables, and finally the meat. Cocido can be found in the most elegant restaurants, such as Lhardy and at the Ritz hotel, as well as the most humble eateries, and is usually offered as a midday selection on Monday or Wednesday. Callos, on the other hand, is a much simpler concoction of veal tripe stewed with tomatoes, onions, and garlic.

Although the countryside near the capital produces some wines, they are not very good. The house wine in nearly all Madrid restaurants is a sturdy, uncomplicated *Valdepeñas* from La Mancha. A traditional, anise-flavored liqueur called *Anís* is manufactured just outside the village of Chinchón.

CATEGORY	COST*
$$$$	over 6,000 ptas.
$$$	4,000–6,000 ptas.
$$	1,800–4,000 ptas.
$	under 1,800 ptas.

per person for three-course meal, excluding drinks, service, and tax

Lodging

Hotel prices in Madrid have come down significantly since the glory days of the early '90s, especially in the upper price brackets. The Ritz and the Villamagna both once charged upward of $600 a night, but they each now offer a room rate comparable to that found in other world capitals—$250 to $300 a night. If that's still too steep, try bargaining. Surveys show that only 15% of hotel guests pay the posted room rate in Madrid. More savvy customers take advantage of a dizzying array of special offers. Be sure to ask for a business or professional discount, which can amount to up to 40% off. Since most hotels cater to business travelers, special weekend rates are widely available. You can generally save 50% on a Friday, Saturday, or Sunday night, and many hotels throw in extras, like meals or museum admissions.

If you're willing to embark on a serious hunt, you can also find *hostals* for 4,000 ptas. or even less. Most of these very cheap rooms are found in tiny hostals on the upper floors of apartment buildings. They are frequently full, however, and don't take reservations, so there is little use in listing them here; you simply have to go door to door and trust your luck. Many such places are concentrated in the old city between the Prado Museum and the Puerta del Sol. Start by looking around the Plaza Santa Ana.

CATEGORY	COST*
$$$$	over 20,000 ptas.
$$$	13,000–20,000 ptas.
$$	9,000–13,000 ptas.
$	under 9,000 ptas.

*per standard double room, excluding tax

Tapas Bars

Madrid offers some of the best tapas bars in Spain. A *tapas* is a bit of food that usually comes free with a drink; it might be a few olives, a mussel in vinaigrette, a sardine, or spicy potatoes. A larger plate of the same sort of food called a *ración* can also be ordered and is meant to be eaten with toothpicks and shared among friends. Tapas bars can be found throughout the city, but the best place to start your tapas tour is in the area of Plaza Santa Ana or at the *mesones* built into the wall beneath the Plaza Mayor along Cava San Miguel. These are among the oldest buildings in the city, and each bar specializes in a different tapas, for example, tortilla, garlicky mushrooms, or sardines.

EXPLORING MADRID

Numbers in the margin correspond to points of interest on the Madrid map.

Madrid is a compact city, and most of the things visitors want to see are concentrated in a downtown area barely a mile across, stretching between the Royal Palace and Retiro Park. Broad *avenidas*, twisting medieval alleys, grand museums, stately gardens, and tiny, tiled taverns are all jumbled together in an area easily explored on foot.

In fact, the texture of Madrid is so rich that walking is the only way to experience those special moments—peeking in on a guitar-maker at work or watching a child dip *churros* into a steamy cup of chocolate—whose images linger long after the holiday photos have faded.

Great Itineraries

Numbers in the text below correspond to numbers in the margin and on the Madrid, Madrid Excursions, and El Escorial maps.

IF YOU HAVE 2 DAYS

On a brief stay, you should limit yourself to only one or two museums, leaving the rest of your time to enjoy the rest of the city. See the works of Spain's great masters at the **Museo del Prado** ⑫; then visit the **Palacio Real** ㉑, for a regal display of art, architecture, and history. The tour includes admission to the Royal Library and Royal Armory, both show stoppers in their own right. Stroll along the Paseo de la Castellana to see **Fuente de la Cibeles** ⑤ and **Fuente de Neptuno** ④. Visit the **Puerta del Sol** ③, then relax at an outdoor cafe on the **Plaza Mayor** ②. Try some of the historic tapa bars along the **Cava de San Miguel** ㉙ street.

IF YOU HAVE 4 DAYS

There will be more time to uncover historic Madrid, visit more museums, and take an excursion outside the city.

Visit the **Centro de Arte Reina Sofía** ⑮, and the **Museo Thyssen-Bornemisza** ⑯ tracing the history of modern art. Do not miss the 16th century **Convento de las Descalzas Reales** ⑲, which has a beautiful, frescoed staircase, paintings by Zurbarán and Titian, as well as a hall of sumptous tapestries. Explore Medieval Madrid, beginning on Calle Mayor to **Plaza de la Villa** ㉘ for examples of Spain's Mudéjar architecture and flamboyant Plateresque style. Turn onto Calle Segovia, one of the main streets during the Middle Ages, and make your way to **Plaza de Paja** ㉚ and Museo de San Isidro, Madrid's patron saint and location of his most famous miracle. Take an excursion outside of Madrid to **El Escorial** ㊲ and the **Real Monasterio de San Lorenzo de El Escorial,** 50 km/31 mi from Madrid in the Guadarrama mountains. Here in the Royal Pantheon, the bodies of most of the kings since Carlos I are buried. A few miles away is Faranco's tomb, **Valle de los Caídos** ㊳, the Valley of the Fallen, built by forced labor of Republican prisoners after the civil war.

Central Madrid

Central Madrid stretches between the Royal Palace on the west and Retiro Park to the East—a distance of about 3 km/2 mi that is loaded with most of the city's museums, monuments, and historic buildings.

A Good Walk

A leisurely walk across town will help you get your bearings while locating many of the major sights of Madrid, which can be visited later. Begin in front of the Royal Palace at the **Plaza de Oriente** ①; then walk east towards the **Plaza Mayor** ②, ending your excursion with a stroll up and down the leafy **Paseo del Prado.**

On the way to the Plàza Mayor walk through the narrow **San Ginés passageway** that runs alongside the 14th-century church of San Ginés, one of the oldest in Madrid. It is one of the more picturesque corners of Madrid. Wooden stalls selling used books and prints of old Madrid are built into the church wall. Across the way is Joy Eslava, one of Madrid's late-night discotheques. Located where the passageway jogs to the right is the **Chocolatería San Ginés,** an institution known for its chocolate and churros, and the final stop on many a night owl's bar crawl.

Leaving the Plaza Mayor wind your way among the crowds on **Carrera San Jerónimo**—a jumble of shops and cafés. At No. 8 peek into the ground-floor delicatessen of **Lhardy,** one of Madrid's oldest and most traditional restaurants. Shoppers stop in here on cold winter mornings for steamy cups of *caldo* (chicken broth). Be sure to have a look at the beautifully tiled and decorated tops of buildings, especially at the corner of Calle Sevilla. The big, white-granite building on the left with the lions out in front is the **Congress,** the lower house of Spain's parliament.

You will reach the wide Paseo del Prado right across from the renowned **Museo del Prado** ⑫. A right turn will take you to the **Atocha train station,** thoroughly restored in 1992. The high-speed train (the AVE) to Seville leaves from here, as do local trains to Toledo and long-distance trains to points south. The immense building of painted tiles and winged statues across the traffic circle currently houses the **Ministerio de Agricultura** (Agriculture Ministry). The **Centro de Arte Reina Sofía** ⑮, home to Picasso's *Guernica,* is housed in the building with the glass elevators on the front.

Stolling back north of the Prado, note the elegant Ritz Hotel and the **Museo Thyssen-Bornemisza** ⑯ across the street. Further along, you can see the ornate **Palacio de Communicaciones** ⑥, or post office, and the grand yellow mansion that was once the home of the Marquis of Salamanca, who, at the turn of the 20th century, built the exclusive shopping and residential neighborhood that bears his name. It now houses the **Banco Argentaria.**

If you should choose to do this walk in reverse, you can head from the Royal Palace to the Parque del Oeste (stop first for a coffee at the Café de Oriente) where you can explore the Egyptian **Templo de Debod.** Hop on the **Telefèric** for a scenic ride to the **Casa de Campo;** visit the zoo and amuse yourself in the **Parque de Atracciones** before winding up your day.

TIMING

This walk covers about 3 km/2 mi and, depending on how often you stop, can be covered in two to three hours.

Plan to devote an entire morning or afternoon for return visits to each of Madrid's main sights: the Royal Palace, the Prado Museum, the Reina Sofía Museum, and the Thyssen-Bournemisza Gallery.

Sights to See

㉕ **Academia de Bellas Artes de San Fernando.** Designed by Churriguera in the early-18th century, the waning years of the Baroque period, this little-visited museum is a showcase of painting and the other plastic arts. The same building houses the **Instituto de Calcografía,** where limited-edition prints from original plates engraved by Spanish artists—including Goya—are sold. ⊠ *Alcalá 13,* ☏ *91/532–1249.* 🎟 *200 ptas.* ☉ *Tues.–Fri. 9–9, Sat.–Mon. 9–2.*

❼ **Banco de España.** Spain's equivalent of the U.S. Federal Reserve, the massive 1884 building takes up an entire city block and where it's said the nation's gold reserves are held in great vaults that stretch under the Plaza de Cibeles traffic circle all the way to the fountain. The bank is not open for visits, but if you want to risk dodging traffic to reach the median strip in front of the bank, you can get a fine photo of the fountain and the palaces with the monumental Puerta de Alcalá arch in the background.

㉔ **Campo del Moro.** Below the Sabatini Gardens, but accessible only by walking around to an entrance on the far side, is the Campo del Moro. This park's clusters of shady trees, winding paths, and long lawn that leads up to the palace offer a prime spot for photographing the building. Even without considering the riches inside, the palace's immense size (twice as large as Buckingham Palace) is awe-inspiring.

❽ **Casa de las Américas.** A cultural center and art gallery focusing on Latin America, it was re-opened in 1992 in the allegedly haunted Palacio de

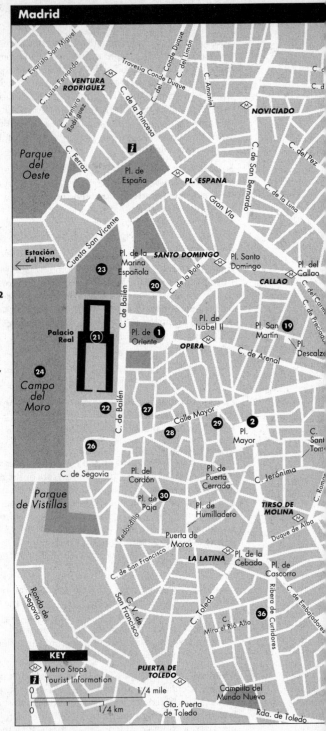

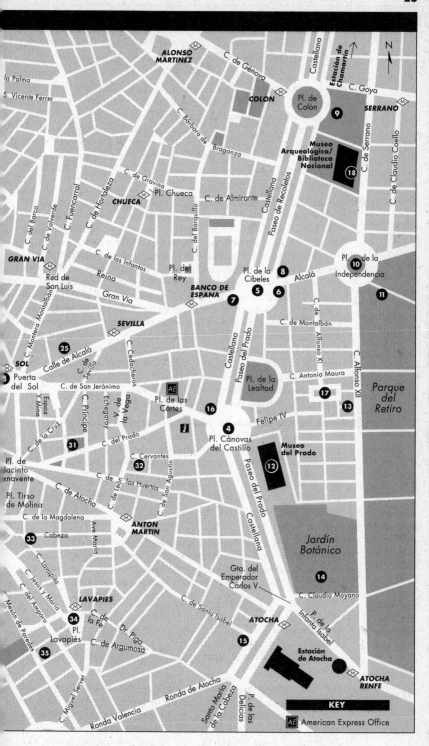

N

C. de la Palma

S. Vicente Ferrer

ALONSO MARTINEZ

C. de Génova

Castellana

Estación de Chamartin

C. Goya

COLON

Pl. de Colón

9

SERRANO

C. de Serrano

C. de Claudio Coello

C. Bárbara de Braganza

C. de Gravina

C. de Hortaleza

C. de Fuencarral

C. de Valverde

C. de Barco

Pl. Chueca

CHUECA

C. del Barquillo

C. de Almirante

Museo Arqueológico/ Biblioteca Nacional

18

C. de las Infantas

Pl. del Rey

Paseo de Recoletos

Castellana

GRAN VIA

Reina

Gran Via

C. Montera

C. Montalbán

Red de San Luis

Pl. de la Cibeles

8

Alcalá

Pl. de la Independencia

10

11

5 **6**

BANCO DE ESPANA

7

Castellana

Paseo del Prado

C. de Montalbán

C. de Alfonso XI

C. Alfonso XII

SEVILLA

Calle de Alcalá

C. Cedaceros

C. de Sevilla

25

SOL

Puerta del Sol

C. de San Jerónimo

C. de San Jerónimo

C. Principe

C. Echegaray

V. de la Vega

C. del Prado

C. de la Cruz

Espoz y Mina

Pl. de las Cortes

AE

16

Pl. de la Lealtad

C. Antonio Maura

17

13

Parque del Retiro

C. Antonio Maura

Felipe IV

31

Pl. de Jacinto Benavente

C. de Cervantes

32

C. de León

las Huertas

i

4

Pl. Cánovas del Castillo

Museo del Prado

12

Paseo del Prado

Pl. Tirso de Molina

C. de Atocha

C. de la Magdalena

Ave María

C. de San Agustín

ANTON MARTIN

Castellana

Jardín Botánico

33

Cabeza

C. Lavapiés

C. Jesús y María

C. del Amparo

Mesón de Paredes

LAVAPIES

C. de la Fe

Dr. Piga

C. de Santa Isabel

Gta. del Emperador Carlos V

C. Claudio Moyano

14

P. de la Infanta Isabel

34

Pl. Lavapiés

C. de Argumosa

ATOCHA

15

Estación de Atocha

ATOCHA RENFE

35

C. Miguel Servet

Ronda de Atocha

Santa María de la Cabeza

P. de las Delicias

Ronda Valencia

KEY

AE American Express Office

Linares, built by a man who made his fortune in the New World and returned to a life of incestuous love and strange deaths. ⊠ *Paseo Recoletos 2,* ☎ *91/595–4800.* ☏ *Palace tour 300 ptas., art gallery free.* ◷ *Palace tour Tues.–Fri. 9–11:30, Sat. 10–1:30; art gallery Tues.–Sat. 11–7, Sun. 11–2.*

⑬ Casón del Buen Retiro. This annex to the Prado museum is just a five minute walk away and can be entered on the same ticket. This building, once a ballroom, and the formal gardens in nearby Retiro Park are all that remains of Madrid's second royal palace complex, which until the early 19th century occupied the entire neighborhood. On exhibit here are 19th-century Spanish painting and sculpture, including works by Sorolla and Rusiñol. ⊠ *C. Alfonso XII s/n,* ☎ *91/420–3662.* ◷ *Tues.–Sat. 9–7, Sun. 9–2.*

㉒ Catedral de la Almudena. The cathedral building adjoins the royal palace to the south and, after 110 years of construction, was consecrated by Pope John Paul II in 1993. The first stone was laid in 1883 by King Alfonso XII. At the time it was planned as a Gothic-style structure of needles and spires, but as time ran long and money ran short, the design was simplified by Fernando Chueca Goltia to become the more austere, classical building you see today. The cathedral houses the remains of Madrid's male patron saint, St. Isidro, and a wooden statue of Madrid's female patron saint, the Virgin of Almudena, which was said to have been discovered following the Christian reconquest of Madrid in 1085. Legend has it that a divinely inspired woman named María led authorities to a secret spot in the old wall of the Alcázar (which in Arabic can also be called *almudeyna*), where the statue was found framed by two lit candles inside a grain storage vault. That wall is part of the cathedral's foundation. ⊠ *C. de Bailén s/n,* ☎ *91/542–2200.* ☏ *Free.* ◷ *Daily 10–1:30 and 6–7:45.*

★ **⑮ Centro de Arte Reina Sofía.** Madrid's modern-art museum is housed in a converted hospital, whose classic, granite austerity is somewhat relieved (or ruined, depending upon who you ask) by the two transparent-glass elevator shafts that have been added to the facade.

The collection focuses on three great, Spanish modern masters: Pablo Picasso, Salvador Dalí, and Joan Miró. Take the elevator to the second floor to see the permanent collections; the other floors house visiting exhibits.

The first rooms are dedicated to the beginnings of Spain's modern-art movement and contain paintings completed around the turn of the century. The focal point is Picasso's 1901 *Woman in Blue*—hardly beautiful, but surprisingly representational compared to his later works.

Moving on to the **Cubist collection,** which includes nine works by Juan Gris, be sure to see the splintered, blue-gray *Self-Portrait* by Dalí, in which he painted his favorite things, a morning newspaper and a pack of cigarettes. The other highlight here is Picasso's *Musical Instruments on a Table,* one of many variations on this theme created by the Spanish-born artist.

The museum's showpiece is Picasso's famous ***Guernica***, which occupies the center hall and is surrounded by dozens of studies for individual figures within it. It depicts the horror of the Nazi Condor Legion's bombing of the ancient Basque town of Guernica in 1937, which helped bring Spanish dictator Francisco Franco to power. The work, in many ways a 20th-century version of Goya's *3rd of May,* is something of a national shrine, as evidenced by the solemnity of Spaniards viewing it. The painting was not brought into Spain until

1981. Picasso, an ardent anti-fascist, refused to allow it to enter the country while Franco was alive.

The room in front of *Guernica* contains a collection of **surrealist works,** including six canvases by Miró, known for his childlike graphicism. Opposite *Guernica* is a hall dedicated to the surrealist Salvador Dalí and hung with paintings bequeathed to the government in the artist's will. Although Dalí is perhaps best known for works of a somewhat whimsical tone, many of these canvases are dark and haunting and bursting with symbolism. Among the best known are *The Great Masturbator* (1929) and *The Enigma of Hitler* (1939), with its broken, dripping telephone.

The rest of the museum is devoted to more recent art, including the massive, gravity-defying sculpture *Toki Egin* by Eduardo Chillida, considered Spain's greatest living sculptor, and five textural paintings by Barcelona artist Antoní Tàpies, who incorporates materials such as wrinkled sheets and straw into his works. ⊠ *Santa Isabel 52,* ☎ *91/467–5062.* ⊠ *400 ptas., free Sat. 2:30–9 and Sun.* ⊘ *Mon. and Wed.–Sat. 10–9, Sun. 10–2:30.*

⑳ **Convento de la Encarnación** (Convent of the Incarnation of the Augustinian order). Once connected to the Royal Palace by an underground passageway, this convent was founded in 1611 by the wife of Felipe III. It houses many artistic treasures, but the convent's biggest attraction is the reliquary chamber where among the sacred bones is a vial containing the dried blood of St. Pantaleón, which is said to liquify every year on July 27. The convent can be entered on the same ticket as the Convent of Descalzas Reales. ⊠ *Plaza de la Encarnación 1,* ☎ *91/547–0510.* ⊠ *400 ptas.* ⊘ *Wed. and Sat. 10:30–1 and 4–5:30, Sun. 11–1:30.*

⑲ **Convento de las Descalzas Reales** (Convent of the Royal Barefoot Nuns). This 16th-century building was restricted for 200 years to women of royal blood, and its plain, brick-and-stone facade hides a treasure trove of riches. Inside there are paintings by Zurbarán, Titian, and Breughel the Elder, as well as a hall of sumptuous tapestries crafted from drawings by Rubens. The convent was founded in 1559 by Juana of Austria, whose daughter shut herself up here rather than endure marriage to Felipe II. A handful of nuns (not necessarily royal) still live here, cultivating their own vegetables in the convent's garden. Unfortunately you must visit as part of a tour, which is conducted only in Spanish. ⊠ *Plaza de las Descalzas Reales 3,* ☎ *91/542–0059.* ⊠ *650 ptas.* ⊘ *Tues.–Thurs. and Sat. 10:30–12:30 and 4–5:30, Fri. 10:30–12:30, Sun. 11–1:30.*

❺ **Fuente de la Cibeles.** A landscaped walkway runs down the center of the Paseo del Prado to the Plaza de la Cibeles, which is home to this famous fountain depicting Sybil, the wife of Saturn, driving a chariot drawn by lions. Even more than the officially designated bear and the strawberry tree, this monument, beautifully lit at night, has come to symbolize Madrid—so much so that during the civil war, patriotic citizens risked life and limb sand-bagging it as Nationalist aircraft bombed the city.

❹ **Fuente de Neptuno** (Neptune's fountain). Located just outside the Palace Hotel and the boutique-filled Galerias del Prado shopping center on the Plaza Canovas del Castillo, this plaza is the hub of Madrid's so-called "golden triangle of art," made up of the red-brick Prado Museum spreading out along the east side of the boulevard, the Thyssen-Bornemisza Museum across the plaza, and, five blocks to the south, the Reina Sofía art center.

⑭ **Jardín Botánico** (Botanical Gardens). Just south of the Prado Museum, the gardens provide a pleasant place to stroll or sit under the trees. True to the wishes of King Carlos III, the garden holds an array of plants, flowers, and cacti from around the world. ⊠ *Plaza de Murillo 2,* ☎ *91/585–4700.* ⊞ *200 ptas.* ⊙ *Summer, daily 10–9; winter, daily 10–6.*

㉓ **Jardines Sabatini** (Sabatini Gardens). The formal gardens to the north of the Royal Palace, are crawling with stray cats, but are a pleasant place for a rest and a good spot from which to watch the sunset.

⑱ **Museo Arqueológico** (Archeology Museum). The museum shares the same neoclassical building with the **Biblioteca Nacional** (National Library). The biggest attraction here is a replica of the prehistoric Altamira cave paintings, located underground in the garden. Inside the museum, look for the *Dama de Elche,* a bust of a wealthy woman of the 4th-century Iberian culture. Notice how her headgear is a rough precursor to the mantillas and hair combs still associated with traditional Spanish costumes. Be sure to see the ancient Visigothic votive crowns discovered in 1859 near Toledo and believed to date back to the 8th century. ⊠ *C. Serrano 13,* ☎ *91/577–7912.* ⊞ *400 ptas.* ⊙ *Tues.–Sat. 9:30–8:30, Sun. 9:30–2:30.*

⑰ **Museo del Ejército** (Army Museum). A real treat for the arms and armor buffs, it is located along the "museum mile." Among the 27,000 items on view are a sword allegedly belonging to Spanish hero El Cid, suits of armor, bizarre-looking pistols with barrels capable of holding scores of bullets, Moorish tents, and a cross carried by Christopher Columbus. This is an unusually entertaining museum of its genre. ⊠ *Mendez Nuñez 1,* ☎ *91/522–8977.* ⊞ *50 ptas.* ⊙ *Tues.–Sun. 10–2.*

★ ⑫ **Museo del Prado** (Prado Museum). This museum was first commissioned in 1785 by King Carlos III and originally meant to be a natural-science museum. The king, popularly remembered as "Madrid's best mayor," intended the museum, the adjoining botanical gardens, and the elegant Paseo del Prado to serve as a center of scientific enlightenment for his subjects. By the time the building was completed in 1819, its purpose had been changed to exhibiting the vast collection of art gathered by Spanish royalty since the time of Ferdinand and Isabella.

Painting represents one of Spain's greatest contributions to world culture, and the jewels of the Prado are the works of the nation's three great masters: Francisco Goya, Diego Velázquez, and El Greco. The museum also contains masterpieces of Flemish and Italian artists, collected when those lands were part of the Spanish Empire. The museum benefited greatly from anticlerical laws in 1836, which forced monasteries, convents, and churches to turn over many of their art treasures so that they could be enjoyed by the general public.

The visit begins on the upper floor (primera planta) of the museum, where you enter through a series of halls dedicated to **Renaissance painters.** While many visitors hurry through these rooms to get to the Spanish canvases, don't miss the *Portrait of Emperor Charles V* by Titian, and Raphael's exquisite *Portrait of a Cardinal.*

Next comes a hall filled with the passionately spiritual works of **El Greco** (Doménikos Theotokópoulos, 1541–1614). This Greek-born artist, who lived and worked in Toledo, is known for his mystical, elongated faces. His style was quite shocking to a public accustomed to strict, representational realism; and as he intended his art to provoke emotion, El Greco is sometimes called the world's first "modern" painter. *The Resurrection* and the *Adoration of the Shepherds,* considered two of his greatest paintings, are on view here.

Velázquez (1599–1660): The artist's meticulous brushwork is visible in numerous portraits of kings and queens. Be sure to look for the magnificent painting *Las Hilanderas* (*The Spinners*)—evidence of the artist's talent for painting light. One hall is reserved exclusively for the Prado's most famous canvas, Velázquez's *Las Meninas* (*The Maids of Honor*). It combines a self-portrait of the artist at work with a mirror reflection of the king and queen in an astounding interplay of space and perspectives. Picasso was obsessed with this work and painted numerous copies of it in his own abstract style, which can be seen in the Picasso Museum in Barcelona.

The south end of the first floor (primera planta) is reserved for **Goya** (1746–1828), whose works span a staggering range of tone, from bucolic to horrific. Among his early masterpieces are numerous portraits of the family of King Carlos IV, to whom he was court painter. A glance at their unflattering and imbecilic expressions, especially in the painting *The Family of Carlos IV*, reveals the loathing Goya developed for these self-indulgent and reactionary rulers. His famous side-by-side canvases, *The Clothed Maja* and *The Nude Maja,* may or may not represent the young duchess of Alba, whom Goya adored and frequently painted. It is not known whether she ever returned his affection. Adjacent rooms house a series of bucolic scenes of Spaniards at play, painted by Goya as designs for tapestries.

His paintings take on political purpose starting in 1808, when the population of Madrid rose up against occupying French troops. The *2nd of May* portrays the insurrection at the Puerta del Sol, and the even more terrifying companion piece, *3rd of May,* depicts the nighttime executions of patriots who had rebelled the day before. The garish lighting effects of this work typify the romantic style, which favors drama over detail, and make it one of the most powerful indictments of violence ever committed to canvas.

Downstairs you'll find the extreme of Goya's range in a hall that features his "black paintings"—dark, disturbing works completed late in his life that reflect the inner turmoil he suffered after losing his hearing and his deep embitterment over the bloody War of Independence. The rest of the ground floor is taken up with Flemish paintings, including the bizarre masterpiece, *Garden of Earthly Delights* by Hieronymous Bosch. ✉ *Paseo del Prado s/n,* ☎ 91/420–3662. 🎟 *400 ptas.* ◷ *Tues.–Sat. 9–7, Sun. 9–2.*

NEED A
BREAK?
> **La Dolores** (✉ Plaza de Jesús 4) is one of Madrid's most atmospheric, old, tiled bars and the perfect place for a beer or glass of wine and a plate of olives. It's a great alternative to the Prado Museum's so-so basement cafeteria and is just across the paseo, one block up on Calle Lope de Vega to the tiny Plaza.

---

⑯ **Museo Thyssen-Bornemisza.** Madrid's third and newest art center, elegantly renovated to include lots of airy space and natural light, opened in 1992 in the Villahermosa Palace. This ambitious collection of 800 paintings attempts to trace the history of Western art with examples from all the important movements, beginning with 13th-century Italy.

The artworks were gathered over the past 70 years by industrialist Baron Hans Heinrich Thyssen-Bornemisza and his father. At the urging of his Spanish wife, a former Miss Spain, the baron agreed to donate the collection to Spain. While the museum itself is beautiful, and its Impressionist paintings are the only ones on exhibit in the country, critics have characterized the collection as the minor works of major artists and the major works of minor artists.

Among the museum's gems are the *Portrait of Henry VIII* by Hans Holbein (purchased from Princess Diana's grandfather, who used the money to buy a new Bugatti sports car). American artists are also well represented. Look for the Gilbert Stuart portrait of George Washington's black cook, and note how much the composition and rendering resembles the artist's famous painting of the Founding Father himself. Two halls are devoted to the Impressionists and Post-impressionists, including many works by Pissarro, and a few each by Renoir, Monet, Degas, Van Gogh, and Cézanne.

Of 20th-century art, the baron shows a weakness for terror-filled (albeit dynamic and colorful) German Expressionism, but there are also soothing paintings by Georgia O'Keeffe and Andrew Wyeth. ⊠ *Paseo del Prado 8,* ☎ *91/361–0151.* 💷 *600 ptas.* ☉ *Tues.–Sun. 10–7.*

❻ Palacio de Comunicaciones. On the southeast side of Cibeles plaza, this ornate building is otherwise known as the main post office. ☉ *Stamps weekdays 9 AM–10 PM, Sat. 9–8, Sun. 10–1; telephone, telex, telegrams, and fax weekdays 8 AM–midnight, weekends 8 AM–10 PM.*

★ ㉑ Palacio Real (Royal Palace). Standing on the same strategic spot where Madrid's first Alcázar or Arab fortress was built in the 9th century, the Royal Palace was commissioned in the early 1700s by the first of Spain's Bourbon rulers, Felipe V.

Before entering, take time to walk around the graceful **Patio de Armas** and admire the classical French architecture. It's clear that King Felipe was inspired by his childhood days spent with his grandfather, Louis XIV, at Versailles. Look for the stone statues of Inca Prince Atahualpa and Aztec King Montezuma, perhaps the only tributes in Spain to these pre-Columbian, American rulers. Notice how the steep bluff drops down to the Manzanares River to the west. On a clear day this vantage point also commands a good view of the mountain passes leading into Madrid from Old Castile, and it becomes obvious why the Moors picked this particular spot for a fortress.

Inside, the palace's 2,800 rooms compete with each other for over-the-top opulence. A nearly two-hour guided tour in English winds a mile-long path through the palace. Highlights include the **Salón de Gasparini,** King Carlos III's private apartments—a riot of Rococo decoration, with swirling, inlaid floors; curlicued, ceramic wall and ceiling decoration all glistening in the light of a 2-ton crystal chandelier; the **Salón del Trono,** an exceedingly grand throne room that contains the royal seats of King Juan Carlos and Queen Sofía; and the **banquet hall,** which is the palace's largest room and seats up to 140 people for state dinners. No monarch has lived here since 1931, when Alfonso XIII was hounded out of the country by a populace fed up with centuries of royal oppression. The current king and queen live in the far simpler Zarzuela Palace on the outskirts of Madrid, using this Royal Palace only for state functions and official occasions, such as the first Middle East peace talks in 1991.

Within the palace you can also visit the **Biblioteca Real** (Royal Library), which has a first edition of Cervantes's *Don Quixote*; the **Museo de Música** (Music Museum), where the five stringed instruments by Stradivarius make up the world's largest collection; the **Armería Real** (Royal Armory), with its vast array of historic suits of armor and some frightening medieval torture implements; and the **Real Oficina de Farmacía** (Royal Pharmacy), boasting an assortment of vials and flasks used for concocting the king's medicines. ⊠ *C. Bailén s/n,* ☎ *91/559–7404.* 💷 *850 ptas.* ☉ *Mon.–Sat. 9:30–6, Sun. 9–3; closed during official receptions.*

★ ⑪ **Parque del Retiro** (Retiro Park). Once royalty's private playground, the park is a vast expanse of green that includes formal gardens, fountains, lakes (complete with rentable rowboats), exhibition halls, children's play areas, and a **Puppet Theater,** featuring slapstick routines that even non-Spanish speakers will enjoy. Shows take place on Saturday at 1 and on Sunday at 1, 6, and 7. Admission is free. The park is especially lively here on weekends, when it fills with street musicians, jugglers, clowns, gypsy fortune-tellers, and sidewalk painters, along with hundreds of Spanish families out for a walk. During May the park hosts a month-long book fair, and in summer flamenco concerts often take place here.

From the entrance at the Puerta de Alcalá, head straight toward the center of Retiro park and you'll find the **Estanque** (lake), presided over by a grandiose equestrian statue of King Alfonso XII, erected by his mother. One of the best of the many cafés within the park is behind the lake, just north of the statue. If you're feeling more energetic, you can rent a boat and work up an appetite rowing around the lake.

The 19th-century **Palacio de Cristal** (Crystal Palace), southeast of the Estanque, was built to house a collection of exotic plants from the Philippines, a Spanish possession at the time. This airy marvel of steel and glass sits on a base of decorative tile and is now undergoing a long-overdue renovation. A small lake with ducks and swans is next door. At the south end of the park along the Paseo del Uruguay is the **Rosaleda** (rose garden), an English garden bursting with color and heavy with the scent of flowers for most of the summer. West of the Rosaleda, look for a statue called the **Ángel Caído** (fallen angel), which Madrileños claim is the only one in the world depicting the prince of darkness before—during, actually—his fall from grace.

❾ **Plaza Colón.** The modern plaza is named for Christopher Columbus. A statue of the explorer (identical to one in the port of Barcelona) looks west from atop a high tower in the middle of the square. The airport bus leaves from here every 15 minutes via the underground parking. Behind Plaza Colón is **Calle Serrano,** the city's number-one shopping street (think Gucci, Prada, and Loewe). Take a stroll in either direction on Serrano for some window shopping.

NEED A BREAK?
Decorated in the style of Belle Epoque Paris, **El Espejo** is the ideal place to rest your feet and sip a cup of coffee or a beer. You can pull up a chair on the shady terrace or inside the air-conditioned, stained-glass bar. Located right in the center of the paseo, at the Paza Colon. ✉ *Paseo Recoletos 31,* ☎ *91/308–2347,* ⊘ *Daily 10 AM–2 AM.*

❶ **Plaza de Oriente.** The stately plaza in front of the Royal Palace, is surrounded by stone statues of all the Spanish kings from Ataulfo to Fernando VI. These massive sculptures were meant to be mounted on the railing atop the palace, where there are now stone urns. But Queen Isabel de Farnesio, one of the first royals to inhabit the palace, had them taken off because she was afraid their enormous weight would bring the roof down. At least that's what she *said.* Palace insiders reported the queen wanted the statues removed because her own likeness had not been placed front and center.

The statue of King Felipe IV in the center of the plaza was the first equestrian bronze ever to be cast of a horse rearing up. This action pose comes from a painting of the king by Velázquez by which the monarch was so smitten that in 1641 he commissioned an Italian artist, Pietro de Tacca, to turn it into a sculpture. De Tacca enlisted the help of the scientist Galileo to figure out the feat of engineering that keeps the statue from falling over.

In the minds of most Madrileños, the Plaza de Oriente is forever linked with Francisco Franco. The *generalissimo* liked to make speeches from the roof of the Royal Palace to his thousands of followers crammed into the plaza below. Even now, on the November anniversary of Franco's death, the plaza fills with his supporters, most of whom are old-timers, although lately the occasion has also drawn Nazi flag–waving skinheads from other European countries in a chilling, pro-fascist tribute.

NEED A
BREAK?

Taberna del Alabardero. Stop for a drink or a snack in the Royal Palace neighborhood. Named for a regiment of the king's guards, this cozy bar stocks a dozen types of tapas. Try the garlicky *patatas à la pobre* (poor man's potatoes). ⊠ *C. Felipe V, 6.*

② **Plaza Mayor.** This arcaded square is the very heart of Madrid. Austere, grand—and surprisingly quiet compared to the rest of the city— the Plaza Mayor has seen it all: *autos da fe* (public burnings of heretics); the canonization of saints; criminal executions; royal marriages, such as that of Princess María and the King of Hungary in 1629; bullfights (until 1847); masked balls; fireworks displays, and all manner of events and celebrations.

Measuring 360 by 300 feet, this is one of the largest public squares in Europe and considered by many to be one of the most beautiful. It was designed by Juan de Herrera, the architect to Felipe II and the same man who designed the forbidding El Escorial monastery outside Madrid. Construction of the plaza lasted just two years and was completed in 1620 during the reign of Felipe III, whose **equestrian statue** stands in the center of the plaza. The inauguration ceremonies included celebrating the canonization of four Spanish saints: Teresa of Ávila, Ignatius of Loyola, Isidro (Madrid's male patron saint), and Francis Xavier.

Prior to becoming the Plaza Mayor, this space was occupied by a city market, and many of the surrounding streets retain the names of the trades and foodstuffs once ensconsed there. Nearby are Calle de Cuchilleros (Knife Makers' Street), Calle de Lechuga (Lettuce Street), Calle de Fresa (Strawberry Street), and Calle de Botoneros (Button Makers' Street). The oldest building on the plaza is the one with the brightly painted murals and the gray spires, Casa de la Panadería (the bakery) in honor of the bread shop on top of which it was built. Opposite it is the Casa de la Carniceria (the butcher shop), which now houses a police station.

The plaza is closed to motorized traffic, making this a pleasant place to sit in the sun or to while away a warm, summer evening at one of the sidewalk cafés, watching alfresco portrait artists, street musicians, and Madrileños from all walks of life. At Christmas the plaza fills with stalls selling trees, ornaments, and nativity scenes, as well as all types of practical jokes and tricks to be used on December 28, the *Día de los Inocentes,* a Spanish version of April Fool's Day.

⑩ **Puerta de Alcalá.** Marking the spot of the ancient city gates, this triumphal arch was built by Carlos III in 1778. Bomb damage inflicted on the arch during the civil war is still visible.

③ **Puerta del Sol.** Always crowded with people and exhaust fumes, the plaza is Madrid's traffic nerve center. The city's main subway interchange is located below, and buses fan out through the city from here. A brass plaque in the sidewalk on the south side of the plaza marks Kilometer 0, the spot from which all distances in Spain are measured.

The restored 1756 French neoclassical building by the marker now houses government offices, but during the Franco period it was used as a political prison and is still known as the "house of screams." Across the square is a bronze statue of Madrid's official symbol, a bear and a *madroño* (strawberry) tree.

Teatro Real (Royal Theater). This neoclassical theater was built in about 1850 and was once the center of Madrid's cultural society. It has been closed for renovations and is set to reopen as the city's opera house by the end of 1996. ⊠ *Plaza de Isabel II.*

Teléfèric (cable car). Children love the cable car that takes you from just above the Rosaleda gardens in the Parque del Oeste to the center of Casa de Campo. Be warned, however, that it's at least a mile from where the cable car drops you off to both the zoo and the amusement park, and you'll have to ask directions. ⊠ *Estación Terminal Telefèico, Jardines Rosaleda,* ☎ *91/541–7440.* ☒ *470 ptas.* ☉ *Apr.–Sept., daily noon–sundown; Oct.–Mar., weekends noon–sundown.*

OFF THE
BEATEN PATH

CASA DE CAMPO – The Casa de Campo contains a zoo, an amusement park, a convention center, major outdoor concerts, and a half-dozen cafés. Pintor Rosales ends at Paseo de Moret, where you'll turn right to climb up the hill that follows the hilly Parque del Oeste (West Park), a perfect place for a picnic. At the top of the hill you'll come into the Moncloa traffic circle.

Templo de Debod (Debod Temple). An authentic 4th-century BC Egyptian temple donated to the Spanish in recognition of their engineering help during the construction of the Aswan Dam, it sits near the site of the former Montaña barracks, where Madrileños bloodily crushed the beginnings of a Francoist uprising in 1936. ⊠ *Atop hill in Parque de la Montaña, near Estación del Norte train station,* ☎ *91/409–6165.* ☒ *300 ptas.* ☉ *Tues.–Fri. 10–1 and 4–7, weekends 10–1.*

Medieval Madrid

Through the narrow streets of medieval Madrid, trace the city's history from its beginnings as an Arab fortress. Madrid's historic quarters are not so readily apparent as the ancient neighborhoods that characterize Toledo, Segovia, and Ávila, nor are they so grand. But the visitor who takes time to explore the quiet, winding streets of medieval Madrid will be rewarded with an impression of the city that is light-years away from today's traffic-clogged avenues.

A Good Walk

The walk begins near the Royal Palace at the 8th-century **Arab Wall** ㉖ on Cuesta de la Vega street. Traveling west on Calle Mayor to **Plaza de la Villa** ㉘, you find examples of the Spanish Mudéjar architecture, and old family crests carved above doorways. Passing below the Plaza Mayor on **Cava de San Miguel** ㉙ street are Madrid's oldest tapas bars, taverns, and restaurants.

From the Puerta Cerrada, the Calle Segovia guides you to ramped alleyways that lead to **Plaza de Paja** ㉚, the heart of the old city where peasants in the Middle Ages would deposit their crops as tithings to the church. Here you can visit the **Museo de San Isidro,** the site where Madrid's patron saint performed his most famous miracle.

Walk west from the Plaza de Paja on Calle de la Redondilla for one block to the **Plaza Morería,** which is really no more than a wide spot in the street. This neighborhood was once the home of Moors who had chosen to stay in Madrid after the Christian reconquest. Although most of the buildings date from the 18th and 19th centuries, the steep, narrow streets and twisting alleyways are reminiscent of the much older *medina.*

Climb the stairway and cross Calle Bailén near the **Viaduct,** a metal bridge that spans a ravine 100 feet above Calle Segovia. The viaduct has won grisly fame as the preferred spot in Madrid for suicides.

Across the street on Calle Bailen is the neighborhood known as **Las Vistillas,** named for the pleasant park on the bluffs that overlooks Madrid's western edge. A great place to watch the sun go down or catch a cool breeze on a sweltering, summer's night, the best thing to do here is find an empty outdoor table and order a drink and some tapas.

TIMING

This three-hour walk covers 2½ km/1½ mi and requires some short, uphill climbs through the narrow, winding streets. Give yourself ample time for frequent stops to appreciate the old world charm (especially during the summer months when heat will be a factor).

Sights to See

㉖ Arab Wall. The city of Madrid was founded on Calle Cuesta de la Vega at the ruins of the wall which protected a fortress built on this site in the 8th century by Emir Mohammed I. In addition to being an excellent defensive position, the site had plentiful water and was called *Mayrit,* which is Arabic for "water source" and the likely origin of the city's name. All that remains of the Arab *medina* or early city that formed within the walls of the fortress is this neighborhood's crazy quilt of streets and plazas, which likely follow the same layout as they did more than 1,100 years ago. The park **Emir Mohammed I** (⊠ Cuesta de la Vega, s/n), alongside the wall, is a venue for summertime concerts and plays.

★ ㉙ Cava de San Miguel. The narrow, picturesque streets behind the Plaza de la Villa are well worth exploring. From Calle Mayor turn onto the Plaza de San Miguel and continue down the Cava de San Miguel street. With the Plaza Mayor on your left and the iron-and-glass San Miguel market on your right, walk downhill past the row of **ancient tapas bars** built right into the retaining wall of the plaza above. Each one specializes in something different: Mesón de Champiñones has mushrooms; Mesón de Boquerones serves anchovies; Mesón de Tortilla cooks up excellent Spanish omelettes, and so on. Madrileños and tourists flock here each evening to sample the food and sing along with raucous musicians, who delight in playing foreign tunes for tourists.

Costanilla de San Andrés. The ramped street leads to the heart of the old city. To find it, follow Calle Segovia from the Plaza Puerta Cerrada until you reach Plaza Cruz Verde, and turn left up the ramped street. Halfway up the hill, look left down the narrow Calle Principe Anglona for a good view of the Mudéjar tower of the **church of San Pedro el Viejo,** which, after San Nicolás, is one of the city's oldest. The brick tower is believed to have been built in 1354 following the Christian reconquest of Algeciras, in southern Spain. Be sure to notice the tiny defensive slits designed to accommodate crossbows.

Cuevas de Luis Candelas. The oldest of Madrid's taverns, about halfway down the street of Cava San Miguel, is named for a 19th-century Madrid version of Robin Hood who was famous for his ingenious ways of tricking the rich out of their money and jewels. As the same street changes names to Calle Cuchilleros, on the left is **Casa Botín** (☞ Dining, *below*), Madrid's oldest restaurant and a favorite haunt of Ernest Hemingway. The curving street of Cuchilleros was once a moat just outside the walls of old Madrid. The plaza with the bright murals at the intersection of Calle Segovia is called the **Puerta Cerrada** (⊠ Cava San Miguel and Cuchilleros), or Closed Gate, named for the entrance to the city that once stood here.

㉗ Iglesia de San Nicolás de las Servitas (Church of St. Nicholas). The church tower is one of the oldest buildings in Madrid, and there's some debate over whether it once formed part of an Arab mosque. More likely it was built after the Christian reconquest of Madrid in 1085, but the brick-work and horseshoe arches are clear evidence that it was crafted by either Moorish workers or Spaniards well versed in the style. Inside the church are exhibits detailing the Islamic history of early Madrid. ⊠ *Near the Plaza de San Nicolás,* ☎ *91/559–4064.* ⊡ *100 ptas.* ☉ *Tues.–Sun. 6:30–8:30 or by appointment.*

Museo de San Isidro. Just behind San Andres Church, you can visit the site of St. Isidro's most famous miracle. Housed in the newly opened museum is the original *pozo milagroso* (miracle well). It is said, Isidro's infant son Illán fell into the well one day and to save the child, Isidro raised the water level so that his son floated up to the top and could be pulled out. ⊠ *Plaza San Isidro s/n,* ☎ *91/522–5732.* ⊡ *Free.* ☉ *Aug.–June, Tues.–Sun. 10–2.*

Palacio de la Nunciatura (Palace of the Nunciat). Although it's not open to the public, you can peek inside the Renaissance garden of this mansion that once housed the Pope's ambassadors to Spain and is now the official residence of the Archbishop of Madrid. It's near the Plaza Puerta Cerrada off Calle Segovia, one of the main streets of Madrid during the Middle Middle Ages. ⊠ *Costanilla del Nuncio s/n.*

NEED A BREAK? The **Café del Nuncio** (⊠ Costanilla del Nuncio, s/n) on the corner of Calle Segovia is a relaxing Old World–style spot for coffee or a beer where classical music plays in the background.

㉘ Plaza de la Villa. A medieval-looking complex of buildings, it is now Madrid's city hall, located just two blocks west of the Plaza Mayor on Calle Mayor. Once called the Plaza de San Salvador for a church that used to stand here, this site has been the meeting place for the town council since the Middle Ages. **Casa de los Lujanes** is the oldest building in the Plaza de la Villa. It is the one with the Mudéjar tower on the east side of the plaza. Built as a family home in the late 15th century, the Lujanes crest can be seen over the main doorway. On the east side of Plaza de la Villa is the **Casa de la Villa,** built in 1629. This brick-and-stone building is a classic example of Madrid design with its clean lines and spire-topped, corner towers. Connected by an overhead walkway, the **Casa de Cisneros** was commissioned in 1537 by the nephew of Cardinal Cisneros. The building is one of Madrid's rare examples of the flamboyant Plateresque style, which has been likened to splashing water—liquid exuberance wrought in stone. ⊠ *C. Mayor.* ☉ *Spanish guided tour Mon. at 5.*

㉚ Plaza de Paja. Located at the top of the hill on Costanillo San Andres street, is the most important square of medieval Madrid. Although a few upscale restaurants have moved in, the small plaza remains atmospheric. The jewel of Plaza de Paja square is the **Capilla del Obispo** (Bishop's Chapel), built between 1520 and 1530. This was where peasants deposited their tithes, called *diezmas,* literally one-tenth of their crop. Reference to this is made by the stacks of wheat shown on the ceramic tiles on the chapel. Architecturally, the chapel marks a transition from the blockish Gothic period—the basic shape of this structure—to the Renaissance, as evidenced by its decorations. Try to get inside to see the intricately carved, polychrome altarpiece by Francisco

Giralta, featuring scenes from the life of Christ. Opening hours of the chapel are erratic; the best time to visit is during mass or on feast days.

The chapel forms part of the complex of the **church of San Andres,** whose dome was raised to house the remains of Madrid's male patron saint, San Isidro Labrador. Isidro was a peasant who worked fields belonging to the Vargas family. The 16th-century **Vargas palace** (⊠ Plaza de Paja, s/n) forms the eastern side of the Plaza de Paja. According to legend, St. Isidro actually worked little but thanks to many hours spent in prayer had the best-tended fields. When Señor Vargas came out to investigate the phenomenon, Isidro made a spring of sweet water spurt from the ground to quench his master's thirst. Because St. Isidro's power had to do with water, in times of drought his remains were paraded through the city to bring rain (even as recently as the turn of the century).

Castizo Madrid

Castizo is a Spanish word that means authentic, and while there are few "sights" in the usual sense on this tour, our walk wanders through some of the most traditional and lively neighborhoods of Madrid.

A Good Walk

On this walk we explore the humble but vibrant neighborhoods known as *castizo* or "authentic" Madrid, where Miguel de Cervantes once lived and where today poets, musicians, and average people still do.

Begin at **Plaza Santa Ana** ③, which was the hub of the theater district in the 17th century, and today is recognized for its a lively nightlife. Around the Plaza there are many noteworthy sights, such as the **Teatro Español,** and the tile facade of the **Casa de Guadalajara,** one of the most beautiful buildings in Madrid. Walk east two blocks on Calle del Prado; then turn right on Calle Leon, named for a lion kept here long ago by a resident Moor. One block on this street brings you to the corner of **Calle Cervantes,** where a plaque marks the spot where the author of *Don Quixote* lived (**Home of Cervantes** ㉜).

Continuing down Calle Leon on block, turn left on Calle Huertas, the premier street of bars in bar-bespotted Madrid. One block down Huertas turn right onto **Calle Amor de Dios,** the center of the city's flamenco community. Look for the music shops and guitar makers.

Follow Calle Amor de Dios until it ends at the busy Calle Atocha. Across the street you will see the church, **Iglesia San Nicolás.** Next door is the **Pasaje Doré,** home to a colorful assortment of market stalls typical of most Madrid neighborhoods.

Cross the street and walk down Calle de la Rosa, which turns into Calle de la Cabeza. This is the beginning of the **Barrio Lavapíes**—the old *judería* (Jewish Quarter). Today it remains one of the most typical or castizo of all working-class Madrid neighborhoods, although there are some recent signs of creeping gentrification. Don't be surprised to see graffiti reading "Yuppies No!" Explore the area by strolling south on Calle Lavapíes until you reach the heart of the neighborhood, **Plaza Lavapíes** ㉞.

Leave the Plaza heading southwest on Calle Sombrerete two blocks until you reach the intersection of Calle Mesón de Paredes. On the corner you'll see a lovingly preserved example of a popular Madrid architecture called the **Corrala building** ㉟. Life in this type of balconied apartment building is lived very publicly, with laundry flapping in the breeze, babies crying, and old ladies dressed in black gossiping over the railings. In the past, common kitchen and bathroom facilities in the patio were shared among neighbors.

Work your way west, crossing Calle de Embajadores into the neighborhood known as **El Rastro** ㊱. This is a shopper's paradise, with streets of small family shops selling furniture, antiques, and a cornucopia of used junk (some of it highly overpriced). On Sundays, El Rastro becomes a flea market and Calle de Ribera de Curtidores, the main thoroughfare is closed to traffic, jammed with outdoor booths and shoppers.

TIMING

One of the main attractions of this walk is simply the "castizo" atmosphere that you encounter. Therefore, you should plan on spending at least three hours. A good time to visit is on a weekday morning, when the markets are bustling.

Plaza Santa Ana is an interesting area to explore at night with some of Madrid's best tapas bars and nightspots. **El Rastro** can be saved for a Sunday morning if you decide to brave the crowds at the flea market.

Sights to See

Barrio Lavapiés. The Barrio Lavapiés is the old judería (Jewish Quarter). Jews, as well as Moors, were forced to live outside the city walls in old Madrid, and this was one of the suburbs they founded.

㉝ Cárcel de la Inquisición (Inquisition Jail). For a chilling reminder of the depth of Catholic Spain's intolerance, stop at the southeast corner of Calle Cabeza and Calle Lavapiés. Unmarked by any historical plaque, today the building serves as a lumber warehouse. Here Jews, Moors, and others designated as unrepentant heathens and sinners suffered the many tortures devised by the merciless inquisitors.

NEED A BREAK?

Taberna de Antonio Sánchez. Drop in at Madrid's oldest bar for a glass of wine and some tapas or just a peek inside. The dark walls, lined with bullfighting paintings, zinc bar, and pulley system used to lift casks of wine from the cellar, look much the same as they did when the place was first opened in 1830. Meals are also served in a dining room in back. Specialties include *rabo de buey* (bull's-tail stew) and *morcillo al horno* (a beef stew). ⊠ *Mesón de Paredes 13.*

㉜ Home of Cervantes. A plaque marks the house where the author of *Don Quixote* lived and died. Miguel de Cervantes's 1605 epic story of the man with the impossible dream is said to be the world's second-most-widely translated and read book, after the *Bible.* ⊠ *Calles Cervantes and Leon.*

Cine Doré. A rare example of Art Nouveau architecture in Madrid, the theater shows movies from the Spanish National Film Archives and eclectic foreign films, usually in the original version. Showtimes are listed under FILMOTECA in the newspaper. ⊠ *C. Santa Isabel, 3.* ☉ *Tues.–Sun.*

㉟ Corrala building. This building is not unlike the corrales that were used as the city's early theater venues, and there is a plaque to remind us that the setting for the famous 19th-century *zarzuela* or light opera called *La Revoltosa* was a *corrala* like this one. In summer, city-sponsored musical theater events are occasionally held here. The ruins across the street were once the Escalopios de San Fernando—another church and parochial school that fell victim to anti-Catholic sentiments in this neighborhood during the civil war. ⊠ *Calle Mesón de Paredes and C. Sombrerete.*

36 **El Rastro.** Filled with tiny shops selling antiques and all types of used stuff (some of it junk), the rastro becomes an overcrowded flea market on Sunday morning from 10 to 2. The best time for exploring is any other morning, when a little browsing and bargaining are likely to turn up such treasures as old iron grillwork, marble tabletops, or gilt picture frames. The main street of the rastro is Ribera de Curtidores, and the best streets for shopping are the ones to the west.

Home of Lope de Vega. The home of Lope de Vega, a contemporary of Cervantes, has been turned into a museum that shows how a typical home of the period was furnished. Considered the Shakespeare of Spanish literature, Lope de Vega (1562–1635) wrote some 1,800 plays and enjoyed huge success during his lifetime. ⊠ *C. Cervantes 11,* ☎ *91/429–9216.* ⊠ *200 ptas.* ⊙ *Weekdays 9:30–3, Sat. 10–2.*

Iglesia San Nicolás. A plain, modern church noteworthy for its history, the burning of this church in 1936 is vividly described by writer Arturo Barea in his autobiographical *The Forge.* Like many other churches during that turbulent period, the original building here fell victim to the wrath of working-class crowds who felt themselves to be the victims of centuries of clerical oppression. ⊠ *C. Atocha and Plaza Anton Martín.*

34 **Plaza Lavapiés.** This is the heart of this historic neighborhood. To the left is the Calle de la Fe (Street of Faith), which was called Calle Synagogue up until the expulsion of the Jews in 1492. The **Church of San Pedro el Real** was built on the site of the razed synagogue. Legend has it that Jews and Moors who accepted baptism over exile were forced to walk up this street barefoot to be baptized in the church, as a demonstration of the sincerity of their newly found faith. ⊠ *Top of Calle de la Fe.*

31 **Plaza Santa Ana.** This Plaza is the heart of the theater district in the 17th century—the Golden Age of Spanish Literature—and today the center of Madrid's thriving nightlife. In the plaza is a statue of playwright Pedro Calderón de la Barca on a base depicting scenes from his works. His likeness faces the **Teatro Español,** which is adorned with the names of Spain's greatest playwrights. The theater, rebuilt in 1980 following a fire, stands in the same spot in which plays were performed as early as the 16th century, at that time in a rowdy outdoor setting called a *corrala.* These makeshift theaters were usually installed in a vacant lot between two apartment buildings, and families with balconies overlooking the action rented out seats to wealthy patrons of the arts. The **Casa de Guadalajara** with its ceramic-tile facade is one of the most beautiful buildings in Madrid and currently a popular nightspot. It faces the Teatro Español on the opposite side of the plaza Santa Ana. The recently refurbished **Hotel Victoria** on Plaza Santa Ana, is now an upscale establishment but was once a rundown residence frequented by famous and not-so-famous bullfighters, including Manolete.

To the side of the hotel is the diminutive **Plaza del Ángel,** home of one of the city's best jazz clubs, the Café Central. Back on Plaza Santa Ana is one of Madrid's most famous cafés, the **Cervecería Alemana.** Another Hemingway haunt, the café still attracts struggling writers, poets, and beer lovers.

DINING

Madrileños tend to eat their meals even later than other Spaniards. Restaurants generally open for lunch at 1:30 and fill up by 3. Dinnertime begins at 9, but reservations for 11 are common. A meal in Madrid is usually a lengthy (up to three hours) and rather formal affair, even at inexpensive places. Restaurants are at their best at midday, when most places offer a *menú del día* (daily special), a main course, dessert, wine, and coffee.

Dinner, on the other hand, can present something of a problem if you don't want to eat such a big meal so late. One solution is to take your evening meal at one of Madrid's many foreign restaurants. Good-quality Italian, Mexican, Russian, Argentine, and American places abound and on the whole tend to be less formal, more lively, and open earlier.

What to Wear

Dress in most Madrid restaurants and tapas bars is stylish but casual. The more expensive places tend to be a bit more formal; men generally wear jackets and ties, and women wear skirts.

$$$$ ✕ **Horcher.** Housed in a luxurious mansion at the edge of Retiro Park, ★ this classic restaurant is renowned for its hearty but elegant fare served with impeccable style. Specialties include the types of game dishes favored by Spanish aristocracy. Try the wild boar, venison, or roast wild duck with almond croquettes. The star appetizer is lobster salad with truffles. Offerings like stroganoff with mustard, pork chops with sauerkraut, and *baumkuchen,* a chocolate-covered, fruit and cake dessert, reflect the restaurant's Germanic roots. (The Horcher family operated a restaurant in Berlin at the turn of the century.) The intimate dining room is decorated with antique Austrian porcelains and rust-colored, brocade fabric on the walls. A wide selection of French and German wines rounds out the menu. ⊠ *Alfonso XII 6,* ☎ *91/522–0731. Reservations essential. AE, DC, MC, V. Closed Sun.*

$$$$ ✕ **Lhardy.** Serving Madrid specialties from the same central-city locale for more than 150 years, Lhardy's, with its dark-wood paneling, brass chandeliers, and red-velvet chairs, looks pretty much the same as it must have on day one. The menu features international fare, but most diners come for the traditional cocido madrileño and callos madrileño. Sea bass in champagne sauce, game, and dessert soufflés are also very well prepared. The dining rooms are upstairs, and the ground-floor entryway doubles as a delicatessen and stand-up coffee bar that, on chilly winter mornings, is filled with shivering souls sipping *caldo* (chicken broth) ladled steaming hot from silver urns. ⊠ *Carrera de San Jerónimo 8,* ☎ *91/521–3385. AE, DC, MC, V. Closed holidays. No dinner Sun.*

$$$$ ✕ **Viridiana.** The trendiest of Madrid's gourmet restaurants, Viridiana has the relaxed atmosphere of a bistro and black-and-white decor punctuated by prints from Luis Buñuel's classic, anti-clerical film after which this establishment is named. Iconoclast chef Abraham Garcia says "market-based" is too narrow a description for his creative menu, though the list does change every two weeks depending on what's locally available. Offerings include such varied fare as red onions stuffed with *morcilla* (black pudding); soft flour tortillas wrapped around marinated fresh tuna, and filet mignon in white truffle sauce. If it's available, be sure to try the superb duck pâté drizzled with sherry and served with Tokay wine. The tangy grapefruit sherbet is a marvel. ⊠ *Juan de Mena 14,* ☎ *91/531–5222. Reservations essential. No credit cards. Closed Sun., Easter wk, and Aug.*

$$$$ ✕ **Zalacaín.** The deep-apricot color scheme, set off by dark wood and ★ gleaming silver, suggests the atmosphere of an exclusive villa. One of only two Spanish restaurants to be awarded three Michelin stars, Zalacaín introduced nouvelle cuisine to Spain and continues to set the pace after 20 years at the top. Splurge on prawn salad in avocado vinaigrette,

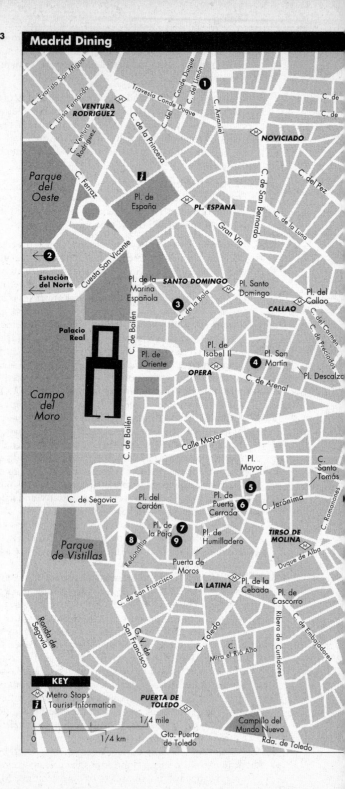

Madrid Dining

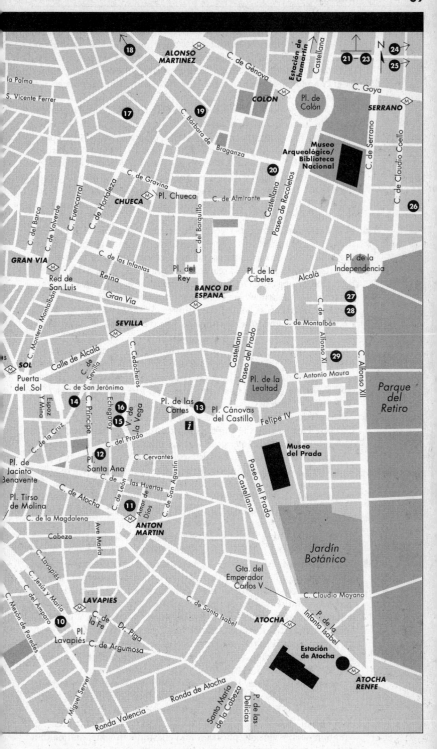

scallops and leeks in Albariño wine, and roast pheasant with truffles. Service is correct but somewhat stuffy. A fixed-price tasting menu allows you to sample the best of Zalacaín for about 6,500 ptas. ⊠ *Alvarez de Baena 4,* ☎ *91/561–5935. Reservations essential. AE, DC, V. Closed Easter wk and Aug. No lunch Sat.*

$$$ ✕ **El Cenador del Prado.** A mecca for those with gourmet palates, Cenador features an innovative menu with French and Asian touches and some exotic Spanish dishes not often found in restaurants. Dine in the baroque, salmon-and-gold salon or the less formal, plant-filled conservatory. The house specialty is *patatas a la importancia* (sliced potatoes fried in a sauce of garlic, parsley, and clams). Equally rewarding are the shellfish consommé with ginger raviolis, veal and eggplant in béchamel, or wild boar with prunes. For dessert try *cañas fritas* (a cream-filled pastry treat once served only at Spanish weddings). ⊠ *C. del Prado 4,* ☎ *91/429–1561. AE, DC, MC, V. Closed Sun., Easter wk, and 1st ½ of Aug. No lunch Sat.*

$$$ ✕ **El Pescador.** Spaniards swear that the seafood in Madrid is fresher
★ than in the coastal towns where it was caught. That's probably an exaggeration, but it *seems* plausible, at least judging from El Pescador, one of Madrid's best-loved seafood restaurants. Stop for a drink at the bar before sitting down to dinner, and take in the delicious aromas wafting from the kitchen, where skilled chefs dressed in fishermen's smocks prepare shellfish just behind the counter. As tapas at the bar or as a first course of your meal, definitely try the incredible *salpicón de mariscos* (mussels, lobster, shrimp, and onions in vinaigrette). Named for the restaurant's owner, the *lenguado Evaristo* (grilled sole) is the best dish on the menu. The place is cheerful and noisy, and the decor is "dockside rustic," with lobster-pot lamps, red-and-white-checked tablecloths, and rough-hewn posts and beams. ⊠ *José Ortega y Gasset 75,* ☎ *91/402–1290. MC, V. Closed Sun. and Aug.*

$$$ ✕ **Gure-Etxea.** Located in the heart of medieval Madrid on the trendy
★ Plaza de Paja, this is the capital's most authentic Basque restaurant. The ground-floor dining room is airy, high-ceilinged, and elegant, while brick walls lining the downstairs eating area give it a rustic, farmhouse feel. As in the Basque country (but uncommon elsewhere in Europe), you are waited on by women. Classic dishes here include *bacalao pil-pil* (spicy cod fried in garlic and oil, making the "pil-pil" sound), *rape en salsa verde* (monkfish in green parsley sauce), and for dessert *leche frita* (fried custard). On weekdays a hearty and inexpensive plate of the day is added to the lunchtime menu. ⊠ *Plaza de Paja 12,* ☎ *91/365–6149. AE, DC, V. Closed Sun., Aug., and Easter wk.*

$$$ ✕ **La Trainera.** Fresh seafood—the best quality money can buy—is what La Trainera is all about. For decades this informal restaurant, with its nautical decor and maze of little dining rooms, has reigned as the queen of Madrid's seafood houses. Crab, lobster, shrimp, mussels, and a dozen other types of shellfish are served by weight. While most Spanish diners share several plates of these delicacies as their entire meal, the grilled hake, sole, or turbot make an unbeatable second course. Skip the listless house wine and go for a bottle from the cellar. ⊠ *Lagasca 60,* ☎ *91/576–8035. AE, MC, V. Closed Sun. and Aug.*

$$$ ✕ **Mentidero de la Villa.** The decor of this intimate eatery is a bewitching blend of pastel colors, pale wood, and candlelight, with fanciful, rough-hewn, rocking-horse sculptures. The menu is adventuresome—the chef's salad mixes fresh kelp and lettuce. Specialties include breast of squab in cherry vinegar, pheasant and chestnuts in wine, and halibut with a black-olive sauce. Apropos of the restaurant's moniker (the name means "gossip shop"), service is informal and chatty. ⊠ *Santo Tomé 6,* ☎ *91/308–1285. AE, MC, V. Closed Sun. and Aug. No lunch Sat.*

$$ ✕ **Brasserie de Lista.** For a gourmet meal in a comfortable, informal setting this bistro-style spot in a neighborhood of designer boutiques can't be beat. A long, marble bar, lots of brass, and frosted glass create a turn-of-the-century ambience. Waiters in long white aprons serve Spanish specialties with nouvelle touches, such as grilled monkfish with toasted garlic or steak with *cabrales* (blue cheese sauce). The varied menu also includes international fare such as chicken and avocado salad with chutney, and beef carpaccio. The weekday lunchtime special is a good value. ✉ *Ortega y Gasset 6,* ☎ *91/435–2818. AE, MC, V.*

$$ ✕ **Café Balear.** A sophisticated yet informal eatery that attracts a crowd of creative types from the fashion and advertising worlds, the Café Balear serves some of the best paella in Madrid. Art prints and potted palms are the only nods to decoration in the stark, white dining room. Specialties include paella *centolla* (with crab) and *arroz negro* (rice with squid in its ink). The perfectly prepared paella *mixta* combines seafood, pork, and vegetables. ✉ *Sagunto 18,* ☎ *91/447–9115. AE, V. No dinner Sun. or Mon.*

$$ ✕ **Cañas y Barro.** Hidden away on an unspoiled plaza that was the 19th-century center of Madrid's university, this Valencian restaurant specializes in rice dishes with flair. The most popular is *arroz à la banda* (rice with peeled shrimp cooked in seafood broth). Another good choice is the paella Valenciana, made with chicken, rabbit, and vegetables. The service is friendly and unpretentious, and white-plaster friezes lend the pink dining room a touch of elegance. ✉ *Amaniel 23,* ☎ *91/542–4798. AE, DC, MC, V. Closed Mon. and Aug. No dinner Sun.*

$$ ✕ **Casa Botín.** The *Guinness Book of Records* calls this the world's
★ oldest restaurant (1725), and Hemingway called it the best. The latter claim may contain a bit of hyperbole, but the restaurant *is* excellent and extremely charming, despite the hordes of tourists. There are four floors of tiled and wood-beamed dining rooms, and ovens dating back several centuries—which you'll pass if you're seated upstairs. There are also visits from traditionally garbed musical groups called *tunas*. Must-try specialties are *cochinillo asado* (roast suckling pig) and *cordero asado* (roast lamb). It is said Francesco Goya was a dishwasher here before he became successful as a painter. ✉ *Cuchilleros 17, off Plaza Mayor,* ☎ *91/366–4217. AE, DC, MC, V.*

$$ ✕ **Casa Paco.** This is a popular Castilian tavern that wouldn't have
★ looked out of place two or three centuries ago. Squeeze your way past the old, zinc-topped bar, always crowded with Madrileños downing shots of red wine, and into the tiled dining rooms. People come here to feast on thick slabs of red meat, served sizzling on plates so hot that it continues to cook at your table. The beef is superb, and the Spanish consider overcooking a sin, so if you ask for your meat well done, be prepared for nasty glares. You order the meat by weight, so remember that a *medio kilo* is more than a pound. For starters try the *pisto manchego* (the La Mancha version of ratatouille). ✉ *Puerta Cerrada 11,* ☎ *91/366–3166. DC. Closed Sun. and Aug.*

$$ ✕ **Casa Vallejo.** With its homey dining room, friendly staff, creative menu, and reasonable prices, this restaurant is the well-kept secret of Madrid's budget gourmets. Try the tomato, zucchini, and cheese tart or artichokes and clams for starters, then follow up with duck breast in prune sauce or meatballs made with lamb, almonds, and pine nuts. The fudge and raspberry pie alone makes it worth the trip. ✉ *San Lorenzo 9,* ☎ *91/308–6158. Reservations essential. AE, MC, V. Closed Sun. No lunch Mon.*

$$ ✕ **Ciao Madrid.** Always noisy and packed with happy diners, Ciao Madrid is the city's best Italian restaurant. Homemade pastas like tagliatelle with wild mushrooms or *panzerotti* stuffed with spinach and ricotta are popular as inexpensive main courses, but the kitchen also turns out credible versions of osso buco and veal scaloppine, accompanied by a good selection of Italian wines. The decor—mirrored walls and sleek, black furniture—convincingly evokes fashionable Milan. A second location (⊠ Apodaca 20, ☎ 91/447–0036), run by the owner's sons and daughter, also serves pizza. ⊠ *Argensola 7, ☎ 91/308–2519. Reservations essential. AE, DC, MC, V. Closed Sun. No lunch Sat.*

$$ ✕ **Cornucopia en Descalzas.** Run by former Boston caterer Deborah Hansen and her Madrid-born husband, Julio de Haro, this young and friendly restaurant on the first floor of an old mansion just off the historic Plaza de las Descalzas Reales features a creative blend of nouvelle Spanish and American dishes. The menu changes with the seasons: In winter expect dishes like duck soup with duck meatballs, roast pork loin stuffed with apricots, or scallops in wine and cream; the lighter summer menu includes cold almond and garlic soup and grilled calamares with garlic mayonnaise. The mustard-and-burgundy-colored dining room is a tad ornate. ⊠ *Flora 1, ☎ 91/547–6465. AE, MC, V. Closed Mon. and Aug. 15–Sept. 15. No lunch weekends.*

$$ ✕ **El Cosaco.** This romantic, candlelit, Russian restaurant, tucked away
★ on the ancient Plaza de Paja, is a favorite of young couples in love. While they may only have eyes for each other, the food here is definitely worth a look—savory blini stuffed with caviar, smoked trout, or salmon, and hearty beef dishes like stroganoff. The dining rooms are decorated with paisley wallpaper and dark-red linens, and if the crackling fireplace's cheery glow in winter isn't enough to warm you, there are eight types of vodka that ought to do the trick. ⊠ *Plaza de Paja 2, ☎ 91/365–3548. AE, DC. No lunch Mon.–Sat.*

$$ ✕ **La Bola.** First opened as a *botellería* (wine shop) in 1802, La Bola
★ developed slowly into a tapas bar and eventually a full-fledged restaurant. Tradition is what La Bola offers, from the blood-red paneling outside to the original bar and cozy dining nooks decorated with polished wood, Spanish tile, and lace curtains inside. It still belongs to the founding family, with the seventh generation currently in training to take over. Although it's open for dinner, La Bola's specialty is that quintessential Madrid meal, cocido madrileño, which is served only at lunch, and accompanied by crusty bread and a hearty red wine. ⊠ *Bola 5, ☎ 91/547–6930. No credit cards. Closed Sun.*

$$ ✕ **La Cacharrería.** The name of this restaurant in medieval Madrid means junkyard, and it's reflected in the funky decor—a mix of dusty calico, old lace, and gilt mirrors. The cooking, however, is decidedly upscale, with a market-based menu that changes daily and an excellent selection of wines. Venison stew and fresh tuna steaks with cava and leeks were among the specialties on a recent visit. Whatever else you order, save room for the homemade lemon tart. ⊠ *Moreiria 9, ☎ 91/365–3930. AE, DC, MC, V. Closed Sun.*

$$ ✕ **La Galette.** Located just one block from Madrid's main shopping street, Calle Serrano, this is an intimate restaurant for a romantic lunch or supper by candlelight. The menu is primarily vegetarian but includes some inventive meat dishes. Avoid the tasteless onion soup and go straight for the *Pimiento Persa* (green pepper stuffed with vegetables, rice, and cheese) or the *Cocotte Rusia* (beef stewed with laurel and plums, served over basmati rice). Luscious fruit tarts and brownies de Boston are irresistible dessert choices. ⊠ *Conde de Aranda 11, ☎ 91/576–0641. AE, V. Closed Sun.*

$$ ✕ **La Gamella.** American-born chef Dick Stephens has created a new,
★ reasonably priced menu at this hugely popular dining spot. The sophisticated, rust-red dining room, batik tablecloths, oversize plates, and attentive service remain the same, but much of the nouvelle cuisine has been replaced by more traditional fare, such as chicken in garlic, beef bourguignonne, and steak tartar à la Jack Daniels. A few of the old-

favorite signature dishes like sausage and red pepper quiche and bittersweet chocolate pâté remain. The lunchtime menú del día is a great value at 1,700 ptas. ⊠ *Alfonso XII 4,* ☎ *91/532–4509. AE, DC, MC, V. Closed Sun., Mon., and Aug. 15–30.*

$$ ✗ **La Pampa.** This excellent Argentine restaurant is secluded on a side
★ street in the Lavapíes neighborhood. As you enter there's a small eating area to the left, but most patrons prefer to sit in the rustic dining room to the right. The massive and delicious *bife* La Pampa is the specialty of the house (enough steak, fried eggs, peas, and tomatoes for two light eaters) and contains sufficient protein for a week. Pasta dishes, such as cannelloni Rossini, are also good. ⊠ *Amparo 61,* ☎ *91/528–0449. AE, DC, MC, V. Closed Mon.*

$$ ✗ **Sí Señor.** One of Madrid's new crop of entertaining restaurants, Sí Señor specializes in Mexican food and tequila slammers. There's a big bar in the entryway, which serves Mexican-style tapas (quesadillas or chips with guacamole). The huge, noisy dining hall is lined with oversize paintings, artfully executed in a unique, Mexican pop-art style. While the drinks here are far better than the food, do try the beef enchiladas or *pollo pibil,* a spicy Yucatan-style chicken dish. ⊠ *Paseo de la Castellana 128,* ☎ *91/564–0604. AE, DC, MC, V.*

$ ✗ **Café La Plaza.** Strategically positioned between the Prado and Thyssen-Bornemisza art museums and open 10 AM to midnight, the Café La Plaza is an indispensable rest stop for tourists exploring Madrid. This is an upscale, self-service restaurant with a green-and-white, garden-party decor, situated among the exclusive boutiques of the Galerias del Prado shopping center. Food is arranged on several circular tables. There's a do-it-yourself salad bar, a pasta bar, and an economical menú del día, which, depending on the day, might be Spanish-style chicken, breaded fish, or beef stew served with vegetables, bread, and wine. Breakfast, including bacon and eggs, is available until 12:30 PM, and the café is also a good place to remember for afternoon coffee and pastries. ⊠ *Plaza de las Cortes 7,* ☎ *91/429–6537. AE, V. Closed Sun.*

$ ✗ **Casa Mingo.** Resembling an Asturian cider tavern, Casa Mingo is built
★ into a stone wall beneath the Estación del Norte train station, across the street from the hermitage of San Antonio de la Florida. It's a bustling place where you'll share long, plank tables with other diners, and the only dishes offered are succulent roast chicken, salad, and sausages, all to be washed down with numerous bottles of *sidra* (hard cider). In summer small tables are set up on the sidewalk. ⊠ *Paseo de la Florida 2,* ☎ *91/547–7918. Reservations not accepted. No credit cards.*

$ ✗ **Inti de Oro.** This Peruvian restaurant, located on one of Madrid's premier restaurant streets, is a big hit, thanks largely to the care the owners put into such traditional specialties of their native Peru as *cebiche de camarones* (shrimp in lime juice), *conejo con maní* (rabbit in peanut sauce), and *seco de cabrito* (goat meat stew). The dining room is light, and the walls are adorned with handicrafts. ⊠ *Ventura de la Vega 12,* ☎ *91/429–6703. AE, DC, V.*

$ ✗ **Puebla.** Although the dining room decor lacks charm (the fake wood beams fooling no one), you'd be hard-pressed to find better-prepared food at such affordable prices anywhere else in Madrid. Puebla opened in 1992 and is always crowded with bankers and congressmen from the nearby Cortes. There are two prices ranges for the menú del día, with more than a dozen choices in each. The selection changes frequently, but be sure to try the *berenjenas a la romana* (batter-fried eggplant) if it's offered. The soups are always great, and other dishes include roast lamb, trout, calamari, and chicken. ⊠ *Ventura de la Vega 12,* ☎ *91/429–6713. AE, DC, MC, V. Closed Sun.*

$ ✕ Sanabresa. You can tell by the clientele what a find this place is. Working men and women who demand quality but don't want to spend much money come here daily, as does an international assortment of starving students from the nearby flamenco school. The menu is classic Spanish fare—hearty, wholesome meals like *pechuga villaroy* (chicken breast in béchamel, breaded and fried) and paella (Thursday and Sunday lunch only). The functional, green-tiled dining room is always crowded, so be sure to arrive by 1:30. ⊠ *Amor de Dios 12, no phone. Reservations not accepted. No credit cards. Closed Aug. No dinner Sun.*

LODGING

There are booking services at the airport and the Chamartín and Atocha train stations. You can also contact the La Brujula agency (⊠ Torre de Madrid, 6th floor, Plaza de España, ☎ 91/559–9705); the fee's a modest 250 ptas. The staff speaks English and can book rooms and tours all over Spain. All the rooms listed below have baths.

$$$$ 🏨 Palace. Built in 1912, this enormous, Belle Epoque, grand hotel is
★ a creation of Alfonso XIII. At less than two-thirds the price of the nearby Ritz, the Palace is a pleasure, though its attractions are concentrated in the opulent public areas, including a large cupola with a stained-glass ceiling. The rooms aren't impressive for a hotel of this caliber—they're plain and often small, with a pronounced 1960s, American flavor. Bathrooms are spacious, however, with double sinks, tubs and separate shower stalls, and other welcome touches such as bathrobes and magnifying mirrors. ⊠ *Plaza de las Cortes 7, 28014, ☎ 91/429–7551, ℻ 91/429–8266. 436 rooms, 20 suites. Restaurant, bar, beauty salon, parking. AE, DC, MC, V.*

$$$$ 🏨 Ritz. When Alfonso XIII was preparing for his marriage to the
★ granddaughter of Queen Victoria of England, he realized, to his dismay, that Madrid had not a single hotel that could meet the exacting standards of his royal guests. Thus, the Ritz was born. Opened in 1910 by the king, who had personally overseen its construction, the Ritz is a monument to the Belle Epoque, furnished with rare antiques in every public room, hand-embroidered linens from Robinson and Cleaver of London, and all manner of other luxurious details. The rooms are carpeted, hung with chandeliers, and decorated in pastel colors; many have good views of the Prado or the Castellana. Visit the garden terrace even if you're not staying here. ⊠ *Plaza de Lealtad 5, 28014, ☎ 91/521–2857, ℻ 91/532–8776. 158 rooms. Restaurant, bar, beauty salon, health club, parking. AE, DC, MC, V.*

$$$$ 🏨 Santo Mauro. A turn-of-the-century mansion that once housed the Canadian embassy was opened in 1992 as an intimate luxury hotel. The neoclassical architecture is complemented by contemporary furnishings such as suede armchairs, and sofas in such colors as mustard, teal, and eggplant. Twelve of the rooms are in the main building, which also houses a popular gourmet restaurant. Other rooms are in a new annex, are all split-level, and have stereo systems and VCRs. ⊠ *Zurbano 36, 28010, ☎ 91/319–6900, ℻ 91/308–5477. 37 rooms. Restaurant, bar, parking. AE, DC, MC, V.*

$$$$ 🏨 Villa Real. If you're looking for a luxury hotel that combines elegance, modern amenities, and great location, this is the ticket. A simulated 19th-century facade gives way to lobbies dotted with potted palms. Each room has a character of its own, albeit with an overall French feel; some suites have both saunas and whirlpool tubs. The hotel, opened in 1989, faces the Cortes and is convenient to almost everything. Staff is very friendly.

⊠ *Plaza de las Cortes 10, 28014,* ☎ *91/420–3767,* FAX *91/420–2547. 94 rooms, 20 suites. Bar. AE, DC, MC, V.*

$$$$ 🖭 **Villamagna.** Favored by visiting financiers and reclusive rock stars, the modern Villamagna ranks among Madrid's most exclusive hotels and boasts a staff dedicated to personal attention. Its green-and-white lobby exudes elegance, and a pianist provides soothing music in the lounge at lunchtime and during the cocktail hour. Rooms all have desks and working space, as well as luxury details, such as hidden TVs, VCRs, and green plants in the bathrooms. The restaurant, Berceo, has cozy, walnut paneling and the feel of an English library; its garden terrace is open for dinner in warm weather. ⊠ *Paseo de la Castellana 22, 28046,* ☎ *91/576–7500,* FAX *91/575–9504. 164 rooms, 18 suites. Restaurant, bar, beauty salon, parking. AE, DC, MC, V.*

$$$ 🖭 **El Prado.** Wedged in between the classic buildings of Old Madrid, this skinny, new hotel is within stumbling distance of the city's best bars and nightclubs. Rooms are surprisingly spacious and are virtually soundproofed from street noise by double-paned windows. Decorative touches include pastel, floral prints and gleaming, marble baths. ⊠ *C. Prado 11, 28014,* ☎ *91/369–0234,* FAX *91/429–2829. 50 rooms. Cafeteria, parking. AE, DC, MC, V.*

$$$ 🖭 **Fenix.** A magnificent, marble lobby greets guests at this Madrid institution, overlooking Plaza de Colón on the Castellana, where a giant monument to the discoverers of the New World rises. The hotel is also just a few steps from the posh shopping street of Serrano. Its spacious rooms, decorated in beiges and golds, are carpeted and amply furnished. Flowers abound. ⊠ *Hermosilla 2, 28001,* ☎ *91/431–6700,* FAX *91/576– 0661. 204 rooms, 12 suites. Café, bar, beauty salon. AE, DC, MC, V.*

$$$ 🖭 **Hotel Santo Domingo.** An intimate hotel that artfully blends the best of classical and modern design, the Santo Domingo opened in 1994 and is about 10 minutes' walk from the Puerta del Sol, just off Gran Vía. Rooms are decorated in soft tones of peach and ocher, and all feature telephones with personal answering machines, and double-paned windows for soundproofing. An especially friendly and well-trained staff gives this place a personal feel. ⊠ *Plaza Santo Domingo 13, 28013,* ☎ *91/547–9800,* FAX *91/547–5995. 120 rooms. Restaurant, bar, parking. AE, DC, MC, V.*

$$$ 🖭 **Lagasca.** Opened in 1993 in the heart of the elegant Salamanca neighborhood, this hotel combines large, brightly decorated rooms with an unbeatable location two blocks from Madrid's main shopping street, Calle Serrano. The marble lobbies border on the coldly functional but are fine to use as a meeting place. ⊠ *Lagasca 64, 28001,* ☎ *91/575–4606,* FAX *91/575–1694. 100 rooms. Restaurant, bar, parking. AE, DC, MC, V.*

$$$ 🖭 **Reina Victoria.** The Tryp chain recently bought and extensively ren-
★ ovated what is one of Madrid's most historic and loved hotels. Now, besides the attractive exterior and great location facing one of Madrid's most charming squares, the Victoria boasts a far more upscale clientele than in the era when it served down-at-the-heels bullfighters and American writers such as Ernest Hemingway (in fact, rather well-heeled bullfighters still frequent the place). Once past the fairly charmless lobby and public rooms, the hotel becomes quite attractive, with handsome details and an overall stately decor in the hallways and the big, bright, airy guest rooms. The best rooms overlook Plaza Santa Ana. Reservations usually are needed because the hotel is becoming very popular. ⊠ *Plaza del Ángel 7, 28014,* ☎ *91/531–4500,* FAX *91/522–0307. 110 rooms. Restaurant, bar, parking. AE, DC, MC, V.*

$$$ 🖭 **Suecia.** The chief attraction of the Suecia is its location right next to the super-chic Círculo de Bellas Artes (arts society/café/movie/theater complex). Though recently remodeled, its lobby is still somewhat soulless. The rooms are trendy, with modern art on the walls and futuristic light fixtures. ⊠ *Marqués de Riera 4, 28014,* ☎ *91/531–*

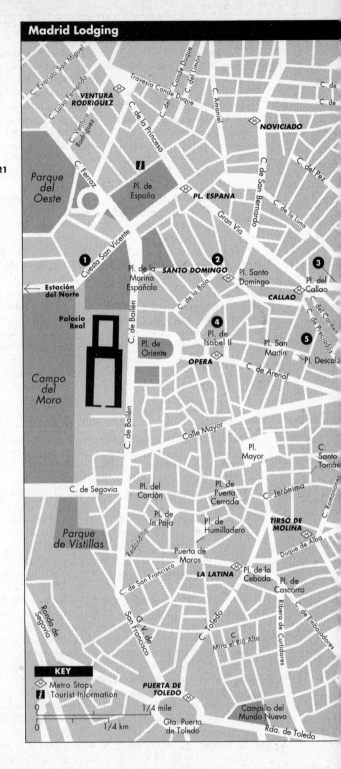

Madrid Lodging

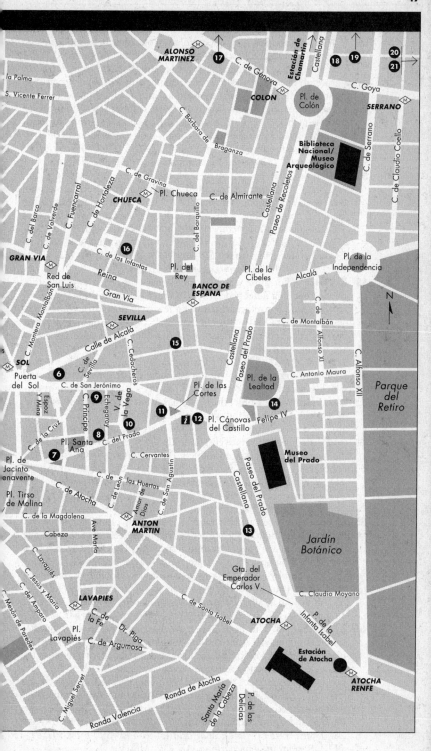

6900, FAX *91/521–7141. 119 rooms, 9 suites. 2 restaurants, bar. AE, DC, MC, V.*

$$$ 🏨 **Tryp Ambassador.** Ideally located on an old street between Gran Vía
★ and the Royal Palace, this hotel opened in 1991 in the renovated 19th-century palace of the Dukes of Granada. A magnificent front door and a graceful, three-story staircase are reminders of the building's aristocratic past; the rest has been transformed into an elegant hotel favored by business executives. Bedrooms are large, with separate sitting areas, and have mahogany furnishings and floral drapes and bedspreads. A greenhouse bar filled with plants and songbirds is especially pleasant on cold days. ✉ *Cuesta Santo Domingo 5 and 7, 28013,* ☎ *91/541–6700,* FAX *91/559–1040. 182 rooms. Restaurant, bar, parking. AE, DC, MC, V.*

$$ 🏨 **Atlántico.** Don't be put off by the location on a noisy stretch of Gran Vía, or by the rather shabby third-floor lobby. Bright, clean accommodations at good prices is what the Atlántico is all about. Rooms are small but comfortable, with fabric wall coverings and new furniture. All have tile baths. A member of the Best Western chain, this hotel is a favorite with British travelers and is almost always full, so it's a good idea to book well in advance. ✉ *Gran Vía 38, 28013,* ☎ *91/522–6480,* FAX *91/531–0210. 80 rooms. Snack bar. AE, MC, V.*

$$ 🏨 **Carlos V.** For those who like to be right in the center of things, this classic hotel in a quiet pedestrian zone may be one of the best options for value and convenience. It's just a few steps away from the Puerta del Sol and Plaza Mayor. A suit of armor decorates the tiny lobby, while crystal chandeliers add elegance to a second-floor guest lounge. All rooms are bright and carpeted. ✉ *Maestro Victoria 5, 28013,* ☎ *91/531–4100,* FAX *91/531–3761. 67 rooms. AE, MC, V.*

$$ 🏨 **Inglés.** Virginia Woolf was one of the first discoverers of this hotel, which is smack in the center of the old city's bar and restaurant district. Since Woolf's time, the Inglés has attracted more than its share of less-famous artists and writers. The public areas and guest rooms are faded—bordering on dreary—and need renovation, but the guest rooms *are* big and a relatively good value. (Suites cost what you'd normally pay for a standard double.) The balconies overlooking Calle Echegaray give you an unusual view of the medieval look of the old city from the air, all red Mediterranean tiles and ramshackle gables. ✉ *Echegaray 8, 28014,* ☎ *91/429–6551,* FAX *91/420–2423. 58 rooms. Cafeteria, bar, exercise room, parking. AE, DC, MC, V.*

$$ 🏨 **Paris.** For a remarkably fair price, the Paris offers delightful Old
★ World charm, right at the corner of the busy Puerta del Sol and Calle de Alcalá; you can't get more central than this. The odd-shaped rooms are clean, spacious, and decorated with orange bedspreads and curtains. The lobby is dark, woody, and somehow redolent of times long past. There's no bar, but three meals are served in a bright second-floor restaurant. All in all, the Paris is an unusual deal. ✉ *Alcalá 2, 28014,* ☎ *91/521–6496,* FAX *91/531–0188. 114 rooms. Restaurant. MC, V.*

$$ 🏨 **Príncipe Pío.** This hotel appears to have seen better days, but despite the fading velveteen-and-linoleum look of the lobby, it's convenient to much of Madrid's west side: the Royal Palace and its gardens, Plaza de España, and the Norte railway station. The rooms are surprisingly pleasant once you're past the lobby; they're bright, with fine views of the Royal Palace, and furnished with white bedside tables and orange carpeting. Also offered are "apartosuites," complete with kitchen and up to two bedrooms. ✉ *Cuesta de San Vicente 14–16, 28008,* ☎ *91/547–0800; apartosuites, 91/542–5900;* FAX *91/541–1117. Restaurant, bar, parking. AE, DC, MC, V.*

$ 🏨 **Lisboa.** Clean, small, and central, the Lisboa has for years been a well-kept secret just off the Plaza Santa Ana. It offers no frills but is in a marvelous location on a busy bar and restaurant street and is easy on most budgets. Past a tiny lobby, the rooms tend to vary greatly in size and quality. Most of them are sparsely furnished, with tile floors and papered walls, and the linen doesn't always match; but they are clean and functional. ✉ *Ventura de la Vega 17, 28014,* ☎ ﬀ *91/429–9894. 22 rooms. AE, DC, MC, V.*

$ 🏨 **Monaco.** Just a few steps from the tiny Plaza de Chueca, the Monaco is an eccentrically opulent delight. The lobby is resplendent with red-carpeted stairs, potted plants, brass rails, and mirrors—and the rooms are similar, with Louis XIV–style furniture and mirrored walls. The owner is Portuguese and very gracious. ✉ *Barbieri 5, 28004,* ☎ *91/522–4630,* ﬀ *91/521–1601. 33 rooms. Cafeteria, bar. AE, MC, V.*

$ 🏨 **Mora.** Directly across the Paseo del Prado from the Botanical Gar-
★ dens, the Mora underwent a complete renovation in 1994 and now offers a sparkling, faux-marble lobby and bright, carpeted hallways. The guest rooms are modestly decorated but large and comfortable; those on the street side have great views of the gardens and Prado Museum (and they're also fairly quiet, thanks to double-paned windows). ✉ *Paseo del Prado 32, 28014,* ☎ *91/420–1569,* ﬀ *91/420–0564. 61 rooms. AE, DC, MC, V.*

$ 🏨 **Ramón de la Cruz.** If you don't mind a longish metro ride from the center, this medium-size hotel is a find. The rooms are large, with modern bathrooms, and the lobby is spacious and stone-floored. Given Madrid prices, it's a bargain. ✉ *Don Ramón de la Cruz 94, 28006,* ☎ *91/401–7200,* ﬀ *91/402–2126. 103 rooms. Cafeteria. MC, V.*

NIGHTLIFE AND THE ARTS

The Arts

Madrid's cultural scene is so lively that it's hard to keep pace with the constantly changing offerings and venues. As its reputation has sky-rocketed in recent years, artists and performers of all kinds are coming here. The best way to stay abreast of events is through the weekly *Guía de Ocio* (published Monday) or daily listings in the leading newspaper, *El País.* Both sources are relatively easy to figure out, even if you don't read Spanish. Tickets to performances usually are best purchased at the venues themselves; in the case of major popular concerts, the large Corte Inglés department stores have **Discoplay** outlets that sell advance tickets.

The city puts on major arts festivals in each of the four seasons. While you'll have to look up ever-changing details, events include world-class jazz, salsa, African music, and rock; arts exhibitions of all kinds; movie festivals; and more—all at more than reasonable prices. The venues are more often than not outdoors in city parks and amphitheaters.

Concerts

Opened in 1988, the **Auditorio Nacional de Música** (✉ Príncipe de Vergara 136, ☎ 91/337–0100) is Madrid's principal concert hall for classical music, and regularly hosts major orchestras from around the world.

Film

Almost a dozen theaters regularly show undubbed foreign films, the majority of them English-language. These are listed in newspapers and in the *Guía de Ocio* under "V.O."—meaning original version. Leading V.O. theaters include the **Alphaville** and **Renoir,** both on Martín de los Heros, just off Plaza de España, and each with four theaters. The city offers excellent, classic V.O. films that change daily at the **Filmoteca Cine Doré** (✉ Santa Isabel 3).

Theater

English-speaking performances are a rarity, and when they do come to town, they may play on any of a dozen Madrid stages; you'll have to check local newspapers. One you won't need the language for is the **Teatro de la Zarzuela** (⊠ Jovellanos 4, ☎ 91/524–5400), which puts on the traditional Spanish operettas known as *zarzuela,* a kind of bawdy comedy. The **Teatro Español** (⊠ Príncipe 25, ☎ 91/429–6297) specializes in Spanish Golden Age classics.

Nightlife

It's legendary in Spain that Madrileños hardly sleep, and that's largely because of the amount of time they spend in bars—not drunk, but socializing in the easy, sophisticated way that is unique to the capital. This is true of old as well as young, though the streets that are famous for their bars tend to be patronized by a younger clientele. (These include Huertas, Moratín, Segovia, Victoria, and the areas around Plaza Santa Ana, Plaza de Anton Martin.) Adventuresome travelers may want to explore the scruffier bar scene around the Plaza Dos de Mayo in the Malasaña neighborhood, where trendy, smoke-filled places line both sides of Calle San Vicente Ferrer.

Bars

There are countless bars in Madrid, and while almost all offer something to eat, some are known more for their atmosphere than their food. Some recommendations:

Cafe del Nuncio. A cozy antique bar with red-velvet walls and outdoor tables on a cobblestone stairway during the summer months. ⊠ *Segovia 9,* ☎ *91/366–0853.*

Cafe Gijón (⊠ Paseo de Recoletos 24, ☎ 91/521–5425) may be Madrid's most famous café-bar. For more than a century, it's been the venue of the city's most highfalutin' *tertulias* (discussion groups that meet regularly to muse on all manner of topics).

Casa Pueblo (⊠ C.s del Prado and León, no phone) stays open later than most (4 AM on weekends) and has a wonderful Jazz Age feel to it.

Cervantes (⊠ León 8, ☎ 91/429–6093) is a bright, tiled bar where you can also get a pizza or pasta in a small dining room at the back. It caters to a young neighborhood crowd.

Chicote (⊠ Gran Vía 12, ☎ 91/532–6737) was immortalized in several Hemingway short stories of the Spanish civil war and still makes an interesting stop.

Hard Rock Cafe (⊠ Paseo Castellana 2, ☎ 91/435–0200) is wildly popular with young Spaniards. Madrid's version of this U.S. classic opened in 1994 and serves up the usual drinks, burgers, and salads with a heavy dose of loud music.

Hermanos Muñiz (⊠ Huertas 29, ☎ 91/429–5452) is the quintessential Spanish neighborhood bar, neither trendy nor touristy. The tapas here are uniformly excellent, and the men who serve them both friendly and superbly professional.

La Champañería Gala (⊠ Moratín 24, ☎ 91/429–2562) is one of the city's better-known champagne bars, offering especially good Catalan *cavas* (Spanish champagnes).

La Venencia (⊠ Echegaray 7, ☎ 91/429–7313) is a trendy but engaging sherry bar in a rustic, 19th-century setting. Examples of the best sherries, both sweet and dry, are available.

Los Gabrieles (⊠ Echegaray 17, ☎ 91/429–6261) is featured in most of the tourist literature on Madrid for its remarkable tile walls, but the place's clientele is mostly hip Spaniards, not foreigners.

Palacio de Gaviria (⌧ Arenal 9, ☎ 91/526–8089) is an impeccably restored, 19th-century, baroque palace hidden away on the upper floors of a tawdry commercial street between Puerta del Sol and the Royal Palace. Allegedly built to house one of the queen's lovers, the palace now serves drinks in an elegant setting with live jazz late at night.
Taberna de Antonio Sanchez (⌧ Mesón de Paredes 13, ☎ 91/539–7826) is reputedly the oldest bar in Madrid—the proprietors claim it's been in business since 1830. Order wine and tapas at the old, zinc bar in front; head to the back to order a full meal.
Viva Madrid (⌧ Manuel Fernández y González 7, ☎ 91/410–5535) is an extremely popular and atmospheric bar with a Brassai motif. Packed with Spaniards and foreigners, it has become something of a hip singles scene recently. There are tables—and food served—in the rear.

Cabaret
If you're looking for Las Vegas–style topless revues, head for **La Scala Melía**, a cabaret in the gigantic Melía Castilla Hotel (⌧ Rosario Pino 7, ☎ 91/571–4411).

Casino
Casino Gran Madrid, 29 km/18 mi northwest of the capital on N VI, is said to handle more money per year than any of its counterparts at Monte Carlo, Deauville, and Baden Baden. The casino, with a nightclub, three restaurants, and four bars, is open daily from 5 PM to 4 AM. Men are required to wear jackets and ties, October to April. Free buses to the casino depart from in front of Plaza de España 6 at 4:30, 6, 7:30, and 9, with return trips at 8, 10, 1:30 AM, 5:30 AM. Bring your passport. ☎ 91/856–1100. ⌧ 500 ptas.

Discos
Madrid's hippest new club is a three-story bar, discotheque, and cabaret theater housed in a converted embassy called **Bagelus** (⌧ María de Molina 25, ☎ 91/561–6100). **Joy Eslava** (⌧ Arenal 11, ☎ 91/366–3733), a downtown disco in a converted theater, remains popular, as does **Pacha** (⌧ Barceló 11, ☎ 91/466–0137); the well-heeled crowd likes to be seen at **Archy's** (⌧ Marqués de Riscal 11, ☎ 91/308–3162). Salsa music has become a permanent fixture of the Spanish capital, and the best place to dance to these Latin-American rhythms is the **Café del Mercado** (⌧ Ronda de Toledo 1, ☎ 91/365–8739).

Flamenco
Madrid is not a great city for flamenco, but for those who aren't traveling south, here are a few possibilities:

Café de Chinitas (⌧ Torija 7, ☎ 91/547–1502) is the city's best-known show, and the tourists it draws have included such diplomatic guests as former Nicaraguan president Daniel Ortega. It's expensive, but the food and dancing are good. Plan to reserve in advance; it often sells out.
Corral de la Morería (⌧ Morería 17, ☎ 91/365–8446) serves dinners à la carte and features well-known flamenco stars who perform along with the resident group.
Corral de la Pacheca (⌧ Juan Ramon Jiménez 26, ☎ 91/359–2660) offers good performances, if a little touristy, and the prices are more reasonable than those of Chinitas.

Nightclubs
Jazz, rock, flamenco, and classical music are all popular in the many small clubs that dot the city. Here are a few of the more interesting:

Café Central (✉ Plaza de Ángel 10, ☎ 91/369–4143), the city's best-known jazz venue, is chic and well run. The musicians are often very good, with performances generally beginning at 10 PM.

Cafe del Foro (✉ San Andrés 38, ☎ 91/448–9464) is a funky, friendly club on the edge of the Malasaña neighborhood with live music every night starting at 11:30.

Café Jazz Populart (✉ Huertas 22, ☎ 91/429–8407) is a club featuring blues, Brazilian music, reggae, and salsa.

Cafe Manuela (✉ San Vicente Ferrer 29, Bilbao and Tribunal, ☎ 91/531–7037) is a smoky, literary cafe with big, gilt mirrors on the walls.

Clamores (✉ Albuquerque 14, ☎ 91/445–7939), another famous jazz club, offers a wide selection of French and Spanish champagnes.

La Fídula (✉ Huertas 57, ☎ 91/429–4431) features nightly chamber music (starting at about 11:30 PM) in a subdued and pleasant setting.

Teatriz (✉ Hermosilla 15, ☎ 91/577–5379) is a restaurant that converts to a sophisticated nightspot after hours. Its theatrical decor is entertaining in and of itself, plus the place includes a tiny discotheque.

Torero (✉ Cruz 26, ☎ 91/523–1129), a thoroughly modern club despite the name, is one of Madrid's chicest spots. You'll have to come looking good, though—a doorman ensures that only those judged *gente guapa* (beautiful people) may enter.

Tapas Bars

Spending the early evening hours going from bar to bar and eating tapas is so popular that the Spanish have a verb to describe it: *tapear*. The selection is endless and the best-known tapas bars are the *cuevas* that cluster around Cava de San Miguel (☞ Medieval Madrid, *above*). Here are a few more suggestions:

Bocaíto (✉ Libertad 6, ☎ 91/532–1219) is said by some to serve the best tapas in all of Madrid—a heady claim. In any case, you can have a full meal here or just partake of a few tapas before heading on to the many other fine places in the immediate vicinity.

Casa Alberto (✉ Huertas 18, ☎ 91/429–9356) is an atmospheric place with a pewter-and-marble bar, beautifully carved, wooden ceilings, and some great tapas. As at many other Madrid bars, there's no seating—you're meant to stand while you imbibe.

El Rey de Pimiento (✉ Plaza Puerta Cerrada, no phone) serves some 40 different kinds of tapas including pimientos peppers—the roasted red variety, as well as the intermittently hot pimientos *de padrón*.

El Ventorrillo (✉ Bailén 14, ☎ 91/366–3578) is a place to go between May and October, when tables are set up in the shady park of Las Vistillas overlooking the city's western edge. Specialties include croquettes and mushrooms. This is Madrid's premier spot from which to watch the sun go down.

La Chuleta (✉ Echegaray 20, ☎ 91/429–3729) is a cheery corner bar hung with bullfight memorabilia and offering a colorful selection of tapas on the bar. You *can* sit down here.

La Dolores (✉ Plaza de Jesús 4, ☎ 91/429–2243) is a crowded, noisy, and wonderful place that's rightly reputed to serve the best draft beer in Madrid. Located just behind the Palace Hotel, it offers a very few tables in the back.

La Trucha (✉ Manuel Fernández y González 3, ☎ 91/532–0890) is hung with hams and garlic and has the feel of an inn of the Middle Ages. It's also a restaurant, but the wonderful tapas that line its aging bar are a far better bet.

Las Bravas (✉ Alvarez Gato 3, ☎ 91/532–2620), hidden away in an alley off the Plaza Santa Ana, isn't much to look at, but it's here that *patatas bravas* (potatoes in a spicy tomato sauce) were invented. They're now classic Spanish tapas.

Mesón Gallego (⊠ León 4, ☎ 91/429–8997) is a hole in the wall that serves a wonderfully hearty Galician potato soup (a famous cure for those who've drunk too much) called *caldo gallego*. Not for everyone is the *ribeira* (the somewhat acidic white wine made with grapes from Galician riverbanks).

The Reporter (⊠ Fúcar 6, ☎ 91/429–3922), true to its English name, is hung with great Spanish and world news photos. Its other great attraction is a garden terrace shaded by a grapevine trellis. The raciones are very good, and the pâté plate is terrific.

Taberna de Cien Vinos (⊠ Nuncio 17, ☎ 91/365–4704) is the latest addition to Madrid's tapas route. It is in an atmospheric old house, with wooden shutters and stone columns. A wide selection of Spanish wines is available by the glass and the raciones border on the gourmet.

Taberna del Alabardero (⊠ Felipe V 6, ☎ 91/574–2577) is an upscale and cheerful bar with a twin in Washington, DC. Its specialty is garlicky *patatas à la pobre*.

SHOPPING

Beyond the popular Lladró porcelains, castanets, and bullfight posters, Madrid offers a great selection of gift items and unique souvenirs. In recent years Spain has achieved recognition as one of the world's top design centers. You'll have no trouble finding traditional crafts, such as ceramics, guitars, and leather goods, but don't stop there. Madrid is famous for contemporary furniture and decorator items, as well as chic clothing, shoes, and jewelry. Most major credit cards are accepted at all shops.

Department Stores

El Corte Inglés. The largest of the Spanish department store chains offers the best selection of everything from auto parts to groceries to the latest designer fashions. ⊠ Goya 76, ☎ 91/577–7171; ⊠ Goya 87, ☎ 91/432–9300; ⊠ Preciados 3, ☎ 91/532–8100; ⊠ Princesa 42, ☎ 91/542–4800; ⊠ Serrano 47, ☎ 432–5490; ⊠ La Vaguada Mall, ☎ 91/387–4000; ⊠ Parquesur Mall, ☎ 91/558–4400; ⊠ Raimundo Fernández Villaverde 79, ☎ 91/556–2300.

Marks and Spencer. "Marks and Sparks" is famous for its British woolens and underwear, but most shoppers head straight for the gourmet-food shop in the basement. ⊠ *Serrano 52,* ☎ *91/431–6760.*

Zara. For those with young tastes and slim pocketbooks (think hip, throw-away-at-the-end-of-the-season clothes), Zara offers the latest fads for men, women, and children. In central Madrid, you'll find Zara at the following addresses: ⊠ Carretas 10; ⊠ Gran Vía 32; ⊠ Narvaez 20; ⊠ Preciados 20; ⊠ Princesa 45; and ⊠ Conde de Peñalver 4.

Flea Market

El Rastro (☞ Castizo Madrid, *above*). On Sunday, Calle de Ribera de Curtidores, the main thoroughfare of the Rastro market, is closed to traffic and absolutely jammed with outdoor booths selling all manner of objects. The crowds grow so thick on Sundays that it takes a while to advance just a few feet amid the hawkers and the gawkers. A word of warning: Hang on to your purse and wallet, and be especially careful if you choose to bring a camera—pickpockets abound. The flea market sprawls into most of the surrounding streets, with certain areas specializing in one product or another. Many of the goods sold here are wildly overpriced.

But what goods! You'll find everything from antique furniture to exotic parrots and cuddly puppies; from pirated cassette tapes of flamenco music to keychains emblazoned with symbols of the old anarchist trade union, the CNT; there are paintings, colorful Gypsy oxen yokes, heraldic iron gates, new and used clothes, and even hashish for sale.

Off the Ribera are two *galerías,* courtyards where small shops offer higher-quality, higher-priced antiques and other goods. The whole spectacle shuts down around 2 PM.

Shopping Districts

Madrid has two main centers of shopping. The first is around the **Puerta del Sol** in the center of town and includes the major department stores (El Corte Inglés, the French music-and-book chain Fnac, etc.) and a large number of midline shops in the streets nearby. The second area, far more elegant and expensive, is in the northwest **Salamanca district,** bounded, roughly, by Serrano, Goya, and Conde de Peñalver. An old factory building has been renovated into the **Mercado Puerta de Toledo** (⊠ Ronda de Toledo 1), south of the city center. It is a government-subsidized, ultra-slick mall of dozens of shops that market only the most upscale goods, at prices to match. **Galerias del Prado** (⊠ Plaza de las Cortes, 7) is another attractive mall located underneath the Palace Hotel on the Paseo del Prado. Stores in this elegant, two-story complex include fine shops for books, gourmet foods, clothing, leather goods, art, and more. The latest to open is a four-story mall located in the beautifully renovated, 19th century **Centro Comercial ABC** (⊠ Paseo de la Castellana, 34), named for the daily newspaper which started there. The building is a Madrid landmark with an ornate, tile facade. Inside, the mall opens-up to a large café in the center surounded by balconies of shops including, leather goods, hair dressers, bath supplies, a travel agency, party shop, and music-video Virgin Megastore. The fourth-floor coffee shop has an outdoor terrace on the roof with scenic views of the city.

Specialty Stores

Ceramics
Antigua Casa Talavera (⊠ Isabel la Católica 2, ☎ 91/542–3417) is the best of Madrid's numerous ceramics shops. Despite its name, the finest ware sold here is from Manises, near Valencia, although the blue-and-yellow Talavera ceramics are first-rate, too.
Cerámica El Alfar (⊠ Claudio Coello 112, ☎ 91/411–3587) has shelves laden with pottery from all corners of Spain.
Sagardelos (⊠ Zurbano 46, ☎ 91/310–4830) specializes in distinctive, modern Spanish ceramics made in Galicia and has an excellent selection of breakfast sets, coffee pots, and objets d'art.

Clothing
Adolfo Domínguez (⊠ Serrano 96, ☎ 91/576–7053) is one of the many fashion designers concentrated in Madrid's Salamanca district, especially along Calle Serrano and its side streets. Domínguez is one of the best-known Spanish designers, creating fashions for both men and women.
Del Valle (⊠ Conde Xiqueno 2, ☎ 91/531–1587; ⊠ Princesa 47, ☎ 91/547–1216; ⊠ Galerias del Prado, ☎ 91/420–2182) is an upscale women's boutique with a tasteful collection of evening and casual wear and an emphasis on leather.
Seseña (⊠ De la Cruz 23, ☎ 91/531–6840; ⊠ Argensola 2, no phone; ⊠ Mercado Puerta de Toledo, ☎ 91/366–6980) has outfitted Hollywood stars (and Hillary Rodham Clinton) and famous painters since

the turn of the century, with capes in wool or velvet, some lined with red satin.

Sybilla (✉ Jorge Juan 8, ☎ 91/578–1322) is the studio of the best-known woman designer in Spain. Her fluid garments come in natural colors and fabrics.

Crafts

Artespaña (✉ Hermosilla 14, ☎ 91/435–0221) is a store run by the government to encourage Spanish craftsmanship and stylishly displays the best decorator crafts, such as furniture, lamps, and rugs.

El Arco (✉ Plaza Mayor 9, ☎ 91/365–2680) has a good selection of contemporary handicrafts from all over Spain, including modern ceramics, handblown glassware, jewelry, and leather items, as well as a whimsical collection of pendulum clocks.

Fans

Casa de Diego (✉ Puerta del Sol 12, ☎ 91/522–6643) offers an overwhelming selection of these quintessentially Spanish accessories.

Guitars

Conde Hermanos (✉ Felipe II 2, ☎ 91/547–0612) is a workshop where three generations of the same family have been building and selling professional guitars since 1917.

José Ramirez (✉ Concepción Jerónimo 2, ☎ 91/369–2211) was founded in 1882 and has been exporting guitars around the world ever since. Prices start at 15,000 ptas., and the shop includes a museum of antique instruments.

Hats

Casa Yustas (✉ Plaza Mayor 30, ☎ 91/366–5084) is a century-old shop featuring every type of headgear, from the old Guardia Civil tricornered, patent-leather hat to the berets sported by the Guardia's frequent enemy, the Basques. These berets are much wider than those worn by the French and make excellent gifts.

Leather Goods

Caligae (✉ Augusto Figueroa 27, ☎ 91/531–5343) is located on a street of bargain shoe stores, called *muestrarios,* and is probably the best of the bunch, offering closeout prices on the avant-garde designs of Parisian Stephane Kélian.

Duna (✉ Lagasca 7, ☎ 91/435–2061) offers the best prices in town on famous Spanish leather clothing and shoes, but the selection is somewhat limited.

Loewe (✉ Serrano 26, ☎ 91/577–6056; ✉ Gran Vía 8, ☎ 91/522–6815; ✉ Palace Hotel, ☎ 91/429–8530) features ultra-high-quality, designer purses, accessories, and clothing made of buttery-soft leather, dyed in jewel-like colors. Prices often hit the stratosphere.

Piamonte (✉ Piamonte 16, ☎ 91/365–2878) falls somewhere in the mid-range category, turning out excellent quality purses and leather accessories in original designs with moderate prices.

Tenorio (✉ Plaza de la Provincia 6, no phone) is where you can find those fine old boots of Spanish leather, made to order, with quality that should last a lifetime.

OUTDOOR ACTIVITIES AND SPORTS

Participant Sports

Horseback Riding

On the other side of Casa de Campo, **Club El Trebol** (☎ 91/518–1066) rents both animals and equipment to the public at reasonable prices.

Jogging

The best bet is **Retiro Park,** where one path makes the circumference of the entire park, and numerous others weave their way under trees and through formal gardens. **Casa de Campo** is crisscrossed by numerous, less shady trails.

Swimming

Madrid has devised a perfect antidote to the sometimes intense, dry heat of the summer months—a superb system of clean, popular, and well-run municipal swimming pools (admission about 350 ptas.; there are several reduced-price, multiple-ticket options). There are pools in most neighborhoods, but the biggest and best is in the **Casa de Campo** (take the metro to the Lago stop and walk up the hill a few yards to the entrance). **La Elipa** (⊠ Avda. de la Paz s/n) has a nude sunbathing area. More expensive, and fitted with a comfortable, tree-shaded restaurant by the pool, is the private **Piscina El Lago** (⊠ Avda. de Valladolid 37), a trendy young people's hangout.

Tennis

Club de Tenis Chamartín (⊠ Federico Salmon 2, ☎ 91/345–2500), with 28 courts, is open to the public. There are also public courts in the **Casa de Campo** and on the Avenida de Vírgen del Puerto, behind the Palacio Real. (Ask for details at the tourist office.)

Spectator Sports

Bullfighting

For better or for worse, bullfighting is a spectacle, not a sport. Nevertheless, for those not turned off by the death of six bulls each Sunday afternoon from April to early November, it has all the elements of any major stadium event. Nowhere in the world is bullfighting better than at Madrid's **Las Ventas** (formally called the Plaza de Toros Monumental (⊠ C. Alcalá 231; Metro Las Ventas). The city's sophisticated audience that follows the bulls intensely is more critical in Madrid than anywhere, and you'll be amazed at how confusing their reactions to the fights are; cheers and hoots are difficult at first to distinguish, and it takes years to understand what has prompted the wrath of this most difficult-to-please audience. Tickets may be purchased at the ring or, for a 20% surcharge, at the agencies on Calle Victoria, just off the Puerta del Sol. Most fights start in the late afternoon, and the best of all—the world's top venue of bullfighting—come during the three weeks of consecutive daily fights in May marking the festival of San Isídro. Tickets can be tough to get through normal channels, but they'll always be available from scalpers in the Calle Victoria and at the stadium. You can bargain, but even Spaniards pay prices of perhaps 10 times the face value, up to 10,000 ptas. or even more.

Soccer

Spain's number-one sport is soccer, or *fútbol,* as it's known locally. Madrid has two teams, both of them among Europe's best, and two stadia to match. The 130,000-spectator **Santiago Bernabeu Stadium** (⊠ Paseo de la Castellana 140) is home to the more popular Real Madrid, while the **Vicente Calderón Stadium** (⊠ Paseo de Melancólicos s/n), located on the outskirts of town, is where Atlético Madrid defends. Generally you'll have to stand in line at the stadia to get tickets, but for many major games tickets are available at agencies inside the Corte Inglés department stores (☞ Shopping, *above*).

SIDE TRIPS

El Escorial

③⑦ *50 km (31 mi) northwest of Madrid.*

Felipe II was certainly one of history's most deeply religious and forbidding monarchs—not to mention one of its most powerful—and the great granite monastery he had constructed in a remarkable 21 years (1563–84) offers enduring testimony to that austere character. Severe, rectilinear, and unforgiving, the **Real Monasterio de San Lorenzo de El Escorial** (El Escorial Monastery) stands 50 km/31 mi from Madrid on the slopes of the Guadarrama Mountains, one of the most massive yet simple examples of architecture on the Iberian Peninsula.

Felipe built the monastery in the village of San Lorenzo de El Escorial to commemorate Spain's crushing victory over the French at Saint-Quentin on August 10, 1557, and as a final resting place for his all-powerful father, the emperor Carlos V. The vast rectangle it traces, along with 16 courts, is modeled on the red-hot grille upon which San Lorenzo was martyred—appropriate, given that August 10 was the saint's day. (It's also said that Felipe's troops accidentally destroyed a church dedicated to the saint during the battle, and he sought to make amends.) A Spanish psycho-historian recently theorized that it is actually shaped like a prone woman, an unintended emblem of Felipe's sexual repression. Perhaps most surprising is not the fact that this thesis was put forward by a serious academic but that it provoked several heady newspaper articles and other commentary.

El Escorial can be easily reached by car, train, bus, or organized tour; simply inquire at a travel agency or the appropriate station. While the building and its adjuncts—a palace, museum, church, and more—can take hours or even days to tour, you should be able to include a visit to the Valley of the Fallen, where General Franco is buried, in a day trip. At the monastery, be prepared for the mobs of tourists who visit daily, especially during the summer.

The Escorial was begun by Juan Bautista de Toledo but finished in 1584 by Juan de Herrera, who was to give his name to a major Spanish architectural school. It was completed just in time for Felipe to die here, gangrenous and in great pain from the gout that had plagued him for years, in the tiny, sparsely furnished bedroom that resembled a monk's cell more than the resting place of a great monarch. It is in this bedroom—which looks out, through a private entrance, into the royal chapel—that one most appreciates the spartan nature of this man. Later, Bourbon kings, such as Carlos III and Carlos IV, had clearly different tastes, and their apartments, connected to Felipe's by the Hall of Battles, are far more luxurious.

Perhaps the most interesting spot in the entire Escorial is the **Royal Pantheon**, which contains the body of every king since Carlos I save three—Felipe V (buried at La Granja palace), Ferdinand VI (in Madrid), and Amadeus of Savoy (in Italy). The body of Alfonso XIII, who died in Rome in 1941, was brought to the Escorial only in January 1980. The bodies of the rulers lie in 26 sumptuous, marble and bronze sarcophagi that line the walls (three of which are empty, awaiting future rulers). Only those queens who bore sons later crowned lie in the same crypt; the others, along with royal sons and daughters who never ruled, lie nearby in the **Pantheon of the Infantes.** Many of the child infantes are in a single, circular tomb made of Carrara marble.

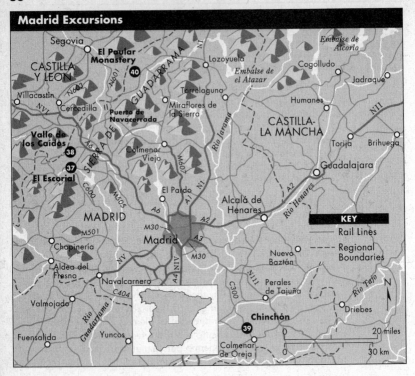

Madrid Excursions

Another highlight is the uncharacteristically lavish and beautiful **library,** with 40,000 rare manuscripts, codices, and ancient books, including St. Teresa of Ávila's diary and the gold-lettered, illuminated *Codex Aureus.* **Tapestries,** woven from cartoons by Goya, Rubens, and El Greco, cover almost every inch of wall space in huge sections of the building, and extraordinary canvases by Velázquez, El Greco, David, Ribera, Tintoretto, Rubens, and other masters have been collected from around the monastery and are now displayed in the New Museums. In the **basilica,** don't miss the fresco over the choir depicting heaven or Titian's fresco of *The Martyrdom of St. Lawrence,* showing the saint being roasted alive. ⊠ *San Lorenzo de El Escorial,* ☎ 91/890–5905. ☒ *800 ptas.* ☉ *Apr.–Sept., Tues.–Sun. 10–6; Oct.–Mar., Tues.–Sun. 10–5.*

NEED A BREAK?	Many Madrileños consider El Escorial the perfect place for a huge weekend lunch. Topping the list of favorite eating spots is the outdoor terrace of **Charoles** (⊠ Floridablanca 24, ☎ 91/890–5975), where imaginative, seasonal specialties round out a menu of Spanish favorites like bacalao al pil-pil and grilled *chuletón* (steak).

Valle de los Caídos (The Valley of the Fallen)

38 *North of El Escorial on the C600.*

Just a few miles north of El Escorial is the Valle de los Caídos (Valley of the Fallen). You'll drive through a pine-studded state park to this massive basilica, which is carved out inside a hill of solid granite and commands magnificent views to the east. Topped with a cross nearly 500 feet high, this is the tomb of both Franco and José Antonio Primo de Rivera, founder of the Spanish Falange. It was built with the forced labor

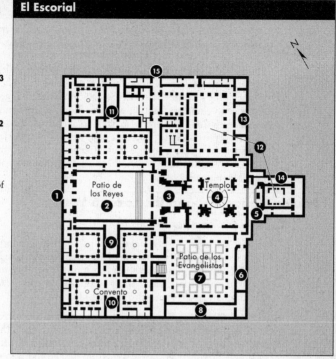

El Escorial

of Republican prisoners after the civil war and dedicated rather disingenuously to *all* those who died in the three-year conflict. The inside of this gigantic hall is more reminiscent of the palace of the Wizard of Oz than of anything else, with every footstep resounding loudly off its stone walls. Tapestries of the Apocalypse add to the generally terrifying flavor of the place. ☎ 91/890–5611. ✉ 600 ptas., funicular 300 ptas. ☉ Apr.–Sept., Tues.–Sun. 10–7; Oct.–Mar., Tues.–Sun. 10–6.

Chinchón

39 *54 km (28 mi) southeast of Madrid, off the N III highway to Valencia on the C300 local road.*

The picturesque village of Chinchón, a true Castilian town, seems a good four centuries away in time. It's an ideal place for a day trip and lunch at one of its many rustic restaurants—the only down side being that swarms of Madrileños have the very same idea, so it's often difficult to find a table for lunch on weekends.

The high point of Chinchón is its charming Plaza Mayor, an uneven circle of ancient three- and four-story houses embellished with wooden balconies resting on granite columns. It's reminiscent of an open-air Elizabethan theater, but with a Spanish flavor. In fact, the entire plaza is converted to a bullring from time to time, with temporary bleachers erected in the center and seats on the privately owned balconies being rented out for a splendid view of the festivities. (It should be noted that these fights are rare, and tickets hard to come by, as they are snatched up by Spanish tourists as soon as they go on sale.)

NEED A BREAK? Two of the best and most popular restaurants on Chinchón's arcaded plaza are **Mesón de la Virreina** (✉ Plaza Mayor 21, ☎ 91/894–0015) and **Café de la Iberia** (✉ Plaza Mayor 17, ☎ 91/894–0998). Both have balconies for dining outside, and it's a good idea to call and reserve an outdoor table ahead of time. The food in each is hearty Castilian fare such as roast lamb and suckling pig or thick steaks.

On the way back to Madrid, you'll pass through the valley of Jarama, just at the point where C300 joins the main highway. This is the scene of one of the bloodiest battles in which the Abraham Lincoln Brigade, American volunteers fighting with the Republicans against Franco in the Spanish Civil War, played a major role (immortalized by folksinger Pete Seeger, who sang, "There's a valley in Spain called Jarama . . ."). Until just a few years ago, you could find bones and rusty military hardware in the fields here; today, there are still a number of clearly discernible trenches.

El Paular Monastery and the Lozoya Valley

40   *100 km (62 mi) north of Madrid.*

Behind the great meseta where Madrid sits, the Guadarrama Mountains rise like a dark, jagged shield that separates New and Old Castile. The mountains, snowcapped for much of the year, are indeed rough-hewn in many spots, particularly so on their northern face, but there is a dramatic exception—the Valley of Lozoya.

About 100 km/62 mi north of the capital, this valley of pine, poplar, and babbling brooks is a cool and green retreat from the often searing heat of the plain. In it, Madrileños often take a day for a picnic or a simple driving tour, rarely joined by foreign tourists, to whom the area is virtually unknown.

A car is required for visiting this place, but the drive will be a pleasant one. Take the A6 motorway northwest from the city, exiting at signs for the Navacerrada Pass on the N601 highway. As you climb toward the 6,100-foot mountain pass, you'll come to a road bearing off to the left toward Cercedilla. This little village, also reachable by train from Madrid, is a favorite spot for mountain hikers. Just above the town an old Roman road leads up to the ridge of the Guadarrama, where an ancient fountain, known as Fuenfría, long provided the spring water that fed the Roman aqueduct of Segovia (☞ Chapter 3). The path traced by this cobble road is very close to the route Hemingway had his hero Robert Jordan take in his novel of the civil war, *For Whom the Bell Tolls*; eventually it will take you near the bridge that Jordan blew up in the novel.

If you continue past the Cercedilla road, you'll come to a ski resort at the highest point of the Navacerrada Pass. Take a right here on the C604 and you'll follow the ridge of the mountains for a few miles before descending into the **Lozoya Valley**.

The **El Paular Monastery** (☎ 91/869–1425) will loom up on your left as you approach the valley floor. This was the first Carthusian monastery in Castile, built by King Juan I in 1390, but it has been badly neglected since the Disentailment of 1836. Fewer than a dozen Benedictine monks still live here, eating and praying exactly as their predecessors did centuries ago. One of them gives tours—as well as abundant advice on the state of your soul—at noon, 1, and 5.

The monastery is physically connected to the Santa María del Paular hotel (☎ 91/869–1011, FAX 91/869–1006). This hotel is tastefully furnished and charming but very expensive and not as grand as similarly priced paradors.

The valley is filled with spots to picnic along the Lozoya River, including several campgrounds. Afterward, take the C604 north a few kilometers to Rascafria, where you turn right on a smaller road marked for Miraflores de la Sierra. In that town you'll turn right again, following signs for Colmenar Viejo, where you pick up a short expressway back to Madrid.

MADRID A TO Z

Arriving and Departing

By Bus

Madrid has no central bus station, and, in general, buses are less popular than trains (though they can be faster). Most of southern Spain is served by the **Estación del Sur** (✉ Canarias 17, ☎ 91/468–4200), while buses for much of the rest of the peninsula, including Cuenca, Extremadura, Salamanca, and Valencia, depart from the **Auto Res Station** (✉ Plaza Conde de Casal 6, ☎ 91/551–7200). There are several other smaller stations, however, so inquire at travel agencies for the one for your destination.

Other bus companies of interest include **La Sepulvedana** (✉ Paseo de la Florida 11, near Norte Station, ☎ 91/527–9537), serving Segovia, Ávila, and La Granja; **Herranz** (departures from Fernández de los Ríos s/n, ☎ 91/543–8167; Metro Moncloa), for the Escorial and Valle de los Caidos; **Continental Auto** (✉ Alenza 20, ☎ 91/533–0400; Metro Ríos Rosas), serving Cantabria and the Basque region; and **La Veloz** (✉ Mediterraneo 49, ☎ 91/409–7602; Metro Conde de Casal), with service to Chinchón.

By Car

Felipe II made Madrid the capital of Spain because it was at the geographic center of his peninsular domains, and today many of the nation's highways radiate out from it like the spokes of a wheel. Originating at Kilometer 0, marked by a brass plaque on the sidewalk of the central Puerta del Sol, these highways include A6 (Segovia, Salamanca, Galicia); A1 (Burgos and the Basque Country); the N II (Guadalajara, Barcelona, France); the N III (Cuenca, Valencia, the Mediterranean Coast); the A4 (Aranjuez, La Mancha, Granada, Seville); N401 (Toledo); and the N V (Talavera de la Reina, Portugal). The city is surrounded by M30, the inner ring road, and M40, the outer ring road, from which most of these highways are easily picked up.

By Plane

Madrid is served by **Barajas Airport,** 12 km/7 mi east of the city; it's a rather grim-looking facility, although the national terminal was recently renovated. Major carriers, including American, Delta, TWA, Iberia, and United, provide regular service to the United States. Most connections are through Miami, Washington, or New York, but American offers daily direct flights to and from Dallas-Fort Worth International Airport; (reserve well in advance because they're very popular). Many carriers serve London and other European capitals daily, but if you shop around at Madrid travel agencies, you'll generally find better deals than those available abroad (especially to and from Great Britain). For more information on getting to Madrid by air, *see* Important Contacts A to Z. For general information and information on flight delays, call the airport (☎ 91/305–8343, 91/305–8344, or 91/305–8345).

BETWEEN THE AIRPORT AND DOWNTOWN

For a mere 360 ptas., there's a convenient **bus** to the central Plaza Colón, where taxis wait to take you to your hotel. The buses run between 5:40

AM and 2 AM, leaving every 15 minutes—slightly less often very early or late in the day. Be sure to watch your belongings, as the underground Plaza Colón bus station is one of the favorite haunts of purse snatchers and con artists. **Taxis** are usually waiting outside the airport terminal near the clearly marked bus stop. Expect to pay up to 2,000 ptas., or even more in heavy traffic, plus small holiday, late-night, and luggage surcharges. Make sure the driver works on the meter—off-the-meter "deals" almost always cost more.

By Train

Madrid has three train stations: Chamartín, Atocha, and Norte. **Chamartín** Station, near the northern tip of the Paseo Castellana, serves trains heading for points north, including Barcelona, France, San Sebastián, Burgos, León, Oviedo, La Coruña, Segovia, Salamanca, and Portugal. The **Atocha** Station, at the southern end of the Paseo del Prado, was renovated in honor of the inauguration of high-speed, AVE train service in 1992, and serves points south and east, including Seville, Málaga, Córdoba, Valencia, Castellon, and Toledo. The **Norte** Station is used primarily as a terminal for local trains serving Madrid's western suburbs, including El Escorial. For schedules and reservations call RENFE (☎ 91/328–9020), or go to the information counter in any of the train stations. Reservations can be made by phone, and tickets can be charged on a credit card and delivered to your hotel. Most major travel agencies can also provide information and tickets.

Getting Around

Madrid has a distinctly different feel depending on the neighborhood—from winding, medieval streets to superchic, shopping boulevards; regal, formal parks to seedy, red-light districts. While you will probably want to start out in the old city, where the majority of attractions are clustered, further adventures are likely to call you to other parts of town.

By Bus

Red city buses run between 6 AM and midnight and cost 130 ptas. per ride. Signs listing stops by street name are located at every stop but are hard to comprehend if you don't know the city well. Pick up a free route map from EMT kiosks on the Plaza de Cibeles or the Puerta del Sol, where you can also buy a 10-ride ticket (*bonobus*, 645 ptas.). If you speak Spanish, you can call for information (☎ 91/401–9900).

Drivers will make change for you, generally up to a 2,000-pta note. If you've bought a 10-ride ticket, step up just behind the driver and insert it in the ticket-punching machine you see there until you hear the mechanism make a "ding."

By Car

Driving automobiles in Madrid is best avoided by all but the most adventurous. Parking is nightmarish; traffic extremely heavy almost all the time, and the city's drivers can be frightening. An exception may be August, when the streets are largely emptied by the mass exodus of Madrileños on vacation.

By Metro

The metro is quick, frequent, and, at 130 ptas. no matter how far you travel, cheap. Vastly cheaper is the 10-ride *billete de diez,* which costs 645 ptas. and has the added merit of being accepted by automatic turnstiles; (lines at ticket booths can be long). The system is open from 6 AM to 1:30 AM, although a few entrances close earlier. Ten metro lines crisscross the city, and there are system maps in every station. Note the end station of the line you need, and just follow the signs to the correct

Madrid Metro

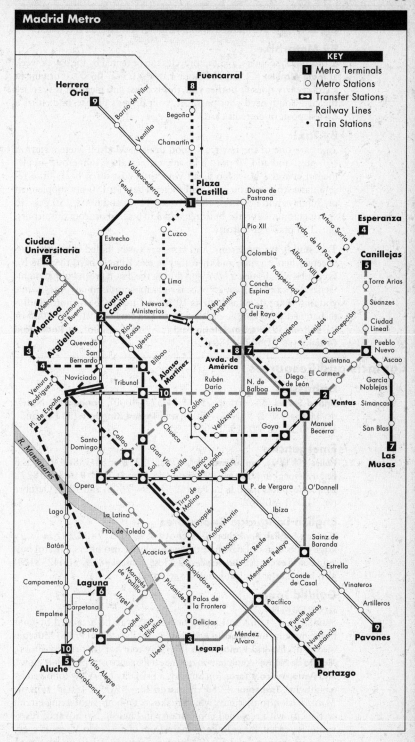

KEY

- **1** Metro Terminals
- ○ Metro Stations
- ⬛ Transfer Stations
- —— Railway Lines
- • Train Stations

end station of the line you need, and just follow the signs to the correct corridor. Exits are marked *salida*. Crime is still rare on the system.

By Motorbike

Motorbikes, scooters, and motorcycles can be rented by the day or week at **Moto Alquiler** (⊠ Conde Duque 13, ☎ 91/542–0657). If driving in a strange city doesn't bother you, this is a fast and pleasant way to see the city. You'll need your passport, your driver's license, and either a cash deposit or a credit card.

By Taxi

Taxis are one of the few truly good deals in Madrid. Meters start at 170 ptas. and add 70 ptas. a kilometer thereafter; numerous supplemental charges, however, mean your total cost often bears little resemblance to what you see on the meter. There's a 150-pta supplement on Sundays and holidays, and between 11 PM and 6 AM; 150 ptas. to sports stadiums and the bullring; and 350 ptas. to or from the airport, plus 150 ptas. per suitcase.

Taxi stands are numerous, and taxis are easily hailed in the street—except when it rains, and then they're exceedingly hard to come by. Free cabs will display a *libre* sign during the day, a green light at night. Generally, a tip of about 25 ptas. is right for shorter in-city rides, while you may want to go as high as 10% for a trip to the airport. Radio-dispatched taxis can be ordered from **Tele-Taxi** (☎ 91/445–9008 or 91/448–4259), **Radioteléfono Taxi** (☎ 91/547–8200), or **Radio Taxi Gremial** (☎ 91/447–5180).

Contacts and Resources

Embassies

United States (⊠ Serrano 75, ☎ 91/577–4000), **Canada** (⊠ Nuñez de Balboa 35, ☎ 91/431–4300), and **United Kingdom** (⊠ Fernando el Santo 16, ☎ 91/319–0200).

Emergencies

Police (☎ 091), **ambulance** (☎ 91/522–2222 or 91/588–4400), and English-speaking **doctors** (⊠ Conde de Aranda 7, ☎ 91/435–1823). Major **hospitals** include La Paz (☎ 91/358–2600) and 12 de Octubre (☎ 91/390–8000).

English-Language Bookstores

Turner's English Bookshop (⊠ Génova 3, ☎ 91/319–0926) has a very large collection of English-language books. It also offers a useful bulletin board exchange. **Booksellers** (⊠ José Abascal 48, ☎ 91/442–8104) also has a large English-language selection.

Guided Tours

ORIENTATION

Standard city tours, in English or Spanish, can be arranged by your hotel; most include **Madrid Artístico** (Royal Palace and Prado Museum included), **Madrid Panorámico** (half-day tour for first-time visitors), **Madrid de Noche** (combinations include a flamenco or a nightclub show), and **Panorámico y Toros** (on Sunday, a brief city overview followed by a bullfight). **Trapsatur** (⊠ San Bernardo 23, ☎ 91/302–6039) runs the *Madridvision* tourist bus, which makes a 1½-hour sightseeing circuit of the city with recorded commentary in English. No advance reservation is needed. Buses leave from the front of the Prado Museum every 1½ hours, beginning at 12:30 Monday–Saturday, 10:30 on Sunday. A round-trip ticket costs 1,500 ptas., while a day pass, which allows you to get on and off at various attractions, is 2,000 ptas.

PERSONAL GUIDES

Contact the **Asociación Profesional de Informadores** (✉ Ferraz 82, ☎ 91/542–1214 or 91/541–1221) if you wish to hire a personal guide to take you around the city.

Late-Night Pharmacies

Emergency pharmacies are required by law to be open 24 hours a day, on a rotating basis. Listings of those pharmacies are found in all major daily newspapers.

Travel Agencies

Travel agencies, found almost everywhere in Madrid, are generally the best bet for obtaining deals, tickets, and information without hassles. Some major agencies: **American Express,** located next door to the Cortés, the parliament building on Génova (✉ Plaza de las Cortés 2, ☎ 91/322–5445); **Carlson Wagons-Lits** (✉ Paseo de la Castellana 96, ☎ 91/563–1202); and **Pullmantur,** across the street from the Royal Palace (✉ Plaza de Oriente 8, ☎ 91/541–1807).

Visitor Information

There are four provincial tourist offices in Madrid, but the best is on the ground floor of the Torre Madrid building, on the **Plaza España.** ✉ Princesa 1, ☎ 91/541–2325; ☉ Weekdays 9 AM–7 PM, Sat. 9:30–1:30, closed holidays. Others are at **Barajas Airport** ☎ 91/305–8656. ☉ Weekdays 8 AM–8 PM, Sat. 9–1); the **Chamartín railroad station** ☎ 91/315–9976. ☉ Weekdays 8–8, Sat. 9–1; and **Duque de Medinaceli 2** ☎ 91/429–4951. ☉ Weekdays 9–7, Sat. 9–1. The city tourism office on the Plaza Mayor is good for little save a few pamphlets ☎ 91/366–5477. ☉ Weekdays 10–8, Sat. 10–2).

3 Around Madrid

The area around Madrid, Castile, is a vast, wind-swept plateau, with clear skies and endless vistas. Outstanding Roman monuments and a fairy-tale castle make Segovia one of the most popular excursions from Madrid. The walled city of Ávila has relics of St. Teresa, the female patron saint of Spain; Salamanca, a university town, is a showpiece of the Spanish Renaissance. The contrast between Aranjuez, with its French-style elegance and Bourbon palace, and nearby Toledo, dramatic and austere with a rich Moorish legacy, is marked.

FOR ALL THE MANY FACETS that make up the surroundings of Madrid, there is an underlying unity. The region covered in this section is Castile—more accurately Old and New Castile, the former north of Madrid, the latter south (and known as "New" because it was captured from the Moors at a slightly later date). Castile is essentially a vast, windswept plateau, famed for clear skies and endless vistas. Over the centuries poets and others have characterized it as austere and melancholy, most notably Antonio Machado, whose experiences early this century at Soria inspired his memorable and haunting *Campos de Castilla* (Fields of Castile).

By Michael Jacobs

Updated by Nancy Hennessey

Stone is one of the dominant elements of the Castilian countryside and it has, to a large extent, molded the character of the region. Gaunt mountain ranges frame the horizons, gorges and rocky outcrops break up many a flat expanse, and the fields around Ávila and Segovia are littered with giant boulders. The villages are predominantly of granite, and their solid, formidable look contrasts markedly with the whitewashed walls of most of southern Spain. The presence of so much stone perhaps helps to explain the rich sculptural tradition of this region— few parts of Europe have such a wealth of outstanding sculptural treasures as does Castile, a wealth testified to by the unrivaled National Museum of Sculpture at Valladolid.

Whereas southern Spaniards are traditionally passive and peace loving, Castilians have been a race of soldiers. The very name of the region refers to the great line of castles and fortified towns built in the 12th century between Salamanca in the west and Soria in the east. The Alcázar at Segovia, the intact surrounding walls of Ávila, and countless other military monuments are among the greatest tourist attractions of Castile, and some of them—for instance, the castles at Sigüenza and Ciudad Rodrigo—are also splendid hotels.

Faced with the austerity of the Castilian environment, many here have taken refuge in the worlds of the spirit and the imagination. Ávila is closely associated with two of the most renowned of Europe's mystics, St. Teresa and her disciple St. John of the Cross; Toledo, meanwhile, was the main home of one of the most spiritual of all western painters, El Greco. As for the escape into fantasy, this is famously illustrated by Cervantes's hero Don Quixote, in whose formidable imagination even the dreary expanse of La Mancha—one of the bleakest parts of Spain—could be transformed into something magical. A similarly fanciful mind has characterized many of the region's architects. Castile in the 15th and 16th centuries was the center of the Plateresque, a style of ornamentation of extraordinary intricacy and fantasy, suggestive of silverwork. Developed in Toledo and Valladolid, it reached its exuberant climax in the university town of Salamanca.

Pleasures and Pastimes

Dining

The classic dishes of Castile are *cordero* (lamb) and *cochinillo* (suckling pig) roasted in a wood oven. These are specialties of Segovia, widely thought of as the gastronomic capital of Castile, thanks largely to the international reputation of such long-established restaurants as the Mesón de Cándido and the Mesón Duque. In the Segovian village of Pedraza, superb roast lamb is served with hearty red wine.

The mountainous districts of Salamanca are renowned for their hams and sausage products—in particular, the villages of Guijuelo and Candelario. Bean dishes are a specialty of El Barco (Ávila) and La Granja (Segovia), while *trucha* (trout) and *cangrejos de río* (river crab) are common to Guadalajara province. Game is abundant throughout Castile, two famous dishes being *perdiz en escabeche* (the marinated partridges of Soria) and *perdiz estofada a la Toledana* (the stewed partridges of Toledo). The most exotic and complex cuisine in Castile is perhaps that of Cuenca, where you will find two outstanding restaurants, Figon de Pedro and Los Claveles. A strong Moorish influence prevails here—for instance, in gazpacho *pastor* (a hot terrine made with a variety of game, topped with grapes).

Among the region's sweets are the *yemas* (sugared egg yolks) of Ávila, *almendras garrapiñadas* (candied almonds) of Alcalá de Henares, *mazapan* (marzipans) of Toledo, and *ponche Segovia* (egg toddy of Segovia). La Mancha is the main area for cheeses, while Aranjuez is famous for its strawberries and asparagus.

Much of the cheap wine in Spain comes from La Mancha, south of Toledo. Far better in quality, and indeed among the most superior Spanish wines, are those from the Duero Valley, around Valladolid. Look for the Marqués de Riscal whites from Rueda and the Vega Sicilia reds from Valbuena; Peñafiel is the most common of the Duero wines. An excellent, if extremely sweet, Castilian liqueur is the *resolí* from Cuenca made from aquavit, coffee, vanilla, orange peel, and sugar and often sold in bottles in the shape of Cuenca's Casas Colgadas.

CATEGORY	COST*
$$$$	over 6,500 ptas.
$$$	4,000–6,500 ptas.
$$	2,500–4,000 ptas.
$	under 2,500 ptas.

per person for a three-course meal, including wine, excluding tax

Lodging

The most stylish of Spain's hotels are usually the paradors. Though this holds true in the region around Madrid, the oldest and most beautiful of the paradors here are generally found in the lesser towns, such as Ciudad Real and Sigüenza, rather than in major tourist centers. The paradors at Salamanca, Toledo, Segovia, and Soria are all in ugly or nondescript modern buildings, albeit with magnificent views. Fortunately, the region has many memorable alternatives to paradors, such as the centrally situated Los Linajes in Segovia, the Palacio de Valderrábanos in Ávila (a 15th-century palace next to the cathedral), and Cuenca's Posada San José, a 16th-century convent.

CATEGORY	COST*
$$$$	over 13,000 ptas.
$$$	8,000–13,000 ptas.
$$	4,000–8,000 ptas.
$	under 4,000 ptas.

per standard double room, excluding tax.

Exploring Around Madrid

Two main regions surround Madrid—Castille and León to the north and west, and Castille—La Mancha to the south and east. Numerous cities and towns in both regions are deserving of your visit. Beginning with Segovia to the north and culminating with Toledo to the south, the most notable will be described in detail in this section.

Great Itineraries

Aranjuez, Ávila, Segovia, and Toledo tend to be visited by tourists on day trips from Madrid. Salamanca and the other major places discussed in this section can also be seen on a day's outing from the capital, but you'll find yourself spending more time traveling than actually being there. Ideally, especially if you have a car, undertake at least a four-day trip around the area, staying in Toledo, Segovia, and Salamanca and passing through Ávila. Both Toledo and Segovia have an extra charm at night, not only because their monuments are so beautifully illuminated but also because they are free of the great crowds of tourists that congest them by day. To visit all the main sights around Madrid would require at least another three to six days and feature overnight stays as well in Zamora, Soria, Sigüenza, and Cuenca.

Numbers in the text below correspond to numbers in the margin and on the maps.

IF YOU HAVE 3 DAYS

🏛 **Toledo** ㊿–㊺, which was for many years the intellectual and spiritual capital of Spain, is a must-see. Spend a night and visit El Greco's former stomping grounds, before moving on to the royal palace, the summer retreat of the Bourbon monarchy in **Aranjuez** ㊾. Next, head north of Madrid and visit 🏛 **Segovia** ①–⑬, famous for its Roman aqueduct and countless Romanesque churches. On your last day, try to catch the incredible fountain display in the gardens of **El Palacio de La Granja** ⑭, before heading back to Madrid.

IF YOU HAVE 4 DAYS

Visit the **El Palacio de La Granja** ⑭ on the way to 🏛 **Segovia** ①–⑬. After admiring the Roman aqueduct and other monuments, visit the famous medieval sight at **Castillo de Coca** ⑰. From there, go to 🏛 **Salamanca** ㉒–㉝ and enjoy one of Spain's architectural treasures while soaking up the university atmosphere. On the following day, spend some time in **Ávila** ⑱, famous for its medieval walls and the legacy left behind by St. Teresa, the female patron saint of Spain who lived most of her life here. Finally, arrive in 🏛 **Toledo** ㊿–㊺, where you may wonder if you've landed back in the Middle Ages.

When to Tour Around Madrid

The best time to tour Around Madrid is between May and October, when the weather is nice. All the restaurants and cafés have sidewalk terraces where you can relax and enjoy the pastime of people-watching. Be warned however, that July and August can be brutally hot at times, especially south of Madrid. If possible, arrange to spend at least one weekend night in Salamanca, where the atmosphere is something to delight in. November through February can be rather cold, especially north and west of Madrid in the Sierra.If you don't mind touring in a winter coat, however, the Christmas holidays can be a nice time to visit, with the streets livened up by decorative lights and colorful processions. Lastly, many museums in all areas around Madrid are closed on Monday, so you may want to spend the day in places where museum visiting will not be your main focus.

SEGOVIA AND ITS PROVINCE

Segovia, El Palacio de la Granja, Pedraza, Sepúlveda, and Castillo de Coca

Discover the rich and varied hostory north of Madrid, from the famous Roman aqueduct in Segovia to the small 16th-century village of Pedraza, either of which would make an enjoyable place to spend the night. Other towns worth a visit include Sepúlveda and Castillo de Coca for their medieval monuments and La Granja, where the impressive gardens are made even more spectacular on those occassions when the fountains are turned on creating a Versaille-like atmosphere.

Numbers in the margin correspond to points of interest on the Around Madrid and Segovia maps.

Segovia★

● *87 km (54 mi) west of Madrid.*

Outstanding Roman and medieval monuments, embroideries and textiles, and excellent cuisine make beautifully situated Segovia one of the most popular destinations for excursions from Madrid. An important military town in Roman times, Segovia was later established by the Arabs as a major textile center. Captured by the Christians in 1085, the town was enriched by a royal residence, and indeed, in 1474 the half sister of Henry IV, Isabella the Catholic (Isabel la Católica, of Castile, wife of Ferdinand of Aragón), was proclaimed queen of Castile here. By that time Segovia was a bustling city of about 60,000 inhabitants (there are 54,000 today), but its importance was soon to diminish as a result of its taking the side of the Comuneros in the popular revolt against the emperor Charles V. Though the construction in the 18th century of a royal palace at nearby La Granja helped somewhat to revive its fortunes, it was never to recover its former vitality. At the turn of the century, its sleepy charm came to be appreciated by numerous artists and writers—for instance the painter Ignacio Zuloaga and the poet Antonio Machado. Today it swarms with tourists and day-trippers from Madrid, and you may want to avoid it in the summer months, especially on weekends or public holidays. On weekdays in the winter you can appreciate fully the haunting peace of the town.

When you approach Segovia driving west from Madrid along N603, the first building that you see is the cathedral, which seems from here to rise directly above the fields. Between you and Segovia lies, in fact, a steep and narrow valley, which shields the old town from view. Only when you descend into this valley does the spectacular position of the old town begin to become apparent, rising as it does on top of a narrow rock ledge shaped like a ship. As soon as you reach the modern outskirts of Segovia, turn left onto the Paseo E. Gonzalez and follow the road marked **"Ruta Panorámica."** Soon you will find yourself descending on the narrow and winding Cuesta de los Hoyos, a road that takes you to the bottom of the wooded valley that dips to the south of the old town. Above, in the old town, you can see the Romanesque church of San Martín to the right; the cathedral in the middle; and on the far left, at the point where the rock ledge tapers out, the turrets, spires, and battlements of the castle, known as the Alcázar.

Worth a quick detour from the Cuestra de los Hoyos, the church of ❷ **Vera Cruz,** is on the northern outskirts of Segovia on the Carretera de Zamarramala. This isolated, Romanesque structure, made of the warm orange stone of the area, was built in 1208 for the Knights Templar. Like other buildings associated with this order, it is round, inspired by the Holy Sepulcher in Jerusalem. A visit here is rewarded by the climb up the bell tower for a view of the whole town profiled against the Sierra de Guadarrama, which in the winter is capped with snow. ☎ 911/ 431475. ▣ 150 ptas. ☉ May–Sept., Tues.–Sun. 10:30–1:30 and 3:30– 7; Oct.–Apr., Tues.–Sun. 10:30–1:30 and 3:30–6.

Just south of the River Eresma, on Calle de la Moneda, take note of the 15th-century building that functioned from 1455 until 1730 as the **3** **mint** where all Spanish coinage was struck. Also on Calle de la Moneda is the **Convento de la Santa Cruz.** The church was established in the 13th century, near a cave inhabited by Santo Domingo de Guzmán, the founder of the Dominican order, and rebuilt in the 15th century by Ferdinand and Isabella.

5 Segovia's leading monument, the **Roman aqueduct,** ranks with the Pont du Gard in France as one of the greatest surviving examples of Roman engineering. Spanning the dip that stretches from the walls of the old town to the lower slopes of the Sierra de Guadarrama, it is about 2,952 feet long, and—above the square to which Avenida Fernández Ladreda leads—rises in two tiers to a height of 115 feet. The raised section of stonework in the center originally carried an inscription, of which only the holes for the bronze letters remain. The massive, granite blocks that make up the vast structure are held up by neither mortar nor clamps. Nonetheless, the aqueduct has managed to remain standing from the time of the emperor Augustus (3rd century BC), and the only damage it has suffered is the demolition of 35 of its arches by the Moors (these were later replaced on the orders of Ferdinand and Isabella). Steps at the side of the aqueduct lead up to the walls of the old town, offering at the top a breathtaking side view of the structure.

Just up Calle de Cervantes from the Roman aqueduct, you'll find the **6** late-15th-century **Casa de los Picos,** so called because its walls are studded with diamond shapes. The Calle de Juan Bravo, a pedestrian shopping street, leads from here toward the center of the old town. The Late **7** Gothic **Palacio de los Condes de Alpuente** (Palace of the Counts of Alpuente), covered with plasterwork incised with regular patterns, is a few meters away from Casa de los Picos. This type of plasterwork, known as *esgrafiado,* is characteristic of the buildings of Segovia and was probably introduced by the Moors. While walking Calle Juan Bravo, notice the small, delightful Plaza Martín, on which rises another por- **8** ticoed Romanesque church, **San Martín.**

The Paseo de Salón, a small promenade at the foot of the town's southern walls was very popular with Spain's 19th-century queen, Isabel II; it offers good views over the wooded valley to the south and toward the Guadarrama range.

The lively Plaza Mayor, lined with bars and terraces, makes an ideal place for a lunch break or early evening drink. You can watch the paseo **9** of the arcaded main square, on which stand the 17th-century **Ayuntamiento** (Town Hall), the tourist office, and the cathedral.

10 The **cathedral** was begun in 1525 to replace an earlier one near the Alcázar that was destroyed during the revolt of the Comuneros. Completed only 65 years later, it is one of the most harmonious in Spain, and one of the last great examples of the Gothic style in the country. The designs were drawn up by the leading Late Gothicist Juan Gil de Hontañon but executed by his son Rodrigo, in whose work can be seen a transition between the Gothic and Renaissance styles. The tall proportions and buttressing are pure Gothic, but much of the detailing— for instance, on the crossing tower—is classical. The golden interior, illuminated by 16th-century Flemish windows, is remarkably light and uncluttered, the one major, distracting detail being the wooden, neoclassical choir. You enter the building through the north transept, which is marked MUSEO, and the first chapel you come to on the right has a lamentation group in polychromed wood by the Baroque sculptor Gregorio Fernández.

Around Madrid

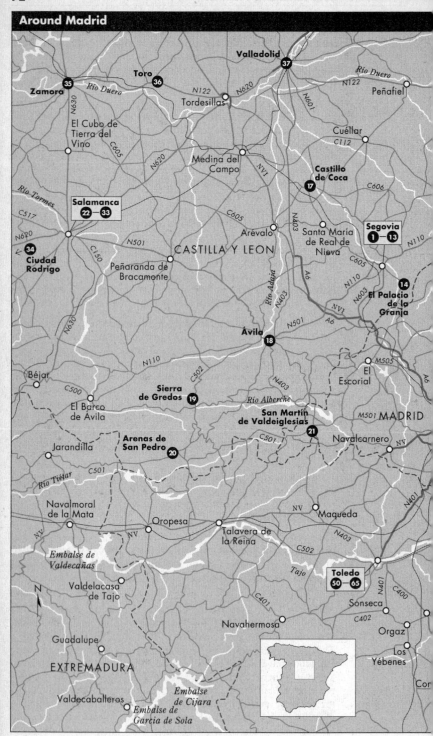

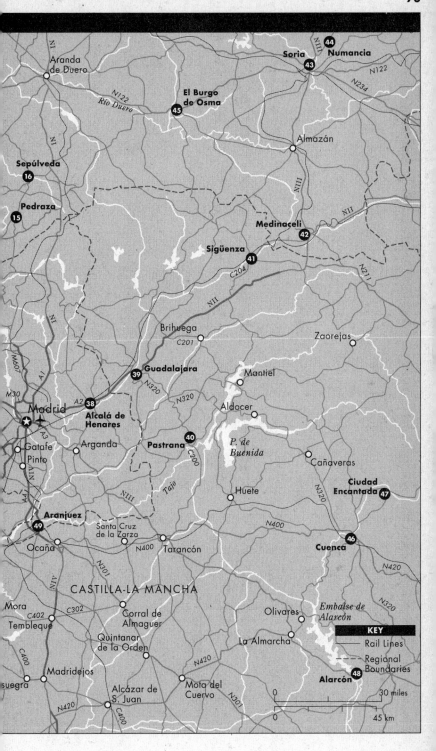

Segovia

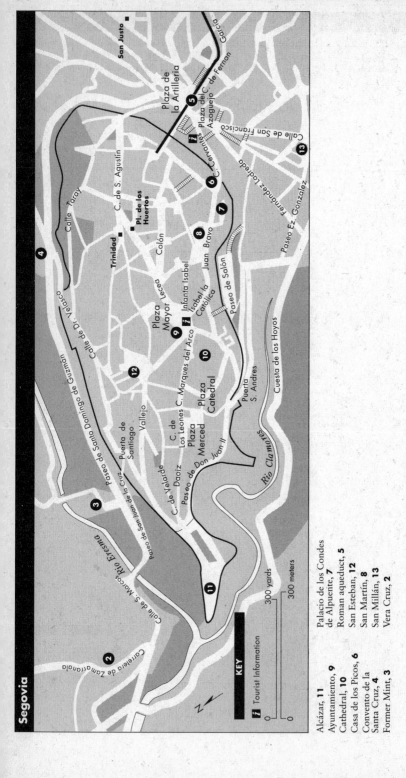

San Justo

Plaza de
la Artillería

Plaza del
Azoguejo

Calle de San Francisco

C. de Cervantes

Plaza del
C. de Fernan García

C. de S. Agustín

Calle Taray

Pl. de los
Huertos

Trinidad

Colón

Paseo de Santo Domingo de Guzmán

Calle de Dr. Velasco

Plaza
Mayor

Lecea

Infanta Isabel

Isabel la
Católica

Paseo de Salón

Paseo de San Juan de la Cruz

Puerta de
Santiago

Vallejo

C. de
Los Leones C. Marqués del Arco

Plaza
Merced

Paseo de Don Juan II

Puerta
S. Andrés

Cuesta de los Hoyos

C. de Velarde

Daoiz

Plaza
Catedral

Río Clamores

Carretera de Zamarramala

Paseo Ez. González

Fernández Ladreda

Calle de San Francisco

Río Eresma

Calle de S. Marcos

KEY

i Tourist Information

0   300 yards

0   300 meters

Alcázar, **11**
Ayuntamiento, **9**
Cathedral, **10**
Casa de los Picos, **6**
Convento de la
Santa Cruz, **4**
Former Mint, **3**

Palacio de los Condes
de Alpuente, **7**
Roman aqueduct, **5**
San Esteban, **12**
San Martín, **8**
San Millán, **13**
Vera Cruz, **2**

On the southern transept is a door opening into the Late Gothic cloister; this and the elaborate door leading into it were transported from the old cathedral and are the work of Juan Guas, architect of the church of San Juan de Los Reyes, in Toledo. Under the pavement immediately inside the cloisters are the tombs of Juan and Rodrigo Gil de Hontañon: That these two men should lie in a space designed by Guas is appropriate, for these three men together dominated the last phase of the Gothic style in Spain. Off the cloister a small museum of religious art, installed partly in the first-floor chapter house, is worth a visit for the white-and-gold-paneled ceiling of the 17th century, a late and splendid example of Mudéjar *artesonado* work. ☎ 911/435325 ☒ *Museum 250 ptas.* ☉ *June–Sept., daily 9–7; Oct.–May, daily 9:30–6.*

The Calle de Los Leones, lined with tourist shops, slopes gently down from the cathedral toward the western extremity of the old town's ridge. From the partially shaded Plaza del Alcázar, there are excellent views to the north and south. At the western end of the square is the famous

⓫ **Alcázar,** which dates possibly to Roman times but was considerably expanded in the 14th century, remodeled in the 15th, altered again toward the end of the following century, and completely redone after being gutted by a fire in 1862, when the building was used as an artillery school. The exterior, especially when seen from the Ruta Panorámica, is certainly imposing, but it is little more than a medieval sham, with the exception of the keep through which you enter, the last remnant of the original structure. Crowned by crenellated towers that seem to have been carved out of icing sugar, the keep can be climbed and offers superb views. The rest of the garishly colored interior of the Alcázar is disappointing. ☎ 911/460759. ☒ *375 ptas.* ☉ *May–Sept., daily 10–7; Oct.–Apr., daily 10–6.*

⓬ Just north of the cathedral, visit the porticoed church of **San Esteban,** the third of Segovia's major Romanesque monuments. Though the interior has a Baroque facing, the exterior has kept some splendid capitals, as well as an exceptionally tall and elegant tower. Due east of the attractive square on which the church stands is the **Capilla de San Juan de Dios,** next to which is the former pension where the poet Antonio Machado spent his last years in Spain. The family who looked after him still owns the building and will show you on request the poet's room, with its paraffin stove, iron bed, and round table. The church is open for mass only.

⓭ The 12th-century church of **San Millán,** a five-minute walk outside the walls of on Fernández Ladreda, is a perfect example of the Segovian Romanesque and perhaps the finest church in town, apart from the cathedral. The exterior is notable for its arcaded porch, where church meetings were once held. The virtually untouched Romanesque interior is dominated by massive columns supporting capitals carved with such scenes as the Flight into Egypt and the Adoration of the Magi; the vaulting of the crossing shows Moorish influence on Spanish medieval architecture. ☉ *For mass only, daily 8–10 AM and 7–9 PM.*

Dining and Lodging

$$$ ✕ **Casa Duque.** Founded by Dionisio Duque in 1895 and still in the family, this is the second-most famous restaurant in town. The intimate interior, homey, wood-beam decoration, and plethora of beautiful and fascinating objects hanging everywhere give it a look similar to Cándido's. It is smaller and friendlier, though, and benefits greatly from the charismatic presence of Julian Duque, the owner. Never still for a moment, Duque attends to all his clients with eccentric but not obsequious charm. Roasts are the specialty, but you should also try the *judiones de La Granja Duque*—the excellent kidney beans from

nearby La Granja, served with sausages. ⊠ *Cervantes 12,* ☎ *921/ 430537. Reservations essential. AE, DC, MC, V.*

$$$ ✕ **Mesón de Cándido.** More than a restaurant, this was declared a na-
★ tional monument in 1941. Situated under the aqueduct and compris-
ing a quaint medley of small, irregular dining rooms covered with
memorabilia, it has served as an inn since at least the 18th century. Cán-
dido took over the running in 1931 and, with his energy and flair for
publicity, managed to make it the Spanish restaurant best known
abroad: Hung everywhere are photographs of countless celebrities
who have been here, from Salvador Dalí to Princess Grace of Monaco.
Cándido passed away several years ago; the place is now run by his
son. First-time visitors are virtually obliged to eat the cochinillo, the
delicacy of which used to be attested by Cándido's slicing it with the
edge of a plate; the trout here is also renowned. ⊠ *Plaza de Azoguejo
5,* ☎ *921/425911. Reservations essential. AE, DC, MC, V.*

$$$ ✕ **Mesón de José María.** The exceptionally lively bar through which
★ you must pass to reach the restaurant augurs well for the rest of the
establishment. Though of relatively recent date in Segovian terms, this
place has already surpassed its formidable rivals and deserves to be considered one of Spain's finest restaurants. The hospitable and passionately dedicated owner is devoted to maintaining the traditional specialties
of his region while making innovations of his own. The emphasis is
on freshness and quality of produce, and the menu changes constantly.
The large, old-style, brightly lit dining room is often packed, and the
waiters are uncommonly friendly. Although a bit touristy, with a set
menu in English, it's also a favorite of the locals. ⊠ *Cronista Lecea
11,* ☎ *921/461111. AE, DC, MC, V.*

$$$$ ✕⌸ **Parador Nacional de Segovia.** Architecturally one of the most interesting and beautiful of the modern paradors, this low building is spa-
ciously arranged amid greenery on a hillside. The rooms are light, with
generous amounts of glass. The panorama of Segovia and its aqueduct
is unbeatable, but there are disadvantages in staying so far from the
town center. The restaurant serves traditional Segovian and international dishes—for instance, *lomo de merluza al aroma de estragón* (hake
fillet with tarragon and shrimp). ⊠ *Carretera de Valladolid s/n, 40003,*
☎ *921/443737,* ⅎⅫ *921/437362. 103 rooms with bath. Restaurant, pool,
meeting room. AE, DC, MC, V.*

$$$ ✕⌸ **Los Arcos.** The comfortable accommodations at this modern hotel,
located a 5- to 10-minute walk from the Roman aqueduct, are a fa-
vorite with business travelers. The staff is friendly and very willing to
assist in whatever ways they can. The rooms are brightly decorated,
and many include a small sitting area. The hotel's restaurant is attractive
with hardwood floors and arched red-brick doorways. Specialties in-
clude cochinillo and *lechazo* (baby lamb). ⊠ *Paseo Ezequiel González,
26, 40002,* ☎ *921/437462,* ⅎⅫ *921/428161. 60 rooms with bath.
Restaurant, bar. AE, DC, MC, V.*

$$$ ⌸ **Infanta Isabel.** This small, 4-year old hotel is in a recently restored
★ building with a Victorian feel. You can't beat the location: It's just 2
steps off the Plaza Mayor and offers great views of Segovia's cathedral. The rooms are spacious, feminine, and light, with painted, white
furnishings. ⊠ *Plaza Mayor s/n, 40001,* ☎ *921/443105,* ⅎⅫ *921/433240.
29 rooms with bath. Coffee shop. AE, DC, MC, V.*

Shopping

After Toledo, **Segovia province** ranks next in importance for its crafts.
Glass and **crystal** are a specialty of **La Granja,** while **ironwork, lace,**
and **embroidery** are famous in Segovia itself. In search of the old, au-

thentic article, go to **San Martín 4** (✉ Plaza San Martín 4, Segovia), an excellent **antiques** shop. You can buy good **lace** from the Gypsies in Segovia's **Plaza del Alcázar,** but be prepared for a lot of strenuous bargaining and never offer more than half the opening price.

Numbers in the margin correspond to points of interest on the Around Madrid map.

El Palacio (Royal Palace) de La Granja

⑭ *11 km (7 mi) southeast of Segovia on the N601.*

Without question the major attraction within the immediate vicinity of Segovia, **El Palacio de La Granja** is built in the town of La Granja de San Ildefonso on the northern slopes of the Guadarrama range. It stands on a site previously occupied by a hunting lodge and a shrine to San Ildefonso administered by Hieronymite monks from the Segovian monastery of El Parral. Commissioned by the Bourbon king Philip V in 1719, the palace has sometimes been described as the first great building of the Spanish Bourbon dynasty. The English 19th-century writer Richard Ford likened it to "a theatrical French château, the antithesis of the proud, gloomy Escorial, on which it turns its back." The architects who brought the building to completion in 1739 and gave it its distinction were, in fact, not French but Italian—Juvarra and Sachetti. They were responsible for the imposing garden facade, a Late Baroque masterpiece articulated throughout its whole length by a giant order of columns. The interior has been badly gutted by fire, and the few rooms that were undamaged are heavy and monotonous; the main interest is the collection of 15th to 18th-century tapestries, gathered together in a special museum. It is the **gardens of La Granja** that you come to see. Terraces, ornamental ponds, lakes, classical statuary, woods, and Late Baroque fountains dot the slopes of the Guadarrama. On Wednesday, Saturday, and Sunday evenings in the summer (from 6 to 7, May–Sept.), the fountains are turned on, one by one, creating one of the most exciting spectacles to be seen in Europe. Note: The hours of the fountains are known to change on a whim; call to check the times. ☎ 921/470020. ▦ *Palace 650 ptas., garden free.* ☉ *Palace Oct.–May, Tues.–Sat. 10–1:30 and 3–5, Sun. 10–2 (10–6 Apr. and May); June–Sept., Tues.–Sun. 10–6. Garden daily 10–sunset.*

Pedraza

⑮ *30 km (19 mi) northeast of Segovia.*

Though it has been commercialized and over-prettified in recent years, Pedraza is still a striking, 16th-century village. Crowning a rocky outcrop and completely encircled by its walls, it is perfectly preserved, with wonderful views of the Guadarrama Mountains. Farther up, at the very top of the tiny village, is a Renaissance castle, which was bought in this century as a private residence by the painter Ignacio Zuloaga. Two sons of the French king Francis I were kept hostage here after the Battle of Pavia, together with their majordomo, the father of the Renaissance poet Pierre de Ronsard. In the center of the village is the attractive main square, irregularly shaped, lined with rustic, wooden porticoes, and dominated by a Romanesque bell tower.

Dining and Lodging

$$$ ✗ **El Yantar de Pedraza.** This traditional establishment, with wooden tables and beamed ceilings on the village's enchanting main square, is famous for roast meats. It is the place to come to for that most celebrated of Pedraza's specialties—*corderito lechal en horno de leña* (baby lamb roasted in a wood oven). ⊠ *Plaza Mayor,* ☏ *921/509842. AE, DC, MC, V. Closed Mon. No dinner Sept. 15–July 15.*

$$$ 🏨 **La Posada de Don Mariano.** This hotel was originally a farmer's home. Each room in the picturesque, old building has been decorated in a different style with rustic furniture and antiques. The atmosphere is intimate, but prices are grand. ⊠ *Plaza Mayor 14, 40172,* ☏ ꜰᴀx *921/ 509886. 18 rooms with bath. AE, DC, MC, V.*

Sepúlveda

⑯   *24 km (15 mi) north of Pedraza, 60 km (37 mi) northeast of Segovia.*

A walled village with a commanding position, Sepúlveda, has a charming main square, but its principal attraction is the **11th-century Church of El Salvador,** the highest monument within the walled perimeter. Older than any of Segovia's Romanesque churches, it has a crude but amusing example of porches found in later Segovia buildings: The carvings of its oversize capitals, probably the work of a Moorish convert, are fantastical and have little to do with Christianity.

Castillo de Coca

⑰   *52 km (32 mi) northwest of Segovia.*

Perhaps the most famous medieval sight in the Segovia area is the Castillo de Coca. Situated near recently planted forests, this castle merits a detour between Segovia or Ávila and Valladolid. Built in the 15th century for Archbishop Alonso de Fonseca I, the castle is a turreted structure in plaster and red brick, surrounded by a deep moat. It looks like a stage set for a fairy tale and, indeed, was intended not for any defensive function but as a place for the notoriously pleasure-loving Archbishop Fonseca to hold riotous parties. The interior, now taken over by a forestry school, can be visited only with special permission. The once-lavish rooms have been modernized, with only fragments of the original decoration preserved.

ÁVILA AND THE SIERRA DE GREDOS

Ávila, Sierra de Gredos, Arenas de San Pedro, San Martín de Valdeiglesias

From the spectacular medieval walls of Ávila to the mountains of the Sierra de Gredos, this area yields more than just spectacular views. In Ávila, trace the history of St. Teresa who spent much of her life here. For those looking for outdoor activities, the Sierra de Gredos provides ideal opportunities for hiking and skiing. Other charms of this region include the small, attractive villages near Arenas de San Pedro and the ancient stone bulls found in San Martín de Valdeiglesias.

Ávila★

⑱   *107 km (66 mi) northwest of Madrid.*

In the middle of a windswept plateau littered with giant boulders, Ávila looks wild and sinister. Ugly, modern development on the outskirts of the town partially obscures Ávila's intact surrounding **walls.** Restored in parts, these walls look exactly as they would have in the Middle Ages. Begun in 1090, shortly after the town had been reclaimed from the Moors, they were completed in only nine years—a feat accomplished by the daily employment of an estimated 1,900 men. Featuring nine gates and 88 cylindrical towers bunched together, these walls are unique to Spain in form and unlike the Moorish defense system that the Christians adapted elsewhere. For the most extensive view, cross the Adaja River and walk to a large cross off the Salamanca road.

The walls of Ávila are a reflection of the town's importance in the Middle Ages. Populated by Alfonso VI mainly with Christians from Asturias, the town came to be known as "Ávila of the Knights," on account of the high proportion of nobles. Decline set in at the beginning of the 15th century, with the gradual departure of the nobility to the court of Charles V at Toledo. Ávila's fame in later years was due largely to St. Teresa, the female patron saint of Spain (St. James, the apostle, is Spain's male patron saint). Born here in 1515, she spent much of her life in Ávila, leaving a legacy of various convents and the ubiquitous yemas, originally distributed free to the poor but now sold for high prices to tourists. Ávila today is well preserved, but with a sad, austere, and slightly desolate atmosphere.

The battlemented apse of the **cathedral** forms the most impressive part of the town's walls. The apse was built mainly in the late 12th century, but the construction of the rest of the cathedral continued until the 18th century. Entering the town gate to the right of the apse, you'll reach the sculpted north portal (originally the west portal until it was moved in 1455 by the architect Juan Guas) by turning left and walking a few steps. The present west portal, flanked by 18th-century towers, is notable for the crude carvings of hairy, male figures on each side. These figures, known as "wild men," are often found in Castilian palaces of this period but are of disputed significance.

The Transitional Gothic interior, with its granite nave, is heavy and austere. The Lisbon earthquake of 1755 deprived the building of its Flemish stained glass, so the main note of color appears in the mottled stone in the apse, tinted yellow and red. Elaborate, Plateresque choir stalls built in 1547 complement the powerful, high altar of circa 1504 by painters Juan de Borgoña and Pedro Berruguete. On the wall of the ambulatory, look for the early 16th-century marble sepulcher of Bishop Alonso de Madrigal, a remarkably lifelike representation of the bishop seated at his writing table. Known as "El Tostado" for his swarthy complexion, the bishop was a tiny man of enormous intellect, the author of 54 books. When on one occasion Pope Eugenius IV ordered him to stand—mistakenly thinking him to be still on his knees—the bishop indicated the space between his eyebrows and hairline, retorting, "A man's stature is to be measured from here to here!" ☎ 920/211641. ▨ 200 ptas. ☉ Daily 10–2 and 4:30–8.

The 15th-century **Casa de Deanes** (Dean's House) is now a cheerful, provincial museum of local archaeology and folklore. It's just a few minutes' walk to the east of the cathedral apse. ☎ 920/211003. ▨ 200 ptas., weekends free. ☉ Tues.–Sat. 10:30–2 and 5–7:30, Sun. 11–2.

Also east of the cathedral, the museum in the **Convento de San José** (or de Las Madres), displays the musical instruments used by Saint Teresa and her nuns at Christmas; she herself specialized in percussion. ☎ 920/222127. ▨ 50 ptas. ☉ Daily 10–1:30 and 3–6.

Just north of the cathedral on the Plaza de San Vincente, visit the Romanesque **Basílica de San Vicente** (Basilica of St. Vincent), a much-venerated church founded on the supposed site where St. Vincent was martyred in 303, together with his sisters Saints Sabina and Cristeta. The west front, shielded by a narthex, has damaged but expressive, Romanesque carvings featuring the death of Lazarus and the parable of the rich man's table. The sarcophagus of St. Vincent, surrounded with delicate carvings of this period, forms the centerpiece of the basilica's Romanesque interior; the extraordinary, Asian-looking canopy that rises over the sarcophagus is a 15th-century addition, paid for by the Knights of Ávila. ☎ *920/255230.* 🎫 *50 ptas.* 🕑 *Daily 10–2 and 4–7:15.*

On Calle de Lopez Nuñez, at the **Capilla de Mosen Rubi,** try to persuade the nuns in the adjoining convent to let you inside the particularly elegant chapel (circa 1516), illuminated by Renaissance stained glass by Nicolás de Holanda.

At the bottom of the walls, just above the river, is the small Romanesque structure of the **Ermita de San Secundo** (Hermitage of St. Secundus). It's in an enchanting farmyard, almost hidden by poplars. Founded on the site where the remains of St. Secundus, a follower of St. Peter, were reputedly found, the hermitage houses a realistic marble monument to the saint, carved by Juan de Juni. 🎫 *Tip caretaker in adjoining house, where you may have to ask for key.* 🕑 *Summer, daily noon–2 and 4–6; winter, daily 10–1 and 4:30–6.*

Inside the south wall on Calle Dama, the **Convento de Santa Teresa** was founded in the 17th century on the site of the saint's birthplace. Her famous written account of an ecstatic vision she had, involving an angel piercing her heart, was to influence many Baroque artists, including the Italian Bernini. There are three small museums dedicated to the saint in Ávila alone, one of which is in this convent; you can also see the small and rather gloomy garden where Teresa—the daughter of a noble family of Jewish origin—played as a child. ☎ *920/211030.* 🎫 *Free.* 🕑 *Daily 9:30–1:30 and 3:30–7:30.*

The **Convento de la Encarnación** is where Saint Teresa first took orders, and where she was to remain based for more than 30 years. Its museum has an interesting drawing of the crucifixion by her disciple, St. John of the Cross, and a reconstruction of the cell used when she was a prioress here. It's outside the walls in the north part of town on the Paseo de la Encarnación. ☎ *920/211212.* 🎫 *100 ptas.* 🕑 *May–Sept., daily 9:30–1 and 4–7; Oct.–Apr., daily 9:30–1:30 and 3:30–6.*

On the town's outskirts the chief monument of architectural interest is the **Monasterio de Santo Tomás.** The monastery's location, a good 10-minute walk from the walls among blackened housing projects, is not where you would expect to find one of the most important religious institutions in Castile. The founders were Ferdinand and Isabella, assisted financially by the notorious Inquisitor-General Tomás de Torquemada, buried in the sacristy here; further funds were provided by the confiscated property of converted Jews who fell foul of the Inquisition. Three decorated cloisters lead you to the church. Inside, a masterly, high altar (circa 1506) by Pedro Berruguete overlooks a serene, marble tomb by the Italian artist Domenico Fancelli. This influential work was one of the earliest examples of the Italian Renaissance style in Spain; it was made for Prince Juan, only son of Ferdinand and Isabella, who died at 19 while at Salamanca University. After his burial here, his heartbroken parents found themselves unable to return to the institution that they had founded. In happier times, they had frequently attended mass in the church, seated in the upper choir behind a balustrade exquisitely carved with their coats of arms; the choir can be reached from the upper part of the Kings' Cloister. The Museum of Easter Art contains works collected in Dominican missions in Vietnam. ☎ *920/220400.* 🎫 *Cloister 50 ptas., Museum of Eastern Art 100 ptas.* 🕑 *Cloister daily 10–1 and 4–8, museum daily 11–1 and 4–7.*

Dining and Lodging

$$ ✕ **El Molino de la Losa.** Few restaurants could have a better or more
★ exciting situation than this one. Standing in the middle of the River
Adaja, with one of the best views of the town's walls, it occupies a 15th-
century mill, the working mechanism of which has been well pre-
served and provides much distraction for those seated in the animated
bar. Lamb is roasted in a medieval wood oven, and fish is freshly
caught from the river; this is also a good place to try the beans from
nearby El Barco (*judías de El Barco*). In the beautiful garden outside
is a small playground for children. ✉ *Bajada de la Losa 12,* ☎ *920/
211101 or 920/211102. AE, MC, V. Closed Mon. in winter.*

$$ ✕ **Mesón del Rastro.** This restaurant occupies a wing of the medieval
Abrantes Palace and has an attractive, old-style interior. Once again,
try the lamb and the El Barco beans; also good is the *caldereta de cabrito*
(goat stew). The place suffers somewhat from its popularity with tour
buses, and service is sometimes slow and impersonal. ✉ *Plaza Rastro
4,* ☎ *920/211218. AE, DC, MC, V.*

$$$$ ✕⌂ **Meliá Palacio de los Velada.** Ávila's top hotel opened in April, 1995,
★ in a beautifully restored 16th-century palace. In the heart of the city beside the cathedral, the hotel is the perfect spot to relax between sightseeing excursions. The lovely courtyard has become a popular meeting
place for guests and locals. Rooms are modern and comfortable. ✉ *Plaza
de la Catedral 10, 05001,* ☎ *920/255100,* FAX *920/254900. 85 rooms
with bath. Restaurant, bar, meeting rooms. AE, DC, MC, V.*

$$$ ✕⌂ **Parador Nacional Raimundo de Borgoña.** This largely rebuilt, me-
dieval castle attached to the town walls has the advantage of a beauti-
ful garden, from which you can climb up onto the town's ramparts. ✉
Marqués de Canales de Chozas 2, 05001, ☎ *920/211340,* FAX *920/226166.
62 rooms with bath. Restaurant, meeting room. AE, DC, MC, V.*

Sierra de Gredos

⑲ *79 km (9 mi) southwest of Ávila.*

In winter, the Sierra de Gredos, the most dramatic mountain range in
Castile, provides a majestic, snowy backdrop to Sierra de Gredos.
From the **Puerto del Pico** (4,435 feet) you can enjoy extensive views.
The small C502 route from Ávila follows a road dating to Roman times,
when it was used for the transport of oil and flour from Ávila in ex-
change for potatoes and wood. Soon after descending from the Puerto
del Pico, you can see below a perfectly preserved stretch of the Roman
road, zigzagging down into the valley and crossing the modern road
every now and then. Today it is used by hikers, as well as by shepherds
transporting their flocks to lower pastures in early December.

Lodging

$$$ ✕⌂ **Parador Nacional de Gredos.** Built in 1926 on a site chosen by
Alfonso XIII, this was the first of the parador chain. It was enlarged
once in 1941, and again in 1975. Though modern, the stone architecture
has a sturdy, traditional look and blends well with the magnificent surroundings. The rooms are standard parador, with heavy, dark furniture and light walls. It has excellent views of the Gredos range and is
the ideal base for a hiking or climbing holiday. ✉ *Carretera Barraco-
Béjar, 05132,* ☎ *920/348048,* FAX *920/348205. 77 rooms with bath.
Restaurant, meeting room. AE, DC, MC, V.*

Outdoor Activities and Sports

HIKING AND MOUNTAINEERING

The best area for both hiking and mountaineering is the Sierra de Gredos, and you could base yourself here at the Parador Nacional de Gre-

dos (☞ *above*). The range has 6 mountain huts with limited accommodations and facilities; for information on these and on mountaineering in general, contact the **Federación Española de Montañismo** (✉ Alberto Aguilera 3, 28015 Madrid, ☎ 91/445–1382).

SKIING

Skiing is popular in the Sierra de Gredos and in the Guadarrama resorts of La Pinilla (Segovia), Navacerrada (Madrid), Valdesquí (Madrid), and Valcotos (Madrid). Information on ski conditions can be obtained from **ATUDEM** (☎ 91/350–2020), although it's better to call the slope you'll visit; general information is available from **Federación Española de Deportes de Invierno** (☎ 91/344–0944).

Arenas de San Pedro

㉔ *143 km (89 mi) west of Madrid.*

This medieval town is surrounded by pretty villages, such as Mombeltrán, Guisando, and Candeleda, where wooden balconies are decorated with flowers. A colorful sight in Candeleda is wicker baskets with pimiento for sale. Guisando, incidentally, has nothing to do with the famous stone bulls of that name, situated 60 km/37 mi to the east.

San Martín de Valdeiglesias

㉑ *73 km (45 mi) west of Madrid.*

To see the bulls, head back east from Arenas on the C501 to this town; it's a pleasant drive through fertile countryside bordered to the north by the Gredos range. Just 6 km/3¾ mi before San Martín, on the right side of the road, is a stone inscription in front of a hedge; this marks the site where in 1468 Isabella the Catholic was acknowledged as rightful successor to Henry IV by the assembled Castilian nobility. On the other side of the hedge stand the forlorn stone bulls of Guisando, now a symbol of the Spanish Tourist Board. These are just three of many such bulls that once were scattered around the Castilian countryside; probably they marked the frontier of a Celto-Iberian tribe. The three here, in their evocative, rustic setting, have an undoubted pathos and power.

SALAMANCA AND ITS PROVINCE

Salamanca and Ciudad Rodrigo

One of the prettiest cities in Spain, Salamanca charms tourists with its beautifully colored sandstone buildings and Plaza Mayor. Today, like centuries ago, the university predominates and provides a stimulating atmosphere for those who spend a night or two in its midst. About an hour away, you can visit the preserved medieval walls at Ciudad Rodrigo, an interesting town with fewer tourists.

Salamanca ★

㉒ *205 km (125 mi) northwest of Madrid.*

Approached from Ávila and Madrid, Salamanca is first seen rising up on the northern banks of the wide and murky River Tormes. In the foreground is its sturdy 15-arch Roman bridge, while, above this, dominating the view, soars the bulk of the old and new cathedrals. Piercing the skyline to the right is the Renaissance monastery and church of San Esteban, the second most prominent ecclesiastical structure in Salamanca. Behind San Esteban and the cathedrals, and largely out of sight from the river, extends a stunning series of palaces, convents, and university buildings, culminating in the Plaza Mayor, one of the most elegant squares in Spain. Despite considerable damage over the centuries, Salamanca remains one of Spain's greatest cities architecturally and one of the showpieces of the Spanish Renaissance. The beauty of its buildings is enhanced by the color of the soft sandstone that has worn over the centuries to a golden, reddish brown.

Already an important settlement in Iberian times, Salamanca was captured by Hannibal in 217 BC and later flourished as a major Roman station on the road between Mérida and Astorga. Converted to Christianity by at least the end of the 6th century, it later passed back and forth between Christians and Moors and began to experience a long period of stability only after the Reconquest of Toledo in 1085. The later importance of the town was due largely to its university, which grew out of a college founded around 1220 by Alfonso IV of León.

Salamanca thrived in the 15th and early 16th centuries, and the number of students at its university rose to almost 10,000. Its greatest royal benefactor was Isabella the Catholic, who generously financed both the magnificent New Cathedral and the rebuilding of the university. A dual portrait of her and her husband, incorporated into the façade of the main university building, commemorates her patronage.

The other outstanding buildings of Renaissance Salamanca nearly all bear the five-star crest of the all-powerful, ostentatious Fonseca family. Alonso de Fonseca I, the most famous of the Fonsecas, was archbishop of Santiago and then of Seville; Alonso was also a notorious womanizer and one of the patrons of the Spanish Renaissance.

Salamanca and its university began to decline in the early 17th century, corrupted by ultraclericalism and devastated by a flood in 1626. Some of the town's former glory was recovered in the 18th century with the construction of the Plaza Mayor by the Churrigueras; natives of Salamanca, they were among the most influential architects of the Spanish Baroque. The town suffered in the Peninsular War of the early 19th century and was damaged by ugly, modern development initiated by Franco after the civil war. The university has revived in recent years and is again one of the most prestigious in Europe.

Numbers in the margin correspond to points of interest on the Salamanca map.

㉓ Both chronologically and in terms of available parking space, the well-preserved **Puente Romano** (Roman Bridge) makes a good starting point for a tour of Salamanca. This is a quiet, evocatively decayed part of town, with strong rural character. Next to the bridge is an Iberian stone bull, and, opposite the bull, a statue commemorating Lazarillo de Tormes, the young hero of an anonymous 16th-century work that is one of the masterpieces of Spanish literature.

㉔ Salamanca is unique in that it has two distinct **cathedrals,** old and new, side by side. For a complete tour of the buildings' exterior (an arduous 10-minute walk), circle the complex in a counterclockwise direction. Nearest the river stands the **Catedral Vieja** (Old Cathedral), built in the late 12th century. It is one of the most interesting examples of the Spanish Romanesque. Because the dome of the crossing tower features strange, plumelike ribbing, it is known as the Torre del Gallo (the rooster's tower). The much larger **Catedral Nueva** (New Cathedral) dates mainly from the 16th century, though some parts, including the dome over the crossing and the bell tower attached to the west facade, had to be rebuilt after the Lisbon earthquake of 1755. Work was begun in 1513 under the direction of the distinguished, Late Gothic

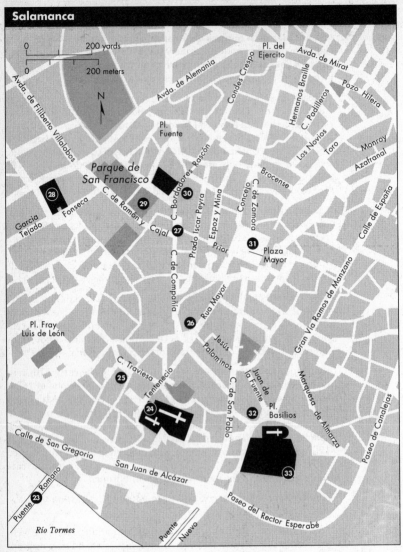

Salamanca

architect Juan Gil de Hontañon. As at Segovia cathedral, Juan's son Rodrigo took over the work after his father's death in 1526. Of the many outstanding architects active in 16th-century Salamanca, Rodrigo Gil de Hontañon left the greatest mark, becoming one of the leading exponents of the Classical Plateresque. The New Cathedral's north facade (where the main entrance is) is ornamental enough, but the west facade is dazzling in its sculptural complexity. Come here in the late afternoon, when the sun shines directly on it.

The interior of the New Cathedral is as light and harmonious as that of Segovia cathedral, but larger. Furthermore, you are treated to a triumphant, Baroque conception designed by the Churrigueras. From a door in the south aisle, steps descend into the Old Cathedral, where boldly carved capitals supporting the vaulting feature a range of foliage, strange animals, and touches of pure fantasy. Then comes the crossing of the dome, which seems to owe much to Byzantine architecture: It is a remarkably light structure raised on two tiers of arcaded openings. Not the least of the Old Cathedral's attractions are its furnishings, including sepulchers of the 12th and 13th centuries and a curved, high altar, comprising 53 colorful and delicate scenes by the mid-15th-century artist Nicolás Florentino. In the apse above, Florentino painted an astonishingly fresh Last Judgment fresco.

From the south transept of the Old Cathedral, a door leads into the cloister, begun in 1177. From about 1230 until the construction of the main university building in the early 15th century, the chapels around the cloister served as classrooms for the university students. In the chapel of St. Barbara, on the eastern side, theology students answered the grueling questions put to them by their doctoral examiners. The chair in which they sat is still there, in front of a recumbent effigy of Bishop Juan Lucero, on whose head the students would place their feet for inspiration. Also attached to the cloister is a small cathedral museum with a 15th-century triptych of St. Catherine by Salamanca's greatest native artist, Fernando Gallego. ☎ 923/217476. 🎟 *New cathedral free, old cathedral 300 ptas.* ◐ *New cathedral daily 10–1 and 4–6, old cathedral daily 10–12:30 and 4–5:30.*

㉕ The back of the main building of the **universidad** (university) faces the New Cathedral's west facade. Its walls, like those of the cathedral and other structures in Salamanca, are covered with large, ocher lettering recording the names of famous university graduates—it is this golden coloring, which seems to glow throughout the city, that you will remember above all things after leaving Salamanca. The earliest names are said to have been written in the blood of the bulls killed celebrating the successful completion of a doctorate. To reach the main facade, walk along Calle Calderón, then turn right into the enchanting quadrangle known as the **Patio de Las Escuelas** (Schools' Square). The main university building (Escuelas Mayores) is to your right, while adjacent to it, on the southern side of the square, is the Escuelas Menores, built in the early 16th century as a secondary school preparing candidates for the university proper. In the middle of the square is a modern statue of the 16th-century poet and philosopher Fray Luis de León, one of the greatest teachers in the history of the university.

The **Escuelas Mayores,** dates to 1415, but it was not until more than 100 years later that an unknown architect provided the building with its gloriously elaborate frontispiece, generally acknowledged as one of the finest works of the Classical Plateresque. Immediately above the main door is the famous double portrait of Isabella and Ferdinand, surrounded by ornamentation that makes much play on the yoke-and-arrow heraldic motifs of the two monarchs. The double-eagle crest of Charles

V flanked by portraits of the emperor and empress in classical guise dominates the middle layer of the frontispiece. On the highest layer is a panel recently identified as representing Pope Martin V (one of the greatest benefactors of Salamanca University), accompanied by cardinals and university rectors. The whole is crowned by a characteristically elaborate, Plateresque balustrade.

The interior of the Escuelas Mayores, which has been drastically restored in parts, comes as a slight disappointment after the splendor of the facade. But the aula (lecture hall) of Fray Luis de León, the place where Cervantes, Calderón de la Barca, and numerous other luminaries of Spain's Golden Age sat, is of particular interest. Here Fray Luis, returning after five years' imprisonment for having translated the *Song of Solomon* into Spanish, began his lecture, "As I was saying yesterday . . ."

Your ticket to visit the Escuelas Mayores permits entrance to the **Escuelas Menores** nearby. Passing through a gate crowned with the double-eagle crest of Charles V, you'll come to a green, on the other side of which is a modern building housing a fascinating ceiling fresco of the zodiac, originally in the library of the main university building. This painting, a fragment of a much larger whole, is generally attributed to Fernando Gallego. ☎ 923/294400, Ext. 1150. ☞ *300 ptas.* ☼ *Weekdays 9:30–1:30 and 4–7:30, Sat. 9:30–1:30 and 4–7, Sun. 10–1:30.*

You might like to visit the **Museo de Salamanca** (also Museo Bellas Artes), on the west side of the Patio de Las Escuelas. Consisting mainly of minor 17th- and 18th-century paintings, it is interesting for the 15th-century building, which belonged to the physician of Isabella the Catholic, Alvárez Abarca. ☎ 923/212235. ☞ *200 ptas.* ☼ *Tues.–Fri. 9:30–2 and 4:30–8, Sat. 10–2 and 4:30–7:30, Sun. 10–2.*

㉖ **Casa de Las Conchas** (House of Shells) was built around 1500 for Dr. Rodrigo Maldonado de Talavera, a professor of medicine at the university and a doctor at the court of Isabella. You can't help but notice it if you walk north from the Patio de Las Escuelas on the Calles Libreros and San Isidro. The scallop shell motif was a reference to Talavera's having been made chancellor of the Order of Santiago, whose symbol is the shell. Among the playful, Plateresque details, note the lions over the main entrance in a fearful tug-of-war with the Talavera crest. The interior has been converted into a tourist office. You can also visit the courtyard, which has an upper balustrade carved with virtuoso intricacy in imitation of basketwork. ☎ 923/269317. ☞ *Free.* ☼ *Weekdays 9–9, Sat. 9–2 and 4–7, Sun. 10–2 and 4–7.*

㉗ The **Palacio de Monterrey** (Palace of Monterrey), was built after 1538 by Rodrigo Gil de Hontañón for an illegitimate son of Alonso de Fonseca I. Only one of its four wings was completed, but this alone makes the palace one of the most imposing in Salamanca. As in Rodrigo's other palaces in this town, the building is flanked on each side by towers and has an open, arcaded gallery running the whole length of the upper level. Such galleries—which, in Italy, you would expect to see on the ground floor of a building—are common features in Spanish Renaissance palaces and were intended as areas where the women of the house could exercise unseen and undisturbed; they also had the advantage of cooling the floor below during the summer months. The palace is privately owned and not open for visitors, but you can stroll around the exterior. To get there, turn left at the Casa de Las Conchas and head north along the Calle de Compañía.

㉘ The **Colegio de Los Irlandeses** was founded in 1521 by Alonso de Fonseca II and is referred to as the Irish College because it served at one time as an institution for the training of young, Irish priests. Today it is a residence hall for guest lecturers at the university. The surroundings are not attractive; this part of town was the most severely damaged during the Peninsular War and still has a slightly derelict character. The interior of the building, however, is a treat. Immediately inside to the right is an elegant and spacious, Late Gothic chapel, while beyond is one of the most classical and genuinely Italianate of Salamanca's many beautiful courtyards; the architect was possibly Diego de Siloe, Spain's answer to Michelangelo. It's located several blocks northwest of the Plaza Mayor on Calle Fonseca, off Calle Ramón y Cajal. ☎ 923/294570. ☞ 100 ptas. ☉ Daily 10–2 and 4–6.

㉙ The **Convento de Las Ursulas** (Convent of the Ursulines) was built during the first half of the 16th century. Archbishop Alonso de Fonseca I lies buried here, in a splendid marble tomb by Diego de Siloe. It's located near the Palacio de Monterrey on the corner of Calle Ursulas and Calle Bordadores. ☎ 923/219877. ☞ 100 ptas. ☉ Daily 10–1 and 4:30–7.

㉚ Just across the street from the Convento de las Ursulas on Calle Bordadores you'll find the bizarre **Casa de Las Muertes** (House of the Dead). Built in about 1513 for the majordomo of Alonso de Fonseca II, the house received its name on account of four small skulls that decorate the facade. Alonso de Fonseca II had them put there to commemorate his deceased uncle, the licentious archbishop who lies in the Convento de las Ursulas, across the small square. For this reason, too, the facade bears a portrait of the archbishop. The square on which the House of the Dead stands was a favorite haunt of the poet, philosopher, and university rector Miguel de Unamuno, whose statue stands here. At the outbreak of the civil war of 1936–39, Unamuno supported the Nationalists under Franco but then turned against them. Placed under virtual house arrest, he died in the house adjacent in 1938. During the Franco period, his statue was frequently daubed red by students, as a symbol that his heart still bled for Spain.

㉛ One of the largest squares in Spain and thought by many to be the most beautiful, the **Plaza Mayor** was built in the 1730s by Alberto and Nicolás Churriguera. It is dominated on its northern side by the grandly elegant, pinkish **Ayuntamiento** (Town Hall). The square is in the center of town, about a five-minute walk east of the Palacio de Monterrey, along Calle Prior. The arcades and traffic-free center of the square are popular gathering spots for most of Salamantine society.

NEED A BREAK? The Plaza Mayor and its surroundings offer innumerable possibilities for a leisurely drink, a snack, or a full meal. One of the most popular cafés is the **Café Novelty** (Number 2). With turn of the century decor and a constant parade of folks coming and going, this is a great place to savor the character of one of Spain's finest squares.

Near the Plaza Mayor, on Calle de San Pablo, is the **Torre del Clavero,** a late-15th-century tower topped by fantastic battlements built for the *clavero* (key warden) of the order of Alcántara. On Calle San Pablo, the **Palacio de La Salina** is another Fonseca palace designed by Rodrigo Gil de Hontañón. Try to pop inside to have a glimpse of the courtyard, where you will find a projecting gallery supported by wooden consoles carved with expressive nudes and other dynamic forms.

㉜ Founded in 1419, the Dominican **Convento de las Dueñas** (Convent of Las Dueñas) contains a 16th-century cloister that is the most fantastically decorated in Salamanca, if not in the whole of Spain. The capitals of its two, superimposed, Salamantine arcades are crowded with a baffling profusion of grotesques that could absorb you for hours. There is another good reason for visiting this convent: The nuns here make excellent sweets and pastries. The Convent is due south of the Plaza Mayor, near the end of Calle de San Pablo. ☎ 923/215442. ☞ 100 ptas. ⊙ Daily 10:30–1 and 4:15–5:30 (until 7 in summer).

③ Facing Las Dueñas, atop a monumental flight of steps, is the church and monastery of **San Esteban.** The vast size of this building is a measure of its importance in the history of the town: Its monks were among the most enlightened teachers at the university, among the first to take Columbus's ideas seriously (hence his statue in the square below), and helpful in gaining his introduction to Isabella the Catholic. The architecture of San Esteban was the work of one of its monks, Juan de Alava. The door to the right of the west facade leads you into a gloomy cloister with Gothic arcading, interrupted by tall, spindly columns adorned with classical motifs. From the cloister, you enter the church at its eastern end. The interior is unified and uncluttered, but also dark and severe. The one note of color is provided by the sumptuously ornate and gilded high altar of 1692, a Baroque masterpiece by José Churriguera. The most exciting feature of San Esteban, though, is the massive, west facade, a thrilling Plateresque work in which sculpted figures and ornamentation are piled up to a height of more than 98 feet. ☎ 923/215000. ☞ 200 ptas. ⊙ Daily 9–1 and 4–7.

Dining and Lodging

$$$ ✗ **Chez Victor.** If you are tired of traditional Castilian cuisine, this chic restaurant is the place to go. Owner and cook, Victoriano Salvador, learned his trade in France and adapts French food to Spanish taste, with whimsical touches quite his own—for instance, *sesos de cordero al vinagre de frambuesa* (lamb brains in raspberry vinegar) and raviolis *rellenos de marisco* (stuffed with shellfish). Desserts are outstanding—in particular, the chocolate ones. ⊠ *Espoz y Mina 26,* ☎ 923/213123. *AE, DC, MC, V. Closed Mon. and Aug. No dinner Sun.*

$$ ✗ **Río de la Plata.** This tiny, basement restaurant, dating back to 1958, has a friendly, old-fashioned character. The elegant, gilded decor is a pleasant change from the ubiquitous, Castilian-style interiors typical of this region. The food is simple but carefully prepared, with good-quality fish and meat. ⊠ *Plaza Peso 1,* ☎ 923/219005. *AE, MC, V. Closed Mon. and July.*

$$$$ ✗🏨 **Gran Hotel.** The grande dame of Salamanca's hotels got a facelift in 1994 and now offers stylishly baroque lounges and refurbished, yet old-fashioned, oversize rooms. It is just steps from the Plaza Mayor. ⊠ *Plaza Poeta Iglesias 3, 37001,* ☎ 923/213500, 🆉 923/213501. *140 rooms with bath. Restaurant, bar. AE, DC, MC, V.*

$$$$ ✗🏨 **Palacio del Castellanos.** Opened in 1992 in an immaculately restored, 15th-century palace, this hotel offers a much-needed alternative to Salamanca's national parador (probably the ugliest in the chain). This palacio has an exquisite interior patio and an equally beautiful restaurant. There is also a lovely terrace which overlooks San Esteban. ⊠ *San Pablo 58,* ☎ 923/261818, 🆉 923/261819. *69 rooms with bath. Restaurant. AE, DC, MC, V.*

Nightlife

The main area for nightclubs is around Calle Bermejeros, but for a fashionable bar-discotheque, try **Camelot,** on Calle Bordadores.

Shopping

Salamanca has a reputation for **leatherwork**; the most traditional shop in town is **Salón Campero** (⊠ Plaza Corrillo 5).

Numbers in the margin correspond to points of interest on the Around Madrid map.

Ciudad Rodrigo

34 *88 km (54 mi) west of Salamanca.*

The most interesting town in the Salamanca province outside the capital, this city is surrounded by its medieval walls. Surveying the fertile valley of the River Agueda, this small town (which makes an excellent overnight stop on the way between Spain and Portugal) has numerous, well-preserved palaces and churches.

The **cathedral** is a combination of Romanesque and Transitional Gothic styles, with much fine sculpture. The early 16th-century choir stalls by Rodrigo Alemán, elaborately carved with entertaining grotesques, deserve attention. The cloister has carved capitals, and the cypresses in its center contribute to its tranquillity. The cathedral's outer walls are still scarred by cannonballs fired during the Peninsular War. ✉ *Cathedral free, museum 200 ptas. ☉ Daily 10–1 and 4–6.*

Besides the cathedral, the town's other chief monument is its sturdy, medieval **castillo** (fortress), part of which has been turned into a parador. From here, you can climb the town's battlements.

Dining and Lodging

$–$$ ✕ **Mayton.** This restaurant has a most engaging, wood-beamed interior, bursting with a wonderful and eccentric collection of antiques, ranging from pestles and mortars to Portuguese yokes and old typewriters. In contrast to the decor, the emphasis of the cooking is on simple preparation; the specialties are fish, seafood, goat, and lamb. ✉ *La Colada 9,* ☎ *923/460720. AE, DC, MC, V.*

$$$–$$$$ ✕⊞ **Parador Nacional Enrique II.** Occupying part of the magnificent castle built by Enrique II of Trastamara to guard over the Agueda Valley, this parador is a series of small, white rooms along the sturdy and gently sloping outer walls of the building; ask for room No. 10 if you want one with original vaulting. A special feature throughout the hotel is the under-floor heating in the bathrooms. Some rooms, as well as the restaurant, overlook a beautiful garden that runs down to the River Agueda; beyond the river the view surveys fertile plains. ✉ *Plaza Castillo 1, 37500,* ☎ *923/460150,* ℻ *923/460404. 27 rooms with bath. Restaurant, bar, meeting room. AE, DC, MC, V.*

PROVINCE OF ZAMORA AND CITY OF VALLADOLID

Zamora, Toro, and Valladolid

The province of Zamora is densely fertile country, divided by the River Duero into two distinct zones: the "land of bread" to the north and the "land of wine" to the south. The province is of interest, above all, for its Romanesque churches, the finest of which are concentrated in the towns of Zamora and Toro. The city of Valladolid, by contrast, is one of the flattest and dreariest parts of the Castillian countryside. But is is home to the National Museum of Religious Sculpture, and it is also filled with some interesting history.

Zamora

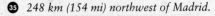

③⑤ *248 km (154 mi) northwest of Madrid.*

On a bluff above the Duero, Zamora is not conventionally beautiful, as its many interesting monuments are isolated from one another by ramshackle 19th- and 20th-century development. It does have lively, old-fashioned character, making it a pleasant stop for a night or two.

In the medieval center of town, on the south side of the Plaza Mayor, is the Romanesque **Church of San Juan,** remarkable for its elaborate rose window. The church is open for mass only. North of the Plaza Mayor, at the end of Calle Reina, is one of the surviving medieval gates of the town, and nearby you will find Santa María, one of the many Romanesque churches in the area.

Zamora is famous for its Holy Week celebrations, and the **Museo de Semana Santa** houses the processional sculptures paraded around the streets during that week. These works, of relatively recent date, have an appealing, provincial quality. You'll find, for instance, a Crucifixion group filled with apparently all the real contents of a hardware shop, including bales of rope, a saw, a spade, and numerous nails. The museum, inside a hideous modern building, is next to the Church of Santa María. ☒ *200 ptas.* ☉ *Mon.–Sat. 10–2 and 4–7 (until 8 in summer).*

Zamora's **cathedral** is in a hauntingly attractive square, situated at the highest and westernmost point of old Zamora. The bulk of the cathedral is Romanesque, and the most remarkable feature of the exterior is its dome, which is flanked by turrets, articulated by spiny ribs, and covered in overlapping stones like scales. The dark interior is notable for its early 16th-century choir stalls. The austere late-16th-century cloister has a small museum upstairs, with an intricate *custodia* (monstrance, or receptacle for the Host) by Juan de Arce and some badly displayed but intriguing Flemish tapestries of the 15th and 16th centuries. ☒ *200 ptas.* ☉ *Mon. 4:30–6:30, Tues.–Sat. 10:30–1:30 and 4:30–6:30 (until 7:30 in summer), Sun. 10:30–1:30.*

Surrounding the cathedral to the north is an attractive park incorporating the town's much-restored **castle.** The Calle Trascastillo, which descends south from the cathedral to the river, affords views of the fertile countryside to the south and of the town's **old Roman bridge.** Climb up to the **parador,** which is located in a Renaissance palace, with excellent views and a patio adorned with classical medallions of mythological and historical personages (☞ Lodging, *below*). The main entrance to this building overlooks the principal street through old Zamora.

Lodging

$$$$ ✕🏨 **Parador Nacional Condes de Alba y Aliste.** This establishment offers a central but quiet location, a historic building with a distinctive Renaissance patio, good views, and a friendly and intelligent staff. ☒ *Plaza Viriato 5, 49001,* ☎ *980/514497,* 🅵🅰🆇 *980/530063. 27 rooms with bath. Restaurant, bar, pool. AE, DC, MC, V.*

Toro

③⑥ *33 km (20 mi) east of Zamora, 272 km (169 mi) northwest of Madrid.*

Standing above a loop of the River Duero and commanding extensive views over the vast plain to the south, Toro, too, was at one time a provincial capital. In 1833, however, it was absorbed into the Zamora province in a loss of status that in some ways was to its advantage. Zamora developed into a thriving, modern town, but Toro slumbered and preserved its old appearance. The town is crowded with Romanesque churches, of which the most important is the **Colegiata,** begun in 1160. The protected west portal (the Portico de La Gloria) has colorfully painted, early 13th-century statuary that is perfectly preserved. Famous, too, is its Serbian-Byzantine dome. In the sacristy is an anonymous, 15th-century painting of the Virgin: This touching work, in a so-called Hispano-Flemish style, is called The Virgin of the Fly because of the fly painted on the Virgin's robe, a most unusual detail. ☎ *Free.* ☉ *Summer, Tues.–Sun. 11–1:30 and 5–7:30; winter, Tues.–Sun. 11:30–1:15 and 7:30–8:30; Mon. open only during mass.*

Valladolid

❸❼ *96 km (60 mi) east of Zamora, 193 km (120 mi) northwest of Madrid.*

Valladolid is a large, dirty, and singularly ugly, modern-looking town in the middle of one of the flattest and dreariest parts of the Castilian
★ countryside. It has one outstanding attraction, however—the **Museo Nacional de Escultura Religiosa** (National Museum of Religious Sculpture)—as well as many other interesting sights. It is also historically one of the most important Spanish towns. Ferdinand and Isabella were married here, Philip II was born and baptized here, and Philip III turned the town, for six years, into the capital of Spain.

To cope with this chaotic city, take a taxi—from the bus station, railway station, or wherever you parked your car—and head for the National Museum of Religious Sculpture, in the northernmost part of the old town. The late-15th-century Colegio de San Gregorio in which this museum is housed is a masterpiece of the so-called Isabelline or Gothic Plateresque, an ornamental style of exceptional intricacy featuring playful, naturalistic detail. The retable facade is especially fantastic, with ribs in the form of pollarded trees, branches sprouting, and—to accentuate this forest imagery—a row of wild men bearing mighty clubs.

The museum is arranged in rooms off an elaborate, arcaded courtyard. Its collections do for Spanish sculpture what those in the Prado do for Spanish painting. The only difference between the museums is that while most people have heard of Velázquez, El Greco, Goya, and Murillo, few know of Alonso de Berruguete, Juan de Juni, and Gregorio Fernández, the three great names represented here.

Arrows and attendants encourage you to tour the museum in a chronological order, beginning on the ground floor with Alonso de Berruguete's remarkable sculptures from the dismantled high altar in the Valladolid church of San Benito (1532). Berruguete, who trained in Italy under Michelangelo, is the most widely appreciated of Spain's postmedieval sculptors. He strove for pathos rather than realism, and his works have an extraordinarily expressive quality. The San Benito altar was the most important commission of his life, and fragments in this museum at least allow one to study, at close hand, his powerful and emotional art. In the museum's elegant chapel (which you normally see at the end of the tour) is a retable by him, dated 1526, his first known work. On either side of Berruguete's retable kneel gilt, bronze figures by the Italian-born Pompeo Leoni, whose polished and very decorative art is diametrically opposed to that of Berruguete.

To many critics of Spanish sculpture, decline set in with the late-16th-century artist Juan de Juni, who used glass for eyes, and pearls for tears. But to his many admirers, the sculptor's works are intensely exciting; they comprise the highlights of the museum's upper floor. Many of the 16th-, 17th-, and 18th-century sculptures on this floor were originally paraded around the streets during Valladolid's celebrated Easter processions; should you ever attend one of these thrilling pageants, the power of Spanish Baroque sculpture will become evident to you.

Dominating Castilian sculpture of the 17th century was the Galician-born Gregorio Fernández, in whose works the dividing line between sculpture and theater becomes tenuous. Respect for Fernández has been diminished by the number of vulgar imitators that his work has spawned, up to the present day. At Valladolid you see his art at its best, and the enormous, dramatic, and moving sculptural groups that have been assembled in the museum's last series of rooms (on the ground floor near the entrance) form a suitably spectacular climax to this impressive collection. ⊠ *C. Cadenas San Gregorio 1,* ☎ *983/250375.* ▨ *400 ptas.* ☉ *Tues.–Sat. 10–2 and 4–6, Sun. 10–2.*

Felipe II's birthplace is the brick mansion on the Plaza de San Pable at the corner of Calle Angustias. The late-15th-century **Church of San Pablo** has another overwhelmingly elaborate retable facade. The city's **cathedral,** however, is disappointing. Though its foundations were laid in Late Gothic times, the building owes much of its appearance to designs executed in the late 16th century by Juan de Herrera, the architect of the Escorial; further work was carried out by Alberto de Churriguera in the early 18th century, but even so, the building remains only a fraction of its intended size. The altarpiece by Juni is the one bit of color and life in an otherwise cold and intimidatingly severe place. ☎ *983/ 304362.* ▨ *Cathedral free, museum 250 ptas.* ☉ *Tues.–Fri. 10–1:30 and 4:30–7, weekends 10–2.*

Far more appealing is the main **university** building, on the southern side of the verdant space south of the cathedral. The exuberant and dynamic, Late Baroque frontispiece is by Narciso Tomé, creator of the remarkable *Transparente* in the Toledo cathedral. The Calle Librería leads south from the main university building to the magnificent **Colegio de Santa Cruz,** a large university college begun in 1487 in the Gothic style and completed in 1491 by Lorenzo Vázquez in a tentative and pioneering Renaissance mode; inside is a harmonious courtyard.

You can see the extensively rebuilt house where Columbus died in 1506; within is the excellent **Museo de Colón,** featuring a well-arranged collection of objects, models, and information panels relating to the life and times of the explorer. ⊠ *C. Colón,* ☎ *983/291353.* ▨ *Free.* ☉ *Tues.–Sat. 10–2 and 4–6, Sun. 10:30–2.*

A more interesting survival from Spain's Golden Age is the tiny house where the writer Miguel de Cervantes lived from 1603 to 1606, **Casa de Cervantes.** A haven of peace set back from a noisy thoroughfare, this house is far from other main monuments in town and is best reached by taxi. Furnished in the early 20th century in a pseudo-Renaissance style by the Marquis of Valle-Inclan—the creator of the El Greco Museum in Toledo—it has a cozy atmosphere. ⊠ *C. Rastro s/n,* ☎ *983/308810.* ▨ *400 ptas.* ☉ *Tues.–Sat. 9:30–3:30, Sun. 10–3.*

Dining and Lodging

$$$ ✕ **La Fragua.** In a modern building with a traditional Castilian interior of white walls and wood-beam ceilings, Valladolid's most famous and stylish restaurant counts members of the Spanish royal family among its patrons. Specialties include meat roasted in a wood oven and imaginative dishes such as *rape Castellano Gran Mesón* (breaded skate served with clams and peppers) and *lengua empiñonada* (tongue coated in pine nuts). ⊠ *Paseo Zorrilla 10,* ☎ *983/337102. AE, DC, MC, V. Closed Mon. No dinner Sun.*

$$$$ ⊡ **Valladolid Meliá.** Although it's situated in the middle of one of Valladolid's most attractive, old districts, this hotel is on a characterless, modern block. The building was erected in the early 1970s, and its pale-green curtains and dark, heavy furniture have a somewhat dated look. The ground and first floors, however, have been dramatically remodeled and given a marbled, pristine elegance. ⊠ *Plaza de San Miguel 10, 47003,* ☎ *983/357200,* ⅢX *983/336828. 226 rooms with bath. Beauty salon, meeting room. AE, DC, MC, V.*

Nightlife

Valladolid has a wide choice of places to go to at night. The Zona Francisco Suarez and the Zona Iglesia La Antigua are two districts popular with students. Livelier and more fashionable are the Zona Cantarranas (in particular, the **Inoxidable**) and around the Plaza Mayor.

NORTHEAST OF MADRID

Alcalá de Henares, Guadalajara, Pastrana, Sigüenza, Medinaceli, and Soria, Numancia, El Burgo de Osma

Though off the main tourist routes, the provinces of Guadalajara and Soria have much to offer and are—for a change—easily accessible by train. The line from Madrid to Zaragoza passes through the towns mentioned above, making possible a manageable and interesting excursion of two to three days. If you travel by car, you can extend this trip by detouring into beautiful, unspoiled countryside.

Alcalá de Henares

38   *30 km (19 mi) east of Madrid.*

Alcalá de Henares' fame in the past was due largely to its university, founded in 1498 by Cardinal Cisneros. In 1836 the university was moved to Madrid, and Alcalá's decline was hastened. The civil war destroyed much of the town's artistic and architectural heritage, and in recent years Alcalá has emerged as a dormitory town of Madrid. Nevertheless, enough survives of old Alcalá to give a good impression of what it must have been like during its Golden Age heyday.

The town's main monument of interest is its enormous Universidad Complutense (university) building, constructed between 1537 and 1553 by the great Rodrigo Gil de Hontañón. Though it is one of the earliest and most important examples in Spain of a building in an Italian Renaissance style, most Italian architects of the time would probably have had a fit had they seen its principal facade. The use of the classical order is all wrong; the main block is out of line with the two that flank it, and the whole is crowned by a heavy and elaborate gallery. All this is typically Spanish, as is the prominence given to the massive crest of Cardinal Cisneros and to the ironwork, both of which form an integral part of the powerful overall design. Inside are three patios, of which the most impressive is the first, comprising three superimposed arcades. A guided tour of the interior will take you to a delightfully decorated room where exams were once held and to the chapel of San Ildefonso, with its richly sculpted Renaissance mausoleum of Cardinal Cisneros. ⊠ *Plaza San Diego s/n.* ⊡ *250 ptas.* ☉ *Tues.–Fri. 11:30–1:30 and 5–6, weekends 11–2 and 4–7.*

On one side of the university square is the **Convento de San Diego,** where Clarissan nuns make and sell the almendras garrapiñadas that are a specialty of the town. The other side adjoins the large and arcaded **Plaza de Cervantes,** the animated center of Alcalá. Off this runs the arcaded Calle Mayor, which still has much of the appearance that it had in the 16th and 17th centuries.

Miguel de Cervantes y Saavedra was born in a house on this street in 1547; a charming replica, **Casa de Cervantes,** built in 1955, contains a small Cervantes museum. ⊠ *Mayor 48.* ☎ *Free.* ☉ *Tues.–Fri. 10–2 and 4–7, weekends 10–2.*

Dining

$$ ✕ **Hostería del Estudiante.** One of the original buildings acquired by Spain's parador chain, this restaurant is magnificently set around a 15th-century cloister and features wood-beam ceilings, a large and splendid fireplace, and glass-and-tin lanterns. Appropriate to such a traditional setting is the good and simple Castilian food, a particular specialty being roast lamb. ⊠ *Los Colegios 3,* ☎ *91/888–0330. AE, DC, MC, V.*

Guadalajara

39 *17 km (10 mi) east of Alcalá, 55 km (34 mi) northeast of Madrid.*

In this provincial capital, which was severely damaged in the civil war of 1936–39, you'll find the **Palacio del Infantado.** Built between 1461 and 1492 by Juan Guas, it's one of the most important palaces of its period in Spain, a bizarre and potent mix of Gothic, classical, and Mudéjar influences. The main facade is rich, the lower floors studded with diamond shapes, and the whole crowned by a complex, Gothic gallery supported on a frieze pitted with intricate, Moorish cellular work (honeycomb motif). Inside is a fanciful and exciting courtyard, though little else; the magnificent, Renaissance frescoes that once covered the palace's rooms having largely been obliterated in the civil war. On the ground floor is a modest, provincial art gallery. ☎ *200 ptas.* ☉ *Tues.–Sat. 10:30–2 and 4:15–7, Sun. 10:30–2.*

En Route East of Guadalajara extends the Alcarria, an area of high plateau intercut with rivers forming verdant valleys. It was made famous in the 1950s by one of the great classics of Spanish travel literature, Camilo José Cela's *Journey to the Alcarria.* Cela evoked the backwardness and remoteness of an area barely an hour from Madrid. Even today you can feel far removed from the modern world here.

Pastrana

40 *42 km (26 mi) southeast of Guadalajara.*

High on a hill, Pastrana's narrow lanes merge into the landscape. It is a pretty village of Roman origin, once capital of a small duchy. The tiny museum attached to its Collegiate Church displays a glorious series of Gothic tapestries. ☎ *125 ptas.* ☉ *Weekends 1–3 and 4–6.*

Sigüenza

41 *86 km (54 mi) northeast of Guadalajara.*

The next major stop on the journey east from Madrid, Sigüenza is one of the most beautiful of all the Castilian towns. Begun around 1150 and not completed until the early 16th century, Sigüenza's remarkable **cathedral** presents an anthology of Spanish architecture from the Romanesque period to the Renaissance. The sturdy, west front has a forbidding, fortress-like appearance. It contains, however, a wealth of ornamental and artistic masterpieces. Go directly to the sacristan (the Sacristy is at the north end of the ambulatory) for an informative guided tour of the building; he will turn on lights and unlock doors for you. The Sacristy is an outstanding Renaissance structure, covered in a barrel vault designed by the great Alonso de Covarrubias; its coffering is studded with hundreds of portrait heads, which stare at you disarmingly. The tour will take you into the Late-Gothic cloister, off which is situated a room lined with Flemish 17th-century tapestries. You will also have illuminated for you the ornate late-15th-century sepulcher of Dom Fadrique of Portugal (in the north transept), an early example of the Classical Plateresque. The cathedral's high point is the Chapel of the Doncel (to the right of the sanctuary), in which is to be found the most celebrated of Spain's funerary monuments, the tomb of Don Martín Vázquez de Arca, commissioned by Isabella the Catholic, to whom Don Martín served as *doncel* (page) before dying young at the gates of Granada in 1486. The reclining Don Martín is portrayed in a lifelike way, an open book in his hands and a wistful melancholy in his eyes. More than a memorial to an individual, this tomb, with its surrounding Late-Gothic foliage and tiny mourners, is like an epitaph of the Age of Chivalry, a final flowering of the Gothic spirit. ▩ *300 ptas.* ☼ *Daily 11–1 and 4–6 (until 7 in summer).*

In a refurbished early 19th-century house, adjacent to the cathedral's west facade, the **Museo Diocesano de Arte Sacro** (Diocesan Art Museum) contains a prehistoric section and much religious art from the 12th to the 18th century.▩ *200 ptas.* ☼ *Tues.–Sun. 11–2 and 4:30–6:30 (until 7:30 in summer).*

The south side of the cathedral overlooks the arcaded Plaza Mayor, a harmonious Renaissance square commissioned by Cardinal Mendoza. The small palaces and cobbled alleys in the area mark the virtually intact Old Quarter. Along the Calle Mayor, you'll find the palace that belonged to the doncel's family. The enchanting **castle** at the top of the street, above Sigüenza and overlooking wild, hilly countryside, is now a parador (☞ Lodging, *below*). Founded by the Romans but rebuilt at various later periods, most of the present structure was put up in the 14th century, when it was transformed into a residence for the queen of Castile, Doña Blanca de Borbón, who was banished here by her husband, Peter the Cruel.

Lodging

$$$–$$$$ ✕▣ **Parador Nacional Castillo de Sigüenza.** Of the many castles be-
★ longing to the parador chain, this is one of the most impressive and historically important. At the very top of the beautiful town of Sigüenza, this mighty, crenellated structure has hosted royalty over the centuries, from Ferdinand and Isabella right up to the present king, Juan Carlos. Some of the rooms have 4-poster beds and balconies perched over the wild landscape. ⬜ *Plaza del Castillo s/n, 19250,* ☎ *949/390100,* ℻ *949/391364. 77 rooms with bath. Restaurant, meeting room, parking. AE, DC, MC, V.*

Medinaceli

🟤 *32 km (20 mi) northeast of Sigüenza.*

The original village of Medinaceli commands an exhilarating position on top of a long, steep ridge. Dominating the skyline is a Roman triumphal arch of the 2nd or 3rd century AD, the only triple archway of this period to survive in Spain. (The arch's silhouette is now featured in signposts to national monuments throughout the country.) The surrounding village, once the seat of one of Spain's most powerful dukes, had virtually been abandoned by its inhabitants by the end of the 19th century, and if you come here during the week, you will find yourself in almost a ghost town. Numerous Madrileños have weekend houses here, and there are also various Americans in part-time residence. It is undeniably beautiful, with extensive views, picturesquely overgrown houses, and unpaved lanes leading directly into wild countryside. The former palace of the dukes of Medinaceli is currently undergoing restoration, and Roman excavations are also being carried out in one of the squares.

Soria

43 *74 km (46 mi) north of Medinaceli, 234 km (145 mi) northeast of Madrid.*

This provincial capital, which has prospered for centuries as a center of sheep farming, has been spoiled by modern development and is frequently beset by biting cold winds. Yet its situation in the wooded valley of the Duero is splendid, and it has a number of fascinating Romanesque buildings.

Soria has strong connections with Antonio Machado, Spain's most popular 20th-century poet after García Lorca. The Seville-born poet lived a bohemian life in Paris for many years but returned to Spain and worked as a French teacher in Soria from 1909 to 1911. A large, bronze head of the poet is displayed outside the **school** where he taught; and, in the room where he taught (now called the Aula Machado), there's a tiny collection of memorabilia relating to him. In Soria he fell in love with and married the 16-year-old daughter of his landlady. When she died only two years later, the heartbroken poet felt he could no longer stay in this town so full of her memories. He moved on to Baeza in his native Andalucía and then went to Segovia, where he spent his last years in Spain (he died early in the civil war, shortly after escaping to France). His most successful work, the Campos de Castilla, was greatly inspired by Soria and by his dead wife, Leonor; the town and this woman both haunted him until his death.

The main roads to Soria converge onto the wide modern promenade called El Espolón, where you will find the **Museo Numantino.** The museum, founded in 1919, contains a collection of local archaeological finds. Few other museums in Spain are laid out quite as well or as spaciously as this; the collections are rich in prehistoric and Iberian finds, and there is one section—on the top floor—dedicated to the important Iberian-Roman settlement at nearby Numancia (☞ *below*). ☎ 975/221397. 🖃 200 ptas. ⊙ *May–Sept., Tues.–Sat. 10–2 and 5–9, Sun. 10–2; Oct.–Apr., Tues.–Sat. 9:30–7:30, Sun. 10–2.*

At the top of the **Calle Aduana Vieja** is the late-12th-century church of **San Domingo,** with its richly carved, Romanesque, west facade. The imposing, 16th-century palace of the counts of Gomara (now a law court) is on Calle Estudios. Dominating the hill just south of the River Dueron is the parador Antonio Machado (☞ Dining and Lodging, *below*), which stands in a park that also contains the ruins of the town's castle. Antonio Machado loved the views of the town and valley from this hill. Calle de Santiago, which leads to the parador, passes on its way the church and cemetery of El Espino, where Machado's wife Leonor is buried. Just before the river stands the **cathedral**—a Late Gothic, hall church attached to a large, Romanesque cloister.

Across the River Dueron from Soria, in a wooded setting overlooking the river, is the deconsecrated church of **San Juan de Duero,** once the property of the Knights Hospitalers. Outside the church are the curious ruins of a Romanesque cloister, featuring a rare Spanish example of interlaced arching; the church itself, now looked after by the Museo Numantino, is a small, didactic museum of Romanesque art and architecture. ☎ *100 ptas.* ☉ *Winter, Tues.–Sat. 10–2 and 4–6, Sun. 10–2; summer, Tues.–Sat. 10–2 and 5–9, Sun. 10–2.*

It is an evocative, half-hour walk along the Duero River to the **Ermita de San Saturio.** A riverside path (accessible by car) lined by poplars leads to the hermitage, which was built above a cave where the Anchorite San Saturius fasted and prayed. Entering the cave, you can climb up to the 18th-century hermitage. ☎ *Free.* ☉ *Winter, daily 10:30–2 and 3:30-6; summer, daily 10:30–2 and 5–9.*

Dining and Lodging

$$ ✕ **Mesón Castellano.** The most traditional restaurant in town, this cozy establishment has a large, open fire over which succulent *chuletón de ternera* (veal chops) are cooked. Another specialty is its *migas pastoriles* (soaked bread crumbs fried with peppers and bacon), a local dish. ⊠ *Plaza Mayor 2,* ☎ *975/213045. AE, DC, MC, V.*

$$$ ✕▥ **Parador Nacional Antonio Machado.** This modern building has a superb, hilltop setting, surrounded by trees and parkland, and excellent views of the hilly Duero Valley. It is named after the poet who came often to this site for inspiration. ⊠ *Parque del Castillo, 42005,* ☎ *975/213445,* ℻ *975/212849. 34 rooms with bath. Restaurant. AE, DC, MC, V.*

Numancia

④④ *7 km (4 mi) north of Soria.*

The bleak, hilltop ruins of Numancia, an important Iberian settlement, are just a few minutes from Soria and accessible by car only. Viciously besieged by the Romans in 135–134 BC, the inhabitants chose death rather than surrender. Most of the foundations that have been unearthed are from the time of the Roman occupation. ☎ *100 ptas.* ☉ *Winter, Tues.–Sat. 10–2 and 4–6, Sun. 10–2; summer, Tues.–Sat. 10–2 and 5–9, Sun. 10–2.*

El Burgo de Osma

④⑤ *56 km (35 mi) west of Soria.*

El Burgo de Osma is a medieval and Renaissance town, dominated by a Gothic cathedral and a Baroque bell tower.

Dining and Lodging

$$–$$$ ✕ **Virrey Palafox.** One of Castile's famed restaurants, this is a family-run establishment set in a modern building. Inside, decor is traditional Castilian style, complete with white walls and a timber-beamed ceiling. The long dining room, adorned with old furnishings, is divided into smoking and no-smoking sections. The emphasis is on fresh, seasonal produce. Vegetables are home-grown, and there is excellent local game throughout the year. The specialty of the house is fish, in particular merluza Virrey (hake stuffed with eels and salmon). On February and March weekends, a pig is slaughtered and a marvelous and very popular banquet is held; admission is about 5,000 pesetas. ⊠ *Universidad 7,* ☎ *975/340222. AE, DC, MC, V. Closed Sun. fall–spring and Dec. 22–Jan. 10.*

$$$ ✕▥ **Virrey II.** Twenty clean, modest, and inexpensive rooms are found above the famous restaurant of this name. For more stylish accommodation, try this new hotel, opened by the same management in 1990 a few hundred yards away. Situated on the village's main square, it adjoins the 16th-century Convent of San Agustín and appears to form

part of it. Though of recent construction, the hotel is built with traditional materials and has an Old World look. The rooms, most of which overlook the square, have marble floors, stone walls, and tastefully simple decoration. ⊠ *C. Mayor 2, 42300,* ☎ *975/341311,* 𝔽𝔸𝕏 *975/340855. 52 rooms with bath. Dining room, meeting room. AE, DC, MC, V.*

SOUTHEAST OF MADRID

Cuenca, Ciudad Encantada, Alarcón

Dramatic landscapes are the main attraction of this region which lies to the southeast of Madrid. The rocky countryside and magnificent gorges of the rivers Huécar and Júcar provide spectacular views. Cuenca offers a museum devoted to abstract art—impressive both for its content as well as its setting. Nearby towns like Ciudad Encntada, with its rock formations, and Alarcón, home to a medieval castle, make for pleasant excursions.

Cuenca

46 *167 km (104 mi) southeast of Madrid.*

Situated in wild and rocky countryside intercut with dramatic gorges, Cuenca offers a haunting atmosphere and outstanding cuisine. On the north side of the River Huécar, the old town rises steeply, hugging a spine of rock thrust up between the gorges of the Huécar and the Júcar and bordered on two sides by sheer precipices, over which soars the odd hawk or eagle. The lower half of the old town is a maze of tiny streets, any of which will take you up to the Plaza del Carmen. From here the town narrows, and just a single street, the Calle Alfonso VIII, continues the ascent up to the Plaza Mayor, which you reach after passing under the arch of the Town Hall.

Just off Calle San Pedro, clinging to the western edge of Cuenca, you'll find the tiny **Plaza San Nicolás,** a picturesquely dilapidated square. Nearby, the unpaved Ronda del Júcar, hovers over the Júcar gorge and commands remarkable views over the mountainous landscape. The best views of the mountaines climes are from the square in front of the **castle,** at the very top of Cuenca, where the town tapers out to the narrowest of ledges. Gorges are on each side of you, while directly in front, old houses sweep down toward a distant plateau. The castle itself, which for many years served as the town prison, has been converted into a parador.

The **Museo Diocesano de Arte Sacro** (Diocesan Museum of Sacred Art) has recently been installed in what were formerly the cellars of the Bishop's Palace; in its beautifully clear display you will find a jewel-encrusted, Byzantine diptych of the 13th century, a Crucifixion by the 15th-century Flemish artist Gerard David, and two small El Grecos. It's located in the former cellars of the Bishop's Palace. From the Plaza Mayor, take the Calle Obispo Valero and follow signs pointing toward the Casa Colgadas. ☎ *969/212011.* 🎟 *200 ptas.* ☉ *Tues.–Fri. 11–2 and 4–6, Sat. 11–2 and 4–8, Sun. 11–2.*

★ Housed in the most famous of Cuenca's buildings, the **Casas Colgadas** (Hanging Houses) is one of the finest and most curious of Spain's museums. This group of joined houses, literally projecting over the town's eastern precipice, originally formed a 15th-century palace; later they served as a town hall, before falling into disuse and decay in the 19th century. During the restoration campaign of 1927, the cantilevered balconies that had once hung over the gorge were rebuilt. Finally, in 1966, the painter

Fernando Zóbel decided to create inside them the first museum in the world devoted exclusively to abstract art. The works he gathered are almost all by the remarkable generation of Spanish abstract artists who grew up in the 1950s and were forced to live abroad. The major names include Carlos Saura, Eduardo Chillida, Muñoz, Millares, Antoni Tàpies, and Zóbel. Even if you have had no previous interest in abstract art, this museum is likely to win you over, with its honeycomb of dazzlingly white rooms and vistas of sky and gorge. ☏ *300 ptas.* ☉ *Tues.–Fri. 11–2 and 4–6, Sat. 11–2 and 4–8, Sun. 11–2:30.*

An iron footbridge over the Huécar gorge, the **Puente de San Pablo** was built in 1903 for the convenience of the Dominican monks of San Pablo, who live on the other side. If you've no fear of heights, cross the narrow bridge to take in the vertiginous view down to the river below and equally thrilling panorama of the Casas Colgadas. A path from the bridge descends to the bottom of the gorge, landing you by the bridge that you crossed to enter the old town.

Dining and Lodging

$$$ ✕ **Figón de Pedro.** The owner of this restaurant, Pedro Torres Pacheco,
★ is one of the famed restaurateurs of Spain and has done much to promote the excellence of Cuenca cuisine. In this pleasantly low-key establishment in the lively heart of the modern town, you can try such unusual local specialties as gazpacho pastor, *ajo arriero* (a paste made with pounded salt cod), and *alaju* (a sweet of Moorish origin consisting of honey, bread crumbs, almonds, and orange water). You can finish off your meal with resolí, the Cuenca liqueur. ✉ *Cervantes 13,* ☎ *969/224511. AE, DC, MC, V. Closed Mon. No dinner Sun.*

$$$ ✕ **Mesón Casas Colgadas.** Run by the management of the Figón de Pedro, it offers much the same fare, but more pretentiously, in an ultramodern, white dining room in the spectacularly sited Casas Colgadas, next to the Museum of Abstract Art. ✉ *Canónigos s/n,* ☎ *969/223509. Reservations essential. AE, DC, MC, V. No dinner Tues.*

$$ ✕ **Los Claveles.** In a quiet and attractive part of the new town, with a
★ colorful, homey interior filled with curiosities and posters (even on the ceiling), this is, in many ways, one of the most agreeable restaurants in Castile. The present owner's father bought the establishment in 1950, following a drunken spree after a bullfight; he realized what he had done only the next day, but fortunately persevered with the place and soon helped win for it a great local popularity. His widow still does the cooking, which is every bit as good as that of El Figón, with perhaps a more authentic character: You feel that she is perpetuating family traditions that go back centuries. All the Cuenca specialties can be found here, including *morteruelo* (an even richer and more elaborate version of gazpacho pastor, containing liver and ham). ✉ *Torres 28,* ☎ *969/213824. AE, MC, V. Closed Thurs. and Sept.*

$$$ ✕🏨 **Parador de Cuenca.** Spain's newest parador (opened in 1993) is in an exquisitely restored, 16th-century monastery in the gorge below Cuenca's famous hanging houses. The guest rooms are furnished in a lighter and more luxurious style than one usually finds in Castilian houses of the same vintage. ✉ *Paseo Hoz de Huecar s/n, 16001,* ☎ *969/232320,* FAX *969/232534. 124 rooms with bath. Restaurant, bar, indoor pool, tennis court. AE, DC, MC, V.*

$$$ 🏨 **Cueva del Fraile.** This luxurious hotel, 7 km/4½ mi out of town on the Buenache road, occupies a 16th-century building in dramatic surroundings. The white rooms have reproduction traditional furniture, stone floors, and some wood ceilings. ✉ *Ctra. Cuenca-Buenache,*

16001, ☎ 969/211571, ℻ 969/256047. *54 rooms with bath. Pool, tennis courts, meeting room. Closed Jan. and Feb.*

$$ ▥ **Posada San José.** This is still the only hotel in the Old Town, and
★ it's just as good, if somewhat more modest, than the nearby parador. Tastefully installed in a 16th-century convent, it clings to the top of the Huécar gorge, which most of its rooms overlook. The furnishings are traditional and in the spirit of the building. The atmosphere is friendly and intimate. Reservations are essential and should be made well in advance of your visit. ⊠ *Julián Romero 4, 16001,* ☎ *969/211300. 25 rooms, 16 with bath. Bar. AE, DC, MC, V.*

Ciudad Encantada

47 *35 km (21 mi) north of Cuenca.*

This "Enchanted City" comprises a series of large and fantastic rock formations erupting in a landscape of pines. If you like to explore on foot, this town is well worth a visit. There's a footpath which will guide you through striking outcrops with names like "El Tobagón" (The Toboggan) and "Mar de Piedras" (Sea of Stones).

Alarcón

48 *69 km (43 mi) south of Cuenca.*

This fortified village on the edge of the great plains of La Mancha stands impressively on a high spur of land encircled almost entirely by a bend of the the River Júcar. The principal monument is its **castle,** which dates to Visigothic times; in the 14th century it came into the hands of the infante Don Juan Manuel, who wrote a collection of moral tales that rank among the great treasures of Spanish medieval literature. The castle is today one of the finest of Spain's paradors (☞ Dining and Lodging, *below*).

Dining and Lodging

$$$$ ✕▥ **Parador Nacional Marqués de Villena.** As a place to indulge in medieval fantasies, this parador, in a 12th-century castle perched above a gorge, is virtually unrivaled. There are only 13 rooms here, 12 of them quite small (the turret room is large). Some rooms are in the corner towers and have as windows the narrow slots once used to shoot arrows out of; others have window niches where the women of the household would sit to do needlework. Dinners are served in a high-arched baronial hall adorned with shields, armor, and a gigantic fireplace recalling medieval banquets. The nearest train connection to Alarcón is Cuenca, 69 km/43 mi away; a bus to Motilla will leave you a short taxi ride away (☎ 969/331797). ⊠ *Avda. Amigos de los Castillos 3, 16213,* ☎ *969/330315,* ℻ *969/330303. 13 rooms with bath. Restaurant. AE, DC, MC, V.*

SOUTH OF MADRID

Aranjuez and Toledo

The small town of Aranjuez is home to the Palacio Royal, a sumptuously decorated French-style palace. Nearby Toledo, on the other hand, is a study is austerity: as you approach Toledo, the city's battlements rise dramatically from the massive granite escarpment. Explore the mighty Gothic Cathedral and the Tránsito Synagogue or gape at El Grecos' most famous painting *The Burial of Count Orgaz.*

Aranjuez

 47 km (29 mi) south of Madrid.

Once the site of a Habsburg hunting lodge on the banks of the Tajo, in
the 18th century Aranjuez became a favorite summer residence of the
Bourbons, who constructed a large palace and other buildings, created
extensive gardens, and planted woods. In the following century, it developed into a popular retreat for the people of Madrid. Today, the spa-
ciously and regularly laid-out small town that grew up in the vicinity
of the palace retains a faded elegance. The **Palacio Real** (Royal Palace)
itself reflects French grandeur. The high point of the sumptuous interior is a room covered entirely with porcelain; there are also numerous
elaborate clocks and a good museum of costumes. Shaded, riverside gardens, full of statuary and fountains, afford pleasant relaxation after the
palace tour. ☎ *91/891–1344.* ⌂ *Palace 600 ptas., gardens free.* ☉ *Palace
May–Sept., Tues.–Sun. 10–6:15; Oct.–Apr., Tues.–Sun. 10–5:15. Gardens May–Sept., daily 8–6:30; Oct.–Apr., daily 8–8:30.*

The charming **Casa del Labrador** (Farmer's Cottage), a small, intimate
palace at the eastern end of Aranjuez, built by Carlos IV in 1804, has
a jewel-like interior bursting with color and crowded with delicate objects. Between the Royal Palace and the Casa del Labrador is the **Casa
de Marinos** (Sailors' House), where you'll see a gondola that belonged
to Felipe V and other decorated pleasure boats that once plied the river.
⌂ *Casa del Labrador 425 ptas., Casa de Marinos 325 ptas.* ☉ *May–
Sept., Tues.–Sun. 10–6:30; Oct.–Apr., Tues.–Sun. 10–5:30.*

Toledo★

 *35 km (22 mi) southwest of Aranjuez, 71 km (44 mi) southwest of
Madrid.*

The contrast between Aranjuez and nearby Toledo could hardly be more
marked. From the sensuous surroundings and French-style elegance of
the former, you move to a place of drama and austerity, tinged with
mysticism, that was long the spiritual and intellectual capital of Spain.
No matter which route you take from Madrid, your first glimpse of
Toledo will be of its northern gates and battlements rising up on a massive, granite escarpment. The flat countryside comes to an end, and a
steep range of ocher-colored hills rises on each side of the city.

The rock on which Toledo stands was inhabited in prehistoric times,
and there was already an important Iberian settlement here when the
Romans came in 192 BC. On the highest point of the rock—on which
now stands the Alcázar, the dominant building on the Toledo skyline—
the Romans built a large fort, later remodeled by the Visigoths, who
had, by the middle of the 6th century AD, transformed the town into
their capital. In the early 8th century, the Moors arrived.

During their occupation of Toledo, the Moors furthered its reputation
as a great center of learning and religion. Enormous tolerance was shown
toward those who continued to practice Christianity (the so-called
Mozarabs), as well as to the town's exceptionally large Jewish population. Today, the Moorish legacy is evident in the strong crafts tradition here, in the maze-like arrangement of the streets, and in the
predominance of brick rather than stone. To the Moors, beauty was
a quality to be found within and not to be shown on the surface, and
it is significant that even the cathedral of Toledo—one of the most richly
endowed in the whole of Spain—is difficult to see from the outside,
being largely obscured by the warren of houses that surrounds it. Long

after the departure of the Moors, Toledo remained secretive, its life and treasures hidden behind closed doors and austere facades.

Alfonso VI, aided by El Cid, captured Toledo in 1085 and styled himself "Emperor of Toledo." Under the Christians, the strong intellectual life of the town was maintained, and Toledo became famous for its school of translators, who spread to the West a knowledge of Arab medicine, law, culture, and philosophy. Religious tolerance continued, and during the rule of Peter the Cruel (so named because he allegedly had members of his own family murdered to advance himself), a Jewish banker, Samuel Levi, became royal treasurer and one of the wealthiest and most important men in town. By the early 15th century, however, hostility toward both Jews and Arabs grew as Toledo developed more and more into a bastion of the Catholic Church.

As Florence had the Medici and Rome the papacy, so Toledo had its long and distinguished line of cardinals, most notably Mendoza, Tavera, and Cisneros. Under these great patrons of the arts, Renaissance Toledo emerged as a center of humanism. Economically and politically, however, Toledo had already begun to decline in the 16th century. The expulsion of the Jews from Spain in 1492 had particularly serious economic consequences for Toledo; the decision in 1561 to make Madrid the permanent center of the Spanish court led to the town's loss of political importance, and the expulsion from Spain of the converted Arabs (Moriscos) in 1601 resulted in the departure of most of Toledo's celebrated artisan community. The years the painter El Greco spent in Toledo—from 1572 to his death in 1614—were those of the town's decline. Its transformation into a major tourist center started in the late 19th century, when the works of El Greco came to be widely appreciated after years of neglect. Today, Toledo is prosperous and conservative, high priced, silent at night, and closed in atmosphere. Yet Spain has no other town of this size with such a concentration of major monuments and works of art.

Numbers in the margin correspond to points of interest on the Toledo map.

51 On the western edge of the city, the **Puente de San Martín,** a pedestrian bridge, dates to 1203 and features splendid horseshoe arches. High above this, and the most prominent monument in western Toledo, is the late-15th-century church of **San Juan de los Reyes.** A much better and more extensive view of Toledo is to be had from the eastern end of the gorge along the Calle de Circunvalación. Here you can park your car (except in the middle of the day, when buses line up) and look down over almost all the main monuments of Toledo.

52 The oldest of the town's bridges, the **Puente de Alcántara,** is of Roman origin. Next to the bridge is a heavily restored castle built after the Christian capture of 1085, and above this stands a vast and depressingly austere military academy, a typical example of Fascist architecture under Franco.

53 The **Alcázar** is the monument with the earliest opening time. The south facade, the most severe, is the work of Juan de Herrera, of Escorial fame; the east facade, meanwhile, gives a good idea of the building's medieval appearance, incorporating a large section of battlements. The finest of the facades is undoubtedly the northern, one of many works executed in Toledo by Alonso de Covarrubias, who did more than any other architect to introduce the Renaissance style to this town.

Within the building is both a military headquarters and a large military museum—one of Spain's few remaining homages to Francoism,

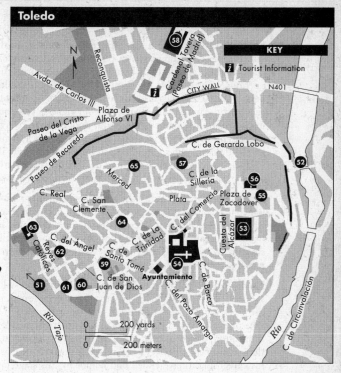

hung with tributes from various right-wing military groups and figures from around the world. Architecturally, its highlight is Covarrubias's harmonious Italianate courtyard, which, like most other parts of the building, was largely rebuilt after the civil war of 1936–39, when the Alcázar was besieged by the Republicans. Though the Nationalists' ranks were depleted, they managed to hold on to the building. Franco later turned the Alcázar into a monument to Nationalist bravery; the office of the Nationalist general who defended the building, General Moscardó, has been left in exactly the same state as it was after the war, complete with peeling ceiling paper and mortar holes. The gloomy tour can continue with a visit to the dark cellars, where living conditions at the time of the siege are evoked.

More cheerful is a ground-floor room full of beautifully crafted swords, a Toledan specialty introduced by the Moorish silver workers. At the top of the grand staircase, which apparently made even Carlos V "feel like an emperor," are rooms displaying a vast collection of toy soldiers. ☎ 925/223038. 🎟 125 ptas. ⊙ Tues.–Sun. 10–1:30 and 4–5:30 (until 6:30 in summer).

From opposite the southwestern corner of the Alcázar, a series of alleys descends to the east end of the **cathedral,** affording good views of the cathedral tower. Make your way around the southern side of the building, passing the mid-15th-century **Puerta de los Leones,** with detailed and realistic carvings by artists of northern descent. Emerging into the small square in front of the cathedral's west facade, you will see to your right the elegant **Ayuntamiento,** begun by the young Herrera and completed by El Greco's son, Jorge Manuel Theotokópoulos. Jorge Manuel was also responsible for the cathedral's Mozarabic chapel, the elongated dome of which crowns the right-hand side of the west facade; the rest of this facade is mainly of the early 15th century and features a representation of the Virgin presenting her robe to Toledo's patron saint, the Visigothic Ildefonsus.

Enter the cathedral from the 14th-century cloisters to the left of the west facade. The primarily 13th-century architecture is inspired by the great Gothic cathedrals of France, such as Chartres; the squat proportions, however, give it a Spanish feel, as do the wealth and heaviness of the furnishings and the location of the elaborate choir in the center of the nave. Immediately to your right as you enter the building is a beautifully carved Plateresque doorway by Covarrubias, marking the entrance to the Treasury. The latter houses a small Crucifixion by the Italian painter Cimabue and an extraordinarily intricate late-15th-century monstrance by Juan del Arfe, a silversmith of German descent; the ceiling is an excellent example of Mudéjar workmanship.

From here, walk around to the ambulatory, off the right-hand side of which is a chapter house featuring a strange and quintessentially Spanish mixture of Italianate frescoes by Juan de Borgoña. In the middle of the ambulatory is a dazzling and famous example of Baroque illusionism by Narciso Tomé, known as the *Transparente,* a blend of painting, stucco, and sculpture.

Finally, off the northern end of the ambulatory, you will come to the sacristy, where a number of El Grecos are to be found, most notably the work known as *El Espolio* (Christ being stripped of his raiment). One of El Greco's earliest works in Toledo, it fell foul of the pedantic Inquisition, which accused the artist of putting Christ on a lower level than some of the onlookers. El Greco was thrown into prison, and there his career might have ended had he not by this stage formed friendships with some of the more enlightened clergy of the town. Before leaving the sacristy, look up at the colorful and spirited Late-Baroque ceiling painting by the Italian Luca Giordano. ☑ *500 ptas.* ۞ *Mon.–Sat. 10:30–1 and 3:30–6 (until 7 in summer), Sun. 10:30–1:30 and 4–6 (until 7 in summer).*

⑤ The town's main square, **Plaza de Zocodover,** was built in the early 17th century as part of an unsuccessful attempt to impose a rigid geometry on the town's chaotic, Moorish ground plan. Nearby, you'll find the Calle del Comercio, the town's narrow and lively pedestrian thoroughfare, lined with bars and shops and shaded in the summer months by awnings suspended from the roofs of tall houses.

NEED A
BREAK?   On the south side of the square, and on the narrow street leading off the middle of it, are numerous bars, cafés, and modest restaurants. Those on the square—one of which features in Luis Buñuel's movie *Tristana*—have chairs and tables outside.

⑤⑥ The **Museo de la Santa Cruz,** displays among others, El Greco's *Assumption* of 1613, the artist's last known work. Unlike the other monuments in town, the museum is open all day without a break and in the early hours of the afternoon is delightfully quiet. One of the joys of this museum is that it is housed in a beautiful Renaissance hospital with a stunning, Classical Plateresque facade. The light and elegant interior has changed little since the 16th century, the main difference being that works of art have replaced the hospital beds. A small **Museo de Arqueología** has been arranged in and around the hospital's delightful cloister, off which a beautifully decorated staircase by Alonso de Covarrubias can also be found. ☎ *925/221036.* ☑ *200 ptas.* ۞ *Mon. 10–2 and 4–6:30, Tues.–Sat. 10–6:30, Sun. 10–2.*

57 The **Capilla del Cristo de la Luz** (Chapel of Christ of the Light) lies behind railings in a small park above the town's northern ramparts. The gardener will open the gate for you and show you around, but if he is not there, inquire at the house opposite. The exposed chapel was originally a tiny Visigothic church, transformed into a mosque during the Moorish occupation; the arches and vaulting of the mosque survive, making this the most important relic of Moorish Toledo. The story behind the chapel's name is that the horse of Alfonso VI, who was riding in triumph into Toledo in 1085, knelt in front of the building; it was then discovered that behind the masonry was a candle that had burned continuously throughout the time that the Infidels had been in power. The first Mass of the Reconquest was said here, and later a Mudéjar apse was added (now shielded by glass). After you have looked at the chapel, the gardener will take you across the ramparts to climb to the top of the Puerta del Sol, a 12th-century, Mudéjar gatehouse. ✉ *Tip to gardener.* ☉ *Any reasonable hr.*

58 Outside the walls beyond Covarrubias's imposing Puerta de Bisagra, Toledo's main northern gate, you'll find the **Hospital de Tavera,** Covarrubias's last work. Unlike the Hospital of Santa Cruz, this complex is unfinished and slightly dilapidated. It is nonetheless full of character and has an evocatively ramshackle museum in its southern wing, looked after by two exceptionally friendly and eccentric women. The most important work in the museum's miscellaneous collection is a painting by the 17th-century artist José Ribera. In the hospital's monumental chapel is the *Baptism of Christ* by El Greco and the exquisitely carved, marble tomb of Cardinal Tavera, the last work of Alonso de Berruguete. Descend into the crypt to experience some bizarre acoustical effects. ☎ *925/220451.* ✉ *500 ptas.* ☉ *Daily 10:30–1:30 and 3:30–6.*

59 El Greco's most famous painting can be found in the church of **Santo Tomé**; ideally, you should get here as soon as it opens in the morning, for later on in the day, especially in the summer months, you may well have to wait in line to get inside. Adorned by an elegant, Mudéjar tower, the specially built chapel houses El Greco's *Burial of Count Orgaz.* The painting—the only one by the artist to have been consistently admired over the centuries—portrays the benefactor of the church being buried with the posthumous assistance of St. Augustine and St. Stephen, who miraculously appeared at the funeral to thank him for all the money he had given to religious institutions named after them. Though the count's burial took place in the 14th century, El Greco painted the onlookers in contemporary costumes and included people he knew; the boy in the foreground is one of El Greco's sons, while the sixth figure on the left is said to be the artist himself. ☎ *925/210209.* ✉ *150 ptas.* ☉ *Daily 10–1:45 and 3:30–5:45 (until 6:45 in summer).*

60 **Casa de El Greco** (El Greco's House), another tourist magnet, is farther down the hill from Santo Tomé, off Calle de San Juan de Dios. The property belonged to Peter the Cruel's Jewish treasurer, Samuel Levi, and the artist once lived in a house owned by this man; whether he lived in this one, however, is pure conjecture. The interior, done up in the late 19th century to resemble a "typical" house of El Greco's time, is a pure fake, albeit quite a pleasant one. The once-drab museum attached to it is currently being restored and remodeled; one of the few works to be seen at present is a large panorama of Toledo by El Greco, featuring in the foreground the Hospital of Tavera. ☎ *925/ 224046.* ✉ *400 ptas.* ☉ *Tues.–Sat. 10–2 and 4–6, Sun. 10–2.*

61 The **Sinagoga del Tránsito** (Tránsito Synagogue), is a 14th-century structure financed by Samuel Levi. Plain on the outside, the walls of this simple, rectangular structure are sumptuously covered inside with intricate Mudéjar decoration, as well as Hebraic inscriptions glorifying God, Peter the Cruel, and Levi himself. The upper, women's gallery has been opened to the public for the first time following restoration; the rooms adjoining the main hall reopened in 1991 as a small museum of Jewish culture in Spain. ☎ 925/223665. ☒ 400 ptas. ☉ Tues.–Sat. 10–2 and 4–6, Sun. 10–2.

㉒ The town's other synagogue, **Santa María la Blanca,** is nearly two centuries older than the Tránsito Synagogue. It has a white interior featuring a forest of columns supporting capitals of the most enchanting filigree workmanship. Stormed in the early 15th century by a Christian mob led by St. Vincent Ferrer, the synagogue was later put to a variety of uses—as a carpenter's workshop, a store, a barracks, and a refuge for reformed prostitutes. ☎ 925/227257. ☒ 150 ptas. ☉ Daily 10–2 and 3:30–6 (until 7 in summer).

A few steps from Santa María la Blanca, at the western end of town, is ㉓ the convent church of **San Juan de los Reyes,** erected by Ferdinand and Isabella to commemorate their victory at the battle of Toro in 1476 and intended originally to be their burial place. The building is largely the work of Juan Guas, who considered it his masterpiece and asked to be buried here himself. Guas, one of the greatest exponents of the Gothic, or Isabelline, was an architect of prolific imagination and great decorative exuberance. The white interior, in true Plateresque fashion, is covered with inscriptions and heraldic motifs. ☎ 925/223802. ☒ 150 ptas. ☉ Daily 10–1:45 and 3:30–5:45 (until 6:45 in summer).

㉔ For a diversion into the virtually unspoiled part of town, visit **San Román,** an early-13th-century Mudéjar church, with extensive remains of frescoes inside; it has been deconsecrated and now serves as a **Museo de los Concilios y de la Cultura Visigoda** (Museum of Visigothic Art), featuring statuary, manuscript illustrations, and delicate jewelry. ☎ 925/ 227872. ☒ 100 ptas. ☉ Tues.–Sat. 10–2 and 4–6:30, Sun. 10–2.

Near the Museo de los Concilios on Calle San Clemente, look at the richly sculpted portal by Covarrubias on the **Convento de San Clemente.** Almost every wall in this quiet part of town belongs to a convent, and the empty streets make for contemplative walks. This was a district loved by the Romantic poet Gustavo Adolfo Bécquer, author of *Rime,* the most popular book of Spanish verse before García Lorca's *Romancero Gitano*. Bécquer's favorite corner was the tiny square in front ㉕ of the 16th-century convent church of **Santo Domingo,** a few minutes' walk to the north of San Román, below the Plazuela de Padilla. You will find here not only the earliest of El Greco's Toledo paintings but also the artist's coffin. The friendly nuns at the convent will show you around an eccentric, little museum, which includes documents bearing El Greco's signature. ☎ 925/222930. ☒ 150 ptas. ☉ Mon.–Sat. 11–1 and 4–7, Sun. 4–7 (weekends only in winter).

Dining and Lodging

$$$ ✕ **Asador Adolfo.** Only a few steps from the cathedral, but discreetly
★   hidden away and making no attempt to attract the passing tourist trade, this is unquestionably the best and most dignified restaurant in town. The modern main entrance shields an old and intimate interior featuring in its principal dining room a wood-beam ceiling with extensive, painted decoration from the 14th century. The emphasis is on freshness of produce and traditional Toledan dishes, but there is also much innovation. Especially good starters are the *pimientos rellenos* (stuffed peppers). For a main course, try the *merluza al azafrán* (hake subtly flavored with saffron from the area). You should finish with another Toledan specialty, *delicias de mazapan* (marzipan), which is cooked here

in a wooden oven and is the finest and lightest to be found in the whole town. ⊠ *Granada 6 and Hombre de Palo 7,* ☎ *925/227321. Reservations essential. AE, DC, MC, V. No dinner Sun.*

$$ ✕ **Hierbabuena.** Dine on an enclosed, Moorish patio with plenty of natural light, at tables covered with crocheted cloths. The food here is just as inviting as the setting, and it is surprisingly reasonably priced; try artichokes stuffed with seafood or steak with blue-cheese sauce. ⊠ *Cristo de la Luz 9, 223463. AE, DC, MC, V.*

$$–$$$ ✕🛏 **Hostal del Cardenal.** Built in the 18th century as a summer palace for Cardinal Lorenzana, this is a quiet and beautiful hotel with light-colored rooms decorated with old furniture; some rooms overlook the hotel's enchanting, wooded garden, which lies at the foot of the town's walls. It is difficult to believe that the main Madrid road is only a short distance away. The restaurant here has a long-standing reputation and is very popular with tourists. The setting is beautifu, and both the food and service are good. The dishes are mainly local, and in season you will find delicious asparagus and strawberries from Aranjuez. ⊠ *Paseo Recaredo 24, 45004,* ☎ *925/224900,* FAX *925/222991. 27 rooms. Restaurant. AE, DC, MC, V.*

$$$$ 🛏 **Parador Nacional Conde de Orgaz.** This modern building on the outskirts of Toledo blends well with its rural surroundings and has an unbeatable panorama of the town. The architecture and furnishings, emphasizing brick and wood, make concessions to the traditional Toledan style. ⊠ *Paseo Emperador s/n, 45001,* ☎ *925/221850,* FAX *925/225166. 77 rooms with bath. Pool. AE, DC, MC, V.*

$$ 🛏 **Pintor El Greco.** Next door to the famous painter's house-museum, this friendly hotel is in what was once a 17th-century bakery. Extensive renovation has resulted in a light and modern interior, with some antique touches, such as exposed brick vaulting. ⊠ *Alamillos del Transito 13, 45002,* ☎ *925/214250,* FAX *925/215819. 35 rooms. AE, DC, MC, V.*

Shopping

The most renowned center for crafts in Castile, if not in the whole of Spain, is **Toledo province.** Here, the Moors established **silverwork, damascene** (metalwork inlaid with gold or silver), **embroidery,** and **pottery** traditions that are still very much alive. Next to the church of San Juan de los Reyes in Toledo is a turn-of-the-century art school that teaches these various crafts and helps to maintain standards. For much cheaper pottery, you would be better off stopping at the large, roadside emporia on the outskirts of the town, on the main road to Madrid. Better still, go to **Talavera la Reina,** 76 km/47 mi west of Toledo, where most of this pottery is made. The finest embroidery in the province is from **Oropesa** and **Lagartera.**

AROUND MADRID A TO Z

Arriving and Departing

By Plane

The only international airport in both Old and New Castile is Madrid Barajas. Valladolid Airport has flights to Barcelona. For information on airlines serving Madrid, *see* Madrid A to Z *in* Chapter 2.

Getting Around

By Bus

The bus connections between Madrid and the two Castiles are excellent. Two of the most popular services with tourists and day-trippers are to Toledo (1 hour) and Segovia (1½ hours); buses to the former leave every half hour from the Estación del Sur (✉ C. Canaria 17, ☎ 91/468–4200) and to the latter every hour from La Sepulvedana (✉ Paseo de la Florida 11, ☎ 91/527–9537). Buses to Soria (3 hours) and Burgo de Osma (2½ hours) leave from Continental Auto (✉ C. Alenza 20, ☎ 91/533–0400), while Auto Res (✉ Plaza Conde de Casal 6, ☎ 91/551–7200) runs services to Cuenca (2 hours, 50 minutes) and Salamanca (3 hours). Services between the provincial towns are not as good as those to and from Madrid: If you are traveling between, say, Cuenca and Toledo, you will find it quicker to return to Madrid and make your way from there. Reservations are rarely necessary; in cases of extra demand, additional buses are usually put into service.

By Car

A series of major roads with extensive stretches of divided highway—the N I, II, III, IV, and V—radiate from Madrid in every direction and make communications with the outlying towns easy; if possible, however, avoid returning to Madrid on these roads at the end of a weekend or public holiday. The side roads are variable in quality and rarely of the high standard that you find, say, in provincial France. Nonetheless, these roads constitute one of the great pleasures of traveling around the Castilian countryside by car—you are constantly coming across unexpected architectural delights and wild and spectacular vistas; above all, you will rarely come across other tourists.

By Train

All the main towns covered in this section are accessible by train from Madrid, and it is quite possible to visit each in separate day trips. There are commuter trains from Madrid to Segovia (2 hours), Alcalá de Henares (45 minutes), Guadalajara (1 hour), and Toledo (1½ hours). Train travel in Spain has improved in recent years, although sometimes it is faster to get to your destination by bus. Trains to Toledo depart from Madrid's Atocha station; trains to Salamanca depart from Chamartín Station; and both stations serve Ávila, Segovia, El Escorial, and Siguenza, although Chamartín may offer more frequent service to some. The one important town that can be reached only by train is Sigüenza. Check with RENFE for details (☎ 91/328–9020).

Contacts and Resources

Car Rental

It is often cheaper to rent cars in advance, while still in the United States, through international firms such as Hertz and Avis (☞ Car Rental *in* Important Contacts A to Z). Spain's leading car-rental agency is **Atesa** (✉ Infanta Mercedes 90, Madrid, ☎ 91/571–2145).

Fishing

The most common fish in Castile's rivers are trout, pike, black bass, and blue carp; among the main trout rivers are the Eresma, Alto Duero, Júcar, Jarama, Manzanares, Tajo, and Tormes. Obtain permits and information from **ICONA** (✉ Gran Vía de San Francisco 4, ☎ 91/347–6000) and from the **Federación Española de Pesca** (✉ Navas de Tolosa 3, 28013 Madrid, ☎ 91/532–8353).

Golf

There are golf courses at Alcalá de Henares, Salamanca, and numerous smaller places in the immediate surroundings of Madrid. For further information, contact the **Real Federación Española de Golf** (⊠ Capitán Haya 9, 28020 Madrid, ☎ 91/555–2682).

Guided Tours

Current information on city tours can be obtained from the local tourist offices, where you can also find out about hiring guides. You should be especially wary of the local guides at Ávila and Toledo; they can be quite ruthless in trying to impose their services on you. Do not buy goods in the shops that they take you to because you will probably end up paying more than the normal prices.

For a special art tour of Castile, including Salamanca, contact **Prospect Music & Art Tours Ltd.** (⊠ 10 Barley Mow Passage, Chiswick, London W4 4PH, ☎ 0181/995–2163). At the same address is by far the best of Great Britain's cultural tour specialists, **Martin Randall Travel** (☎ 0181/994–6477), which offers an excellent five-day trip that includes Madrid and Toledo.

Visitor Information

The main provincial tourist office in Madrid is on the Plaza de España (⊠ Princesa 1, ☎ 91/541–2325). Useful information and excellent town plans can be obtained from the following local offices:

Alcalá de Henares (⊠ Callejón de Santa María, ☎ 91/889–2694), **Aranjuez** (⊠ Plaza San Antonio 9, ☎ 91/891–0427), **Ávila** (⊠ Plaza de la Catedral 4, ☎ 920/211387), **Ciudad Real** (⊠ Avda. Alarcos 21, ☎ 926/212925), **Ciudad Rodrigo** (⊠ Puerta de Amayuelas 5, ☎ 923/460561), **Cuenca** (⊠ Glorieta González Valencia 2, ☎ 969/178800), **Guadalajara** (⊠ Plaza Mayor 7, ☎ 949/220698), **Salamanca** (⊠ Casa de las Conchas, Rúa Mor s/n, ☎ 923/268571), **Segovia** (⊠ Plaza Mayor 10, ☎ 921/460334), **Siguenza** (⊠ Plaza Mayor 1 (949/393251), **Soria** (⊠ Plaza Ramón y Cajal s/n, ☎ 975/212052), **Toledo** (⊠ Puerta de Bisagra s/n, ☎ 925/252648), **Valladolid** (⊠ Plaza de Zorilla), ☎ 983/351801), and **Zamora** (⊠ C. Santa Clara 20, ☎ 980/531845).

4 León, Galicia, and Asturias

The Celtic-flavored provinces of León, Galicia, and Asturias, in the green, rain-swept northwestern climes of Spain, are home to wild mountain scenery and pristine beaches. Visit the city of Santiago de Compostela with its spectacular cathedral; follow the pilgrimage route of St. James; sip hard cider in Villaviciosa, and feast on seafood in La Coruña.

DIVERSE AND FAR-FLUNG, this region includes Spain's wildest mountain scenery in the Picos de Europa and most pristine beaches in the coves of the Lugo coast. It incorporates the ramshackle countryside of Galicia, coal mines, heavy industry, and the lonesome plains of Castile, near León.

By Deborah Luhrman

Updated by Mary Ellen Schultz

Green, rain-swept landscapes are what northwestern Spain is all about. Ancient granite buildings wear a blanket of moss, and even the *horreos* (granaries) are built on stilts above the damp ground. Swirling fog and heavy mist contribute to enduring folk tales of the supernatural. Bagpipes replace flamenco guitar in this part of Spain, evidence of ancient Celtic ties, and even a local folk dance, the muñeira, resembles a combination highland fling and Irish jig.

While Galicia, Asturias, and León are off the beaten track for many visitors to Spain, they are not untouristed. Spanish families flock to the cool northern beaches and mountains each summer. The city of Santiago de Compostela, whose cathedral is said to house the remains of the apostle St. James, has been attracting tourists for more than 900 years, and, in fact, the first guidebook ever published, the Calixtus Codex of 1130, describes the route to Santiago that you can follow to this day. Because of medieval pilgrims who made the journey to Santiago, the region is dotted with churches, shrines, and hospitals. Most monuments in León and Galicia owe their existence to the pilgrimage route.

Asturias, north of the main pilgrimage trail, has always been slightly separate from the rest of the country because of the high mountains encircling it. This is the only region of Spain not conquered by the Moors and there is little Arabic influence in its architecture. It was from their mountain base at Covadonga that the Christians won their first decisive battle against the Moors and launched the reconquest of Spain. Though it took some 700 years, the Reconquest made Spain one of the world's most Roman Catholic countries, a legacy that remains today.

Pleasures and Pastimes

Beaches
After allowing unbridled development to spoil the Costa del Sol, the Spanish government is now promoting the attractions of beaches in the north. The weather in this region is not reliable, but should it be sunny, try one of the following beaches: Llanes, Ribadesella, Cudillero, Santa Ana at Cadavedo, Luarca, Tapia de Casariego, Muros, Noya, El Grove, Islas Cíes, Boa, and Testal. Not recommended because of industrial pollution are San Lorenzo in Gijón and beaches near Avilés. Unfortunately, the beaches of the Rías Bajas also have pollution problems.

Canoes and Kayaking
Ribadesella, in Asturias, is the white-water capital of Spain. An international race in August is the highlight of the season; the race starts at Arriondas and finishes in Ribadesella. There are several other navigable waterways; the tourist office can help you map out a route.

Dining
Galicia and Asturias are famous throughout Spain for their seafood. Specialties include *merluza a la Gallega* (steamed hake in Galician paprika sauce) and *merluza a la sidra* (steamed hake in a tangy Asturian cider sauce). Scallops (*vieira*), the symbol of the pilgrimage to Santiago, are popular in Galicia, where there are also entire bars that serve nothing but wine and *pulpo á feira* (boiled and broiled octopus), or

berberechos (cockles). Ham lovers should try *lacón con grelos* (baked shoulder of pork served with sautéed turnip tops). Cheeses all over the country are delicious; try the fragrant *queso de Cabrales* (blue cheese from Asturias), and the Gallego *queso de tetilla* (a creamy semi-soft cheese in the form of a woman's breast), delicious with *membrillo* (a fruit spread made from quince) for dessert. In Asturias salmon and trout from local rivers are a treat. The region is also famous for hearty stews. In Asturias try *fabada* (butter beans and sausage), and in Galicia sample *caldo Gallego* (stew of potatoes, cabbage, chickpeas, and meat broth). Savory fish or meat pies called empanadas native to Galicia can be eaten out of the hand like a sandwich. In Asturias, try *entrecote con queso cabrales* (a hearty combination of steak topped by a sauce made with the principality's famed blue cheese). The province of León specializes in roast lamb, *afumados* (assorted smoked meats), *morcillas* (varieties of sausages), and *lechón* (suckling pig), and produces a sparkling rosé wine called *bierzo,* similar to the acidic Galician *ribeiro.* The best Galician wine is the smooth, crisp white *albariño,* while Asturias is famous for its *sidra* (hard cider), served either carbonated or still. Brandy aficionados should try Galicia's *queimada,* what superstitious Gallegos claim is a witches' brew, made of potent, grappalike *orujo* mixed with lemon peel and sugar in an earthenware bowl, then set aflame and stirred until the desired amount of alcohol is burned off. While much of this region is rural and remote, restaurant prices are not substantially lower than those in the rest of the country—especially those in Asturias and in Santiago de Compostela.

CATEGORY	COST*
$$$$	over 6,500 ptas.
$$$	4,500–6,500 ptas.
$$	3,000–4,500 ptas.
$	under 3,000 ptas.

per person for three-course meal, excluding drinks, service, and tax

Fiestas

Jan. Visitors to Tordesillas can witness the ritual rooster sacrifice during the feast of San Vincente Martir. The Festa do Chourizo en Sant Anton de Abedes, January 17, in Verin (Orense) includes a parade and sausage festival in honor of the local saint. The Procesión dos Fachos, the night of January 20, in Castro Caldelas in Orense has a torchlight procession commemorating the village's survival of a cholera outbreak in 1753.

March. The Fiesta del Queso, first week in March, Aruza (La Coruña), celebrates folklore and food, with a contest for outstanding cheeses.

May. During San Isidro Labrador, May 15, in Cacabelos (León), villagers parade through town in decorated horse-drawn carriages and on foot carrying flower garlands in honor of the workers' saint.

June. The Fiesta de San Juan, June 23, is a magical night in San Pedro de Manrique (Soria), when residents celebrate the beginning of summer by walking barefoot over smoldering hot coals to help the sun win its battle against the darkness of the shortest night of the year.

July. In Pontevedra, there's the Rapa das Bestas from July 7–8. The apple-scented Cider Festival is held in mid-July in Nava. The Shepherds' Festival, held on July 25 in Cangas de Onís and Covadonga National Park, features regional dances and bagpipe music. The festival commemorating the Día de Santiago (St. James Day) is celebrated on July 25 in Santiago; there are fireworks and mass is celebrated with the *botafumeiro* incense burner.

Aug. The Albariño Wine Festival, the first Sunday in August, takes place in Cambados.

Sept. The Procesión de las Mortajas, in Pobra do Carmiñal (La Coruña), takes place on the third Sunday in September. This tradition dates back to the 15th century, when those who have been cured of ailments, bad luck, or bad loves prepare open coffins, lie in them, and then are carried in a procession around the village.

Oct. Festa do Marisco, second week in October, the town of O Grove, celebrates the bounty of shellfish and seafood. Eat lobster, mussels, clams, *percebes* (goose barnacles that look like mini elephant feet but are, in fact, sugar-sweet), spiny *néora* crabs, shrimp, etc.

Other fiestas: During Carnival, León and nearby La Bañeza are popular for Castilian pre-Lenten partying. During Semana Santa, Easter week, in Viveiro watch a barefoot procession of flagellants, illuminated by hundreds of candles held by spectators and participants.

Lodging

The government-run parador hotel chain has cornered the market on charming places for tourists to stay. Galicia has nine parador hotels, three in elegant manor houses and two in old fortresses. León boasts one of the finest paradors, in a stunning converted convent. Check descriptions before making your choices; some paradors are in modern buildings. Most good-quality hotels are high-rises geared to business travelers or package tour groups. Some rooms, even in the fine hotels, can be suffocatingly small. Reservations are important through the summer season, May–October, but not essential the rest of the year. Another possibility is to contact monasteries in the region that provide simple lodgings at very reasonable prices in some of the more rural areas; contact your local Spanish Tourist Office for a listing.

CATEGORY	COST*
$$$$	over 16,500 ptas.
$$$	12,500–16,500 ptas.
$$	8,500–12,500 ptas.
$	under 8,500 ptas.

*per standard double room, excluding tax and breakfast

Skiing

The three small ski areas in this region cater mostly to families and local residents. The largest is San Isidro, in the Cantabrian Mountains, with one chairlift and 12 slopes. Just east of there is Valgrande Pajares with two chairlifts and eight slopes. West of Orense, in Galicia, Manzaneda has one chairlift and seven slopes. Valgrande Pajares and Manzaneda also have cross-country skiing.

Exploring Galicia, Asturias, and León

Begin your visit in classic, old Castilian León with its austere architecture and Gothic, stained-glass cathedral. Leaving the city, modern day defenders or admirers of the faith can head west toward Galicia and pick up the pilgrim's trail (ticking off the well-marked stops along the way: Astorga, the isolated thatched roof hamlet of O Cebreiro, Samos, and Sarria) along the ancient Camino de Santiago (Way of St. James). Follow the camino to Santiago de Compostela, then travel west to the beach resort of Muros with its arcaded streets and south to Pontevedra and the fishing towns of the Rías Bajas. Venture north again to the thriving port of La Coruña before moving east to Oviedo, capital of emerald-green Asturias, with its apple orchards, cider bars, and some of Spain's most jagged mountains, the Picos de Europa.

Numbers in the text below correspond to numbers in the margin and on the maps.

Great Itineraries

It takes only a few days for the north to cast its spell; the best way to get around is by car. Five days would be enough to get the flavor of each of the three regions. Seven days would allow for more leisurely explorations of the main towns and cities combined with stops here and there in smaller villages to wander through narrow streets. Ten days would mean the opportunity for relaxed landloping through scenic countryside and villages where time appears to have stopped.

No matter how many days you spend here, be prepared to fall in love with this magical region. In the Gallego dialect they call it *morriña,* an indescribable longing for a person or place just out of reach.

IF YOU HAVE 3 DAYS

🏠 **León** ① makes a good starting point. The classy Castilian capital combines the hustle of a modern-day city with the flavor of centuries past.On day two follow the Camino de Santiago pilgrimage route toward Santiago. Head for **Astorga** ② with its Archbishop's Palace designed by Gaudí, then step back into the 17th century in the nearby, stone village of **Castillo de los Polvazares** ③. Wend your way through the hilly countryside past **Ponferrada** ④, stopping to admire the 13th century Castillo de los Templarios (Templar's Castle) on the edge of town, and continue to 🏠 **Villafranco del Bierzo** ⑤, a medieval village in León's wine-growing region. Day three will take you through lovely small towns along the pilgrims' route to 🏠 **Santiago de Compostela** ⑩–⑰. Overnight there, and on day four, explore the impressive soaring Romanesque Catedral, plazas, and old town. Then, take the road north to 🏠 **La Coruña** ㉑, one of Spain's busiest ports. Admire the window-enclosed wooden balconies along the waterfront of the *Ciudad de Cristal* (City of Glass), and visit the Torre de Hercules, the world's oldest functioning Roman lighthouse. Next day, head north for the coast and some of the country's loveliest beaches, stopping for a stroll around the ancient walled town of **Viveiro** ㉔. Continue on to Asturias and **Luarca** ㉞, a cozy village in a cove, and the lively coast city of **Gijón** ㊱. End your tour by driving south to 🏠 **Oviedo** ㉟, capital of the principality.

IF YOU HAVE 7 DAYS

Spend day one exploring 🏠 **León** ①. Next morning, head off for the Camino de Santiago. On your way admire the 13th-century Orbigo Bridge where Quiñónes made his last stand. Set your compass for **Astorga** ② with its recently unearthed Roman ruins and fantastic Gaudí-inspired Archbishop's Palace, the nearby ex-muleteer town of **Castillo de los Polvazares** ③, and medieval 🏠 **Villafranca del Bierzo** ⑤, once home to Grand Inquisitor Torquemada. On day three, continue west through towns dear to pilgrims: **O Cebreiro** ⑥ with its round, thatched-roof huts, Samos, Sarria, **Portomarín** ⑦, **Vilar de Donas** ⑧, **Leboreiro** ⑨, and on to 🏠 **Santiago de Compostela** ⑩–⑰. This city, a World Heritage Site, will be your base for the next two nights. Next day, visit the impressive Cathedral, wander through the old town and visit a museum or two, and make an excursion to the nearby town of **Padrón** ⑲, the birthplace of poet Rosalía de Castro, one of Galicia's literary heroines. On day five, take the road north about 45 minutes to 🏠 **La Coruña** ㉑. On the way, visit **Pazo de Oca** ⑱, a restored manor house, and see how wealthy Gallegos lived. La Coruña is a lively port that combines a medium-size city with a small town atmosphere; see the city and feast on shellfish. The next day head up to the coast, driving through picturesque **Betanzos** ⑳ and **Mondoñedo** ㉓, one of the capitals of ancient Galicia. Along the coast, you'll come to 🖽 **Ribadeo** ㉕, dear to trout and salmon fishermen, with its charming parador. Day seven brings you to the Asturian seacoast towns of **Luarca** ㉞, Avilés, and **Gijón** ㊱, then inland to 🖽 **Oviedo** ㉟, present capital of the principality and the one-time capital of Christian Spain. From there, head to nearby **Cangas de Onís** ㊳ and the famous 8th-century shrine of **Covadonga** ㊵, considered to be the birthplace of Spain.

When to Tour León, Galicia, and Asturias

The most popular and revered festivals take place during the pre-Lenten revels of Carnival (dates vary, but generally any time between end of February and beginning of March) and Easter's Semana Santa. But fairs and festivals can be found in some town or another just about any week of the year (☞ Fiestas *in* Pleasures and Pastimes, *above*).

Summer is best for swimming and water-based sports. Spring and fall are considered by many to be the ideal time to explore, since winters can be bitterly cold (León) or rainy (Galicia and Asturias) to the point of saturation—it's not for nothing that this region is called "Green Spain."

This is still a relatively unknown part of the country for most American travelers. This can be exhilarating or disconcerting, depending on one's sense of adventure.

Numbers in the margin correspond to points of interest on the León, Galicia, and Asturias map.

THE CAMINO DE SANTIAGO (WAY OF ST. JAMES)

In the Middle Ages Santiago de Compostela, where the apostle St. James is said to be buried, was considered the third most important shrine in the Christian world, after Jerusalem and Rome. Making the difficult pilgrimage all but ensured the faithful a spot in heaven. At peak periods in the 12th century, as many as 2 million people a year traveled the road to Santiago from all over Europe. It was crowded with thieves and knights to protect the travelers from them, innkeepers who grew wealthy on the tourist trade, and even souvenir sellers who provided the scallop shells worn by the pilgrims as a symbol of St. James, the fisherman.

The main pilgrimage route traverses the Pyrenees at Roncesvalles and extends across northern Spain to Santiago. Picking up the Way of St. James in León and following it to Santiago will give you plenty to see.

León

❶ *333 km (207 mi) northwest of Madrid, 334 km (208 mi) east of La Coruña, 277 km (172 mi) east of Santiago de Compostela.*

León, capital of the province of Castilla y León, sits on the banks of the Benesga River in the high plains of Old Castile. Founded as a permanent camp for the Roman legions in AD70, today's historians say the city's name has nothing to do with the proud lion that has been its emblem for centuries but is instead a corruption of the Roman word *legio* (legion).

León, Galicia, and Asturias

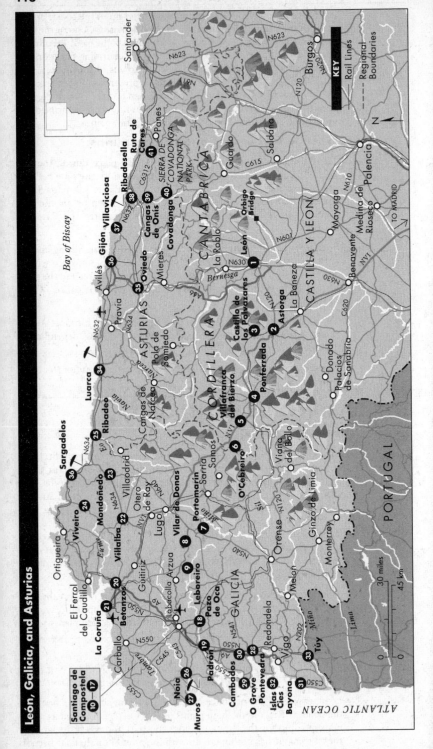

Santiago de Compostela
⑩ — ⑰

KEY
Rail Lines
Regional Boundaries

N

Bay of Biscay

ATLANTIC OCEAN

PORTUGAL

GALICIA

ASTURIAS

CANTÁBRICA

CORDILLERA

CASTILLA Y LEÓN

TO MADRID

30 miles

45 km

The capital of Christian Spain was moved south to León from Oviedo in 914 as the Reconquest spread, launching the city's richest era. Walls were built around the old Roman town, and parts of the 6-foot-thick medieval ramparts are still visible in the middle of the modern city.

Today, León is a wealthy provincial capital. The wide avenues are lined with shops, while a half-timbered old town remains.

★ León is proudest of its soaring Gothic **cathedral,** on the Plaza de Regla. Outside, notice the flying buttresses used to support walls that are built with more windows than stone. The front of the cathedral is decorated with three weather-worn, arched doorways, the center one adorned with slender statues of the apostles.

The cathedral, begun in 1205, contains 125 stained-glass windows plus three giant rose windows. The glass casts bejeweled shafts of light throughout the lofty interior; a clear glass door on the choir permits an unobstructed view to the altar and apse windows. You'll see little 13th-century faces looking at you amid a kaleidoscope of colors from the lower-level windows. The cathedral also contains the sculpted tomb of King Ordoño II, who moved the capital of Christian Spain to León. Inside the cathedral museum, look for the carved wood Mudéjar archives, with a letter of the alphabet above each door. It's one of the world's oldest file cabinets. ✉ *Plaza de Regla,* ☎ *987/230060.* 🗓 *Museum 350 ptas.* ⊘ *July and Aug., weekdays 10–1:30 and 4–6, Sat. 10–1:30; Sept.–June, weekdays 9:30–1:30 and 4–7, Sat. 9:30–1:30.*

The 19th-century **Farmacia Marino,** opened in 1827, offers a glimpse into a Spanish drugstore from long ago. The ceiling is richly carved, as are the walls, which include a niche for each apothecary jar. Only the medicines have changed since it opened. It's down the street from the the Cathedral on Avenida Generalísimo Franco.

The arcaded **Plaza Mayor** in the heart of León's old town, is surrounded by simple, half-timbered houses. If it is Wednesday or Saturday, the plaza will be bustling with farmers selling produce and cheeses. Look at their feet; many still wear a type of wooden shoes called *madreñas,* which are raised on three heels, two in the front and one in the back.

As you're wandering the streets of the old town, look down occasionally and you just might notice small, **brass scallop shells** set into the street. These were installed by the town government to mark the path for modern-day pilgrims on their way to Santiago.

The 12th-century **Plaza San Martín** is where most of León's tapas bars are located. This area is called the Barrio Húmedo (Wet Neighborhood) because of all the wine poured every evening.

NEED A BREAK?   In a corner of Plaza San Martín is the cozy **Prada a Tope** bar (☎ 987/225987), which serves the region's Bierzo wine out of a big barrel. The locale doubles as a gourmet food shop showcasing local products, and the friendly staff may offer you samples of roasted red peppers, potent brandy-soaked cherries, or candied chestnuts. Three other recommended spots in the same plaza are **Rancho Chico** (☎ 987/256047), **Nuevo Racimo de Oro** (☎ 987/254100), and **La Bicha** (☎ 987/256518).

☾ If you're traveling with children, León has a long **park** on the banks of the Bernesga River, with playground equipment every 100 feet or so.

In the center of of the modern city, you'll see the **Casa de Botines,** a multigabled and turreted behemoth designed at the end of the 19th century by controversial Catalan architect Antonio Gaudí. It now houses a bank.

The basilica of **San Isidoro el Real,** on Calle Cid, was built into the side of the city wall in 1063 and rebuilt in the 12th century. Adjoin-

★ ing the Basílica of San Isidro, the **Panteón de los Reyes (Royal Pantheon)** is sometimes called the Sistine Chapel of Romanesque art. The vibrant frescoes painted in the 12th century on the pillars and ceiling have been remarkably preserved. The pantheon was the first building in Spain to be decorated with scenes from the New Testament. Look for the agricultural calendar painted on one archway, showing which farming task should be performed each month. Twenty-three kings and queens were once buried here, but their tombs were destroyed by French troops during the Napoleonic Wars. The museum tastefully displays San Isidoro's treasures, including a jewel-encrusted agate chalice, a richly illustrated hand-written Bible, and an enormous collection of polychrome wood statues of the Virgin Mary. ⊠ *Plaza de San Isidoro,* ☎ *987/229608.* ▱ *Royal Pantheon 325 ptas.* ☉ *July and Aug., Mon.–Sat. 10–1:30 and 3–8:30, Sun. 9–2; Sept.–June, Tues.–Sat. 10–1:30 and 4–6:30, Sun. 10–1:30.*

Visit the sumptuous **Antiguo Monasterio de San Marcos,** a former monastery that is now a five-star hotel named the Hostal San Marcos (☞ Dining and Lodging, *below*). Originally a home for knights of the Order of Santiago, who patrolled the Way of St. James, and a stopping place for weary pilgrims, the monastery you see today was begun in 1513 by the head of the order, King Ferdinand, who felt knights deserved something better. Finished at the height of the Renaissance, the building's Plateresque facade is a sea of small sculptures, many of knights and lords. Inside is an elegant staircase and a cloister full of medieval statues. Enjoy a drink in the bar; the tiny windows are the original defensive slits. The building also houses the **Museo Arqueológico** (Archaeology Museum) famous for its 11th-century, ivory Carrizo crucifix. ⊠ *Plaza de San Marcos,* ☎ *987/245061 or 987/236405.* ▱ *Museum 300 ptas.* ☉ *July and Aug., Tues.–Sat. 10–2 and 4:30–8, Sun. 10–2; Sept.–June, Tues.–Sat. 10–2 and 4–7:30, Sun. 10–2.*

Bars and Cafés

The **Plaza Mayor** and the 12th-century **Plaza San Martín** are where most of León's tapas bars are located. Spots to sample tapas include Universal, Mesón de Don Quijote, Casa Benito, and Bar La Plaza Mayor in the Plaza Mayor; in the Plaza San Martín have a *pinchito* (tidbit) at the cozy Prada a Tope bar, which serves the region's Bierzo wine out of a big barrel, Rancho Chico, Nuevo Racimo de Oro, and La Bicha.

Dining and Lodging

$$ ✕ **Adonias.** Enter through the ground-floor bar and climb one flight up to the softly lit, green dining room, furnished with rustic tables and colorful ceramics. The cuisine is based on regional products such as cured hams, roast peppers, and chorizo. Try the grilled sea bream, the roast suckling pig, and the homemade banana pudding with chocolate sauce. ⊠ *Santa Nonia 16,* ☎ *987/206768. AE, DC, MC, V. Closed last 2 weeks of July.*

$$ ✕ **Casa Pozo.** This longtime favorite is across from city hall on the historic Plaza de San Marcelo. The bright dining rooms are furnished with heavy Castilian furniture. Owner Gabriel del Pozo Alvarez, called Pin, supervises the busy kitchen and attentive service. Specialties include fresh peas with ham, roast lamb, and deep-fried hake. ⊠ *Plaza de San Marcelo 15,* ☎ *987/223039 or 987/237103. AE, DC, V. Closed Sun., 1st 2 weeks of July, and 2 weeks at Christmas.*

$$ ✕ **Nuevo Racimo de Oro.** On the second floor of a ramshackle, 12th-century tavern in the heart of the old town, this restaurant specializes in roast suckling lamb cooked in a wood-fired, clay oven. Try the spicy *sopa de ajo* (Castilian garlic soup) served in a wooden bowl with a wooden spoon or the medieval-style spinach with raisins and pine nuts. ⊠ *Plaza San Martín 8,* ☎ *987/214767. Reservations not accepted. MC, V. No dinner Sun. Closed Tues.*

$$$$ ✕▦ **Hotel San Marcos.** This magnificent parador is a restored 16th-
★ century monastery built by King Ferdinand to shelter pilgrims walking the route of Santiago. The Plateresque facade is longer than a football field: A church and an archaeology museum are housed here. Rooms have antiques and high-quality reproductions. A modern addition with a pool has been built. If you enjoy medieval luxury, ask for a room in the old section. The elegant dining room overlooking the Bernesga River serves braised baby lamb chops, *congrío con patatas al arriero* (river eel stewed with potatoes), *cecina* (smoked beef), and sole with raisin and pine-nut sauce. Top off the meal with *leche quemada* (a light egg custard with a topping of caramelized sugar) or *arroz con leche* (rice pudding dusted ith cinnamon). ⊠ *Plaza de San Marcos 7, 24001,* ☎ *987/237300,* ℻ *987/233458. 258 rooms with bath. Restaurant, bar, pool, beauty salon. AE, DC, MC, V.*

$ ✕▦ **Hotel Riosol.** This modern high-rise is across the river from town and not far from the train station. The comfortable carpeted rooms, decorated with black-lacquer furniture and gold wallpaper, are a frequent choice of business travelers. ⊠ *Avda. de Palencia 3, 24001,* ☎ *987/216650,* ℻ *987/216997. 141 rooms with bath. Restaurant, coffee shop. AE, DC, MC, V.*

Shopping

ARTS AND CRAFTS

In Villar de Mazarife (22 km/15 mi, west of León on the way to Astorga), **Monseñor** (⊠ Camino de León 21, ☎ 987/300338) paints adaptations of Roman archeological finds and makes ceramic tile reproductions of the frescoes found in the San Isidro Pantheon.

CHILDREN'S CLOTHING

For unique, Spanish-designed children's outfits, try **Oliver** (⊠ Sanjurjo 21, no phone).

FOOD

Tasty treats to spend your pesetas on include the regional specialities, such as roast red peppers, potent brandy-soaked cherries, and candied chestnuts. You can find them in food shops all over the city, or shop while "doing" tapas at **Prado A Tope** (⊠ Plaza San Martín 1), where they are packaged by the house.

En Route   Leaving León, follow signs to the N120 and head southwest; stop to admire the 13th-century Orbigo Bridge, 23 km/14 mi outside the city, where Quiñones made his stand. Legend has it that the knight Quiñones was the toughest hombre on the Way of St. James. In the year 1434, he staked out his turf on this bridge, and for a month challenged all the other knights who policed the route. You are now on the Camino de Santiago, marked with large signs for motorists and small signs for the pilgrims who make the journey each year on foot.

Astorga

❷ *46 km (29 mi) southwest of León.*

Astorga, where the pilgrimage roads from France and Portugal merged, once boasted 22 hospitals to lodge and care for travelers. Today the only one left is the **Hospital of Astorga,** adjacent to the cathedral. The **cathedral** is a huge 15th-century building with Baroque decorations, with four statues of St. James.

★ The drabness of the town is relieved by the fairy-tale, neo-Gothic **Palacio Episcopal (Archbishop's Palace),** designed for a Catalan cleric by Gaudí just before the turn of the century. No expense was spared in creating this fanciful building, which houses the **Museo del Camino** (Museum of the Way). Note the standard pilgrim costume: heavy black cloak, staff hung with gourds, and wide-brim hat bedecked with scallop shells. ⊠ *Adjacent to cathedral.* ☎ *300 ptas.* ☉ *Apr.–Sept., daily 10–1 and 4–8; Oct.–Mar., Tues.–Sun. 11–1 and 3:30–6:30.*

NEED A BREAK?	Before you leave town, you might want to buy a box of the pastries that every Spaniard associates with Astorga. The rich *mantecadas* (tea cakes) are sold in shops near the cathedral.

Castillo de los Polvazares

❸ *51 km (32 mi) west of León, 5 km (3 mi) west of Astorga.*

A short walk or a 15-minute drive from Astorga, is Castillo de los Polvazares, a 17th-century village built on the site of a Roman fortified settlement. The 30-odd inhabitants of this city occupy stone houses emblazoned with crests above green doorways. Walk down the stone streets—there are no sidewalks and no asphalt—and look for storks' nests on top of the village church. Telephone wires are the only indication of modernity.

Castrillo is in León's *Maragatería* region, populated by those believed to be a mixture of the Celts and Phoenicians who resisted the Roman invasion of the Iberian Peninsula. They reached the height of their trading prowess in the 18th and 19th centuries as muleteers (hence the wide doorways in the town), transporting gold from America to the royal court in Madrid.

NEED A BREAK?	If your appetite is whet from exploring the village, head to Calle Real. **El Arriero, La Magdalena,** and **Cuca La Vaina** are recommended mesones (taverns). The village specialty is *cocido al Maragato* (a hearty stew of pork, beef, veal, and chickpeas). If you're not hungry, have a cup of coffee or a hot chocolate.

Ponferrada

❹ *115 km (71 mi) west of León, 64 km (40 mi) west of Astorga; follow the Madrid-La Coruña highway, N-VI, west.*

Ponferrada, nestled in a hilly region with beautiful, fertile valleys, is a mining and industrial center that gets its name from an iron toll bridge built by a local bishop in the 1100s. The tall, slim turrets of the 13th-century **Castillo de los Templarios (Templars' Castle)** on the western edge of town command sweeping views of the countryside and may have once been used by the knights of the Order of St. James to police the route. ⊠ *Florez Osorio 4, no phone.* ☎ *Free.* ☉ *Apr.–Sept., Wed.–Mon. 9–1 and 4–7; Oct.–Mar., Wed.–Mon. 9–1 and 3–6.*

Villafranca del Bierzo

❺ *135 km (84 mi) west of León, 20 km (12 mi) west of Ponferrada.*

After crossing the grape-growing region of León, where the slightly acidic Bierzo wine is produced, you will arrive in Villafranca del Bierzo. The medieval village is dominated by a massive feudal fortress, still inhabited. Villafranca was an important stopping place for pilgrims. Visit the Romanesque **church of Santiago** here and see the door of pardon, a sort of spiritual consolation prize for weak pilgrims who couldn't make it over the mountains. Stroll the streets and look for the crests on the old manor houses; seek out the one-time **dwelling of the infamous Grand Inquisitor, Torquemada.** Wine can be purchased at the **Cooperativo Villafranquina** on the highway.

Dining and Lodging

$–$$ ✕🏨 **Parador de Villafranca del Bierzo.** This modern, two-story hotel sits on a hilltop overlooking the Bierzo valley. Ample rooms have heavy wood furniture, window shutters, and large baths. The brick and wrought-iron dining room serves fresh Bierzo trout and *chanfaina barciana* (fried liver and bread crumbs) and chorizo *con alubias* (a hearty dish of white beans and sausage). Try the local Bierzo wine. ✉ *Calvo Sotelo s/n, 24500,* ☎ *987/540175,* FAX *987/540001. 40 rooms with bath. Restaurant, bar. AE, DC, MC, V.*

En Route   The Way of St. James veers left, to the south, from NVI at the pass of Pedrafita. Climb the steep, narrow road and you'll arrive at one of the most unusual hamlets in Spain, O Cebreiro.

O Cebreiro

❻ *32 km (20 mi) from Villafranca del Bierzo.*

In O Cebreiro, round, thatched-roof stone huts called *pallozas* have been preserved in a sort of monument to the way the people in these windswept Galician mountains lived until just a few decades ago. One hut is now a **museum** of the region's Celtic heritage. The village, at 3,648 feet, also contains a rustic **sanctuary** from the 9th century.

En Route   Continue along the mountain road to the town of Samos, with its Benedictine monastery. From Samos head to Sarria, a medieval village with the pilgrim's hospital of La Magdalena.

Portomarín

❼ *40 km (25 mi) from Lugo.*

In Portomarín, on the Miño River, the **Romanesque church** was moved, stone by stone, before the town was flooded by a new dam.

Vilar de Donas

❽ *Approximately 25 minutes from Portomarín.*

Farther on from Portomarín, stop at the church in Vilar de Donas to pay tribute to the knights of St. James, whose tombs line the inside walls. Portraits of the two medieval noblewomen who built the church are included among those of the apostles in the 15th-century frescoes adorning the apse.

Leboreiro

❾ *Approximately a half hour from Vilar de Donas.*

From Vilar de Donas, the countryside flattens out and you can stop at Leboreiro, a village with simple medieval stone houses surrounding a Romanesque church. A stretch of the ancient road, paved with granite boulders, is still surprisingly intact.

Santiago de Compostela

❿ *277 km (172 mi) west of León, 650 km (403 mi) northwest of Madrid.*

Numbers in the margin correspond to points of interest on the Santiago de Compostela map.

Santiago de Compostela was built to impress. Imagine pilgrims walking across Spain for 30 days and finally arriving at the foot of the great cathedral. The sheer size of the opulent building is awe-inspiring, with its main entrance raised two stories above the spacious Plaza del Obradoiro. Its twin towers give a sense of harmony, and a benign St. James, dressed in pilgrim's costume, smiles down from his perch.

One starry night in the year 813, a hermit was directed by a divine light to a field just outside present-day Santiago de Compostela. Digging began, and religious leaders unearthed a sarcophagus said to contain the remains of St. James. The name Compostela is believed to have come from the Latin *campus stellae* (field of the stars). How the apostle's remains got to Galicia is somewhat of a mystery. One legend says that after St. James was beheaded by King Herod in Jerusalem, his headless body was smuggled to Spain, where it lay hidden for centuries.

The discovery came at an opportune moment, when the Moors had overrun most of the country, and only a fragment of the Christian army remained. Those Christian soldiers said St. James, armed with a great sword and riding a white charger, led them to their first victory against the Moors in Clavijo in 844. He earned himself the nickname Santiago Matamoros (St. James the Moor Slayer) and became the patron saint of Spain. Carrying his powerful banner throughout the Reconquest, the Christians went on to expel the Moors from Spain and conquer much of the Americas.

⓫ Climb the two flights of steps to the main doorway of the **cathedral,** and inside you'll see the finest creation of Romanesque sculpture, the 12th-century **Pórtico de la Gloria.** This is the original entrance, completed in 1188 by Maestro Mateo. Its three arches are carved with biblical figures from the Last Judgment and Purgatory. In the center, Christ is flanked by his apostles and the 24 Elders of the Apocalypse playing celestial instruments. Just below Christ is a serene St. James, poised atop a carved column that includes the humble face of Maestro Mateo at the bottom. Look carefully at this pillar and you'll see five indentations made over the centuries by the millions of pilgrims who have placed their hands here as they leaned forward to touch foreheads with Maestro Mateo, in tribute to his genius.

The gold and silver **high altar** is presided over by a statue of St. James dressed in a sumptuous jeweled cloak. Climb the stairs behind the altar and you will be standing at the focal point of the cathedral, surrounded by a dazzling array of decoration, sculptures, and drapery. At this point, pilgrims kiss the cloak of St. James—the grand finale of a spiritual journey. Beneath the altar in the crypt are the alleged remains of St. James and two of his disciples, St. Theodore and St. Athanasius.

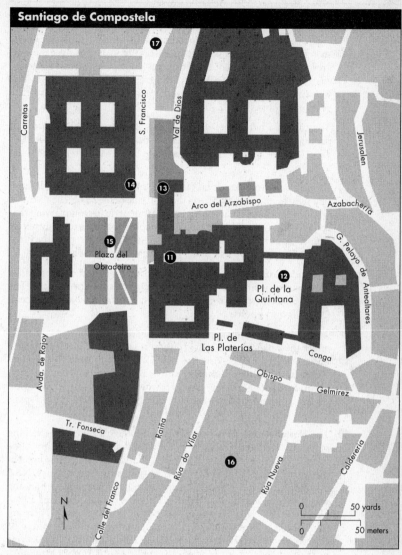

Santiago de Compostela

Carretas
S. Francisco
Val de Dios
Jerusalen
Azabachería
Arco del Arzobispo
G. Pelayo de Antealtares
Plaza del Obradoiro
Pl. de la Quintana
Pl. de Las Platerías
Avda. de Rajoy
Conga
Obispo
Gelmírez
Tr. Fonseca
Raiña
Rúa do Vilar
Rúa Nueva
Caldereria
Calle del Franco

N

0   50 yards
0   50 meters

Cathedral, **11**
Centro Gallego
de Arte
Contemporánea, **17**
Hostal de los Reyes
Católicos, **14**
Old town, **16**

Palacio Gelmírez, **13**
Plaza de la
Quintana, **12**
Plaza del
Obradoiro, **15**

Pilgrims' masses are sung in the cathedral every day at noon. On special occasions a huge incense burner is attached to the thick ropes hanging from the ceiling and anchored against the wall. Eight strong priests swing the *botafumeiro* (a large incensory) in wide arcs over the congregation. In earlier centuries, this was one of the original air fresheners; by the time many pilgrims reached Santiago, they smelled, shall we say, "ripe." National television broadcasts the ceremony live each year on St. James's Day, July 25.

You can see a botafumeiro and the rest of the cathedral's treasure in the **museums.** ☎ *981/572300.* ☒ *400 ptas.* ☉ *July–Oct., Mon.–Sat. 10–1 and 4–7, Sun. 10–1; Nov.–June, Mon.–Sat. 10–1 and 4–6, Sun. 10–1.*

Exit through the **Puerta de las Platerías** (named for the silversmith shops that used to line the square), on the right side of the nave. The so-called silversmith's door is named for the intricate style of stone carving that completely covers the entryway. The double doorway is the only purely Romanesque part of the cathedral's exterior and opens onto the **Plaza de las Platerías,** with its graceful fountain, a favorite photo spot.

⑫ The wide **Plaza de la Quintana,** on the other side of the Cathedral, is the haunt of young travelers and musicians during the summer. The **Puerta Santa** on this plaza is only opened in years in which St. James's Day falls on a Sunday.

Take in the surrounding, handsome complex of buildings. As you pass under the Arco del Arzobispo (Bishop's Arch) and arrive back at the
⑬ Plaza del Obradoiro, visit the rich 12th-century **Palacio Gelmírez (Palace of Archbishop Gelmírez)** with its Baroque apartments and a lavish 30-meter-long meeting room crowned by a carved ceiling depicting the marriage of King Alfonso IX. ☎ *981/572300.* ☒ *175 ptas.* ☉ *May–Oct., Mon.–Sat. 10–1 and 4–7, Sun 10–1.*

⑭ The **Hostal de los Reyes Católicos** is Santiago's other eye-catching building, constructed in 1499 by Ferdinand and Isabella in gratitude to Santiago for having finally expelled the Moors. The oldest hotel in the world has been fortifying travelers for nearly five centuries. Now a parador (☞ Dining and Lodging, *below*), the magnificent building was a hospital for those who fell ill along the road. It remained a hospital until 1953, when it was converted to shameless luxury. There are four arcaded patios with fountains and gargoyle rainspouts said to be caricatures of the 16th-century townsfolk. The public is allowed to visit in the company of an official city guide. ☒ *Plaza del Obradoiro,* ☎ *981/582200.* ☒ *Free.* ☉ *Daily 10–1 and 4–6.*

⑮ As you stand in the middle of the **Plaza del Obradoiro,** the building directly opposite the cathedral is the **Palacio de Rajoy** (Rajoy Palace), now the city hall, and the fourth side is enclosed by the **Colegio de San Jerónimo** (San Jerónimo College).

Santiago de Compostela has many old manor houses, convents, and churches that in most towns would receive headline attention. But the
⑯ best way to spend your remaining time here is to walk around the **old town,** losing yourself in the maze of plazas and narrow streets. The most beautiful Santiago streets are the arcaded Rúa do Vilar, Calle del Franco, and Rúa Nova. You'll notice that all the streets, archways, and buildings are constructed with big granite blocks, tinted green with the moss that flourishes in this rainy climate. The people of Santiago never go anywhere without an umbrella.

This mystical, spiritual, and historical city has long been open to all byways and cultures. It is now also connected to present-day creativity in **El Centro Gallego de Arte Contemporánea (Contemporary Art Center of Galicia),** a home for modern art. The recently opened museum, near the old town, highlights works from regional, national, and international artists. ⊠ *Rúa Valle Inclán s/n,* ☎ *981/546621,* ☒ *Free.* ◷ *Tues.–Sat. 11–8, Sun. 11–2.*

NEED A BREAK?

Santiago's most unusual wine bar is the **Bodega Abrigadoiro** (⊠ Carrera del Conde 5, ☎ 981/563163) in the old town that is decorated with a working waterwheel which cools the bottles of young, local Ribeiro wine. Your order of *tetilla* (the creamy regional cheese) or a plate of grilled chorizo comes with a basket of country bread. Ask for your wine in a *taza* (a white, footed ceramic cup that is traditional in these parts).

⑱ Twenty-seven kilometers (17 miles) southeast of Santiago is **Pazo de Oca,** a Galician-style country manor house. The feudal barons who controlled the peasant society of the kingdom of Galicia lived in *pazos* (homes like this), once sprinkled throughout the region. Walk through the gardens to the lily pond and lake, where a stone boat stays miraculously afloat. ☎ *981/570761.* ☒ *175 ptas.* ◷ *Apr.–Sept., daily 9–1 and 4–8; Oct.–Mar., daily 10–1 and 3–6.*

Dining and Lodging

$$$ ✕ **Anexo Vilas.** Owner Moncho Vilas likes to mingle with his happy
★ customers and loves to promote Galician cuisine. His expertise in the kitchen has won acclaim from Spanish gourmets, and he even prepared the banquet when Pope John Paul II visited Santiago in 1989. Specialties include salmon with clams, hake à la Gallega (with paprika sauce) or à la Vasca (in a green sauce), and a tender steak with garlicky potatos. Anexo Vilas is a little outside town but worth the walk. ⊠ *Avda. Villagarcia 21,* ☎ *981/598387. AE, MC, V. Closed Mon.*

$$$ ✕ **Don Gaiferos.** Named for a mythical medieval minstrel who used to roam the trail to Santiago, Don Gaiferos is in the old section of town. Stone walls, modern furnishings, and indirect lighting enhance the international cuisine. Selections include mixed seafood cocktail, pepper steak, and sole cooked in wine with béchamel sauce and Parmesan cheese. ⊠ *Rúa Nova 23,* ☎ *981/593894. AE, MC, V. Closed Sun.*

$$ ✕ **San Clemente.** On a tiny square off the Plaza del Obradoiro, this restaurant offers high-quality seafood at just about any time of the day or night. Walk past the long bar in the front room to the large dining room in back, and feast on scallops, shrimp, sole, hake, percebes, or the famous Galician pulpo a feira. ⊠ *San Clemente 6,* ☎ *981/565426. AE, DC, MC, V.*

$$$$ ✕▥ **Araguaney.** This glass-and-chrome palace was built by an Arab who came to Santiago as a medical student and fell in love with the daughter of a wealthy Galician family. The rooms are spacious. The disco, built underneath the glass-bottom pool, is one of the trendiest night spots in town. ⊠ *Alfredo Brañas 5, 15701,* ☎ *981/595900,* FAX *981/590287. 65 rooms with bath. Restaurant, bar, pool, beauty salon, sauna, dance club. AE, DC, MC, V.*

$$$$ ✕▥ **Hostal de los Reyes Católicos.** A converted 15th-century hospi-
★ tal, this is one of Santiago's main tourist attractions (☞ *above*). Behind a two-story-high Plateresque facade are four interior patios with formal gardens, fountains, and carved stone arcades. The large rooms are furnished with antiques that span five centuries and include regal

canopy beds. The luxurious, high-ceilinged dining room offers regional specialities; try the *lubina con setas y gambas* (sea bass with mushrooms and shrimp) or entrecote *a la gallega* (filet of beef broiled with oil, and garlic, usually served with boiled potatoes), or *lacó con grelos y cachelos* (fresh ham with chard and boiled potatoes). For dessert, try the gallego treat *filloas* (apple pancakes) with whipped cream. ⊠ *Plaza del Obradoiro, 15705,* ☎ *981/582200,* FAX *981/563094. 136 rooms with bath. Restaurant, bar, beauty salon. AE, DC, MC, V.*

$$ ✕⊡ **Peregrino.** The best of the moderately priced lodgings in Santiago is a relatively new motel-style inn that is a 15-minute walk from the center of town near Anexo Vilas (☞ *above*). The airy, modern rooms have bright accents and large baths. ⊠ *Rosalía de Castro s/n, 15706,* ☎ *981/521850,* FAX *981/521777. 148 rooms with bath. Pool, dance club. AE, DC, MC, V.*

Nightlife and the Arts

Bars line the streets of the old town; the **Calle del Franco, Raiña,** and **Vilar** streets near the cathedral are full of places with lots of *ambiente* (atmosphere) and good tapas. The most popular disco is at the **Araguaney Hotel** (☞ Dining and Lodging, *above*).

Concerts by internationally known orchestras and solo artists take place at the **Auditorium of Galicia.** A schedule of events is available at the tourist office.

The **Hostal de los Reyes Católicos,** in Santiago, holds a classical music course from July 20 to August 10 each summer. Some 150 musicians from many countries participate, and free **concerts** are given in the beautiful hotel performance hall every night.

Shopping

ARTS AND CRAFTS

Galicia is famous throughout Spain for its distinctive blue-and-white **ceramics** with bold modern designs that are made in Sargadelos and O Castro. There is a shop with a wide selection of these pieces at **Sargadelos** (⊠ Rúa Nueva 16, ☎ 981/581905).

Beautifully crafted black stone **jewelry,** called *azabache* (jet), can be found at **Fernando Mayer** (⊠ Plaza de las Platerías 6, ☎ 981/585077).

The women of the fishing town of Camariñas fashion exquisite handmade **lace** collars and scarves, as well as table linens. Some of the best places to buy their work here are **Vainica** (⊠ Rúa do Vilar 58, ☎ 981/566722) and **Dosel** (⊠ Rúa Nova 26, ☎ 981/566078).

FOOD

Individual-size Santiago **almond cakes** are sold at **Confitería Vilas** (⊠ Rosalía de Castro 70, Santiago, ☎ 981/596858)—the same ones served at Anexo Vilas restaurant (☞ Dining and Lodging, *above*).

THE NORTHERN GALICIAN COAST

Santiago, Padrón, Pazo de Oca, Betanzos, La Coruña, Villalba, Mondoñedo, Ribadeo

The rain- and wind-swept northern coast of Galicia has inspired local poets to wax lyrical about raindrops continuously falling on one's head. The sun does shine here, though, suffusing town and country with a bright, golden glow. Either way, prepare to be enthralled with the grandeur of Santiago de Compostela and the quieter beauty of the ancient kingdom of Mondoñedo.

Urban beauty exists here, too, in the many-paned *miradores* (glass galleries) lining La Coruña's waterfront, the charming gazebo in the center of Betanzos, and the tiny castle hotel in Villalba.

Padrón

⑲ *18 km (11 mi) south of Santiago.*

Numbers in the margin correspond to points of interest on the León, Galicia, and Asturias map.

Padrón grew up beside the Roman port of Iria Flavia and is the birthplace of one of Galicia's heroines, the 19th-century poet Rosalía de Castro. But the town is probably best-known for its delicious pimientos *de Padrón* (tiny green peppers fried and sprinkled with sea salt). The fun in eating them is that one in five or so is spicy hot.

Betanzos

⑳ *65 km (40 mi) northeast of Santiago, 25 km (15 mi) east of La Coruña.*

In the medieval town of Betanzos, parts of the old walls still stand, and you enter through one of the old gateways. The 12th-century **San Francisco church** contains the remains of Fernán Perez de Andrade, one of Galicia's feudal nobles. The 15th-century **Santa María de Azogue Church** was built by the mariners' guild, while the tailors' guild put up the Gothic-style **Santiago Church,** which includes a Door of Glory inspired by the original in Santiago Cathedral.

Shopping
Throughout Galicia, you will hear the haunting tones of the bagpipe, a fond token of the area's Celtic past. In Betanzos, outside La Coruña, you can visit a **bagpipe workshop** and buy the real thing at **Sellas y Gaitas** (✉ Cerca s/n), open weekdays 10–1 and 5–8.

La Coruña

㉑ *57 km (26 mi) north of Santiago.*

La Coruña is one of Spain's busiest ports. The weather here can be fierce, wet, and windy, giving this stretch of the Galician seaboard the nickname Coast of Death. Climate explains the enclosed, wood balconies called *miradores* on the tall, harbor houses: Small panes of glass provide protection from the gales and capture the warmth of the sun when it shines.

La Coruña is built on a narrow strip of land jutting out to sea. Out on the tip of the peninsula is the **Torre de Hercules** lighthouse. The lighthouse was originally built during the reign of Trajan, the Roman emperor born in Spain in AD 98. It was rebuilt in the 18th century, and all that remains from Roman times are inscribed foundation stones. Huff and puff your way up the 242 steps, and you'll be rewarded with superb views of the city and coastline. Imagine what it must have been like on July 11, 1544, when Spain's Prince Philip set sail with a fleet of 78 vessels for his wedding to Mary Tudor, the daughter of Henry VIII and Catherine of Aragón. In June, 1588, King Felipe II assembled another fleet at La Coruña, and the "invincible" Spanish Armada sailed from here to conquer England. It might have succeeded if not for a ferocious storm that scattered the fleet. The surviving ships limped back into La Coruña a month later. The spirit of Spain had been badly shaken, and to make matters worse, England's notorious Sir Francis Drake sacked the town the following year. The damage done by the English would have been much worse if not for the heroism of a local housewife, María Pita. She saw Drake's men climb the hill into the old town and at great risk fired a cannon to warn the residents.

The small **Museo de la Torre de Hercules** (Tower of Hercules Museum), which opened in 1995 after several years of excavation and renovation, is an open-air museum, displaying items dug up during the restoration of the ancient Roman lighthouse and surrounding area. ✉ *Carretera de la Torre s/n, no phone.* 🎫 *Free.* 🕙 *Tues.–Sun. 10–2.*

NEED A
BREAK?
> The **Plaza de María Pita** (named after the heroic 16th-century housewife who performed admirable damage control against Sir Francis Drake's navy; ☞ *above*), at the edge of the old town, is a beautiful square with many open-air bars and restaurants in the summer. City Hall dominates one side of the square. The cafés Plaza or Río Tinto are fine for a drink or snack before exploring the old town.

At the northeastern tip of the old town is the **Castillo de San Antón (Castle of San Antón),** formerly a 16th-century fort. It now houses the **Archaeology Museum,** where you can see remnants of the prehistoric Celtic culture that once thrived in this region. There are silver artifacts and pieces of the Celtic stone forts called *castros.* ☎ 981/205994. 🎫 *250 ptas.* 🕙 *June–Sept., daily 10–2 and 4:30–7:30; Oct.–May, daily 10–2 and 4:30–7.*

The **Museo de Bellas Artes,** occupying two lovely old mansions on the edge of the old town, features paintings and a good collection of Goya etchings. ✉ *Plaza del Pintor Sotomayor,* ☎ 981/205630. 🎫 *450 ptas.* 🕙 *Tues.–Sun. 10–3.*

Up on a hill is the ⚙ **Casa de las Ciencias (Science Museum),** a hands-on place in which children can learn the principles of physics and technology. ✉ *Parque Santa Margarita,* ☎ 981/279156. 🎫 *225 ptas., planetarium 200 ptas.* 🕙 *June–Sept., Tues.–Sat. 11–9, Sun. 11–2:30; Oct.–May, Tues.–Sat. 10–7, Sun. 11–2:30.*

On the other side of town, just off the Playa das Amorosas and near the Torre de Hercules, is Coruña's newest museum, the **Domus/Casa del Hombre.** This extraordinary museum dedicated to the interdisciplinary study of mankind features exhibits ranging from the evolution of a single individual to the study of man's relationship to society. Exhibits are interactive and involve the senses, allowing you to become part of the action. ✉ *Parque de Santa Teresa,* ☎ 981/228947. 🎫 *400 ptas.* 🕙 *June–Sept., Tues.–Sat. 11–9, Sun. 11–2:30; Oct.–May, Tues.–Sat. 10–7, Sun. 11–2:30.*

Dining and Lodging

$$–$$$ ✕ **Casa Pardo.** This chic eatery near the port is an elegant study in soft, ochre tones with perfectly matched wood furniture and cool lighting. Try the *merluza a la cazuela* (bayleaf-scented hake and potatoes drizzled with oil and sprinkled with paprika, baked in a clay casserole). For dessert, splurge on almond cake or chocolate mousse. ✉ *Novoa Santos 15,* ☎ 981/287178. *AE, MC, V. Closed Sun.*

$$–$$$ ✕ **El Coral.** The front window is a high altar of shellfish, with varieties
★   of mollusks and crustaceans you've probably never seen before. Inside, wood-paneled walls, crystal chandeliers, and 12 white-clothed tables provide the setting for an intimate, elegant yet casual meal. Specialties include regional dishes such as *arroz con almejas* (clams and shellfish-scented rice), and *turbante de mariscos* (a platter or literally a "turban" of steamed and boiled shellfish). ✉ *Estrella 2–4,* ☎ 981/221082. *Reservations essential. AE, DC, MC, V. Closed Sun. Oct.–May.*

$–$$ ✕ **La Marina.** One of the most classic coruñés restaurants is on a busy
★ street near the port in a large, converted private home. The many elegant and intimate dining rooms are decorated in a rustic fashion; lots of warm pastel colors and floral chintz radiate an elegant, country charm. Fill your stomach on tasty regional dishes: empanadas with meat or tuna-filling, *lacón* (fresh country ham), or one of the house specialties, *croquetas de mariscos* (seafood croquettes). Soothe your stomach afterward with a light dessert of *natillas* (cream custard). ✉ *Avda. de la Marina 14,* ☎ *981/223914. AE, MC, V.*

$$$ ✕🔲 **Finisterre.** This superbly-located high-rise where the old town joins the bay has its own sports complex and four pools. Long a favorite with businesspeople and families visiting La Coruña, Finisterre has comfortable, carpeted rooms with modern, wood furnishings and brightly colored upholstery. Ask for one of the many rooms overlooking the bay. ✉ *Paseo del Parrote, 15314,* ☎ *981/205400,* ᶠᴬˣ *981/208462. 127 rooms with bath. Restaurant, bar, 4 pools, tennis court, health club, playground. AE, DC, MC, V.*

Nightlife and the Arts

Wander along **Calle Estrella, Calle de los Olmos,** and **La Galera** for tapas and local ribeiro wine served in tazas. Serious night owls head for the area around **Orzan beach, the Marina,** or the **streets of old town.**

If you feel like gambling, head for the **Casino del Atlántico** (✉ Jardines de Médez Nuñez, ☎ 981/221600).

Shopping

ARTS AND CRAFTS

You'll find the famous blue-and-white pottery at the factory, museum, and showroom in nearby Cervo on the Lugo coast at **Cerámica de Sargadelos** (✉ Carretera Paraña s/n, ☎ 982/557841 or 982/557600), open weekdays 8:30–1 and 4:30–6. A wide choice is also available in nearby Sada at the combination factory and museum **Cerámicas del Castro** (✉ Carretera Sada-La Coruña s/n, ☎ 981/620225).

Glazed terracotta ceramics from Buño (40 km, or 25 mi, west of La Coruña on C552) are highly prized. Stop by **Alfaería y Cerámica de Buño** (✉ C. Barreiros s/n, Buño, ☎ 981/711251) for a selection of vases, plates, and wine jugs based on traditional designs.

One of the best places to buy the famous **Camariñas lace** is at **Carmina Touriña** (✉ Panaderas 19, La Coruña, ☎ 981/206290).

CLOTHING

Galicia boasts some of Spain's top fashion designers, notably **Adolfo Dominguez** (✉ Finisterre 3, ☎ 981/251539).

For **berets,** the traditional male headgear of the region (and the country), try **Luis Tomé Pérez Fábrica de Gorras y Boinas** (✉ Linares Rivas 52, ☎ 981/232014) in Coruña, an old-world hat and cap emporium.

FOOD

Want to take home some local culinary specialties? Try the *supermercado* (supermarket) floor of **El Corte Inglés** department stores for vacuum-packed food items that U.S. customs will not be forced to remove from your luggage. (✉ C. Ramón y Cajal 57–59, ☎ 981/290011).

SPORTING GOODS

In Xubia, along the Calle de Castilla road between Coruña and El Ferrol, **Armería Domingo** (✉ C. de Castilla 982, ☎ 981/302018) is an old-fashioned sporting-goods store (rumored to have been one of

Franco's favorite places to browse) that sells fishing rods, all-weather gear, and camping knives for roadside picnics.

Villalba

㉒ *70 km (43 mi) east of La Coruña.*

This part of Galicia is called *Terra Cha* (Flat Land). Known as the Galician Mesopotamia, it's where several rivers have their source, most notably, the Miño, which flows down into Portugal (where it's known as the Minho). The countryside is pretty, with gentle hills and knolls adding texture to the plain. The largest city in this area is Villalba, which has a tiny parador in a castle associated with the same Andrade family that wielded considerable power here over the centuries.

Dining and Lodging

$$$ ✕🏠 **Parador Condes de Villalba.** This tiny parador is in a 15th-century tower that was once a fortress belonging to the powerful, local Andrade family. A drawbridge leads to the two-story lobby, hung with medieval-style tapestries. The three large octagonal rooms in the massive tower and the three in a lower building have beamed ceilings and hardwood floors, hand-carved, Spanish-style furniture, and wood chandeliers. The dining room's specialty is empanadas (try the empanada *de Rax,* which is made of beef loin, or try the traditional *atún,* or tuna). For dessert, sample the region's renowned *San Simón* (cone-shaped, birch-smoked cheese with apples or pears). ✉ *Valeriano Valdesuso, 27800,* ☎ *982/510011,* 🆂🆇 *982/510090. 6 rooms with bath. Restaurant, bar. AE, DC, MC, V.*

Mondoñedo

㉓ *122 km (76 mi) northeast of La Coruña, 52 km (32 mi) northeast of Villalba.*

This dignified town, founded in AD 1156, was one of the seven original capitals of the kingdom of Galicia from the 16th to early 19th century. The most impressive building here is the **Cathedral,** consecrated in 1248. The surrounding peaceful streets and squares are filled with old buildings, monasteries, churches, and an old Jewish quarter.

En Route   Instead of Mondoñedo, you could continue along a winding 81-km/50-mi road past Villalba on N634 and return to the coast. Spain's cleanest and least crowded beaches are north of here.

Viveiro

㉔ *184 km (114 mi) northeast of La Coruña, 81 km (50 mi) northeast of Villalba.*

Stroll the narrow streets of this ancient town whose once-turreted walls are still partially intact. During Easter's Semana Santa, you can see penitents following religious processions on bloodied knees.

OFF THE   **CERVO –** If the weather is good, you may want to do some beach explor-
BEATEN PATH ing or visit the town of Cervo (10 km, or 6 mi), and visit the Sargadelos factory and store where Spain's most distinctive blue-, white-, and red-glazed modern-design ceramics are made.

Ribadeo

㉕ *25 km (16 mi) east of Cervo, 81 km (50 mi) northeast of Villalba, 113 km (70 mi) northwest of Mondoñedo.*

Ribadeo, on the broad *ría* (estuary) of the same name, is the last coastal town before Asturias; the view of Castropol, on the other side of the ría is marvelous. Walk out to the **estuary lighthouse,** where you can watch waves crash against the rocks and fishermen haul in their catch. Upriver is a favorite haunt for salmon and trout fishermen.

Just 2 km/1 mi outside Ribadeo is the **Santa Cruz hill,** with more sweeping views and a monument to the bagpipe, the most common folk instrument in Galicia and Asturias.

Dining and Lodging

$$ ✕ **O Xardin.** Renovations have freshened the charm of this old-fashioned garden restaurant. Specialties include mint-scented vegetable pudding, casserole of monkfish and scallops, and sole with wild mushroom and albariño wine sauce. ⊠ *Reinante 20,* ☎ *982/110222. Reservations not accepted. DC, MC, V. Closed Mon. winter–spring.*

$$ ✕⊞ **Parador de Ribadeo.** This modern parador on the banks of the Eo River has views across to Asturias. Gleaming hardwood floors and hefty rafters convey a feeling of warmth in this whitewashed hotel. Rooms have Castilian-style furniture, artisan rugs, and large baths. The estuary provides a cornucopia of shellfish for the dining room, including cockles, clams, and oysters. Try the chocolate mousse for dessert. ⊠ *Amador Fernández, 27700,* ☎ *982/100825,* ℻ *982/100346. 47 rooms with bath. Restaurant. AE, DC, MC, V.*

SOUTHWESTERN GALICIA AND THE ATLANTIC COAST

Noia, Muros, Pontevedra, O Grove, Bayona, Túy

If you love beaches, head due west from Santiago along scenic C543 toward the Galician coast, sliced by a series of wide estuaries called the Rías Altas and Rías Bajas. The hilly drive takes you through countryside dotted with tiny farms and horreos. Even the vineyards are staked with granite posts. You are likely to see stout, black-clad peasant women gracefully carrying heavy loads on their heads.

Noia

㉖ *36 km (22 mi) west of Santiago.*

A 45-minute drive from Santiago along the curving, scenic C543 brings you to Noia, a historic town with the Gothic **church of San Martín** facing resolutely out to sea and mysterious Celtic inscriptions on the gravestones in the medieval cemetery. The best places to swim and sun are Testal and Boa beaches.

En Route   Cross the narrow neck of the Tambre River and head up the other side of the ría to Muros.

Muros

㉗ *30 km (19 mi) west of Noia, 65 km (40 mi) southwest of Santiago, 75 km (47 mi) southwest of La Coruña.*

The cheerful harbor town of Muros is a popular summer resort with lovely, Gothic-arched, arcaded streets and good beaches nearby on Point Louro. Try Praia de San Francisco or Praia de Area. Notice all the mussel-breeding platforms in the bay.

Pontevedra

㉘ *55 km (34 mi) southeast of Noia, 59 km (37 mi) south of Santiago, 28 km (17 mi) south of Padrón, 120 km (75 mi) south of La Coruña.*

South of Santiago, Pontevedra is the next largest city south on the way to Portugal after La Coruña. You've probably noticed that road signs are difficult to read in Galicia because most have been spray-painted over with place names in the regional language, Gallego, which is actually an offshoot of Portuguese and sounds very different from Spanish.

A charming old town is preserved in Pontevedra, similar in style to Santiago but practically undiscovered by tourists. On the edge of the maze of granite-block streets and plazas is the seamans' 16th-century **Santa María Mayor church,** which has a beautifully carved facade in the intricate Plateresque style.

The **Museo Provincial (Provincial Museum)** is in two 18th-century mansions. The medieval statues within were removed from the Door of Glory in Santiago's cathedral when the new facade was built. ✉ *Sarmiento 51,* ☎ *986/851455.* ✐ *275 ptas.* ☉ *Daily 11–1:30 and 5–8.*

Dining and Lodging

$$ ✗ **Casa Solla.** Owner Pepe Solla makes the most of the bountiful har-
★ vest from local coasts and vineyards at his terraced garden restaurant, 2 km/1¼ mi outside town on the highway to O Grove. Try the sole in albariño wine sauce, filet mignon in red wine, and, in summer, fresh figs with Cabrales cheese. ✉ *Carretera O Grove, Km 2,* ☎ *986/852678. MC, V. No dinner Sun. Closed Thurs.*

$$$ ✗▥ **Casa del Barón.** A 16th-century manor house (built over the foundations of an ancient Roman villa) in the heart of Pontevedra, this parador hotel has a baronial stone stairway that winds into the front lobby. The rooms have antique reproductions and face a rose garden. The dining room is full of antique mirrors, candelabras, portraits of personages who look vaguely familiar, and a kitchen that prepares tasty seafood, shellfish, and meat dishes. Try grilled squid with garlic and parsley. ✉ *Maceda s/n, 36002,* ☎ *986/855800,* 𝔽𝔸𝕏 *986/852195. 47 rooms with bath. Restaurant, library. AE, DC, MC, V.*

En Route   Driving west on C550 from Pontevedra, you see the albariño vineyards, which produce the region's best and rarest wine, which some connoisseurs claim beats out the much revered rioja.

O Grove

㉙ *20 km (12 mi) west of Pontevedra, 75 km (47 mi) south of Santiago, 138 km (86 mi) south of La Coruña.*

The gourmet paradise of O Grove, on the peninsula, throws a shellfish festival the second week of October. But you can enjoy the day's catch in taverns and restaurants year-round.

Dining

$$ ✗ **Posada del Mar.** Overlooking the channel that separates O Grove from the island of La Toja, the dining room is decorated with a collection of ceramics from all parts of Spain. Expertly prepared seafood is king here. Try the monkfish in garlic butter or the fish soup thick with chunks of sugar-sweet turbot. ✉ *Castelao 202,* ☎ *986/730106. AE, MC, V. Closed mid-Dec.–Jan.*

Cambados

㉚ *34 km (21 mi) from Pontevedra; 53 km (33 mi) from Santiago.*

The town of Cambados has colorfully painted houses in its old town, and the imposing 17th-century Fefiñanes palace occupying almost half of the town square (named after the owners of the palace). Nearby is the wooded **island of La Toja,** with its luxury spa hotel and golf course (☞ Dining and Lodging, *below*). Legend has it that a man abandoned a donkey here, and upon his return, found it up on all fours and rejuvenated. Hence, the fame of restorative powers of the place.

Dining and Lodging

$$$$ ✕🏨 **Gran Hotel de la Toja.** This sybaritic Spanish version of Belle Epoque elegance is surrounded by a pine forest. Rooms are simple and have a slightly faded charm compared to the grandiose formality of the spa hotel's public salons and foyers. Dining areas have expansive sea views, and special diet menus are available. ⊠ *36991 Isla de la Toja,* ☎ *986/730025,* ℻ *986/730026. 201 rooms with bath. Restaurant, pool, spa, 9-hole golf course, tennis court, health club, horseback riding, beach, casino, dance club. AE, DC, MC, V.*

$$ ✕🏨 **Parador El Albariño.** Built in 1966 in the style of an old manor house, this parador faces the Atlantic. The lobby has heavy, leather furniture and beamed ceilings. Rooms are simply furnished with wrought-iron lamps, handmade rugs, and ceiling-high, wood shutters over small-paned windows. The dining room serves such Galician dishes as lacón con grelos. Be sure to order a bottle of local albariño wine. ⊠ *Paseo de Cervantes s/n, 36630, Cambados,* ☎ *986/542250,* ℻ *986/542068. 63 rooms with bath. Restaurant, bar, tennis court. AE, DC, MC, V.*

Nightlife and the Arts

There is a casino on La Toja: **Casino La Toja** (⊠ La Toja, ☎ 986/731000).

Bayona

㉛ *30 km (19 mi) south of Pontevedra, 128 km (80 mi) south of Santiago, 160 km (100 mi) south of La Coruña.*

The A9 expressway takes you from Pontevedra to the industrial center of Vigo in about half an hour. Bayona is on the southern bank of the Río Vigo on the cape. This was the first town to receive news of the discovery of the New World when one of Columbus's ships, the *Pinta,* landed here in 1493. **Monte Real,** a hilltop castle-fortress, is one of Spain's most popular parador hotels. Walk around the battlements for superb views. Be sure to check out the graceful Roman bridge on your way in or out of town.

Dining and Lodging

$$$ ✕🏨 **Parador Conde de Gondomar.** A modern hotel has been constructed inside the walls of a medieval castle. Rooms are furnished with period reproductions; some have balconies, with views of the sea from a hilltop fortified since 200 BC. The dining room serves regional specialties; try *entremeses variados* (mixed appetizers) for a sampler of typical seafoods; for a main dish perhaps the *robalo con navallas* (sea bass with razor clams). ⊠ *Carretera de Bayona, 36300,* ☎ *986/355000,* ℻ *986/355076. 124 rooms with bath. Restaurant, bar, pool, tennis court, health club, beach, playground. AE, DC, MC, V.*

Shopping

There is a branch of the department store chain **El Corte Inglés** in nearby Vigo (⊠ Avda. Gran Vía 25–27, ☎ 986/415111).

Islas Cies

32 *About 35 km (21 mi) out from Vigo in Altantic Ocean.*

The Islas Cies (pronounced *see*-ace), or Cies Islands, are one of the last unspoiled refuges on the Spanish coast. From July to September, about eight boats a day leave from Vigo harbor, returning later in the day. Round-trip fare is about $20. The 45-minute ride brings you to fine white-sand beaches. This is a nature reserve; birds abound, and the only land transportation is your own two feet. It takes about an hour to hike across the main island. For camping reservations (required), call Camping Islas Cies (☎ 986/438358).

Túy

33 *14 km (9 mi) south of Bayona, 50 km (31 mi) south of Pontevedra, 200 km (124 mi) south of La Coruña.*

Follow coastal road C550 around the peninsula and up the banks of the Miño River, which separates Spain from Portugal, and you come to the town of Túy. Túy was an important defensive position during the medieval wars between Castile and Portugal—which explains why the 13th-century **cathedral** has the look of a fortress. The steep, narrow streets are rich with ancient, crested mansions, evidence of Túy's former stature as one of the seven capitals of the Galician kingdom. Today it is important as a border town with Portugal.

Dining and Lodging

$$ ✕▦ **Parador San Telmo.** On the bluffs overlooking the Miño River, the granite and chestnut wood hotel is modeled after a pazo. Paintings by local artists and rural antiques decorate the lobbies. Rooms are furnished with convincing reproductions. Good views of the surrounding woods can be had from the windows of the dining room, where regional specialties include river salmon, lamprey eel, and trout. For dessert, try the almond *pececitos* (almond cookie-like pastries made by local convent nuns). ✉ 36700 Túy, ☎ 986/600309, FAX 986/602163. *22 rooms with bath. Restaurant, bar, pool. AE, DC, MC, V.*

OVIEDO AND THE PRINCIPALITY OF ASTURIAS

Luarca, Cudillero, Giýn, Villaviciosa, Cangas de Onís, Cavadonga, Ribadesella

As you cross the border into the Pricipality of Asturias, you'll notice how the same intense green countryside as in Galicia continues, belying the fact that this is a major mining region (ancient Romans conquerors coveted the iron- and gold-rich earth). Spaniards call the two regions *primos hermanos* (cousins) because the geographical resemblance is so strong. But Asturias is more mountainous, bordered on the south by the imposing snowcapped Picos de Europa mountains, the Cantabrian Sea and its enviable long and wide beaches to the north, the Deva River to the east, and the Eo River to the west. Listen closely and, as in Galicia, you might just hear the mournful notes of the *gaita*, bagpipe, souvenir of the Celts.

Luarca

34 *75 km (47 mi) east of Ribadeo, 92 km (57 mi) northeast of Oviedo, 95 km (59 mi) west of Gijón.*

The N634 road wanders through the far western reaches of Asturias into Oviedo. On the way, stop at the village of Luarca, tucked into a cove with a sparkling bay and a fishing port. It's a maze of cobbled streets, stone stairways, and whitewashed houses, with painted flowerpots decorating the edge of the harbor. The tantalizing smells wafting from the many bars and restaurants will tempt you to stay awhile and sample the freshly caught seafood.

Dining and Lodging

\$\$ ✗ **Leonés.** Medieval images are evoked by large, iron chandeliers and rural antiques that line the walls. Try peppers stuffed with shellfish or fabada, and for dessert, apple sherbet. If you don't use a credit card, you can order from a cheaper menu. ⊠ *Paseo Alfonso X el Sabio,* ☏ *98/564–0995. Reservations not accepted. AE, DC, MC, V.*

\$\$ ✗⊞ **Gayoso.** This comfortable, old and charming hotel has been run by the same family for more than 120 years. It has spacious rooms and wooden balconies with views of the Black River. Five of the hotel's 60 rooms have been upgraded to three-star status and cost almost twice as much as the others. ✗ *Paseo de Gómez 4, 33700,* ☏ *98/564–0050,* 𝔽𝔸𝕏 *98/547–0271. AE, DC, MC, V.*

En Route The coast road leads to Cudillero, a town 35 km/22 mi east of Luarca, that rises up an incline from a tiny port. On a sunny day, the emerald green of the surrounding hills, the bright blue of the sparkling water, the white of the houses, and the smell of the sea might make you want to buy a boat and settle down for a while.

Oviedo

③⑤ *92 km (57 mi) southeast of Luarca, 50 km (31 mi) southeast of Cudillero, 30 km (19 mi) south of Gijó.*

As you continue inland, you'll notice that the countryside begins to look a bit more prosperous. Wooden, thatched-roof horreos strung with golden bundles of drying corn replace the stark, granite sheds of Galicia. Drive through the rolling hills and industrialized valleys and soon you'll arrive in Oviedo, the Asturian capital.

★ Start your visit to Oviedo just outside the city on the slopes of Mt. Naranco, with its two exquisite 9th-century chapels. The church of **Santa Maria del Naranco,** with its superb views, and its plainer sister, **San Miguel de Lillo,** 300 yards uphill, are the jewels of an early architectural style called Asturian Pre-Romanesque, which was centuries ahead of its time. The carved hunting scenes and ceiling vaulting, art and architecture didn't show up in the rest of Europe for another 200 years. These masterpieces were commissioned as part of a summer palace by King Ramiro I when Oviedo was the capital of Christian Spain. They have survived more than 1,000 years, and you can still enjoy them today in the same natural setting for which they were designed. From the arched porches of Santa María, the valley of Oviedo is spread out at your feet. On a clear day the mighty, snowcapped Picos de Europa gleam in the distance. ⊠ *Carretera de los Monumentos, 2 km (1¼ mi) outside town,* ☏ *98/529–6755.* ▦ *300 ptas., free Mon.* ☉ *Apr.–Sept., Mon.–Sat. 10–1 and 3–7, Sun. 10–1; Oct.–Mar., Mon.–Sat. 10–1 and 3–5, Sun. 10–1.*

The tallest building in the skyline is the Gothic **cathedral,** built from the 14th to the 16th century around Oviedo's most cherished monument, the **Cámara Santa** (Holy Chamber). King Ramiro's predecessor, Alfonso the Chaste (792–842), erected the Cámara Santa to hide the treasures of Christian Spain during the long struggle with the Moors. The chamber was heavily damaged during the Spanish civil war but has now been rebuilt. Inside is the gold-leaf **Cross of the Angels,** encrusted with pearls and jewels. It was commissioned by Alfonso the Chaste in 808 and is inscribed with the warning: "May anyone who dares to remove me from the place I have been willingly donated be struck down by a bolt of divine lightning." On the left is the more elegant **Victory Cross,** actually a jeweled sheath crafted in AD 908 to cover the oak cross used by Pelayo in the battle of Covadonga (☞ *Covadonga, below*). Despite the warning, the crosses and other treasures were stolen from the cathedral in 1977 but were recovered relatively intact as thieves tried to spirit them out of Europe through Portugal. ⊠ *Plaza Alfonso II El Casto,* ☎ *98/522–1033.* ☑ *375 ptas.* ☉ *May–Oct., Mon.–Sat. 10–1 and 4–7; Nov.–Apr., Mon.–Sat. 10–1 and 4–6.*

NEED A BREAK?   Oviedo has an outstanding tapas bar called **Cabo Peñas** (⊠ Melquiades Alvarez 24) that shouldn't be missed. It's a huge brick place, bedecked with hams and corn and stacked to the ceiling with wine barrels. You sit on stools at high tables and order plates of salad, sausage, cheese, and seafood from high-speed waiters.

Look directly across the Plaza Alfonso from the cathedral for the 15th-century **Palacio de la Rúa;** it is the oldest palace in town and is still inhabited. The beautifully cleaned 16th-century **Antigua Universidad de Oviedo** is across from the Palacio de la Rúa.

Behind the cathedral, the **Museo Arqueológico,** housed in the splendid Monastery of San Vicente and containing fragments of pre-Romanesque buildings. ⊠ *San Vicente 3,* ☎ *98/512–5405.* ☑ *Free.* ☉ *Tues.–Sat. 10–1:30 and 4–6, Sun. 11–1.*

If you've got a taste for Asturian art, visit the **Santullano Church,** which was built in the 9th century. ⊠ *Plaza Santullano.* ☑ *Free.* ☉ *May–Oct., Tues.–Sun. 11–1 and 4:30–6; Nov.–Apr., Tues.–Sun. noon–1 and 4–5.*

If you are a fan of exquisite hotels, take a peek at the **Hotel de la Reconquista** (☞ *Dining and Lodging, below*), a former 18th-century hospice with an imposing Baroque shield on the front. The Spanish crown prince, who carries the title Prince of Asturias, presents an award for world achievement each year from the ornate hotel chapel.

NEED A BREAK?   In the center of Oviedo is the **Campo de San Francisco** park, with swans and ducks to feed, and ice-cream vendors on hot summer days.

Dining and Lodging

$$$ ✕ **Casa Fermín.** This sophisticated pink-and-granite restaurant, with ★   its plants and skylights, has an air of modernity that belies more than 50 years of experience in the kitchen. Founder Luis Gil has introduced traditional Asturian cuisine in seminars around the world. The wine cellar is extensive. Specialties include fabada, wild game in season, hake in cider, and a tortilla de angulas. ⊠ *San Francisco 8,* ☎ *98/521–6452. AE, DC, MC, V. No dinner Sun. except in May and Sept.*

$$$ ✕ **La Boca Mar.** Award-winning, nouvelle Spanish cuisine is presented ★   with flair at this unusual restaurant. Tucked into a vine-covered building in the plaza that houses Oviedo's fish market, La Boca Mar is a jumble of cozy wooden booths. Try fried prawns, filet mignon with sweet mustard, or *angulas* (spaghetti-thin baby eels). ⊠ *Plaza Trascorrales 14,* ☎ *98/520–4126. AE, DC, MC, V. Closed Sun.*

$$ ✕ **El Raitan.** Owned by the same family as La Boca Mar, and just across the plaza, El Raitan is perfect for a big appetite. The restaurant is styled like an old-fashioned kitchen, with an antique cookstove in the entrance.

At lunch, there's no menu; everyone is served the same nine dishes, all Asturian specialties: seafood soup, crab bisque, vegetable and bean stew, fabada, potatoes stuffed with meat, onions filled with tomatoes, rice pudding, crepes, and nut pastries. ⊠ *Plaza Trascorrales 6,* ☎ *98/521–4218. AE, DC, MC, V. No dinner Sun.*

$ ✕ **La Máquina.** To sample the best fabada in Asturias, head 6 km/4 mi
★ outside Oviedo on the road to Avilés. Stop when you see the farmhouse with the miniature locomotive out front. The L-shape, whitewashed dining room has been attracting customers from all over Spain for 50 years, some of whom think nothing of making a weekend trip solely for the purpose of eating here. The memorable rice pudding is topped with a crisp layer of hot caramel. ⊠ *Avda. de Santa Bárbara 59,* ☎ *98/526–0019. AE, MC. No dinner. Closed Sun.*

$$$$ ✕🖭 **Hotel de la Reconquista.** Housed in an 18th-century hospice em-
★ blazoned with a huge, stone coat of arms, the Reconquista is run by the Spanish Occidental chain. The wide lobby is circled by a balcony and has 18th-century paintings and velvet upholstery. A pianist entertains nightly. The rooms are large and modern, with comfortable beds and big armchairs. ⊠ *Gil de Jaz 16, 33004,* ☎ *98/524–1100,* ᶠᴬˣ *98/524–1166. 142 rooms with bath. Restaurant, bar, coffee shop, beauty salon, men's sauna. AE, DC, MC, V.*

$$ ✕🖭 **Hotel Principado.** If you value friendliness over flash, try the Principado, between the old town and park. The lobby resembles a comfortable living room. ⊠ *San Francisco 6, 33003,* ☎ *98/521–7792,* ᶠᴬˣ *98/521–3946. 70 rooms with bath. Restaurant, bar. AE, MC, V.*

Nightlife and the Arts

You can get a nightcap at the plant-filled **Sidrería Venicia** (⊠ Doctor Casal 13), or enjoy loud rock music at the brass-and-glass **La Loggia** across the street from the cathedral.

Plays and concerts are presented at the Municipal Theater in Oviedo; check newspapers for schedules.

Shopping

ARTS AND CRAFTS

The typical and unusual **black pottery** in these parts can be found at **Esacanda** (⊠ Jovellanos 5, no phone).

FOOD

If you like fabada, you can take home a do-it-yourself kit complete with beans and meat conserved in a vacuum pack from **Casa Veneranda** (⊠ Melquiades Alvarez 23, ☎ 98/521–2454).

JEWELRY

Throughout the city are shops where you can find beautiful jewelry made of azabache (jet).

Gijón

㊱ *30 km (19 mi) north of Oviedo, 95 km (59 mi) east of Luarca, 50 km (31 mi) east of Cudillero.*

The lively city of Gijón (pronounced he-*hone*) is part fishing port and part summer-holiday resort. It is also a university town and jam-packed with inviting cafés and noisy night spots. There's a promenade along **San Lorenzo Beach,** which extends from one end of town to the other; summer swimming is often prohibited because of pollution. Across the narrow peninsula is the harbor, where the fishing fleet comes in with the day's catch; on the hill at the tip is the old fishermen's quarter, **Cimadevilla,** the hub of the city's nightlife. The **Roman**

Baths (⊠ Campo Valdez), dating back to the time of Emperor Augustus, are closed for excavations and can no longer be visited. The **Parque Isabel la Católica** at the eastern edge of town, is home to the **Museo de la Gaita** (Bagpipe Museum), which has a collection of bagpipes from all over the world and craft workshops. The museum is in a park called the **Pueblo de Asturias,** containing interesting examples of typical Asturian country houses and horreos, in need of better care. ⊠ *Bagpipe Museum,* ☎ 98/533–2244. ⬛ *Free.* ☉ *Tues.–Sat. 10–1 and 5–8, Sun. and holidays 11–1.*

Dining and Lodging

$$ ✕ **Casa Victor.** Owner Victor Bango runs an inventive seafood restaurant that modernizes traditional Asturian dishes. The bright and noisy dining room is always packed; service is friendly. Try the hake in leek sauce, clams with asparagus, or the house variation of *caldereta* (fish stew). ⊠ *Carmen 11,* ☎ *98/535–0093. AE, DC, MC, V. No dinner Sun. Closed Thurs. and Nov.*

$$ ✕⬛ **Parador Molino Viejo.** The only parador in Asturias is one of the simplest and friendliest in the chain. The modern rooms are small, with bleached-wood floors and thick, pine shutters. Ask for a view of the city park, a favorite with joggers and children. The dining room and garden cider bar are popular with locals. Try the *tigres* (spicy stuffed mussels), pimientos *de piquillos rellenos de champiñones* (green peppers stuffed with squid, mushrooms, and rice), or the *oricios* (sea urchins), raw or served steamed with lemon juice or a spicy sauce. For dessert, try fresh figs (in season) with *cabrales* (regional blue) cheese. ⊠ *Parque de Isabel la Católica, 36980,* ☎ *98/537–0511,* FAX *98/537–0233. 40 rooms with bath. Restaurant. AE, DC, MC, V.*

En Route   Eastward from Gijón on N632 is the apple orchard country that produces the famous hard cider of Asturias. Rolling hills, cows, and white chalets make this place look more like Switzerland than Spain.

Villaviciosa

❸❼ *32 km (20 mi) east of Gijón, 45 km (28 mi) northeast of Oviedo, 125 km (78 mi) east of Luarca.*

The cider capital of Villaviciosa has a big dairy and several cider-bottling plants, as well as a picturesque old quarter. Emperor Charles V first set foot in Spain just down the road from here.

NEED A BREAK?   One of the best cider bars lining the main square in Villaviciosa is **El Furacu** (⊠ Plaza Generalísimo 26). The waiter will bring you a full bottle of cider, raise it high above his head, and hold your glass down by his knees. Then he'll pour, looking straight ahead. Of course, some of the cider splashes on the sawdust-covered floor. The locals claim their flat cider is aerated this way and tastes better.

Shopping

You'll find the beautiful stone, azabache jewelry at **Adolfo Cayado Alonso** (⊠ C. Vedriñana) or at **José Ordieres Rodríguez** (⊠ C. Arguero).

Ribadesella

❸❽ *38 km (24 mi) east of Gijón, 48 km (30 mi) northeast of Oviedo, 128 km (80 mi) east of Luarca.*

The fishing village-cum-beach resort of Ribadesella is famous for international canoe races held on the Sella River the first Saturday of August; plentiful, fresh seafood; and the **Tito Bustillo Cave.** The cave was discovered in 1968 by Señor Bustillo; the 20,000-year-old paintings in it are on par with those in Lascaux, France, and Altamira. Giant horses and deer prance about the walls. To protect the paintings, no more than 400 visitors a day are allowed inside. Guided tours are given in Spanish. ☎ 98/586–1118 or 98/586–1120. 🖭 *400 ptas., free Tues.* ☉ *Daily 10–1 and 3:30–5:15 except Sun. July and Aug.*

OFF THE BEATEN PATH	**LLANES** – Llanes is a pretty town on the Costa Verde (Green Coast), 40 km/25 mi east of Ribadesella on the way to Santander. Stretch your legs and go for an invigorating, cliffside stroll along the seaside.

Dining

$ ✕ **El Repollu.** This small, homey grill specializes in fish dishes. Try the fresh-grilled turbot and the house Cabrales cheese, or sugar-sweet grilled *gambas* (shrimp). ⊠ *Santa Marina 2,* ☎ *98/586–0734. Reservations not accepted. AE, DC, MC, V. Closed Oct.*

Cangas de Onís

㊳ *25 km (16 mi) south of Ribadesella, 70 km (43 mi) east of Oviedo.*

Cangas de Onís lies in the narrow valley carved by the Sella River. This town was the first capital of Christian Spain and has the feel of a bracing, mountain village. The hump-backed, ivy-covered **Roman bridge** that spans the Sella River Gorge is a favorite spot for picture taking.

En Route   To the east of Cangas de Onís, on the C6312 road, is the turnoff for the imposing Peña Santa peak (8,488 feet). At the end of the winding road is the famous shrine of Covadonga.

Covadonga

㊵ *84 km (52 mi) from Oviedo.*

★ The **shrine** of Covadonga is considered the birthplace of Spain. Here, in AD 718, a handful of sturdy Asturian Christians, led by Don Pelayo, took refuge in the Cave of St. Mary, about halfway up a cliff, where they prayed to the Virgin Mary to give them strength to turn back the Moors. Pelayo and his followers resisted the superior Moorish forces and set up a Christian kingdom that eventually led to the Reconquest. Covadonga itself has a basilica in a magnificent, mountain setting and a shrine in the legendary cave, which includes an 18th-century statue of the Virgin and Don Pelayo's grave. The museum displays the treasures donated to the Virgin of the Cave, including a crown studded with more than 1,000 diamonds. ☎ 98/584–6077 or 98/524–1412. 🖭 *Suggested admission 150 ptas.* ☉ *Mar.–June, daily 11–2 and 4–6; July–Sept., daily 10:30–2 and 4–7:30; Oct., daily 11:30–2 and 4–6; Nov.–Mar., weekends 11:30–2 and 4–6.*

Covadonga is connected to the **Sierra de Covadonga National Park** by a narrow lane. Don't miss the two alpine lakes at the top of the road, Lake Enol and Lake Ercina. Wild horses can be seen grazing nearby. Pope John Paul II was brought here to picnic during his tour of Galicia and Asturias in 1989. Head uphill for a spectacular view all the way to the ocean from the **Mirador de la Reina.**

Ruta de Cares

㊶ *Between Cangas de Onís and Panes.*

Wind back toward Cangas de Onís, but when you reach C6312, turn east toward Panes. This 55-km/34-mi drive between Cangas de Onís and Panes, called the Ruta de Cares (Cares Route), is the most beautiful in Asturias. The road passes through the towns of Benia and Carreña, with crested houses, to arrive in **Arenas de Cabrales.** This is the area where the popular Cabrales blue cheese is made. From here, a branch of the road heads into the mountains, and you can follow the Cares River toward the toothlike **Naranjo de Bulnes** (8,264 feet). Hiking trails begin here for treks to the villages of Carmarmeña and Bulnes and the spectacular Cares Gorge. From the town of Arenas, follow the road east to Panes, and from there you can head for the coast.

Dining and Lodging

$$ ✕🏠 **La Pousada de Babel.** This exquisite family-run inn provides plenty of personal attention and roaring fires in the public rooms. One of the bedrooms is in a converted granary. ✉ *La Pereda, 33509,* ☎ *98/540–2525. 8 rooms with bath. Restaurant, bar, horseback riding, bicycles, library. MC, V.*

$$ ✕🏠 **La Tiendona.** This restored roadhouse is strategically located halfway between the mountains of Cangas de Onís and the beaches of Ribadesella. Rooms have country-style furnishings. The dining room emphasizes regional specialties such as smoked salmon, fabada, and cider. ✉ *Ctra. Nac. Arriondas-Ribadesella,* ☎ *98/584–0474,* FAX *98/ 584–1316. 18 rooms. Restaurant, bar. AE, V.*

LEÓN, GALICIA, AND ASTURIAS A TO Z

Arriving and Departing

By Bus

ALSA runs daily buses to Galicia and Asturias from Madrid and has weekly service from Paris, Brussels, Zurich, Nîmes, Toulouse, and Lyon. Several other companies operate between the region and major Spanish cities. Contact the bus stations for information in **León** (✉ Cardenal Lorenzana s/n, ☎ 987/211000), **Oviedo** (✉ Plaza Primo de Rivera 1, ☎ 98/528–1200), and **Santiago** (✉ San Cayetano, ☎ 981/ 587700).

By Car

The **NVI,** also called the La Coruña Highway, links Spain's northwestern region with Madrid. Although it is a four-lane expressway for the first 90 km/56 mi out of the capital, the rest of the road is two or three lanes. Be warned that it is heavily traveled by slow-moving trucks. Distance between Madrid and La Coruña is 609 km/378 mi, between Madrid and Leó (via the NVI highway to Benavente, where you pick up the N630) is 333 km/207 mi. Good highways connect Santiago and La Coruña, Ferrol and Vigo, Caraballo and La Coruña, and Vigo and Túy (on the border with Portugal).

Although distances are great in Galicia and Asturias, travel by car is really the best way to appreciate the countryside.

By Plane

Galicia is served by an international airport 12 km/7 mi east of **Santiago de Compostela** at Labacolla (☎ 981/597400), with daily flights on Iberia to London, Paris, Zurich, Geneva, and Frankfurt. Regular domestic flights connect Santiago with the rest of Spain, including daily service to Madrid and Barcelona. The region's other two domestic airports are in **La Coruña** (☎ 981/232240) and in Asturias, near **San Esteban de Pravia,** 47 km/29 mi north of Oviedo (☎ 98/554–7733).

Iberia has ticket offices in **Gijón** (✉ Alfredo Truán 8, ☎ 98/535–1846), **La Coruña** (✉ Plaza de Galicia 6, ☎ 981/228730), **Oviedo** (✉ Uria

21, ☎ 98/524–0250), and **Santiago de Compostela** (✉ Calvo Sotelo 25, ☎ 981/572028).

Airport buses leave from in front of the Iberia office and the bus station (☞ *above*) in Santiago. The Asturias airport can be reached by buses that leave from the Iberia office in Gijón and the Iberia terminal in Oviedo (✉ Marqués de Pidal 20).

By Train
RENFE runs several trains a day from Madrid to León (4 hours), Oviedo (7 hours), and Gijón (8 hours), while a separate RENFE line serves Galicia (11 hours to Santiago). Daytime first-class and second-class cars are available, as is an overnight train with sleeping compartments. RENFE ticket windows are at the stations in **Gijón** (☎ 98/517–0202), **La Coruña** (☎ 981/150202), **León** (☎ 987/270202), **Oviedo** (☎ 98/525–0202), and **Santiago de Compostela** (☎ 981/520202).

Getting Around

By Bus
For information on the numerous local bus routes, contact the tourist offices or bus stations (☞ Arriving and Departing by Bus, *above*).

By Car
A four-lane, divided highway links León with Oviedo and Gijón—the fastest way to cross the Cantabrian Mountains. A north-south Galician expressway was completed in 1992, shortening the travel time between La Coruña, Santiago, Pontevedra, and Vigo. Elsewhere roads wind along the coast or climb over hills, always slow-going and seldom direct. Allow more time than you think it will take.

By Train
Local trains connect all the small towns with the major cities of Galicia and Asturias, but be prepared for dozens of stops.

Narrow-gauge **FEVE trains** clatter across northern Spain, connecting Galicia and Asturias with Santander, Bilbao, and Irún, on the French border. Tickets can be purchased at the train stations or the main office in Oviedo (✉ Avda. Santander s/n, ☎ 98/529–0104).

Contacts and Resources

Car Rentals
Hertz has a main reservation office at the airport in Madrid (☎ 91/305–8457). Other offices include: León (✉ C. Santiro 20, ☎ 987/231999); Santiago (✉ airport, ☎ 981/598893); La Coruña (✉ Ronda de Nelle s/n, ☎ 981/245424); and Oviedo (✉ C. Ventura Rodríguez 4, ☎ 985/270824).

Budget has a main reservation office in Madrid at the Hotel Diana (✉ 27 Bajo, Centro Comercial, ☎ 91/329–5048. Other offices: No office in León; La Coruña (✉ C. Fleming 16-Bajo, ☎ 981/151112); and Oviedo (✉ C. Arquitecto Regueira 5, ☎ 985/507751).

Avis has an office in Madrid at the airport (☎ 91/305–8532). Other offices: León (✉ Paseo de la Condesa s/n, ☎ 987/270075); Santiago (✉ airport, ☎ 981/596101); La Coruña (✉ Plaza de Vigo 5, ☎ 981/121201); and Oviedo (✉ airport, ☎ 985/562111).

Golf
Asturias has two good golf courses, the **Club de Golf de Castiello** in Gijón (☎ 98/536–6313) and **La Barganiza** in Siero (☎ 98/522–4965). León's **Club de Golf León** (✉ San Miguel del Camino, ☎ 987/303400) is 15 km/9 mi from the city. Galician courses include **Monte la Zap-**

ateira (✉ C. Zapateira s/n, 15310 La Coruña, ☎ 981/285200), 11 km/7 mi from the city; **Domaio** (✉ Domaio, Pontevedra, ☎ 986/330386); **La Toja** (✉ Isla La Toja, Pontevedra, ☎ 986/730818); and **Padrón** (✉ Padrón, La Coruña, ☎ 981/598891). Santiago's links are near the airport, **Campo de Golf del Aero Club Labacolla** (☎ 981/888406). Call the club a day in advance to reserve equipment.

Guided Tours

The **Transcantábrico narrow-gauge train tour** offered by FEVE is an eight-day, 1,000-km/600-mi journey through Basque country, Galicia, and Asturias, with English-speaking guides and a private bus that takes the group from train stations to regional artistic and natural attractions. Passengers sleep on the train and dine on local specialties. Trains run from June through September; the cost is approximately $1,575 per person, all-inclusive. Contact **Transcántabrico** (✉ General Rodrigo 6, 28003 Madrid, ☎ 91/553–7656), **E.C. Tours** (✉ 10153½ Riverside Dr., Toluca Lake, CA 91602, ☎ 213/874–3848 or 800/388–0877), **Conference Travel Int'l.** (✉ 157 Glen Head Rd., Glen Head, NY 11545, ☎ 516/671–5298 or 800/527–4852), or **Marsans** (✉ 66 Whitmore St., London W1H 9LG, ☎ 0171/224–0504).

Trastur, in Oviedo, (✉ Muñalen, 33873 Tineo, ☎ 98/580–6036) offers wilderness trips on horseback through the remote valleys of western Asturias. The five- to 10-day trips are designed for beginners and experienced cowboys; mountain cabins provide shelter along the trail. Tours begin and end in Oviedo and cost approximately $100 a day, all-inclusive. In Galicia, try **Galiciaventura** (✉ C. Manuel Pereira 10-Bajo, 32003 Orense, ☎ 986/235374). The **Centro Hípico de Turismo Ecuestre y de Aventuras "Granjo O Castelo"** in Galicia (✉ Rúa Urzaiz 91-5A, 36201 Vigo, ☎ 986/425937) conducts horseback-riding excursions along the pilgrimage routes to Santiago from Pedrafita do Cebreiro and from Braga (in Portugal). **Reatur** (✉ Rúa Castelao 11-1, 3266 Allariz, Orense, ☎ 988/442066) offers guided historical and cultural walks, some of which include hiking, horseback riding, mountain biking, and canoeing in the surrounding areas.

In Santiago, walking tours with multilingual guides are organized by the tourist office (✉ Rúa do Vilar 43, ☎ 981/584081) during peak travel periods. The three-hour tour covers all the major monuments and costs approximately $12.

Hiking and Climbing

The Picos de Europa and the Covadonga National Park are excellent hiking areas. One of the most popular walks is the **Cares Gorge.** The tourist offices in Oviedo and Cangas de Onís can help you organize your trek, but for more technical climbing, contact **Servicio de Guías de Montaña** (✉ Cangas de Onís, ☎ 98/584–8916). **Mazaneda Estación de Montaña** in Orense (✉ 31875 Pobra de Trives, ☎ 988/308767) is a full-service resort with mountaineering, biking, and skiing programs. **Nortrak** in La Coruña (✉ Rúa Inés de Castro 7–B, 15005, ☎ 981/151674) has activities ranging from mountain excursions and trekking to paragliding and bungee jumping.

Skiing

The three small ski areas in this region cater mostly to families and local residents. The largest is **San Isidro** (☎ 987/731115 or 987/721118), in the Cantabrian Mountains, with one chairlift and 12 slopes. Just east of there is **Valgrande Pajares** (☎ 98/549–6123), with two chairlifts and eight slopes. West of Orense, in Galicia, **Manzaneda** (☎ 988/310875) has one chairlift and seven slopes. Valgrande Pajares and Manzaneda also have cross-country skiing.

Visitor Information

Tourist offices are usually open 9–2 or 3 and 5–7. For information about the city and province of **León,** contact the **Oficina de Turismo de León** (✉ Plaza de Regla 3, 24003 León, ☎ 987/237082); for information about **Galicia** and the city of Santiago de Compostela, contact the **Oficina de Turismo** (✉ Rúa do Vilar 43, 15705 Santiago de Compostela, ☎ 981/584081), and about the principality of **Asturias,** contact the **Oficina de Turismo** (✉ Plaza de la Catedral 6, 33007 Oviedo, ☎ 98/521–3385).

Other tourist offices in towns covered in this chapter are **Astorga** (✉ Plaza de España, ☎ 987/615205), **Cangas de Onís** (✉ Emilio Laria 2, ☎ 98/584–8005), **El Grove** (✉ Plaza Corgo, ☎ 986/730975), **Gijón** (✉ Marqués de San Esteban 1, ☎ 98/534–6046), **La Coruña** (✉ Dársena de la Marina, ☎ 981/221822), **Ponferrada** (✉ next to castle, ☎ 987/424236), **Pontevedra** (✉ General Mola 2, ☎ 986/850814), **Ribadeo** (✉ Plaza de España, ☎ 982/110689), **Ribadesella** (✉ Carretera Piconera, ☎ 98/586–0038), **Túy** (✉ Puente Tripes, ☎ 986/601785), and **Vigo** (✉ Jardines de las Avenidas, de las Avenidas, ☎ 986/430577).

5 Burgos, Santander, and the Basque Country

Bilbao, Guernica, and Pamplona

Burgos, home of legendary hero El Cid, is a somber city in a parched landscape of stone villages; Santander is a very Spanish beach resort flanked by the Cantabrian cordillera; while the Basque country, with its own language, moist green hills, and rugged coast, has a large population devoted to gastronomy, sports, and rural culture and a small population that wants independence from Spain.

By George
Semler

THIS CHAPTER EXPLORES three very different destinations in northern Spain. Burgos, at the edge of the central meseta, is one of the most Castilian cities; Santander (Cantabria), once the seaport for Old Castile on the Bay of Biscay, is a beach resort and mountainous zone wedged between the Basques to the east and the Asturians to the west; and the Basque country (Euskadi in its own mysterious, non-Indo-European language), with its moist, green hills and rugged coastline, is a distinct and semi-autonomous, national and cultural entity within the Spanish state.

Burgos was the 11th-century capital of Castile and the native city of El Cid, or "lord conqueror," Spain's legendary hero of the Christian reconquest of the Iberian Peninsula from Moorish domination. Franco's wartime headquarters were established at Burgos during the 1936–39 Spanish Civil War, possibly as much for symbolic as for strategic reasons. Even today the army and the clergy seem to set the tone in this somber city, which sprawls in the shadow of one of Europe's finest Gothic cathedrals.

Santander and the Cantabrian region are traditionally a Castilian or Spanish stronghold with sandy beaches, the peaks of the Cantabrian mountain chain, tiny highland towns, and colorful fishing villages.

The Basque country is more a country within a country, or a nation within a state (the semantics are much debated, even today) with a language of its own: Euskera. In contrast to the traditionally individualistic and passionate Latin peoples who have been their neighbors, the Basques have often been regarded as more collective-minded and practical. They are also known to love competition—it has been said that Basques will bet on anything that has numbers on it and moves. Such traditional rural sports as chopping mammoth tree trunks, lifting boulders, and scything grass reflect the Basques' traditional attachment to the land and farm life as well as an ingrained admiration for feats of strength and endurance. Even poetry and gastronomy become contests in Euskadi, as *bertsolaris* (amateur poets) improvise duels of (often very witty) verse, and men-only *sociedades gastronómicas* compete in cooking contests to see who can make the best *marmitako* (tuna stew).

The much-reported Basque independence movement is made up of a small but radical sector of the political spectrum. The underground organization known as ETA, or Euskadi Ta Askatasuna (Basque Homeland and Liberty), has claimed more than 700 victims in more than 25 years of terrorist activity. While this continuing problem is extremely unlikely to affect or endanger the visitor, it will be inescapably apparent in the political graffiti—of an unusually colorful and photogenic variety—that adorn nearly every free inch of wall space from San Sebastián to Bilbao to Pamplona.

The Basque country also has long-time connections with both Britain and the United States. Bilbao and its province of Vizcaya, in particular, were the source of most of the iron used by the English during the Industrial Revolution. The region as a whole, poor before industry made it a center of productivity on the peninsula, has long sent out wave upon wave of immigrants to the New World. Perhaps as a result, the Basques are unusually friendly to both Americans and the British—often friendlier, in fact, than they are to Spaniards from Madrid and points south, who are still widely seen as unwelcome interlopers.

Pleasures and Pastimes

Beaches

In Santander there are three excellent sandy beaches: Magdalena, nearest to town; El Sardinero, the most elegant and well-equipped; and Matalenas, near the camping site of Bellavista. In San Sebastián, the La Concha and Ondarreta beaches, directly in front of the city, are beautiful and clean but packed wall to wall for the entire summer holiday season. The beach on the northern side of the Urumea River, known as the Playa de Gros, is less crowded; surfers gather for the big breakers. The wide expanse of beach at Zarauz, 22 km/14 mi west of San Sebastián, is another good choice, as are the smaller beaches at Guetaria and Zumaya. The beach at Lequeitio is particularly beautiful.

Dining

If your taste is for traditional Spain and the roasts and hearty soups of Castilla, concentrate on the rustic taverns and *mesones,* or inns, of Burgos at the edge of the famous Spanish plain, the central meseta. Roast lamb and suckling pig are local specialties. Santander offers mountain cooking such as roast kid and lamb or *cocidos* (bean stews) in the highlands and fresh seafood along the coast. Try the *soropotun,* Santander's bonito, potato and vegetable stew. Navarra is famous for beef, lamb and vegetable dishes such as the *menestra de habas* (broad beans cooked with garlic, mint, artichoke hearts, white wine, and thyme). The Basque cuisine in and around San Sebastián is generally considered the best in Spain, combining the fresh fish of the Atlantic with a love of sauces that is rare south of the Pyrenees—a result, no doubt, of the region's proximity to France. In recent years, *nueva cocina vasca* (new Basque cooking) has introduced exciting new elements. In San Sebastián it's nearly impossible to have anything other than a superlative gastronomical experience no matter where you tuck in and pull up to a table. *Don't* miss the chance for a *besugo al horno* (roast sea bream) or a *txuleta de buey* (beef steak). Wines are not a strong point along the northern coast although the local *txakolí,* a young, white wine made from tart grapes, is a refreshing accompaniment to both seafood and meats. The Rioja wine-growing region is at the southern edge of the Basque country and provides all the autochthonous wine power Basque cuisine needs, while Navarra produces some fine vintages, especially rosés and reds (and in such quantity that churches in the villages of Allo, Peralta, and other towns as well were actually constructed with a mortar mixed with wine instead of water).

Food is not cheap in Basque country. But for your money, you'll taste some of the most superb creations in Europe, in an ambience that ranges from the traditional hewn beams and stone walls of old farmhouses and Castilian mesones to international of settings.

Casual dress is acceptable in most restaurants of the region. However, some of the more expensive ones will expect more formal wear: A jacket and tie, though never required, will always suffice for men.

CATEGORY	MAJOR CITIES*	OTHER AREAS*
$$$$	over 8,000 ptas.	over 6,000 ptas.
$$$	5,000–8,000 ptas.	4,000–6,000 ptas.
$$	2,500–5,000 ptas.	2,000–4,000 ptas.
$	under 2,500 ptas.	under 2,000 ptas.

per person for a three-course meal, excluding drinks, service, and tax

Fiestas

Pamplona is home to one of Spain's most famous celebrations, the festival of San Fermín, made famous by Ernest Hemingway in *The Sun Also Rises*. The festival, which takes place July 6-14, triples the population of this town; if you plan to attend, reserve a room months in advance. The coastal town of Lequeitio is famous for its highly unusual September 1–18 fiestas, when men dangle for as long as they can from the necks of dead geese!

Hiking and Walking

This three-in-one chapter offers more varieties of hiking and exploring on foot than you can cover in a lifetime, much less a two-week visit. From the Cordillera Cantábrica to the Pyrenees or along the Basque coast there are well-marked footpaths between towns and over mountains from one fishing village to another with scenery, exercise and appetites head and shoulders above those available via motor travel. Try the walks around Zumaya, or the walk over Jaizkibel between San Sebastián and the French border. Check with local tourist offices for recommendations on routes of the length and intensity you desire.

Lodging

The largely industrial and well-to-do north is a relatively expensive region of Spain, and this is nowhere more apparent than in lodging prices. San Sebastián is particularly pricey, especially in the summer, and Pamplona rates double or triple during the San Fermín fiesta in July. Staying in Basque farmhouses included in the *Agroturismo* network of lodging establishments is economical, authentic, and beautiful. However, the quality of hotels, service, and connected restaurants is quite high. Reserve ahead in Bilbao, which fills up year-round with business conventions, and nearly everywhere during the summer.

CATEGORY	MAJOR CITIES*	OTHER AREAS*
$$$$	over 20,000 ptas.	over 15,000 ptas.
$$$	12,000–20,000 ptas.	9,000–15,000 ptas.
$$	7,500–12,000 ptas.	6,000–9,000 ptas.
$	under 7,500 ptas.	under 6,000 ptas.

per standard double room, excluding breakfast and tax.

Monasteries

For a brief stay among the present-day masters of the Gregorian chant, the double platinum-selling monks who recorded *Chant* and *Chant Noel,* stop in the town of Santo Domingo de Silos, 58 km/36 mi southeast of Burgos. Single men can stay in the monastery for a maximum of 10 days. Guests are expected to be at breakfast, lunch, and dinner but are otherwise left to their own devices. If the monastery is full, as it often is these days, try to stay for a vespers service. Closer to Burgos (10 km/6 mi) is the Monastery of San Pedro de Cardeña, also offering lodging, but for couples and even families as well, possibly as a result of the monastery's importance in the story of El Cid, the medieval Spanish hero, who left his wife and children there when sent into exile.

Outdoor Activities and Sports

Basques tend to be most passionate about sport and food. From Jai-Alai to horse racing or soccer, this part of Spain has much to offer in spectator or participant sporting activities.

PELOTA AND OTHER BASQUE SPORTS

Pelota is the Basque national sport, and most towns of any size have a local *frontón* (arena). Games normally start at 4 or 4:30. Other traditional Basque sports (*herrikirolak*) include *sokatiri* (tug-of-war), *aizkolaris* (contests by woodchoppers), ram-butting, and scything competitions. But the most bizarre, and interesting, of the local competitions is the *harrijasotazailes* (the raising of huge rocks by stone-lifters). Events are posted locally, or ask at the tourist office.

SOCCER

Although Athletic de Bilbao is the area's soccer giant, with San Sebastián's Real Sociedad just behind, there are also first-division teams in Santander, Pamplona, and—-more often than not—Burgos. Inquire at tourist offices or hotels for information on matches and tickets.

Exploring Burgos, Santander, and the Basque Country

The radical geographical and cultural contrasts included in this chapter are those of Spain itself: the meseta, the Pyrenees, the Cantabrian Cordillera, and the Bay of Biscay; Castilians, Cantabrians, and Basques. And then there is landlocked Navarra, part Basque and part Navarrese. Each is described and explored in the sections that follow.

Great Itineraries

This area on the map may not seem like much compared to the Iberian Peninsula as a whole, but the best roads to explore are also the slowest, and any one of the four main entities—Burgos, Santander, the Basque Country, Navarra—has enough hills, streams, and villages (not to mention the cities of Burgos, Vitoria, Bilbao, San Sebastián and Pamplona) to spend a lifetime discovering.

Ten days to two weeks would be a fair time frame for seeing all of this area, although all of that time could very happily be spent in the tiniest of the villages or the smallest fishing port. In five days you could cover the high points and come away with an overall impression and some objectives for future visits. Three days is barely more than a drive-through, but it's time to at least lay eyes on it all.

Numbers in the text below correspond to numbers in the margin and on the maps.

IF YOU HAVE 3 DAYS

If three days is all you can manage, make a quick tour of the **Burgos** ①–⑦ with its splendid cathedral and drive through the Picos de Europa to ⊞ **Santander** ⑧ on day one. You might even manage to stop in Santillana del Mar and see the cave paintings at **Altamira** ⑨, or at least the museum and the video since a visit to the actual caves requires a permit requested months in advance. Follow the Basque coast to ⊞ **San Sebastián** ㉑ on the second day, stopping for lunch in the fishing port of **Guetaria** ⑳. Drive through **Pamplona** ㉔ and Navarra on the third day, approaching either from the north if you are continuing across Spain, or from the west (and then north) if you are headed for France.

IF YOU HAVE 5 DAYS

If you have five days, start in **Burgos** ①–⑦ and visit the cathedral before driving up into the mountains for lunch on your way down to the coast. Stop at **Altamira** ⑨ for a look at the caves, the splendid national parador, and the tiny village houses. In ⊞ **Santander** ⑧, get the feel of beach life along the Playa de la Magdalena and El Sardinero and browse around the Plaza Porticada. On the second day, explore ⊞ **Laredo** ⑩ and **Castro-Urdiales** ⑪, both port towns with lovely old quarters. **Bilbao** ⑫ could be bypassed as the giant industrial behemoth that it is, but it offers exquisite, sybaritic consolation for its many discomforts and inconveniences. Art buffs should not miss the new

Guggenheim Museum, designed by American Frank Gehry, which is scheduled to open in 1997. The third day should be devoted to exploring the Basque Coast from Bilbao to San Sebastián. **Bermeo** ⑮, **Elanchove** ⑯, **Lequeitio** ⑰, **Ondárroa** ⑱, **Guetaria** ⑳, Zarauz: each of these fishing ports outdoes the other in hustle, bustle, color, and cuisine. Day four is for ⊞ **San Sebastián** ㉑ and its delicious (though, in summer, overpopulous) La Concha beach. **Pasajes** ㉒ (to be approached by launch from Pasajes de San Pedro on the San Sebastian side of the straits) is a lovely village for lunch. **Fuenterrabía** ㉓, on the Bidasoa river border with France, is another indispensable visit. The fifth day could be spent at ⊞ **Pamplona** ㉔ and the province of Navarra, taking care not to miss the upland towns of the Baztán valley (☞ Chapter 6).

IF YOU HAVE 10 DAYS

If you have 10 days, spend more time in ⊞ **Burgos** ①–⑦, see the cathedral, and get the feel of this city and its clerical and military austerity. Wander around the Espolón and visit the Casa del Cordón and the Cartuja de Miraflores. See the monastery at ⊞ **Santo Domingo de Silos** or the closer-by ⊞ **San Pedro de Cardeña.** Spend the night at one of these monasteries, if you can, or start toward **Santander** ⑧. Spend a day exploring the mountains between Burgos and Santander. Have a look at the highland town of Reinosa and drive down N611 along the river Saja past semi-abandoned villages such as Cabuerniga Mayor. Plan to spend the night near the **Altamira Caves** ⑨ at ⊞ **Santillana del Mar** in the excellent parador. On the third day, drive to **Santander** ⑧, get settled and explore the beaches and the Plaza Porticada. See what's going on at the Universidad Internacional Menéndez y Pelayo if it's summertime. The next day will allow time to investigate the towns of **Laredo** ⑩ and **Castro-Urdiales** ⑪, walking their old quarters and trying one of their excellent taverns, on the way to ⊞ **Bilbao** ⑫. Settle in for a night in Bilbao if you feel ready for an urban experience. Visit the new Guggenheim Museum (if it has, in fact, opened) on the morning of your fifth day, then head up the Basque coast for a night in some fishing village between **Bermeo** ⑮ and Zarauz. Take a walk around Zumaya. Walk up the Urola river estuary to the quayside Bedua restaurant for a *tortilla de merluza* (codfish omelet), or have lunch in **Guetaria** ⑳ after walking over from Zumaya through Askizu. Day six can be dedicated to ⊞ **San Sebastián** ㉑, exploring the three beaches and the Parte Vieja. The seventh day is a good chance to visit **Pasajes** ㉒ (Donibane in Basque). Spend that night in a *caserío* such as the Artzu that overlooks the Atlantic and the town of **Fuenterrabía** ㉓. The eighth day is a chance to see the charming town of Fuenterrabía. Take the launch to Hendaye in France. Spend the night at the El Emperador parador, before heading up the Bidasoa river into the foothills of the Pyrenees. Explore the Baztán valley (☞ Chapter 6) on the ninth day, sleeping in one of the little towns like ⊞ Elizondo and save the 10th day for **Pamplona** ㉔. If it's during Pamplona's famous sanfermines, try a smaller and saner version of this legendary fiesta at the village of Lesaka.

When to Tour Burgos, Santander, and the Basque Country

June or September or even May or October would be the best months to combine good weather and avoid the tourist crush of summer, especially in August. The Basque Country is characteristically rainy, and in winter, more so. Summer temperatures are fairly temperate, which is why Sebastián became the favored summer watering hole for the Madrid aristocracy. The longer hours of daylight during the month of June, combined with the absence of tourists and the sweet temperatures would make this the best month to explore this part of Spain.

BURGOS, SANTANDER, LAREDO, AND CASTRO-URDIALES

After a day in Burgos, or lunch and a look at the cathedral, either take the relatively poor and slow N623 through the Cantabrian Mountains to Santander (156 km/97 mi), or skip Cantabria and head straight for Bilbao (159 km/99 mi) on the A1 and A68 toll roads.

Numbers in the margin correspond to points of interest on the Basque Country and Burgos maps.

Burgos

❶ *240 km (150 mi) north of Madrid.*

Set on the banks of the Arlanzón River, Burgos is a small city that boasts some of the most outstanding Spanish architecture of the Middle Ages. Reached by a relatively good road from Madrid, the city first presents the twin spires of its magnificent cathedral, which rises headily above the main bridge and gate into the old city center. The second glory of Burgos lies in its heritage as the city of El Cid, the part-historical, part-mythical hero of the Christian Reconquest of Spain.

Burgos has been known for centuries as a center of militarism and religion, and even today you will see more nuns and military officers on the streets than almost anywhere else in Spain. The city was born as a military camp in 884, a fortress built on the orders of the Christian king Alfonso III, who was having a hard time defending the upper reaches of Old Castile from the constant forays of the Arabs. It quickly became a key in the defense of Christian Spain. The ruins of the castle erected then still overlook Burgos.

Burgos's religious identity as an early outpost of Christianity was consolidated with the founding of the Royal Convent of Las Huelgas in 1187. The city also became an important station on the Way of St. James, a place where religious pilgrims stopped for rest and sustenance throughout the Middle Ages.

★ ❷ Start at the **cathedral,** the city's high point, which contains such a wealth of art and other treasures that jealous Burgos residents actually lynched their civil governor on the morning of January 25, 1869, for trying to make an inventory. The proud Burgalese apparently feared the poor man was preparing to remove the treasures.

Most of the outside of the cathedral is sculpted in flamboyant Gothic style. The cornerstone of the building was laid in 1221, and by the middle of the 14th century, the cathedral's twin, 84-meter/275-foot towers were completed; the final chapel was not finished until 1731. The interior boasts 13 chapels, the most elaborate of which is the hexagonal Condestable Chapel. You will also find the **tomb of El Cid** (1026–99) and his wife, Ximena, under the transept. El Cid, whose real name was Rodrigo Díaz de Vivar, was a mercenary warrior whose victories over the Moors made him famous; the medieval *Song of My Cid* transformed him into a Spanish national hero.

At the other end of the cathedral, high above the West Door, is the **Papamoscas (Flycatcher) clock,** so named for the sculptured bird that opens its mouth as the mechanism marks every hour. Some of the finest wrought-iron work in central Spain is to be seen in the grilles, and the choir features 103 delicately carved walnut stalls, no two alike. The 13th-century stained-glass windows that once shed a beautiful, filtered light in the cathedral were destroyed in 1813—yet another Spanish treasure destroyed by Napoleon's retreating troops. ⊠ *Plaza del Rey San Fernando,* ☎ *947/204712.* ▣ *Cathedral museum and cloister 400 ptas.; in groups, 250 ptas.* ☉ *Daily 9:30–1 and 4–7.*

❸ Across the Plaza del Rey San Fernando from the cathedral is the city's main gate, the **Arco de Santa María.** Walk through it toward the river and look up above the arch—the 16th-century statues are of the first Castilian judges, El Cid, Spain's patron saint James, and King Charles I of Spain.

❹ The Arco de Santa María gate fronts the city's loveliest promenade, the **Espolón.** The walkway follows the riverbank and is shaded with pollarded sycamores.

NEED A
BREAK? Take in the city's most pleasant aspects at any of the cool outdoor *terrazas* (terraces) that line the Espolón.

❺ The **Casa del Cordón,** a 15th-century palace on the Plaza de Calvo Sotelo, is where the Catholic Monarchs received Columbus after his second voyage to the New World. Today, it is a bank building and can only be viewed from the outside.

❻ Three km/1¾ mi east of town, at the end of a poplar- and elm-lined drive, is the **Cartuja de Miraflores,** which has an unusual link to the Americas. Founded in 1441, this florid, Gothic charterhouse has an Isabelline church boasting an altarpiece by Gil de Siloe, which is said to be gilded with the first gold brought back from the New World. To get there, follow signs from the city's main gate. ▣ *Free.* ☉ *Church open for mass Mon.–Sat. at 9 AM, Sun. and holidays 7:30 and 10:15 AM; main building open Mon.–Sat. 10:15–3 and 4–6, Sun. and holidays 11:20–12:30, 1–3, and 4–6.*

❼ On the western edge of town—a long walk if you're not driving—is the **Monasterio de Las Huelgas Reales,** still run by nuns who live hidden away behind a double iron grille. Founded in 1187 by King Alfonso VIII and his wife, Eleanor, daughter of Henry II of England, this convent for noble ladies was unprecedented in the 12th century for the powers it gave to the women running it. The present building was originally a summer palace for the kings of Castile and in 1988 underwent major renovations in connection with its 800th anniversary. The convent was conceived in Romanesque style and housed a royal mausoleum; the tombs of its founders are still there. All but one of the royal coffins kept at Las Huelgas were desecrated by Napoleon's soldiers, but this last contained clothes that form the basis of the medieval textile museum housed in part of the convent complex. Don't miss the Chapel of St. James, where Castilian noblemen came to be knighted by the articulated statue of Spain's patron saint; the figure lowered its sword arm, dubbing the candidates knights with a tap on the shoulder. ⊠ *1.6 km/1 mi southwest of town, along the Paseo de la Isla and left across the Malatos Bridge,* ☎ *947/201630.* ▣ *450 ptas.; in groups, 300 ptas.; free Wed.* ☉ *Tues.–Sat. 11–1:15 and 4–5:15, Sun. 11–1:15.*

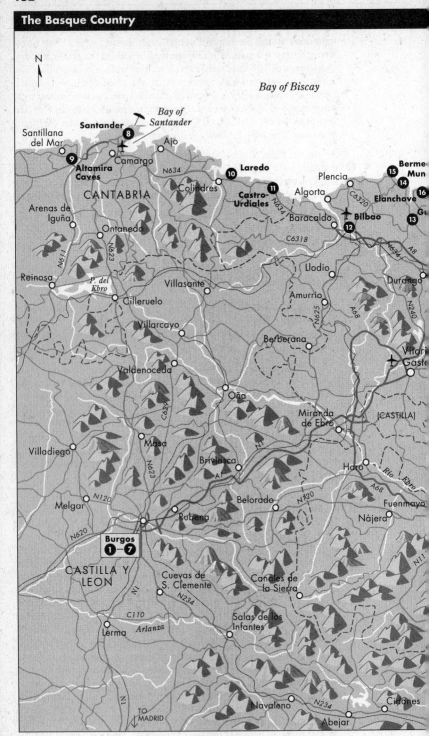

N

Bay of Biscay

Bay of Santander

Santander ⑧

Ajo

Santillana del Mar

Altamira Caves ⑨

Camargo

Laredo ⑩

N634

Colindres

Berme Mun ⑮

⑭

Plencia

Algorta

CANTABRIA

Castro-Urdiales ⑪

Baracaldo

Bilbao ⑫

Elanchove

⑯

C6320

Gu ⑬

Arenas de Iguña

Ontaneda

C6318

N634

A8

N634

Reinosa

N611

N623

P. del Ebro

Villasante

Amurrio

N625

Llodio

Durango

N240

Cilleruelo

Villarcayo

Berberana

A68

Vitori Gaste

Valdenoceda

C629

Oña

Miranda de Ebro

[CASTILLA]

Villadiego

Masa

N623

Briviesca

A1

N1

Haro

Rio Ebro

A68

Fuenmayo

Melgar

N120

Rubena

Belorado

N120

Nájera

N620

Burgos ①—⑦

N1

CASTILLA Y LEON

N1

Cuevas de S. Clemente

N234

Canales de la Sierra

N11

C110

Arlanza

Lerma

Salas de los Infantes

TO MADRID

Navaleno

N234

Cidones

Abejar

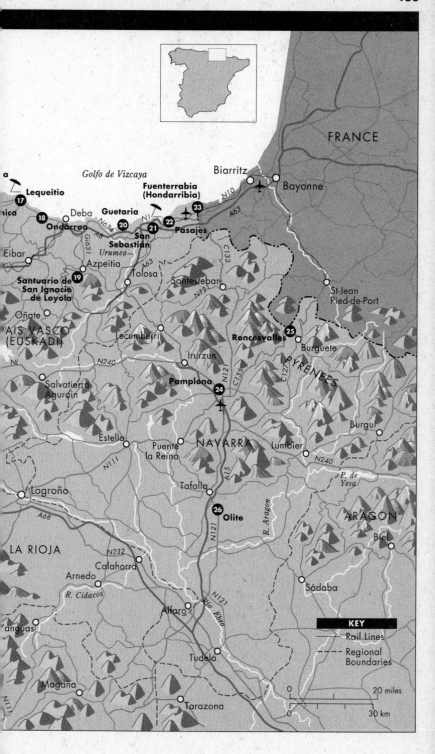

FRANCE

Golfo de Vizcaya

a

Lequeitio

17

Deba

nica

18

Ondárroa

N634

Eibar

Gió31

A8

Guetaria

20

Urumea

A63

Azpeitia

19

Santuario de San Ignacio de Loyola

Oñate

Tolosa

N1

San Sebastián

21

22

Pasajes

Fuenterrabía (Hondarribia)

23

Biarritz

N10

A63

Bayonne

C133

Santesteban

N121

St-Jean Pied-de-Port

AIS VASCO (EUSKADI)

NI

N240

Lecumberri

Irurzun

N121

Roncesvalles

25

Burguete

PYRENEES

Salvatierra-Aguráin

Pamplona

24

C135

C127

Burgui

Estella

N111

Puente la Reina

NAVARRA

A15

Lumbier

N240

P. de Yesa

Logroño

A68

Tafalla

R. Aragón

ARAGON

Biel

LA RIOJA

N232

Olite

26

N121

Calahorra

Arnedo

R. Cidacos

Alfaro

N121

Río Ebro

Sádaba

anguas

Magaña

Tudela

Tarazona

NII)

Burgos

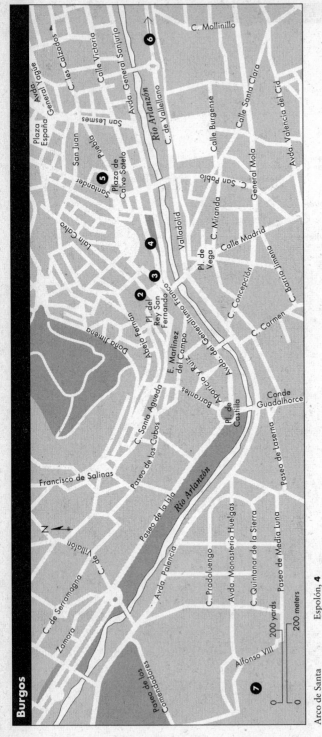

Arco de Santa María, **3**
Cartuja de Miraflores, **6**
Casa del Cordón, **5**
Cathedral, **2**

Espolón, **4**
Monasterio de Las Huelgas Reales, **7**

Dining and Lodging

$$$ ✕🗊 **Mesón del Cid.** In a 15th-century building that once housed one
★ of the first printing presses in Spain, this family-run restaurant has been
offering traditional Burgalese cooking for four generations. The sec-
ond- and third-floor dining rooms are framed with handhewn beams,
and many tables have a spectacular view of the cathedral. The *pimien-
tos rellenos* (peppers stuffed with meat) are succulent as are the *pisto
Don Diego* (vegetable stew with egg) and the Doña Jimenez soup (a
garlic soup with bread and egg). A very comfortable hotel is attached.
⊠ *Plaza Santa María 8, 48383,* ☎ *947/205971; closed Sun. evening.
Hotel,* ☎ *947/208715,* 🅵🅰🆇 *947/269460. 29 rooms. AE, DC, MC, V.*

Shopping

Burgos is famous all over Spain for its wide variety of **cheeses,** known
simply as *queso de Burgos* (cheese from Burgos). Pick some up at the
Casa Quintanilla (⊠ Calle Paloma 17).

*Numbers in the margin correspond to points of interest on the Basque
Country map.*

Santander

★ ❽ *390 km (240 mi) north of Madrid; 116 km (72 mi) west of Bilbao.*

Santander is one of the great Bay of Biscay ports, and the first thing
that will strike you about it is its situation on the western edge of the
Bay of Santander. A major northern beach resort—especially for Span-
ish tourists from the south—the city is surrounded by beaches that hap-
pily lack the package-tour feel of most Mediterranean resorts. A huge
fire in 1941 destroyed most of the old town; the city may now be the
most modern in Spain. It is a lively place, but unusually conservative,
especially next to its liberal neighbor, the Basque country. It is one of
the few places in Spain that didn't topple its statue of General Franco
after he died in 1975. The province, renamed Cantabria from Santander
in 1984, when it became an official autonomous region, is historically
part of Old Castile.

The origins of Santander are obscure, but it was already a busy port
in the 11th century and enjoyed a thriving commercial life between the
13th and 16th centuries. The waning of Spain's naval power and a se-
ries of deadly plagues during the reign of Felipe II, however, caused
the city's fortunes to plummet. It came back to life commercially only
in the 18th century, when it was finally allowed by Madrid to engage
in trading with the Americas. In 1910 a summer residence, the **Pala-
cio de la Magdalena,** was built by popular subscription as a gift to Al-
fonso XIII and his queen, Victoria Eugenia. Thus the city gained status
as one of the royal residences of Spain, but even this failed to make it
thrive like San Sebastián. Today, it still suffers from second-best sta-
tus among northern cities.

Apart from beaches, Santander benefits from promenades and gardens,
most of them facing the bay. Walk east along the Paseo de Pereda, the
main boulevard, to the **Puerto Chico,** a small yacht harbor.

Past the Puerto Chico, follow Avenida Reina Victoria and you'll come
to the tree-lined park paths above the first of the city's beaches, the
Playa de la Magdalena. Walk onto the Magdalena Peninsula to the **Mag-
dalena Palace,** today the summer seat of the University of Menéndez
y Pelayo, which offers Spanish-language and culture courses for for-
eigners. The grounds offer dramatic views of the bay.

Beyond the Magdalena Peninsula, wealthy locals have built mansions
facing the long stretch of shoreline known as **El Sardinero,** the city's

best beach. The heart of the neighborhood is the Belle Epoque **Gran Casino del Sardinero,** an elegant, twin-tower casino and restaurant worth a quick visit, even if gaming tables hold no charms for you. A white building fronted with red awnings in a small park set with sycamores, it lies at the center of the vacationer's Santander, surrounded by expensive hotels and some of the finest restaurants in the area. These specialize in the fresh seafood for which Cantabria is famous.

In the old city, the center of life is the **Plaza Porticada,** officially called the Plaza Velarde. This rather unassuming little square is the seat of Santander's annual star event, the International Festival of Music and Dance, a series of outdoor performances in August. Across the Avenida de Calvo Sotelo from the Plaza Porticada is the blockish **Buen Pastor Cathedral** (✉ Somorrostro s/n), a building marking the transition between Romanesque and Gothic. It was badly damaged in the 1941 fire and then largely rebuilt. The chief item of interest here is the tomb of Marcelino Menéndez y Pelayo (1856–1912), the city's most famous literary figure.

Visit the **Museo Municipal de Bellas Artes** for a look at works by Flemish, Italian, and Spanish artists. Noteworthy is Goya's portrait of the absolutist King Fernando VII; the smirking face of the lion at the king's feet gives you a clue to the feelings Goya had toward his patron. The same building holds the **Biblioteca Menéndez y Pelayo,** a library housing some 50,000 volumes and the study of the writer, kept as it was in his day. ✉ *City Fine Arts Museum, Calle Rubio s/n,* ☎ *942/239485.* ▨ *Free;* ⊙ *Tues.–Fri. 10–1 and 5–8, Sat. 10–1; Biblioteca:* ☎ *942/ 234534;* ▨ *Free.* ⊙ *Weekdays 9–2 and 4–9:30, Sat. 9–1:30).*

Dining and Lodging

$$ ✕ **Bodega del Riojano.** The paintings on wine- barrel ends that deco-
★   rate this restaurant have given it the sobriquet Museo Redondo (Round Museum), but this is not its only charm. The building dates back to the 16th century, when it was a wine cellar, and the atmosphere is carried on in dark wood beams and tables. The menu changes daily and seasonally, but try the fish of the day, always a sure bet on the Cantabrian coast. Desserts are homemade. ✉ *Río de la Pila 5,* ☎ *942/216750. AE, DC, MC, V. Closed Sun. evening in winter.*

$$ ✕ **Rhin.** On the El Sardinero Beach, next to the casino, this restaurant offers views from every seat and dining on a large terrace in summer. The Rhin is somewhat touristy, however, and the food is not the best in town. Among the better dishes are *lomos de merluza con setas* (hake fillets with wild mushrooms) or, if you miss meat, the *lomo de añojo al queso de Tresviso* (steak with Tresviso cheese). ✉ *Plaza de Italia,* ☎ *942/273034. AE, DC, MC, V.*

$$–$$$ ▥ **Las Brisas.** Jesús García and his wife, Teresa, have managed to turn
★   this 75-year-old mansion into a ritzy, cottage-style hotel by the sea. If you value homey atmosphere and personality, this is the place for you. Each room is different, from dollhouse alcoves to an odd but attractive two-story family room. The basement bar and breakfast room is especially cozy. Just a few hundred feet from the beach, the house offers many rooms with fine views. ✉ *Travesía de los Castros 14, 39005,* ☎ *942/ 270991 or 942/275011. 14 rooms with bath. AE, DC, MC, V.*

$ ▥ **México.** Don't be put off by the modest exterior. The personal
★   touch still counts in this family-run establishment, and the breakfast room is elegant, with Queen Anne chairs, inlaid porcelain rosettes, and oak wainscoting. The rooms are pleasant, with high ceilings and the glassed-in balconies. Reserve in advance because word of this good deal has gotten around. ✉ *Calderón de la Barca 3, 39002,* ☎ *942/212450,* FAX *942/229238. 34 rooms with bath or shower. MC, V.*

Nightlife and the Arts

Santander's big event is the **International Music and Dance Festival,** which attracts leading international artists throughout August. Many of the events are in the city's main square, Plaza Porticada. The backdrops for many other performances are local monasteries, palaces, and churches. You'll find information at the tourist office and at seasonal box offices in the Plaza Porticada and the Jardines de Pereda park. The city's **Teatro Coliseum** (✉ Plaza de los Remedios 1, ☎ 942/211460) is normally a movie theater but hosts a summer theater.

Shopping

Santander is known as a **ceramics** center. There are several touristy retailers on the Calle Arrabal downtown, but La Muralla, at No. 17, is known locally as the best bet.

Altamira Caves

❾ *29 km (18 mi) west of Santander; 3 km (2 mi) from the medieval town of Santillana del Mar.*

The world-famous Altamira Caves are known as the "Sistine Chapel of Rupestrian Art" for the beauty of the drawings, judged to be some 13,000 years old. The caves, first uncovered in 1875, are testimony to early humans' love of beauty and to their skill—especially in the use of the forms of the rock to accentuate perspective. The floods of tourists led to serious deterioration; visitors must now apply in advance to be among the 25 people allowed in daily. There is an adjoining museum and a cave with interesting rock formations that can be visited freely. To see the drawings, write for permission, including the names and number of people in your group, and what date you hope to visit. A waiting list of 8–10 months is normal. ✉ *Centro de Investigación de Altamira, 39330 Santillana del Mar;* ☎ *942/818005.*

Dining and Lodging

$$–$$$ ✕🏨 **Parador de Santillana del Mar.** Built in the 16th century, this lovely
★ parador occupies what was once the summer home of the Barreda-Bracho family. ✉ *Plaza Ramón Pelayo 8, 39330,* ☎ *942/818000,* FAX *942/818391. 56 rooms. Restaurant, bar. AE, DC, MC, V.*

Laredo

❿ *Leaving Santander en route to the Basque country, take the N635 southeast and then the N634 east to Laredo (49 km/30 mi).*

Although you would hardly know it today, Laredo was an early home port of the Spanish Armada and remained the chief harbor in the north until the French sacked it in the 18th century and Santander became the regional capital. This little town witnessed the visits of the most powerful of Spanish royalty, including Isabella the Catholic (Isabel la Católica) and Charles I of Spain, better known as the Holy Roman Emperor Charles V (Carlos V). When Charles, the most powerful monarch in European history, stopped by in 1556, he donated two brass choir desks in the shape of eagles that can still be seen today in the parish **Iglesia de Asunción** (Church of the Assumption) in the center of the town's tiny Old Quarter. Walk through the **Old Quarter;** ancient mansions with heraldic coats of arms are commonplace.

Dining and Lodging

$$ ✕🏨 **Risco.** *Risco* means "cliff" in Spanish, an appropriate name for this hotel-restaurant built into the craggy slope overlooking the historic port of Laredo. The food is renowned as an ingenious mixture of classical and more nouvelle Cantabrian cuisine. Try the *pimientos* *rellenos de cangrejo y de buey de mar* (peppers stuffed with crab and fish). Every room has a spectacular view of the town and cove below. ✉ *La Arenosa 2, 39770,* ☎ *942/605030,* FAX *942/605055. 25 rooms with bath. Hotel reservations required July and Aug. Restaurant. AE, DC, MC, V. Restaurant closed Wed., except July and Aug.*

Castro-Urdiales

⑪ *34 km (21 mi) northwest of Bilbao.*

The N634 winds up into the hills behind Laredo, with views of the Bay of Santoña over your shoulder. A short drive, parts of it within sight of the coast, takes you into the fishing village of Castro-Urdiales, believed to be the oldest settlement on the Cantabrian coast. Called Flaviobriga by the Romans, it became the region's leading whaling port in the 13th and 14th centuries, with almost three times today's 13,000 residents. Overlooking the town is the **Santa María Church,** revered as a Gothic work of art; just behind the church is an ancient **castle** to which has been added a modern lighthouse. Aside from its arcaded main plaza and the narrow streets of its **Old Quarter** (much of which burned on May 11, 1813), Castro-Urdiales is famous for seafood.

Dining

$$ ✕ **Mesón Marinero.** This pearl of a tavern and restaurant is a gastro-
★ nomic delight, where local fishermen rub elbows with visiting elites. The array of tapas spread out on the bar will tempt you to forgo the main meal and *tapear* (munch tapas) away your dinner hour; but if you don't succumb, you'll be in for a treat in the elegant, second-floor dining room overlooking Castro's weathered fishing port. An un-beatable dessert is the *tostada de leche frita* (a milk-based custard con-coction). ✉ *Correría 23,* ☎ *942/860005. AE, DC, MC, V.*

En Route   The 45-minute drive from Castro-Urdiales on the N634 to Bilbao takes you through some of the sprawling, industrial development that mars much of Vizcaya, the westernmost of the Basque provinces.

Bilbao

⑫ *34 km (21 mi) southeast of Castro-Urdiales; 116 km (72 mi) east of Santander.*

Bilbao (Bilbo, in Euskera), Spain's sixth-largest city and the commercial capital of the Basque country, with its surrounding industrial sub-urbs, takes in some 430,000 people. The Vizcaya province now has nearly 1.2 million inhabitants, over half of the Basque country's total population of 2,150,000. The River Nervión, on which it is built, is lined with huge industrial cranes, steel mills, shipyards, and smaller, heavy industries, many in grave decline, contributing to the political and social malaise of the region. Water and air pollution are problems. Signposts are in the Basque language, as well as Spanish (very often with the Spanish blotted out by nationalist spray painters).

Bilbao's treasures, perching giddily on the steep hills rising from the river, include a **Casco Viejo** (Old Quarter), also known as Siete Calles, and a number of wide boulevards that date from the late 19th century (especially **Gran Vía,** the main shopping artery). The city is also rich in cultural institutions, including a major fine arts museum of its own and the new **Guggenheim Museum** scheduled (very tentatively) to open by summer of 1997. Many devotees of Bilbao consider it one of the best culinary cities on the Iberian peninsula.

Founded in 1300 by a Vizcayan noble, Diego López de Haro, Bilbao was predated by settlements of primitive tribes. Only in the mid-19th century did the city become an important industrial center, thanks mainly to the wealth of minerals in the surrounding hills. A wealthy industrial class grew up here as did the working-class suburbs like Portugalete and Baracaldo that line the Margen Izquierda (Left Bank) of the Nervión estuary. Many of the wealthy have left in the last 25 years—the fear of kidnapping and the extortion of ETA's so-called revolutionary tax has driven them to Madrid. The rightbank suburb of Getxo, for instance, is remarkable for its abandoned mansions.

What's marked on most maps as the **Puente de Vizcaya** is known as the **Puente Colgante** (Hanging Bridge)—an 85-year-old symbol of Bilbao industry. The bridge, a transporter hung from cables, ferries cars and passengers across the Nervión, uniting two distinct worlds: exclusive, quiet Las Arenas and Portugalete, a much older, working-class town, now filled with jobless steelworkers (Dolores Ibarruri, the famous Republican orator of the Spanish civil war known as *La Pasionaria,* was born here). Portugalete is a 15-minute walk from Santurce, where the quayside Hogar del Pescador serves simple and ample fish specialties. Besugo (sea bream) is the traditional choice, but fresh grilled sardines are hard to surpass.

In Siete Calles, on the river's right bank, by the Arenal Bridge, you will see Bilbao's rustcolored river, the beautifully refurbished **Teatro Arriaga** (built in 1890), and the train that runs along the riverbank. The Old Quarter, walled until the 19th century, lies around the **Santiago Cathedral** (open during Mass). This church was a stop for pilgrims on one of the routes to Santiago; work on the structure began in 1379, but fire destroyed most of it in 1571. It has a notable outdoor arcade. Visit the **Old Quarter,** where you will see ancient mansions and fine ironwork on many balconies. The quarter received a major facelift after the devastating floods of August, 1983 and is now an upscale shopping district, replete with bars, restaurants, and a bustling nightlife. The most interesting square is the 64-arch **Plaza Nueva,** where a street market is pitched every Sunday morning.

Near the Ayuntamiento Bridge is the riverside **Ayuntamiento** (City Hall), built in 1892. Stop before reaching the neoclassical Ayuntamiento and take the elevator at Calle Esperanza 6. This will bring you to the **Basílica de Begoña,** the huge church from which you have a stunning view of Bilbao, with the Nervión winding through it. Its Gothic hulk was begun in 1519 on the spot where the Virgin Mary had supposedly appeared long before.

NEED A BREAK?
In the modern district, a 20-minute walk from the Old Quarter, the **Café Gran Vía** (⊠ Gran Vía 40) is a good place for a tapas and something to drink. Near the Carlton Hotel, it has long been a favorite watering hole for the city's movers and shakers.

Don't miss the ★**Museo de Bellas Artes** (Fine Arts Museum) in the Doña Casilda Iturriza Park, a half-hour walk west of the Old Quarter. It offers a large collection of the works of Flemish, French, Italian, and Spanish painters, including El Greco, Goya, Velázquez, Zurbarán, and Rivera, as well as modern Basque artists. ☎ 94/441–0154 or 94/441–9536. ⊡ Free. ◷ Tues.–Sat. 10–1:30 and 4–7:30, Sun. 10–2.

For local history, stop by the **Museo Arqueológico** (Museum of Basque Archaeology, Ethnology, and History. It houses items related to Basque crafts, fishing, and agriculture. ⊠ Calle Cruz 4, ☎ 94/415–5423. ⊡ Free. ◷ Tues.–Sat. 10:30–1:30 and 4–7, Sun. 10:30–1.

Dining and Lodging

$$$ ✕ **Goizeko Kabi.** Here you can choose your own crab or crayfish. The dining rooms are of brick and wood paneling, and set off with Persian rugs and tapestry-upholstered chairs. Chef Fernando Canales's creations include *alcachofas rellenos de verdura* (artichokes stuffed with vegetables, sweetbreads, and goose liver) and *capricho de bacalao y caracoles* (cod fried in garlic with snails and served in pastry). ✉ *Particular de Estraunza 4 y 6,* ☎ *94/442–1129. Reservations essential. AE, DC, MC, V. Closed Sun.*

$$ ✕ **Ariatza.** The upstairs dining room, all wallpaper and dark-wood floor-
★ ing, is homey yet elegant. There's an intriguing and delicious selection of traditional and nouvelle elements here: In the former category, try *merluza a la koskera* (hake in a green sauce of clams and asparagus); in the latter, *pastel de verduras* (an aspiclike vegetable delight that looks like a painting and tastes better). One imaginative dessert is *gratinado de frutas* (fruits in a sweet, white sauce). ✉ *Somera 1,* ☎ *94/415–9674. AE, DC, MC, V. Closed Sun. evening and Mon.*

$$ ✕ **Retolaza.** Bilbao's movers and shakers have been coming to this restau-
★ rant since 1906. Operated by the third generation of the founding family, this typical *mesón* has wood beams and low ceilings. Classic Vizcayan fare includes *sopa de aluvias* (red beans and sausage) or *bacalao pilpil* (cod fried with garlic and served in a white sauce). ✉ *Tendería 1,* ☎ *94/415–0643. Reservations not accepted. MC, V. Closed holiday evenings, Sun., Mon.; July 24–Aug. 23; Easter wk.*

$$ ✕ **Victor Montes.** Widely respected as one of Bilbao's top spots for tapeo,
★ ranging from wild mushrooms to sausage or cheese along with splashes of wine, this well-stocked counter should not be missed. ✉ *Plaza Nueva 8,* ☎ *94/415–7067.*

$$$ ✕⌂ **Carlton.** The luminaries who have trod the halls of this grand old but recently refurbished hotel include Orson Welles, Ava Gardner, Ernest Hemingway, Lauren Bacall, and most of Spain's great bullfighters. During the Spanish civil war, it was the seat of the Republican Basque government; later, it housed many Nationalist generals. It is still elegant and well attended. ✉ *Federico Moyúa 2, 48009,* ☎ *94/416–2200,* FAX *94/416–4628. 148 rooms with bath. Restaurant, bar, meeting rooms. AE, DC, MC, V.*

$$$ ✕⌂ **Hotel Ercilla.** This modern hot spot fills with the taurine crowd during Bilbao's *semana grande* in early August, partly because of its proximity to the bullring and partly because it has taken over the Carlton as the place to see and be seen in Bilbao. Its impeccable rooms, facilities, and services have also helped its reputation. This might not be the place to stay if you're looking for a quiet getaway. ✉ *Calle Ercilla 3739, 48009,* ☎ *94/410–2020,* FAX *94/443–9335. 346 rooms. Restaurant, bar, cafeteria. AE, DC, MC, V.*

$ ⌂ **Caserío Gurutzelarreta.** Come here for good prices in a charming Basque farmhouse 10 minutes outside of Bilbao toward the airport; there are only two rooms and beds for four. ✉ *Erandio,* ☎ *94/453–1885. No credit cards.*

Nightlife and the Arts

Bilbao hosts an **August music festival;** again, ask at the tourist office, as venues change. The city's most prized possession, a magnificently restored building on the Nervión River, is the **Teatro Arriaga** (✉ Plaza Arriaga s/n, ☎ 94/416–3244). The theater consistently draws world-class ballet, theater, concerts, opera, and *zarzuela* (comic opera). Opera and zarzuela also is frequently on offer at the **Teatro Coliseo Alvia**

(⌗ Alameda Urquijo 13, ☎ 94/415–3954); information on opera is available at ⌗ *Rodríguez Arias 3,* ☎ *94/415–5490.*

Shopping

The *txapelas* (berets) of the Basque country are famous worldwide and make fine gifts: They are best when waterproofed and keep you remarkably warm in rain and mist. In the Old Quarter of Bilbao, try Sombreros Gorostiaga (⌗ Calle Victor, ☎ 94/416–1276), a shop that sells the most famous line of berets, Elosegui.

En Route   From Bilbao, pick up the A8 toll road and follow signs to the Guernica (Gernika, in Euskera) exit; from there, the Bi 635, a good road through the coastal hills of Vizcaya, takes you north to Guernica.

THE BASQUE COAST, FROM GUERNICA TO GUETARIA AND ZARAUZ

This colorful stretch of coast winds along the edges of the hills of the Basque country, dipping into protected fishing port towns.

Guernica

⑬   *15 km (9 mi) east of Bilbao.*

On Monday, April 26, 1937, market day, Guernica suffered history's second terror bombing against a civilian population (the first, much less famous, was against neighboring Durango, about a month earlier). The planes of the Nazi Luftwaffe were sent with the blessings of General Franco to experiment with saturation bombing of civilian targets and, in the bargain, decimate the traditional seat of Basque autonomy. Since the Middle Ages, Spanish sovereigns had sworn under the ancient **oak tree of Guernica** to respect Basque *fueros* (special local rights—just the kind of local autonomy inimical to the centralist generalíssimo and his "national movement" of Iberian unity). More than a thousand people were killed in the bombing, and today Guernica remains a symbol of independence in the heart of every Basque, known to the world through Picasso's famous painting (now in Madrid's Centro de Arte Reina Sofía).

The city was destroyed—though miraculously the oak tree emerged unscathed—and has been rebuilt as a modern, unattractive place. One point of interest, however, is the stump of the sacred oak, which finally died several decades ago, in the courtyard of the **Casa de Juntas** (a new oak has been planted alongside the old one); it is the object of many pilgrimages. Nearby is the stunning **Ría de Guernica estuary,** a stone's throw from some of the most colorful fishing towns.

Dining and Lodging

$$ ✕ **Baserri Maitea.** This is your chance to see the inside of one of the
★   traditional *caseríos* (farmhouses) of the Basque country. Strings of red peppers and garlic hang from wooden beams in the cathedral-like interior of this 300-year-old building; the driveway leading to it from the Guernica-Bermeo road is well marked. Entrées include the *pescado del día* (fish of the day) and *cordero de leche asado al horno de leña* (milk-fed lamb roasted in a woodburning oven). The pastries are homemade. ⌗ *Bi 635 road to Bermeo, Km 2,* ☎ *94/625–3408. AE, DC, MC, V. Closed Sun. evening, except in summer.*

$ ⊞ **Boliña.** Not far from the famous oak in downtown Guernica, the
★   Boliña is pleasant, friendly, and modern—a good base for exploring the Vizcayan coast. Rooms are smallish but comfortable. ⌗ *Bar-*

renkale 3, 48300, ☎ and FAX 94/625–0300. 16 rooms with bath. Restaurant, bar. AE, DC, MC, V.

En Route From Guernica follow signs for Bermeo, but before you get there, be sure to stop at the Mirador de Portuondo, a roadside lookout with an excellent view of the estuary (at kilometer post 43 on Bi 635).

Mundaca

⑭ 45 km (28 mi) northeast of Bilbao.

Mundaca (Mundaka, in Euskera) is a tiny town that draws surfers from all over the world, especially in the November-to-February season.

Dining and Lodging

$$ ✕ **Casino José Mari.** Constructed in 1818 as the local fishermen's guild auction house, this building, with wonderful views of Mundaca's beach, is now a local eating club, but the public is welcome. It is a super lunch stop in summer, when you can sit in the glassed-in, upper-floor porch. Very much a local haunt, the club serves excellent fish caught, more often than not, by members. ⊠ In the park at the center of town, ☎ 94/687–6005. Reservations not accepted. AE, MC, V.

$$ ▦ **Atalaya.** This 1911 landmark is a private house tastefully redone as a hotel. The rooms are charming and comfortable, and those upstairs have balconies with marvelous views. Room No. 12 is the best in the house. The breakfast room is cheerful and light. ⊠ Itxaropen Kalea 1, Villa María Luisa Esperanza, 48360, ☎ 94/687–6888, FAX 94/687–6899. 15 rooms. Bar. AE, DC, MC, V.

Bermeo

★ ⑮ 3 km (2 mi) west of Mundaca.

Bermeo, just beyond Mundaca, claims the largest fishing fleet in Spain, 62 long-distance boats of more than 150 tons and 121 smaller craft that specialize in hake. Bermeo was long a whaling port; in the 16th century, local whalers had to donate the tongue of every whale to help raise money for the church. Bermeo still has one of only two wooden shipyards on the northern coast, and the boats that fill its harbor form a cheerful picture. Drive to the top of the town's windswept hill, where the cemetery overlooks the crashing waves of the coast below and where at sunset townspeople tend family tombs.

Dining

$$ ✕ **Jokin.** There's a good view of the Puerto Viejo from this cheerful, strategically located restaurant. Fish come directly off the boats you see in the harbor below. Try the rape Jokin (angler in a clam and crayfish sauce) or chipirones en su tinta (small squid in its own ink) and, for dessert, the tarta de naranja (orange cake). ⊠ Eupeme Duna 13, ☎ 94/688–4089. AE, DC, MC, V. Closed Sun. evening.

En Route From Bermeo you can now head back on the Bi 635, passing Guernica, toward Lequeitio (Lekeitio, in Euskera). For a rewarding side trip, turn left at Muretagana and follow the signs to the road's end in Elanchove (Elantxobe, in Euskera).

Elanchove

⑯ 27 km (17 mi) from Bermeo.

This tiny fishing village is nestled amid huge, steep cliffs, with a small breakwater protecting its fleet from the storms of the Bay of Biscay. The view of the port from the upper village, which is quite unused to tourists, is breathtaking; if you take the lower fork in the road, you will drive into the port itself.

NEED A BREAK? In the upper town, stop in at the rustic **Bar Itxasmin,** which has a small restaurant just off the plaza where the road ends.

Dining and Lodging

$ ╳🏠 **Arboliz Jatetxea.** Set on a bluff overlooking the coast, about a mile outside Elanchove on the road to Lequeitio, this rustic inn is isolated yet pleasant. Rooms are simple, modern, and well kept; several have balconies. ✉ *Arboliz 12, 48311 Ibarranguelua,* ☎ *94/627–6283. 9 rooms, 3 with bath. Restaurant. AE, MC, V.*

Lequeitio

⑰   *59 km (37 mi) east of Bilbao; 61 km (38 mi) west of San Sebastián.*

This bright, little town is similar to Bermeo but has two wide, sandy beaches right by the harbor. Soaring over the Gothic Santa María church (open for mass only) is a graceful set of flying buttresses. Lequeitio is famous for its September 1–18 fiestas, which include a gruesome event in which men dangle for as long as they can from the necks of dead geese tied to a cable over the inlet while the cable is whipped in and out of the water by crowds of burly men at either end.

OFF THE BEATEN PATH **SANTIMAMIÑE CAVERNS –**Some prehistoric cave paintings are in the Santimamiñe caverns (guided visits offered Tuesday–Sunday at 10:30, noon, 4, and 5:30) on the road to Elanchove.

Ondárroa

⑱   *61 km (38 mi) east of Bilbao; 49 km (30 mi) west of San Sebastián.*

Farther east along the coast from Lequeitio, Ondárroa is another gem of a fishing town; like its neighbors, it has a major fishing fleet painted in red, green, and white, which are the colors of the *Ikurriña,* the Basque national flag.

En Route   Continuing along the coastal road through Motrico and Deva, you approach some of the prettiest fishing ports and culinary spots in the Basque country. Before reaching them, however, as you come into Zumaya you will see the turnoff up to Azpeitia, the birthplace of one of Spain's greatest religious figures, St. Ignatius of Loyola, founder of the Jesuits and spiritual architect of the Catholic Reformation. A half-hour trip up the Gi 631 will take you to this colossal structure.

Sanctuary of San Ignacio de Loyola

★ **⑲**   *Cestona is 34 km (21 mi) southwest of San Sebastián.*

The Santuario de San Ignacio de Loyola (Sanctuary of St. Ignatius of Loyola) was erected in honor of Iñigo Lopez (1491–1556) after he was sainted in 1622 as Ignacio de Loyola for his defense of the Catholic Church against the tides of Luther's Reformation. Iñigo for many years sought earthly glory in the fratricidal struggles that characterized the Basque country at the time. But after being badly wounded at Pamplona and returning to his family's ancestral home to recover, he abandoned war and took up religion. Almost two centuries later, the Roman architect Carlos Fontana designed the basilica that was to memorialize the saint, after whom five major universities in the United States and Canada and many others worldwide have been named. The basilica is Baroque in style—it's a severe Baroque that does justice to the austere saint's memory. Inside, however, it is rich with polychrome marble, ornate altarwork, and a huge but delicate dome. The old family tower house, a fortress-like structure adjoining the basilica, contains the room where Iñigo gave himself to religion. The massive chest was carved by Indians in Spain's Paraguayan missions.

On the coast road, you will find **Zumaya**—a cozy little port and summer resort with the fjord-like estuary of the Urola river flowing (back and forth, according to the tides) through town.

Dining and Lodging

$$ X☐ **Arocena.** One of the European spa hotels so popular around the ★ turn of the century, the Arocena has free bus service to the nearby springs, whose medicinal waters are still used to treat liver-related diseases. The rooms facing away from the road have especially fine views of the mountains behind. The common rooms, including an elegant restaurant and the lobby, faithfully retain the hotel's Belle Epoque flavor. ⊠ *San Juan 12, 20740, Cestona (10 min from Loyola),* ☎ *943/147040,* FAX *943/ 147978. 109 rooms with bath. Restaurant, bar, pool, tennis court, playground, chapel. AE, DC, MC, V.*

Guetaria

⑳ *22 km (14 mi) from San Sebastián.*

From Zumaya, there are several perfect walking excursions, one of them over to Guetaria, the next town, known as *la cocina de guipúzcoa* (the kitchen of Guipúzcoa province) for its surfeit of restaurants and taverns. Guetaria is the birthplace of Juan Sebastián Elcano (1460–1526), the first circumnavigator of the globe and Spain's most emblematic naval hero. Elcano took command of and completed Magellan's voyage after Magellan was killed in the Phillipines in 1521. Declared a national monument, Guetaria's galleon-like church with its sloping, wooden decks, is a must, while the Iribar restaurant across the street is the best place for *besugo* cooked over coals.

Zarauz, the next town over, is another beauty with a wide beach, taverns, and cafés.

Dining and Lodging

$$ X☐ **Iribar.** The Iribar has been grilling fish and beef over coals in the street outside the restaurant next to the church for over half a century, raising havoc, no doubt, with the fasting faithful within. While Kaia and Kai-pe in the port are also excellent choices, with views of the fleet of colorful fishing boats in the harbor, the Iribar has a warm, family feel about it that makes it the top choice in Guetaria. ⊠ *Kale Nagusia, 38. E-20808 Guetaria.*☎ *943/140406. MC, V.*

En Route Heading east toward San Sebastián, you have a choice of the toll road or the coastal N634 highway. The former is quick and scenic (44 km/27 mi), but the latter will take you through the village of Orio past a few more tempting inns and restaurants, not the least of which is the Sidrería Ugarte at Usurbil.

SAN SEBASTIÁN TO FUENTERRABÍA (HONDARRIBIA)

Relax on the beach in the beautiful and sophisticated city of San Sebastián. As you head east from here you'll pass through Pasajes, from where Lafayette once set out to fight in the American Revolution. Before reaching the French border, you'll reach Fuenterrabía (Hondarribia, in Euskera) a quaint but touristy port town.

San Sebastián

★ ㉑ *119 km (74 mi) east of Bilbao.*

San Sebastián is a sophisticated city that arcs around one of the finest urban beaches in the world, **La Concha** (Conch), so named for its almost perfect resemblance to the shape of a scallop shell.

The best way to see this city, another center of Basque nationalism, is simply to walk around. San Sebastián is full of promenades and pathways, several leading up the hills that surround it; it is a metropolis built for the enjoyment of the eye and spirit.

The first records of San Sebastián date to the 11th century. For centuries a backwater, the city had the good fortune in 1845 to attract Queen Isabella II, seeking relief from a skin ailment in its balmy waters. Her arrival was followed by that of much of the aristocracy of the time, and the city became a favored spot for the wealthy. San Sebastián is laid out in a remarkably modern way, with wide streets on a grid pattern, thanks mainly to the 12 different times it has been largely destroyed by fire. The latest occurred after the French were expelled in 1813; English-Portuguese forces occupied the city, badly abused the population, and then proceeded to torch it. Today, San Sebastián is a seaside resort in a class with Nice and Monte Carlo. The city is probably the most expensive in Spain in summer, when it is a favorite destination for French tourists (and the seasonal seat of the Spanish government); accommodations are scarce.

In the middle of the entrance to the bay, tiny **Santa Clara Island** protects the city from Bay of Biscay storms, making La Concha one of the calmest beaches on the entire northern coast of Spain. A large hill dominates each side of the cove's entrance, and a visit to **Monte Igueldo,** on the southwest side, is a must. (You can drive up for a toll of 90 ptas. per person or take the cable car—funicular—for 130 ptas. roundtrip; open 10–8 in summer, 11–6 in winter; departures every 15 minutes.) From here, you see the remarkable panorama for which San Sebastián is famous: a view of gardens, parks, wide, tree-lined boulevards, and Belle Epoque buildings.

Every Spaniard will tell you that his or her native town is where you will eat best in Spain; but most will agree that San Sebastián is second best. Many of the city's restaurants—along with scores of private, all-male eating societies—are in the **Parte Vieja** (Old Quarter), beyond the elegant **Casa Consistorial** (City Hall). This building, next to the formal **Alderdi Eder gardens,** began life in 1887 as a casino. After gambling was outlawed early in this century, the town council decided to move there from the Plaza de la Constitución, the main square in the Old Quarter.

San Sebastián is divided by the **Urumea River,** which is crossed by three bridges inspired by French architecture of the late 19th century. At the mouth of the Urumea, the incoming surf smashes the rocks with such force that waves erupt to heights of as much as five stories.

Be sure to visit the moumental **Buen Pastor (Good Shepherd) Cathedral,** near the beachfront. The **Basílica de Santa María** is considered the first church of the city and located in the Old Quarter.

NEED A BREAK? Take the funicular to the top of Monte Igueldo, overlooking San Sebastián, for the **amusement park.** The park is open Easter–August, daily

10–10; early spring and late fall, daily 10–8; winter, Monday–Saturday 11–6, Sunday and holidays 10–8.

Dining and Lodging

$$$$ ✕ **Akelarre.** This restaurant is set on the slopes of Monte Igueldo, with spectacular views of La Concha Bay and San Sebastián. Chef Pedro Subijana is known for, among other things, his *lubina a la pimienta verde* (sea bass with green pepper) and Basque classics like squid in a sauce of its own ink. ⊠ *Barrio de Igueldo*, ☎ *943/212052 or 943/214086. Reservations essential. AE, DC, MC, V. Closed Sun. evening, Mon., 1st 2 wks of June, and Dec.*

$$$ ✕ **Arzak.** Renowned chef Juan Marí Arzak's restaurant, on the city's
★ outskirts on the road to Fuenterrabía, is in an intimate, cottage setting. But the place is internationally famous, so reserve well ahead. The entire menu is a wonder, with traditional Basque preparations and more recent creations. The pastries are extremely light and wonderful. Prices are very fair. ⊠ *Alto de Miracruz 2*, ☎ *943/285593 or 943/278465. Reservations essential. AE, DC, MC, V. Closed Sun. evening, Mon., last 2 wks in June and 2 wks in Nov.*

$$$ ✕ **Panier Fleuri.** One of the most select wine lists in Spain complements the food here, served in a sober dining room overlooking the crashing surf at the mouth of the Urumea River. Chef Tatus Fombellida is a winner of Spain's national gastronomy prize, no mean feat. Try his *faisan* (pheasant) or the *supremas de lenguado a la florentina* (sole baked with spinach and served with hollandaise sauce) and for dessert, the lemon sorbet with champagne. ⊠ *Paseo de Salamanca 1*, ☎ *943/424205. Reservations essential. AE, DC, MC, V. Closed Sun. evening, Wed., last 2 wks of Dec., 3 wks in June, Christmas wk.*

$$ ✕ **Salduba.** Javier Arbizu is the cook for the Spanish national soccer team. His restaurant is built of ancient, oak beams and heavy, wooden furniture, a bastion of sound cooking and service in the middle of Sab Sebastian's teeming *parte vieja*. ⊠ *Calle Pescadería 2*, ☎ *943/425627. AE, DC, MC, V.*

$$ ✕ **Urepel.** Both the cuisine and the sense of interior design here balance classical and modern elements in a felicitous way. The *chicharro al escama dorada* (a deboned, skinned mackerel served under a layer of goldenbrown slices of potato) is a typical Urepel invention. There is no principal chef; the kitchen staff works as a team in prototypically Basque egalitarianism. ⊠ *Paseo de Salamanca 3*, ☎ *943/424040. AE, DC, MC, V. Closed Sun. and Tues. evening.*

$ ✕ **Casa Vallés.** Just a two-minute walk from the back of San Sebastián's cathedral, this fine little tapas bar-restaurant displays some 30 to 40 different, freshly prepared and irresistible creations at midday and again in the early evening. Famous among locals, Casa Vallés combines excellent offerings with top value. ⊠ *Reyes Católicos 10*, ☎ *943/452210. AE, DC, MC, V. Closed Wed. and June 15–30.*

$$$$ ✕▥ **Maria Cristina.** The graceful beauty of the Belle Epoque is evoked by San Sebastián's top luxury hotel, which sits like the queen it's named after on the elegant west bank of the Urumea River. The grandeur continues inside the entrance; in salons filled with Oriental rugs, potted palms, and Carrara marble columns; and in bedrooms to match. ⊠ *Paseo República Argentina s/n, 20004*, ☎ *943/424900, FAX 943/423914. 139 rooms with bath. Restaurant, bar, beauty salon, shops, meeting rooms. AE, DC, MC, V.*

$$$ ✕▥ **Londres y Inglaterra.** This stately hotel has a privileged position on the promenade above the main La Concha beach. It also offers a quiet lobby with chandeliers, fine rooms, and attentive, warm service. Its bar faces the bay. ⌧ *Zubieta 2, 20007,* ☎ *943/426989,* Ⓕⓐⓧ *943/420031. 130 rooms with bath. Restaurant, bar, casino. AE, DC, MC, V.*

$$ ⊞ **Bahía.** A two-minute walk from the beach, this hotel is small but appealing. It has a welcoming lobby, with a cute minibar and salon, and its rooms are comfortable and modern. ⌧ *San Martín 54 Bis, 20007,* ☎ *943/469211,* Ⓕⓐⓧ *943/463914. 60 rooms with bath. MC, V.*

Nightlife and the Arts

San Sebastián's film festival is held in the second half of September, although exact dates vary; ask at the tourist office or read the local press for details and ticket information. The same is true of the **jazz festival** in late July, an event that draws many of the world's top performers. A varied program of theater, dance, and other events is offered year-round at the beautiful **Teatro Victoria Eugenia** (⌧ Reina Regente s/n, ☎ 943/481155 or 943/481160).

Shopping

Ponsol (⌧ Calle Narrica 4, ☎ 943/420876) is the best place to buy the Basque berets called boinas. The Leclerq family business has been hatting *donostiarras* (residents of *donosti*, San Sebastián, in Euskera) for three generations. Stop in at **Juncal** (⌧ Avenida Libertad 32) for a fabulous selection of chocolates.

Pasajes

㉒ *10 km (6 mi) east of San Sebastián.*

The historic port of Pasajes (Pasaia, in Euskera) is whence Lafayette set out to aid the rebels of the American Revolution. It is actually three towns in one large bay: **Pasajes Ancho,** an industrial port; **Pasajes de San Pedro,** a large fishing harbor; and **Pasajes de San Juan.** This last is a tiny settlement of 18th and 19th-century buildings along a single street that fronts the bay's outlet to the sea. It is best reached by driving into Pasajes de San Pedro and catching a launch that takes you across the mouth of the harbor (about 100 pesetas, depending on the time of day). The town is famous for its fine restaurants.

Dining

$$ ✕ **Casa Cámara.** Four generations ago, Pablo Camara turned this old
★ fishing wharf on Pasajes Bay into a first-class restaurant. The dining room has lovely views and a pit from which lobsters and crayfish are hauled up for inspection by diners. Try *cangrejo del mar* (spider crab with vegetable sauce) or the superb hake in green sauce. ⌧ *Pasajes de San Juan,* ☎ *943/523699 or 943/517874. Reservations essential. V. Closed Sun. evening and Mon.*

Fuenterrabía

㉓ *12 km (8 mi) east of Pasajes.*

A final fishing port before you reach the French border is Fuenterrabía (Hondarribia, in Euskera). The harbor, lined with fishermen's homes and small fishing boats, is a beautiful but rather touristy spot. If you have a taste for history, follow signs up the hill to the medieval bastion and one-time castle of Charles V, today a national parador.

Dining and Lodging

$$$ ✕ **Ramón Roteta.** Set in a beautiful, old villa with an informal garden, this restaurant offers excellent food, making it *the* choice for anyone staying at the local parador. Sample the garlic and shrimp pastries or the rice with vegetables and clams. The pastry is all homemade. ⊠ *Villa Ainara, Calle Irún 2,* ☎ *943/641693. AE, DC, MC, V. Closed Sun. evening and Thurs., except in summer.*

$ ✕ **La Hermandad de Pescadores.** This centrally located "brotherhood" is owned by the local fishermen's guild and serves simple and hearty fare at reasonable prices. Try the *sopa de pescado* (fish soup) or the *almejas a la marinera* (clams in a creamy sauce). If you come outside of peak hours (2–4 and 9–11), you'll find room at the long communal boards. ⊠ *Calle Zuloaga s/n,* ☎ *943/642738. AE, DC, MC, V. Closed Tues. evening and Wed.*

$ ✕🏠 **Caserio "Artzu."** This family farmhouse, with its classical low, wide roof-line, has been here, in one form or another, for some 800 years. Just west of the Nuestra Señora de Guadalupe hermitage, Artzu offers dinner and lodging in modernized accomodations in a setting overlooking the junction of the Bidasoa estuary and the Atlantic. ⊠ *Barrio Montaña, 20280 Hondarribia.*☎ *943/640530. 5 rooms with shared bath, 1 with bath. Restaurant No credit cards.*

$$$ 🏠 **Parador El Emperador.** This parador, replete with suits of armor and other chivalric bric-a-brac is a superb medieval bastion that dates back to the 10th century and was the residence of Carlos V in the 16th century. Many rooms have gorgeous views of the Bidasoa River and estuary, which is dotted with colorful fishing boats. Be sure to reserve ahead. Ask for one of the three "special" rooms; they're worth the extra $30. ⊠ *Plaza Armas de Castillo, 20005,* ☎ *943/645500,* 🖷 *943/642153. 36 rooms with bath. Bar. AE, DC, MC, V.*

En Route   Either of two routes from the northeast corner of the Basque country to Pamplona is a dramatic drive, taking you through spectacular mountains that are snowcapped and often impassable in the winter months. The fastest way is by the major highway from San Sebastián to Tolosa, a busy industrial stretch, and then on N240 into the mountains, finally descending into Pamplona. A somewhat prettier drive (134 km/83 mi), if slower and more tortuous, is by C133, which starts out near the French border (and Fuenterrabía); catch the N121 about halfway, and continue on to Pamplona, the ancient capital of Navarra (Navarre).

PAMPLONA, BAZTÁN, RONCESVALLES, AND OLITE

Run with the bulls during Pamplona's annual festival of St. Fermín. Or, should you seek quieter climes, head for the mountain pass of Roncesvalles or explore a French-style castle in Olite.

Pamplona

㉔   *91 km (56 mi) southeast of San Sebastián.*

Pamplona is known the world over for the event made famous by Ernest Hemingway in *The Sun Also Rises*—the running of the bulls during the festival of San Fermín, July 6–14. The population triples during the fiesta, and rooms must be reserved months in advance (hotel prices almost triple for the event), though some 700 private rooms are also rented out. Tickets to the bullfights, as opposed to the running (to which access is free), can be difficult to obtain. Every morning at 7 sharp a skyrocket is shot off, and the bulls kept overnight in the corral are loosed through a series of closed-off streets leading to the bullring, a 902-yard dash. Running before them are Spaniards and foreigners feeling festive enough to risk a goring, wearing the traditional white shirts and trousers with red neckerchiefs and carrying rolled-up newspapers to swat the bulls with. If all goes well—no serious gorings or even deaths—the bulls arrive in the ring in just 2½ minutes.

Pamplona was founded by the Roman emperor Pompey as Pompaelo or Pameiopolis and was successively taken by the Franks, the Goths, and the Moors. The Pamplonans managed to expel the Arabs temporarily in 750, putting themselves under the protection of Charlemagne. But the foreign commander took advantage of this trust to destroy the city walls, so that when he was driven again from the area by the Moors, the Navarrese took their revenge, ambushing and slaughtering the retreating Frankish army as it fled over the Pyrenees through the mountain pass of Roncesvalles in 778. This is the episode depicted in the *Song of Roland,* although the author chose to cast the aggressors as Moors. For centuries after that event, Pamplona remained as three argumentative towns, until they were forcibly incorporated into one city by Carlos III (the Noble, 1387–1425) of Navarra.

The **Pamplona Cathedral,** set near the portion of the ancient walls rebuilt in the 17th century, is one of the most important religious buildings in Spain because of its fine Gothic cloister. Inside are the tombs of Charles III and his wife, marked by an alabaster sculpture. The **Museo Diocesano** houses religious art spanning the period from the Middle Ages to the Renaissance. ⊠ *Calle Curia s/n.* ⊠ *Free.*

★ On Calle Santo Domingo, in a 16th-century building that once served as a hospital for pilgrims on their way to Santiago, is the **Museo de Navarra** (⊠ Calle Jaranta s/n, ☎ 948/227831), which houses a collection of local archaeological artifacts and historical costumes. Admission is 300 pesetas, and the museum is open Tuesday–Saturday 9–2 and 5–7, Sun. 9–2. with a collection of local archaeological artifacts and historical costumes. The most remarkable civil architecture in the city is the ornate **Ayuntamiento (city hall),** on the Plaza Consistorial; this 18th-century structure is unusual for the blackish color it has acquired over the years, set off against its gilded balconies. Stop for a look at its wood-and-marble interior.

NEED A BREAK?

In the central Plaza del Castillo, the gentry of Pamplona have been flocking to the ornate, French-style **Café Iruña** since 1888. The bar and salons are sumptuously paneled in dark woods; if you walk through, past the stand-up bar, you reach the attached bingo hall (you must be 18 to play). ⊠ *Plaza del Castillo 44.* ⊙ *Daily 5 PM–3 AM).*

One of Pamplona's main charms is the warren of small streets near the **Plaza del Castillo** (especially Calle San Nicolás), which are filled with restaurants, taverns, and bars. Pamplonans, a hardy sort, are known far and wide for their eagerness and capacity to eat and drink.

The central **Ciudadela,** an ancient fortress, today is a parkland of promenades and pools; walk through in the late afternoon, the time of the *paseo* (traditional stroll), for a taste of city life.

Dining and Lodging

$$$ ✕ **Josetxo.** Pamplonans consider this one of their city's finest restaurants. It's a homey, warm place, run by a family whose specialties include, for starters, *hojaldre de marisco* (shellfish pastry) and, for an entrée, *ensalada de langosta* (spiny lobster salad). ⊠ *Príncipe de Viana 1,* ☎ 948/222097. AE, DC, V. Closed Aug. and Sun., except in May and during San Fermín.

$$ ✕ **Erburu.** In the heart of the nightlife district, this dark, wood-beamed
★ restaurant is frequented by Pamplonans in the know—a true "find."
Come here to eat or just to sample tapas at the bar. Try the *merluza
con salsa verde* (hake in green sauce), a Basque classic, or any of a whole
range of dishes made with *alcochofas* (artichokes). ✉ *San Lorenzo 1921,
☎ 948/225169. AE, DC, MC, V. Closed Mon. and 2nd half of July.*

$$$$ ✕🏨 **Los Tres Reyes.** If you come to the San Fermín blowout (July 6–
14) you can arrange to be very comfortable at this wonderful place.
Pool, piano bar, restaurant: everything you need is here, just a step from
all the action. Prices double here during *sanfermines.* ✉ *Calle de la
Taconera s/n, 31001, ☎ 948/226600, FAX 948/222930. 168 rooms
with bath. Restaurant, piano bar, cafeteria, pool, beauty salon, car rental.
AE, DC, MC, V.*

$ ✕🏨 **Casa Otano.** This friendly and tumultuous boarding house or
hostal is simple and well placed, right in the middle of the tapas and
wine circuit and just a few paces from Pamplona's central square. The
restaurant downstairs will keep you well fed. The general atmosphere
of the Otano is compatible with the San Fermín madness that will be
raging in the street if you are there during fiestas (July 6–15). ✉ *San
Nicolas 5, 31001, ☎ 948/225095, FAX 948/212012. 15 rooms with bath.
AE, DC, MC, V. Closed (usually) July 16–31.*

$$$–$$$$ 🏨 **La Perla.** Hemingway and Henry Cabot Lodge slept here, but then
so did many other famous people who happened to be passing through.
At 126, La Perla is the oldest, though far from the best, hotel in town.
The founder's son was a bullfighter, and two of the beasts he slew pre-
side over the salon. It's a bit faded but very charming, right on the main
plaza. ✉ *Plaza del Castillo 1, 31001, ☎ 948/227706, FAX 948/211566.
67 rooms, 45 with bath. AE, DC, MC, V.*

$$–$$$$ 🏨 **Hotel Yoldi.** This hotel is much-frequented haunt by the (you read
it here) somewhat snooty, foreign *afición,* that is, old-hand bullfight
fans. Still, anthropologically they're fun to peruse; the hotel is always
boiling with in-the-know looking Hemingwayoids debating taurine es-
oterica such as the exact placement, angle, intent, and esthetic of the
third sword thrust on the second bull of the fifth corrida of the third
feria of the last decade. Who could ask for more? ✉ *Avenida San Ignacio 11 31002, ☎ 948/224800, FAX 948/212045. 50 rooms with bath.
Bar, cafeteria. AE, DC, MC, V.*

Nightlife and the Arts

Pamplona also has a varied summer program of theater, zarzuela, ballet, and concerts. For information, contact the **Teatro Gayarre** (✉
Avenida Carlos III Noble 1, ☎ 948/220139). In August, the **Festivales
de Navarra** includes theater and other events.

Shopping

Botas are the wineskins from which Basques typically drink while at
bullfights or during fiestas. The art is in drinking a stream of wine while
the bota is held at arm's length—without spilling a drop, if you intend
to maintain your honor before hypercritical Basque onlookers. Botas
can be bought in any Basque town, but an especially fine brand, ZZZ,
is sold at Anel (✉ Calle Comedías 7) in Pamplona. The **neckerchiefs**
worn during the running of the bulls are available in Pamplona shops;
the same shops sell *gerrikos,* the wide belts worn by Basque sports-
men during contests of strength to hold in overstressed organs.

For **sweets,** try Salcedo (✉ Calle Estafeta 37), open since 1800, which
invented, and still sells, almond-based *mantecadas* (powder cakes), as
well as *coronillas* (a delightful almond and cream concoction). Also

stop in at Hijas de C. Lozano, at ⊠ *Calle Zapatería 11, which offers the café y leche (coffee and milk) toffees that are prized all over Spain.*

Roncesvalles

★ ㉕ *48 km (30 mi) north of Pamplona.*

The 3,468-foot mountain pass of Roncesvalles is one of the most beautiful routes into France. A simple **cross** marks the site of the legendary battle where Roland fell after calling for help on his Sicilian, ivory, battle horn. In the tiny town—a short drive down the mountain (population about 100)—you'll find the **chapel of Santiago,** the first church on the Spanish section of the Way of St. James. Walk into the **Colegiata** (Royal Collegiate Church), built at the orders of King Sancho the Strong (open irregular hours); inside is the king's tomb, measuring 7 feet 4 inches, for the monarch was a giant, and two thorns that are said to have come from the crown worn by Christ.

En Route   Return to Pamplona to catch the A15 toll road to Olite. The route, largely through wine country, is a stark contrast to any area yet seen on this itinerary; in spring it is particularly beautiful, with fields full of wildflowers.

Olite

★ ㉖ *41 km (25 mi) south of Pamplona.*

Much of Olite is ancient and a pleasure to walk through. The 11th-century **San Pedro church** is interesting for its finely worked Romanesque cloisters and portal. The town has a national parador that is part of a **castle** restored by Carlos III in the French style, a fantasy structure of ramparts, crenellated walls, and watchtowers. You can walk the ramparts in the part not occupied by the parador. ▨ *300 ptas.* ☉ *Daily 10–2 and 4–5.*

Dining and Lodging

$$ ✕⊞ **Parador Príncipe de Viana.** This is a fantasy palace-castle, named
★   for the grandson of Carlos III, who spent his life here. The parador is part of the castle complex for which Olite is famous. The chivalric atmosphere is well preserved, with grand salons, secret stairways, heraldic tapestries, and the odd suit of armor. ⊠ *Plaza de los Teobaldos 2, 31390,* ☎ *948/740000,* ☒ *948/740201. 43 rooms with bath. Restaurant, bar. AE, DC, MC, V.*

BURGOS, SANTANDER, AND THE BASQUE COUNTRY A TO Z

Arriving and Departing

By Boat

Santander is linked to Plymouth, England, by a twice-weekly car ferry that operates year-round. For information, contact **Brittany Ferries** (⊠ Paseo de Pereda 27, Santander, ☎ 942/220000 or 942/214500); or **Brittany's offices in England** (⊠ Millbay Docks, Plymouth, PL1 3EW, ☎ 0990/360360); or go through travel agencies in Spain or Britain. Be sure to book at least six weeks in advance in summer because the 24-hour passages are often sold out. Another option is the ferry that travels between Bilbao and Portsmouth, England; there are two sailings each week. Contact **Ferries Golfo de Vizcaya** (⊠ Cosme Etxevarrieta 1, 48009 Bilbao, ☎ 94/423–4477, ☒ 94/423–5496).

By Bus

Daily bus service connects all the major cities of the region to Madrid, with several departures a day in some cases. San Sebastián and Bilbao are especially well connected with the capital. In Madrid, try getting through to **Continental Auto bus company** for information (☎ 91/533–0400), or go right to the station at Calle Alenza 20.

By Car

Traveling by car is the best way to see Burgos, Santander, and the Basque country, the remotest point of which is an easy, one-day drive from Madrid. From the capital, it's 242 km/150 mi on the N I (or the A1 toll road) to Burgos, and 396 km/246 mi if you continue on the N623 to Santander. Driving direct from Madrid to Bilbao will take you 401 km/247 mi: Follow the NI or A1 past Burgos to Miranda del Ebro, where you pick up the A68 into Bilbao. From Madrid, San Sebastián is 472 km/293 mi if you travel the fastest route, via Bilbao, and take the A8 toll road from there.

By Plane

The major airport serving the region is 11 km/7 mi outside Bilbao; Iberia has regular connections between there and England, France, Madrid, and Barcelona. Smaller, less convenient airports serve Santander, San Sebastián, and Pamplona, less frequent service to Madrid and Barcelona.

By Train

Burgos, Santander, Bilbao, and San Sebastián are all well served by trains direct from the Chamartín Station in Madrid or, with some changes, from virtually every major city in Spain. If you're leaving from Madrid, call **RENFE** for information (☎ 91/563–0202).

Getting Around

By Bus

Bus service among the main cities and most smaller towns is comprehensive, but few have main bus stations where information can be obtained; most have numerous bus companies serving different routes and leaving from different points. Ask at travel agencies or local tourist offices. The following do have central bus stations: **Burgos** (✉ Calle Miranda 4, ☎ 947/265565), **Santander** (✉ Calle Navas de Tolosa s/n, ☎ 942/211995), **Pamplona** (✉ Calle Conde Oliveto 8, ☎ 948/223854), and **San Sebastián** (✉ Calle Sancho el Sabio 33, ☎ 943/463974).

By Car

Because so many of the north's attractions are rural landscapes and relatively small towns, a car is the ideal mode of transportation. Some distances within this relatively small area are Burgos–Bilbao, 159 km/99 mi; Santander–Bilbao, 107 km/66 mi; Bilbao–San Sebastián, 119 km/71 mi; and San Sebastián–Pamplona, 91 km/56 mi. This region has the best road system in Spain. The NI from the French border to San Sebastián and Vitoria is packed with tourists in July and August, however, and should be avoided then at all costs. In addition, the N634 from Santander to Bilbao snakes through mountainous country and can be very slow going because of trucks; however, a new four-lane highway has dramatically improved that trip.

By Train

Trains are not the ideal way to travel the region, although many major cities are connected by rail. The main train stations in the region belong to the RENFE system. They are **Burgos** (✉ end of Avenida Conde de Guadalhorce, ☎ 947/203560; ✉ RENFE agent, Calle La Moneda 21, ☎ 947/209131), **Santander** (✉ Calle Rodriguez near center of town, ☎ 942/210211; ✉ RENFE office, Paseo de Pereda 25, ☎ 942/212387 or 942/218567), **Bilbao** (⊠ Estación del Abando, Calle Hurtado de Amezaga, ☎ 94/423–8623 or 94/423–8636), **San Sebastián** (⊠ Estación del Norte, Avenida de Francia, ☎ 943/283089 or 943/283599; ⊠ RENFE's main office, Calle Camino 1, ☎ 943/426430), and **Pamplona** (⊠ on road to San Sebastián, ☎ 948/130202). In addition, the regional FEVE train company (⊠ Estación de FEVE, next to Estación de Abando, Bilbao, ☎ 94/423–2266) runs a delightful, narrow-gauge train that winds through stunning landscapes. From San Sebastián, lines west to Bilbao and east to Hendaye depart from the Estación de Amara (⊠ Plaza Easo 9, ☎ 943/450131 or 943/471852).

Contacts and Resources

Consulates

Bilbao: Great Britain (⊠ Calle Alameda Urquijo 2, 8th floor, ☎ 94/415–7600 or 94/415–7722), United States (⊠ Avenida Lehendakari Aguirre 11, 3rd floor, ☎ 94/475–8300 or 94/475–8308).

Emergencies

Police: ☎ 091.

Guided Tours

There are no regularly organized tours in the region, but travel agencies in major cities will know of those offered by local firms, usually during the summer. In Pamplona, the tourist office keeps a list of private guides and interpreters for hire.

Jai-Alai

The best local frontón, from which the finest players depart for Miami and other U.S. jai-alai frontones, is **Guernica** Jai-Alai. In **Pamplona,** try EuskalJai Berri (⊠ 6 km/4 mi out in Huarte, ☎ 948/331159 or 943/331160) or, in **San Sebastián,** Galarreta JaiAlai (⊠ on highway to Hernani, ☎ 943/551023), both of which host games Thursdays and weekends.

Monastery Visits

Contact the **Monasterio de Santo Domingo de Silos** (⊠ Santo Domingo de Silos, Burgos, ☎ 947/390068) or **Monasterio de San Pedro de Cardeña** (⊠ Cardeña, Burgos, ☎ 947/290033).

Visitor Information

General information and pamphlets on the Basque provinces (Alava, Vizcaya, and Guipúzcoa) are available in the regional government building in **Vitoria** (⊠ Parque de la Florida, Vitoria, ☎ 945/131321) and at the **San sebastián** tourist office (⊠ Calle Fueros 1, San Sebastián, ☎ 943/426282).

Bilbao's official city tourism office is on the ground floor of the Teatro Arriaga downtown (⊠ Plaza Arriaga, ☎ 94/416–0022 or 94/416–0288); the regional tourism office (☎ 94/4242277) is at Gran Via 441 Izquierda. **Burgos** (⊠ Plaza Alonso Martínez 7, ☎ 947/203125). **Guernica** (⊠ Artekale 5, ☎ 94/625–5892). **Pamplona** (⊠ Calle Duque de Ahumada 3, ☎ 948/220741). **San Sebastián** (⊠ Calle Reina Regente s/n, ☎ 943/481166). **Santander** (⊠ Estación Marítimo, at ferry landing, ☎ 942/310708). **Vitoria** (⊠ Edificio Europa, Av. Gasteiz, ☎ 945/161261).

6 The Pyrenees

The Pyrenees, snowcapped mountains that have historically sealed off the Iberian Peninsula from the rest of Western Europe, are a source of much fascination, legend, and superstition. They have protected within their meadows and valleys the last vestiges of several ancient cultures. Thoroughly exploring any one of these valleys—its flora and fauna, gastronomy and architecture, remote glacial lakes and streams, and Romanesque art, hidden in a thousand chapels and hermitages—could take a lifetime.

By George
Semler

FOR BETTER OR FOR WORSE, the Pyrenees have historically sealed off the Iberian Peninsula from the rest of Western Europe, helping to shape a trans-Pyrenean culture distinct from that of neighboring France. The tribes in the prehistoric Pyrenees—originally cave dwellers, later shepherds and farmers—saw the first invaders arrive by ship across the Mediterranean when the Greeks landed at Empúries in the 6th century BC. The seagoing Carthaginians colonized Spain in the 3rd century BC, and their great general Hannibal surprised the Romans by crossing the Oriental (eastern) Pyrenees in 218 BC. After defeating the Carthaginians, the Romans built roads through the mountains: Via Augusta at Portus, Strata Ceretana through Llivia and La Seu d'Urgell to Lleida, Summus Pyrenaecus at Somport to Jaca and Zaragoza, and the route through Roncesvalles to Pamplona in the western Pyrenees.

After the fall of Rome, the Iberian Peninsula was the last of the empire to be overtaken by the Visigoths, who crossed the Pyrenees in AD 409. In the 8th century, the northern tribes were met by Moorish invaders from the south. Although Moorish influence was weaker in the Pyrenees and only briefly pushed past the mountains into the rest of Europe, at the end of the first millennium the region was a crossroads of Arab, Greek, and European culture. Toulouse was the melting pot of these influences, the medieval artistic and literary center. Christianity survived the Moors' invasion and occupation largely by fleeing to the hills, dotting the Pyrenees with Romanesque art and architecture. When Christian crusaders reconquered Spain, the Pyrenees were divided among three feudal kingdoms: Catalunya, Aragón, and Navarra, proud and independent entities with their respective spiritual "cradles" in the mountains at the Romanesque monasteries of Ripoll, San Juan de la Peña, and San Salvador de Leyre.

Through the centuries, the barrier of the Pyrenees remained an obstacle to be reckoned with. Napoléon never completed his conquest of the Iberian Peninsula largely as a result of communications and supply problems over the Pyrenees. The German Third Reich chose not to attempt to use post-civil war Spain as a base camp for its African campaign. Franco's Spain aided many Jews fleeing the holocaust to safety over the Pyrenees chain.

The Pyrenees stretch 435 km/270 mi along Spain's border with France. There are three main ranges: the Catalan Pyrenees, the central Pyrenees (in Aragón), and the Basque Pyrenees, which fall gently westward through the Basque country to the Bay of Biscay. The highest peaks are in Aragón—Aneto in the Maladeta ridge, Posets, and Monte Perdido, all of which are around 3,400 meters or 11,000 feet above sea level.

These snowcapped mountains have always been a magical realm, the source of legend and superstition, of myth and mystical religious significance. They have protected within their own meadows and valleys the last vestiges of numerous ancient cultures. Each mountain system is drained by rivers forming a series of some three dozen valleys, between the Mediterranean and the Atlantic, that, especially until the 10th century, were all but completely isolated. The local languages range from Castilian Spanish to Euskera (Basque) in upper Navarra; to dialects such as Grausín, Chistavino, Cheso, Patués, or Benasqués in Aragón; to Aranés, a dialect of Gascon French, in the Vall d'Aran; and Catalan in the Cerdanya, the Vall de Camprodón, and east to the Mediterranean.

Thoroughly exploring any of these valleys—the flora and fauna, the local gastronomy, the peaks and upper meadows, the remote glacial lakes and streams, the Romanesque art hidden in a thousand chapels and hermitages—is a lifetime project. The five tours suggested here are introductions to some of Spain's richest and most remote combinations of geography and civilization.

Pleasures and Pastimes

Dining

Pyrenean cuisine is characterized by thick soups, stews, and the use of local ingredients prepared in many different ways in each valley, village, and kitchen from the Atlantic to the Mediterranean. The three main, Pyrenean culinary schools are obviously those corresponding to the three principal, regional and cultural identities—Catalan, Aragonese, and Basque—but within these are further subdivisions such as the Vall d'Aran, Benasque, Roncal, or Baztán. Game is common throughout. Trout (once supplied by anglers, now often raised in lakes and ponds fed by mountain streams), wild goat, deer, boar, partridge, rabbit, duck, and quail are roasted over coals or cooked in aromatic stews called *civets* in Catalonia and *estofadas* in Aragón and Navarra. Fish and meat are often seared on slabs of slate (*a la llosa* in Catalan, *a la piedra* in Castilian). Wild mushrooms are another important local specialty when in season, as are wild asparagus, leeks, and herbs such as marjoram, sage, thyme and rosemary.

CATEGORY	COST*
$$$$	over 6,000 ptas.
$$$	5,000–6,000 ptas.
$$	3,000–5,000 ptas.
$	1,500–3,000 ptas.

per person for a three-course meal, including tax, house wine, and service

Fishing

Well populated with trout, Pyrenean streams provide excellent angling from the third Sunday in March to the end of August. The River Segre has fine trout fishing down as far as Ponts. Although most rivers and streams flowing from the Pyrenees are good habitats for fish—and fisherman—the Garonne, Aragón, Gállego, Noguera Pallaresa, Arga, and Esca are notable. For information on fishing licenses, *see* the Pyrenees A to Z, *below.*)

Hiking and Walking

In summer, mountain climbing and hiking are fundamental Pyrenean activities. Walking the crest of the Sierra Catllar above Setcases, scaling the Cadí over the Cerdanya, and climbing from Benasque to the highest peaks are typical excursions. Local *excursionista* clubs, especially, the Centro Excursionista de Catalunya in Barcelona, can advise climbers and hikers. Local and trans-Pyrenean paths and trails crisscross the region offering unforgettable views. Wild-mushroom-hunting rambles through the piny, hillside meadows are a way of life for many, combining walking, questing, and eating. (Be 100% certain of any wild mushroom you consume; consult with experts.) There are also opportunities for equestrian outings and four-wheel-drive excursions to the upper Pyrenees. Try a fly-fishing tour of the high streams and lakes on horseback from Llívia in the Cerdanya or a fall hike through the beeches of the Irati Forest in upper Navarra.

Lodging

Hotels in the Pyrenees feel informal and outdoorsy and usually have a fireplace in the public rooms. They often blend with the surrounding mountains and are frequently built of wood and slate, typically with steep roofs. The comfortable and protected but not luxurious atmosphere found in most hotels here reflects the tastes of the visitors—mostly skiers and hikers. Options include friendly, family establishments, such as the Güell in Camprodón or the Hotel Llívia in the Spanish enclave at Llívia; grand-luxe places such as Torre del Remei in the Cerdanya Valley; rural accommodations in Basque *caseríos* (farmhouses) like the Iratxeko Berea in Vera de Bidasoa on the upper reaches of the Bidasoa River in Navarra; and town houses such as La Tuca in the Canfranc ski station of Aragon in the central Pyrenees.

CATEGORY	COST*
$$$$	over 15,000 ptas.
$$$	10,000–15,000 ptas.
$$	5,000–10,000 ptas.
$	under 5,000 ptas.

per standard double room, including service and tax

Romanesque Art and Architecture

The treasury of Romanesque chapels, monasteries, hermitages, and cathedrals sprinkled across the Pyrenees is important enough to organize a trip around. The tiny chapel at Beget above Camprodón, the superb rose window and 50 carved capitals of La Seu d'Urgell's Santa Maria Cathedral, the matched set of churches and bell towers of the Noguera de Tor Valley below the Vall d'Aran, the San Juan de la Peña or Siresa monasteries west of Jaca, and the village churches of the Baztán Valley of Navarra are among the best examples of more than a thousand Romanesque pieces of art and architecture found in the region.

Winter Sports

Skiing is the main sport in the Pyrenees, with Baqueira-Beret as the leading resort. Owing to the increasing reliance on artificial snow machines, there is usually fine skiing from December through March at more than 20 resorts—from Vallter 2000 at Setcases in the Camprodón Valley, west to Isaba and Burguete in the province of Navarra. Although weekend skiing can be crowded in the eastern valleys, Catalunya's western Pyrenees, especially Baqueira-Beret in the Vall d'Aran, rank among Spain's best winter-sports centers. Cerler-Benasque, Panticosa, Formigal, Astun, and Candanchú are the major ski areas in Huesca. There are opportunities for helicopter skiing and Nordic skiing at numerous resorts. Lles in the Cerdanya; Salardú and Beret in the Vall d'Aran; and Panticosa, Benasque, and Candanchú in Aragón are among the leading Nordic ski areas. Jaca, Puigcerdà, and Viella☎ have hockey programs, figure skating classes, and public skating sessions. *El País,* Spain's daily newspaper prints complete ski information every Friday during winter (☞ Outdoor Activities and Sports *in* the Pyrenees A to Z, *below*).

Exploring the Pyrenees

Traversing the Pyrenees from the Mediterranean to the Atlantic is a pilgrimage of deep cultural and telluric significance. A six- to seven-week hike on foot, the crossing can be accomplished in 10 days to two weeks by automobile. The main geographical units are the valleys of Camprodón, Cerdanya, Aran, Benasque, Tena, Canfranc, Roncal, and Baztán.

Great Itineraries

Barcelona is the hub closest to the mountains. A trip through the Oriental Pyrenees would be a good introduction to an important third of the chain. Five days is enough time to reach the Vall d'Aran and the

Noguera de Tor Valley and its Romanesque churches before heading back to Barcelona or farther west. Such a trip is probably the most cost-effective in terms of time, terrain, art, and architecture. A 10-day trip permits the satisfaction of a sea-to-sea crossing, though nearly all of this time would be spent in an automobile.

IF YOU HAVE 3 DAYS
Numbers in the text below correspond to numbers in the margin and on the maps.

Begin in Barcelona, the major urban area with the best communications to the Pyrenees. On the first day, explore the ⛰ **Camprodón Valley** and a night at the Hotel Güell. Spend the second day in the ⛰ **Cerdanya Valley.** On the third day, drive west down the valley through **La Seu d'Urgell** ⑪ and back to Barcelona.

IF YOU HAVE 5 DAYS
If you have five days, beginning from Barcelona or from the Costa Brava, go through the ⛰ **Camprodón Valley** on day one; see the **Cerdanya** on day two; drive down to **La Seu d'Urgell** ⑪ (with a break for climbing **Prat d'Aguiló** ⑩) for the third night. Spend the fourth night in the ⛰ **Vall d'Aran** and spend day five driving through the Noguera de Tor Valley to see the Romanesque churches. If you have time, go through **Aigües Tortes National Park** ⑮.

IF YOU HAVE 10 DAYS
If you have 10 days, the complete crossing is within reach. From Barcelona, or from the Costa Brava, begin by wading in the Mediterranean at Cap de Creus (☞ Barcelona Side Trips *in* Chapter 7), peninsular Spain's easternmost point, just north of Cadaqués, and then cross westward to Fuenterrabía (☞ Burgos, Santander, and the Basque Country *in* Chapter 5) to do the same at the Cabo Higuer lighthouse in the Bay of Biscay; or travel in the opposite direction, reversing the order of this chapter. On the westbound trip, a day's drive up through Figueres and Olot (☞ Barcelona Side Trips *in* Chapter 7) will bring you to the Camprodón Valley, the Vall de Camprodón, and its unspoiled mountain towns, skiing, and wildlife. The next stop is the widest, sunniest valley in the Pyrenees, La Cerdanya. From there move westward through **La Seu D'Urgell** ⑪ to the Vall d'Aran, **Aigües Tortes National Park** ⑮, and the winter-sports center of Baqueira-Beret. Don't miss the Romanesque churches of the Noguera de Tor Valley. Farther west, explore the remote valleys of Alto Aragón, the **Parque Nacional de Ordesa y Monte Perdido** ㉗, and **Jaca** ㉙, the region's most important town. Finally, move through western Aragón into the Basque Pyrenees to visit the Irati Forest, climb over the Velate Pass, explore the **Baztán Valley** ㉟ and follow the Bidasoa River to the Atlantic Bay of Biscay at Fuenterrabía.

When to Tour the Pyrenees
For skiing, tour the Pyrenees between December and April. If hiking is your thing, stick to June through September with a definite emphasis on July, when the weather is better and there is less chance of a blizzard or daily lightning storms at high altitudes. October is nice for the still-green valleys and wild-mushroom hunting. November is the month for changing leaves, the last wild mushrooms, and the first frosts.

THE ORIENTAL PYRENEES

Numbers in the margin correspond to points of interest on the Catalan Pyrenees map.

Catalunya's easternmost Pyrenean valley, the Vall de Camprodón, can be reached from Barcelona by way of N152 through Vic and Ripoll; from the Costa Brava by way of Figueres and Olot; or from France through the Col (Pass) d'Ares, which enters the head of the valley at an altitude of 5,280 feet from the French Vallespir and Amélieles-Bains. This valley has several exquisite towns and churches; a ski area; and peaks and bowls, such as the Sierra de Catllar, where mountain goat, snow partridge, and wild boar abound.

Camprodón

❶ *127 km (80 mi) northwest of Barcelona.*

Camprodón, the capital of the *comarca* (county), lies at the junction of the Rivers Ter and Ritort—excellent trout streams. The rivers flow by, through, and under much of the town, giving it a waterfront character, as well as a long history of flooding. The town owes much of its opulence to the summer residents from Barcelona who have constructed important mansions along the leafy, tree-lined promenade, **Passeig Maristany**, at the northern edge of town. Camprodón's best-known symbol is the elegant **12th-century stone bridge** that broadly spans the River Ter in the center of town. It consists of a wide arch with a graceful angle descending outward from a central peak. Camprodón is also known for its **sausages** of every imaginable size, shape, and consistency and for its two cookie factories, Birbas and Pujol, locked in eternal competition. (Birbas is better and has an image of the bridge on the box.)

Lodging

$$ 🏨 **Hotel Güell.** Owned and managed by the charming Güell family, this elegant glass, wood, and stone structure is home to skiers and enthusiasts of the Camprodón Valley. Rooms are simple but tasteful with heavy Pyrenean wood furniture. ⊠ *Plaça d'Espanya 8, 17867,* ☎ *972/740011,* 𝖥𝖠𝖷 *972/741112. 38 rooms. V.*

Shopping

Don't miss **Cal Xec,** the sausage store at the end of the emblematic Camprodón Bridge. Along with every kind of charcuterie ever conceived, Birbas and Pujol cookies are sold.

En Route   From Camprodón take C151 north toward the French border at Col d'Ares and turn east toward Rocabruna, a village of crisp, clean Pyrenean stone at the source of the crystalline River Beget.

Beget

❷ *17 km (11 mi) east of Camprodón.*

The village of Beget, considered Catalunya's *més bufó* (cutest), was connected to the rest of the world by asphalt roadway only in 1980 and until the mid-60s was completely cut off from motorized transportation. Beget's 30 houses are eccentric, stone structures with heavy, wood doors and an unusual golden tone peculiar to the Camprodón Valley. Graceful stone bridges span the stream in which protected trout feast. The 11th-century **Sant Cristófol Church** has a diminutive bell tower and a 6-foot Majestat, a polychrome wood carving of Christ in a head-to-foot tunic, dating from the 12th or early 13th century. The church is usually closed, but townsfolk can direct you to the keeper of the key.

Dining

$$ ✗ **Can Po.** Perched over a deep gulley, Can Po serves first-rate cuisine in an ancient, ivy-covered, stone and mortar farmhouse. Specialties include *peu de porc* (pigs' feet) and *anec amb peras* (duck prepared with

Catalan Pyrenees

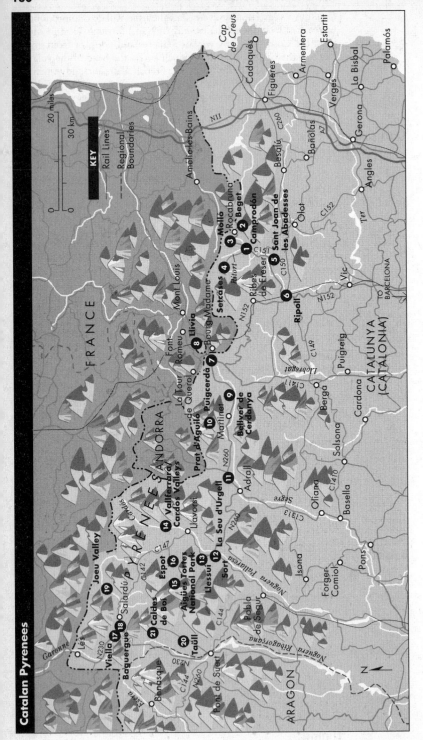

stewed pears). ✉ *Carretera de Beget s/n, 17867,* ☎ *972/741045. MC,
V. Closed Mon.–Thurs.*

Molló

❸ *135 km (84 mi) northwest of Barcelona.*

Molló lies on route C151 on the Ritort stream toward Col d'Ares. Molló
is the site of a **12th-century Romanesque church** of exceptional balance and simplicity, with a delicate, Romanesque bell tower that seems
set into the building and the surrounding countryside like a half-
hidden Pyrenean mushroom.

Setcases

❹ *91 km (57 mi) northwest of Gerona; 11 km (7 mi) northwest of Camprodón.*

This tiny village is nestled at the head of the valley. Although Setcases
(literally, "seven houses") is somewhat larger than its name would imply,
the town has a distinct, mountain spirit, a gravelly roughness, perhaps
owing to the torrents flowing through and over the streets of town en
route to the River Ter.

The **Vallter ski area** above Setcases, built into a glacial cirque reaching a height of 8,216 feet, has a dozen lifts and, on very clear days,
views east from the top all the way to the Bay of Roses and Cap de
Creus on the Costa Brava.

On the road back down the valley from Setcases, **Llanars,** just short
of Camprodón, has a **12th-century church** in a rare shade of ocher. The
wood-and-ironwork portal depicts the martyrdom of St. Steven.

Sant Joan de les Abadesses

❺ *21 km (13 mi) southeast of Setcases; 14 km (9 mi) south of Camprodón.*

South of Camprodón, Sant Joan de les Abadesses—named for the 9th-
century abbess Emma, daughter of Guifré el Pilós, the founder of the
Catalonian nation and medieval hero of the Christian Reconquest of
Ripoll—is the site of the important, **12th-century church of Sant Joan.**
The altarpiece is a 13th-century polychrome wood sculpture of the Descent from the Cross, one of the most expressive and human of that
epoch. The town's **porticoed main square** has a medieval look and feel;
the **12th-century bridge** over the Ter is wide and graceful.

Ripoll

❻ *65 km (40 mi) southeast of Puigcerdà.*

Ripoll, one of the first Christian strongholds of the Reconquest and
an important center of religious erudition during the Middle Ages, is
known as the *bressol* (cradle) of Catalonian nationhood. A dark, mysterious country town built around a **9th-century Benedictine monastery,**
Ripoll was a focal point of culture throughout the Rousillon (French
Catalonia and the Pyrenees) from the monastery's founding in 888 until
the mid-19th century.

The 12th-century **Santa Maria Church** doorway is one of Catalunya's
great works of Romanesque art. Designed as a triumphal arch, its sculptures portray the glory of God and his creatures from the creation onward. A guide to the figures on the portal, the work of stone masons
and sculptors of the Rousillon school, is available at the church or at

the information kiosk nearby. ✉ *Cloister 250 ptas., museum 350 ptas.* ☉ *Tues.–Sun. 10–2 and 3–7.*

North of Ripoll, the cogwheel train from Ribes up to Nuria offers one of Catalunya's most unusual excursions. Known as the *cremallera* (zipper), the cogwheel line was constructed in 1917 to connect Ribes with the **sanctuary of La Mare de Deu de Nuria** (Mother of God of Nuria). (The ride takes 45 minutes and costs 1,500 ptas. round-trip.) Nuria, at an altitude of 6,562 feet at the foot of Puigmal, is a **ski area**, and site of some of Spain's earliest ice hockey activity, starting in the 1950s.

The legend of Nuria, a Marian religious retreat, is based on the story of Sant Gil of Nîmes, who did penance in the valley of Nuria during the 7th century, leaving behind a wooden statue of the Virgin Mary, a bell he used to summon shepherds to prayer, and a cooking pot. Three centuries later, a pilgrim found these treasures in the sanctuary at Nuria. The **bell and the pot** came to have special importance to barren women, who were enabled to bear as many children as they wished by placing their heads in the pot and ringing the bell, each peal of the bell meaning another child. ✉ *Free.* ☉ *Open daily except during religious celebrations.*

En Route   It is a 63-km/39-mi drive on Route N152 from Ripoll through Ribes de Freser and over the Collada de Toses (Tosses Pass) to Puigcerdà. Above Ribes, the road winds to the top of the pass over a sheer drop down to the Freser stream. From here, even during the driest months, emerald-green pastures remain moist in shaded corners—a sharp contrast to the shale and brown peaks above the tree line. In early spring the climate can range from showers at Ribes to a blizzard at Tosses.

This traditional approach to the Cerdanya has been all but replaced by the road through Manresa, Berga, and the Túnel del Cadí (Cadí tunnel). Tosses was a barrier for centuries, until the railroad connected Puigcerdà to Barcelona in 1924. The 32 km/20 mi of switchback curves between Ribes and La Molina kept many in Barcelona until the tunnel cut the driving time from more than three hours to less than two and all but eliminated the danger factor.

LA CERDANYA

The Pyrenees's widest, sunniest valley—said to be in the shape of the handprint of God—La Cerdanya is an alpine paradise. High pastureland bordered north and south by snow-covered peaks, the valley starts in France at Mont Louis and ends at Martinet in the Spanish province of Lleida. Split into two countries and subdivided into two more provinces, the Cerdanya is nevertheless an autonomous geographical and cultural unit with an identity of its own.

"Meitat de França, meitat d'Espanya, no hi ha altra terra com la Cerdanya" ("Half France, half Spain, there's no country like the Cerdanya"): The Cerdanya Valley straddles the border that meanders through the rich valley floor no more purposefully than the River Segre itself. Inhabitants on both sides of the border speak Catalan, a Romance language derived from early Provençal French, and regard the valley's international division with undisguised hilarity.

The Cerdanya, unlike any other valley in the upper Pyrenees, runs east–west, and thus has a record annual number of hours of sun. Two solar stations collect and store energy at Font Romeu, while in Mont Louis, also on the French side of the valley, there is a medieval solar oven once used for baking bread.

Puigcerdà

❼ *65 km (40 mi) northwest of Ripoll.*

Puigcerdà (*puig* means "hill"; *cerdà* derives from "Cerdanya") is the valley's largest town. From the small piece of high ground upon which it stands, the views across the meadows and into the Pyrenees inspire sensations of both height and humility. The **Romanesque bell tower** and the **sunny sidewalk café** beside it are among Puigcerdà's prettiest spots, along with the Gothic **Santa Maria Church** and its long square, the **Plaça del Cuartel,** where Sunday markets offer shoppers from both sides of the border clothes, cheeses, fruits, vegetables, and wild mushrooms.

The **Plaça Cabrinetty,** with its porticoes and covered walks, has a sunny, northeast corner where farmers in for the Sunday market gather to discuss life. This square is protected from the wind and ringed by two- and three-story houses of various pastel colors, some with engraved decorative designs, all with balconies. Leaving the lower end of Plaça Cabrinetty, Carrer Font d'en Llanas winds down to the *font* (spring) where *Voldria*, a haunting verse by the Cerdanya's greatest poet, Magdalena Masip (1890–1970), is inscribed on a plaque over the fountain: *I wish . . . and I wish that I could have/my house beneath a fir tree/with all the woods for a garden/ and all the sky for a roof./And flee from the world around me/that overwhelms and confuses me/and stay there quiet like that/drinking the woods in great gulps/with clods of earth for a pillow/and a bed of golden leaves.*

A 300-yard walk around to the right from the font of **Voldria** will bring you to the stairs leading up from the train station to the balcony in front of the town hall. From this *mirador,* an ample view of the Cerdanya Valley stretches all the way past Bellver de Cerdanya down to the rock walls of the Sierra del Cadí above Martinet and the end of the valley itself.

NEED A BREAK?

The **Madrigal** (✉ Alfons I 1), the best tapas restaurant in Puigcerdà, is next to the town hall square. Owner-manager Pere Compte serves delicacies ranging from hot mushrooms to squid to Serrano ham on *pa amb tomaquet* (toasted bread with oil, garlic, and tomato paste) from 9 AM to well after midnight.

To explore the **Cerdanya Valley floor,** walk from Puigcerdà north to La Tour de Querol in France or out to Aja and Vilallovent to the southeast on roads that wind through green fields filled in spring with foals and calves. You could also the train to Alp or Urtg or up to La Tour de Querol and walk back to Puigcerdà.

Le petit train jaune (little yellow train) leaves daily from La Tour de Querol or from Bourg-Madame, a short walk from Puigcerdà, winding through the Cerdanya to the walled city of Vilafranca de Conflent. The *carrilet* (narrow-gauge railway) is the last in the Pyrenees and is used for tours as well as for getting around the valley. The 63 km/39 mi tour can take most of a day, especially if you stop to browse through Mont Louis or Vilafranca. The train resembles an illustration from a Dr. Seuss story and is popular with children and adults. ⊞ *2,000 ptas. (100 frs.) per person in groups of 10 or more, 3,000 ptas. (150 frs.) singly; boarding at SNCF stations at Bourg-Madame or La Tour de Querol, payable in French frs. only.* ☉ *Schedules at Touring travel agency or Turismo Office, Puigcerdà; or at RENFE station below Puigcerdà.*

Dining and Lodging

$$–$$$ ✗ **La Tieta.** A nearly 500 year-old, restored town house built into the original walls of Puigcerdà, this is the town's top restaurant. Its garden is an ideal place for a late-night drink in summer, and the menu has mountain specialties such as *trinxat de Cerdanya* (roast kid over coals) and a rib-sticking purée of cabbage and potatoes mixed with bits of fried salt pork or bacon. ✉ *Carrer de les Ferrers 20,* ☎ *972/880156. MC, V.*

$ ✗ **Madrigal.** This popular bar-restaurant is near the Puigcerdà town hall. The low-ceilinged, wood-trimmed dining room upstairs is filled with tables and benches. Selections include tapas or a meal of assorted specialties such as calamares a la *romana,* quail, Serrano ham, *albóndigas* (meatballs), *caracoles* (snails), *esqueixada* (raw codfish with peppers and onion), or wild mushrooms in season. Pere Compte, proprietor and host, is always helpful in suggesting selections. ✉ *Alfons I 1,* ☎ *972/880860. MC, V.*

$$$$ ✗▥ **La Torre del Remei.** Two miles west of Puigcerdà, this splendid,
★   mansion built in 1910 has been brilliantly restored by José María and Loles Boix of Can Boix (☞ *below*). Everything about the Torre del Remei, from the Belle Epoque luxury of the manor house to the redesigned rooms, heated bathroom floors, huge bathtubs, the bottle of Moët & Chandon on ice upon arrival, and, of course, the cuisine, is superb. Reserve well in advance. ✉ *Camí Reial s/n, Bolvir de Cerdanya, 17463,* ☎ *972/140182,* ℻ *972/140449. 11 rooms. Restaurant, pool, 2 putting greens. AE, DC, MC, V.*

$$ ✗▥ **Hotel Maria Victoria.** This comfortable perch overlooking the Cerdanya Valley is a relaxed and convenient in-town base. The staff is friendly and helpful; the rooms, charmingly lived-in, have creaky, wooden floors, flowered wallpaper, and panoramic views to the Sierra del Cadí. The glassed-in restaurant is warmed by the sun in winter, breezy and open in summer. The house specialty is *escudella* (a country stew of meats and vegetables). ✉ *Querol 9, 17520,* ☎ ℻ *972/880300. 50 rooms. Restaurant. AE, MC, V.*

Nightlife and the Arts

Clubs such as **N'Ho Sé, Transit, Gatzara,** and **De Nit** (5 km/3 mi from Puigcerdà near Caixans on the road to Alp) are filled with young French and Spanish until dawn on weekends and holidays.

Shopping

Look for local specialties, such as herbs, goat cheese, wild mushrooms, honey, and basketry, found in the Sunday markets held in most towns. The **Puigcerdà Sunday market** is as social as it is commercial. The long square in front of the church and former military barracks, known as the Plaça del Cuartel, fills with people and produce of all kinds, a great chance to learn about wild mushrooms of autumn.

Llívia

❽   *6 km (4 mi) northeast of Puigcerdà.*

Llívia is a Spanish enclave in French territory. Marooned by the 1659 Peace of the Pyrenees treaty that ceded 33 villages to France, Llívia, incorporated as a *vila* (town) by royal decree of Carlos V—who spent a night there in 1528 and was impressed by its beauty and the hospitality of its inhabitants—remained Spanish. Llívia's **fortified church** is an acoustical gem. The **ancient pharmacy,** now a museum, was founded in 1415 and is considered Europe's oldest.

Dining and Lodging

$$ ✕ **Can Ventura.** Built into a 17th-century farmhouse, this superb
★ restaurant is the best around Puigcerdà for decor, cuisine, and value.
Trout or beef cooked a la llosa is one of the house specialties; the *en-
tretenimientos* (a wide selection of hors d'oeuvres) are delicious. ⊠ *Plaça
Major 1,* ☎ *972/896178. Reservations essential. MC, V. Closed Tues.
and Oct.*

$$ ✕▥ **Hotel Llívia.** An ideal base of operations for skiing in France, Andorra, or Spain, the Hotel Llívia is owned and operated by the warm,
generous Pous family, the proprietors of Can Ventura (☞ *above*). A
spacious structure with large fireplaces and a glass-wall dining room
nearly as scenic as a picnic in a Pyrenean meadow, the hotel runs
transports to nearby ski resorts and can organize tours, excursions, riding, or trout fishing. ⊠ *Av. de Catalunya s/n, 17527,* ☎ *972/896000,*
FAX *972/146000. 78 rooms and apartments. Restaurant, pool, tennis
court. DC, MC, V.*

Bellver de Cerdanya

➒ *20 minutes west of Puigcerdà on N260.*

Bellver de Cerdanya has conserved its slate-roof and fieldstone, Pyrenean architecture more successfully than many of the larger towns in
the Cerdanya. Perched on a promontory over the **River Segre,** which
folds neatly around the town, Bellver is a fishing village. The river is
the town's main event; discussions about how much water is coming
down and whether it is low or high, muddy or clear, warm or cold replace the weather as a topic of conversation. Bellver's **Gothic church**
and **porticoed square** in the upper part of town are lovely examples of
traditional, Pyrenean mountain-village design.

Dining

$$$ ✕ **Can Boix.** Although the Lego-blocky, modern building doesn't look
★ like much from the outside, this restaurant 10 km/6 mi from Bellver is
one of the Cerdanya's premier establishments. (First prize goes to Can
Boix owners' La Torre del Remei; ☞ *above*.) José María Boix and his
wife, Loles, prepare a mix of Catalan and French cuisine, featuring *setas*
(wild mushrooms) in season and surprising specialties such as *canard
magret amb mel* (duck breasts with honey) or *trinxat rostit* (chopped
potato and cauliflower prepared with bacon). ⊠ *Ctra. Nacional, km
204, 25724,* ☎ *973/515050,* FAX *973/515268. AE, DC, MC, V.*

$$ ✕ **Grau de l'Os.** This cozy mountain retreat—"Bear Cave" is the
translation—has simple, rough-hewn carpentry. The typical Catalan
cuisine features combinations such as roast rabbit with *all i oli* (olive
oil and garlic sauce), civet de jabalí, and quail, partridge, trout, and
lamb. ⊠ *Jaume II de Mallorca 5,* ☎ *973/510046. AE, DC, MC, V.
Closed Tues.*

Prat d'Aguiló

➓ *An hour's drive above Martinet up a dirt road that is rough but navigable by normal automobile.*

The spectacular Prat d'Aguiló (Eagle's Meadow) is one of the highest
points in the Cerdanya accessible without recourse to a Jeep or a hike.
Another seemingly short climb (which will take about three hours) to
the top of the sheer rock wall of the Cadí range, reaches an altitude of
nearly 8,000 feet. On a clear day you can see Puigcerdà and beyond;
the River Segre seems no more than a thin, silver ribbon on the valley
floor.

La Seu d'Urgell

★ **⓫** *20 km (12 mi) from Andorra la Vieja; 45-minute drive from Puigcerdà past Bellver and Martinet along the River Segre.*

La Seu d'Urgell is an ancient town tucked under the Sierra del Cadí. Its historical importance as the seat of the regional archbishopric since the Middle Ages has left the city with a rich legacy of art and architecture. The mountain *ambiente* of the streets, the dark balconies and porticoes, overhanging galleries, and colonnaded porches make La Seu d'Urgell memorable.

The 12th-century ★**Santa Maria Cathedral,** smaller than Barcelona's Santa Maria del Mar, is similarly graceful in line and proportion. Sunlight gleaming through the rich reds and blues of Santa Maria's southeast-facing rose window over the transept's deep gloom is among the most moving sights in the Pyrenees. The 13th-century cloister, with its 50 columns and their individually carved capitals—sculpted by the Rousillon school of masons who carved the Santa Maria monastery doorway in Ripoll—is an elaborate, intricate work of art, as is the elegant 11th-century Sant Miquel Chapel. In May of 1996, archaeologists discovered Roman tombs in the ground just beside the cathedral—an astounding find that may change perspectives about La Seu d'Urgell's role in the early history of the region. ☒ *300 ptas.* ☉ *Daily 9–1 and 4–8.*

Dining and Lodging

$$ ✕▥ **El Castell.** This wood-and-slate structure is one of the area's finest dining and lodging spots. Rooms on the second floor have balconies overlooking the river; third-floor rooms have slanted ceilings and dormer windows; suites consist of room and salon. The restaurant specializes in mountain cuisine, such as civet de jabalí and *llom de cordet* (lamb cooked over coals). Reservations are required for lodging. ☒ *Ctra. de Lleida, K129, Apdo. 53, 25700,* ☎ *973/350704,* ℻ *973/351574. 38 rooms, 4 suites. Restaurant. AE, DC, MC, V.*

THE WESTERN CATALAN PYRENEES

The town of Sort is a haven for skiers, fishermen, and white-water kayakers. Explore the rugged terrain within the Aigües Tortes National Park, ski the slopes at Espot, or visit the area's many Romanesque churches.

Sort

★ **⓬** *From La Seu d'Urgell, take N260 toward Lleida, head west at Adrall, and drive 53 km (33 mi) over the Cantó Pass to Sort.*

Sort, the capital of the Pallars Sobirà (Upper Pallars Valley), is a sports center for skiing, fishing, and white-water kayaking. Don't be content with the Sort you see from the main road; a block back the town is honeycombed with tiny streets and protected corners built against heavy winter weather. Sort is also the origin of the road into the unspoiled **Assua Valley,** a hidden pocket of untouched mountain villages, such as Saury and Olp.

Llesui

⓭ *15 km (9 mi) north of Sort.*

The **Romanesque church of Sant Pere,** in Llessuí at the head of the Upper Pallars Valley, is topped with a bell tower resembling a pointed witch's hat, characteristic of the Vall d'Aran and its environs. The **ski area** at Llessuí presides over the valley, along the slopes of the Altars peak above.

Vallferrera/Cardós Valleys

⓮ *From Llavorsí, 14 km (9 mi) on C147 from Sort, at the junction of the Noguera Pallaresa and Cardós rivers, the road up to the valleys of Cardós and Vallferrera branches off to the northeast.*

A trip up the Vallferrera Valley is a good way to get into some unfrequented countryside, explore icy trout streams, or browse through the Romanesque and pre-Romanesque buildings scattered in and around the village of **Alins** under Catalunya's highest mountain, the Pica d'Estats. In the neighboring Cardós Valley, the svelte, Romanesque bell tower of the **Santa Maria Church** rises amid the greens of alfalfa and early wheat and the bright red splashes of poppies in May.

Aigües Tortes National Park

⓯ *After Escaló, 12 km (8 mi) from Llavorsí, the road to Espot and the Aigües Tortes National Park veers west.*

This wild domain of meadows and woods in the shadow of the twin peaks of Els Encantats has more than 50 lakes (the beautiful **Sant Maurici** among them) as well as streams, waterfalls, and marshes. Forested by pines, firs, beech, and silver birches, it has ample pastureland inhabited by Pyrenean chamois, capercaillie, golden eagle, and ptarmigan. The park has strict rules: no camping, no fires, no vehicles beyond certain points, no loose pets. Access to the park is free, however, and shelters equipped with bunks and mattresses provide overnight accommodations. For information and reservations contact the park administration (✉ Camp de Mart, 35, 25004, Lleida, ☎ 973/246650).

Lodging

The **Ernest Mallafré Refugio** (shelter) at the foot of Els Encantats near lake Sant Maurici (☎ 973/624009); the shelter sleeps 36 and is open February–December. Also try the **L'Estany Llong Refugio** (☎ 973/690284) in the Sant Nicolau Valley; it is open mid-June–mid-October and sleeps 57.

Espot

⓰ *Next to the entrance to the Aigües Tortes park.*

Espot, which has a **ski area** (Super-Espot), nestles at the floor of the valley along a clear, aquamarine stream. **La Capella Bridge,** a perfect, mossy arch over the flow, looks as if it may have sprouted directly from the Pyrenean slate.

En Route From Esterri d'Aneu, C142 reaches the Mare de Deu de Ares sanctuary, a hermitage and refugio at an altitude of 4,600 feet, and the 6,798-foot Bonaigua Pass, offering a dizzying look back at the Pallars Mountains and ahead to the Vall d'Aran and the Maladeta Massif shimmering in its white glacial frosting.

VALL D'ARAN AND ENVIRONS

The Vall d'Aran is at the western edge of the Catalan Pyrenees and the northwestern corner of Catalunya. North of the main Pyrenean axis, it is the Catalan Pyrenees' only Atlantic valley, opening into the plains of Aquitania and drained by the Garonne, which flows into the Atlantic Ocean north of Bordeaux. The 48 km/30 mi drive from the

Bonaigua Pass to the Pont del Rei border with France faithfully follows the riverbed.

The Atlantic personality of the valley is manifested in its climate—wetter and colder—and its language: The 6,000 inhabitants speak Aranés, a dialect of Gascon French that can, with difficulty, be understood by speakers of Catalan and French.

Originally part of the Aquitanian county of Comenge, the Vall d'Aran maintained feudal ties to the Pyrenees of Spanish Aragón and, from the 12th century, became part of the Catalonia-Aragón realm. In 1389 the valley was assigned to Catalunya.

The Vall d'Aran, neither as wide as the Cerdanya nor as oppressively narrow and vertical as Andorra, has a sense of well-being and order, an architectural consonance unique in Catalunya. The clusters iron-gray, slate roofs, the lush vegetation, the dormer windows—a clear manifestation of French influence—all make the Vall d'Aran a distinct geographic and cultural pocket that happens to have washed up on the Spanish side of the border. Hiking and climbing opportunities abound here. Guides are available year-round and have an office in Viella.

Viella

🟢 *79 km (49 mi) northwest of Sort.*

Viella (*vielha*, in Aranés), the capital of the Vall d'Aran, is a lively crossroads vitally involved in the Aranese movement to defend and reconstruct the valley's architectural, institutional, and linguistic heritage. The **Romanesque Sant Miquel parish church** has an octagonal, 14th-century bell tower that is one of the town's trademarks, as is the 15th-century Gothic altar. The partly damaged 12th-century *Cristo de Mig Aran* polychrome wood carving, displayed under glass at Sant Miquel Church, evokes an intensely emotional sense of mortality and humanity rarely achieved by medieval sculptors.

From Viella you can visit **Salardú,** with its porticoed central *plaça* and an especially tall, graceful bell tower.

The village of **Tredós,** site of the **Church of Santa Maria de Cap d'Aran,** symbol of the Aranese independence movement and, until 1827, meeting place for the valley's governing body, the Consell General, lies just east of Salardú.

Dining and Lodging

$$ ✕ **Era Mola.** Also known as Restaurante Gustavo y María José, this ★ restored stable with wood beams and whitewashed walls serves Aranese cuisine with a French flair. The *confite de pato* (duck stewed with apple) and *magret de pato* (breast of duck served rare with *carradetas,* wild mushrooms from the valley) are favorites. ✉ *Carrer Marrec s/n,* ☎ *973/640868. Reservations essential. MC, V.*

$$$ ✕🏨 **Parador Nacional Valle de Aran.** This modern granite structure has large windows that overlook the Maladeta peaks. Rooms are furnished with traditional, carved Spanish furniture and floor-to-ceiling curtains. The restaurant serves Catalan cuisine, such as *entremeses Parador* (a selection of hors d'oeuvres, including sausage, asparagus, pâtés, and hams) and *espinacas a la catalana* (spinach cooked in olive oil with pine nuts, raisins, and garlic). ✉ *Ctra. del Túnel s/n, 25530,* ☎ *973/640100,* ℻ *973/641100. 135 rooms. Restaurant. AE, MC, V.*

$$ 🏨 **Residencia d'Aran.** On the left side of the road entering Viella, this modern hotel commands some of the best views in town. Rooms are bright and simply furnished. The cozy sitting room and the charming family who manage the hotel make a stay here delightful. Book ahead during ski season; you are 15 minutes from the slopes. ✉ *Ctra. del Túnel s/n, 25530,* ☎ *973/640075,* FAX *973/642295. 40 rooms with bath. AE, DC, MC, V.*

Baguergue

🔟 *Salardú is 9 km (6 mi) from Viella.*

The town of Baguergue is 12 km/7½ mi below the sanctuary of **Santa Maria de Montgarri.** This partly ruined, 11th-century structure was once an important way station on the route into the Vall d'Aran from France. The beveled, hexagonal bell tower's spire and the rounded brook bottom stones give the structure a speckled sharpness not unlike the coloring of the Pyrenean trout.

Dining

$ ✗ **Casa Rufus.** In the tiny, gray-stone village of Gessa, between Viella and Salardú, Casa Rufus is cozily furnished with pine and checked tablecloths. Rufus himself, who also runs the ski school at Baqueira, specializes in local country cooking; try the *conejo relleno de ternera* (rabbit stuffed with veal). ✉ *Sant Jaume 8,* ☎ *973/645246 or 973/645872. MC, V.* ⊙ *Closed May–July, Sept., Nov., and Sun.*

Outdoor Activities and Sports

DOGSLEDDING

The Pyrenean version of the Iditarod, **La Pirena,** runs from Panticosa to La Molina, February 1–15. Contact Oficina de Turismo de Jaca (☎ 974/360098).

HORSE RACES

The Vall d'Aran's most extraordinary winter-sports event is the **Rally Hipic Internacional Sobre Neu,** a horse race held every February on a 16 km/10 mi course of packed snow. Contact the Centro Internacional Turístico del Val d'Aran (☎ 973/640979) for information.

Joeu Valley

🔟 *9 km/6 mi west of Viella.*

The Joeu Valley, above the town of Les Bordes, provides a surprising look into the Vall d'Aran's water-drainage system. One of the two main sources of the Garonne, the Joeu River at Artiga de Lin cascades down the Barrancs waterfalls, disappears underground into the Aigüalluts tunnel and reappears 4 km/2½ mi later at Güell d'Et Joeu, flowing north toward the Garonne and, eventually, the Atlantic.

The **Baqueira-Beret and Tuca-Betrén winter-sport centers,** visited annually by King Juan Carlos I and the royal family, provide Catalunya's most varied and reliable skiing.

En Route The 6-km/4-mi Viella tunnel under the Maladeta peak connects the Vall d'Aran with the Alta Ribagorça Oriental.

ALTA RIBAGORÇA ORIENTAL

This valley includes the east bank of the Noguera Ribagorçana River and the Llevata and Noguera de Tor valleys; the latter has the Pyrenees' richest concentration of medieval art and architecture.

Route N230 runs south from Viella, 33 km/20 mi to the intersection with N260, which goes west to the Fadas Pass. Four km/2½ mi farther, the road up the Noguera de Tor Valley turns to the northeast, 2 km/1½ mi short of Pont de Suert.

The quality and unity of design apparent of the Romanesque churches in the villages along the Noguera de Tor are the result of the protection of the counts of Erill. The Erill knights, away fighting the Moors in distant theaters of the Reconquest, left women behind to support the creation of the religious structures here. They brought in the leading masters—architects, masons, sculptors, and painters—to build and decorate the churches. To what extent a single eye and sensibility was responsible for the extraordinarily harmonious and coherent set of churches along the Noguera de Tor River may never be known. They all share definite characteristics: a miniaturistic tightness; an eccentric or irregular design; and square and slender bell towers at once light and forceful, perfectly balanced against the rocky background.

Taüll

㉑ *58 km (36 mi) south of Viella.*

Taüll, a town of narrow streets and tight mountain design—wooden balconies, steep slate roofs—now has a ski resort, **Boí Taüll,** at the head of the Sant Nicolau Valley.

The **church of Sant Climent,** at the edge of town, was built in 1123. This three-naved basilica has a six-story belfry. The proportions, the Pyrenean stone, changing hues in the light, and the intimacy of the place create an exceptional balance and harmony. The church's murals, including the famous *Pantocrator,* the work of the "Master of Taüll," were moved to Barcelona's Museu Nacional d'Art de Catalunya (MNAC) in 1922; reproductions have been installed in Sant Climent. ⊠ *400 ptas.* ⊙ *Daily 9–2 and 4–8.*

Although Sant Climent is the best known of these Romanesque gems, other important churches in this area include **Sant Feliu,** at Barruera; **Sant Joan Baptista,** at Boí; **Santa Maria,** at Cardet; **Santa Maria,** at Col; **Santa Eulàlia,** at Erill-la-vall; **La Nativitat de la Mare de Deu** and **Sant Quirze,** at Durro; **Sant Llorenç,** at Sarais; and **Sant Nicolau,** in the Sant Nicolau Valley, at the entrance to the Aigües Tortes National Park.

Caldes de Boí

㉒ *6 km (4 mi) north of Taüll.*

The thermal baths at Caldes de Boí include, between hot and cold sources, 40 springs. The caves inside the area of the baths, with thermal steam seeping through the cracks in the rock, are a singular natural phenomenon. Take advantage of the therapeutic qualities of these baths at either the Hotel Sallent-Caldes or the Hotel Manantial. Services range from a thermal bath costing 1,000–1,500 ptas. to a 3,000 ptas. underwater body massage; arthritic patients are frequent visitors. ⊠ *Hotel Caldes,* ☎ *973/696230;* ⊠ *Hotel Manantial,* ☎ *973/690191.* ⊙ *June 24–Sept.*

En Route   The western end of the Aigües Tortes National Park (☞ *above*) can be reached through the Sant Nicolau Valley to the east; to the west, 7 km/4½ mi north of Pont de Suert, N260 turns toward the Benasque Valley and the Central Pyrenees of Aragón.

ARAGÓN AND THE CENTRAL PYRENEES

Numbers in the margin correspond to points of interest on the Central and Western Pyrenees map.

In Alto Aragón (Upper Aragón), the northern part of the province of Huesca, the Maladeta (11,165 feet), Posets (11,070 feet), and Monte Perdido (11,004 feet) massifs are the highest points in the Pyrenean chain. The north–south valleys were formed by glaciers at their headlands; the lower deep canyons and gorges were cut by rivers swollen by rainfalls and heavy snow runoff.

Communications in this area were all but nonexistent until recently. Four-fifths of the region had never seen a motorized vehicle of any kind until the beginning of the century, while the 150 km/93 mi of border with France between Portalet de Aneu and Vall d'Aran never had an international crossing. The high peaks, deep defiles, and lack of communication has produced some of the Iberian Peninsula's most isolated towns and valleys. The inhabitants of much of Alto Aragón speak dialects such as Grausín or Benasqués and have variations on the typical Aragonese folk dance, the *jota*, and different kinds of folkloric costumes. The unspoiled setting provides a habitat for a wide variety of Pyrenean wildlife, including several strains of mountain goat; deer; and, in Ordesa and Monte Perdido National Park, the Pyrenean brown bear.

The Noguera Ribagorçana River is the border between Catalunya and Aragón, everything west of the river forming part of the Aragonese Ribagorza. Seventy km/43 mi west on N260 off the road from Viella to Pont de Suert is Castejón de Sos and the Esera River, leading north beside C139 up into the islandlike Benasque Valley. It shares the Maladeta Massif with the Vall d'Aran.

Benasque

★ ㉒ *79 km (49 mi) southwest of Viella.*

Benasque, as Aragón's easternmost town, has always been an important link between Catalunya and Aragón. The 13th-century **Santa Maria Mayor Church** and the ancient, dignified manor houses of the old families of Benasque, such as the **palace of the counts of Ribagorza** on Calle Mayor, are among the notable structures in this town of 1,000 inhabitants. From Benasque you can make excursions to the Maladeta Massif, the Refugio de la Renclusa, and the Pico de Aneto.

The stone farmhouses of **Anciles**, 2 km/1¼ mi south of Benasque, are sturdy examples of mountain design.

The **Cerler** ski area (☏ 974/551012), 6 km/3¾ mi from Benasque, has lifts on the slopes of the Cogulla peak east of town. Built on a shelf over the valley at an altitude of 5,051 feet, Cerler has 26 ski runs, 3 lifts, and a helicopter service, with guides, to drop you at the highest peaks.

Dining and Lodging

$ ✕▥ **Hotel Aneto.** This stone structure, surrounded by the highest crests in the Pyrenees, makes an excellent base camp. The decor and ambience are distinctly Castilian, with a predominantly wood interior and traditional furniture. The restaurant's Aragonese mountain cuisine features such specialties as the *sopa Benasquesa* (a hearty, highland stew) and *crepas Aneto* (crepes filled with ham, mushrooms, and béchamel sauce). ✉ *Carretera de Anciles, 22440,* ☏ *974/551061,* ℻ *974/551509. 38 rooms. Restaurant, sauna, gymnasium. AE, MC, V. Closed Oct.–Dec. 23.*

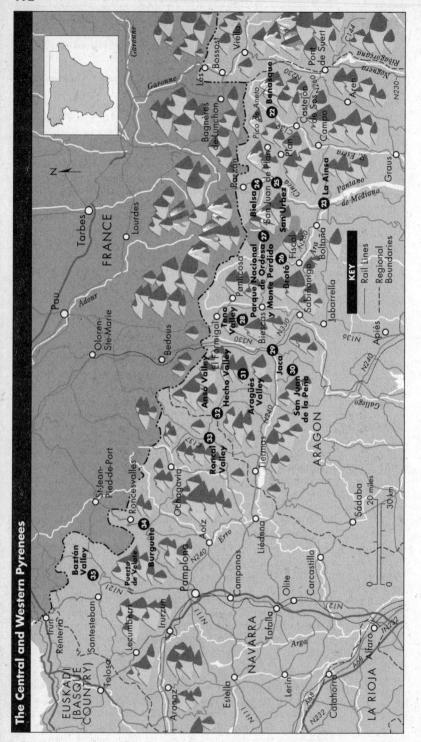

The Central and Western Pyrenees

En Route South of Castejón de Sos, down the Esera Valley, through the Congosto de Ventamillo—a sheer slice through the rock made by the Esera River—a turn west on N260 cuts over to La Aínsa at the junction of the Rivers Cinca and Ara.

La Aínsa

㉓ *66 km (41 mi) southwest of Benasque.*

La Aínsa's **arcaded central plaza** and **old part of town** are classic examples of medieval village design, with heavy, stone archways and tiny windows. In contrast, the **12th-century Romanesque church** has a quadruple-vaulted door. ⊞ *Free.* ⊙ *Daily 9–2 and 4–8.*

Explore the **Cinca Valley** from the river's source at the head of the valley above Bielsa, at the Parador Nacional Monte Perdido overlooking the Pineta Reservoir and the Ordesa and Monte Perdido National Park.

Bielsa

㉔ *34 km (21 mi) northeast of La Aínsa.*

Bielsa, at the confluence of the Cinca and Barrosa rivers, is a busy summer resort with archaic, **porticoed plazas** and **medieval, mountain architecture.**

Northwest of Bielsa the **Monte Perdido glacier** and the icy **Marbore Lake** drain into the **Pineta Valley** and the Pineta Reservoir. You can take three- or four-hour walks from the parador up to the Larri, Munia, or Marbore lakes among remote peaks.

North of Bielsa, the road leading to the French border reaches **Parzán,** in the Barrosa Valley, with trails up to Chisagües and Urdiceto.

OFF THE
BEATEN PATH **GISTAÍN VALLEY** – This rewarding detour rises to the east of Salinas 7 km/4½ mi toward La Aínsa. The Cinqueta River drains the Gistaín Valley, flowing through the mountain villages of Sin, Senes, and Serveta. The towns of **Plan** and **San Juan de Plan** preside from the head of the valley. San Juan de Plan has become a guardian of local folklore. An **Ethnographic Museum** (⊙ Daily 9–2 and 4–8; ⊞ 350 ptas.) and a dance ensemble have been founded.

San Urbez

㉕ *On the road to La Aínsa, the Añisclo Canyon is 5 km/3 mi above the town of Escalona. An asphalt road to the right runs 14 km/8½ mi along the edge of the sheer rock divide to Urbez.*

As you drive into town, you'll see the **ancient stone bridge.** On the far bank of the river is the **cave chapel** named for San Urbez, a hermit monk from Bordeaux who lived there in the 8th century.

Brotó

㉖ *From La Aínsa, turn west on N260 for the 48 km/30 mi drive through Boltaña to Brotó.*

This exemplary, Aragonese mountain town is home to a **16th-century Gothic church.** Brotó also has many satellite villages such as **Oto,** which has several stately manor houses with classical local features: oversize windows and entryways, conical chimneys, and wooden galleries.

Parque Nacional de Ordesa y Monte Perdido

★ ㉗ *2 km (1.2 mi) from Brotó.*

The entrance to the Parque Nacional de Ordesa y Monte Perdido (Ordesa and Monte Perdido National Park), next to the town of Torla, lies under the vertical walls of the Mondarruego Mountain, source of the Ara River and its tributary, the Arazas, which forms the famous Ordesa Valley.

The park, founded by royal decree in 1918 to protect the natural integrity of the Central Pyrenees, has increased from 4,940 to 56,810 acres as provincial and national authorities have added the Monte Perdido Massif, the head of the Pineta Valley, and Escuain and Añisclo canyons. Defined by the Ara and Arazas rivers, the Ordesa Valley is endowed with pine, fir, larch, beech, and poplar forests; lakes, waterfalls, and high mountain meadows; and protected wildlife, including boar, chamois, and the *Capra Pyrenaica* mountain goat.

Hikes through the park on well-marked and maintained mountain trails lead to waterfalls, caves, and vantage points. There are a few spots that, while not physically difficult, are precarious. Information and guidebooks are available at the booth on the way into the park. The best time to visit is from the beginning of May to the middle of November, but check conditions in regional tourist offices before either driving into a blizzard in May or missing *el veranillo de San Martín* (Indian summer) in the fall.

En Route   Follow N260 over the Cotefablo Pass from Torla to Biescas.

Tena Valley

㉘ *40 km (25 mi) from Ordesa.*

The Tena Valley, a north–south hexagon of 400 sq km/248 sq mi, is formed by the Gállego River and its two tributaries, the Aguaslimpias and the Caldares. A glacial valley surrounded by peaks rising to more than 10,000 feet (such as the 10,900-foot Vignemale), Tena is a busy winter-sport and hiking center. Starting from the top, **Sallent de Gállego**, at the head of the valley, has long been a jumping-off point for excursions to **Aguaslimpias**, **Piedrafita**, and the meadows of the Gállego headwaters at **El Formigal** (a major ski area) and **Portalet**. The Pyrenean *ibon* (glacial lake) of **Respumoso**, accessible by walking 2½ hours above the old road from Sallent to Formigal, is a peaceful and perfectly horizontal expanse amid all that vertical Pyrenean landscape.

Dining and Lodging

$$ ✕🏠 **Parador Nacional Monte Perdido.** This modern structure of glass, steel, and stone overlooks the national park, the peak of Monte Perdido, and the source of the Cinca River. Rooms are decorated in bright wood, but the best part is the proximity to the park and the views. The restaurant specializes in Aragonese mountain dishes such as *pucherete de Parzán* (a stew with beans, sausage, and an assortment of vegetables). *Migas Aragonesas* (a combination of bread, grapes, and sausage) is another local dish. ✉ *Bielsa, 22350,* ☎ *974/501011,* 🖷 *974/501188. 24 rooms. Restaurant. AE, DC, MC, V.*

$-$$ ✕🏠 **Morlans.** The rooms here are warm and well equipped with views south over the town of Panticosa's ski area and mountains beyond. The ground-floor restaurant specializes in roast lamb, goat, and suckling pig. The upper restaurant serves civets of deer, boar, and mountain goat, as well as such Upper Aragonese favorites as *pochas* (bean soup with sausage). ✉ *Calle de San Miguel, Barriada de la Cruz, 22066,* ☎ *974/487057,* 🖷 *974/487386. 25 rooms, 2 restaurants. MC, V.*

Jaca

㉙ *Down the Tena Valley through Biescas, a westward turn at Sabiñánigo onto N330 leaves a 14 km/9 mi drive to Jaca.*

Jaca, the most important municipal center in Alto Aragón, with a population of more than 15,000, is anything but a sleepy town. Bursting with ambition and blessed with the natural resources to exploit their relentless drive, Jacetanos are determined to host a Winter Olympics.

Jaca hosts or has hosted a Summer University, the Center for Pyrenean Studies, the biannual Pyrenean Folklore Festival, the Winter Games of the Pyrenees, and the World University Winter Games. World and National Figure Skating Championships are held nearly every year, and the national ice hockey King's Cup is often played on Jaca's **Olympic-size ice rink**. Jaca's ice-hockey program is one of Spain's best, along with San Sebastián's Txuri Urdiñ and another Pyrenees club, Puigcerdà in the Catalan Cerdanya.

NEED A BREAK?	One of Jaca's most emblematic restaurants is **La Campanilla** (⊠ Escuelas Pías 8), behind the Town Hall. La Campanilla's baked potatoes with garlic and olive oil are an institution in Jaca, unchanged for as far back as anyone can remember.

Once the capital of the 11th-century kingdom of Jacetania and an important stop on the pilgrimage to Santiago de Compostela, Jaca has an **11th-century cathedral** that is one of Spain's oldest. The **Museo Episcopal** (☉ Daily 11–1:30 and 4:30–6:30; ☎ 350 ptas.) is filled with excellent Romanesque and Gothic murals. The **Ciutadella** (☉ Oct.–Mar., daily 11–2 and 4–5, and April–Sept., daily 5–6; ☎ Free) in town is a good example of 17th-century, military architecture. The **Rapitán Garrison,** (☉ July and Aug., Mon.–Sat. 5–8, Sun. and holidays 11–1; ☎ Free) outside town, is known for its military architecture, as well. The **Ayuntamiento door** is a notable Renaissance design.

The ski areas of **Candanchú** and **Astún** are 32 km/20 mi north on the road to Somport and the French border.

Dining and Lodging

$$ ✕ **Casa Paco.** Cozy Casa Paco, furnished with bright wood and checked tablecloths, is one of Jaca's best restaurants. The fresh and innovative cuisine features venison, wild boar, partridge, and duck. The current chef is a specialist in Basque cuisine, giving Casa Paco an extra dimension to accompany local Aragonese home cooking. ⊠ *La Salud 10,* ☎ *974/361618. AE, DC, MC, V.*

$$ ✕🏨 **Gran Hotel.** This rambling, wood, stone, and glass structure has a garden and a separate dining room wing. It is central to life and tourism in Jaca. Rooms are comfortable, decorated in rich colors, with practical wood furniture. ⊠ *Paseo de la Constitución I, 22700,* ☎ *974/360900,* ℻ *974/364061. 166 rooms. Restaurant, pool, meeting rooms. AE, DC, MC, V.*

Nightlife and the Arts

Discos such as Dimensión and Oroel are thronged with skiers and hockey players in season (Oct.–April). But the so-called *bares musicales* (music bars), not quite as hard-core, loud or smoky as the discos, are the main nocturnal attraction. Nearly all of these are in the old part of Jaca around the Plaza Ramiro I and along Calle Gil Verges and Calle Bellido.

WEST OF JACA, NAVARRA AND THE BASQUE COUNTRY

The western Aragonese valleys of Hecho and Ansa are among the most pristine enclaves in the Pyrenees, while Navarra's Irati Forest, the Baztán Valley, and the route down to the Atlantic along the Bidasoa River have rich combinations of natural, human, and historical resources.

San Juan de la Peña

30 *Reached by driving south to the town of Bernués (16 km/10 mi), where a right turn leads 12 km/7 mi to the monastery.*

Before starting west through the Aragonese valleys of Hecho and Ansó, you might want to take a loop south to visit the monastery of San Juan de la Peña, a site connected to the legend of the Holy Grail as well as a symbol of Christian resistance during the Moorish invasion of Spain between the 8th and 15th centuries. Its origin is traced to the 9th century, when a hermit monk named Juan settled on the *peña* (cliff) on the Paño Mountain. A monastery was founded at that spot in 920. In 1071 Sancho Ramirez, son of King Ramiro I, founded the Benedictine monastery of San Juan de la Peña, making use of the previous monastery built into the rock wall of the mountain. The **cloister**, tucked under the cliff, was constructed during the 12th century and features carved capitals depicting biblical scenes. ☺ *Oct.–Mar., Wed.–Sun. 11–1:30 and 4–6; Apr.–Sept., Tues.–Sun. 10–1:30 and 4–7.*

En Route   The Aragüés, Hecho, and Ansó are the last three Aragonese valleys. From Jaca, head west on N240 and take a hard right at Puente de la Reina, after turning right to cross the bridge, and continue north along the Aragón-Subordán River. The first right after 15 km/9 mi leads into the Aragüés Valley along the Osia River to Aisa and then Jasa.

Aragüés Valley

31 *Aragüés del Puerto is 2 km (1¼ mi) from Jasa.*

Above Aragüés del Puerto is the **Bisaurín Peak,** at 8,638 feet, one of the highest in the area. **Aragüés del Puerto** is a tidy mountain village with stone houses and diminutive nooks and crannies. The distinctive folk dance in Aragüés is the *Palotiau,* a special variation of the jota performed only in this village. At the source of the River Osia, the **Lizara** cross-country ski area is in a flat between the Aragüés and Jasa valleys where you can find dolmens left from the megalithic period.

Hecho and Ansó Valleys

32 *Hecho is 49 km (30 mi) from Jaca.*

The Hecho Valley can be reached by returning to the valley of the Aragón-Subordan and turning north again. The **Siresa Monastery,** above the town of Hecho, is the area's most important monument, a 9th-century retreat of which only the 11th-century church remains. The Cheso dialect is still alive in the Hecho Valley and is still used by some writers and poets. The **Selva de Oza** (Oza Forest), at the head of the valley, is the natural pièce de résistance, reachable only after passing through the **Boca del Infierno** (Mouth of Hell), a tight draw where the road and the river pass. On the other side of the Selva de Oza is a **Roman road** that, before the 4th century, was used to reach France through the El Palo Pass and became one of the first routes across the border on the pilgrimage to Santiago de Compostela in northwestern Spain.

The **Ansó Valley** is Aragón's western limit. Rich in fauna (mountain goats, wild boar, even a bear or two), the Ansó Valley follows the Veral River up to Zuriza. Above Zuriza there are three cross-country ski areas known as the **Pistas de Linza.** Near Fago is the **sanctuary of Virgen de Puyeta**, patron saint of the valley. From the town of **Ansó**, travel west to Roncal on a difficult but beautiful road through the Sierra de San Miguel.

Lodging

$$ 🏨 **Hotel Usón.** If you want to see more of the upper Hecho Valley and explore the Selva de Ozo forest, stay here. This friendly little Pyrenean inn will rent you a bicycle, find you a trout fishing permit, or orient your climbing or hiking. ✉ *Ctra. Selva de Ozo, Km. 7, 22720,* ☎ *974/375358. 14 rooms. MC, V.*

En Route The Basque Pyrenees extend west from Roncal, at the border with Aragón, to Vera de Bidasoa, where the Bidasoa River, the border between France and Spain, flows down through the western Pyrenean foothills to the Bay of Biscay. From the peaks of Anie (8,213 feet) and Ori (6,616 feet) and the plateau of the Tres Reyes (7,984 feet), the mountains descend to the Pyrenees' last height, Larrún (2,952 feet), in the west.

Roncal Valley

③③ *Take N240 from Jaca west along the Aragón River; a right turn north on NA137 follows the Esca River from the head of the Yesa Reservoir up the Roncal Valley.*

The Roncal Valley is famous for its sheep's milk cheese and as the birthplace of Julián Gayarre (1844–90), the leading tenor of his time. The 34 km/21 mi drive through the towns of **Burgui** and **Roncal** to the capital at **Isaba** winds through green hillsides and Basque caseríos housing farmers and their livestock. Burgui's red-tile roofs backed by rolling pastures contrast with the vertical rock and steep, slate roofs of the Aragonese and Catalan Pyrenees, while Isaba's wide-arched bridge across the Esca is a reminder of Roman engineering influence on later construction. Try to be in the Roncal Valley for the celebration of the Tribute of the Three Cows, held every July 13 since 1375. The mayors of the valley's villages, dressed in distinctive traditional gowns, gather at the San Martín peak to receive the symbolic payment of three cows from their French counterparts, in memory of the settlement of ancient border disputes over rights to high pastures and water sources. The road west (NA140) to Ochagavia through the Lazar Pass offers views of the peaks of Anie and Ori towering over the French border.

Two km/1¼ mi south of Ochagavia, at Escároz, a small secondary roadway winds 22 km/14 mi over the Abaurrea heights to Aribe. From Aribe, a 15 km/9 mi detour through the town of Orbaiceta up to the headwaters of the Irati River at the Irabia Reservoir provides a good look at the **Selva de Irati.**

The Selva de Irati (Irati Forest) is one of the major beech forests in Europe. It is said, though not widely believed, that before the construction of the 16th-century Spanish Armada depleted Spain's forests beyond repair, a squirrel could cross the Iberian Peninsula without touching the ground.

Burguete

③④ *120 km (75 mi) northwest of Jaca.*

South of Roncesvalles (☞ Chapter 5) Burguete lies between two mountain streams forming the headwaters of the Urobi River. The town became famous in 1926 when Ernest Hemingway published *The Sun Also Rises,* with its evocative description of trout-fishing in an ice-cold stream above a moist, Navarran village called Burguete. Travelers to Burguete and to Roncesvalles attempt to recreate the mood of this happy parenthesis in the novel.

Dining and Lodging

$$ ✕⊡ **Hostal Burguete.** This is the inn where Hemingway's character Jake spent a few days clearing his head in the cool streams of Navarra before plunging back into the psychodrama of the San Fermín festival and his impossible love with Lady Brett Ashton. It still works for this sort of thing, although there don't seem to be as many trout around as there were in the 1920s. Good value and simple Navarran cooking make this a good place to stop for a meal or a night. ⊠ *Calle Unica 51, 31540,* ☎ *948/760005. 22 rooms. Restaurant. Closed Feb. and Mar. MC, V.*

En Route   From Burguete continue 21 km/13 mi southwest on C135 until you reach a small road on the right to Saigos, Urtason, Iragui, Egozcue and Olagüe, where it connects with N121 some 20 km north of Pamplona. Turn north and climb over the Puerto de Velate (Velate Pass) to the turn for Elizondo and the Baztán Valley.

Baztán Valley

㉟   *Lesaka is 39 km (24 mi) east of San Sebastián.*

Tucked neatly over the headwaters of the Bidasoa River and under the peak of the 1,081 meter Garramendi Mountain looming over the border with France, the Baztán Valley's rounded, green hills are an ideal halfway stop between the rocky crags of the central Pyrenees and the flat expanse of the Atlantic Ocean below. Each village in this enchanted valley seems smaller and simpler than the next, tiny clusters of red-tile-roofed, whitewashed mortar and stone grouped around the town *frontón* (handball court).

If you are coming through this area during Pamplona's San Fermín festival (July 6–15), stop at **Lesaka,** just 2 km/1¼ mi off the main road (4 km/2½ mi before Vera de Bidasoa). Lesaka's patron saint is also San Fermín, and its *"sanfermines txikos"* ("miniature San Fermín festival") may more closely resemble the one described in *The Sun Also Rises* than the Pamplona beerbust of today.

OFF THE   **CABO HIGUER** – Follow the Bidasoa River down through Vera de Bida-
BEATEN PATH   soa to Irún, Fuenterrabía, and, for its symbolic value as well as for the
                 view out into the Atlantic, Cabo Higuer, the other geographical bookend
                 of this trans-Pyrenean trek begun at Cap Creus on the Mediterranean.

Dining and Lodging

$$ ✕ **Galarza.** This stone town house overlooks the Baztán River in the
★   town of Elizondo and serves excellent Basque fare with a Navarran emphasis on vegetables. Try the *txuritabel* (roast lamb in season with a special stuffing of egg and vegetables) and *txuleta de ternera* (veal raised in the valley). ⊠ *Calle Santiago 1,* ☎ *948/580101. MC, V.*

$ ✕⊡ **Fonda Etxeberria.** This tiny inn, in the town of Arizcun in the Baztán
★   Valley, is an old farmhouse with creaky floorboards and oak doors. The rooms are small but handsomely decorated; not all have private baths. The restaurant serves simple country dishes, such as bean stew and roast lamb. ⊠ *Next to frontón in Arizcun,* ☎ *948/453013. 16 rooms. Restaurant. MC, V.*

THE PYRENEES A TO Z

Arriving and Departing

By Plane

El Prat International Airport at Barcelona is the center for transportation to and from the Pyrenees. El Prat is a 15-minute and 2,500-pta. taxi ride from the center of Barcelona, 30 minutes and considerably cheaper (400 ptas.) by train or bus. There are also airports at Zaragoza, Pamplona, and Fuenterrabia serving the Pyrenees of Aragon, Navarra, and the Basque Country.

To travel from Madrid to a jumping-off point for the Pyrenees, take the shuttle (Puente Aéreo) to Barcelona or go by a scheduled flight to the Hondarribia airport at Fuenterrabía, 20 minutes from San Sebastián.

By Train

The overnight train from Madrid's Chamartín Station to Barcelona or San Sebastián offers several advantages: You leave late (9:15 PM–11 PM) and arrive early (7:30 AM–8:30 AM), thus losing no daytime activities at either end; you may sleep well and save time and money.

Getting Around

By Car

The only practical way to tour the Pyrenees—short of hiking—is by car. The most difficult road into the Oriental Pyrenees is over the Tosses Pass to Puigcerdà, but it's free and the scenery is spectacular. Safer, faster, more expensive but somewhat less scenic (you will have a great view of the Montserrat Massif) is the approach through the Cadí Tunnel. The wide, two-lane roads of the Cerdanya are new and well paved. Moving west, roads may be more difficult to navigate, but they are rapidly being improved. Car rentals are available at airports at both ends of the Pyrenees (☞ Chapters 5 and 7).

By Train

Three railheads have been established in the Pyrenees, at Puigcerdà in the Cerdanya, Pobla de Segur in the Noguera Pallaresa Valley, and Canfranc north of Jaca below the ski resorts of Candanchú and Astún.

Contacts and Resources

Emergencies

Barcelona: Red Cross (☎ 93/2051414). **Province of Gerona:** Red Cross (☎ 972/200415); Guardia Civil (☎ 972/201381). **Province of Huesca:** Red Cross (☎ 974/221186); Guardia Civil (☎ 974/244711). **Province of Lleida:** Red Cross (☎ 973/267011); Guardia Civil (☎ 973/245012). **Province of Navarra:** Red Cross (☎ 948/226404); Guardia Civil (☎ 948/237000).

Fishing Licenses

Season licenses for fishing for each autonomous region (Catalunya, Aragón, Navarra) can be purchased at local rod and gun clubs (*Asociaciones de Pesca, Caza*), at the Federació Catalana de Pesca (✉ Av. Madrid 118, Barcelona, ☎ 93/330–4818), or from the regional fishing authorities: Servei Territorial d'Agricultura, Ramaderia, i Pesca de Barcelona (✉ Carrer Sabí d'Arana 2224, Barcelona, ☎ 93/330–6451).

Golf

The Cerdanya has two golf courses, at **Puigcerdà** (☎ 972/880950) and at **Font Romeu** (☎ 968/303809) in France. Greens fees are 6,500 ptas. at Puigcerdà and 250 frs. at Font Romeu.

Guided Tours

The **Touring travel agency** (☎ 972/880602 or 972/881450, FAX 972/881939) in Puigcerdà can assist in arranging routes, guides, horses, or Jeeps for treks to upper lakes, peaks, and meadows. Local *excursionista* clubs and, especially, the Centro Excursionista de Catalunya in Barcelona (✉ Carrer Paradís 10, ☎ 93/3152311) can advise climbers and hikers.

Outdoor Activities and Sports

Jaca (☎ 974/361032), Puigcerdà (☎ 972/880243), and Viella (☎ 973/642864) have excellent **ice rinks** where there are hockey programs, figure skating classes, and public skating sessions. Spain's daily newspaper, *El País,* prints complete ski information every Friday during the winter-sports season. For up-to-the-minute information, contact the hot line in Barcelona (☎ 93/416–0194). For further information, contact the Federació Catalana Esports d'Hivern (✉ Carrer Casp 38, Barcelona, ☎ 93/302–7040).

Visitor Information

The regional tourist offices for the areas covered in this chapter are **Oficina de Turismo de Barcelona** (✉ Gran Via de les Corts Catalanes 658, Barcelona, ☎ 93/301–7443) for Catalunya; **Oficina de Información y Turismo** (✉ Coso Alto 23, Huesca, ☎ 974/212583) for Aragón; and **Oficina de Información Turística** (✉ Duque de Ahumada 3, Pamplona, Navarra, ☎ 948/211287) for Navarra.

Local tourist offices in major towns covered in this chapter are **Aínsa** (✉ Avenida Pirenaica 1, Aínsa, Huesca, ☎ 974/500767); **Benasque** (✉ Plaza Mayor 5, Benasque, Huesca, ☎ 974/551289); **Camprodón** (✉ Plaça Espanya 1, Camprodón, Gerona, ☎ 972/740010); **Jaca** (✉ Avenida Rgto. Galicia, Jaca, Huesca, ☎ 974/360098); **Puigcerdà** (✉ Carrer Querol 1, Puigcerdà, Gerona, ☎ 972/880542); **Seu d'Urgell** (✉ Avinguda Valira s/n, Seu d'Urgell, Lleida, ☎ 973/351511); and **Viella** (✉ Avenida Castiero 15, Viella, Lleida, ☎ 973/640979).

7 Barcelona and Northern Catalunya

Barcelona is one of Europe's most vital cities: Few places can rival the medieval atmosphere of the Gothic Quarter's narrow alleys or the elegance of the Moderniste Eixample's boulevards. Artists such as Miró, Picasso, and Dalí have links to this vibrant city, which has a strong Catalan identity. During the 40-year, post-civil-war Franco regime the Catalan language and culture were suppressed, but after home rule was granted in 1975 Catalan returned as never before. Now this ancient Romance language is heard in every street and is, along with Castilian Spanish, Barcelona's co-official language.

By Philip Eade
and George
Semler

Updated by
George Semler

CAPITAL OF CATALUNYA, 2,000-year-old Barcelona has long rivaled, even surpassed, Madrid in industrial muscle and business acumen. Though Madrid has now finally well and truly taken up the mantle of capital city, Barcelona has relinquished none of its former power. The city witnessed a massive building program in anticipation of the long-cherished goal of hosting the Olympics. It ranks as one of Europe's most beautiful cities: Few places can rival the narrow alleys of the Gothic Quarter for medieval atmosphere or the elegance and distinction of the boulevards in its Moderniste Eixample.

Barcelona enjoys an active cultural life and heritage. It was the home of the architect Antoni Gaudí (1852–1926), whose buildings form the most startling statements of Modernisme, a Spanish and mainly Catalan offshoot of Art Nouveau, of which other leading exponents were the architects Lluís Domènech i Muntaner and Josep Puig i Cadafalch. The painters Joan Miró (1893–1983) and Antoni Tàpies (born 1923) also began their careers here. It was in Barcelona where Pablo Picasso spent his formative years, and one of the city's treasures is a museum devoted to his works. Catalonia's capital until recently claimed Spain's oldest and best opera house, the Liceu (which burned down in 1994 and is being rebuilt and restored), and acknowledges with pride contributions to the arts of such native Catalans as cellist Pablo (Pau, in Catalán) Casals (1876–1973), surrealist Salvador Dalí (1904–89), and opera singers Montserrat Caballé and Josep (José) Carreras. It flaunts a fashion industry hard on the heels of those of Paris and Milan, as well as one of the world's most glamorous soccer clubs.

In 133 BC the Romans conquered the city built by the Iberian tribe known as the Laietans and founded a colony they called Colonia Favencia Julia Augusta Paterna Barcino. In the 5th century, Barcelona was established as the Visigothic capital; the Moors invaded during the 8th century; and in 801, the Franks under Charlemagne captured Barcelona and made it their frontier with the Moorish empire on the Iberian Peninsula. By 988, the autonomous Catalonian counties had gained independence from the Franks, and in 1137 they were united through marriage with the House of Aragón. In 1474 the marriage of Ferdinand of Aragón and Isabella of Castile brought Aragón and Catalonia into a united Spain. As the capital of Aragón's Mediterranean empire, Barcelona grew in importance between the 12th and the 14th centuries and began to falter only when maritime emphasis shifted to the Atlantic after 1492. Despite Madrid's confirmation as permanent seat of government in 1562, Catalonia continued to enjoy autonomous rights and privileges until 1714, when, in reprisal for having backed the Austrian Habsburg pretender to the Spanish throne, all institutions and expressions of Catalonian nationalism were suppressed by the triumphant Felip V of the French Bourbon dynasty. Not until the 19th century would Barcelona's industrial growth bring about a *Renaixença* (renaissance) of nationalism and a cultural flowering redolent of the city's former opulence.

The tradition of independence nevertheless survived intact, and on numerous occasions Catalonia has revolted against the central authority of Madrid. During the civil war, Barcelona was a Republican stronghold and base for many anarchists and Communists. As a result, during the Franco dictatorship, Catalan identity and language were both suppressed through such devices as book burning, the renaming of streets and towns, and the banning of the use of Catalan in schools and the media. But this repression had little lasting effect, for the Catalans have jealously guarded their language and culture and generally think of themselves as Catalans first and Spaniards second.

Catalonian home rule was granted after Franco's death in 1975, and in 1980, the ancient Generalitat, Catalunya's autonomous parliament, was reinstated. Catalan is now heard on every street, eagerly promoted through free classes funded by the Generalitat. Street names are now in Catalan, and newspapers, radio stations, and a TV channel publish and broadcast in Catalan. The circular Catalan *sardana* is danced regularly all over town. The triumphant culmination of this rebirth was, of course, the staging of the Olympics in 1992. Stadia and pools were renovated, new harborside promenades created, and an entire set of railway tracks moved to make way for the Olympic Village. Not content to limit themselves to Olympics's building projects, Barcelona's last two mayors have presided over the creation of an architecture student's paradise.

Pleasures and Pastimes

Dining

Barcelona is, without any doubt, a feast for all of the senses, though perhaps principally the visual one. But the others, especially the sense of taste, are not far behind. Music prospers here; the air temperature is almost always about right. Even the fragrance of the Mediterranean is often able to overcome urban fumes on the beach at Barceloneta or in the port. But, from the culinary point of view, the post-Franco renaissance of local Catalan culture brought with it an important renewal of Catalan cuisine. What once seemed a city in which the best policy was to look for Italian or French food or faux-Castilian roasts is now filled with exciting places celebrating local produce from the sea, as well as from inland and upland areas. Catalans are great lovers of fish and vegetables, rabbit, duck, lamb, game and natural ingredients from the Pyrenees or the Mediterranean. The mar i muntanya, a recipe combining seafood with inland or highland products, is a standard specialty on most menus. The influence of nearby France seems to ensure finesse while the Iberian factor discourages pretense. The now-fashionable Mediterranean diet featuring "good" virgin olive oil, seafood, fibrous vegetables, onions, garlic, and red wine is nowhere more exactly and universally present than in Catalonia. Catalan cuisine is wholesome and served in hearty portions. Spicy sauces are more prevalent here than elsewhere in Spain; for instance, you will come across *all i oli,* pure garlic and virgin olive oil (nothing else) beaten to a mayonnaise-like sauce and used to accompany a wide variety of dishes from rabbit to lamb to potatoes and vegetables. Typical entrées include *habas a la catalana* (a spicy broadbean stew), *bullabesa* (fish soup-stew similar to the French bouillabaisse), or *espinacas a la catalana* (spinach cooked in oil, garlic, pine nuts, raisins and bits of bacon). Bread is often doused with olive oil and spread with tomato to make *pa amb tomaquet,* delicious on its own or as an accompaniment. Read Colman Andrews's book *Catalan Cuisine (Europe's Last Culinary Secret),* a classic found on nearly every Catalan gourmet's bedside table, for a more complete rundown on the products and practices of Catalan chefs.

Catalan wines from the nearby Penedès region, especially the local *méthode champenoise* (sparkling white wine known in Catalonia as *cava*) more than adequately accompany all regional cuisine.

Barcelona

Avda. Diagonal

Avda. de Pedralbes

Passeig de Manuel Girona

Plaça Prat de la Riba

Ronda del General Mitre

C. de les Escales

C. de Modolell

Via Augusta

Plaça Pius XII

Plaça de la Reina Maria Cristina

C. de Calvet

C. de Muntaner

Via de Carles III

C. de Numància

Avda. de Sarrià

Travessera de les Corts

Pl. de Francesc Macià

Avda. de Madrid

C. de Brasil

Gran

C. de Joan Güell

C. del Vallespir

C. de Berlin

Avda. de Josep Tarradellas

C. de París

C. de Villarroel

Avda.

C. de Sants

C. de Corsega

C. de Muntaner

C. d'Aribau

Estació Sants

C. del Rosello

C. de Casanova

C. d'Antoni de Capmany

Pl. Països Catalans

C. de Provença

C. del Comte d'Urgell

C. de

C. de la Creu Coberta

Avda. de Roma

C. de Villarroel

C. de Mallo

C. de Valencia

Entença

Rocafort

C. de Calabria

C. de Viladomat

C. del Comte Borrell

C. d'Arago

C. de Vilamari

C. de

la Diputació

Plaça Universitat

Gran Vía de les Corts Catalanes

Plaça d'Espanya

Plaça Universitat

C. de Sepulveda

Avda. de Mistral

C. de Floridablanca

Plaça de Sant Jordi

Pl. de les Cascades

Avda. Reina M. Cristina

Avda. del Paral·lel

C. de Tamarit

C. de Manso

Joaquin Costa

C. del

Pg. de les Cascades

C. de Lleida

C. de Hospita

Palou Nacional

C. de Sant Pau

Jardins de Joan Maragall

C. de Blai

Les Flores

C. de Sant Pau

C. la Unió

C. Nou de la Rambla

Estadi Olimpic

Avda. de Miramar

C. de Magalhaes

Rda. de Sant Pau

Carretes

Cami dels Tres Pins

Pg. de Montjuïc

Plaça Portal de la Pau

KEY

◇ Metro Stations
— Railway Lines
◆◆◆ Funicular
••••• Telefèric

Parc de Montjuïc

C. dels Mondials

Jardins de Miramar

Moll de Sant Bertrán

TORRE DE JAUME

N

Castell de Montjuïc

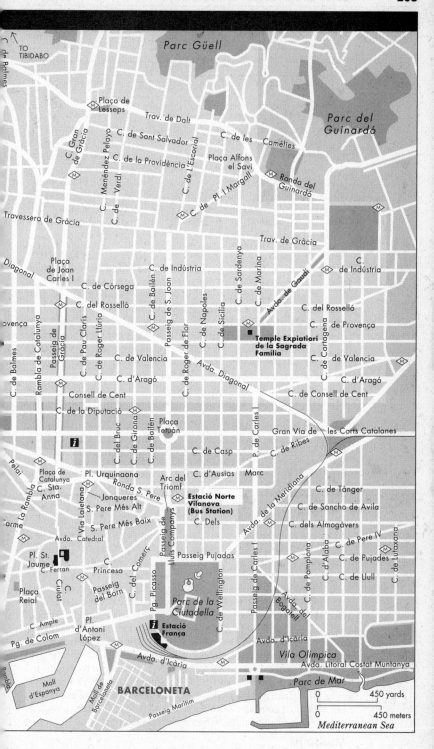

TO TIBIDABO

Parc Güell

Parc del Guinardó

Plaça de Lesseps

Trav. de Dalt

C. de Sant Salvador

C. de les Camèlies

C. Gran de Gràcia

C. Menéndez Pelayo

C. de la Providència

C. de l'Escorial

Plaça Alfons el Savi

Ronda del Guinardó

C. de Verdi

C. de Pl. I Margall

C. de

Travessera de Gràcia

Trav. de Gràcia

Diagonal

Plaça de Joan Carles I

C. de Còrsega

C. de Indústria

C. de Bailén

Passeig de S. Joan

C. de Sardenya

C. de Marina

Avda. de Gaudí

C. de Indústria

C. del Rosselló

C. de Pau Claris

C. de Roger L'Lúria

C. de Nápoles

C. de Sicília

C. del Rosselló

C. de Provença

Temple Expiatori de la Sagrada Família

C. de Cartagena

C. de Balmes

Rambla de Catalunya

Passeig de Gràcia

C. de Valencia

C. de Roger de Flor

Avda. Diagonal

C. de Valencia

C. d'Aragó

C. d'Aragó

C. d'Aragó

ovença

Consell de Cent

C. de Consell de Cent

C. de la Diputació

C. del Bruc

C. de Girona

C. de Bailén

Plaça Tetuán

P. de Carles I

Gran Vía de   les Corts Catalanes

ℹ

C. de Casp

C. de Ribes

Pelai.

Plaça de Catalunya

Pl. Urquinaona

C. d'Ausias   Marc

Avda. de la Meridiana

C. de Tànger

C. Sta. Anna

Ronda S. Pere

Arc del Triomf

C. de Sancho de Avila

la Rambla

Jonqueres

S. Pere Més Alt

Estació Norte Vilanova (Bus Station)

C. dels Almogàvers

Via Laietana

S. Pere Més Baix

C. Dels

Passeig de Lluís Companys

Passeig de Carles I

C. de Pamplona

C. d'Alaba

C. de Pere IV

C. de Lutxana

arme

Avda. Catedral

Passeig Pujadas

C. de Pujades

Pl. St. Jaume

C. Ferran

C. Princesa

C. del Comerç

Pg. Picasso

C. de Llull

C. Ciutat

Passeig del Born

Parc de la Ciutadella

Avda. del Bogatell

Plaça Reial

C. Ample

Pl. d'Antoni López

ℹ Estació França

C. de Wellington

Avda. d'Icària

Pg. de Colom

Vila Olímpica

Avda. d'Icària

Avda. Litoral Costat Muntanya

rambla

Moll d'Espanya

Moll de Barceloneta

BARCELONETA

Parc de Mar

Passeig Marítim

0   450 yards

0   450 meters

Mediterranean Sea

CATEGORY	COST*
$$$$	over 6,000 ptas.
$$$	4,500–6,000 ptas.
$$	2,500–4,500 ptas.
$	under 2,500 ptas.

per person for a three-course meal, excluding drinks, service, and tax

Lodging

Barcelona's 1992 Olympic Games caused a massive boom in hotel construction. New hotels shot up, and existing ones underwent renovations. The most spectacular new hotels in Barcelona are the Hotel Arts and the Hotel Rey Juan Carlos I, which joins (or possibly eclipses) the Princesa Sofía as the Barcelona luxury hotel closest to the airport. Room rates have increased well above the rate of inflation in recent years, meaning that there are very few real bargains left. Don't give up too easily, however, as most receptionists will become flexible about rates if they suspect you might leave in search of cheaper accommodations. Write or fax ahead asking for a discount; you may be pleasantly surprised.

Generally speaking, hotels in the Gothic Quarter and the Rambla are convenient for sightseeing, have plenty of Old World charm, but, with some notable exceptions, are not as strong on creature comforts. Those in the Eixample are generally set in late-19th-century to 1950s town houses, often Moderniste in design; they all offer a choice between street and inner courtyard rooms, so be sure to specify when you book. The newest hotels, with the widest range of facilities and the least sense of being in Barcelona (or anywhere in particular), are out to the west along the Diagonal. Reservations are a good idea, if only to make your bid for a good rate, but the pre-Olympics hotel-shortage days are over, and in the forseeable future there will be few times when lodging cannot be found with relative ease. Ask for weekend rates, which are often half-price.

CATEGORY	COST*
$$$$	over 20,000 ptas.
$$$	15,000–20,000 ptas.
$$	8,000–15,000 ptas.
$	under 8,000 ptas.

per standard double room, excluding tax.

Modernisme

Barcelona is the city most filled with the buildings and various manifestations of the late 19th-century artistic and architectural movement known as art nouveau in France, *jugendstil,* in Germany, *sezessionstil* in Austria, liberty or *floreale* in Italy, modernismo in the rest of Spain and "modern style" in English-speaking countries. This movement was, in many ways, analogous to the "greening of America" spirit of the American 1960's in that it represented a disillusionment with the fruits of technology and industry and a return to more natural shapes and aesthetic values. The curved line replaced the straight line, flowers and fruits and wild mushrooms were sculpted into facades. The pragmatic gave way to ornamental excess. Modernisme is everywhere in Barcelona, not only because it tapped into the playfulness of the Catalan artistic impulse (as evidenced in the works of Gaudí, Picasso, Miró, Dalí and others), but because it coincided with Barcelona's late-19th-century industrial prosperity and an upsurge of nationalistic sentiment.

Museums

Barcelona's museums ofer a wide and constantly self-renewing range of attractions. The Picasso Museum probably gets more acclaim and attention than it strictly deserves, and, though we are certainly not suggesting you skip the Picasso, there are much better permananent collections of art in Barcelona. The best of these is the Romanesque exhibit at the Palau Nacional on Montjuïc. Other less well-known gems are the Thyssen-Bornemisza Collection at the Monasterio de Pedralbes above Sarriàa and the collection of Catalan impressionists at the Museu d'Art Modern in the Ciutadella. The Fundació "la Caixa" at Passeig de Sant Joan 108 frequently offers excellent itinerant shows that have, in the past, ranged from Kandinsky to William Blake. Gaudí's famous Pedrera house on the Passeig de Gràcia also has frequent exhibits as do the new museums, the CCCB and the MACBA in the Raval. Other museums with excellent offerings are the Museu de la Ciencia in upper Barcelona, the Museu d'Història de la Ciutat in the Plaça del Rei, and the Museu d'Història de Catalunya in the Port Vell's Palau de Mar.

EXPLORING BARCELONA

Barcelona is made up of two principal and contrasting parts. The old city lies between Plaça de Catalunya and the port. Above it is the grid-patterned extension built after the city's third set of walls were torn down in 1860, known as the Eixample, where most of the Moderniste architecture is to be found. Farther out are the former outlying towns of Gràcia and Sarrià, the Pedralbes zone and the Collserola hills behind the city.

Great Itineraries

The Rambla and the Gothic Quarter and all of the old parts of Barcelona produce constant surprises, even for longtime Barcelona residents. The markets such as the Boqueria, on the Rambla, or the Mercat de Sant Antoni in the Raval, or Barcelona's flea market known as Els Encants are always good browsing and grazing grounds, well-seeded with cafés, bars, patios, and terraces for mid-itinerary breaks. Balancing the joys of aimless wandering with those of searching out and studying key objectives is the recommended approach.

Three days in Barcelona would be sufficient to explore the Rambla and the Gothic Quarter, see the Sagrada Família and the main moderniste sights, go to one or two of the most important museums, and take in a concert or two. Five days would allow time for a more thorough exploration of the city, as well as an opportunity to see more museums and explore Barceloneta and the Collserola hills. A week-long stay would give you time to become familiar with the authentic rhythms and resources of Barcelona, check the daily papers for art gallery openings and concerts, make a sidetrip to Sitges, Montserrat or the Costa Brava, and to see virtually all of the components that makes this the biggest and busiest city on the Mediterranean.

IF YOU HAVE 3 DAYS

Stroll the Rambla and then cut over to the **Catedral de la Seu** ① and walk around the Mons Taber, the high ground upon which the original Roman settlement was established some 2000 years ago, the area enclosed within Barcelona's first set of walls. Go through **Plaça del Rei** ③ to the **Plaça Sant Jaume** ⑦ where the Catalonian seat of government, **Palau de la Generalitat,** faces across the square to the Town Hall, or **Ajuntament.** From there it is not far to the **Museu Picasso** ⑤, **Santa Maria del Mar** ⑥ church, **Cal Pep** in Plaça de les Olles (for the best tapas in Barcelona) or Set Portes for lunch or even dinner. Try to catch an evening concert at the **Palau de la Música** ㉚. Day two might be a Gaudí day, spending the morning at the **Temple Expiatori de la Sagrada Família** cathedral ㉓, midday at **Parc Güell** ㉕ and the afternoon walking down past **Casa Vicens** in Gràcia, **La Pedrera** and **Casa Batlló** on Passeig de

Gràcia, and the **Palau Güell** ⑪ just off the lower Rambla. The morning of the third day would be a chance to see the best Romanesque art collection in the world at the **Museu Nacional d'Art de Catalunya** ㊷ in the Palau Nacional on Montjuïc, as well as to get at least a glimpse of Montjuïc's other important attractions, such as the **Fundació Miró** ㊶, the **Poble Espanyol** ㊹, or the Olympic facilities, especially Izosaki's superb Palau Sant Jordi and the restored Olympic Stadium. Take the cable car across the port for a late paella at Barceloneta.

IF YOU HAVE 5 DAYS
Walk the Rambla, the **Boqueria market** ⑭, Plaça del Pi and the Barri Gòtic around the cathedral on the first day. On the second day take a couple of hours to see the **Museu Picasso** ⑤ and the **Santa Maria del Mar** ⑥ church nearby. Walk through Barceloneta and down to the Olympic port, or out the rompeolas into the Mediterranean and back. On the third morning you can explore the Raval, to the right of the Rambla, and see the new contemporary art museum, the **Museu d'Art Contemporani de Barcelona (MACB)** ⑰, and the Center for Contemporary Culture, the CCCB, as well as the medieval hospital and Barcelona's earliest church, Sant Pau del Camp. If you have time, you can have a look at the **Museu Marítim** ⑩ in the Reial Drassanes, the medieval shipyards. In the afternoon you can take a guided tour of the **Palau de la Música** ㉚. While you're there, pick up tickets to a concert. The fourth day can be your Gaudí day, taking in the **Temple Expiatori de la Sagrada Família** ㉓ in the morning and **Parc Güell** ㉕ after lunch. In the late afternoon, walk down through Gràcia and see Gaudí's first house, Casa Vicens. Farther down on Passeig de Gràcia you can walk past La Pedrera and Casa Batlló in the heart of the city's grid square Eixample and see yet another early Gaudí structure, the **Palau Güell** ⑪, just off the Rambla on Carrer Nou de la Rambla. The fifth and last day in Barcelona is a chance to explore Montjuïc, visit the **Museu Nacional d'Art de Catalunya** ㊷ in the Palacio Nacional, see the **Fundació Miró** ㊶, the **Poble Espanyol** ㊹, and the Olympic facilities: the Palau Sant Jordi and the Estadio Olímpico. In the afternoon, take the cable car across the port and have a paella in Barceloneta at one of the outdoor terraces along Passeig Joan de Borbó.

Barri Gòtic (The Gothic Quarter)

This walk explores Barcelona's Gothic Quarter, a quiet warren of medieval buildings, among them the cathedral and the Picasso Museum. Parts of the Barri Gòtic and the Barri Xinès (or Barrio Chino), Barcelona's notorious red-light district, received a major sprucing up as part of the Olympic preparations. Wandering off into the heart of the quarter, you will come across squares freshly begot by the demolition of whole blocks and the planting of fully grown palms. Bag-snatching, alas, is not uncommon in these parts, so it's highly advisable not to carry one.

A Good Walk

Numbers in the margin correspond to points of interest on the Barri Gòtic; La Rambla (Les Rambles); Eixample; Parc Güell, Tibidabo, and Pedralbes; Ciutadella and Barceloneta; Montjuïc; and Barcelona Excursions maps.

A good walk through the Barri Gòtic could begin at **Catedral de la Seu** ① and move through and around the cathedral to the left to the **Museu Frederic Marès** ② (and its little café-terrace surrounded by Roman walls); next, pass the patio of the Arxi de la Corona d'Aragó (Archives of the House of Aragón), then turn left again and down into **Plaça del Rei** ③. Leaving Plaça del Rei, on the left is the **Museu d'Història de la**

Ciutat ④ (City History Museum). Crossing Via Laetana pass through the Plaça del Angel and walk down Carrer Princesa will take you to Carrer Montcada and a right turn to the **Museu Picasso** ⑤. Continuing down Carrer Montcada you will pass some of Barcelona's most elegant medieval palaces before emerging into the Passeig del Born. Take a walk down to the Born itself, once one of Barcelona's major produce markets, now used for theatrical and musical events. Next, walk back to **Santa Maria del Mar** ⑥ church just past the Carrer Montcada end of the Passeig del Born. After spending some time in Santa Maria del Mar, walk around the left side of the church through the Fossar de les Moreres. A ten minute walk up Carrer Argenteria and back across Via Laetana to Carrer Ferran will take you to the **Plaça Sant Jaume** ⑦ where the seats of government of both Catalonia and Barcelona face each other in (at the moment) political discord. Try to arrange visits to these buildings, both of which are lavishly endowed with works of art. Finally, walk down Carrer Ferran to **Plaça Reial** ⑧, one of Barcelona's few neoclassical squares.

TIMING
This walk covers some 2 km (1¼ mi) and, depending on stops, should take about three hours (including an hour in the Picasso Museum).

Sights to See

★ ❶ **Catedral de la Seu.** The Cathedral at Plaça de la Seu is the much heralded and magical spot where on Saturday afternoon and Sunday morning the citizens of Barcelona gather to dance the *sardana,* a somewhat demure circular dance and a great symbol of Catalan pride. Climb the steps to the magnificent Gothic cathedral, built from 1298 to 1450. (The spire and neoGothic facade were added in 1892.) Architects of Catalan Gothic churches strove to make the high altar visible to the entire congregation; hence, the unusually wide central nave and slender side columns. Highlights are the beautifully carved choir stalls, Santa Eulàlia's tomb in the crypt, the battle-scarred crucifix in the Lepanto Chapel, the intimate Santa Llucia chapel on the front right corner, and the tall cloisters surrounding a tropical garden. ☉ *Daily 7:45–1:30 and 4–7:45.*

Fossar de les Moreres (Cemetery of the Mulberry Trees). The Fossar de les Moreres is in the open space along the eastern side of Santa Maria del Mar. This low, marble monument honors the defenders of Barcelona who gave their lives in the 1714 siege that ended the War of the Spanish Succession and established Felipe V on the Spanish throne. The inscription on the low, elongated marble (EN EL FOSSAR DE LES MORERES NO S'HI ENTERRA CAP TRAIDOR, or IN THE CEMETERY OF THE MULBERRY TREES NO TRAITOR LIES) refers to the story of the graveyard keeper who refused to bury anyone who fought on the invading side, even one of them who turned out to be his son.

❹ **Museu d'Història de la Ciutat** (City History Museum). This museum allows you to trace the evolution of the city from its first Iberian settlement. Founded by a Carthaginian, Hamilcar Barca, in about 230 BC, Barcelona shortly passed into the hands of the Romans during the Punic Wars. It didn't expand much until the Middle Ages, when trading links with Genoa and Venice began its long and illustrious mercantile tradition. Look for the plans submitted for the 19th-century extension, Eixample, to see how different the city would have looked had the radial plan of Antoni Rovira Trias not been blocked by cost-conscious bureaucrats in Madrid. Downstairs are some well-lighted Roman excavations. ⊠ *Palau Padellàs, Carrer del Veguer 2.* 🎟 *400 ptas.* ☉ *Mon. 3:30–8, Tues.–Sat. 9–8, Sun. 9–1:30.*

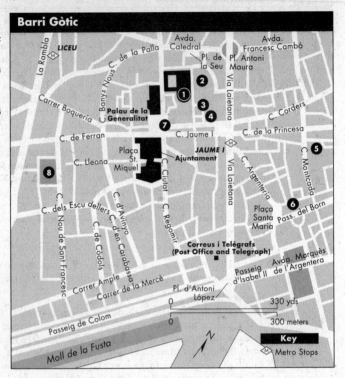

Barri Gòtic

② **Museu Frederic Marès** (Frederic Marès Museum). The Frederic Marès Museum is off the left (north) side of the cathedral. Here you can browse for hours among the miscellany assembled by sculptor-collector Frederic Marès. Displayed here are everything from paintings and polychrome crucifixes to pipes and walking sticks. ⊠ *Plaça Sant Iu 5.* ☎ *350 ptas.* ☉ *Tues.–Sun. 10–7:30.*

★ **⑤** **Museu Picasso** (Picasso Museum). The Picasso Museum is across Via Laietana, down Carrer de la Princesa and just to the right on Carrer Montcada from the Museu Frederic Marès. This narrow street contains some of Barcelona's most elegant medieval palaces, including the Picasso Museum. Two 15th-century palaces provide a handsome setting for collections donated in 1963 and 1970, first by Picasso's secretary, and then by the artist himself. Although it contains very few of his major works, there is plenty here to warrant a visit, including childhood sketches, pictures from his Blue Period, and his famous, 1950s Cubist variations on Velázquez's Las Meninas. ⊠ *Carrer Montcada 1519.* ☎ *650 ptas., ½ price Wed., free 1st Sun. of month.* ☉ *Tues.–Sat. 10–8, Sun. 10–3.*

Passeig del Born. The Passeig was once the site of medieval jousting meets, is at the end of Carrer Montcada, a long and narrow "square" lined with late-night cocktail bars and miniature restaurants with tiny, spiral stairways and intimate corners.

❸ **Plaça del Rei.** This plaza is widely thought of as the oldest and most beautiful space in the Gothic Quarter. After Columbus's first voyage to America, the Catholic Monarchs received him on the stairs fanning out and in the Saló del Tinell, a magnificent banquet hall built in 1362. Other ancient buildings around the square are the Palau del Lloctinent (Lieutenant's Palace), the 14th-century chapel of Santa Àgata, and the Palau Padellàs.

⑧ Plaça Reial. The Royal Plaza is an elegant and symmetrical, 19th-century, arcaded square. The newly repainted yellow houses around the open space overlook the wrought-iron Fountain of the Three Graces and lampposts designed by a young Gaudí in 1879. Sidewalk cafés line the whole square. It has acquired quite a reputation for drug-pushers and the homeless, who occupy the benches on sunny days. The most colorful time to come is on Sunday morning when crowds gather at the stamp and coin stalls and, in times past, listened to soapbox orators. At night it is the center for downtown nightlife. Bar Glaciar on the top Rambla corner is a booming beer place for young internationals.

⑦ Plaça Sant Jaume. This central square is the site of the seats of government for both Barcelona and Catalonia, and it occupies the high ground behind the cathedral. Located in the heart of the Gothic Quarter, the Plaça Sant Jaume was built in the 1840s. The two imposing buildings facing each other across the square are much older. The 15th-century **Ajuntament** (City Hall) to the left has an impressive black-and-burnished-gold mural (1928) by Josep Maria Sert and the famous Saló de Cent, from which the Council of One Hundred ruled the city between 1372 and 1714. You can wander into the courtyard, but to visit the interior, you will need to arrange for a tour in the office beforehand. The **Palau de la Generalitat,** opposite, seat of the autonomous Catalan government, is an elegant, 15th-century palace with a lovely courtyard and first-floor patio with orange trees. The room whose windows you can see at the front is the Saló de Sant Jordi (St. George), dragon-slaying patron saint of Catalunya as well as of England. Normally you can visit the Generalitat only on the day of Sant Jordi, April 23, but check with the protocol office.

NEED A
BREAK?

At the bottom of Carrer Montcada, a cluster of leather wineskins announces **Xampanyet** (✉ Montcada 22), a traditional, tiled bar, popular for its house cava and delicious Catalan tapas. Even better is **Euskal Etxea** (✉ Placeta Montcada 13), which serves Basque tapas.

★ **⑥ Santa Maria del Mar.** Santa Maria del Mar, the most perfect of all Barcelona's Gothic churches, is on the Carrer Montcada end of Passeig del Born. This simple and elegant structure, something of an oddity in Moderniste Barcelona, was built from 1329 to 1383 in fulfillment of a vow made a century earlier by Jaume I to build a church for the Virgin of the Sailors. Its stark beauty is enhanced by a lovely rose window, soaring columns, and unusually wide vaulting. It is a fashionable place for concerts and weddings, and if you pass by on a Saturday afternoon, you are very likely to see a couple exchanging vows eternal. ⊙ *Weekdays 9–12:30 and 5–8.*

OFF THE
BEATEN PATH

MUSEUM DEL CALÇAT – Hunt out the tiny Shoe Museum in a hidden corner of the Gothic Quarter, between the cathedral and the Bishop's Palace. The collection includes a pair of clown's shoes and a pair worn by Pablo Casals. The tiny square, originally a graveyard, is probably more interesting than the museum, with its bullet- or shrapnel-pocked walls and quiet, central fountain. ✉ *Plaça de Sant Felip Neri.* ▣ *300 ptas.* ⊙ *Tues.–Sun. 11–2.*

La Rambla and the Raval

Barcelona's most famous street is a snaking avenue of 24-hour newspaper kiosks, flower stalls, and bird-sellers, along which traffic plays second fiddle to the endless *paseo* (stroll) of locals and visitors alike; it is the street that Federico García Lorca called the only one in the world he wished would never end. The whole avenue is referred to as Les Rambles (in Catalan) or La Rambla, but each section has its own name: Rambla Santa Monica is at the southern end; Rambla de les Flors in the middle, and Rambla dels Estudis at the top leading down from Plaça de Catalunya. A complete macro-Rambla hike could begin at the Diagonal and continue down Rambla Catalunya, through the Rambla proper between Plaça de Catalunya and the Columbus monument, and across the port on the wooden boardwalk Rambla de Mar. El Raval is the area to the right (west) of the Rambla, originally a slum stuck outside of Barcelona's second set of walls, which ran down the left side of the Rambla.

A Good Walk

Our Rambla walk will start on the Rambla opposite Plaça Reial and proceed down the Rambla toward the sea, the **Monument a Colom** ⑨ (Columbus monument), the Rambla de Mar, and the Port Vell's new attractions, especially the aquarium. Moving back to the Columbus monument, the medieval shipyards are a convenient visit as you start back up the Rambla. Gaudí's **Palau Güell** ⑪ on Carrer Nou de la Rambla is the next stop before going by the **Gran Teatre del Liceu** ⑫ (Liceu Opera house) (which will probably still be in the process of rebuilding). At the Miró mosaic at Pla de la Boqueria, cut in to the right to the Plaça del Pi and the church of **Santa Maria del Pi** ⑬. Back on the Rambla, stroll through the **Boqueria** food market ⑭, through the Virreina exhibition center next door and then cut around the medieval Hospital de la Santa Creu. Next visit the new museums and cultural centers, the **MACB** ⑰ and the CCCB on Carrer Montalegre, before hooking back into the Rambla along Carrer Tallers, ending up in **Plaça de Catalunya** ⑲.

TIMING

This walk covers about 2 km (1¼ mi). Allow three hours including stops and visits to complete the suggested itinerary.

Sights to See

⑯ **Antic Hospital de la Santa Creu.** This medieval hospital, surrounded by a cluster of other 15th-century buildings is today home to a number of libraries and cultural and educational institutions. The Hospital can be approached from the back door of the Boqueria (where Petràs and his display of wild mushrooms are a must), either from Carrer del Carme or from Carrer Hospital. Particularly impressive and lovely is the courtyard of the Casa de Convalescència, with its Renaissance columns and scenes of the life of Saint Paul portrayed in *azulejos* (ceramic tiles).

Antigua Casa Figueres. This Moderniste grocery and pastry store is on the corner of Petxina and has a splendid, mosaic facade and exquisite, old fittings.

Barri Xinès. South from Plaça Reial toward the sea, the Barri Xinès (normally referred to in Castilian Spanish as the Barrio Chino), the notorious red-light district, is on your right. The Chinese never had much of a presence there (the name rather a generic reference to foreigners of all kinds); and the area, though ill-famed for prostitutes, drug pushers, and street thieves, is not particularly dangerous compared to cities in other parts of the world. In fact, the reinforced police presence here probably makes it safer than other parts of the Gothic Quarter.

⑭ **Boqueria market.** Barcelona's most spectacular food market is the Boqueria, also known as the Mercat de Sant Josep, an important explosion of life and color complete with delicious spots for coffees and the

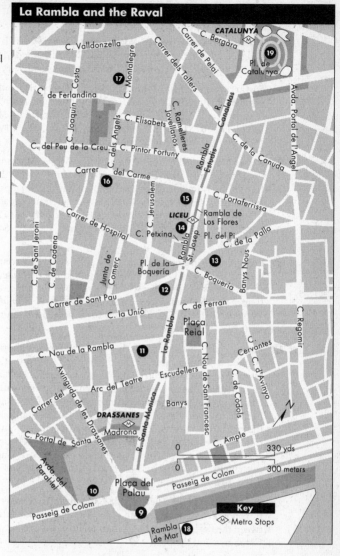

La Rambla and the Raval

odd snack or even a meal at **Pinotxo,** the little bar that could make an international name for itself as a gourmet sanctuary.

12 Gran Teatre del Liceu. Barcelona's once and future opera house, the Gran Teatre del Liceu is on the Rambla at the corner of Carrer de Sant Pau. Long one of Barcelona's most cherished cultural gemstones, the Liceu was gutted by fire in early 1994. Montserrat Caballé stood on the Rambla in tears as this beloved venue was consumed by a mid-morning fire, the origins of which have been the subject of much speculation. The restoration of this landmark, one of the world's oldest and most beautiful opera houses, will continue through most or even all of 1997. Check for tours of undamaged rooms.

9 Monument a Colom (Columbus Monument). At the foot of the Rambla, take an elevator to the top of the Monument a Colom for a breathtaking view over the city. The entrance is on the harbor side of the monument. 📧 *350 ptas.* ⊘ *June 24–Sept. 24, daily 9–9; Sept. 25–June 23, Tues.–Sat. 10–2 and 4–8, Sun. 10–7.*

⑰ Museu d'Art Contemporani de Barcelona. The new MACB building was designed by American architect Richard Meier. ✉ *Plaça dels Angels,* ☎ *93/412–0810.* 📧 *450 ptas.* ⊘ *Tues.–Sat. 10–2 and 4–8, Sun. 10–2.*

Farther up on Carrer Montalegre 5 is the **Centre de Cultura Contemporànea de Barcelona** (CCCB), in the restored and renovated Casa de la Caritat, a former medieval convent and hospital. ✉ *Montalegre 5,* ☎ *93/412–0781.* 📧 *350–650 ptas.* ⊘ *Tues.–Fri. 11–2 and 4–8, Wed. and Sat. 11–8, Sun. and holidays 10–3.*

⑩ Museu Marítim (Maritime Museum). The Museu Marítim is housed in the 13th-century **Drassanes Reials** (Royal Shipyards) to the right at the foot of the Rambla. This superb museum is full of ships, including a spectacular, lifesize, reconstructed galley, figureheads, nautical gear, and several early navigational charts. ✉ *Plaça Portal de la Pau 1.* 📧 *500 ptas., ½ price Wed., free 1st Sun. of month.* ⊘ *Tues.–Sat. 10–2 and 4–7, Sun. 10–2.*

⑮ Palau de la Virreina. The neoclassical Palau de la Virreina, built by a viceroy to Peru in 1778, is now a major exhibition center; you should check out what's showing while you're here. The Tourist Information Center and the bookstore are also useful stops. ✉ *Rambla de les Flors 99,* ☎ *93/301–7775.* ⊘ *Tues.–Sat. 10–2 and 4:30–9, Sun. 10–2, Mon. 4:30–9.*

★ **⑪ Palau Güell.** This mansion is just up the Rambla at Number 3, Carrer Nou de la Rambla. Antoni Gaudí built this mansion in 1886–89 for his patron, a textile baron named Count Eusebi de Güell, and was soon launched into the international limelight. The prominent Catalan emblem between the parabolic entrance gates attests to the nationalist leanings that Gaudí shared with Güell. The facade is a dramatic foil for the treasure house inside, where spear-shaped Art Nouveau columns frame the windows and prop up a series of minutely detailed, wood ceilings. On the roof you can see good examples of Gaudí's decorative chimneys. 📧 *450 ptas., ½ price Wed., free 1st Sun. of month.* ⊘ *Tues.–Sat. 10–2 and 4–7, Sun. 10–2.*

⑲ Plaça de Catalunya. The Plaça de Catalunya, Barcelona's banking and transport center, is at the head of the Rambla, marking the frontier between the new, upper urbanization and the old city between Plaça de Catalunya and the port.

⑱ The Port. In the port beyond the Columbus monument, behind the ornate Duana, or former customs building, now headquarters for the Barcelona Port authority, is the **Rambla de Mar,** a sliding boardwalk (with drawbridge) taken up at night to allow boats in and out of the inner harbor. The Rambla de Mar extends out to the **Moll d'Espanya** with its Maremagnum shopping center, IMAX theater, and new aquarium, a loop that can easily take a few hours to explore. Here you can board a Golondrina boat for a tour of the port or, from the Moll de Barcelona on the right, take a cable car to Montjüic or Barceloneta. On the Moll de Barcelona is the passengerboat station where Trasmediterranea ferries leave for Italy and the Balearic Islands. At the end of the quay is Barcelona's World Trade Center.

⑬ Santa Maria del Pi. The colorful paving stones at mid-Rambla in the Pla de la Boqueria were designed by Joan Miró. Nearby are the adjoining squares **Plaça del Pi** and **Plaça de Sant Josep Oriol,** among the Gothic Quarter's most tranquil. The church of Santa Maria del Pi is another good example of Catalan Gothic. Its gigantic rose window is especially impressive overlooking its diminutive square.

NEED A BREAK? The **Bar del Pi** is a stylish and popular venue for bohemians from the world over. The chairs outside move from one square to another, following the sun, and are particularly popular on a Sunday morning.

The Moderniste Eixample

Above the Plaça de Catalunya, is an elegant area known as the Eixample. With the dismantling of the city walls in 1860, Barcelona embarked upon a vast expansion scheme, fueled by the return of rich colonials from America and an influx of provincial aristocrats who had sold their estates after the debilitating second Carlist War (1847–49) (☞ Chronology *in* Chapter 16). The grid street-plan was the work of Ildefons Cerdà. Much of the building here was done at the height of the Modernisme movement. The principal thoroughfares of the Eixample are the Rambla de Catalunya and the Passeig de Gràcia, where some of the city's most elegant shops and cafés are to be found.

A Good Walk

Starting in the Plaça de Catalunya ⑲ walk up Passeig de Gràcia until you reach the corner of Consell de Cent. Take a deep breath. You are about to head into the Bermuda Triangle of Moderniste architecture, the much-heralded **Manzana de la Discordia** ⑳, the "block" or "apple" of discord (the pun only works in Spanish), where the three great figures of Barcelona's late-19th-century art nouveau (Moderniste) movement—Gaudí, Domènech i Muntaner, and Puig i Cadafalch—went hand to hand. Next is the Tápies Foundation on Carrer Aragó, and Gaudí's Pedrera farther up Passeig de Gràcia. Next hike (or taxi) to the **Temple Expiatori de la Sagrada Família church** ㉓ for an exploration of this mighty symbol of Barcelona. Afterwards stroll over to Domènech i Muntaner's **Hospital de Sant Pau** ㉔.

TIMING

Depending on how much taxi transport you use, this is a two to three hour walk. Add another two hours for a thorough exploration of the Sagrada Familia.

Sights to See

★ ㉒ **Casa Milà.** Gaudí's Casa Milà, nicknamed La Pedrera (the Quarry), has a remarkable, curving, stone facade with ornamental balconies that actually ripples its way around the corner of the block. In 1910, Barcelona's bourgeoisie were quite taken aback by the appearance of these cave-like apartments on their most fashionable street. From the roof, you have as good an opportunity as any of peering into the courtyards of Eixample blocks. ☒ *Passeig de Gràcia 92.* ☒ *Free.* ☉ *Guided visits Tues.–Sat. at 10, 11, noon, 1, and 4.*

㉑ **Casa Montaner i Simó.** This former publishing house (at nearby Carrer Aragó, 255) has been beautifully converted to hold the work of the preeminent contemporary Catalan painter Antoni Tàpies. Atop the building, Tàpies has added a tangled, metal hairdo, entitled *Núvol i cadira* (Cloud and Chair). The airy, split-level Fundació Tàpies has temporary exhibitions and a library strong on Tàpies and Asian art. ☒ *550 ptas.* ☉ *Tues.–Sun. 11–8.*

㉔ **Hospital de Sant Pau.** The Hospital de Sant Pau is at the end of Avinguda Gaudí, just a 15-minute walk from the Sagrada Família. This brick

The Moderniste Eixample

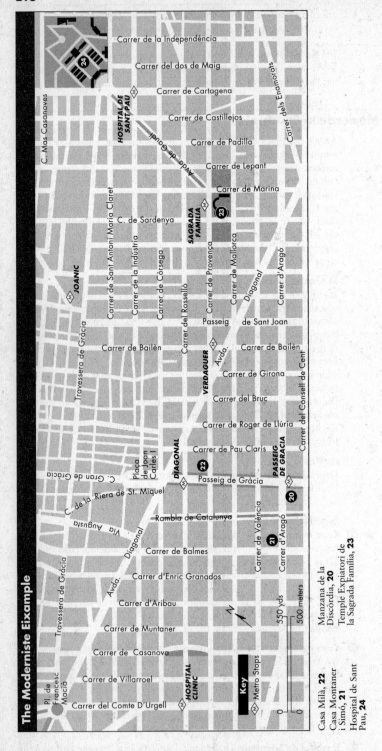

Carrer de la Independència

Carrer del dos de Maig

Carrer de Cartagena

Carrer de Castillejos

Carrer de Padilla

Carrer de Lepant

Carrer de Marina

HOSPITAL DE SANT PAU

Avda. de Gaudí

C. Mas Casanoves

SAGRADA FAMÍLIA

C. de Sardenya

Carrer de Sant Antoni Maria Claret

Carrer de la Indústria

Carrer de Còrsega

Carrer del Rosselló

Carrer de Provença

Carrer de Mallorca

Diagonal

Carrer d'Aragó

Carrer dels Enamorats

JOANIC

Travessera de Gràcia

Carrer de Bailèn

Passeig de Sant Joan

Avda.

Carrer de Bailèn

Carrer de Girona

Carrer del Bruc

Carrer de Roger de Llúria

Carrer de Pau Claris

Carrer del Consell de Cent

VERDAGUER

DIAGONAL

Plaça de Joan Carles I

C. Gran de Gràcia

Gran de Gràcia

Passeig de Gràcia

PASSEIG DE GRACIA

C. de la Riera de St. Miquel

Rambla de Catalunya

Via Augusta

Diagonal

Avda.

Carrer de Balmes

Carrer d'Enric Granados

Carrer d'Aribau

Carrer de Muntaner

Carrer de Casanova

Carrer de Villarroel

Carrer del Comte D'Urgell

Carrer de València

Carrer d'Aragó

HOSPITAL CLINIC

Travessera de Gràcia

Pl. de Francesc Macià

Key

Ⓜ Metro Stops

N

550 yds

500 meters

Casa Milà, **22**
Casa Montaner
i Simó, **21**
Hospital de Sant
Pau, **24**

Manzana de la
Discòrdia, **20**
Temple Expiatori de
la Sagrada Família, **23**

structure is notable for its Mudéjar motifs and wards set among the gardens. You can board the metro here back to Diagonal.

㉒ Manzana de la Discordia. The Manzana de la Discordia is between Consell de Cent and Aragó. Its name is a pun on the word *manzana,* which means both "block" and "apple," alluding to the architectural counterpoint on the block and to the classical myth of the Apple of Discord. The houses here are quite fantastic: The floral Casa Lleó Morera (Number 35) was extensively rebuilt (1902–06) by Domènech i Muntaner, and with permission you can visit the ornate interior. The pseudo-Gothic, pseudo-Flemish Casa Amatller (Number 41) is by Puig i Cadafalch and features a terraced gable. Next door is Gaudí's Casa Batlló, with a mottled facade that resembles nearly anything you want it to. Nationalist symbolism is at work here: The scaly roof line represents St. George's dragon with his cross stuck into its tail.

★ ㉓ Temple Expiatori de la Sagrada Família. The Sagrada Família church is Barcelona's most emblematic landmark. Antoni Gaudí's Temple Expiatori de la Sagrada Família (Expiatory Temple of the Holy Family) is still under construction. Unfinished at his untimely death—Gaudí was run over by a tram and, unrecognized for several days, died in a pauper's ward in 1926—this striking and surreal creation will cause consternation or wonder, howls of protest, shrieks of derision, or cries of rapture. One way or another, it occupies space in an exceptional, possibly unique manner. During the 1936–39 Spanish Civil War, even Barcelona's most radical anticlerical elements loved their idiosyncratic temple enough to spare it from the flames that engulfed nearly all the other churches (La Seu cathedral also escaped). Gaudí envisaged three facades: Faith, Hope, and Charity, each with four towers collectively representing the 12 apostles. These, in turn, would be dwarfed by a giant central dome some 500 feet high, still unfinished (in fact, not started) today. An elevator (150 ptas.) takes visitors to the top of the east towers (although the stairway is a better way to get a real feel for this structure) for a spectacular bird's-eye view. Construction began again in 1940 but faltered due to confusion over Gaudí's plans. Current controversy centers on sculptor Josep Maria Subirach's angular figures on the western facade, condemned by the city's intellectual elite as kitsch and the antithesis of Gaudí's lyrical style, and by religious leaders for depicting Christ in the nude.

The Sagrada Família crypt, offers a museum of Gaudí's scale models, photographs showing the progress of construction, and photographs of Gaudí's multitudinous funeral. Gaudí, 74 when he died, is buried here. ☎ 93/455–0247, ▨ 800 ptas. ☉ Nov.–Mar., daily 9–6; Apr.–June, Sept., and Oct., daily 9–7; July and Aug., daily 8–9 PM.

Upper Barcelona: Parc Güell, Tibidabo, Sarrià, and Pedralbes

A Good Walk

These Barcelona visits are really four neighborhoods spread across the upper reaches of the city. Connecting them on foot, a one-to-two-hour hike, would mean leaving the back entrance of Parc Güell ㉕, crossing the Vallcarca viaduct and walking up to the bottom of Avda. del Tibidabo at Plaça J.F. Kennedy. From there, the Passeig de Sant Gervasi leads over to Plaça Bonanova, where it becomes Passeig de la Bonanova over to Plaça Sarrià. After exploring Sarrià ㉗, it is just a 15-minute walk to the Monasterio de Pedralbes ㉘.

TIMING

Allowing time for exploring the Güell Park, Sarrià, the Pedralbes Monastery and its Thyssen-Bornemisza collection, this is a good four hour outing that will necessarily end when they close the monastery at 2. Add another two hours for going up to Tibidabo and the Collserola Tower.

Sights to See

Collserola Tower. The Collserola Tower that now dwarfs Tibidabo is an architectural triumph erected during the 1992 Olympics amid a certain amount of controversy over the defacement of the traditional Collserola skyline. What is incontrovertible is the splendid panorama over the city that this lookout point provides. To reach the tower, take the funicular up to Tibidabo; there is free transport to the tower from Plaza Tibidabo. ☎ *93/211–7942.* ✉ *600 ptas.* ☉ *Weekdays 11–2:30 and 4–6, weekends and holidays 11–7.*

㉘ Monasterio de Pedralbes. This monastery, even without its Thyssen-Bornemisza collection of Italian masters, is one of Barcelona's finest semi-secret gems. Founded by Reina Elisenda for Clarist nuns in 1326, the convent has a triple-story Gothic cloister that is the finest in Barcelona. In the chapel are a beautiful stained-glass rose window and famous murals painted in 1346 by Ferrer Bassa, a Catalan much influenced by the Italian Renaissance. You can also visit the medieval living quarters. The monastery alone was already one of Barcelona's finest semisecret delights, but the new **Thyssen-Bornemisza Collection,** installed in what was once the dormitory of the nuns of the Order of St. Clare, has become one of the city's great treasures. The canvases by Tiepolo, Tintoretto, Rubens, and Velázquez surrounded by 14th-century windows and pointed arches should not be missed. ✉ *Monastery 350 ptas., Wed. 175 ptas., free 1st Sun. of month; Thyssen-Bornemisza Collection 350 ptas.; combined ticket 575 ptas.* ☉ *Tues.–Sun. 10–2, Sat. 10–5.*

㉙ Palau Reial de Pedralbes. This palace, built in the 1920s for King Alfonso XII, is now home to the **Ceramics Museum.** A 20-minute walk downhill from the monastery, this museum provides a look at a wide sweep of Spanish ceramic art from the 14th to the 18th century, with the influence of Moorish design techniques carefully documented. ☎ *93/280–1621.* ✉ *550 ptas., free 1st Sun. of month.* ☉ *Daily 10–3.*

OFF THE
BEATEN PATH

F.C. BARCELONA SOCCER TEAM – Go to see the soccer club F.C. Barcelona play, preferably against Real Madrid. The massive Camp Nou stadium seats 130,000 spectators, and crowds frequently number more than 100,000. Look in the museum, with its impressive array of trophies and five-screen video showing memorable goals in the history of one of Europe's most glamorous soccer clubs. From here you can board the metro (Palau Reial, green line) back to the center of town. ✉ *Arístides Maillol,* ☎ *93/330–9411.* ✉ *Museum 500 ptas.* ☉ *Oct.–Mar., Tues.–Fri. 10–1 and 4–6, weekends 10–1 and 3–6; Apr.–Sept., Mon.–Sat. 10–1 and 3–6.*

㉕ Parc Güell. The Parc Güell is one of Gaudí's, and Barcelona's, most delightful resources. Whereas the Sagrada Família can be tiring in its massive energy and complexity, Parc Güell is light and playful, always uplifting and restorative. To get there, take the metro to Lesseps, where you can walk 10 minutes uphill or catch Bus 24 to the park entrance. Named after Gaudí's main patron, it was originally intended as a hillside garden suburb on the English model, but only two of the houses were ever built. It is an Art Nouveau extravaganza, with a mosaic pagoda,

Parc Güell, Tibidabo, and Pedralbes

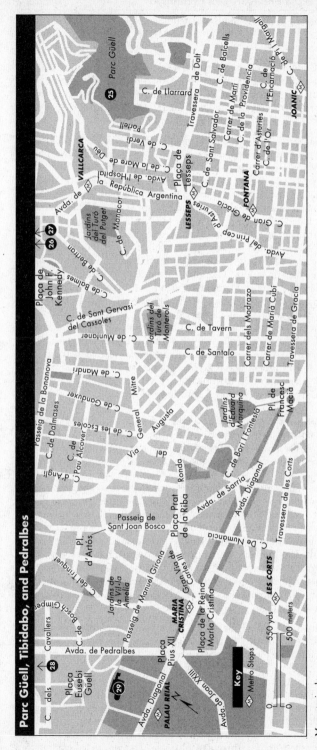

Parc Güell

C. de Llarrard

de Dalt

C. de Balcells

C. de Martí

Carrer de la Providència

C. de l'Encarnació

C. de l'Or

JOANIC

Carrer d'Astúries

Carrer de Marti

C. de Sant Salvador

Travessera

VALLCARCA

C. de Verdi

C. de la Mare de Déu

Avda. de l'Hospital

Plaça de Lesseps

C. de Manacor

Avda. de la República Argentina

LESSEPS

C. d'Astúries

Gran de Gràcia

FONTANA

Jardins del Turó del Putget

C. de Bertran

C. de balmes

Avda. del Príncep d'Astúries

Plaça de John F. Kennedy

C. de Sant Gervasi del Cassoles

Jardins del Turó de Monterols

C. de Tavern

Carrer dels Madrazo

Carrer de María Cubí

Travessera de Gràcia

C. de Muntaner

C. de Santalo

Passeig de la Bonanova

Mitre

C. de Mandri

C. de Ganduxer

Pl. de Francesc Macià

Jardins d'Eduard Marquina

C. de Dalmases

C. de les Escoles

Via

General

Augusta

del

C. de Bori i Fontestà

C. d'Angli

C. de Pau Alcover

Ronda

Plaça Prat de la Riba

Avda. de Sarrià

Avda. Diagonal

Travessera de les Corts

Passeig de Sant Joan Bosco

C. De Numància

Pl. d'Artós

Jardins de la Vil·la Amèlia

Passeig de Manuel Girona

Gran Via de Carles III

LES CORTS

Bosch Gimpera

C. del Tinquel

Plaça de la Reina Maria Cristina

MARIA CRISTINA

Cavallers

C. de

Avda. de Pedralbes

Plaça Pius XII

PALAU REIAL

Avda. Diagonal

Avda. de Pius XII

Plaça Eusebi Güell

C. dels

N

Key
◇ Metro Stops

550 yds
500 meters

Monasterio de
Pedralbes and
Thyssen–Bornemisza
Collection, 28

Palau Reial de
Pedralbes, 29

Parc Güell, 25

Sarrià, 27

Tibidabo, 26

undulating benches, and large, multicolored lizards guarding a Moderniste grotto. ☉ *Oct.–Mar., daily 10–6; Apr.–June, daily 10–7; July–Sept., daily 10–9.*

The **Gaudí Museum** in Parc Güell is up the hill to the right of the main entrance. This small museum is in an Alice-in-Wonderland house where Gaudí lived from 1906 to 1926, and contains some of his eccentric furniture, decoration, and drawings. 🖂 *450 ptas.* ☉ *Apr.–Oct., daily 10–2 and 4–7; Nov.–Mar., daily 10–2 and 4–6:30.*

㉗ Sarrià. Sarrià, a 1,000-year-old village that once overlooked Barcelona from the distance, is now a village-like enclave of tranquillity surrounded by the roaring metropolis. From Avinguda de Tibidabo (Plaça John F. Kennedy), take Bus 22 to Sarrià. Your stop will leave you in the Plaça Sarrià, the town's central square and the site of many antique and artesan markets, sardana dancing, and Christmas fairs. The Romanesque church belfry, illuminated at night, towers above. Sarrià's choice corners include the produce market across from the church and tiny Plaça Sant Gaietà behind it. Moving downhill, cut through the Placeta del Roser around the left side of the church to reach the elegant town hall in the Plaça de la Vila. Take tiny Carrer dels Paletes out to Major de Sarrià and continue downhill through this (intermittently pedestrian-only) street to the bougainvillea- and honeysuckle-lined Carrer Canet with its tiny, cottage-like artesans' quarters. Next go right on Carrer Cornet i Mas and walk down to Carrer Jaume Piquet. A quick probe to the left to No.30 will give you a look at Barcelona's most perfect and smallest Moderniste house, now a *parvulario* (kindergarten). Next stop down Cornet i Mas is Sarrià's prettiest square, Plaça Sant Vicenç, where an image of the patron saint of Sarrià stands high over this leafy space surrounded by typical old village houses.

NEED A
BREAK?
> **Bar Tomás** just out on Major de Sarrià on the corner of Jaume Piquet, is all but a Barcelona institution, home of the finest potatoes and all i oli in town. Order the famous *doble mixta* of potatoes and a potent blend of all i oli and hot sauce. Draft beer (ask for a *caña*) is the de rigueur beverage.

Other important Sarrià landmarks include the two **Foix** pastry stores, one on Plaça Sarrià at Nos. 9 and 10 and the other on Major de Sarrià at No.57 on the corner above Bar Tomás. Both have excellent pastries, artisanal breads and produce of all sorts, including cold cava, and remain open until 9 PM on Sundays. More important still is the fact that the late J.V. Foix, son of the store's original founders, was one of the great Catalan poets of the 20th century, doing much to keep the Catalan language alive during the 40-year Franco regime that systematically suppressed local customs and culture, the language foremost among them.

㉖ Tibidabo. Tibidabo is Barcelona's other (with Montjuïc) promontory overlooking the city. To get there, you can use the subway, which has a Tibidibao branch off the Sarrià train, a combination of Buses 24 and 22, or a taxi. At Avinguda Tibidabo, catch the Tramvia Blau, which connects with the funicular (☞ *Getting Around, below*) to the summit. The views from this hill are legendary, but clear days are few and far between in fin-de-millennium Barcelona. The shapes that distinguish Tibidabo from below turn out to be an unprepossessing, commercialized church, a vast radio mast, and the new 850-foot communications tower, the Mirador Torre de Collserola. The misguided exploitation of this natural vantage point is completed by a noisy amusement park. All in all, taking a miss on Tibidabo might not be a bad idea, although the views from the Torre de Collserola are, as advertised, the most panoramic views in Catalunya. If the northwest wind has blown the air pollution out to sea on a day following some rain, it might be worth thinking about. La Venta restaurant at the base of the funicular is excellent and a fine place to sit in the sun during cool weather (the establishment traditionally provides straw sun hats). The Mirablau bar is also a popular hangout for evening drinks overlooking the lights of Barcelona.

OFF THE
BEATEN PATH **MUSEUM DE LA CIÈNCIA –** Young scientific minds work overtime in the Science Museum, just below Tibidabo, many of whose displays and activities are designed for children (over age 7). ⊠ *Teodor Roviralta 55,* ☎ *93/212–6050.* ☑ *500 ptas.* ⊙ *Tues.–Sun. 10–8. Metro: Avinguda de Tibidabo and Tramvia Blau halfway.*

Sant Pere, La Ribera, La Ciutadella and Barceloneta

Barcelona's early textile neighborhood around the Sant Pere church includes the flagship of the city's Moderniste architecture, the Palau de la Música. The Ribera, the Ciutadella, and Barceloneta complete this walk which traces Barcelona's 13th-century walls.

A Good Walk

This neighborhood, or series of neighborhoods, lies generally to the left (north and east) of the Gothic Quarter. The area runs from the medieval, textile Sant Pere district to the early waterfront, later silted and filled in to create La Barceloneta. Beginning in **Plaça de Catalunya,** ⑲ it is no more than a 10-minute walk over to the **Palau de la Música** ㉚, taking your first left off the Rambla. After an inspection of the palau (guided tours can be concerted on weekdays), continue along Carrer Sant Pere Més Alt to the Plaça Sant Pere on your way past the Sant Pere de les Puelles church and out to the **Arc del Triomf** ㉛ on Passeig de Sant Joan. From there, walk through the Parc de la Ciutadella and the Estació de Francia to the edge of the port, through **Barceloneta** ㊲ and along the beach to the **Port Olímpic** ㊳.

TIMING

Depending on the number of stops, this could take a complete morning or afternoon. Count on about two hours of actual walking time.

Sights to See

㉛ **Arc del Triomf.** This imposing, exposed-red-brick arch was built by Josep Vilaseca as the grand entrance for the 1888 exhibition, *L'Exposició Universal,* held in Barcelona.

㊲ **Barceloneta.** Interior Barceloneta still retains the colorful ambience of what was once Barcelona's pungent fishing port and waterfront district, a pretty walk through narrow streets with lines of laundry snapping in the breeze overhead. Stop in Plaça de la Barceloneta and have a close look at the baroque Sant Miquel del Port church with its somewhat outsized new sculpture of the saint in the alcove on the facade. Try the tapas bar on the sea side of the square.

The Barcelona beach, a little dusty, often crowded in summer, is much improved over recent years and can actually be used for swimming purposes, provided the winds and currents haven't created some unseemly back-up of sewage. Take a close look at the water before you dive in.

NEED A
BREAK? The **Gato Negro Chiringuito,** a portable restaurant usually planted in the middle of the beach during warm weather, is a good place for a beverage.

Ciutadella and Barceloneta

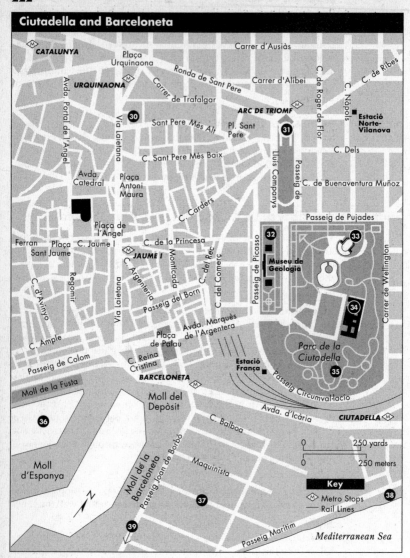

Arc del Triomf, 31
Barceloneta, 37
Castell dels Tres
Dragons, 32
Font de la Senyoreta
del Paraigua/Font
d'Aurora, 33

Palau de la
Ciutadella, 34
Palau de la
Música, 30
Port Olímpic, 38
Port Vell, 36
Telefèric, 39
Zoo, 35

③ Castell dels Tres Dragons (Castle of the Three Dragons). This castle built by Domènech i Muntaner as the café for the 1888 exhibition is the arresting building you will see as you enter the park from Passeig Lluí Companys. This became a workshop where Moderniste architects met to experiment with traditional crafts and exchange ideas. It is now home to the Zoological Museum. ⊡ *450 ptas.* ☉ *Tues.–Sun. 9–2.*

Estació de Francia. The elegantly restored Estació de França, Barcelona's main railroad station until about 1980 and even now the destination for certain trains from France, is outside the west gate of the Ciutadella park. This structure is worth having a walk through, for a sense of the old-world romance of Europe's traditional railroads and stations.

NEED A BREAK?

You are just a step from Barcelona's best tapas at **Cal Pep** (⊠ Plaça de les Olles 8). Try the *gambitas* (baby shrimp). (Don't give up if you have to wait for a while; they'll feed you wine while you wait; it's fun and well worth it. For a slightly younger crowd, **Cal Paixano,** across the Pla del Palau behind the Restaurant Set Portes (⊠ 13 Reina Cristina), is legendary for its inexpensive (though not very good) cavas, tapas, sales of good wines, cheeses and sausages, and a bar tightly packed with young bodies. Have a close look at the spectacular wooden door.

③ Font de la Senyoreta Paraigua (Fountain of the Lady with the Umbrella). Escape the sight and sound of the city by the lake and Font de la Senyoreta del Paraigua (Fountain of the Lady with the Umbrella) and behind it the monumental *Cascada,* by Josep Fontserè, designed for the 1888 exhibition. The rocks of the waterfall are known to be the work of a young student of architecture named Antoni Gaudí, his first public works, appropriately natural and organic and certainly a hint of things to come.

Geology Museum. The Geology Museum is next to the Castell dels Tres Dragons, along with the beautiful Umbracle, whose black slats help create a jungle light for the valuable collection of tropical plants growing here.

③ Palau de la Ciutadella. This is the only surviving remnant of Felipe V's fortress, now shared by the Catalan Parliament and the Museu d'Art Modern (Museum of Modern Art). This collection of late-19th- and early-20th-century paintings and sculptures by Catalan artists, such as Isidro Nonell, Ramon Casas, and Marià Fortuny, is one of Barcelona's artistic treasures. A stroll through this collection will make it very clear that Catalonia's universally famous artists, Gaudí, Picasso, Dalí, and Miró, emerged as no surprise at all, from an exceptionally rich artistic context. ⊡ *500 ptas.* ☉ *Wed.–Mon. 9–9.*

★ **③ Palau de la Música.** The Palau de la Música on Carrer Amadeus Vives, just off the top of Via Laietana (Metro: Urquinaona) is a fantastic and flamboyant tour de force designed by Domènech i Muntaner (1908) that is considered the flagship of Moderniste architecture in Barcelona. The tiny ticket booths in the richly embellished columns are sadly now out of use. Try to get to a concert here, if only to see the interior, with its inverted, stained-glass cupola (☞ Nightlife and The Arts, *below*). Otherwise you can make an appointment to see inside on Tuesday, Thursday, or Saturday (☏ 93/268–1000).

Parc de la Ciutadella (Citadel). Ths park, once a fortress designed to consolidate Madrid's military occupation of Barcelona, is now the city's main downtown park. The clearing dates from shortly after the War of the Spanish Succession, when Felipe V demolished some 2,000 houses in what was then the Barrio de la Ribera (waterfront neighborhood) to build a fortress and barracks for his soldiers and fields of fire for his artillery. The fortress walls were pulled down in 1868 and replaced by gardens laid out by Josep Fontserè. In the park are a cluster of museums, the Catalan Parliament, and a zoo.

③⑧ Port Olímpic. This area, choked with yachts, restaurants and tapas bars of all kinds, is just a mile north up the beach, marked by the mammoth Frank Gehry-designed goldfish sculpture in front of Barcelona's first real skyscraper, the Hotel Arts. The Port Olímpic rages on Friday and Saturday nights, especially in summer, with hundreds of young people of all nationalities circling and grazing until dawn.

③⑥ Port Vell. From Pla del Palau cross to the edge of the port where the Moll d'Espanya, the Moll de la Fusta, and the Moll de Barceloneta meet. The modern wonders of the new Port Vell complex—the IMAX theater, the aquarium, and the Maremagnum shopping mall—loom seaward on the Moll d'Espanya. The Palau de Mar with its five, quayside, terrace restaurants stretches down along the Moll de Barceloneta. (Try Llevataps or the establishment on the far corner, the Merendero de la Mari.) Take a stroll through the Museu de Historia de Catalunya (MHC) in the Palau de Mar for a look at a purely Catalonian view of its national history. Along the Passeig Joan de Borbó are a dozen more traditional Barceloneta paella and seafood specialists.

Sant Pere de les Puelles. Sant Pere de les Puelles, one of the oldest medieval churches in Barcelona, has been destroyed and restored so many times that there is little left worth seeing. It's stark interior is highlighted by a beautiful, stained-glass window. The word *Puelles* is from the Latin for girl *puella*. The convent here was known for the beauty and nobility of its young women and was the setting for some of medieval Barcelona's most tragic stories of impossible loves and romantic agony.

③⑨ Telefèric (cable car). The cable car at the end of Passeig Joan de Borbócan take you across to Montjuïc. Alternately, you can walk to the end of the rompeolas, a mile and a half out to sea, where you can catch a Golondrinas boat back into the port. ☜ *Cable car 400 ptas.* ☼ *Oct.–June 21, weekends 11–2:45 and 4–7:30; June 22–Sept., daily 11:30–9.*

✋ ③⑤ Zoo. The excellent zoo, home to Snowflake, the world's only captive albino gorilla, occupies the whole bottom section of the park. ☜ *1,100 ptas.* ☼ *Oct.–Apr., daily 10–6; May–Oct., daily 9:30–7:30.*

Montjuïc

Montjuïc, the hill to the south of town, is thought to have been named for the Jewish cemetery once located on its slopes, although an alternate explanation has it named for the Roman deity Jove or Jupiter. The most dramatic approach is by way of the cross-harbor telefèric, but you can reach it from the Paral.lel or from Plaça Espanya.

A Good Walk

Walking from sight to sight on Montjuïc is possible but not recommended. The things to see on Montjuïc, especially the Romanesque art collection in the Palau Nacional and, to a lesser but still significant degree, the Miró Foundation and the Olympic facilities, are very much worth fresh eyes, backs and feet.

The telefèric drops you at the Jardins de Miramar, a 10-minute walk from the Plaça de Dante and the entrance to the amusement park. If you are nostalgic for the days of rock and roll, you may want to look up Chus Martínez, one-time colleague of Bill Haley and Eddie Cochrane, who runs the Bali restaurant here. It's not unheard of for him to give an impromptu concert for his guests. From here, another small cable car takes you up to the **Castell de Montjuïc** ㊵. The **Fundació Miró** ㊶ is a just a few minutes' walk from the bottom cable car station. The Estadi Olímpic (Olympic stadium) is the next attraction. From there, on foot, cut straight down to the Palau Nacional and the **Museu Nacional d'Art de Catalunya** ㊷. From here, a wide stairway leads down toward Plaça de Espanya.

TIMING

With unhurried visits to the Miró Foundation and the Romanesque exhibit in the Palau Nacional, this is a four-hour sortie. Lunch afterwards in the Poble Espanyol.

Sights to See

㊵ **Castell de Montjuïc.** Built in 1640 by rebels against Felipe IV, the castle has been stormed several times, most famously in 1705 by Lord Peterborough for Archduke Carlos of Austria. In 1808, during the Peninsular War, the castle was seized by the French under General Dufresne. Later, during an 1842 civil disturbance, Barcelona was bombed by a Spanish artillery battery from its heights. The moat has been made into attractive gardens, with one side given over to an archery range. From the various terraces, there are panoramic views over the city and out to sea. The castle now functions as a military museum housing the weapons collection of Frederic Marès. ▨ *350 ptas.* ☉ *Oct.–Mar., Tues.–Sat. 10–2 and 4–7, Sun. 10–2; Apr.–Sept., Tues.–Sat. 10–2 and 4–7, Sun. 10–8.*

★ **Estadi Olímpic** (Olympic Stadium). The Olympic Stadium was originally built for the Great Exhibition of 1929, with the idea that Barcelona would then host the 1936 Olympics (ultimately staged in Hitler's Berlin). After twice failing to gain the nomination, Barcelona celebrated the attainment of its long-cherished goal by renovating the semi-derelict stadium in time for 1992, providing a seating capacity of 70,000. Next door and just downhill stands the futuristic Palau Sant Jordi Sports Palace, designed by the Japanese architect Arata Isozaki. The structure has no pillars nor beams obstructing view, and built from the roof downward; that is, the roof was built first and then hydraulically lifted into place. ☎ *93/424–0508.* ☉ *Weekdays 10–2 and 4–7, weekends 10–6.*

★ ㊶ **Fundació Miró** (Miró Foundation). The Miró Foundation was a gift from the artist Joan Miró to his native city and is one of Barcelona's most exciting contemporary art galleries. The white, airy building was designed by Josep Lluís Sert and opened in 1975; an extension was added by Sert's pupil, Jaume Freixa, in 1988. Miró himself now rests in the cemetery on the southern slopes of Montjuïc. During the Franco regime, which he strongly opposed, Miró lived in self-imposed exile in Paris and in 1956 moved to Mallorca. When he died in 1983, the Catalans gave him a send-off amounting to a state funeral. ▨ *650 ptas.* ☉ *Tues., Wed., Fri., and Sat. 11–7; Thurs. 11–9:30; Sun. 10:30–2:30.*

㊺ **Mies van der Rohe Pavilion.** The reconstructed Mies van der Rohe Pavilion, was the German contribution to the 1929 Exhibition, has interlocking planes of white marble, green onyx, and glass. ☉ *Daily 10–6.*

㊸ **Museu Arqueològic** (Archaeological Museum). Just downhill to the right of the Palau Nacional, the Archaeological Museum contains many important finds from the Greek ruins at Empúries on the Costa Brava. These are exhibited, along with fascinating objects from, and explanations of, Megalithic Spain. ▨ *500 ptas.* ☉ *Tues.–Sat. 9:30–1 and 4–7, Sun. 9:30–1.*

★ ㊷ **Museu Nacional d'Art de Catalunya** (National Museum of Catalan Art). This museum, in the imposing **Palau Nacional**, was built in 1929 and

Montjuïc

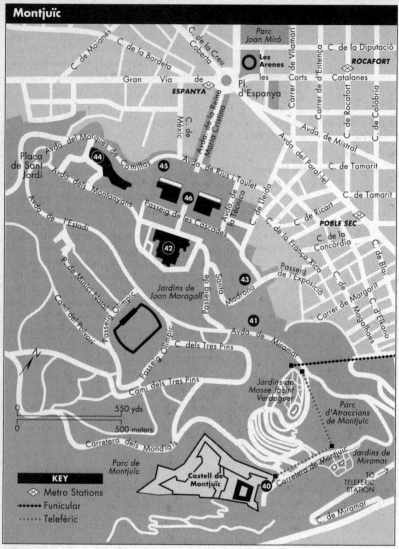

Parc Joan Miró
C. de la Diputació
ROCAFORT
Les Arenes
les Corts Catalanes
C. de la Creu Coberta
C. de la Bordeta
C. de Moianès
Gran Via de
ESPANYA
Pl. d'Espanya
C. de Vilamarí
Carrer de d'Entença
Carrer de Rocafort
C. de Calàbria
C. de Mèxic
Avda. de la Reina Maria Cristina
Avda. del Marquès de Comillas
Avda. de Mistral
C. de Tamarit
Avda. del Paral·lel
Plaça de Sant Jordi
Avda. dels Montanyans
44
45
Avda. de Rius I Taulet
46
Passeig de les Cascades
Avda. de la Tècnica
C. de Lleida
C. de Tamarit
C. de Ricart
POBLE SEC
Avda. de l'Estadi
42
C. de la França Xica
C. de la Concòrdia
C. de Blai
Passeig de l'Exposició
Jardins de Joan Maragall
43
Passeig de Santa Madrona
Carrer de Margarit
C. d'Elkano
Carrer de Magallues
P. de Minici Natal
Passeig Olímpic
41
Avda. de Miramar
Cami del Polvori
C. dels Tres Pins
Passeig Olímpic
Cami dels Tres Pins
Jardins de Mossè Jacint Verdaguer
Parc d'Atraccions de Montjuïc

0   550 yds
0   500 meters

Carretera dels Mondia'ls
Parc de Montjuïc
Castell de Montjuïc
40
Carretera de Montjuïc
Jardins de Miramar
TO TELEFERIC STATION
C. de Miramar

KEY
◈ Metro Stations
•••••• Funicular
•••••• Teleféric

Castell de Montjuïc, **40**
Fundació Miró, **41**
Mies van der Rohe Pavilion, **45**
Museu Arqueològic, **43**

Museu Nacional d'Art de Catalunya, **42**
Plaça de les Cascades, **46**
Poble Espanyol, **44**

recently renovated by Gae Aulenti, architect of the Musée d'Orsay in Paris. The Romanesque and Gothic art treasures, medieval frescoes, and altarpieces here are simply staggering. Most were removed from small churches and chapels in the Pyrenees during the 1920s to ward off the threat of exportation by art dealers. When possible, the works are being returned to their original homes or are being replicated, as with the famous *Pantocrator* fresco, a copy of which is now back in the Church of Sant Climent de Taüll (☞ Chapter 6). The museum also contains works by El Greco, Velázquez, and Zurbarán. ▦ *750 ptas.* ⊙ *Tues.–Sun. 9–2.*

㊻ Plaça de les Cascades. Upon exiting the Mies van der Rohe Pavilion, you'll see the multicolored fountain in the Plaça de les Cascades. Stroll down the wide esplanade past the exhibition halls used for Barcelona fairs and conventions to the large and frenetic **Plaça d'Espanya.** Across the square is Les Arenes bullring, now the venue for theater performances and political rallies rather than bullfights. From here, you can take the metro or Bus 38 back to Plaça de Catalunya.

㊹ Poble Espanyol (Spanish Village). The Spanish Village was created for the 1929 Exhibition. This enclave, possibly somewhat too artificial to successfully compete with other Montjuïc options and opportunities, is a kind of Spain-in-a-bottle, with the local architectural styles of each province faithfully reproduced, enabling you to wander from the walls of Ávila to the wine cellars of Jerez. The liveliest time to come is at night, for a concert or flamenco show. ▦ *850 ptas.* ⊙ *Mon. 9–8, Tues.–Thurs. 9–2, weekends 9–4.*

BARS AND CAFÉS

Barcelona abounds in colorful tapas bars; smart, trendy cafés; and a whole range of stylish, in-vogue bars with titles ranging from *coctelerias* (cocktail bars) and *whiskerias* (often singles bars with professional escorts), to *xampanyerias* (champagne bars). Below, we list just a few; it is best to wander at will and try out any that take your fancy. Most stay open till 2:30 AM (*see* Nightlife and The Arts, *below,* for later-closing spots).

Cafés

Café de l'Acadèmia. Said to serve the best *bocadillos* (French-bread sandwiches) in town, this is a sophisto-rustic spot with wicker chairs and stone walls, frequented by politicians from the nearby Generalitat who come here to listen to classical music. The cuisine is excellent, so don't think of it as only a sandwich spot. ⊠ *Lledó 1,* ☎ *93/319–8253.* ⊙ *Daily 9–4 and 9–11:30.*

Café de l'Opera. Right opposite the Liceu, the high-ceilinged Art Nouveau interior played host to opera-goers and performers before the theater's fire. It's also right on the tourist trail, so you won't be alone. ⊠ *Ramblas 74.* ⊙ *Apr.–Sept.; Oct.–Mar., daily 10–2.*

Café Zurich. Few avoid a drink in Barcelona's best-known meeting place, a sea of alfresco tables perfectly placed to watch the world emerge from the top end of the Ramblas. ⊠ *Pelai and Plaça de Catalunya.* ⊙ *Daily 10 AM–midnight.*

Els Quatre Gats. This is the café where Picasso staged his first exhibition and met fellow Modernistes. Don't confuse it with the modern one next door. The restaurant serves respectable cuisine and snacks, such as different variations of *pa torrat* (slabs of country bread with tomato, olive oil and anything from anchovies to cheese to cured ham or omelets). ⊠ *Montsió 3.* ⊙ *Daily 8 AM–3 PM.*

Espai Barroc. This unusual "space" (*espai*), filled with baroque decor and music, is located in Carrer Montcada's most beautiful patio. The 15th-century Palau Dalmases is one of the houses built by powerful Barcelona families between the 13th and 18th centuries. The stairway, decorated with sculptures portraying the rape of Europa and Neptune's chariot, leads up to the Omnium Cultural, one of the major disseminators of Catalonian history and culture. This quiet spot serves drinks only.⊠ *Carrer Montcada 20.* ☎ *93/310–0673. AE, DC, MC, V.* ☉ *Tues.–Sun. 4–midnight.*

Coctelerías

El Copetín. On Barcelona's best-known cocktail avenue, this bar has exciting decor and good cocktails. ⊠ *Passeig del Born 19.* ☉ *Daily 7 PM–3 AM.*

El Paraigua. Behind the Ajuntament, this rather pricey bar serves cocktails in a stylish setting with classical music. ⊠ *Plaça Sant Miquel.* ☉ *Daily 7 PM–1 AM.*

Miramelindo. This bar offers a large selection of herbal liquors, fruit cocktails, pâtés, cheeses, and music, usually jazz. ⊠ *Passeig del Born 15.* ☉ *Daily 8 PM–3 AM.*

Tapas Bars

Bar Rodrigo. Next to the church of Santa Maria del Mar is this popular tapas bar of mirrors, marbletop tables, and steel columns. The specialty is the *vermut* (vermouth) cocktail. There is also a good-value menu for lunch. ⊠ *L'Argenteria 67.* ☉ *Fri.–Tues. 8 AM–1 AM.*

Cal Pep. This lively spot has Barcelona's best and freshest selection of tapas served piping hot amid a booming and boisterous ambiance. ⊠ *Plaça de les Olles 8. Closed Sun. No lunch Mon.*

Casa Tejada. The charismatic owner, Mr. Tejada, a former professional soccer star for FC Barcelona, seems to have a photographic memory for everyone who has ever snapped tapas in his seminal contribution to this gastronomical genre. Though a little out of the way, Casa Tejada is handy to the boiling music-bar scene on nearby Marià Cubí. ⊠ *Tenor Viñas 3.*

El Rosal. Just across from the giant steel hangar of the one-time Born market at the end of the Passeig del Born, this sweet little spot is a good place for tapas, sandwiches, beer, wine or an espresso anytime of day or night. A minute's walk from the basilica of Santa Maria del Mar or the Picasso Museum, within sight of the Estació de França train station, El Rosal is worth keeping in mind when you're in this part of Barcelona. ⊠ *Passeig del Born 27, at Carrer de Comerç,* ☎ *93/319–5081.* ☉ *Tues.–Sun. 8 AM–1 AM.*

La Palma. Between the Ajuntament and Via Laietana, this café has marble tables reminiscent of a Paris bistro, tapas to nibble, and newspapers to read. ⊠ *Palma Sant Just 7.* ☉ *Daily 7 AM–10 PM.*

Xampanyerias

El Xampanyet. Just down the street from the Picasso Museum, hanging *botas* (leather wineskins) announce one of Barcelona's liveliest xampanyerias, packed full most of the time. The house cava, cider, and pan con tomate are served on marbletop tables surrounded by barrels and walls decorated with azulejos and fading yellow paint. ⊠ *Montcada 22.* ☉ *Tues.–Sun. 8:30–4 and 6:30–midnight.*

La Cava del Palau. Very handy for the Palau de la Música, this champagne bar serves a wide selection of cavas, wines, and cocktails, with cheeses, pâtés, smoked fish, and caviar, on a series of stepped balconies adorned with shiny azulejos. ⊠ *Verdaguer i Callis 10.* ☎ *93/310–0938* ⏱ *Mon.–Sat. 7 PM–2:30 AM.*

BEACHES

Topless bathing is fine on all the beaches around Barcelona, but nudists should head up the Costa Brava or down the Costa Dorada.

Barceloneta

This is the city's main beach and has become quite popular since being cleaned up for the Barcelona Olympics of 1992. Now, clean sand, surf, and fairly decent swimming are to be found just a 20-minute walk from the Rambla.

Elsewhere

North of the City

As you go north from Barcelona, the first fine beaches you come to are Arenys, Sant Pol, and Calella, reached by train from Passeig de Gràcia. Sant Pol is the pick, with a sandy, bathing beach and a lovely, old town. Generally, the farther north you go toward the Costa Brava, the better the beaches become.

South of the City

Ten km/6 mi south is the popular day resort of Castelldefels, with a series of handy and happening beachside restaurants and bars and a long, sandy beach for sunning and bathing.

DINING

Barcelona restaurants are so numerous and generally exciting that keeping up with them constitutes a legitimate, ongoing, lifetime project. So don't be discouraged if the selection seems overwhelming. A good policy is to stick with local produce and local cuisine. Roast suckling pig, for example, a Castilian specialty, will nearly always be better in Castilla where the best and freshest piglets prevail. In Barcelona they will probably be frozen, second-tier products. Mediterranean seafood is better consumed on the Mediterranean as it does not travel as well as, say, Cantabrican or Atlantic seafood, which, coming from colder waters, is hardier and travels better. *Menús del día* (menus of the day) offer good value, though they vary in quality and are generally served only at lunchtime. Restaurants usually serve lunch 1–4 and dinner 9–1. It is normal but by no means a requirement to tip; 10% is perfectly acceptable.

$$$$ ✕ **Beltxenea.** Previously a smart Eixample apartment, Beltxenea, es-
★ tablished in 1987, retains an atmosphere of privacy in its elegant dining rooms. In summer you can dine outside in the formal garden. Chef Miguel Ezcurra's outstanding cooking hails from the Basque country. His specialty is *merluza con kokotxas y almejas* (hake fried in garlic, simmered in stock, added to clams, and garnished with parsley). If the wine list defeats you, narrow it down to the Riojas. ⊠ *Mallorca 275,* ☎ *93/215–3024. Reservations essential. AE, DC, MC, V. Closed Sun. and July and Aug. No lunch Sat.*

$$$$ ✕ **Botafumeiro.** On Gràcia's main thoroughfare is Barcelona's finest
★ shellfish restaurant, with dishes prepared according to traditional recipes. The waiters will impress you with their soldierly, white out-

230

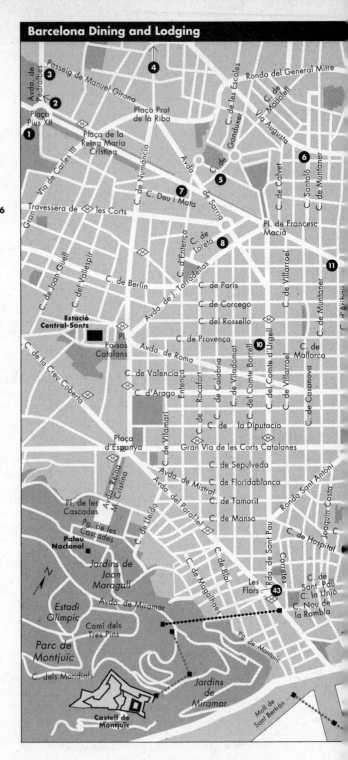

Barcelona Dining and Lodging

Parc Güell

Plaça de Lésseps
Trav. de Dalt

C. de Sant Salvador
C. de les Camèlies

C. Gran de Gracia

C. Menéndez Pelayo
C. de Verdi

C. de la Providència
Plaça Alfons el Savi

C. de l'Escorial
C. de Pl. I Margall
Ronda del Guinardó

13

14

C. de Tuset

Travessera de Gràcia
12

9

Avda. Diagonal

C. d'Aribau

Travessera de Gràcia

C. de Sardenya
C. de Marina
Avda. de Gaudí

Plaça de Joan Carles I
16
C. de Còrcega
15

C. de Bailèn
C. de Indústria

Passeig de S. Joan

C. del Rosselló
17

C. de Provença
18 **19** **20**
C. de Pau Claris
C. de Valencia
21 **22** **23**
C. de Roger Llúria

Rambla de Catalunya
Pg. de Gràcia

C. de Mallorca
Temple Expiatori de la Sagrada Familia

C. de Balmes

24
C. d'Aragó

Consell de Cent

C. de Roger de Flor
Avda. Diagonal
C. de Napoles
C. de Sicilia
C. de Sardenya
Passeig de Carles I

Plaça Universitat
25
C. de la Diputació
Gran Vía de les Corts Catalanes
26

Ronda Universitat
28 **i** **27**

C. del Bruc
C. de Girona
C. de Bailèn

Plaça Tetuán

C. de Casp
C. de Ribes

C. dels Tallers
Pelai
29

Pl. Urquinaona

C. d'Ausias Marc

Pl. de Catalunya

38
Ronda S. Pere
Jonqueres
Arc del Triomf
Estació Vilanova-Norte (Bus Station)

del Carme
30
31 **37**
40
S. Pere Més Alt
39
S. Pere Més Baix

36
Porteferrissa
Via Laietana
41

C. Dels

Passeig de Lluís Companys
Avda. de la Meridiana
Passeig de Carles I

32 **33**
Avda. Catedral
34 **35**
Pl. St. Jaume
Catedral

Passeig Pujadas

42
C. Ferran
48 **49**
Pl. de l'Angel
C. Princesa

44
46 **47**
50

Ciutat
Passeig del Born
Pg. Picasso

45
Plaça Reial
Passeig Isabel II

Parc de la Ciutadella

C. de Wellington

51 **52** **53** **54**
C. Ample
Pl.
55
Avda. M. de l'Argentero

i **Estació Franca**

KEY

Plaça del Palau
Pg. de Colom d'Antoni López
56
Moll de la Fusta

Avda. d'Icària

Metro Stations
Railway Lines
Funicular
Telefèric
i Tourist Information
57

TORRE DE JAUME I
Moll d'Espanya

Passeig D. Joan de Borbó
BARCELONETA

0   450 yards

0   450 meters

fits and super-quick service. The tone is maritime, with white table-cloths and pale, varnished-wood paneling. Highlights are the *mariscos Botafumeiro* (myriad plates of shellfish that arrive one after the other). ⊠ *Gran de Gràcia 81,* ☎ *93/218–4230. AE, DC, MC, V. Closed Mon. No dinner Sun.*

$$$$ ✕ **Jean Luc Figueras.** Jean Luc Figueras's other restaurants (Eldorado
★ Petit, Azulete) instantly shot to the top of all known gourmet listings; this one managed to earn a Michelin star in its first year. Charmingly installed in the Gràcia town house that was once Cristóbal Balenciaga's studio, this exceptional spot makes everyone's short list when choosing Barcelona's best restaurants. Try the *lubina amb tripes de bacalao i botifarra* (sea bass with cod tripe and sausage). ⊠ *C. Santa Teresa 10,* ☎ *93/415–2877. Reservations essential. AE, DC, MC, V. Closed Sun. No lunch Sat.*

$$$$ ✕ **La Dama.** Manager-chef Josep Bullich, previously at Vía Veneto and Agut d'Avignon, has converted a Moderniste house into the most chic restaurant in town, with green walls, orange tablecloths, and a polished-wood floor. The building was designed by the "amateur," Manuel Sayrach, who built only three buildings during his life. His Art Nouveau interior is perfect for Bullich, who likens his cooking to a movement in modern art. Try the *ensalada tibia de cigalas al vinagre de naranja* (langoustine salad with orange vinegar). ⊠ *Diagonal 423/425,* ☎ *93/202–0686. Reservations essential. AE, DC, MC, V.*

$$$$ ✕ **Neichel.** Hailing from Alsace-Lorraine, chef Jean-Louis Neichel is not bashful about his reputation as he explains such French delicacies as the *ensalada de gambas al sésamo con puernas fritas* (shrimp in sesame-seed sauce with fried leeks). The prices fluctuate widely, depending on your choice. The setting is the ground floor of a Pedralbes apartment block, mundane modernity compared with the cooking. ⊠ *C. Bertran i Rozpide 16 bis, off Avda. Pedralbes,* ☎ *93/203–8408. Reservations essential. AE, DC, MC, V. Closed Sun., Christmas wk, Holy Wk, and Aug.*

$$$$ ✕ **Orotava.** A 50th-anniversary painting by Miró and an acclaimed copy of Velázquez's *Los Borrachos* (*The Drunkards*) adorn this intimate, baroque-style dining room. Game is the chef's special drawing card, and he is well supplied by clients who bring back the results of their sport from as far afield as Albacete. In season try the *faisán royal* (roast pheasant in a cream and truffle sauce). ⊠ *Consell de Cent 335,* ☎ *93/302–3128. Reservations essential. AE, DC, MC, V. Closed Sun.; also Sat. June–Sept.*

$$$$ ✕ **Passadis del Pep.** Hidden away through a tiny passageway off the
★ Pla del Palau, this lively bistro serves wine and hot delicacies of all kinds—the best available at that morning's market. Sometime late in the proceedings you may be asked to make a decision about your main course, usually a fish of one kind or another. As long as you do not choose *bogavante* (lobster), criminally expensive in Spain and a favorite number to play on inebriated tourists, everything will be fine. ⊠ *Pla del Palau 2,* ☎ *93/310–1021. AE, DC, MC, V. Closed Sun. and last 2 wks of Aug.*

$$$$ ✕ **Reno.** Fish is smoked on the premises and meat is cooked on charcoal in this respected, haute cuisine restaurant, just north of Diagonal. Game specialties are recommended in season; try the *perdiz a la moda Alcántara* (partridge in wine or port). The tasting (*de gustació*) menu is a treat. Semicircular, black sofas surround white-clothed tables, and dark paneling, interspersed with mirrors, extends to the ceiling. ⊠ *Tuset 27,* ☎ *93/200–1390. Reservations essential. AE, DC, MC, V. No lunch Sat.*

$$$$ ✕ **Vía Veneto.** A Baroque dining room with pink tablecloths, located just above Plaça de Francesc Macià, provides the setting for one of the city's more traditional restaurants. Try the *salmón marinado al vinagre de fram-*

buesa (salmon marinated in raspberry vinegar and aromatic herbs). ⊠ *Ganduxer 1012,* ☎ *93/200–7024. Reservations essential. Jacket and tie. AE, DC, MC, V. Closed Sun. and Aug. 1–20. No lunch Sat.*

$$$ ✕ **Agut d'Avignon.** This venerable Barcelona institution (since 1962) takes a bit of finding; head down Carrer Ferran from the Plaça de Sant Jaume, turn left down Carrer Avinyó, and Carrer Trinitat is the first alley off to the right. White walls, heavy wood tables, and terracotta urns give the place a rustic air; it's a favorite with businesspeople and politicians from across the road in the Generalitat. The cooking is traditional Catalan, and specialties change with the season; from September to May, try the *pato con higos* (roast wild duck in a fig sauce). ⊠ *Trinitat 3,* ☎ *93/302–6034. AE, DC, MC, V.*

$$$ ✕ **Arcs de Sant Gervasi.** Situated up the hill toward Muntaner, Arcs is a modern restaurant that has beige walls with frequently changed artwork, salmon-pink tablecloths, and plentiful mirrors. The cooking is *cuina de mercat* (based upon what fresh produce is available in the market) and includes very good fish. Try the *lenguado a las almendras* (sole with almonds). ⊠ *Santaló 103,* ☎ *93/201–9277. AE, DC, MC, V. Closed Mon.*

$$$ ✕ **Can Isidre.** This small restaurant located just inside the Raval from Avinguda del Paral.lel has a longstanding tradition with Barcelona's artistic elite. Pictures and engravings by Dalí and other prominent artists line the walls. The traditional Catalan cooking with a slight French accent draws on the nearby Boqueria's fresh produce. The homemade foie gras is superb. Come and go by cab at night; the area between Can Isidre and the Rambla is risky. ⊠ *Les Flors 12,* ☎ *93/441–1139. Reservations essential. AE, MC, V. Closed Sun., Holy Wk, and mid-July–mid-Aug.*

$$$ ✕ **El Asador de Aranda.** Few restaurants can compete with the setting here—a large, detached, red-brick castle above the Avenida Tibidabo metro. The dining room is large and airy, with a terracotta floor and traditional Castellano furnishings. The traditional Castilian cooking here has won high praise since the restaurant opened in 1988. Try *pimientos de piquillo* (hot spicy peppers) and then chorizo *de la olla* (chorizo sausage stew). ✕ *Avda. Tibidabo 31,* ☎ *93/417–0115. AE, DC, MC, V. No dinner Sun.*

$$$ ✕ **Jaume de Provença.** People come here because of the very high reputation of the chef, Jaume Bargués. From his haute cuisine repertoire, try the *lenguado relleno de setas* (sole stuffed with mushrooms) or *lubina* (sea bass) soufflé. The restaurant, situated in the Hospital Clinic area of Eixample, has been recently redecorated in a modern black and bottle green. ⊠ *Provença 88,* ☎ *93/430–0029. Reservations essential. AE, DC, MC. Closed Mon. and Aug. No Sun. dinner.*

$$$ ✕ **La Cuineta.** When the Madolell family converted their antiques business into a restaurant in the late 1960s, it soon gained respect for its neo-Baroque elegance, intimacy, and Catalan nouvelle cuisine. The clientele is composed of a wide range of foreigners and locals alike. Fish is the house specialty; try the *bacalao La Cuineta* (cod with spinach, raisins, pine nuts, and white sauce). The restaurant is in two neighboring premises behind the cathedral's apse. ⊠ *Paradís 4,* ☎ *93/315–0111. Closed Mon.* ⊠ *Pietat 12,* ☎ *93/315–4156. Closed Tues. Reservations not accepted. AE, DC, MC, V.*

$$$ ✕ **La Odisea.** The dark-red walls of this small restaurant, near the cathedral front, are crowded with contemporary Catalan paintings, and a colorful portrait of the chef as you enter. The artistic sense translates to the cooking, adventurously concocted from a myriad of Mediterranean ingredients and brought to your table by friendly waiters. Try the *merluza al vapor con salsa de tomate fresco* (steamed sea bass with fresh tomato sauce) or *ensaladilla de higado* (liver salad served with mushrooms and Modena vinegar). ⊠ *Copons 7,* ☎ *93/302–3692. Reservations essential. AE, DC, MC, V. Closed Sun., Holy Wk, and Aug. No lunch Sat.*

\$\$\$ ✕ **Quo Vadis.** Just off the Rambla, near the Boqueria market and Betlem Church, a shiny, gray facade camouflages one of Barcelona's most respected restaurants. A succession of small dining rooms decorated in grays and greens provides an atmosphere of sleek intimacy. Its much-praised cuisine includes *higado de ganso con ciruelas* (fried goose liver with prunes). ⊠ *Carme 7,* ☎ *93/317–7447. AE, DC, MC, V. Closed Sun.*

\$\$\$ ✕ **TramTram.** At the end of the old tram line just uphill from the vil-
★ lage of Sarrià, Isidre Soler and his stunning wife, Reyes, have put together one of the finest and most original of Barcelona's new culinary opportunities. Try the menu de gustació, and you might be lucky enough to get the marinated tuna salad, the cod medallions, and the venison filet mignons, among other tasty creations. Perfect-size portions and the graceful setting—especially in or near the garden out back—make this a popular spot. Although making a reservation is a good idea, Reyes can always invent a table on the spur of the moment, so don't pass up the chance to come for lack of planning. ⊠ *Major de Sarrià 121,* ☎ *93/204–8518. AE, MC, V. Closed Sun. and Dec. 24–Jan. 6.*

\$\$–\$\$\$ ✕ **Los Caracoles.** Just below Plaça Reial, a wall of roasting chickens announces one of Barcelona's most famous tourist haunts, which, despite catering primarily to American and other foreign visitors, has great food and real atmosphere. At night you are likely to be serenaded at your table. The walls are thickly hung with azulejos and photos of bullfighters and visiting celebrities. House specialties are *suquillo de pescadores* (an assortment of fish fried in oil and butter and added to a sauce), paella, *mejillones* (mussels), and, of course, *caracoles* (snails). ⊠ *Escudellers 14,* ☎ *93/302–3185. AE, DC, MC, V.*

\$\$–\$\$\$ ✕ **Set Portes.** A high-ceilinged dining room, black-and-white-marble floor,
★ and numerous mirrors hide behind these seven doors near the waterfront. Going strong since 1836, this festive and elegant restaurant serves continuously from one in the afternoon to one in the morning, seven days a week. The cooking is Catalan; the portions are enormous, and specialties are paella *de peix* (fish) and *sarsuela Set Portes* (seafood casserole). ⊠ *Passeig Isabel II 14,* ☎ *93/319–3033. AE, DC, MC, V.*

\$\$ ✕ **Bilbao.** Located at the corner of Venus and Perill, this cozy bistro is
★ indeed perilous to abstinence of all kinds. The overhanging balcony seems to place all diners on stage, and it gets fun and foolish quickly. The Catalan cuisine is excellent, and the value is among the best in Barcelona. This is a good place for earlyish dining at lunch or dinner. ⊠ *Carrer de Perill 33,* ☎ *93/458–9624. MC, V. Closed Sun. and holidays.*

\$\$ ✕ **Brasserie Flo.** A block above the Palau de la Música, this used to be a textiles factory; you dine in a large, elegantly restored warehouse with arched vaulting, steel columns, and wood paneling. Opened in 1982 by a group of Frenchmen, the Brasserie serves an exciting combination of French and Catalan dishes. Try the freshly made foie gras and *choucroûte.* ⊠ *Jonqueres 10,* ☎ *93/319–3102. AE, DC, MC, V.*

\$\$ ✕ **La Vaqueria.** This onetime cow shed has been wonderfully converted into an unusual eating place where tables for romantic couples and boisterous groups seem to coexist in perfect harmony. The feed bins and watering troughs have been left in place, and the country design has a certain urban elegance, along with a veneer of humor. The food is delicious and, for the most part, uncomplicated. The *solomillo de buey* (filet mignon) can be prepared with wild mushrooms, green peppers, or blue cheese, and is always superb. ⊠ *Deu i Mata 141,* ☎ *93/419–0735. AE, DC, MC, V. Closed Sun. No lunch Sat.*

$ ✕ **Agut.** Wood paneling surmounted by white walls on which hang 1950s
★ canvases forms the setting for the mostly Catalan diners in this homey
restaurant in the lower reaches of the Gothic Quarter. It was founded
in 1924, and its popularity has never waned, not least because the hearty
Catalan fare offers fantastic value. In season (September–May), try the
pato silvestre agridulce (sweet-and-sour wild duck). There's a good selection of wine but no frills such as coffee or liqueurs. ✉ *Gignàs 16,*
☎ *93/315–1709. Reservations not accepted. AE, MC, V. Closed Mon.
and July. No dinner Sun.*

$ ✕ **Egipte.** Hidden away behind the Boqueria market, Egipte has become
more and more popular over the last few years, especially with the young.
The traditional Catalan home cooking (featuring such favorites as
habas a la catalana) emanates from an overstretched but resourceful
kitchen, and the results can be uneven. Nevertheless, the many-tiered
dining rooms with marble-top tables and Egyptian motifs continue to
entice a lively and sophisticated crowd. The best time to come is
lunchtime, when there is a good-value menú del día. There are sister
branches at Jerusalem 3 and Rambla 79. ✉ *Jerusalem 12,* ☎ *93/3177480.
Reservations not accepted. AE, DC, MC, V. Closed Sun.*

$ ✕ **El Glop.** Noisy, hectic, and full of jolly diners from all over Barcelona,
El Glop's specialties are *calçotades* (giant spring onions baked in a clay
oven) and *asados* (barbecued meats). House wine arrives in a porró
(porrón in Spanish; unless you're practiced at pouring wine into your
mouth from some distance, save your blushes by using the wider opening and a glass). Bright and simply furnished, this restaurant is located
a few blocks north of Plaça del Sol in Gràcia. ✉ *Sant Lluís 24,* ☎
93/213–7058. MC, V. Closed Mon.

$ ✕ **La Fonda.** This is one of three Camós family restaurants that offer
top dining value. The other two locations are in neighboring Plaça
Reial: **Les Quinze Nits** (✉ Plaça Reial 6) and **Hostal de Rita** near the
corner of Arago and Pau Claris (✉ Carrer Arago 279). Be early (1 for
lunch, 8 for dinner); no reservations are accepted, and long lines tend
to form. ✉ *Escudellers 10,* ☎ *93/301–7515. AE, DC, MC, V. Closed
Dec. 25.*

$ ✕ **Sopeta Una.** Dining in this delightful, minuscule restaurant, with
old-fashioned, earthy decor and cozy ambience, is more like eating in
a private house. The menu is in Catalan; all the dishes are Catalan,
and everything is very genteel. Try the *cors de carxofes* (artichoke hearts
with prawns and tomato and mayonnaise sauce) and, for dessert, the
traditional Catalan *música,* a plate of raisins, almonds, and dried fruit,
served with a glass of Muscatel. ✉ *Verdaguer i Callis 6,* ☎ *93/319–
6131. Reservations not accepted. AE, V. Closed Sun. and Aug.*

LODGING

Barcelona's hotel selection is, like the restaurant offering, vast. The downtown hotels, such as the Husa Palace (the former Ritz), the Claris, the
Condes de Barcelona, and the Colón, probably best combine comfort
with a sense of where you are, while the sybaritic new palaces, like the
Arts, the Rey Juan Carlos I, the Hilton, and the Princesa Sofía, cater
more to business guests seeking luxury more than geography. Meanwhile, the smaller hotels, such as the Jardí or the España, are less than
half as expensive and more a part of the real life of the city.

$$$$ 🏨 **Avenida Palace.** At the bottom of the Eixample, between the Rambla de Catalunya and Passeig de Gràcia, this hotel manages to convey
a feeling of elegance and antiquated style despite dating only from 1952.
The lobby is wonderfully ornate, with curving staircases leading off in
many directions. Everything is patterned, from the carpets to the plas-

terwork, a style largely echoed in the bedrooms, although some have been modernized and the wallpaper subdued. Nevertheless, if you prefer contemporary simplicity, go elsewhere. ⊠ *Gran Via 605607, 08007,* ☎ *93/301–9600,* FAX *93/318–1234. 160 rooms with bath. Restaurant, bar, health club. AE, DC, MC, V.*

$$$$ 🏨 **Condes de Barcelona.** Installed in the old Batlló house (with an annex ★ across the street in the old Duarella house), this is one of the city's most popular hotels—rooms need to be booked well in advance. The stunning, pentagonal lobby features a marble floor and the columns and courtyard of the original 1891 building. The modern rooms have Jacuzzis and terraces overlooking interior gardens. An affiliated fitness club around the corner offers facilities including squash courts and a pool. ⊠ *Passeig de Gràcia 75, 08008,* ☎ *93/488–2200,* FAX *93/487–1442. 183 rooms with bath. Restaurant, bar, parking. AE, DC, MC, V.*

$$$$ 🏨 **Hotel Arts.** This luxurious, Ritz-Carlton monolith overlooks Barcelona from the new Olympic Port, providing unique views of the Mediterranean, the city and the mountains behind. A short taxi ride from the center of the city, the hotel is virtually a world of its own with three restaurants (one specializing in Californian cuisine), the beach, and an outdoor pool. ⊠ *C. de la Marina 1921, 08005,* ☎ *93/221–1000,* FAX *93/221–1070. 455 rooms and suites. 3 restaurants, bar, pool, beauty salon, beach, parking. AE, DC, MC, V.*

$$$$ 🏨 **Hotel Claris.** Widely considered Barcelona's best hotel, the Claris is a fascinating melange of design and tradition. The rooms come in 60 different layouts, all furnished in classical, 18th-century, English style. There are wood and marble furnishings, a Japanese water garden, a first-rate restaurant, and a roof-top pool, all close to the center of Barcelona. ⊠ *Carrer Pau Claris 150,* ☎ *93/487–6262,* FAX *93/215–7970. 124 rooms and suites. Restaurant, bar, pool. AE, DC, MC, V.*

$$$$ 🏨 **Hotel Rey Juan Carlos I Conrad International.** This modern complex towering over the western end of Barcelona's Avinguda Diagonal is an exciting commercial complex, as well as a luxury hotel. Jewelry, furs, caviar, art, flowers, and fashions; even limousines are for sale or hire here. The lush garden, including a pond complete with swans, is the setting of an Olympic-size swimming pool; the green expanses of Barcelona's finest in-town country club, El Polo, spread luxuriantly out beyond. There are two restaurants: the luxurious Chez Vous featuring French cuisine and the Café Polo, a sumptuous buffet, as well as an American bar. ⊠ *Avinguda Diagonal 661671, 08028,* ☎ *93/448–0808,* FAX *93/448–0607. 375 rooms with bath, 40 suites. 3 restaurants, bar, pool, beauty salon, meeting rooms. AE, DC, MC, V.*

$$$$ 🏨 **Husa Palace** (formerly the Hotel Ritz). Founded in 1919 by Cae- ★ sar Ritz, this grande dame of Barcelona hotels changed ownership and name in early 1996. Extensive refurbishment has restored it to its former splendor. The imperial entrance lobby is awe-inspiring; the rooms contain Regency furniture; some have Roman baths and mosaics, and the service is impeccable. As for the price, you can almost double that of its nearest competitor. 🏨 *Gran Via 668, 08010,* ☎ *93/318–5200,* FAX *93/318–0148. 158 rooms with bath. Restaurant, bar. AE, DC, MC, V.*

$$$$ 🏨 **Le Meridien.** The English-owned and managed Le Meridien vies with the Colón and Rivoli Ramblas as the premier hotel in the Rambla–Barri Gòtic area. Bedrooms are light, spacious, and decorated in pastel shades. The hotel hosts rock stars such as Michael Jackson and is very popular with business people; facsimiles and computers in your room are available on request. A room overlooking the Rambla is worth the extra noise. ⊠ *Rambla 111, 08002,* ☎ *93/318–6200,* FAX *93/301–7776. 209 rooms with bath. Restaurant, bar, parking. AE, DC, MC, V.*

$$$$ ⊞ **Princesa Sofía.** Long regarded as the city's foremost modern hotel despite its slightly out-of-the-way location on Avenida Diagonal, this towering highrise offers a wide range of facilities and everything from shops to three different restaurants, including one of the city's finest, Le Gourmet, and the 19th-floor Top City, with breathtaking views. Modern bedrooms are ultra-comfortable and decorated in soft colors. ⊠ *Plaça Pius XII 4, 08028,* ☎ *93/330–7111,* FAX *93/411–2106. 505 rooms with bath. 3 restaurants, bars, indoor and outdoor pools, beauty salon, health club, sauna, parking. AE, DC, MC, V.*

$$$ ⊞ **Alexandra.** Behind a reconstructed Eixample facade, everything here is slick and contemporary. The rooms are spacious, attractively furnished with dark wood chairs, and thatch screens on the balconies to give privacy to the inward-facing rooms. From the airy, white-marble hall up, the Alexandra is perfectly suited to modern, Martini-sipping folk. ⊠ *Mallorca 251, 08008,* ☎ *93/487–0505,* FAX *93/488–0258. 81 rooms with bath. Restaurant, bar, parking. AE, DC, MC, V.*

$$$ ⊞ **Calderón.** Ideally placed on the chic, uptown extension of the Rambla, this modern highrise possesses the range of facilities normally expected only of those establishments farther out of town. Public rooms are huge, with cool, white-marble floors, a style continued in the bedrooms. Don't forgo one of the higher rooms, from which the views from sea to mountains and over the city are breathtaking. ⊠ *Rambla de Catalunya 26, 08007,* ☎ *93/301–0000,* FAX *TK. 264 rooms with bath. Restaurant, piano bar, indoor and outdoor pools, health club, squash, parking. AE, DC, MC, V.*

$$$ ⊞ **Colón.** This cozy, older, townhouse hotel has a unique charm and
★ intimacy reminiscent of an English country inn. It lays claim to the sightseer's ideal location, with many of the rooms overlooking the floodlit main facade of the cathedral. The rooms are comfortable and tastefully furnished. The ones in the back are, if anything, noisier, as there is no longer any automobile traffic on the front side, and the church bells are equally audible all over the neighborhood. So by all means try to get a room with a view of the cathedral. The Colón was a great favorite of Joan Miró, and for comfort, ambience and location, it's very possibly the best place to be in Barcelona. ⊠ *Avda. Catedral 7, 08002,* ☎ *93/301–1404,* FAX *93/317–2915. 147 rooms with bath. Restaurant, bar. AE, DC, MC, V.*

$$$ ⊞ **Duques de Bergara.** This hotel is set in a stately Moderniste mansion with high ceilings and the full range of Art Nouveau trappings. The public rooms successfully combine old and new, Persian rugs, and glass tables. The bedrooms display restraint and elegance in their mingling of functional contemporary with antiques, though some are smaller and have thinner walls than one would wish. ⊠ *Bergara 11, 08002,* ☎ *93/301–5151,* FAX *93/317–3442. 54 rooms with bath. Restaurant, bar. AE, DC, MC, V.*

$$$ ⊞ **Gran Derby.** Every bedroom in this modern Eixample hotel has its own sitting room, and each is decorated with modern, black-and-white tile floors, plain, light-colored walls, and coral bedspreads. Some have an extra bedroom, making this an ideal choice for a family. If it weren't for the location, some way out (for sightseeing purposes), just below Plaça Francesc Macià, it would be unreservedly recommended. ⊠ *Loreto 28, 08029,* ☎ *93/322–3215,* FAX *93/419–6820. 44 rooms with bath. Café, bar, parking. AE, DC, MC, V.*

$$$ ⊞ **Majestic.** With an unbeatable location on the city's most stylish boulevard and a great, roof-top pool, this is a near-perfect place to stay. The different combinations of wallpaper, pastels, and vintage furniture in the rooms and the leather sofas, marble, and mirrors in the reception area all suit the place well. The building is part Eixample town house and part modern extension, so bear this in mind when booking your room. ✉ *Passeig de Gràcia 70, 08008,* ☎ *93/488–1717,* FAX *93/488–1880. 335 rooms with bath. Restaurant, bar, pool, health club, parking. AE, DC, MC, V.*

$$$ 🏨 **Rivoli Ramblas.** Behind the upper-Rambla facade lies imaginative, slick, modern decor with marble floors, elegant, pastel bedrooms, and a roof-terrace bar with panoramic views. ✉ *Ramblas 128, 08002,* ☎ *93/302–6643,* FAX *93/317–5053. 87 rooms with bath. Restaurant, spa, health club. AE, DC, MC, V.*

$$ 🏨 **España.** They've completely modernized the large bedrooms here—
★   the best and quietest overlook the bright, interior patio—and now this erstwhile budget hotel, with already stunning public rooms, is a real winner. Its main attraction remains the Moderniste ground-floor decor, designed by Domènech i Muntaner, with a superbly sculpted hearth by Eusebi Arnau, elaborate woodwork, and a mermaid-populated, Ramón Casas mural in the breakfast room. Don't miss this lovely concentration of Art Nouveau, even if you only stop in for a meal. ✉ *Sant Pau 911, 08001,* ☎ *93/318–1758,* FAX *93/317–1134. 76 rooms with bath. Restaurant, breakfast room, cafeteria. AE, DC, MC, V.*

$$ 🏨 **Gótico.** Along with the neighboring Rialto and Suizo hotels, this now belongs to the Gargallo group, which has done a good job of renovating these three old favorites, popular with tour groups. Just off Plaça Sant Jaume, the Gótico is central for exploring the Gothic Quarter. The rooms have wood beams, white walls, heavy wood furniture, white tile floors, and walnut doors; ask for an exterior location. ✉ *Jaume I 14, 08002,* ☎ *93/315–2211,* FAX *93/315–3819. 80 rooms with bath. Cafeteria, bar. AE, DC, MC, V.*

$$ 🏨 **Gran Via.** Architectural features are the attraction of this grand, 19th-century town house, close to the main tourist office. The original chapel has been preserved; also, you can have breakfast in a hall of mirrors, climb its elaborate Moderniste staircase, and call from the Belle Epoque phone booths. The rooms have plain, alcoved walls, bottle-green carpets, and Regency-style furniture; those overlooking Gran Via itself have better views but are quite noisy. ✉ *Gran Via 642, 08007,* ☎ *93/318–1900,* FAX *93/318–9997. 53 rooms with bath. Breakfast room, parking. AE, DC, MC, V.*

$$ 🏨 **Metropol.** Located between the lower reaches of the Rambla and Via Laietana, this town house offers easy access to the port while being pleasantly off the tourist trail. Bedrooms are cozily decorated with plain, orange carpets, green bedspreads, and modern prints. ✉ *Ample 31, 08002,* ☎ *93/315–4011,* FAX *93/319–1276. 68 rooms with bath. Cafeteria, bar. AE, DC, MC, V.*

$$ 🏨 **Montecarlo.** Entrance from the Rambla is through an enticing, marble hall, and upstairs is a sumptuous, large reception room with a dark-wood, Moderniste ceiling. The rooms are modern, bright, and functional; ask for a view of the Rambla if you don't mind the higher noise level. ✉ *Rambla 124, 08002,* ☎ *93/412–0404,* FAX *93/318–7323. 76 rooms with bath. Bar, cafeteria, parking. AE, DC, MC, V.*

$$ 🏨 **Nouvel.** Centrally located just below Plaça de Catalunya, this hotel blends white marble, etched glass, elaborate plasterwork, and carved, dark woodwork in its handsome Art Nouveau interior. Bedrooms have pristine, marble floors, firm beds, and smart bathrooms. The narrow street is pedestrian-only and therefore quiet, but views are nonexistent. ✉ *Santa Anna 1820, 08002,* ☎ *93/301–8274,* FAX *93/301–8370. 74 rooms with bath. Breakfast room. AE, MC, V.*

$$ 🏨 **Oriente.** Down toward the seamier end of the Rambla, Barcelona's oldest hotel has nevertheless retained its style and charm. Ornate public rooms and glowing chandeliers recall a bygone era. The only drawback is the somewhat functional decor of the rooms, some of which have an extra bed for families. Popular with businesspeople, the hotel

is just below the Liceu Opera House. ⊠ *Rambla 4547, 08002,* ☎ *93/302–2558,* FAX *93/412–3819. 142 rooms with bath. Restaurant, bar. AE, DC, MC, V.*

$$ 🏨 **Regente.** The Moderniste decor and plentiful, stained glass lend style and charm to this smallish hotel. The public rooms have been renovated over the last two years and are carpeted with many different patterns. The bedrooms, fortunately, are elegantly restrained; the verdant roof-terrace with a pool and the prime position on the Rambla de Catalunya complete the positive verdict. ⊠ *Rambla de Catalunya 76, 08008,* ☎ *93/487–5989,* FAX *93/487–3227. 78 rooms with bath. 2 restaurants, bar, pool. AE, DC, MC, V.*

$$ 🏨 **Rialto.** This hotel seems to have taken a leaf from the paradors' book with its subdued and classy decor of pine floors, white walls, and walnut doors. The rooms (ask for an exterior one) echo this look, with heavy furniture set against light walls, and they have all the same fittings as the Gótico. There is a vaulted bar in the basement and a modern, mirrored *salón* off the lobby. ⊠ *Ferran 42, 08002,* ☎ *93/318–5212,* FAX *93/310–4081. 140 rooms with bath. Cafeteria, bar. AE, DC, MC, V.*

$$ 🏨 **Suizo.** The last of the Gargallo hotels lacks the spacious corridors of the Rialto, but its public rooms are preferable, with elegant, modern seating at the front of the hotel, either near the reception area or one floor up, and good views over the noisy square. The bedrooms have bright walls and either wood or tile floors. ⊠ *Plaça del Àngel 12, 08002,* ☎ *93/315–0461,* FAX *93/310–4081. 50 rooms with bath. Restaurant, cafeteria, bar. AE, DC, MC, V.*

$ 🏨 **Continental.** Something of a legend among cost-conscious travelers, this comfortable hotel with canopied balconies stands at the top of the Rambla, just below Plaça de Catalunya. Everything is cramped, but the bedrooms manage to accommodate large, firm beds. The green, swirly patterns on the walls match those on the fast-fading carpets. Ask for a room on the Rambla side. A good breakfast is served overlooking the famous street. ⊠ *Rambla 138, 08002,* ☎ *93/301–2508,* FAX *93/302–7360. 35 rooms with bath. Breakfast room. AE, DC, MC, V.*

$ 🏨 **Jardí.** With views over the adjoining traffic-free and charming
★ squares, Plaça del Pi and Plaça Sant Josep Oriol, this hotel's newly renovated bedrooms have immaculate, white-tile floors, modern pine furniture, white walls, and powerful, hot showers. Be sure to get an exterior room—they're quiet and represent excellent value. The alfresco tables of the Bar del Pi downstairs are ideal for breakfasting in summer. ⊠ *Plaça Sant Josep Oriol 1, 08002,* ☎ *93/301–5900,* FAX *93/318–3664. 40 rooms with bath. Breakfast room. AE, DC, MC, V.*

$ 🏨 **Paseo de Gràcia.** Formerly a hostel, this hotel has good-quality, plain carpets and sturdy, wooden furniture adorning the soft-color bedrooms. Add to this the location on the handsomest of Eixample's boulevards, and this is an excellent budget option if you want to stay uptown. Half the rooms have superb, roof-top terraces, with great views up to Tibidabo. ⊠ *Passeig de Gràcia 102, 08008,* ☎ *93/215–5828,* FAX *93/215–3724. 33 rooms with bath. Breakfast room, bar. AE, DC, MC, V.*

$ 🏨 **Peninsular.** Built for the 1890 Exposition, this hotel in the Barri Xines
★ features an impressive, coral-marble lobby and an appealing interior courtyard, painted white and pale green and adorned with numerous hanging plants. The bedrooms have tile floors, good showers, and firm beds. Look at a few before choosing because all are different—some have views; others give onto the courtyard. ⊠ *Sant Pau 34, 08001,* ☎ *93/302–3138,* FAX *93/302–3138. 100 rooms, 80 with bath. Breakfast room. MC, V.*

NIGHTLIFE AND THE ARTS

With music halls, theaters, and some of Europe's trendiest nightclubs, Barcelona has a wide-ranging arts and nightlife scene. To find out what's on, look in newspapers or the weekly *Guía Del Ocio,* available from newsstands all over town. *Activitats* is a monthly list of cultural events, published by the Ajuntament and available from its information office in Palau de la Virreina (⊠ Rambla 99).

The Arts

Concerts

Catalans are great music lovers, and their main concert hall is the **Palau de la Música** (⊠ Sant Francesc de Paula 2, ☎ 93/268–1000). The ticket office is open weekdays 11–1 and 5–8, Saturday 5–8 only. Sunday morning concerts at 11 are a popular tradition. Tickets range from 900 to 12,000 ptas. and are best purchased in advance. Concerts are held September–June. Check daily music listings in *El País,* the *Spanish New York Times,* for concerts around town, especially the *Solistas del OBC* series of free performances held in the Barcelona Town Hall's opulent Saló de Cent, a chance to hear world-class chamber music in an incomparable setting. In September the city hosts an **International Music Festival** as part of its celebrations for the festival of the Mercè.

Dance

L'Espai de Dansa i Música de la Generalitat de Catalunya, generally listed as **L'Espai** (⊠ Travessera de Gràcia 63, ☎ 93/414–3133), or the Space, was opened by the Catalonian government in February, 1992, and is now Barcelona's prime venue for ballet, contemporary dance, and musical performances of varying kinds. **El Mercat de les Flors** (⊠ Lleida 59, ☎ 93/426–1875) near Plaça de Espanya, is the more traditional setting for modern dance and theater.

Film

Though some foreign films will be dubbed, there is always a good selection of films showing in their original language. Look in listing magazines for movies marked *v.o.* (*versión original*). The **Filmoteca** (⊠ Avda. Sarrià 33, ☎ 93/430–5007) shows three films daily in v.o., often English. The **Verdi** (⊠ Verdi 32, Gràcia), Arkadin (⊠ Travessera de Gràcia 103, near Gràcia train stop), and the **Rex** (⊠ Gran Via 463) tend to have recent releases in v.o. as do Casablanca (⊠ Passeig de Gràcia 115), Renoir Les Corts (⊠ Eugeni d'Ors 12), and numerous other theaters.

Flamenco

Barcelona is not richly endowed with flamenco spots, as Catalans are only moderately fond of this very Andalusian spectacle. The best place is **El Patio Andaluz** (⊠ Aribau 242, ☎ 93/209–3378), with *sevillanas* rather than flamenco and some audience participation, but it is quite expensive. **El Cordobés** (⊠ Rambla 35, ☎ 93/317–6653) is the place most visited by tour groups, but it can be colorful and fun. Others are **El Tablao de Carmen** (⊠ Poble Espanyol, ☎ 93/325–6895) and **Los Tarantos** (⊠ Plaça Reial 17, ☎ 93/318–3067).

Opera

Barcelona's opulent and beloved **Gran Teatre del Liceu** was gutted by flames in early 1994 and will in all probability not be restored until 1997. The box office, according to present plans, will remain open at San Pau 1 (☎ 93/318–9277); operas and musical events will be staged at the **Palau Sant Jordi** sports hall on Montjuïc, at the **Palacio Nacional** above Plaza España, or at the **Palau de la Música.** Some of the most spectacular halls and rooms of the Liceu were unharmed by the fire, and there may be some tours of these areas during the restoration.

Theater

Most theater performances are in Catalan, but Barcelona is also well known for its mime troupes (**Els Joglars, Els Comediants,** and **La Claca**). An international mime festival is held most years, as is the **Festival de Titeres** (Puppet Festival).

The best-known modern theaters are the **Teatre Lliure** (✉ Montseny 47, Gràcia, ☏ 93/218–9251), **Mercat de les Flors** (✉ Lleida 59, ☏ 93/318–8599), **Teatre Romea** (✉ Hospital 51, ☏ 93/317–7189), **Teatre Tívoli** (✉ Casp 10, ☏ 93/412–2063), and **Teatre Poliorama** (✉ Rambla Estudios 115, ☏ 93/317–7599), all of which offer a dynamic variety of classical, contemporary, and experimental theater.

Many of the older theaters specializing in big musicals are along the Paral.lel. They include **Apolo** (✉ Paral.lel 56, ☏ 93/241–9007) and **Victòria** (✉ Paral.lel 6769, ☏ 93/441–3979). There is an open-air summer theater festival in July and August, when plays, music, song, and dance performances are held in the **Teatre Grec** (Greek Theater) on Montjuïc, as well as in other venues.

Nightlife

Cabaret

Take in the venerable **Bodega Bohemia** (✉ Lancaster 2, ☏ 93/302–5061), where a variety of singers perform to an upright piano, or the minuscule **Bar Pastis** (✉ Santa Mònica 4, ☏ 93/318–7980), where the habitués form the cabaret and a phonograph plays the music of Edith Piaf.

Arnau (✉ Paral.lel 60, ☏ 93/242–2804) and **El Molino** (✉ Vila i Vila 99, ☏ 93/329–8854) are both traditional, old-time music halls that have retained their popularity. **Belle Epoque** (✉ Muntaner 246, ☏ 93/209–7711), a richly decorated music hall, stages the most sophisticated shows.

Casinos

The **Gran Casino de Barcelona** (☏ 93/893–3666), 42 km/26 mi south in Sant Pere de Ribes, near Sitges, also has a dance hall and some excellent international shows in a 19th-century setting. The only others in Catalunya are in **Lloret del Mar** (☏ 972/366512) and **Perelada** (☏ 972/538125), both in Girona province up the coast north of Barcelona.

Jazz Clubs

Try **La Cova del Drac** (✉ Vallmajor 33, ☏ 93/200–7032); **L'Auditori** (✉ Balmes 245); or the Gothic Quarter's **Harlem Jazz Club** (✉ Comtessa Sobradiel 8, ☏ 93/310–0755), which is small but puts on atmospheric bands. The Palau de la Música stages an important **international jazz festival** in November, and the nearby city of Terrassa has its own jazz festival in March. The **Blue Note,** a hot new place in the Port Vell's Maremagnum shopping mall complex, draws a mixture of young and not-so-young nocturnals to musical events and Wednesday night "Friends of the Blue Note" buffets. Food and drinks are served until dawn. ✉ *Maremagnum, Port Vell/across from R.C. Marítim,* ☏ *93/225–8003. AE, DC, MC, V.*

Late-Night Bars

Bar musical is Spanish for any bar that plays modern music loud enough to drown out conversation. The pick of these are **Universal** (✉ Marià Cubí 182184, ☏ 93/200–7470), **Mas i Mas** (✉ Marià Cubí 199, ☏ 93/209–4502), and **Nick Havanna** (✉ Rosselló 208, ☏ 93/215–

6591). **L'Ovella Negra** (⊠ Sitjàs 5) is the top student tavern. **Glaciar** (⊠ Plaça Reial, 13) is *the* spot for young out-of-towners.

For a more laidback locale, tall ceilings, billiards, tapas, and hundreds of students, visit the popular **Velodrom** (⊠ Muntaner 211213, ☎ 93/230–6022), just below Diagonal. Two blocks away is the intriguing *barmuseo* (bar-cum-museum) **La Fira** (⊠ Provença 171, ☎ 93/323–7271). Downtown, deep in the Barrio Chino, try the **London Bar** (⊠ Nou de la Rambla 34, ☎ 93/302–3102), an Art Nouveau old circus haunt with a trapeze suspended above the bar. Don't miss **Bar Almirall** (⊠ Joaquin Costa 33), or **Bar Muy Buenas** (⊠ Carme 63).

For extra-late-night and dawn patrol with spectacular views over Barcelona try **Bar Cel Ona** up on Tibidabo (⊠ Plaça Tibidabo 34).

Nightclubs and Discothèques
Barcelona is currently so hip that it is difficult to keep track of the trendiest places to go at night. Most clubs have a discretionary entrance charge that they like to inflict on foreigners, so dress up and be prepared to talk your way past the doorman. Don't expect much to happen until 1:30 or 2:00.

Top ranked recently has been the prison decor-mimicking **Otto Zutz** (⊠ Lincoln 15, ☎ 93/238–0722), just off Via Augusta. **La Via** (⊠ Marqués de l'Argentera s/n, ☎ 93/319–5356), in the Estació de França, is a new hot spot, while **Fibra Optica** (⊠ Beethoven 9, ☎ 93/209–5281) and the city's nearly classic **Up and Down** (⊠ Numancia 179, ☎ 93/280–2922), pronounced "Pendow," are both anything but calm. **Bikini** (⊠ Deu i Mata 105, at Entença, ☎ 93/322–0005) reopened in 1996 after closing shortly before the 1992 Barcelona Olympics. Enormously popular before and after its parenthetical disappearance, Bikini's only drawback is the line that occasionally forms on particularly festive Saturday nights. **Oliver y Hardy** (⊠ Diagonal 593, ☎ 93/419–3181) next to the Barcelona Hilton is a recent invention more popular with the older set (you won't stand out if you're over 35), while **La Tierra** (⊠ Aribau 230, ☎ 93/200–7346) and **El Otro** (⊠ Valencia 166, ☎ 93/323–6759) also accept postgraduates with open arms. **Zeleste** (⊠ Almogavers 122, ☎ 93/309–1204) is one more standard hangout, especially popular with jazz and rock buffs. **La Boîte** (⊠ Diagonal 477, ☎ 93/419–5950) has live music and a nice balance of insanity and civilization.

For an old-fashioned *sala de baile* (dance hall) with a big band playing tangos, head to **La Paloma** (⊠ Tigre 27, ☎ 93/301–6897); the kitsch 1950s decor creates a peculiar atmosphere that's great fun.

OUTDOOR ACTIVITIES AND SPORTS

Golf

Barcelona is fortunate enough to be ringed by some excellent golf courses; be sure to call ahead to reserve tee times.

Around Barcelona
Reial Club de Golf El Prat (⊠ 08820 El Prat de Llobregat, ☎ 93/379–0278), greens fees 6,000 ptas. and up. **Club de Golf de Sant Cugat** (⊠ 08190 Sant Cugat del Vallès, ☎ 93/674–3958), greens fees 5,000 ptas. **Club de Golf Vallromanes** (⊠ 08188 Vallromanes, ☎ 93/568–0362), greens fees 3,500 ptas. weekdays, 6,000 ptas. weekends. **Club de Golf Terramar** (⊠ 08870 Sitges, ☎ 93/894–0580), greens fees 3,500–5,000 ptas.

Farther Afield
Club de Golf Costa Brava (⊠ La Masía, 17246 Santa Cristina d'Aro, ☏ 972/837150), greens fees 4,000–6,000 ptas. **Club de Golf Pals** (⊠ Platja de Pals, 17256 Pals, ☏ 972/637009), greens fees 7,000 ptas.

Gymnasiums

Catalans are becoming increasingly keen on fitness: You will see gymnasiums everywhere and in the *Páginas Amarillas/Pàgines Grogues (Yellow Pages)* under "Gimnasios/Gimnasis." Recommended is the new and exciting **Crack,** which has gym, sauna, pool, six squash courts, and paddle tennis. ⊠ *Pasaje Domingo 7,* ☏ *93/215–2755.* ⬛ *Day membership 2,000 ptas.; small supplement for courts.*

Hiking

Although you may not have come to Barcelona with the idea of hiking in the mountains, the **Collserola** hills behind the city offer well-marked trails, fresh air, and lovely views. Take the Sabadell or Terrassa FF.CC. train from Plaça de Catalunya and get off at the Baixador de Vallvidrera. The nearby information center can supply you with maps of this surprising mountain woodland just 20 minutes from downtown Barcelona.

Swimming

Indoor
Try the **Club Natació Barceloneta** (⊠ Passeig Marítim, ☏ 93/309–3412) or the **Piscines Pau NegreCan Toda** (⊠ Ramiro de Maetzu, ☏ 93/213–4344). The fee at each is 500 ptas.

Outdoor
Uphill from Parc Güell is the **Parc de la Creueta del Coll** (⊠ Castellterçol, ☏ 93/416–2625), which has a huge outdoor swimming pool. ☞ Tennis, *below.* The fee is 300 ptas.

Tennis

The cheapest place to play tennis is the **Complejo Deportivo Can Caralleu** (Can Caralleu Sports Complex), above Pedralbes. ☏ 93/203–7874. ⬛ *Daytime 700 ptas. per hr, nighttime 1,200 ptas. per hr.* ☽ *Daily 8–11.*

There is also the upscale **Club Vall Parc.** ⊠ *Carretera de la Rabassada 79,* ☏ *93/212–6789.* ⬛ *Daytime 3,000 ptas. per hr, nighttime 3,500 ptas. per hr.* ☽ *Daily 8–midnight.*

SHOPPING

Shopping Districts

Elegant shopping districts are the Passeig de Gràcia, Rambla de Catalunya, and Avinguda Diagonal up as far as Carrer Ganduxer. Try Carrer Tuset, above Diagonal, for small boutiques. For more affordable, more old-fashioned, and typically Spanish-style shops, explore the area between the Rambla and Via Laietana, especially around Carrer de Ferran. The area around Plaça del Pi, from the Boqueria to Carrer Portaferrissa and Carrer de la Canuda, has fashionable stores, jewelry, and gift shops. Most shops are open weekdays 9–1:30 and 5–8; Saturday hours are generally the same, but some don't open in the afternoon; on Sunday virtually all are closed. Check out the Maremagum mall in the new Port Vell.

Specialty Stores

Antiques

Carrer de la Palla and Carrer Banys Nous in the Gothic Quarter are lined with antiques shops full of old maps, books, paintings, and furniture. An antiques market is held every Thursday, 10–8, in Plaça del Pi. The **Centre d'Antiquaris** (⊠ Passeig de Gràcia 57) contains 75 antiques stores. Try **Gothsland** (⊠ Consell de Cent 331) for Moderniste design.

Art

The greatest concentration of prestigious galleries is along Carrer Consell de Cent (and around the corner on Rambla Catalunya) between Passeig de Gràcia and Carrer Balmes. The best known are **Sala Gaspar** at 323 and **Galeria Ciento** at 347. The Joan Gaspart Gallery in Plaça Letamendi is also a major gallery. Carrer Petritxol, which leads down into Plaça del Pi (☞ La Rambla [Les Rambles] *in* Exploring, *above*) is also lined with art galleries, most importantly the dean of Barcelona art galleries, Sala Parès. Carrer Montcada boasts Galeria Maeght and others. The Passeig del Born is another hot gallery area. Galeria Verena Hofer is around the corner on Plaça Comercial, and the happening Metrònom is just across on Carrer Fussina.

Boutiques and Fashion

If you are after fashion and jewelry, you've come to the right place, because Barcelona makes all the headlines on Spain's booming fashion front. Check out **El Bulevard Rosa** (⊠ Passeig de Gràcia 53–55), a collection of boutiques that stock the very latest outfits. Others are on Avinguda Diagonal between Passeig de Gràcia and Carrer Ganduxer. **Adolfo Domínguez,** Spain's top designer, is at Passeig de Gràcia 35 and Diagonal 570; **Toni Miró**'s two **Groc** establishments are at Muntaner 385 and Rambla Catalunya 100, for the latest look for men, women, and children. **Joaquim Berao,** a top jewelry designer, is at Rosselló 277.

Department Stores

The ubiquitous **El Corte Inglés** is now in four locations at Plaça de Catalunya 14, Porta de l'Angel 19, Avda. Francesc Macià 58, and Diagonal 617 (Metro: Maria Cristina). Marks & Spencer is in L'Illa shopping mall at Diagonal 545, along with a full range of outlets ranging from Benetton to Zara.

Design and Interiors

At Passeig de Gràcia 102 is **Gimeno,** whose elegant displays range from unusual suitcases to the latest in furniture design. A couple of doors down, at 96, **Vinçon** is equally chic. Some 50 years old, it has steadily expanded through a rambling Moderniste house that was once the home of Moderniste poet-artist Santiago Rusiñol as well as the site of the studio of his colleague, the painter Ramón Casas. It stocks everything from Filofaxes to handsome kitchenware. **Bd** (Barcelona design), at 291–293 Carrer Mallorca, located in another Moderniste gem, Doménech i Muntaner's Casa Thomas, is another spectacular design store.

Food and Flea Markets

The **Boqueria** market, on the Rambla between Carrer del Carme and Carrer de Hospital, is a colorful and bustling food market, open Monday–Saturday. **Els Encants,** Barcelona's biggest flea market, is held Monday, Wednesday, Friday, and Saturday 8–7, at the end of Dos de Maig, on Plaça de les Glòries (Metro: Glòries, red line). **Sant Antoni** market, at the end of Ronda Sant Antoni, is an old-fashioned food and clothes market, best on Sunday.

SIDE TRIPS

Montserrat

47 *50 km (30 mi) west of Barcelona.*

An almost obligatory side trip while you are in Barcelona is to the shrine of La Moreneta, the Black Virgin of Montserrat, high in the peaks of the Serra de Montserrat. These weird, saw-toothed peaks have given rise to countless legends: Here, Parsifal found the Holy Grail; St. Peter left a statue of the Virgin Mary carved by St. Luke; and Wagner sought inspiration for his opera. A monastery has stood on the site since the early Middle Ages, though the present 19th-century building replaced the rubble left by Napoleon's troops in 1812. Montserrat is a world-famous shrine and one of Catalunya's spiritual sanctuaries. Honeymooning couples flock here by the thousands, seeking La Moreneta's blessing upon their marriages; and twice a year, on April 27 and September 8, the diminutive statue of Montserrat's Black Virgin becomes the object of one of Spain's greatest pilgrimages.

Follow the A2/A7 autopista on the new upper ring road (Ronda de Dalt) or from the western end of Diagonal as far as salida (exit) 25 to Martorell. Bypass this industrial center and follow signs to Montserrat. There are also train and bus service from Sants station to Montserrat, as well as guided tours (Pullmantur and Julià).

Only the basilica and museum are readily open to the public. The **basilica** is dark and ornate, its blackness pierced by the glow of hundreds of votive lamps. Above the high altar stands the famous polychrome statue of the Virgin and Child to which the faithful can pay their respects by way of a separate door. ☉ *Daily 6–10:30 and noon–6:30.*

The monastery's **museum** has two sections: The Secció Antiga (open Tuesday–Saturday 10:30–2) contains old masters, among them paintings by El Greco, Correggio, and Caravaggio, and the amassed gifts to the Virgin; the Secció Moderna (open Tuesday–Saturday 3–6) concentrates on recent Catalan painters.

NEED A BREAK?	Amid a string of overpriced buffet establishments, the pick of lunching spots is the unremarkably named **Montserrat.** ⊠ *Plaça Apòstols. No dinner.*

Montserrat is as memorable for its setting as for its religious treasures, so be sure to explore these strange, pink hills. The vast monastic complex is dwarfed by the grandeur of the jagged peaks, and the crests are dotted with hermitages: **Sant Joan hermitage** can be reached by funicular. The views over the mountains away to the Mediterranean and, on a clear day, to the Pyrenees, are breathtaking, and the rugged, boulder-strewn setting makes for dramatic walking and hiking country.

Sitges, Santes Creus, and Poblet

These three attractions to the south and west of Barcelona can be seen comfortably in a day. Sitges is the prettiest and most popular resort in Barcelona's immediate environs and flaunts, apart from an excellent beach, a picturesque Old Quarter and some interesting Moderniste touches—Sitges is also one of Europe's premier gay resorts. The Cistercian monasteries west of here are characterized by restrained Romanesque architecture and beautiful cloisters.

Head southwest along Gran Via or Passeig de Colón to the freeway that passes the airport on its way to Castelldefels. From here, the new

Barcelona Excursions

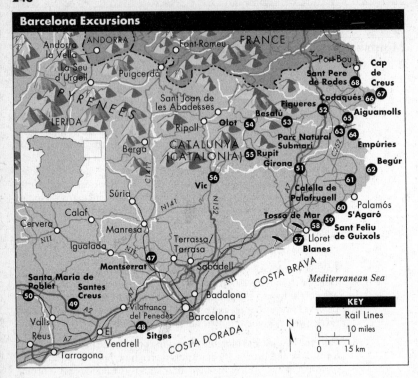

freeway and tunnels will get you to Sitges in 20 minutes. From Sitges, drive inland toward Vilafranca del Penedès and the A7 freeway. The A2 (Lleida) is the road for the monasteries.

Regular trains leave Sants and Passeig de Gràcia for Sitges; the ride takes a half hour. From Sitges, trains go to L'Espluga de Francolí, 4 km/2½ mi from Poblet (Lleida line). For Poblet, stay with the train to Tarragona and catch a bus to the monastery (⊠ Autotransports Perelada, ☎ 973/202058).

Sitges

🕲 *43 km (27 mi) south of Barcelona.*

In Sitges, head for the museums. Most interesting is the **Cau-Ferrat**, founded by the artist Russinyol, which contains some of his own paintings, together with two works by El Greco. Connoisseurs of wrought iron will be delighted to find here a beautiful collection of *cruces terminales*, crosses once erected to mark town boundaries. ⊠ *Fonollar s/n,* ☎ *93/894–0364.* 🎫 *250 ptas., Sun. and holidays free.* ⊙ *Tues.–Sun. 9:30–2.*

NEED A BREAK?	You will find excellent seafood in a nonpareil setting overlooking the sea at **Vivero** ⊠ *Passeig Balmins s/n,* ☎ *93/894–2149. Closed Tues. Dec.–May.*

On leaving Sitges, make straight for the A2 autopista by way of Vilafranca del Penedès. If you are a wine buff, you may want to stop here to taste the excellent Penedès wine. You can visit and taste at the **Bodega Miguel Torres** (⊠ Comercio 22, ☎ 93/890–0100). There's an interesting **Museu del Vi** (Wine Museum) in the Royal Palace, with descriptions of winemaking history. 🎫 *500 ptas.* ⊙ *Tues.–Sun. 10–2 and 4–7.*

Santes Creus

49 *95 km (59 mi) west of Barcelona.*

Santes Creus, founded in 1157, is the first of the monasteries you will find as A2 branches west into the province of Lleida. Three austere aisles and an unusual, 14th-century apse combine with the newly re-stored cloisters and the courtyard of the royal palace. ☎ *450 ptas.* ☼ *Oct.–Mar., daily 10–1 and 3–6; Apr.–Sept., daily 10–1 and 3–7.*

Montblanc is at exit 9 off A2, its ancient gates too narrow for cars. A walk through its tiny streets reveals Gothic churches with intricate, stained-glass windows, a 16th-century hospital, and medieval mansions.

Santa Maria de Poblet

50 *8 km .(5 mi) west of Santes Creus.*

This splendid Cistercian foundation at the foot of the Prades Mountains is the most complete and representative masterpiece of Spanish monastic architecture. The cloister is outstanding for its lightness and severity; on sunny days the shadows across the yellow sandstone managed the difficult task of restoration. Today, monks and novices again pray before the splendid retable over the tombs of Aragonese rulers, restored to their former glory by sculptor Frederic Marés; sleep in the cold, barren dormitory; and eat their frugal meals in the stark refectory. You can join them if you'd like to. There are 18 very comfortable rooms available (for men only). Call Padre Benito (☎ 977/870089) to arrange a stay of up to 15 days, surrounded by the stones and silence of one the most stunning spots on the Iberian Peninsula. ☎ *500 ptas.* ☼ *Guided tour 10–12:30 and 3–6 (until 5:30 Oct.–Mar.).*

Girona and Northern Catalunya

The ancient city of Girona, often ignored by visitors who use its airport for the resorts of the Costa Brava, is full of interest and within easy, day-tripping distance of Barcelona. The narrow, medieval streets, with frequent stairways as required by the steep terrain, are what give Girona much of its charm. The historic buildings here include the cathedral, dominating the city from atop 90 steps; Arab baths; and an antique and charming Jewish Quarter.

Northern Catalunya boasts the green, rolling hills of the Ampurdan, the Alberes mountain range at the eastern tip of the Pyrenees, and the rugged Costa Brava. Sprinkled across the landscape are charming *masías* (farmhouses), whose austere, grayish or pinkish stone, staggered rooftops, and ubiquitous square towers give them a look of fortresses. Churches confer dignity on the villages, and the tiniest of these contains its main arcaded square and rambla where villagers stroll during the sacred evening paseo.

Girona

51 *97 km (60 mi) northeast of Barcelona.*

In Girona you can park in the Plaça Independencia and find your way to the Tourist Information Office at Rambla Llibertat 1. Ask for their *oferta,* a card that will get you discount prices all over town. Then head to the Old Quarter across the River Onyar, past Girona's best-known view: the orange, waterfront houses and their windows, draped with a colorful array of drying laundry, reflected in the waters of the Onyar. Use the cathedral's huge Baroque facade to guide you up through the labyrinth of streets.

At the base of 90 steps, go left through the Sobreportes gate to the **Banys Arabs** (Arab Baths). Built by Morisco craftsmen in the late 12th century, long after Girona's Islamic occupation (795–1015) had ended, the baths are both Romanesque and Moorish in design. ▦ *350 ptas.* ☉ *May–Sept., Tues.–Sat. 10–2 and 4–7, Sun. 10–2; Oct.–Apr., Tues.–Sun. 10–1.*

Cross the River Galligants to visit the church of **Sant Pere** (Holy Father), finished in 1131 and notable for its octagonal, Romanesque belfry and the finely detailed capitals atop the columns of the cloister. Next door is the **Museu Arquaeològic,** which documents the region's history since Paleolithic times. ▦ *Free.* ☉ *Church and museum daily 10–1 and 4:30–7.*

Stroll back to and up the stepped Passeig Arquaeològic, which runs below the Old City walls. Climb to the highest **ramparts** through the Jardins de la Francesa. You get a good view from here of the 11th-century Romanesque Tower of Charlemagne, the oldest part of the cathedral.

Complete the loop around the **cathedral** to visit the interior. Designed by Guillem Bofill in 1416, it is famous for its immense, uncluttered, Gothic naveat, which, at 75 feet, is the widest in the world and the epitome of the goal of Catalan Gothic architects. The cathedral's museum contains the famous *Tapis de la Creació* (Tapestry of Creation) and a 10th-century copy of Beatus's manuscript *Commentary on the Apocalypse.* ▦ *300 ptas.* ☉ *Oct.–June, daily 9:30–1:15 and 3:30–7; July–Sept., daily 9:30–8.*

The adjacent **Palau Episcopal** (Bishop's Palace) houses the **Museu d'Art,** a good mix of Romanesque, Catalan Gothic, and modern art. ▦ *Included in ticket for Arab baths.* ☉ *Tues.–Sat. 10–1 and 4:30–7, Sun. 10–1.*

Leave Plaça dels Apòstols along Carrer Claveria and turn right down Carrer Lluis Batlle i Prats. Plunge right down the tiny Carrer Sant Llorenç, formerly the cramped and squalid center of the 13th-century *Call,* or Jewish Quarter. Halfway down on the left is the small **Monastruc Ça-porta,** a museum of Jewish history (☉ open Tuesday–Saturday 10–2 and 4–7, Sunday 10–2) and the **Pati dels Rabís** (Rabbis' Courtyard).

DINING AND LODGING

$$ ✕ **Alvereda.** Excellent Ampurdan cuisine is served in a bright setting. Try the *galletá con langostinos glaceada* (zucchini bisque with prawns). ✉ *C. Alvereda 7,* ☎ *972/226002. AE, DC, MC. Closed Sun. and holidays.*

$$ 🏨 **Ultonia.** The modern rooms in this centrally located hotel are decorated with attractive wooden furnishings. ✉ *Gran Via Jaume I 22, 08002,* ☎ *972/203850,* FAX *972/203334. 45 roomswith bath. Coffee shop. AE, DC, MC, V.*

Figueres

🔵 *37 km (23 mi) north of Girona.*

Figueres, a bustling country town and the capital of the Alt Empordà (Upper Ampurdan) is 37 km/23 mi north of Girona on the A7 autopista. Walk on the **Figueres Rambla,** scene of the passeig, the constitutional midday or evening stroll, and visit the **Museu Dalí,** a spectacular homage to a unique artist. The museum is installed in a former theater next to the bizarre, ocher-color Torre Galatea where Dalí lived until his death in 1989. The remarkable Dalí collection includes a vintage Cadillac with ivy-cloaked passengers you can water for 25 ptas. Dalí himself is entombed beneath the museum. ▦ *Oct.–May 650 ptas., June–Sept. 1,000 ptas.* ☉ *Oct.–May, Tues.–Sun. 10:30–5:30; June–Sept., Tues.–Sun. 9–7:15.*

DINING

$$$ ✕ **Ampurdan,** 1 ½ km/1 mi north on the N II, and hailed as the birth-place of modern Catalan cuisine, serves hearty portions of superb French/Catalan/Spanish cooking in a simple setting. Try one of the fish mousses. ⊠ *Carretera N II,* ☎ *972/500562. AE, DC, MC, V.*

$$ ✕ **Hotel Duran.** A well-known kitchen for miles around, the Duran restaurant is open every day of the year. Try the *lentilles amb morro de vadella* (lentils with calf snout) or the *mandonguilles amb sepia al estil Anna* (meatballs and cuttlefish), a *mar i muntunya* specialty of the house. ⊠ *C. Lasauca 5, 17600,* ☎ *972/501250,* 𝐅𝐀𝐗 *972/502609. MC, V.*

OFF THE
BEATEN PATH

AMPURDAN UPLANDS – For a trip into the Ampurdan uplands, take the N-II road 10 km/6 mi north of Figueres and turn west on Gi 502 to Darnius. At kilometer two is Robin Townsend's **La Posta restaurant** (⊠ Km 2, Gi 502, 17722 Darnius, ☎ 972/193078) at Mas Salellas, a good stop for lunch and general orientation. American-Catalan photographer/restaurateur Townsend has encyclopedic knowledge of this part of the Ampurdan. Work your way 13 km/6 mi west to the village of Maçanet de Cabrenys, another rustic hamlet. From there, follow signs to the **Santuari de les Salines** where there is a chapel and a tiny restaurant open in summer. Above Salines is one of the greatest beech forests in the Pyrenees. A newer and better road from Maçanet can take you through the village of Tapis and into France at Coustouges.

Besalú

53 *34 km (21 mi) north of Girona.*

Besalú, once capital of a feudal county as part of Charlemagne's 8th- and 9th-century Spanish March, is 25 km/15 mi west of Figueres on C260. This ancient town's most emblematic feature is its **fortified bridge** with crenellated battlements and two **churches,** Sant Vicenç and Sant Pere, are the main sights, along with the ruins of the Santa Maria convent on the hill over the town. The tourist office is in the arcaded Plaça de la Llibertat and can provide the schedule for the opening of the Sant Pere church, as well as keys to the *migwe,* the unusual **Jewish baths** discovered in the 1960s.

Castellfollit de la Roca perches on its prow-like, basalt cliff over the Fluvià River 16 km/10 mi west of Besalu.

Olot

54 *55 km (34 mi) northwest of Girona.*

Olot, the capital of the Garrotxa, is just 5 km/3 mi from Castellfollit de la Roca. Famous for its 19th-century school of landscape painters, Olot has several excellent Art Nouveau buildings, including one with a facade by Domènech i Muntaner. The **Museu Comarcal de la Garrotxa** contains an important assemblage of Moderniste art and design, as well as sculptures by Miquel Blai, creator of the long-tressed maidens who support the balconies along Olot's main boulevard. ⊠ *Carrer Hospici 8.* 🎫 *450 ptas.* ☉ *Mon. and Wed.–Sat. 10–1 and 4–7, Sun. 10–1:30.*

The villages of **Vall d'En Bas** lie south from Olot off Route A153. A new freeway cuts across this countryside to Vic, but you'll miss a lot by taking it. The twisting old road will take you by farmhouses that are characterized by dark wooden balconies bedecked with bright flowers in this rich farmland. Turn off for **Sant Privat d'En Bas** and **Els Hostalets d'En Bas.**

DINING AND LODGING

$$$ ✕ **Restaurante Ramón.** Ramón is so exclusive he adamantly refused to be in this book, so please don't let him see this. Olot's gourmet option par excellence, Ramón is the opposite of rustic: sleek, modern, international, and refined. ⊠ *Plaça Clarà 10,* ☎ *972/261001. Reservations essential. AE, DC, MC, V. Closed Thurs.*

$ ✕⊡ **Hotel La Perla.** Known for its friendly, family ambience, this hotel is always Olot's first to fill up. On the edge of town in the direction of the Vic road, La Perla also has a restaurant and two parks nearby. ⊠ *Avda. Santa Coloma 97, 17800,* ☎ *972/262326,* ℻ *972/270774. 30 rooms, 30 apartments. Restaurant, bar. MC, V.*

$$$ ⊡ **Parador de Vic.** This parador with quiet charm, also known as the Parador del Bac de Sau, is 14 km/8½ mi northeast of town off the Roda de Ter road past the village of Tavernoles. Views are of a stunning mountain and nearly lunar landscape over the Sau reservoir. ⊠ *Carretera VicRoda de Ter, 08500,* ☎ *93/8887311. 36 rooms. Coffee shop, pool, tennis court. MC, V.*

Rupit

⑤ *97 km (60 mi) north of Barcelona.*

Rupit is a spectacular stop for a view of its medieval houses and for a meal of local specialties, such as lamb, duck, and beef-stuffed potatoes. Built into a rocky promontory over a stream in the rugged Collsacabra region, Rupit, about halfway from Olot to Vic, has some of the most esthetically perfect stone houses in Catalonia, some of which have been reproduced in Barcelona's Poble Espanyol.

DINING

$$ ✕ **El Repòs.** Hanging over the river that runs through Rupit, this restaurant serves the best meat-stuffed potatoes. Ordering meals here is easy; you just need to know one word: *patata.* Other specialties include duck and lamb. ⊠ *C. Barbacana 1,* ☎ *93/856–5000. MC, V.*

Vic

⑥ *66 km (41 mi) north of Barcelona.*

Vic rests on a 1,600-foot plateau at the confluence of two rivers and serves as the commercial, industrial, and agricultural hub of the surrounding area. Known for its conservative character and Catalan nationalism, Vic's wide **Plaça Major,** surrounded by Gothic arcades and well supplied with bars and cafés, perfectly expresses the city's personality. Vic's religiosity is demonstrated by its 35 churches, of which the largely neoclassical **cathedral** is the foremost. The 11th-century Romanesque tower, el Cloquer, built by the Abbot Oliva, and the powerful modern murals painted twice by Josep Maria Sert (once in 1930 and again after fire damage in 1945) are the cathedral's most important features. Next door, the **Museu Episcopal** houses a fine collection of religious art and relics. ▣ *450 ptas.* ⊙ *Mon.–Sat. 10–1 and 4–7, Sun. 10–1:30.*

DINING

$$ ✕ **Ca l'U.** Translated as "The One," Ca l'U is, in fact, *the* place in Vic for hearty local cuisine with a minimum of pretense and expense. Try the *llangostinos i llenguado* (prawns and sole) or the regional standard *botifarra i mongetes* (sausage and beans). ⊠ *Plaça Santa Teresa 4 i 5,* ☎ *93/886–3504. MC, V. Closed Mon. No dinner Sun.*

Girona and Northern Catalunya Essentials

ARRIVING AND DEPARTING

By Bus: Sarfa (Estació Norte–Vilanova Calle Alí Bei 80, ☎ 93/265–1158) has buses every 1½ hours to Girona, Figueres, and Cadaqués. For Vic try **Segalés** (✉ Fabra i Puig Metro stop, ☎ 93/231–2756) and for Ripoll call **Teisa** (✉ Pau Claris 118, ☎ 93/488–2837).

By Car: Barcelona is now completely surrounded by a new network of *rondas,* or ring roads, with quick access from every corner of the city. Look for signs for these rondas; then follow signs to France (Francia), Girona, and the A7 autopista, which goes all the way. Leave the autopista at salida 7 for Girona. The 100 km/62 mi to Girona takes about one hour.

By Train: Trains leave **Sants** and **Passeig de Gràcia** every 1½ hours for Girona, Figueres, and Port Bou. Some trains for northern Catalunya and France also leave from the França Station. For Vic and Ripoll, catch a Puigcerdà train (every hour or two) from Sants or Plaça de Catalunya.

GUIDED TOURS

Trenes Turísticos de RENFE (☎ 93/490–0202) operates guided tours to Girona by train May through September, leaving Sants at 10 AM and returning at 7:30 PM. It also has train tours to Vic and Ripoll, leaving Sants at 9 AM and returning at 8:40 PM. The cost for each is 1,500 ptas. Call RENFE to confirm these tours.

The Costa Brava

The Costa Brava (wild coast) is a rocky stretch of shoreline that begins at Blanes and continues north through 135 km/84 mi of coves and beaches to the French border at Port Bou. This tour concentrates on selected pockets—Tossa, Cap de Begur, Cadaqués—where the rocky terrain has discouraged the worst excesses of real estate speculation. In these spots, on a good day, the luminous blue of the sea still contrasts with the red-brown headlands and cliffs; the distant lights of fishing boats reflect across wine-colored waters at dusk; and umbrella pines escort you to the fringes of secluded *calas* (coves) and white, sandy beaches.

Exploring the Costa Brava

57 The closest Costa Brava beaches to Barcelona are at **Blanes,** where between May and October launches (✉ Crucetours, ☎ 972/314969) can take you to Cala de Sant Francesc or the double beach at Santa Cristina.

58 Next stop north from Blanes along the coast road is **Tossa de Mar,** christened "blue paradise" by painter Marc Chagall, who summered here in 1934. The only Chagall painting in Spain is in Tossa's Museu Municipal (☎ 972/340709), or Municipal Museum. The entrance fee is 350 ptas., and the museum is open Tuesday–Sunday 10–1 and 5–8. Tossa's walled medieval town and pristine beaches are considered among the best in Catalonia.

59 **Sant Feliu de Guixols** comes next after Tossa de Mar, after 23 km (15 mi) of hairpin curves over hidden inlets. Tiny turnouts or parking spots along this road are nearly always placed over intimate coves with stone stairways winding down from the road. Visit Sant Feliu's two fine beaches, the church and monastery, the Sunday market, and the lovely Passeig del Mar.

60 **S'Agaró,** one of the Costa Brava's most elegant concentrations of villas and seaside mansions, is just 3 km/2 mi north of Sant Feliu. The 30-minute walk along the sea wall from La Gavina to Sa Conca beach is a delight.

㉖1 Up the coast from S'Agaró a road leads east to **Llafranc,** a small port with quiet waterfront hotels and restaurants, and forks right to **Calella de Palafrugell,** a pretty fishing village known for its July *Habaneras* (Catalan/Cuban sea chanties inspired by the Spanish-American War of 1898) festival. Just south is the panoramic promontory of **Cap Roig,** with its views of the barren Formigues (ants) isles and its fine botanical garden (garden tours are given March–December daily 9–9; the cost is 450 ptas.). The left fork drops down to **Tamariu,** one of the prettiest inlet towns on the Costa Brava. A climb up over the bluff leads down to the Parador Nacional at **Aiguablava,** a modern eyesore overlooking magnificent cliffs and crags.

㉖2 From **Begur,** the next town north of Aiguablava, you can go east through the calas or take the more inland route past the rose-colored, stone houses and ramparts of the restored medieval town of **Pals.** Nearby **Peratallada** is another medieval town with a fortress, castle, tower, palace, and well-preserved walls. North of Pals there are signs for **Ullastret,** an Iberian village that dates to the 5th century BC. **L'Es-**
㉖3 **tartit** is the jumping-off point for spectacular **Parc Natural Submarí,** the underwater park, at the Medes Isles, islands famous for diving and underwater photography.

㉖4 The Greco-Roman ruins at **Empúries** are Catalonia's most important archaeological site: Its port with a breakwater is considered one of the most monumental, ancient engineering feats on the Iberian Peninsula. As the original point of arrival of the Greeks in Spain, Empúries was where the Olympic Flame entered Spain for Barcelona's 1992 Olympic Games.

㉖5 The **Aiguamolls** (marshlands), an important nature reserve filled with migratory waterfowl from all over Europe, lies mainly around **Castelló d'Empúries,** but the principal information center is at El Cortalet on the road in from Sant Pere Pescador. Follow the road from Empúries, crossing the Fluvià river at Sant Pere Pescador, and proceed through the wetlands north to Castelló. From Castelló d'Empúries there are a series of roadways exploring the marshes, as well as footpaths well marked on the maps available at the information center.

㉖6 **Cadaqués,** Spain's easternmost town, still has all of the whitewashed, floral charm that converted this one-time fishing village into an international artists' haunt in the early part of this century. Salvador Dalí's house (not open to the public) still stands at Portlligat, a 30-minute walk north of town. The **Museu Perrot-Moore** in the old town has an important collection of graphic arts dating from the 15th to the 20th century, including works by Dalí. ▨ *400 ptas.* ☺ *June 15–Oct. 15, daily 5–9.*

㉖7 **Cap de Creus,** just north of Cadaqués, the Iberian Peninsula's easternmost point, is a fundamental pilgrimage if only for the symbolic telluric rush. The Pyrenees officially end (or rise) here. New Year's dawn finds mobs of revelers here awaiting the first glimpse of the sun emerging from the Mediterranean. A stroll through knee-deep bushes of rosemary and thyme with the added fragrance of the Mediterranean is an unforgettable sensorial feast.

㉖8 **Sant Pere de Rodes**'s monastery is the last and possibly the most spectacular visit on the Costa Brava. Built in the 10th and early 11th centuries by Benedictine monks, sacked and plundered repeatedly since, this Romanesque monolith commands a breathtaking panorama of the Pyrenees, the Empordà plain, the sweeping curve of the Bay of Roses, and the craggy contours of Cap de Creus.

Dining and Lodging

AIGUABLAVA

$$ ✗🎇 **Parador de la Costa Brava.** This modern parador is on a promontory overlooking sheer cliffs and surging seas. The service is impeccable. ✉ *Parador Nacional Aiguablava, 17255, Begur, Girona,* ☎ *972/622162,* FAX *972/622166. 87 rooms with bath. Restaurant, minibars, pool. AE, DC, MC, V.*

CADAQUÉS

$$$$ ✗ **El Bulli.** El Bullí is in the famous gourmet haven of Roses, which is
★ 7km/4mi (by sea) from Cadaqués and 22km/14 mi by land. Acclaimed without quarter by all European gastronomical reviews, chef Fernando Adrià will astound and delight your palate with his 12-course taster's menu. ✉ *Cala Montjoi, Roses, Girona,* ☎ *972/150457. AE, DC, MC, V. Closed Mon. and Tues.*

$$ ✗ **Can Pelayo.** This tiny, family-run restaurant, hidden behind Plaça Port Alguer, a few minutes' walk south of the center of town, has the best fish in town. ✉ *Carrer Nou 11,* ☎ *972/258356. MC, V. Closed weekdays Oct.–May.*

$$–$$$ ✗🎇 **Hotel Rocamar.** This hotel with splendid views has modern rooms, excellent service, and first-rate cuisine with no gourmet pretensions. ✉ *C. Doctor Bartomeus s/n, 17488 Cadaqués, Girona,* ☎ *972/258150,* FAX *972/258650. 70 rooms with bath. Restaurant, bar, indoor pool, tennis court. AE, DC, MC, V.*

CAP DE CREUS

$ ✗🎇 **Bar Cap de Creus.** This restaurant next to the Cap de Creus lighthouse commands spectacular views. The cuisine is simple and good; the England-born proprietor, Chris Little, rents three apartments above the restaurant. ✉ *Cap de Creus s/n, 17488 Cadaqués, Girona,* ☎ *972/159271. Closed Tues.–Thurs. Oct.–June. MC, V.*

PALAFRUGELL

$$ ✗ **Cypsele.** This restaurant serves local specialties such as *es niu,* an explosive combination of game fowl, fish tripe, pork meatballs, and cuttlefish, stewed in a rich sauce. ✉ *C. Ancha 22,* ☎ *972/300192. MC, V.*

PERETALLADA

$$ ✗ **Can Bonay.** Fine local cuisine served here includes duck with turnips and pigs' feet with snails. The decor is rustic, but the gastonomical quality is first-rate. ✉ *Plaça Espanya 4,* ☎ *972/634034. MC, V.*

S'AGARÓ

$$$$ 🎇 **El Hostal de la Gavina.** At the eastern corner of Sant Pol beach, this hotel is a superb display of design and cuisine founded in 1932 by Josep Ensesa, who invented S'Agaró itself. The Gavina offers complete comfort, superb dining, and tennis, golf, and riding nearby. ✉ *Plaça de la Rosaleda, s/n, 17248,* ☎ *972/321100,* FAX *972/321573. Restaurant AE, DC, MC, V.*

TAMARIU

$$ ✗ **Royal.** This sunny spot serves fisherman-style creations of superb freshness and quality. The *suquet* (the special paella), is especially recommendable at this beachside restaurant. ✉ *Passeig de Mar 9,* ☎ *972/620041. MC, V.*

TOSSA DE MAR

$$–$$$ ✗🎇 **Hotel Mar Menuda.** This modern hideaway on the Costa Brava offers as much peace and quiet or different varieties of water sports as you can possibly handle. Windsurfing, sailing, swimming, and scuba diving are all available, instruction included. The hotel terrace overlooks the coast and the town of Tossa de Mar with its medieval castle and the cobbled streets of its old quarter. ⊠ *Playa Mar Menuda s/n, 17320 Tossa de Mar, Girona,* ☎ *972/341000,* ℻ *972/340087. Restaurant, pool, tennis court. AE, DC, MC, V.*

Costa Brava Essentials

By Bus: Buses to Blanes, Lloret, Sant Feliu de Guixols, Platja d'Aro, Palamos, Begur, Roses and Cadaqués are operated by **Sarfa** (⊠ Estació de Norte-Vilanova, C. Ali-Bei 80, ☎ 93/265–1158; Metro Arc de Triomf).

By Car: From Barcelona, the fastest way to the Costa Brava is to start up the A7 autopista as if to Girona and take Exit 10 for Blanes. Coastal traffic can be slow and frustrating and the coast roads tortuous.

By Train: A local train pokes along the coast to Blanes from Sants and Passeig de Gràcia.

GUIDED TOURS

Between June 1 and September 31, Julià and Pullmantur run coach and cruise tours visiting Empúries, L'Estartit, the Medes Isles underwater natural park, and the medieval town of Pals. Lunch, swimming, and underwater exploring are offered at the Medes Isles stop. Buses leave Barcelona at 9 and return at 6. The price per person is 9,500 ptas. with lunch included, 8,000 ptas. without.

BARCELONA A TO Z

Arriving and Departing

By Bus

Barcelona has no central bus station, but most buses to Spanish destinations operate from the **Estació Norte Vilanova** (⊠ End of Avda. Vilanova, a couple of blocks east of Arc de Triomf, ☎ 93/245–2528). Most international buses arrive at and depart from **Estació Autobuses de Sants** (⊠ Carrer Viriato, next to Sants train station, ☎ 93/490–4000). Scores of independent companies operate from depots dispersed about town (☞ Excursions, *below*).

By Car

Do not be intimidated by either driving or parking in Barcelona. Legal and safe parking places on the street are always available, sooner or later.

By Plane

All international and domestic flights arrive at the stunning glass, steel, and marble **El Prat de Llobregat Airport,** 14 km/8½ mi south of Barcelona, just off the main highway to Castelldefels and Sitges. For information on arrival and departure times, call Iberia at the airport (☎ 93/401–3131, 93/401–3535, or 93/301–3993; international reservations and confirmations, 93/302–7656). The only airlines with direct flights from the United States to Barcelona are TWA and Delta.

Check first to see if your hotel provides a free shuttle service. Otherwise, you have the option of train, bus, taxi, or a rented car to drive yourself in.

BETWEEN THE AIRPORT AND DOWNTOWN

By Bus. The Aerobus leaves the airport for Plaça de Catalunya every 15 minutes (6 AM–11 PM) on weekdays and every 30 minutes (6:30 AM–10:50 PM) on weekends. From Plaça de Catalunya to the airport, it leaves every 15 minutes (5:30 AM–10:05 PM) on weekdays and every 30 minutes (6:30 AM–10:50 PM) on weekends. The fare is 450 ptas.

By Car. By following signs to the Centre Ciutat, you will enter the city along Gran Via. For the port area follow signs for the Ronda Litoral. The journey to the center of town can take anywhere from 15 to 45 minutes depending on traffic conditions.

By Taxi. A cab from the airport to downtown costs about 2,500 ptas.

By Train. The train from the airport to Sants Station in the city leaves every 30 minutes between 6:12 AM and 10:42 PM (Sants Station to the airport 5:40 AM–10:12 PM) and takes 20 minutes. There are also trains every 30 minutes to and from Plaça de Catalunya Station: airport–Plaça de Catalunya 6:12 AM–10:12 PM and Plaça de Catalunya–airport 6:05 AM–10:05 PM. The fare is 400 ptas.

By Train

Almost all long-distance and international trains arrive and depart from **Estació de Sants** (⊠ Sants Station, Plaça Països Catalans, ☎ 93/490–0202). There is another station on Passeig de Gràcia (⊠ at Aragó, ☎ 93/490–0202), where some trains stop before going on to, or after leaving, Sants. The **Estació de França,** near the port, handles long-distance trains to and from France.

Getting Around

Modern Barcelona, above the Plaça de Catalunya, is built on a grid system, though there's no helpful coordinated numbering system. The old town, from the Plaça de Catalunya to the port, is a labyrinth of narrow streets, and you'll need a good street map to get around. Most sightseeing can be done on foot—you won't have any choice in the Gothic Quarter—but you'll need to use the metro or buses to link sightseeing areas. The Dia T1 is valid for one day of unlimited trips on all subway, bus, and the FF. CC. lines. For general information on the city's public transport, call 93/412–0000. Public-transport maps showing bus and metro routes are available free from booths in Plaça de Catalunya.

By Boat

Golondrinas harbor boats operate short harbor trips from the Portal de la Pau, near the Columbus Monument. The fare is 500 ptas. for a half-hour trip. Departures fall and winter, daily 11–5 (until 6 on weekends); spring, daily 11–6 (until 7 on weekends); summer, daily 11–9.

By Bus

City buses run daily from 5:30 AM to 11:30 PM. Fares are 135 ptas. (150 ptas. Sundays and holidays); for multiple journeys purchase a Targeta T1, costing 700 ptas. and good for 10 rides (valid for the same as T2 plus buses). Route maps are displayed at bus stops. Note that those with a red band always have a stop at a central square—Catalunya, Universitat, or Urquinaona—and blue indicates a night bus. From June 12 to October 12 the *Bus Turistic* (9:30–7:30 every 30 minutes) operates on a circuit that takes in all the important sights. A day's ticket, which you can buy on the bus, costs 1,200 ptas. (850 ptas. halfday) and also covers the fare for the Tramvía Blau, funicular, and Montjuïc cable car across the port. The Bus Turistic starts from Plaça de Catalunya.

By Cable Car and Funicular

Montjuïc Funicular is a cog railroad that runs from the junction of Avinguda Paral.lel and Nou de la Rambla to the Miramar Amusement Park on Montjuïc (Paral.lel metro). It operates weekends and fiestas 11 AM–

8 PM in winter, and daily 11 AM–9:30 PM in summer; the fare is 125 ptas. A telefèric then takes you from the amusement park up to Montjuïc Castle. In winter the telefèric operates weekends and fiestas 11–2:45 and 4–7:30; in summer, daily 11:30–9. The fare is 350 ptas.

A Transbordador Aeri Harbor Cable Car runs between Miramar and Montjuïc across the harbor to Torre de Jaume I on Barcelona *moll* (quay), and on to Torre de Sant Sebastià at the end of Passeig Joan de Borbó in Barceloneta. You can board at either stage. The fare is 850 ptas. (1,000 ptas. round-trip), and the cable operates October–June, weekdays noon–5:45, weekends noon–6:15, and July–September daily 11–9.

To reach Tibidabo summit, take the metro to Avinguda de Tibidabo, then the Tramvía Blau (single fare: 250 ptas.) to Peu del Funicular, and the Tibidabo Funicular (single fare: 350 ptas.) from there to the Tibidabo fairground. It runs every 30 minutes, 7:05 AM–9:35 PM ascending, 7:25 AM–9:55 PM descending.

By Metro

The subway is the fastest and cheapest way of getting around, as well as the easiest to use. You pay a flat fare of 135 ptas. no matter how far you travel, but it is more economical to buy a Targeta T2 (valid for metro and FF. CC. Generalitat trains, Tramvía Blau [blue tram], and Montjuïc Funicular; ☞ *above*) costing 700 ptas. for 10 rides. It runs 5 AM–11 PM (until 1 AM on weekends and holidays).

By Taxi

Taxis are black and yellow and, when available for hire, show a green light. The meter starts at 300 ptas. (lasts for six minutes), and there are supplements for luggage, night travel, Sundays and fiestas, rides from a station or to the airport, and for going to or from the bullring or a soccer match. There are cab stands all over town; cabs may also be flagged down on the street. Make sure the driver puts on his meter. To phone a cab, try 93/387–1000, 93/490–2222, or 93/357–7755, 24 hours a day.

Guided Tours

Excursions

These are run by **Julià Tours** and **Pullmantur** and are booked as explained below. The principal trips are either full or half-day tours to Montserrat to visit the monastery and shrine of the famous Moreneta, Catalonia's beloved Black Virgin; or a full-day trip to the Costa Brava resorts, including a boat cruise to the Medes isles.

Orientation

City sightseeing tours are run by **Julià Tours** (⊠ Ronda Universitat 5, ☎ 93/317–6454) and **Pullmantur** (⊠ Gran Via 635, ☎ 93/318–5195). Tours leave from these terminals, though it may be possible to be picked up from your hotel. Prices are 3,300 ptas. (half-day) and 8,000 ptas. (full day).

Personal Guides

Contact the **Barcelona Tourist Guide Association** (☎ 93/345–4221) or the **Barcelona Guide Bureau** (☎ 93/268–2422) for a list of English-speaking guides.

Special-Interest and Walking Tours

The main organization for walking tours is **Terra Endins** (⊠ Ausias Marc 49, ☎ 93/232–2413). Every month this excellent group produces a new agenda of cultural visits. There's usually one visit per day (but not every day), and the cost for nonmembers is 350 ptas. If you are a serious Gaudí enthusiast, contact **Amics de Gaudi** (⊠ Avda. Pedralbes

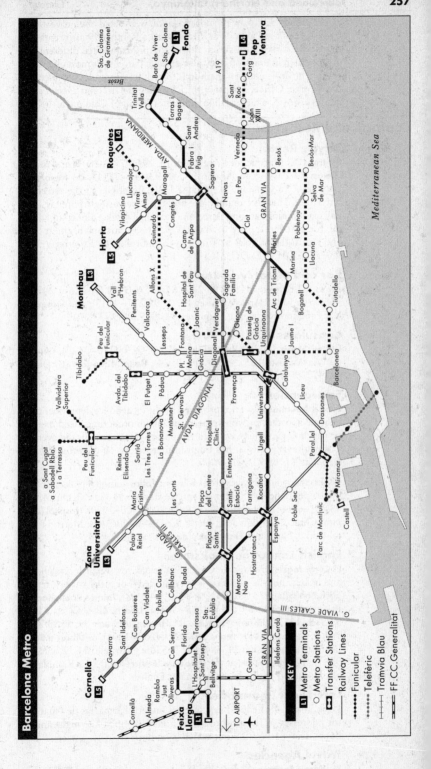

Barcelona Metro

7, ☏ 93/204–5250), or Friends of Gaudí, well ahead of your visit. The bookstore in the Palau de la Virreina at La Rambla 99 also rents cassettes with walking tours that follow footprints, painted different colors for different tours, on sidewalks through Barcelona's most interesting spots. The do-it-yourself method is to pick up the guides produced by the Tourist Office, *Discovering Romanesque Art* and *Discovering Modernist Art,* which outline itineraries for all of Catalunya.

Contacts and Resources

Bicycle Rental

Bicitram (✉ Marquès de l'Argentera 15, ☏ 93/792–2841) and **Los Filicletos** (✉ Passeig de Picasso 38, ☏ 93/319–7811). **Un Menys,** or "one less" in Catalan, means one less automobile in the streets of Barcelona. This bike-rental place organizes increasingly popular Tuesday night outings around Barcelona including drinks, dinner and dancing for an overall price of about $35. The excursions begin at 9 PM and return the bicycles at 1 or 2 in the morning. ✉ *Esparteria 3,* ☏ *93/268–2105. AE, DC, MC, V.*

Car and Motorcycle Rental

Atesa (✉ Balmes 141, ☏ 93/237–8140), **Avis** (✉ Casanova 209, ☏ 93/209–9533), **Hertz** (✉ Tuset 10, ☏ 93/217–3248), and **Vanguard** (cars and motorcycles, ✉ Londres 31, ☏ 93/439–3880).

Consulates

United States (✉ Pg. Reina Elisenda 23, ☏ 93/280–2227), **Canada** (✉ Via Augusta 125, ☏ 93/209–0634), **United Kingdom** (✉ Diagonal 477, ☏ 93/419–9044).

Emergencies

Tourist Attention, a service provided by the local police department will provide assistance if you've been the victim of a crime, need medical or psychological help, or need temporary documents in the event of loss of the originals. It has English interpreters. ✉ *Guardia Urbana, Ramblas 43,* ☏ *93/301–9060.*

Other emergency services are as follows. **Police** (national police, ☏ 091; municipal police, ☏ 092; main police station, ✉ Via Laietana 43, ☏ 93/301–6666). **Ambulance** (Creu Roja, ☏ 93/300–2020). **Hospital** (Hospital Clinic; ✉ Villarroel 170; ☏ 93/454–6000/7000; Metro Hospital Clinic, blue line). **Emergency doctors** (☏ 061).

English-Language Bookstores

El Corte Inglés in Plaça de Catalunya sells a few English guidebooks and novels, but the selection is very limited. For more variety, try **English Bookshop** (✉ Calaf 52, ☏ 93/239–9908), **Jaimes Bookshop** (✉ Passeig de Gràcia 64, ☏ 93/215–3626), **Laie** (✉ Pau Claris 85, ☏ 93/318–1357), **Llibreria Francesa** (✉ Passeig de Gràcia 91, ☏ 93/215–1417), **Come In** (✉ Provença 203, ☏ 93/253–1204), or **Llibreria Bosch** (✉ Ronda Universitat 11, ☏ 93/317–5308; ✉ Rosselló 24, ☏ 93/321–3341). The bookstore at the **Palau de la Virreina** (✉ La Rambla 99) also has good books on Barcelona in English.

Late-Night Pharmacies

Look in any of the local newspapers under "Farmacias de Guardia" for addresses of those whose turn it is to be open late-night and 24 hours. Dial 010 to find out which is on duty.

Travel Agencies

American Express (✉ Rosselló 257, at Passeig de Gràcia, ☏ 93/217–0070), **Iberia** (✉ Passeig de Gràcia 30, ✉ Diputació 258, ☏ 93/410–

3382), **WagonsLits Cook** (⊠ Passeig de Gràcia 8, ☎ 93/317–5500), and **Bestours** (⊠ Diputación 241, ☎ 93/487–8580).

Visitor Information

Tourist offices dealing with Barcelona itself are at **Sants Estació** (open daily 8–8); **Estació França** (open daily 8–8); **Palau de Congressos** (⊠ Avda. María Cristina s/n), open daily 10–8 during trade fares and congresses only; **Ajuntament** (⊠ Plaça Sant Jaume), open June 24–September, weekdays 9–8 and Saturday 8:30–2:30; and **Palau de la Virreina** (⊠ La Rambla 99), open Monday–Saturday 9–9 and Sunday 10–2. Those with information about Catalunya and Spain are at **El Prat Airport** (☎ 93/478–4704), open Monday–Saturday 9:30–8 and Sunday 9:30–3, and **Gran Via de les Corts Catalanes 658** (⊠ near Huse Palace Hotel, ☎ 93/301–7443), open weekdays and Sunday 9–7 and Saturday 9–2. Dial 010 for general information of all kinds.

In summer (July 24–September 15), **tourist information aides** patrol the Gothic Quarter and Ramblas area 9 AM–9 PM; they travel in pairs and are recognizable by their uniforms of red shirts, white trousers or skirts, and badges.

American Visitors' Bureau (⊠ Gran Via 591, between Rambla de Catalunya and Balmes, 3rd floor (☎ 93/301–0150/0032).

8 Southern Catalunya and the Levante

Southern Catalunya's Tarragona province and the Valencia region, known as the Levante, is a landscape of grayish, arid mountains backing a lush coast of sandy beaches often marred by modern tourist developments. Inland, the rugged landscape is dotted with small, fortified towns that were strategically important in medieval times. The Romans left many archaeological reminders, nowhere more so than in Tarragona. Valencia, a rich trove of art and architecture, is Spain's third-largest city.

By Philip Eade

Updated by
George Semler

THIS REGION STRADDLES CATALUNYA (Catalonia) and Valencia, allowing you to sample the differences and similarities between these two feuding Mediterranean cousins. Valencia was part of the House of Aragón, Catalonia's medieval Mediterranean empire, after Jaume I conquered it in the 13th century; staunch Valencia nationalists feel about Catalunya and the Catalan language much as Catalonia feels about Madrid and central Spain. Valencia was incorporated, along with Catalonia, into a united Spanish state in the 15th century, but resentment of the centuries of Catalan imperial domination is still strong amongst the most energetic cultivators of Valencia's separate cultural and linguistic identity. You will note the subtle differences in these two languages as you move south. Catalan prevails in Tarragona, a province of Catalunya, but Valenciano, widely accepted (though generally not by Valencianos themselves) as a dialect of Catalan, is spoken and used in street signs in the Valencian provinces.

The *huerta* (fertile, irrigated coastal plain) is largely devoted to citrus and vegetable farming, which lends color to the landscape and a fragrance to the air. Grayish, arid mountains provide a stark backdrop for the lush coast. These shores have seen Phoenician, Greek, Carthaginian, and Roman visitors. The Romans stayed several centuries, and there are archaeological reminders all the way down the coast, nowhere more so than in Tarragona, which was capital of Rome's Spanish empire by 218 BC. Rome's dominion did not go uncontested, the most serious challenge coming from the Carthaginians of North Africa. The three Punic Wars, fought over this territory between 264 BC and 146 BC, led to the immortalization of Hannibal, the most famous of the Carthaginian generals.

The coastal farmland and beaches that looked so attractive to the ancients have proved similarly popular for today's tourists, and a chain of ugly developments has marred much of the coast. Venturing inland, however, you discover a completely different world, where tourism is not the decisive fact of life and where local authenticity has survived intact. This rugged and often strikingly beautiful landscape is dotted with small, fortified towns, several of which bear the name of Spain's 11th-century national hero, El Cid, as proof of the battles he fought here against the Moors nine centuries ago. Each has its porticoed Plaza Mayor, whitewashed houses, and countless coats of arms as further reminders of the strategic importance of these towns in medieval times.

The city of Valencia, founded originally by the Greeks, was in Moorish hands from 712 to 1238, apart from a brief interlude from 1094 to 1102, when El Cid reconquered the city. The bright blue cupolas atop churches and the *azulejos* (glazed, patterned tiles) reflect Moorish themes and traditions. Also striking are the products of Valencia's 15th-century Golden Age: the Gothic Lonja (Silk Exchange) and mansions, and the Primitive paintings of Jacomart and Juan Reixach in the Fine Arts Museum. The flamboyant, 18th-century Palacio de los Dos Aguas embodies the vitality of Churriguerismo, or early Spanish Baroque.

Pleasures and Pastimes

Beaches

If you've just come from the Costa Brava, you will find the beaches in this area to be quite different, endless strands of fine-grained sand. Salou has the best beaches at the northern end; there's a lively palm-lined promenade. More tranquil are the beaches of the Ebro Delta: The best is the Playa de los Eucaliptos, reached by a pretty road from Amposta via Montells. Peñíscola's beach seems to go on forever; the sand is soft, and the old city rising up out of the sea at one end provides a scenic bonus. Alcocéber has a series of small, uncrowded, sandy crescents. Just to the north is the sophisticated new marina at Las Fuentes. Benicàssim's long, crescent-shaped beach has the most dramatic setting of all, with mountains rising steeply in the background. Valencia itself has a long beach that is great for sunning and for its numerous seaside restaurants, but it's not the best place for swimming. For cleaner water you need to head south as far as El Saler.

Dining

Romesco (a spicy blend of hazelnuts, peppers, and olive oil) hails from Tarragona and is used as a sauce for fish and seafood, and especially in the *calçotada* (spring onion) feasts of February. If you are here during the September Santa Tecla festival, you can try the *espineta amb cargolins* (tuna fish with snails). You can accompany this with excellent wine from the nearby Penedés or Priorato vineyards. The Ebro Delta is renowned for its fresh fish-eels, in particular; *rossejat* (fried rice in a fish broth, dressed with garlic sauce) is another local specialty. *Jamones* (hams), *cecinas* (smoked meats) and *carnes a la brasa* (meats cooked over coals) all feature in Maestrazgan cooking, together with good *trucha* (trout) and *conejo* (rabbit). You should also try the *trufas* (truffles) that grow here. In Valencia and down the coast you are in the land of Spain's national dish, paella *valenciana* (based on rice flavored with saffron and embellished with bits of seafood, poultry, meat, peas, and peppers). Prepared to order in a *caldero* (shallow pan), it takes a good 20 minutes to cook, so it is not for visitors in a hurry. Nor should paella be chosen from a *menú del día*, when it is generally tasteless and disappointing. The alternative is *arroz a la banda,* for which the fish and rice are cooked separately; the fish is fried in garlic, onion, and tomato, after which the rice is boiled in the resulting stock.

CATEGORY	COST*
$$$$	over 6,000 ptas.
$$$	4,000–6,000 ptas.
$$	2,000–4,000 ptas.
$	under 2,000 ptas.

*per person for a three-course meal, excluding drinks, service, and tax

Fiestas

Tarragona's most important fiestas are those of *Sant Magí* (August 19) and *Santa Tecla* (September 23), both characterized by colorful processions. In Valencia, the *Fallas* are held for a week in March and reach their climax on March 19, San José, or St. Joseph's, Day, when families throughout Spain celebrate Father's Day. The fact that St. Joseph is also the patron saint of carpenters is what gave rise to this bizarre and time-honored fiesta. Back in medieval days the guilds of carpenters burned their wood shavings in huge bonfires on St. Joseph's Day. Today Valencia explodes into a week-long celebration of fireworks, flower-strewn floats, carnival processions, top bullfights, and uncontrolled merrymaking to which tourists and Spaniards alike flock. On March 19, the huge and often grotesque satirical effigies of popular and not-so-popular figures are ceremoniously burned in massive bonfires, somehow creating a moving sense of nostalgia and of the ephemerality of life itself. If you are allergic to firecrackers or large crowds, stay away from this one.

Lodging

Tarragona's hotels are fairly uninspiring, but this is well compensated for by the time you reach the Ebro and the Maestrazgo, where antique, one-of-a-kind places are in convenient abundance. Back on the coast, lodgings become more mundane, with modern highrises the predominant style. The selection of hotels elsewhere down the coast is provided more for the convenience of anyone who especially wishes to stop in these places than because the hotels themselves are particularly recommended. Just to the north and south of Valencia, in Puzol and El Saler, are some famous luxury hotels, while in the city itself there is a reasonable range, old and modern, to suit all budgets. If you plan to be in Valencia for its Falla celebrations in mid-March, it is worthwhile to book your accommodations months ahead; prices are sure to rise closer to the festivities.

CATEGORY	COST*
$$$$	over 16,500 ptas.
$$$	9,500–16,500 ptas.
$$	6,000–9,500 ptas.
$	under 6,000 ptas.

*per standard double room, excluding tax

Exploring Tarragona to Valencia

Great Itineraries

Numbers in the text below correspond to numbers in the margin and on the Southern Catalunya and the Levante and Valencia maps.

Mountain villages, wetlands, sweeping beaches, cities filled with art, architecture and archeology: There is much to see and do between Tarragona and Valencia. Tarragona is distinguished by its extremely well preserved Roman remains. The fertile Ebro Delta, rich in fauna and flora, is next, followed by the ancient town of Tortosa, where a splendid night can be spent in the hilltop parador. A rewarding loop inland explores the wild and remote Beceite and Maestrazgo mountains, the highlight being the ancient, contoured town of Morella. The Costa del Azahar (Orange Blossom Coast) down to Valencia is characterized by orange groves against a backdrop of arid hills. Peñíscola, a cluster of white houses on a promontory, is very picturesque, although it is sadly becoming surrounded by tourist development. Farther south, the next stop of architectural note is the Roman town of Sagunto, with its hilltop fortress and amphitheater. Finally, we reach Valencia, a rich trove of art and architecture. Highlights include the Gothic Lonja (Silk Exchange), the striking baroque Palacio Marqués de Dos Aguas, and the superb Fine Arts Museum.

IF YOU HAVE 3 DAYS

If you have three days, see **Tarragona** ① and its Roman ruins, before moving on to the **Delta de l'Ebro** ⑤ for a late lunch at the Estany restaurant-museum near Villafranca del Delta. Next, drive up the Ebro river for a night at the Parador Castillo de la Zuda in ⛨ **Tortosa** ⑥. The second day should be an exploration of the Beceite and Maestrazgo mountains, passing through Miravet, **Gandesa** ⑦, Calaceite, Valderrobres, Beceite, Fredes, and **Morella** ⑩, on the way to coastal Vinaròs and ⛨ **Peñíscola** ⑭, where you can stop for the night. The final day would be devoted to exploring **Valencia** ⑯–㉝.

IF YOU HAVE 5 DAYS

Begin at **Tarragona** ①, and spend the night 'in the ⛨ **Delta de l'Ebro** ⑤. Explore the Delta for a day, not missing a late lunch at the Estany restaurant near Villafranca del Delta, before driving up to ⊞ **Tortosa** ⑥ for night two at the Parador Castillo de la Zuda. Day three can be dedicated to the Beceite mountains, exploring Miravet, **Gandesa** ⑦, Calaceite, Valderrobres, Beceite, and Fredes, before stopping at ⊞ **Morella** ⑩ for the night. On the fourth day, drive through the Maestrazgo mountains for a look at some of the least tourist-oriented valleys and villages on the Iberian Peninsula. Take the slow but scenic CS802 up through Iglesuela del Cid and around to Villafranca del Cid before going through **Ares del Maestre** ⑪, Albocácer, and **San Mateo** ⑫ on your way to ⊞ **Peñíscola** ⑭, where you can spend the night. On the fifth day, travel down through the Costa del Azahar to ⊞ **Valencia** ⑯–㉝.

When to Tour Tarragona to Valencia

It's a good idea to avoid coming to this region in the summer. This is a hot and arid part of Spain, and the beaches are crowded. Fall and Spring are probably the best times, but anyone who has seen the slanting December light in the Delta or the dramatic shadows cast across medieval stone facades in winter will not soon forget it. Remember that timetables for most sights change with the seasons, and many places close as early as 5:30 in winter.

TARRAGONA AND ENVIRONS

Tarragona, less than an hour from Barcelona, offers a bracing melange of fresh provincial capital, ancient outpost of the Roman Empire, pungent fishing port, busy shipping harbor, and vibrant cultural center.

Tarragona

❶ *98 km (60 mi) from Barcelona, 251 km (155 mi) from Valencia.*

The name Tarragona promises rich classical remains, and the city does not disappoint. As capital of the Roman province of Tarraconensis (from 218 BC), Tarraco, as it was then called, formed the empire's principal stronghold in Spain. During the 1st century BC its population was double the present-day figure of 110,000, and the city was regarded as one of the empire's finest urban creations. Its wine was already famous, and the people were the first in Spain to become Roman citizens. St. Paul preached here in AD 58, and the city became the seat of the Christian Church in Spain until it was superseded by Toledo in the 11th century.

Coming into the city from Barcelona, you pass by the **triumphal arch of Berà** (19 km/12 mi north of Tarragona), dating to the 3rd century BC, and from the Lleida road or autopista you can see the 1st-century **Roman Aqueduct** that helped bring fresh water the 32 km/19 mi from the River Gayo. Coming from the south, past the gasworks, you may think that modern Tarragona has forsaken her splendor, but, thankfully, some outstanding monuments remain and have received a valuable facelift as part of the city's ongoing renovation and rediscovery of its archaeological treasures. Tarragona is clearly divided into old and new by the Rambla Vella: The old town and most of the Roman remains are to the north, while modern Tarragona spreads out to the south.

Start your tour of Tarragona at the acacia-lined Rambla Nova, at the end of which is a balcony overlooking the sea, the **Balcó del Mediterràni.** Walking uphill along the Passeig de les Palmeres, you arrive at a clear illustration of the dichotomy between ancient and modern. The ★ remains of Tarragona's **amphitheater** are visible down toward the sea; above stands the modern, semicircular Hotel Imperial Tarraco, artfully echoing the amphitheater's curve. If you descend the steps to the am-

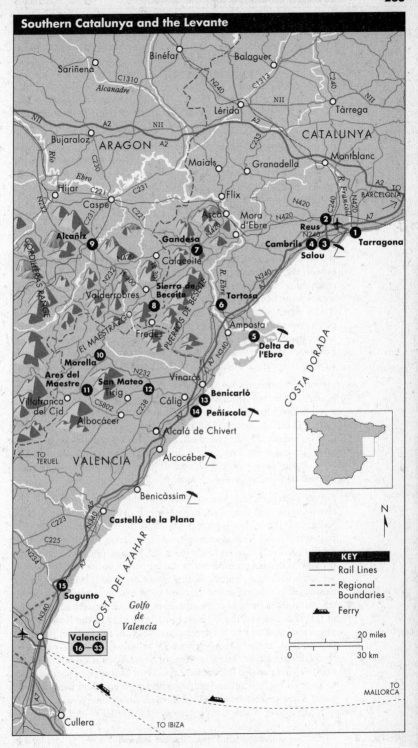

Southern Catalunya and the Levante

phitheater, you will see just how well preserved it is. You are free to wander through the access tunnels and along the seating rows, and sitting with your back to the sea, you may understand why Augustus favored Tarragona as a winter resort. In the center of the amphitheater are the remains of two superimposed churches, the earlier of which was a Visigothic basilica built to mark the bloody martyrdom of Sant Fructuós and his deacons in AD 259. 🎫 *500-pta. pass is valid for all of Tarragona's Roman remains.* ⊙ *Weekdays 10–8 (until 5:30 in winter), weekends 10–3.*

Across the Rambla Vella from the amphitheater, students have excavated the vaults of the 1st century AD Roman **Circus Maximus.** The plans just inside the gate show that the vaults you can see were only a small corner of a vast arena (350 yards long), where 23,000 spectators gathered to watch chariot racing. As medieval Tarragona grew, it gradually swamped the Circus. 🎫 *500-pta. pass is valid for all of Tarragona's Roman remains.* ⊙ *Weekdays 10–5:30, weekends 10–3.*

Around the corner from the Circus Maximus, up Passeig Sant Antoni, is the tall former **Praetorium.** This was Augustus's town house and reputedly the birthplace of Pontius Pilate. It looks Gothic because of extensive alterations in the Middle Ages, when it served as the residence for the kings of Catalunya and Aragón during their visits to Tarragona. It now serves as the **Museu d'Història** (the city's History Museum), with plans showing the evolution of the city. The highlight is the **Hippolytus sarcophagus,** with a bas-relief depicting the legend of Hippolytus and Fraeda, on the first floor. 🎫 *500-pta. pass is valid for all of Tarragona's Roman remains.* ⊙ *Tues.–Sat. 10–1:30 and 4:30–8; closed holidays.*

★ Next door to the History Museum is a 1960s neoclassical building that houses the **Museu Arqueològic** (Archaeological Museum), which has a collection of Roman statuary and domestic fittings. Look for the keys, bells, and belt buckles on the first floor. The beautiful mosaics displayed here include the Head of Medusa, famous for her piercing stare. Don't miss the video on Tarragona's history. 🎫 *125 ptas., free Tues.* ⊙ *Apr.–Sept., Tues.–Sat. 10–1 and 4:30–8, Sun. 10–2; Oct.–Mar., Tues.–Sat. 10–1:30 and 4–7, Sun. 10–2.*

Follow Passeig de Sant Antoni uphill from the Museu Arqueològic, the city walls on your left, to the ornately sculpted **Portal de Sant Antoni,** and go into the cobbled square inside. Walk down Carrer d'en Granada past some lovely, arched entryways to the Carrer Sant Bernat, where a right turn will take you into **Placa del Forum,** once the seat of the provincial Roman authorities. At the far corner of the square you will see signs for the cathedral. Walk down Carrer de la Merceria under the arcade on the right and you will soon reach the stairway leading ★ up into the **Pla de la Seu,** the square in front of the **cathedral.** Begun in the 12th century, the initial rounded placidity of the Romanesque apse later gave way to the spiky restlessness of the Gothic; the result is confused. If there is no service in progress, enter the cathedral through the cloister. The altarpiece of Santa Tecla is the main attraction, a richly detailed depiction of the life of Tarragona's patron saint. Converted by St. Paul and subsequently persecuted by local pagans, Santa Tecla was repeatedly saved through divine intervention. 🎫 *350 ptas., including cloister and museum.* ⊙ *Daily 10–1 and 4–7.*

NEED A BREAK?
At the foot of the cathedral steps, the **Bar Valmoll** is a handy spot for a coffee or a drink.

Continuing down the steps from the cathedral into the Carrer Major, Carrer Cavallers is the second street to the right. But before actually taking this street, continue down to the Plaça del Font for a look at the 19th-century neoclassical **Ajuntament** (Town Hall) at the far end.

After leaving the Plaça del Font and walking back up Carrer Major toward the Cathedral, Carrer Cavallers will take you down to the **Casa Castellarnau,** a Gothic *palacete* or town house built by Tarragona nobility in the 18th century, now a museum. The decor is stunning, dating from the 18th and 19th centuries. The last member of the Castellarnau family vacated the house in 1954. ✉ *500-pta. pass is valid for all of Tarragona's Roman remains.* ☉ *Mon.–Sat. 10–1 and 4–7, Sun. 10–1.*

At the end of Carrer Cavallers is the Plaça Pallol, where, on the right, **Les Voltes,** a Roman Forum with a Gothic upper story added later, is one of the prettiest corners in Tarragona. Through the **Portal del Roser** to the right is the entrance to the **Passeig Arqueólogic,** a path skirting the 3rd-century BC Ibero-Roman ramparts built on even earlier walls of giant rocks. The glacis was added by English military engineers in 1707 during the War of the Spanish Succession. Don't miss the rusted bronze of Romulus and Remus.

Beside the Portal del Roser you can catch Bus 2 to the **Serallo fishing quarter,** where, at the quayside, boats create a hive of activity as they unload their catch. Sneak a look inside the market, where fish are swiftly auctioned off to fishmongers and restaurateurs. Near the fish market, on the Passeig de la Independencia (also on the Bus 2 route), is the **Necròpolis i Museu Paleocristià** (Paleochristian Tomb Museum). Both Christian and pagan tombs have been unearthed on this site. ✉ *Included with Museu Arquelògic ticket, free Tues.* ☉ *Summer, Tues.–Sat. 10–1 and 4:30–8, Sun. 10–2; winter, Tues.–Sat. 10–1:30 and 4–7, Sun. 10–2.*

Dining and Lodging

$$$ ✕ **Sol Ric.** The flagship of the Tomas family restaurants remains the classiest in Tarragona. The menu changes constantly, as the chef experiments with variants of the regional cuisine. Try the *sepia estofada con guisantes* (casserole of cuttlefish with peas). Located 1 km/½ mi out of town along the old Roman road, it has a rustic interior and a leafy terrace. ⊠ *Vía Augusta 227,* ☎ *977/232032. Reservations essential. AE, MC, V. Closed Mon. and Dec. 15–Jan. 15. No dinner Sun.*

$$ ✕ **La Puda.** The quayside location, opposite the fish auction house, guarantees the freshness of seafood here. It is popular with locals but obviously not unaccustomed to foreigners, as the menu appears in several languages. The simple decor includes a tile floor, blue walls, and white tablecloths. ⊠ *Muelle Pescadores 25,* ☎ *977/211511. AE, DC, MC, V. No dinner Sun. Oct.–Mar.*

$$ ✕ **Les Voltes.** Built into the vaults of the original Roman amphithe-
★ ater, this elegant spot is a great favorite of all Tarragona visitors lucky enough to find out about it. The fine cuisine includes local Tarragona specialties as well as international recipes. ⊠ *Carrer Trinquet Vell 12,* ☎ *977/230651. AE, DC, MC, V. Closed Sun. July and Aug. No dinner Sun. No lunch Mon. July and Aug.*

$$$ ✕▥ **Imperial Tarraco.** This large, white, half-moon hotel has a superb position overlooking the sea. The public rooms are large, with cool, marble floors, black leather furniture, marble-top tables, and Oriental rugs. The bedrooms are plain but comfortable, each with a private balcony; insist on a sea view. ⊠ *Rambla Vella 2, 43003 Tarragona,* ☎ *977/233040,* ℻ *977/216566. 170 rooms with bath. Restaurant, bar, pool, beauty salon, tennis court. AE, DC, MC, V.*

$$ ✕▥ **Faristol.** The amiable Agustí Martí and his English wife, Lynne,
★ administer this tiny hotel in the medieval village of Altafulla (11 km/7 mi north of Tarragona). The five bedrooms are decorated with period

furniture from Agustí's family, and the dining room has a terracotta tile floor and murals. Specialties from the kitchen include meats *a la brasa* (cooked over coals). Within easy striking distance of the city, this is *the* place to stay in Tarragona. ⊠ *Carrer Sant Martí 5, Altafulla, 43893 Tarragona,* ☎ *977/650077,* ⅋ *977/228134. 5 rooms with bath. Restaurant. MC, V.*

$ 🏠 **España.** This modern town house offers comfort at a good value. The bedrooms have white walls, shiny tile floors, and functional, 1970s furniture. Each of the exterior rooms has a balcony overlooking the Rambla. ⊠ *Rambla Nova 49, 43003 Tarragona,* ☎ *977/232712. 40 rooms with bath. Breakfast room. AE, DC, MC, V.*

Nightlife and the Arts

Nightlife in Tarragona comes in two versions: older and quieter in the upper city or younger and more raucous down below. There are some lovely, rustic bars in the Casco Viejo, the upper section of old Tarragona. Try **Poetes** (⊠ Sant Llorenç 15), near the cathedral, a music bar set in a bodega-like cellar. Other spots for quiet talking and tippling include **Anticuari, El Mirall,** and **Museum.** In the lower part of town around the train station there are some two dozen music bars and clubs such as **Carpe Diem, Cucudrulus,** and **Toc de Gralla** where younger citizens rage until dawn on Friday and Saturday nights, holiday eves, and during the summer.

The Teatro Metropol (⊠ Rambla Nova 46, ☎ 977/244795) is the center for music, dance, theater and a variety of cultural events ranging from human castle (*casteller*) formations to folk dancing.

Shopping

You will have to be careful with the price hagglers, but Carrer Major in Tarragona has some exciting antiques stores, worth a thorough rummage, because the gems tend to be hidden away. You can also try the shops just in front of the cathedral and in the Plaza la Seu; **Antigüedades Ciria** (⊠ Plaza la Seu 2) has an interesting selection.

SOUTH TOWARD THE MAESTRAZGO

Reus, Salou, Cambrils, Delta de l'Ebro, Tortosa, Gandesa, Alcañiz, Morella, Ares del Maestre, and San Mataeo

This chaotic enumeration truly runs the gamut from the ridiculous, such as the Port Aventura theme park, to the sublime, in the extraordinary natural resources from the Ebro Delta and the Ebro river itself to the Sierra de Beceite and mountain villages such as Morella. This wildly varied route takes you from below sea level in parts of the Delta to high stone villages in the hills, from very wet wetlands to the arid hinterlands of Tarragona.

Reus

➋ *13 km (8 mi) inland from Tarragona, along the N420 highway.*

Reus is an industrial town with the distinction of having been the birthplace of Antoni Gaudí, as well as the longtime home of his fellow Moderniste architect, Lluís Domènech i Montaner. If Moderniste architecture interests you, Domènech's **Casa Navàs** is well worth the short detour. Following signs to the center of town, you arrive in the Plaça del Mercadal, where the Casa Navàs is beside the Ajuntament. The rich interior decoration includes mosaics, stained glass, tiles with characteristic Moderniste floral motifs, and weirdly shaped leather chairs. ⊠ *San Juan 27,* ☎ *977/320349.* ⊘ *Call caretaker or tourist office.*

Nightlife and the Arts

The **Teatre Fortuny** (Plaça Prim 4, ☎ 977/318307) is the region's number one theater and opera venue.

Salou

❸ *10 km (6 mi) southwest of Tarragona.*

Traveling south from Reus, you may want to stop in Salou, a burgeoning beach resort with a long esplanade of young palms. The old port here is where the conquerors of Mallorca set out in 1229.

☾ On the edge of Salou is the macro–theme park **Port Aventura** (⊠ Autovéia Salou/Vila-Seca, Km 2 Apartat 90-43480 Vila-Seca, Tarragona, ☎ 93/400–5555 or 977/779000), which opened in early 1995. It boldly offers "the adventure of your life" to anyone brave enough to shell out $30–$40 for rides, water slides, steam engines, and boat rides through Mexico, China, Polynesia, the American West, and the Mediterranean.

Cambrils

❹ *7 km (4 mi) from Salou, 18 km (11 mi) southwest of Tarragona.*

Cambrils, another coastal town, is a target for gourmets, who come to dine in the Gatell family restaurants (☞ Dining, *below*). Less built-up than Salou, it also has a pretty marina.

Dining

$$$ ✕ **Can Gatell and Casa Gatell.** The two Gatell family restaurants,
★ right next door to one another, are of legendary popularity. Pilar Gatell runs Can Gatell, her sister Fanny, Casa Gatell. The local cuisine is excellent in both eateries. Try the *fideos negros amb sepionets* (paella in ink of baby squid) or *lubina al horno con cebolla y patata* (roast sea bass with onion and potato). ⊠ *Miramar 27; Can Gatell,* ☎ *977/360106; Casa Gatell, 977/360057. AE, DC, MC, V. Closed Oct., 20 days in Feb., and Wed. in winter. No dinner Tues. in winter.*

Delta de l'Ebro

❺ *77 km (46 mi) from Tarragona, 60 km (36 mi) south of Cambrils.*

The Delta de l'Ebro (Ebro Delta), a flat piece of wetlands, redolent of Holland, juts out into and embraces the Mediterranean. Its **Parc Natural del Delta de L'Ebre** is a major stopping and breeding place for more than 200,000 birds of more than 300 species. An impressive 60% of Europe's species are to be found here at some time during the year. To get to the park, take N230 and follow signs to Sant Jaume d'Enveja. At Sant Jaume you can get the ferry across to **Deltebre.** The Park Information Office (⊠ Plaça 20 de Maig, ☎ 977/489679) will tell you how to visit the reserve, which occupies the northern, eastern, and southern tips of the delta. A permit is required for entering the reserve proper.

Tortosa

❻ *80 km (50 mi) southwest of Tarragona.*

The ancient town of Tortosa, which straddles the River Ebro 10 km/6 mi inland, was successively Roman, Visigothic, Moorish, and Christian. The parador here, set in the ruined hilltop castle of **La Zuda,** is worth visiting even if you don't plan to stay here; keep to the left bank of the river and follow the signs. Originally a Templar fortress, the citadel (and town) passed, around 713, into the hands of the Moors, who kept it until its reconquest by Ramón Berenguer IV, count of Barcelona, in 1153. For more than three centuries, Moors, Christians, and Jews lived peacefully together in the town. There are sweeping views from the castle walls across the fertile Ebro Valley to the Beceite Mountains.

Tortosa was the scene of one of the civil war's bloodiest battles. The Republicans, loyal to the democratically elected government and already in control of Catalunya, crossed the Ebro here in July 1936 to attack the rebel Nationalists' rearguard. They got no farther than Tortosa, though, and were pinned down in trenches until they were forced to retreat with the loss of 150,000 lives. A conspicuously Nationalist monument rises from the Ebro to commemorate the victory of Franco's forces.

Look for the **cathedral,** then follow your nose toward it through the warren of streets. On the way, visit the **Renaissance Colegio Sant Lluís,** which has a pretty, arcaded patio, embellished with a frieze depicting the kings of Aragón. The cathedral's main facade is Baroque, although if you enter through the cloister, you can see that behind the facade lies a pure Gothic design. It was common in Spain during the 18th century to tack these exuberant stuccos onto the existing Gothic facade. The name given to the style is Churrigueresque, after its earliest practitioner, José Churriguera. ☉ *Cloister daily; cathedral open for services only.*

Dining and Lodging

$$ ✕ **San Carlos.** Joan Ros, chef-proprietor of this small restaurant on the northern edge of the old town, excels in seafood and freshwater fish from the Ebro Delta. Order *almejas* (marinated clams) or rossejat. ✉ *Rambla Felip Pedrell 19,* ☎ *977/441048. AE, DC, MC, V.*

$$–$$$ ✕🔟 **Parador Castillo de la Zuda.** Few sights near here equal the superb view from this old Arab castle across the Ebro Valley to the Beceite Mountains. Dark shades of mahogany and numerous tapestries evoke a sense of the past. The bedrooms have heavy wood furniture, terracotta floors, rugs, and plain walls. ✉ *Parador Castillo de la Zuda, Tortosa, 43500 Tarragona,* ☎ *977/444450,* 🄵🄰🄷 *977/444458. 82 rooms. Restaurant, bar, pool. AE, DC, MC, V.*

Gandesa

❼ *86 km (53 mi) from Amposta, 87 km (54 mi) west of Tarragona.*

Renowned for its strong wine (up to 16% alcohol), Gandesa also contains two architectural landmarks. Out on the Mora road is the extraordinary **Cooperative Agrícola** (Wine Cooperative), designed by the Moderniste architect Cèsar Martinell in 1919. Its white, Islamic-looking facade does little to prepare you for the remarkable vaulting inside, constructed entirely of small bricks ingeniously arranged to allow for expansion and contraction. It is a working building, and you can buy some of the local wine here for a sleepy picnic on the way to Alcañiz or Beceite. The building is open weekdays 9–2 and 4–8. Also visit the parish church in the center of town, **L'Assumpció,** where the geometric patterns on the otherwise Romanesque doorway are attributed to Moorish influence. The church is open daily.

Dining and Lodging

$ ✕🔟 **Hostal Piqué.** This modern roadhouse, although uninviting from the outside, has a large, smart dining room with a tile floor, pristine white tablecloths, and highly professional service. The menu ranges from everyday local options to more expensive rarities. Rooms are inexpensive and comfortable. ⊠ *Via Catalunya 68, 43780,* ☎ *977/420329,* FAX *977/ 420068. 48 rooms with bath. Restaurant. MC, V.*

Sierra de Beceite

8 *15 km (9 mi) west of Gandesa on N420.*

The Sierra de Beceite offers a beautiful excursion as you leave Gandesa, as long as you (and your car) can handle some bumpy roads. Just after you enter the Aragonese province of Teruel, you'll come to **Calaceite** (on your right). Explore its ancient, labyrinthine streets, which assemble at the arcaded Plaza Porticada. For a closer inspection of the Beceite massif, turn left at the Calaceite crossroads, and drive along TE301. Turn right after 18 km/11 mi at a T-junction to reach **Valderrobres,** where you'll find a fortress palace and a Renaissance town hall that served as the model for Barcelona's Poble Espanyol. Continue to **Beceite,** and follow signs to a *panorama* for a bumpy drive along a track culminating in an impressive vista. Depending on the condition of these forest roads, you can drive all the way to **Fredes,** due south of Beceite. Near here, on the Tossal dels Tres Reis (4,450 feet), the kings of Catalunya, Aragón, and Valencia are said to have met to iron out disputes. The best way to explore these hills is either by hiking or on horseback; a sign on the way into Beceite points you toward the tourist office, which provides maps of trails and arranges horseback riding. From Valderrobres, you can cut back to the Alcañiz road via TE300, which follows the River Matarraña.

Alcañiz

9 *62 km (37 mi) west of Gandesa, 74 km (46 mi) north of Morella.*

Alcañiz lies on a plain and is encircled by the River Guadalope. It is surrounded by ugly, modern apartment blocks, the result of a recent population explosion, stemming from the success of the surrounding olive and almond orchards. The highway (N420) enters the town along a modern street, busy with new construction. For the old town, turn left at the end of this street to Plaza Mayor. On the right is the **Lonja** (Exchange), with pointed arches defining its Gothic origin. Adjoining it on the corner is the Renaissance **Ayuntamiento.** The galleries and overhanging eaves on both these buildings mark them as Aragonese. The **Collegiata Church,** with its rhythmic Baroque façade, looms over the plaza. The ornate portal is very impressive, but the painted interior is disappointing. Next, climb to the **hilltop castle,** seat in the 14th century of the Calatrava knights and now a tiny parador.

Dining and Lodging

$$$ ✕⌂ **Parador de la Concordia.** Installed in the sturdy castle of the Cala-
★ trava Knights, this hotel grandly surveys the surrounding fertile, olive-growing plain and foothills of the Maestrazgo. Bedrooms have terracotta tile floors, patterned rugs, dark furniture, generous beds, and shutters. All have a good view. The restaurant serves *aragonés* specialties such as *cordero chilindrón* (lamb with a sauce of tomato, garlic, and peppers). ⊠ *Castillo de Calatrava, Alcañiz, 44600 Teruel,* ☎ *974/ 830400,* FAX *974/830366. 12 rooms with bath. Restaurant, bar. AE, DC, MC, V. Closed Dec. 15–Jan.*

Morella

★ **10** *74 km (46 mi) south of Alcañiz, 64 km (40 mi) from Benicarló.*

The walled town of Morella stands on a towering crag in Castellón, the northernmost Valencian province. It is not immediately evident if you approach from the north, however, from the south and east the land drops away sharply, rendering it a natural fortress—the scene of several bloody battles. Before you reach the town walls, you pass a well-preserved 14th-century aqueduct. The **castle,** Morella's most prominent feature, can be reached through the gate on Plaza de San Francisco, on the uppermost of the town's contoured streets. Just inside the gate is the ruined cloister of an old Franciscan monastery. The walk up to the summit castle takes a good 15 minutes; the often high winds contribute to its air of impregnability. In 1088 El Cid scaled these walls and wrought havoc among the occupying Moors. During the Carlist Wars, the castle became a stronghold for General Cabrera, who captured Morella in 1838 for the pretender to the Spanish throne, Don Carlos. ⊠ *Free.* ☉ *Oct.–Mar., daily 10–2 and 3–6; Apr.–Sept., daily 10–2 and 3–8.*

The beautiful church of **Santa María la Mayor,** near the castle on Calle Hospital, has a blue-tile dome that lends an exoticism to its otherwise Gothic structure. The larger of its two doorways dates from the 14th century and depicts the Apostles. The raised, flat-vaulted choir is reached by a spiral, marble staircase. The sanctuary has received the full Baroque treatment, as has the high altar, which would glisten were it not for the gloom of the interior. The museum has a painting by Francisco Ribalta and some 15th-century Gothic panels. ⊠ *Free.* ☉ *Daily 10–6.*

Descend the stepped Calle Cuesta de Prades to the arcaded **Calle Don Blasco de Alagón,** the town's main thoroughfare. There are numerous bars here, which are packed on the weekends. If you go right, you soon arrive at the old mansion of **Cardinal Ram,** now a hotel, and continuing uphill brings you into the pretty **Plaza de los Estudios,** whose white houses are distinguished by attractive, wood balconies.

Dining and Lodging

$ ✕ **Mesón del Pastor.** A restored, 14th-century, stone mansion, down
★   a side street off Calle Don Blasco de Alagón, houses this rustic mesón, which combines a family atmosphere with excellent cooking. Chef José Ferrer specializes in Maestrazgan dishes; try the *conejo relleno trufado* (rabbit and truffles enveloped in ham). Desserts, too, are homespun; try the *buñuelos con miel* (fried dumplings with honey). ⊠ *Cuesta Jovaní 3 y 5,* ☎ *964/160249. MC, V. Closed Wed.*

$–$$ ✕🏠 **Cardenal Ram.** Installed in one of Morella's most handsome man-
★   sions, originally Cardenal Ram's 14th-century, ancestral home, this hotel oozes history from its bare, stone walls and ubiquitous coats of arms. The tall lobby has a huge tapestry depicting the arrival of the Antipope Papa Luna in Morella in 1414. The bedrooms, all different, have pine floors; bare, white walls; high, beamed ceilings; and magnificent, heavy furniture. The wide beds are covered with Morellan striped bedspreads. ⊠ *Cuesta Suñer 1, Morella, 12300, Castellón,* ☎ *964/173085,* ℻ *964/ 173218. 19 rooms with bath. Restaurant. MC, V.*

$ ✕🏠 **Elías.** If the Cardenal Ram is full, this friendly *residencia* (inn) in
★   an old town house is an excellent alternative. There is a small, cozy sitting room with an open fire, and the L-shape bedrooms have terracotta tile floors, white walls, heavy wood furniture, and Morellan bedspreads. Ask for room No. 30, which has a good view of the Santa María Basilica. ⊠ *Colomer 7, Morella, 12300 Castellón,* ☎ *and* ℻ *964/160092. 17 rooms, 15 with bath. Restaurant. MC, V.*

Shopping

The Maestrazgo region produces brightly colored, woven, wool textiles. The best buys are the striped *mantas morellanas* (Morellan bedspreads). Morella's calles Blasco de Alagón and Hospital are good places to shop for them.

Ares del Maestre

⑪ *50 km (31 mi) from Morella. Take N232 from Morella. Turn right 2 km (1 mi) just after the 57 km (35 mi) marker. This road may not be signposted, but it does appear on some newer maps. If you get lost, ask for the new road to Villafranca del Cid. After 16 km/9 mi, turn left at a T-junction and quickly left again toward Albocácer (CS802).*

Ares del Maestre occupies the most dramatic site of any village in the area. Like Morella, it rests on a crag, but here the drop is more severe and the vistas are more rewarding. A very steep climb—windy in winter and scorching in summer—takes you to a ruined castle. 🎟 *Free.* ⊙ *Daily.*

NEED A BREAK?	On the mountain pass over which CS802 runs, about 550 yards before you arrive at Ares del Maestre, is **Mesón el Coll** (☎ 964/443088), a family-run restaurant that serves a delicious, set menu of local specialties. Try the *olla de Ares* (a thick stew typical of the Maestrazgo).
OFF THE BEATEN PATH	**TERUEL** – You may want to make the trip (about 110 km/68 mi) from Ares del Maestre to Teruel to see the town's famous Mudéjar architcture. Backtrack on CS802 towards Morella. At Villafranca del Cid get on TE811, which will take you to Teruel via the small towns of La Iglesuela, Mosqueruela, Linares de Mora, Rubielos de Mora, and Mora de Rubielos. Once in Teruel, visit the Mudéjar Towers, built between the 12th and 16th centuries in a style more reminiscent of a Muslim minaret than a Christian belfry. The highlight in the cathedral is the coffered ceiling with 13th-century court and hunting scenes, visible from the upper gallery. You can spend the night in one of the spacious rooms of the rustic Parador de Teruel (✉ Apdo. 67, ☎ 974/601800) and sample the local fare at the restaurant there.

San Mateo

⑫ *26 km (22 mi) west of Benicarló. CS802 from Ares del Maestre to Albocácer, then turn left.*

The small town of San Mateo proudly bears the title Capital del Maestrazgo, because it was from here that King Jaume I set out on his decisive reconquering raids in the 13th century, freeing the region finally from Moorish control. The legacy of its regal past consists of sturdy Gothic mansions near the Plaza Mayor. Visit the Archpriest's Church on the corner of the plaza. Its nave is a fine example of the Catalan Gothic style; the vault covers a wide expanse, dispensing with the need for columns. The coast is now close again, and the nearest place to make for is Benicarló via Cervera del Maestre and Cálig.

THE COSTA DEL AZAHAR
Benicarló, Peñiscola, and Sagunto

Named for the orange blossom and its all-pervading fragrance along this sweet coastal plain, the Costa del Azahar has been hit hard by the tourist building boom of the 60's and 70's. Castellón de la Plana is the northernmost province of the Levante, so-called because the sun rises (*se levanta*) out of the Mediterranean on this eastern coast. Phoenician

(Syrian) trading ships were frequently seen plying these ports some two milleniums ago, and it was the Phoenicians who, patrolling this stretch of coast and gazing uneasily at the menacing backdrop of mountains, are thought to have given the country its name—Spagna, or "hidden land." Benicarló and Peñíscola are, with Vinarós, the northernmost towns on the Costa del Azahar, while Sangunto marks the start of the Costa de Valencia.

Benicarló

⓭ *55 km (34 mi) south of Tortosa.*

Benicarló is a small village that has become an important tourist center. The Benicarló harbor is a lively confusion of fishing and pleasure craft, and the beaches are well stocked with northern European and local visitors most of the year.

Dining and Lodging

$$–$$$ ✕ **Casa Pocho.** This is named after owner Paco Puchal, known as "El Pocho," or "The Tubby One." Wood paneling and maritime motifs set the scene for the famously good seafood prepared here. The *langostinos* (prawns) make the best choice. ⊠ *San Gregorio 49, Vinaròs,* ☎ *964/451095. AE, DC, MC, V. Closed Mon. and Dec. No dinner Sun.*

$$$ ✕🏨 **Parador de la Costa del Azahar.** The main attraction of this modern parador, 6½ km/4 mi north of Peñíscola, is its large, semiformal garden, which runs down to the sea. It is a perfect place to rest up, in peace and quiet, away from the most crowded beaches. The decor doesn't match that of its more atmospheric cousins, but the public rooms are huge, bright, and tasteful, with white-wicker furniture and white walls. The bedrooms have shiny tile floors, white walls, and functional furniture. Ask for a sea view. ⊠ *Avda. Papa Luna 3, Benicarló, 12580 Castellón,* ☎ *964/470100,* 📠 *964/470934, 108 rooms with bath. Restaurant, bar, pool, tennis court, AE, DC, MC, V.*

Peñiscola

⓮ *7 km (4 mi) south of Benicarló, 60 km (37 mi) from Benicàssim.*

Peñíscola owes its foundation to the Phoenicians. It later became the bridgehead by which the Carthaginian Hamilcar (father of Hannibal) imported his elephants and munitions to wage the first of the three Punic Wars. Carthaginian influence in the peninsula rose to its zenith some 20 years later, in 230 BC, but was eroded by Rome's success in the subsequent campaigns.

★ The **old town** is a cluster of white-painted houses and tiny, narrow streets leading up to the castle, whose promontory setting affords a perfect surveillance of the coast. You can drive up to the **castle**, but in summer it would be wiser to leave your car by the town walls and walk. Of chief interest now are the chapel and study of the Antipope Papa Luna, to whom the 14th-century castle passed in the 15th century. Hardly any of his effects remain, but while in his drafty quarters try to imagine this 90-year-old Frenchman, formerly Pope Benedict XIII, passing the last six years of his life attending mass and composing schismatic bulls, while all the time surrounded by hostile Moorish townsfolk. 🎫 *300 ptas.* ☉ *Apr.–Sept., daily 10–8:30; Oct.–Mar., daily 10–1 and 3:15–5:30.*

Dining and Lodging

$$–$$$ ✕🏨 **Hostería del Mar.** A semi-parador, this modern, white hotel next to Peñíscola's long beach fits in with the paradors' high standards. Most of the rooms have balconies overlooking the old town. The rustic, beamed

public rooms surround a leafy pool terrace; the bedrooms have white walls, striped bedspreads, tile floors, and Castellano-style dark wood and leather furniture. ⊠ *Avda. Papa Luna 18, Peñíscola, 12598 Castellón,* ☎ *964/480600,* FAX *964/481363. 86 rooms with bath. Restaurant, bar, pool, tennis court. AE, DC, MC, V.*

Between Peñíscola and Sagunto

Alcalá de Chivert is 49 km (30 mi) north of Castellón de la Plana.

Along the Costa del Azahar are several small towns that merit a stop on your way from Peñíscola to Sagunto. The route is through carob and orange plantations. The autopista is the fasted way of heading south, but N340 shares the same scenery and allows access to places en route. **Alcalá de Chivert** boasts the tallest belfry in the Valencian provinces. The road here is cut off from the sea by the Sierra de Hirta, whose rugged outlines contain some ruined castles easily visible from the road. Next down the coast is **Alcocéber,** an expanding but still quiet holiday town with two good beaches. **Benicàssim** (salida 45 from the autopista or coast road from N340) derives its appeal from the dramatic shapes in its mountainous background. Besides the setting, there is a long, sandy, bathing beach and plenty of disco-type action at night. **Castellón de la Plana,** the provincial capital, has little to warrant the struggle through its suburbs, unless you are an admirer of the Spanish Baroque painter Zurbarán, 10 of whose works are in the Convento de las Religiosas Capuchinas on Calle Nuñez de Arce (open for services).

Dining and Lodging

$$ ✕ **Villa del Mar.** An old, colonial-style house with a verdant terrace for dining, surrounded by palms and pines, forms an elegant and secluded setting. Inside, the decor is modern and the cuisine international as well as regional; try the *arroces Valencianos* (Valencian rice dishes). On summer evenings there is a barbecue in the garden. ⊠ *Paseo Marítimo Pilar Coloma 24, Benicàssim,* ☎ *964/302852. AE, MC, V. Closed Oct.–Easter.*

$$ ✕▦ **Orange.** If facilities are what you're after, this huge, modern, chalet-style hotel possesses the widest range in town. It is centrally located, 150 yards from the beach, and surrounded by a garden and trees. Loud patterns of browns and oranges set the tone in the public rooms, and the plain bedrooms are no more than functional. Ask for a sea view; rooms over the pool may be noisy. ⊠ *Gran Avenida s/n, Benicàssim, 12560 Castellón,* ☎ *964/394400,* FAX *964/301541. 415 rooms with bath. Restaurant, 2 bars, 2 pools, beauty salon, miniature golf, tennis court, dance club. AE, DC, MC, V. Closed Nov.–Feb.*

$$ ✕▦ **Voramar.** At the north end of Benicàssim, right on the beach, this small, white hotel is encircled by classical balconies. It is the nearest thing to an old-fashioned resort hotel in town. The decor, though, is also rather plain and functional, with tile floors, white walls, and 1970s furniture. Ask for a bedroom overlooking the sea; each has a generous balcony. ⊠ *Paseo Pilar Coloma 1, Benicàssim, 12560 Castellón,* ☎ *964/300150,* FAX *964/300526. 55 rooms with bath. Restaurant, tennis court. AE, DC, MC, V. Closed mid-Oct.–Easter.*

Nightlife and the Arts

The top club in Benicàssim is **K'asim,** on Avda. Gimeno Tomas. Things really get going only during the summer months and Holy Week; at other times the atmosphere is decidedly tame.

Sagunto

⑮   *65 km (40 mi) southwest of Benicàssim, 23 km (20 mi) from Valencia.*

Sagunto will ring a bell if you've read Caesar's history; Saguntum, as the Romans called it, was the sparking point for the Second Punic War. When Hannibal laid seige to the town (at that time a port on the coast, from which the sea has since receded), the people heroically held out, faithfully expecting a Roman relief force, and burned the town rather than surrender to the Carthaginians.

★   Rambling Moorish hilltop fortifications dominate the town, and within this citadel earlier Roman remains are now being excavated. On the way up, visit the well-restored **amphitheater** (signposted from the town center), more complete than Tarragona's and a product of the Roman rebuilding five years after Hannibal's siege. Some of the finds from this era are housed in a fascinating and manageable museum just opposite the amphitheater. ▦ *Amphitheater and museum 400 ptas.* ☉ *Tues.–Sat. 10–2 and 4–6, Sun. 10–2.*

Nightlife and the Arts

The festival of classical Mediterranean drama, *Sagunto a Escena,* takes place during the first two weeks of August, when Spanish and international theater groups perform a variety of ancient plays in the authentic setting of Sagunto's Roman amphitheater. For information, contact the tourist office there or in Valencia (✉ Barcas 15, ☎ 96/351–0051).

VALENCIA

Valencia, the third city of Spain and capital of the Levante, is nearly equidistant from Barcelona and Madrid, the two national, metropolitan giants. The city's location, on a fertile huerta, has been fiercely contested ever since its foundation by the Greeks. El Cid captured the city from the Moors in 1094, and in 1099 won his strangest victory here: His corpse was strapped to his saddle and so frightened the waiting Moors as to cause a complete rout. In 1102, his widow, Jimena, was forced to return the city to Moorish rule; Jaume I finally drove them out in 1238.

It is a somewhat confusing place, uneasily poised between old and new, with many of its finer monuments having suffered destruction or damage. The city walls were pulled down late in the 19th century in order to build a ring road and provide employment for the poor, and its river, the Turia, was later diverted to the south to prevent further flood damage, leaving the city's beautiful *puentes* (bridges) to span a municipal park.

Valencia is split up here into two sections: Valencia Center and Outer Valencia.

Exploring

⑯   *23 km (14 mi) south of Sagunto, 351 km (218 mi) from Madrid, 362 km (224 mi) from Barcelona.*

Valencia Center

⑰   Valencia's historic buildings cluster around the 14th-century **cathedral** in the Plaza de Zaragoza, a convenient place to begin your visit. The cathedral can be entered by three portals, respectively Romanesque, Gothic, and Rococo, the last leading off Plaza de Zaragoza. In the interior, Renaissance and Baroque marbles have been removed, as is now the trend in Spanish churches, in a successful restoration of the original, pure Gothic.

In case you want to see the world.

At American Express, we're here to make your journey a smooth one. So we have over 1,700 travel service locations in over 120 countries ready to help. What else would you expect from the world's largest travel agency?

do more ®

Travel

In case you want to be welcomed there.

We're here to see that you're always welcomed at establishments everywhere. That's why millions of people carry the American Express® Card – for peace of mind, confidence, and security, around the world or just around the corner.

do more

Cards

In case you're running low.

We're here to help with more than 118,000 Express Cash locations around the world. In order to enroll, just call American Express before you start your vacation.

do more

Express Cash

And just in case.

We're here with American Express® Travelers Cheques and Cheques *for Two*.® They're the safest way to carry money on your vacation and the surest way to get a refund, practically anywhere, anytime.
Another way we help you...

do more

Travelers Cheques

In a side chapel is a purple, agate chalice, said to be the Holy Grail (Christ's cup at the Last Supper), which, it is claimed, was brought to Spain in the 4th century. The most interesting feature of the museum is Goya's famous painting of St. Francis Borgia surrounded by devils eagerly awaiting his demise, on display in the treasury. ⊠ *250 ptas.* ☉ *Mar.–Oct., daily 10–1 and 4–6; Nov.–Feb., daily 10–1.*

Dominating the cathedral at the near corner is the octagonal **Miguelete Tower,** which you can climb from inside the cathedral for good views over the city; 300 belfries are said to be visible. ⊠ *250 ptas.* ☉ *Daily 10:30–1 and 4:30–6:30.*

⓲ Leaving the cathedral by the Gothic Apostle Door brings you out into the trafficless **Plaza de la Virgen,** a lovely place for a drink in the late afternoon. Next to its portal, market gardeners of the huerta bring their irrigation disputes before the Water Tribunal, which has met every Thursday noon since 1350. Verdicts are given on the spot, and sentences range from fines to deprivation of water.

⓳ To the right of the Plaza de la Virgen, down Calle Almudín, stands the old, 14th-century granary, the **Almudín,** housing the **Museo de Paleontología,** which has an impressive collection of bones (including antediluvian skeletons from Argentina!) and shells. ⊠ *Free.* ☉ *Oct.–May, Tues.–Fri. 10–1 and 4–6:30, weekends 10–1; June–Sept., Tues.–Sun. 10–1.*

⓴ On the left of the Plaza de la Virgen, fronted by orange trees and box hedges, is the elegant east facade of the Gothic **Palau de la Generalitat,** home of the Valencia Cortes (Parliament) until its suppression by Felipe V for supporting the wrong (losing) side during the War of the Spanish Succession. The two *salones* (reception rooms) in the elder of the two towers have superb woodwork on the ceilings. You must obtain permission to enter; call first. ☎ *96/332–0206.* ☉ *Weekdays 9–2.*

Down Calle Caballeros, the main artery of the old part of town leading out of the Plaza de la Virgen, look for high door knockers, which could be reached without dismounting. Go left, down the tiny Calle Abadía San Nicolás (just after Number 41), to reach a small plaza con-
㉑ taining Valencia's oldest church, **San Nicolás,** once the parish of the Borgia Pope Calixtus III. The first portal you come to, with a tacked-on, rococo bas-relief of the Virgin Mary with cherubs, gives a good hint of what's inside, where every inch of the originally Gothic church has been covered with Churrigueresque embellishments.

★ **㉒** Make your way downhill from San Nicolás to the **Lonja de la Seda** (Silk Exchange), on Plaza del Mercado. The 15th-century Lonja is a product of the Golden Era here, when arts came under the patronage of Don Fernando de Antequerra, and it is generally held to be one of Spain's finest Gothic buildings. The perfect Gothic facade, dotted with ghoulish gargoyles, is complemented inside by high vaulting and twisted columns. ⊠ *Free.* ☉ *Tues.–Fri. 10–2 and 4–8, weekends 10–1.*

Opposite the Lonja de la Seda stands the Iglesia de los Santos Juanes, whose interior was destroyed during the civil war, and, next to this, the Modernista Mercado Central (market), constructed entirely of iron and glass. Down Avenida María Cristina from the market is the
㉓ **Plaza del Ayuntamiento.** This is the hub of the city's life, a fact well conveyed by the massiveness of the Baroque facades.

278

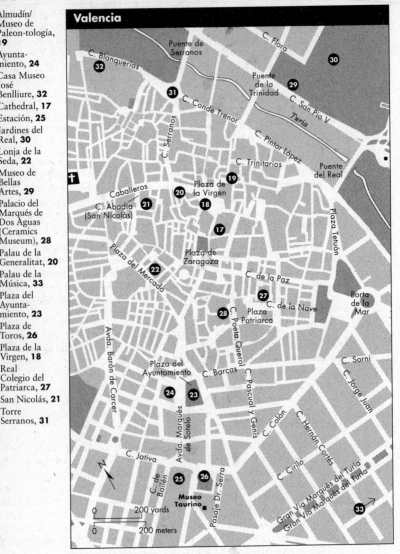

Valencia

NEED A
BREAK?

On the right-hand side of the Plaza del Ayuntamiento, at Number 2, is **Barrachina,** a venerable Valencian institution famous throughout Spain. It is a bar, café, restaurant, and delicatessen.

㉔ Just beyond Barrachina is the **Ayuntamiento** itself, which houses the municipal tourist office and a museum of the city's history. ✉ *Free.* ⊙ *Sun.–Fri. 9–2.*

㉕ The **Estación** (train station), down Avenida Marqués de Sotelo from the Ayuntamiento, is a splendid, Modernista structure. Designed by Demetrio Ribes Mano in 1917, it is replete with citrus motifs to let travelers know where it is they've arrived.

㉖ Adjacent to the Estación stands the **Plaza de Toros** (bullring); the best bullfighters are featured on and around July 25 and during the Fallas in March. The **Museo Taurino,** just beyond, down Pasaje Dr. Serra, is packed with bullfighting memorabilia, bulls' heads, and matadors' swords from this, one of Spain's oldest bullrings. 🔲 *250 ptas.* ☾ *Week-days 10–1:30.*

㉗ Back toward the center of town near the university is the Plaza Patri-arca, on the far side of which stands the **Real Colegio del Patriarca.** Founded by San Juan de Ribera in the 16th century, it has a lovely Re-naissance patio and an ornate church, and its museum contains works by Juan de Juanes, Francisco Ribalta, and El Greco. The entrance is off Calle de la Nave. 🔲 *250 ptas.* ☾ *Daily 11–1:30.*

★ ㉘ After leaving the Plaza Patriarca and crossing the Calle Poeta Querol, which is the first street you will cross moving west, you are soon face-to-face with the elaborate wedding-cake facade of the **Palacio del Mar-qués de Dos Aguas.** The famous, Churrigueresque facade around the corner centers on the figures of the *Dos Aguas* (Two Waters) carved by Ignacio Vergara in the 18th century. The palace contains the Ce-ramics **Museum,** with a magnificent collection of mostly local ware, the highlight being the Valencian kitchen on the second floor. 🔲 *Palace and museum 350 ptas.* ☾ *Tues.–Sat. 10–2 and 4–6, Sun. 10–2.*

Outer Valencia

★ ㉙ Foremost among the sights farther from the city center is the **Museo de Bellas Artes** (Fine Arts Museum), one of Spain's best art galleries. To get there, cross the riverbed by Puente de la Trinidad to No. 9, Calle San Pio V. On the first floor are the Valencian Primitives: In the 15th century Valencia was a thriving center of artistic talent, and many of the best works by Jacomart and Juan Reixach are here. Hieronymus Bosch, or El Bosco, as they call him here, is also represented. Still on the first floor are the murky, 17th-century Tenebrist masterpieces of Fran-cisco Ribalta and his pupil José Ribera, together with a Velázquez self-portrait and a room devoted to Goya. Upstairs, look for Joaquín Sorolla (Gallery 66), the luminous Valencian painter of 19th-century Spanish everyday life. 🔲 *350 ptas.* ☾ *Tues.–Sat. 10–2 and 4–6, Sun. 10–2.*

㉚ Adjacent to the Museo de Bellas Artes are the **Jardines del Real,** or Viveros, a pleasant park with fountains, rose gardens, tree-lined av-enues, and a small zoo. ☾ *Daily 9–dusk.*

㉛ Cross Puente de Serranos to the **Torre Serranos,** a 14th-century, forti-fied gate guarding the entrance to the old city. After you cross the Puente de Serranos, turn right, down Calle Blanquerías, and stop at No. 23, **㉜** the **Casa Museo José Benlliure.** The elegant house of the modern Va-lencian painter–sculptor contains many of his works. 🔲 *Free.* ☾ *Sept.–July, Tues.–Fri. 10–1:30 and 4–6, Sat. 10–1:30; Aug., Tues.–Fri. 10–1:30, Sat. 10–1:30.*

㉝ You can also stroll south down the riverbed park to the modern **Palau de la Música** (Concert Hall, ✉ Paseo de la Alameda 30, ☎ 96/337-5020). For performance listings, look in the *Turia* guide.

Dining and Lodging

$$$$ ✕ **Civera.** Three blocks northwest of the Fine Arts Museum, this restaurant, run by the Civera brothers, enjoys local renown for its fresh fish and seafood, cooked *a la plancha* (grilled), *hervidos* (boiled), or *á la sal* (baked in salt). The decor is marine oriented: white walls, beams, nautical motifs, and sumptuous displays of fish, fruit, and vegetables. ✉ *Lérida 11,* ☎ *96/347–5917. AE, DC, MC, V. Closed Mon. and Aug. No dinner Sun.*

$$$ ✕ **El Timonel.** Decorated to resemble the interior of a yacht, this cen-tral restaurant, two blocks east of the bullring, serves outstanding shellfish. The cooking is simple yet benefits from the freshest ingredients. Try the *salmonetes* (whitebait) or *pescado de roca* (rockfish). The clientele ranges from businesspeople at lunch to well-heeled, fashionable types at night. ⊠ *Félix Pizcueta 13,* ☎ *96/352–6300. AE, DC, MC, V. Closed Mon., Holy Wk, and Aug.*

$$$ ✕ **Eladio.** Some way out of town, this welcoming restaurant has oak and marble in the decor. You can select from Galician fish dishes prepared with a mixture of tradition and invention by chef Eladio Rodríguez; try the *mero a la brasa* (charcoal-grilled grouper), and finish up with a mouth-watering Swiss pastry made by his wife, Violette. ⊠ *Chiva 40,* ☎ *96/384–2244. AE, DC, MC, V. Closed Sun. and Aug.*

$$ ✕ **El Plat.** The local press have dubbed this restaurant *el Rey del Arroz* (Rice, or Paella, King) because it offers a different variant of Valencia's most characteristic dish each day of the week. The simple decor consists of white, alcoved walls adorned with local ceramics, but the lighting is rather bright. The atmosphere is relaxed, the service attentive, and the location ideal should you feel like *marcha* (nightlife) after dinner. ⊠ *Conde de Altea 41,* ☎ *96/395–1511. AE, MC, V. Closed Mon. and Holy Wk. No dinner Sun.*

$$
★ ✕ **Gargantua.** A series of apricot-colored rooms, crowded with pictures, sets the accent in this intimate and chic restaurant located in a 1910 town house. The excellent cooking is nouvelle and imaginative, the menu constantly changing. For a regional dish, try the *esgarrat* (grilled cod with green peppers). ⊠ *Navarro Reverter 18,* ☎ *96/334–6849. DC, MC, V. Closed Mon. No dinner Sun.*

$$ ✕ **La Riuà.** This fine local secret specializes in Valencian cuisine, served in a colorful setting splashed with ceramic tiles. Order a rice dish, fresh fish prepared with *all i pebre* (garlic and pepper), or the *pato guixado con cebollas i pasas* (stewed duck with onions and raisins). ⊠ *C. del Mar 27,* ☎ *96/391–4571. AE, DC, MC, V. Closed Mon. and Aug. No dinner Sun.*

$ ✕ **Patos.** Small and cozy, this restored, 18th-century town house, just north of Calle Paz in the old quarter, is primarily for locals. Terracotta tiles, white tablecloths, wood-paneled walls, and overhead beams lend it an earthy look. In summer you can dine outside. The set menu (at 1,500 ptas. a real bargain) often includes duck (*pato*). It's very popular, so get here by 9:30 PM to be sure of a table. ⊠ *C. del Mar 28,* ☎ *96/392–1522. No reservations. AE, DC, MC, V.*

$$$$
★ ✕🏨 **Monte Picayo.** If you enjoy the proximity of a casino and don't mind looking at the sea from a distance, this is a hotel to consider. Set into a hill, its greenery-draped modern, tiered structure overlooks the huerta and offers a rare degree of luxury. Public areas and bedrooms are spacious and cheerful, each guest room has a balcony, and the service is impeccable. ⊠ *Urbanización Monte Picayo, 46530 Valencia,* ☎ *96/142–0100,* ⨳ *96/142–2168. 83 rooms with bath. Restaurant, 5 bars, 11 pools, sauna, miniature golf, tennis courts, casino, dance club. AE, DC, MC, V.*

$$$$ ✕🏨 **Sidi Saler.** On a stretch of coastline just south of Valencia that suffers from being in mid-development, Sidi Saler's contemporary khaki facade surrounds an oasis of luxury. The bedrooms are modern, bright, and unremarkable, besides giving their inhabitants the impression that the beach belongs to them exclusively. ⊠ *Playa del Saler, 46012 Valencia,* ☎ *96/161–0411,* ⨳ *96/161–0838. 276 rooms with bath. Restaurant, 2 bars, outdoor and indoor pools, beauty salon, massage, sauna. AE, DC, MC, V.*

$$$ ✕🏨 **Meliá Valencia Palace.** This five-star hotel has become Valencia's ultimate refuge, just steps from the Palau de la Música concert hall. The Valencia Palace is filled with state-of-the-art design and an ample staff of hotel professionals who seem truly excited about making every guest happy. ✉ *Alameda 32, 46023,* ☎ *96/337–5037,* FAX *96/337–5532. 200 rooms and suites. Restaurant, bar, room service, pool, sauna, exercise room. AE, DC, MC, V.*

$$$ ✕⌂ **Parador Luis Vives.** Definitely for golf enthusiasts, this modern parador in El Saler boasts a famous course with the first tee just outside the front door. The hotel occupies an exposed position on the edge of a pine forest, fronted by sand dunes. The bright reception rooms are spacious, with cool marble floors, white walls, and baronial furniture. The bedrooms echo this style; insist on a sea view. ✉ *El Saler, 46012 Valencia,* ☎ *96/161–1186,* FAX *96/162–7016. 58 rooms with bath. Restaurant, bar, pool, 18-hole golf course, tennis court. AE, DC, MC, V.*

$$$ ✕⌂ **Reina Victoria.** The grand old lady of Valencia's hotels has recently
★ received a much-needed face-lift, making her an excellent choice for comfort, as well as time-worn charm and centrality. The spacious reception rooms have cool marble floors with rugs to take the chill off; the bedrooms are clothed in green chintz and deep-pile carpets with a subdued pattern. ✉ *Barcas 4, 46002,* ☎ *96/352–0487,* FAX *96/352–0487. 97 rooms with bath. Restaurant, bar. AE, DC, MC, V.*

$$ ✕⌂ **Excelsior.** In a centrally located 1930s building, this hotel provides
★ the best value in this price category. From the Art Deco restaurant-cum-bar, a spiral. marble staircase leads to a dark, wood-paneled salon, with a terrace for the summer. The bedrooms have olive-green carpets; the beds have brass headboards, and old prints hang on the white walls. The atmosphere is very friendly. ✉ *Barcelonina 5, 46002,* ☎ *96/351–4612,* FAX *96/352–3478. 67 rooms with bath. Restaurant, bar. AE, DC, MC, V.*

$$ ✕⌂ **Inglés.** Once the palace of the dukes of Cardona, this hotel stands next door to the Palacio del Marqués de Dos Aguas. There is nothing very grand about it, but it's extremely well located for seeing the old part of town. The polished wood floors and striped Regency chairs in the public rooms look rather more spartan than they must have been in the duke's day. The bedrooms have a jaded appearance, born of the passé modern decor, but are perfectly comfortable. All are exterior; ask for one overlooking Hipolito Roviro's alabaster doorway into the next-door palacio. ✉ *Marqués de Dos Aguas 6, 46002,* ☎ *96/351–6426,* FAX *96/394–0251. 62 rooms with bath. Restaurant, bar. AE, DC, MC, V.*

$$ ⌂ **Bristol.** Central, but hidden away in a narrow street by the church of San Martín, just behind the Inglés hotel, this is an unpretentious but well-maintained hotel. It has little in the way of public rooms, but the bedrooms are perfectly comfortable, with their plain decor and functional furniture. ✉ *Abadía San Martín 3, 46002,* ☎ *96/352–1176,* FAX *96/352–8502. 40 rooms with bath. AE, DC, MC, V.*

$ ⌂ **Continental.** This friendly establishment taking up two floors of a town house, just off the central Plaza del Ayuntamiento, offers excellent value for the money if all you need is a clean and comfortable room. It has a small salon and a restaurant that serves breakfast only. ✉ *Correos 8, 46002,* ☎ *96/351–0926,* FAX *96/351–0926. 46 rooms with bath. Breakfast room. AE, DC, MC, V.*

Nightlife and the Arts

Castellón and Valencia publish *Que y Donde*, the major listings magazine; for Valencia only, there is *Turia*, with events, prices, and reviews.

Throughout July, Valencia hosts a festival of theater; classical, jazz, and pop music; film; and dance. Contact the Ayuntamiento (☎ 96/352–0694). If you're homesick, there is the Instituto Shakespeare (✉ Avda.

Blasco Ibañez 28, ☎ 96/360–1950), which holds performances in English and Spanish.

Sleep seems to be anathema in Valencia. The best time to experience this nocturnal way of life is anytime but summer, when everybody has disappeared on holiday. Plaza Canovas del Castillo and the surrounding streets are the liveliest zone, closely followed by Plaza Xuquer, near the university. For a rougher breed, head to the beach. Calle de Eugenia Viñes is lined with numerous loud discotheques and bars. Try **Casablanca** (⊠ Eugenia Viñes 152, ☎ 96/371–3366) or the aptly named **Vivir Sin Dormir** (⊠ Paseo Neptuno 42, ☎ 96/372–7777), or Live Without Sleeping.

For more sophisticated clubs, try **Belle Epoque** (⊠ Cuba 8) or **Xuquer Palace** (⊠ Plaza Xuquer 8), and for Sevillanas, **Albahaca** (⊠ Almirante Cadarso 30, ☎ 96/334–1484), **Triana** (⊠ Grabador Esteve 11, ☎ 96/374–3001), or **Candela Canovas** (⊠ Plaza Canovas del Castillo 6, ☎ 96/373–1882).

Shopping

Try **Salvador Ribes** (⊠ Vilaragut 7) for top-quality antiques with correspondingly daunting price tags. A local crafts market is held every day (10–8) in Plaza Alfonso Magnánimo at the bottom of Calle de la Paz. A flea market is held every Sunday morning in the streets around the cathedral.

Valencia is a good place to buy the famous Lladró porcelain or the slightly cheaper version, Nao porcelain; both of these are made locally. Check with the tourist office in the Ayuntamiento, which occasionally arranges visits to the factory. In Valencia itself, try **Cerámicas Lladró** (⊠ Poeta Querol 9) for purchases. Manises, 9 km/5½ mi west of Valencia, is another center for Valencian ceramics, especially famous for its azulejos.

SOUTHERN CATALUNYA AND THE LEVANTE A TO Z

Arriving and Departing

By Boat
Trasmediterránea Ferries (⊠ Avda. Manuel Soto 15, ☎ 96/367–6512, FAX 96/367–3345) leave Valencia for Mallorca (Monday–Saturday) and Ibiza (Tuesday and Thursday only). They shuttle from Tarragona to Mallorca and Ibiza daily in July and August only (☎ 977/225506).

By Bus
The connection between Barcelona and Tarragona is easy; nine buses daily leave the Estación Vilanova-Norte in Barcelona. **Bacoma, S.A.** (☎ 93/231–3801) also dispatches buses from Tarragona (⊠ Plaça Imperial Tarraco s/n, ☎ 977/222072). From Valencia, buses continue down the coast and to Madrid. The bus depot is across the river (⊠ Avda. Menendez Pidal 3, ☎ 96/349–7222) and is reached by Bus 8 from Plaza del Ayuntamiento.

By Car
The A7 *autopista* (motorway) provides excellent road access to the region at both ends. Having a car will be extremely valuable, even necessary, if you want to explore the inland areas of the Maestrazgo, where there is some excellent, uncrowded, and scenic motoring.

By Plane

The international airport nearest to the northern end of this tour is in **Barcelona** (☞ Barcelona A to Z *in* Chapter 7), 100 km/65 mi from Tarragona. **Valencia** has an international airport (☎ 96/370–9500) with direct flights to London, Paris, Brussels, Frankfurt, and Milan. It is 8 km/5 mi west of the center of the city and best reached by taxi. For Iberia information, call ☎ 96/351–3739.

By Train

Trains for Tarragona leave Barcelona's Passeig de Gràcia and Sants stations every half hour or so (☞ Barcelona A to Z *in* Chapter 7) or from Zaragoza. The RENFE office in Tarragona is at Rambla Nova 40 (☎ 977/23–25–34); the station is downhill from the Mediterranean balcony, south toward the port (☎ 977/240202). Leaving the region at Valencia, you have a choice of train connections to Madrid, via Cuenca, or Alicante, via Játiva. The main station, Estación del Norte (☎ 96/352–0202), is on Calle Játiva, next to the bullring. It's very centrally located and involves only a short walk or cab ride to most hotels.

Getting Around

By Bus

Connections up and down the coast between Tarragona and Valencia are frequent. Transport inland to Morella and Alcañiz can be arranged from Vinaròs, while Castellón or Sagunto have bus lines west to Teruel.

In Valencia buses provide the main method of public transport, and central services start from Plaza del Ayuntamiento. Services for the beaches and outlying suburbs leave from Plaza Puerta del Mar. The tourist office can supply details of bus routes.

By Car

The roads are generally very good, but the main N340 becomes very clogged, and you're often much better off paying extra to use the autopista. For car rentals in Tarragona, **Avis** is at **Viajes Vibus** (✉ Rambla Nova 125, ☎ 977/219156). In Valencia you have the choice of **Avis** (✉ Isabel la Católica 17, ☎ 96/351–0734), **Europcar** (✉ Antiguo Reino de Valencia 7, ☎ 96/374–1512; ✉ airport, ☎ 96/153–1369), or **Hertz** (✉ Segorbe 7, ☎ 96/341–5036; airport, ☎ 96/152–3791).

By Train

Within the region, trains run more or less down the coast: Tarragona–Salou/Cambrils–Tortosa–Vinaròs–Peñíscola–Benicàssim–Castellón–Sagunto–Valencia. A line also goes from Valencia to Zaragoza by way of Sagunto and Teruel, and local lines go around Valencia from the station on Cronista Rivelles (☎ 96/347–3750).

Contacts and Resources

Consulates

British: Tarragona (✉ C. Real 33, ☎ 977/220812), **U.S.:** Valencia (✉ C. La Paz 6, ☎ 96/351–6973), open weekdays 10–1.

Emergencies

Police: ☎ 091.

Ambulance: Castellón (Servicio Médico Urgencias, ☎ 964/211253), Gandesa (Servei d'Ambulancies, ☎ 977/420390), Morella (Cruz Roja, ☎ 964/160389), Tarragona (Creu Roja, ☎ 977/236511), and Valencia (Cruz Roja, ☎ 96/380–2244).

General medical assistance: Castellón (Hospital Provincial, ☎ 964/210522), Morella (Ambulatorio, ☎ 964/160034), Tarragona (Hospital Joan XXIII, ☎ 977/211554), and Valencia (Hospital Clínico, ☎ 96/368–2600).

Golf

The area is well provided with courses, all of them near or on the coast. Call in advance to reserve tee times. Listed geographically north to south, they are: Club de Golf Costa Dorada (⊠ Apdo. 600, Tarragona, ☎ 977/655416), 9 holes; Club de Golf Costa de Azahar (⊠ Carretera Grao–Benicàssim, Grao de Castellón, ☎ 964/280979), 9 holes; Club de Campo del Mediterráneo (⊠ Urbanización La Coma, Borriol, Castellón, ☎ 964/321227), 18 holes; Club de Campo El Bosque (⊠ Chiva, 31 km/19 mi west of Valencia, ☎ 96/326–3800), 18 holes; Club de Golf Escorpión (⊠ Apdo. 1, Betera, Valencia, ☎ 96/160–1211), 18 holes; Campo de Golf de Manises (⊠ Apdo. 22029, Valencia, ☎ 96/152–3804), 9 holes; Campo de Golf El Saler (⊠ Apdo. 9034, Valencia, ☎ 96/161–1186), 18 holes.

Guided Tours

For a guided tour of Tarragona's sights, contact the municipal tourist office just below the cathedral (⊠ Carrer Major 39, ☎ 977/245203). The tour covers all the important archaeological sites, together with the cathedral.

Servei Turistic Parc (☎ 977/702324) in Amposta operates guided tours of every imaginable variety through the Ebro Delta, Amposta, and Taragona province in general. Vineyards, Templars castles, Cistercian monasteries, gondola-like *perxar* excursions through the canals and lagoons of the Delta, bicycle rentals. Go in and talk it over with official Tarragona Diputació guide Josep Valldeperas.

You can book guided tours of Valencia at the municipal tourist office (⊠ Plaza Ayuntamiento 1, ☎ 96/351–0417). Leaving daily at 10 from the Ayuntamiento, a bilingual guide takes you around the Ayuntamiento itself, the Lonja, the cathedral, the Ceramics Museum, the bullring, the station, the Fine Arts Museum, and Viveros Park.

In summer the municipal tourist office in Valencia (☞ Visitor Information, *below*) organizes tours of the Albufera, the marshlands to the south of Valencia, depending on demand. You tour the port area before continuing south to the Albufera lagoon, where you can visit a traditional *barraca* (thatched farmhouse). You'll end up in the Devesa Gardens, where you can hire boats to explore the canals through the paddy fields.

Late-Night Pharmacies

Pharmacies (*farmacias de guardia*) operate on a rotating basis whereby one stays open 24 hours in every sizable town or city. To find the address of the one whose turn it is, look in the local press or on the door of any pharmacy.

Sailing

The safe waters off the coast make for good sailing conditions. Ask at local tourist offices or just chance upon places where you can rent boats. Some possibilities are Club Náutico Tarragona (⊠ port, ☎ 977/240360), Club Náutico Salou (⊠ Espigón del Muelle, no phone), Club Náutico Castellón (⊠ port, ☎ 964/222764), and Club Náutico Valencia (⊠ Camino del Canal 91, ☎ 96/367–9011).

Travel Agencies

Tarragona: **Vibus SA** (⊠ Rambla Nova 125, ☎ 977/219156); Valencia: **Iberia** office (⊠ Paz 14, ☎ 96/351–7237), and **Viajes Paz** (⊠ Paz 32, ☎ 96/351–8080).

Visitor Information

Tourist offices that offer information covering the whole region are in **Castellón** (✉ Plaza María Agustina 5, ☎ 964/221000), **Tarragona** (✉ Ramon y Cajal 33, ☎ 977/230312), and **Valencia** (✉ Paz 48, ☎ 96/394–2222). Local tourist offices are as follows: **Benicàssim** (✉ Médico Segarra 4, ☎ 964/303851), **Morella** (✉ Torre San Miguel, ☎ 964/173032), **Peñíscola** (✉ Paseo Marítimo, ☎ 964/480208), **Reus** (✉ San Juan 27, ☎ 977/320349), **Sagunto** (✉ Cronista Chabret, ☎ 96/266–2213), **Tarragona** (✉ Major 39, ☎ 977/245203), **Teruel** (✉ Tomás Nogués 1, ☎ 974/602279), **Tortosa** (✉ Plaza España, ☎ 977/440000), and **Valencia** (✉ Paz 48, ☎ 96/394–2798; and Estación RENFE (✉ Játiva 24, ☎ 96/352–8573).

There are information phone lines at Castellón (☎ 964/221000) and Valencia (☎ 96/352–4000); in Valencia (✉ Paz 48), a 24-hour machine dispenses information in exchange for 25-pta coins.

9 The Southeast

The southeastern corner of Spain has a flat, fertile coastal plain that produces oranges, rice paddies that stretch miles down the coast, and mountains that give rise to the strange, almost lunar desert landscape in Almería. But most visitors come to the region for the beaches and striking white architecture that attests to long Moorish occupation.

THE SOUTHEASTERN CORNER OF SPAIN is a land of contrasts. In the north, the flat, fertile *huerta* (coastal plain) produces an orange harvest from late November until the end of April; in spring, you can see fragrant flowers and fruit growing on the same tree. The rice paddies stretching from the Albufera (lagoon) south of Valencia to Gandía are what gave rise to the Valencian specialty, paella. The farther south you go, the drier and more mountainous the country becomes, until you reach the singular desert/lunar landscape of Almería, made famous by the advent of spaghetti-western film crews in the 1960s. The inland province of Albacete, historically part of Murcia, is of interest for having been the scene of Don Quixote's exploits in the Castilian expanses of La Mancha, and for its tiny villages and natural treasures.

By Philip Eade

Updated by
George Semler

The striking architecture that you encounter in most towns attests to the long Moorish occupation. Alicante was in Moorish hands from 718 to 1249; Murcia, from 825 to 1243; and Almería, from 712 to 1489, when it was finally reconquered by Ferdinand and Isabella.

Most visitors come for the beaches, from the crowded Costa Blanca to the nearly deserted stretches around Cabo de Gata in Almería, renowned for its scuba diving. Mild temperatures in spring and fall permit vacationing before or after the worst of the crowds.

South of Valencia (☞ Chapter 8) drive along the thin strip between the sea and the Albufera lagoon, before following the coast around the Cabo de la Nao to the Costa Blanca. Just south of Cullera, head inland through the historic towns of Játiva and Alcoy on the way to Alicante. Alicante, an exotic and bustling Mediterranean port, is worth a day of exploring before moving inland toward Murcia, past the palm forest at Elche and the ancient town of Orihuela. The vast inland areas that fall within the bounds of the Southeast are best placed for travelers approaching Murcia from Madrid or readers of Cervantes keen to explore the setting for *Don Quixote*. Murcia, with its superb cathedral, is an important stop, before proceeding on to the African-looking Almería, by way of Lorca, Mohácar, and the stunning, crowd-free coast around the Cabo de Gata.

Pleasures and Pastimes

Beaches

The Southeast coastline offers abundant variety: from the long stretches of sand dunes north of Denia and south of Alicante to the rocky coves and sweeping crescents of the Costa Blanca. The benign climate means you can be on the beach for most of the year. Major beaches have Red Cross (Cruz Roja) stations with helicopters and flags to warn swimmers of conditions: green for safe, red for danger.

Altea, popular with families, is busy and pebbly, but the old town provides a pretty setting. Benidorm's two, white, crescent-shape beaches extend for more than 5 km/3 mi and are widely considered the best in Spain. For backup entertainment, Benidorm takes all the prizes; however, in summer you will be sunbathing head to toe. Calblanque is on the road between Los Belones and Cape Palos, which takes you down a longish rough track to a succession of nearly deserted beaches frequented by young Murcians. Calpe's beaches have the scenic advantage of the sheer Peñon de Ifach, which stands guard over stretches of sand to either side. Denia and Jávea both have family beaches where children paddle in the relatively safe waters. Gandía's sandy beach is well kept, with bars and restaurants lining the promenade. Although the narrow La Manga del Mar Menor (*Manga* refers to a thin "sleeve" of land), which encloses a huge lagoon, offers some stunning views, it has been ruined by a tasteless sprawl of hotels and holiday apartments. Mojácar has a shingly beach backed by bars and good sports facilities, but if you are mobile, try some of the deserted beaches to the south. Needless to say, there aren't any facilities, bar the odd water tap for campers. Nudity seems quite accepted here, as it does just north of Cullera and at Calblanque. In Moraira, the best is Castillo beach, just outside the center. Santa Pola and Guardamar del Segura are good options, with fine, clean sand and pine trees behind the dunes.

Dining

In the Valencian provinces, rice grows better than anywhere else in Spain—which explains why paella originated here. Another rice dish to try is *arroz a banda* (meat or fish and vegetables cooked over a wood fire). Remember that paella should be eaten directly after cooking, so don't order it from a *menú del día* (menu of the day) before checking its freshness. Alicante and Jijona are famous for their *turrón* (nougat made with almonds and flavored with honey). In Elche you can eat fresh dates. Murcian cooking uses products of the huerta and the sea, with a marked Arab influence in the preparation. Traditionally a fisherman's rice dish, the *caldero de Mar Menor* is cooked in huge iron pots and has a distinctly oily consistency, flavored by fish cooked in its own juices. Delicious as tapas or a first course are *muchirones* (broad beans in a spicy sauce), similar to the Catalan *habas a la catalana,* as well as *cocas* (meat pies similar to empanadas). In Almería, *gazpacho andaluz* (often described as a spicy, liquid salad—and here characterized by the addition of croutons) appears on the menu. It is also the place for *pescaditos fritos* (small fried fish), as well as grapes.

CATEGORY	COST*
$$$$	over 6,500 ptas.
$$$	4,500 ptas.–6,500 ptas.
$$	2,000 ptas.–4,500 ptas.
$	under 2,000 ptas.

per person for a three-course meal, excluding drinks, service, and tax

Fiestas

Local festivals provide excellent entertainment. Here are some standouts: Almería's *Festival Internacional de Títeres* (Puppet Theater Festival) is a lively event held in January. Denia holds a mini *Fallas,* March 16–19. Alcoy's spectacular *Moros y Cristianos* (Moors and Christians) festival takes place April 21–24, a reenactment of the quests and conquests of the Christian battle to dislodge the Moors at the end of the 15th century. The *Semana Santa* (Holy Week) processions in Murcia are among the most famous in Spain. The *Semana Santa* (Holy Week) festivities in Lorca are known for the opulent costumes of both biblical and Roman participants and for the penitents' solemn robes. Don't miss Altea's *Moros y Cristianos* spectacle held on the third Sunday in May, a combination of battle reenactment and pageant with elaborate costumes and the town's youngsters dressed up as knights in shining armor. Alicante's main festival is the *Hogueras de San Juan* (St. John's Day Bonfires), June 21–24. *El Misteri* (The Mystery Play) in Elche is performed in two parts, August 14–15, and preceded by a public dress rehearsal (August 13).

Golf

Spain is Europe's top golfing opportunity, and the southeast's mild climate makes it an excellent choice for winter golfing. The region's golf courses are as follows (listed north to south): El Saler (☞ Southern Catalunya and the Levante A to Z *in* Chapter 8), Club de Golf Jávea, 9 holes; Club de Golf Don Cayo, Altea, 9 holes; Campo de Golf Villa Martín, Torrevieja, 18 holes; La Manga Club de Golf (Los Belones, two 18-hole courses; and Golf Almerimar, 18 holes. Reserve tee times in advance, and expect to pay about 8,000 ptas. for 18 holes, 4,000 ptas. for nine.

Lodging

Many hotels on the coast are modern high-rises. When trying to avoid this, one is often faced with a choice between character and comfort. Paradors have traditionally solved this conundrum, and there are four in the region: Jávea, Puerto Lumbreras (Lorca), Mojácar, and Albacete. The last of these, likely to be off most people's itineraries, is the most representative of the rustic, parador style. The others are tasteful, albeit modern. There are older, one-of-a-kind hotels in Calpe, Alicante, San José, and Almería. Make reservations in advance. Some coastal hotels close for the winter.

CATEGORY	COST*
$$$$	over 18,000 ptas.
$$$	11,500 ptas.–18,000 ptas.
$$	7,000 ptas.–11,500 ptas.
$	under 7,000 ptas.

per standard double room, excluding tax

Exploring the Southeast

From Valencia's Albufera lagoon, inland to Xátiva and Albacete, down the Costa Blanca through Alicante and on to Murcia, Cartagena and Almeria, the southeast has many kinds of natural and man-made phenomena to explore. Beaches, salt lagoons, steppes, mountain villages, and Mediterranean port cities provide abundant opportunities.

Great Itineraries

The southeast offers three different coastal experiences (the lagoon, the populous beaches of the Costa Blanca, and the deserted strands south of Mojácar), two distinct inland programs (the steppe around Albacete and the mountains near Murcia), and four major cities (Alicante, Albacete, Murcia and Almería).

In seven days you could see nearly everything this area has to offer, unless you find the beach or the golf course of your dreams and just stay. Five days would allow a sampling of some beaches, inland villages and the three coastal cities. Three days is time for a beach or two, an inland village, and at least a look at Alicante, Murcia and Almeria.

Numbers in the text below correspond to numbers in the margin and on the maps.

IF YOU HAVE 3 DAYS

Start with the Albufera lagoon and **El Palmar** ① before continuing through **Cullera** ② and **Denia** ④ to the **Cabo de la Nao** ⑥. Plan on spending the night at the Parador de la Costa Blanca at 🏨 **Jávea** ⑤ or in the village of 🏨 **Moraira** ⑦. Begin the next day with a visit to the fishing village of **Altea** ⑨ before heading for **Alicante** ⑰ for lunch and on through **Elche** ⑱ and **Orihuela** ⑲ to 🏨 **Murcia** ㉒ for the night. On the third day see **Lorca** ㉕, Aguilas, **Mojácar** ㉗ and the **Cabo de Gato Nature Reserve** ㉘ on the way to 🏨 **Almería** ㉙ for the night.

IF YOU HAVE 5 DAYS

Explore the Albufera lagoon and **El Palmar** ① before continuing through **Cullera** ② and **Denia** ④ to the **Cabo de la Nao** ⑥. Spend the night at

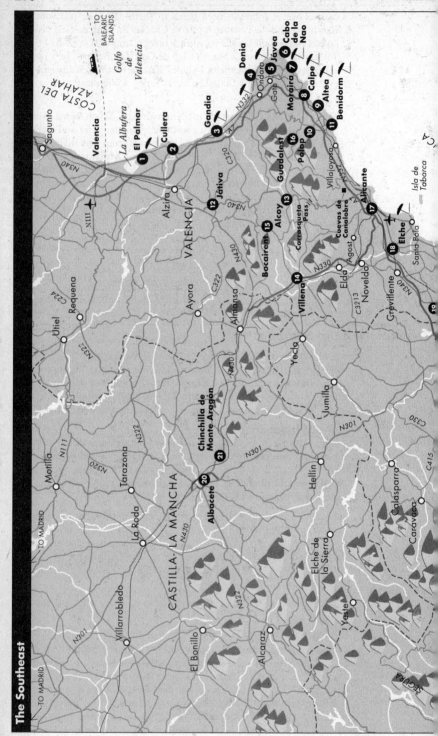

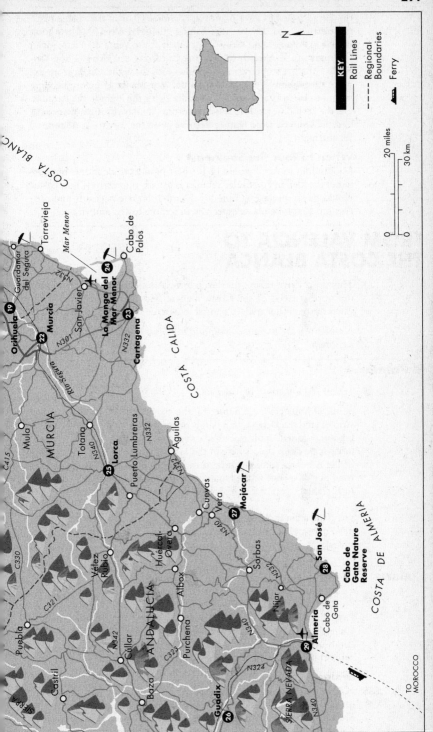

KEY

Rail Lines

Regional Boundaries

Ferry

20 miles
30 km

COSTA BLANCA

Torrevieja

Mar Menor

Cabo de Palos

Guardamar del Segura

N332

Orihuela 19

Murcia 22

San Javier

La Manga del Mar Menor 23

24

N301

N340

Cartagena

N332

COSTA CALIDA

Mula

MURCIA

Totana

Lorca 25

Puerto Lumbreras

N340

N332

Aguilas

C415

Río Segura

N332

Cuevas

Vera

Mojácar 27

Vélez Rubio

Huércal-Overa

26

Albox

N340

Sorbas

N340

N332

San José 28

Cabo de Gata Nature Reserve

C330

C321

Puebla

N342

Cúllar

Purchena

ANDALUCIA

C323

Níjar

Cabo de Gata

COSTA DE ALMERIA

Castril

Baza

Guadix 26

N324

N340

SIERRA NEVADA

Almería 29

TO MOROCCO

SIERRA

the Parador de la Costa Blanca at ▣ **Jávea** ⑤ or in the village of ▣ **Moraira** ⑦. Next day visit the fishing village of **Altea** ⑨. Then hook inland to **Polop** ⑩ and **Alcoy** ⑬ for lunch at the Venta del Pilar. Spend the night in ▣ **Alicante** ⑰. On the third day see **Elche** ⑱ and **Orihuela** ⑲ before stopping in ▣ **Murcia** ㉒ for the night. On day four explore **Cartagena** ㉓ and **La Manga del Mar Menor** ㉔ before heading inland to **Lorca** ㉕ and on to ▣ **Guadix** ㉖ for the night in the Parador. On the fifth day, explore the coast from Aguilas through **Mojácar** ㉗ and the **Cabo de Gato Nature Reserve** ㉘ on the way to ▣ **Almería** ㉙ for the night.

When to Tour the Southeast

Midautumn to April would be the best months to be in this hot corner of the Iberian Peninsula. Summer is usually oppressively hot. Easter would be an interesting time for the often bizarre pageants and processions that take place, especially in remote towns and villages.

FROM VALENCIA TO THE COSTA BLANCA

This short drive takes you through the Albuferas wetlands and into the northern end of the Costa Blanca, known as La Marina Alta. There are many unexploited natural spots to be savored along this stretch.

Numbers in the margin correspond to points of interest on the Southeast map.

El Palmar

❶ *16 km (10 mi) south of Valencia.*

South of Valencia (☞ Chapter 8), the coastal road runs along a thin strip of land (La Dehesa) that barely separates the sea from the **Albufera lagoon,** rimmed with rice fields and shady pine woods. There are large-scale duck shoots here in the fall and winter. For a closer whiff of the Albufera's unique aura, turn right to El Palmar. A single-track road hugs the edge of the lagoon, passing thatched *barracas* (shacks). In El Palmar, you can hire boats to explore the lagoon.

NEED A BREAK? Lining the main street of El Palmar are bars; try the local delicacy, *anguila al allipebre* (eel fried in garlic and served with a hot-pepper sauce).

Cullera

❷ *39 km (24 mi) south of Valencia, 27 km (17 mi) north of Gandía.*

Pass the lighthouse at Cullera; around the rocky point is modern Cullera, a mushrooming resort, marked by futuristic high-rises. The climb up to the **hermitage of Nuestra Señora del Castillo** and **castle ruins** culminates in views of the sea, the huerta, and the mountains.

Dining

$$$ ✕ **Les Mouettes.** On the road up to the castle, this tiny restaurant with
★   only a dozen tables has a lovely terrace with stunning, sea views. The French owner-chef Jacqueline Lagarce prepares secret recipes from home; try the mousse de salmón con coulis de tomate fresco (salmon mousse with slices of tomato). ⊠ *Carretera subida al Castillo,* ☎ *96/172–0010. AE, DC, MC, V. Closed Dec. 15–Feb. 15 and Mon. in winter. No dinner Sun. and no lunch July–Sept.*

Gandía

❸ *30 km (19 mi) northwest of Denia.*

The old town of Gandía lies 4 km/2½ mi inland from the modern beach development. This became the Borgia (Borja, in Spanish) fief after Ferdinand the Catholic granted the duchy to the family in 1485. The canny Borgia pope Alexander VI was one of the most notorious of all Renaissance prelates. The family's reputation was later redeemed, however, by the Jesuit St. Francis Borgia (1510–72), born in Gandía and canonized in 1671.

In Gandía, you can visit the **Palacio de los Duques** (Ducal Palace), signposted from the center. It was founded by St. Francis in 1546 and still serves as a Jesuit college. Elaborate ceilings and brightly colored *azulejos* (tiles) adorn the 17th-century state rooms. ✉ *350 ptas.* ☼ *Guided tours summer, Mon.–Sat. 10, 11, noon, 5, 6, and 7; winter, Mon.–Sat. 11, noon, 4:30, and 5:30; Sun. and fiestas, 10 and 11.*

Dining

$$ ✕ **Mesón Gallego.** This restaurant serving northern cuisine (from Galicia) is a lucky discovery in the port area. The rough and simple decor is a good setting for hearty Gallegan dishes such as *pulpo* (octopus), or fish and meat specialties cooked over coals. Ask for Gallegan, shallow, ceramic bowls for drinking the young *ribeiro* wines. ✉ *Levante 37, Grao de Gandía,* ☎ *96/284–1892. AE, DC, MC, V.*

En Route   As you head south, parchment-colored hills mark the beginning of the province of Alicante. Once past Ondara, which has an unusual, stone bullring, you can detour to the Cueva de las Calaveras (Skull Cave), near Benidoleig, inhabited by prehistoric humans some 40,000 years ago. ☎ *96/640235.* ✉ *400 ptas.* ☼ *Daily 9–7.*

LA COSTA BLANCA

The popular name for the stretch of coast between Cape Nao and Cape Palos is the Costa Blanca, or White Coast. Carnations grow in such abundance here that they even faintly perfume the local wine. The Costa Blanca includes the towns of Alicante and Cartagena, as well as numerous beach resorts, which have expanded at an uncontrolled rate since the 1960s and early '70s.

Gata de Gorgos, the next town, specializes in basketwork. A road branches off to the coastal resorts of Denia and picturesque Jávea.

Denia

❹ *100 km (62 mi) south of Valencia, 8 km (5 mi) from both Jávea and Ondara.*

Denia is a busy tourist town, the northernmost beach resort on the Costa Blanca, known for its fleet of fishing boats and fiestas and celebrations culminating in the midsummer Saint John's fires of 23 June. Backed by the Montgó massif rising to over 2,100 ft to the west, Denia's beaches to the north—Les Marines, Les Bovetes, and Les Deveses are smooth and sandy, while to the south the coast is rocky, forming *calas* (tiny secluded inlets redolent of the Costa Brava north of Barcelona). Denia's most interesting architectural feature is its **Palau del Governador** (Governor's Palace) overlooking the town, with its 12th-century tower and its renaissance bastion, which has a Moorish portal with a lovely, horseshoe arch over it. There are also several interesting churches and convents, such as the **Iglesia de la Asunción.** Known as the "gastronomical capital of the Costa Blanca," Denia is a good place to sample fresh Mediterranean seafood. Try a plate of *picaetes de sepia y calamar* (squid and cuttlefish) or a *suquet de rape* (stewed hake) at any of the town's fine restaurants. Denia has the **closest ferry connection to the Balearic islands** with two companies, Flebasa (☎ 96/578–4011) and Pitra (☎ 96/642–3120) sailing the 3½-hour, 80 km/50 mi crossing to Ibiza daily (more frequently in summer).

Dining

$$ ✕ **Drassanes.** Built into the original medieval shipyards, Drassanes is a well-known place for fresh, local seafood. The decor is maritime, simple and rustic, and the people and fare are authentic and good. *Arroz a la banda* (rice cooked with seafood) is the house specialty. ⊠ *C. Puerto 15,* ☎ *96/578–1118. AE, DC, MC, V. Closed Mon.*

Jávea

❺ *108 km (67 mi) southeast of Valencia, 92 km (57 mi) northeast of Alicante, 8 km (5 mi) south of Denia.*

A labyrinth of tiny streets and houses with arched portals and Gothic windows, Jávea's antique aspect is contrasted by its modern **Santa María de Loreto church. San Bartolomé church-fortress** is Jávea's architectural gem; the **Soler Blasco Ethnological and Archeological Museum** (open mornings only in winter) is another interesting visit. The **Aduanas del Mar area** around the port is well sprinkled with restaurants serving local dishes such as *arroz a la marinera* (paella).

Cabo de la Nao

❻ *East of Jávea.*

Cabo de la Nao (Cape Nao) is a great spur of land that juts out into the Mediterranean toward Ibiza, barely 100 km/62 mi away. As you round the point, you turn from a coast that looks toward Italy to one that mirrors Africa. In the course of a few kilometers, you pass from an agriculture of oranges and rice to one of olives and palms; from a benign, if variable, climate to tawny aridity.

Moraira

❼ *12 km (7 mi) northeast of Calpe, 20 km (12 mi) south of Jávea.*

Moraira has managed to preserve an atmosphere of seclusion in the narrow streets leading down to the harbor. The *casco viejo* (the old part of town) has a good selection of bars and restaurants, while the outskirts of town have been edified with chalets and private residences. The **castle** and **watch tower** overlooking the port were for protection from Mediterranean pirates during the Middle Ages.

Dining and Lodging

$$$$ ✕ **El Girasol.** An elegant, ivy-cloaked villa on the Calpe road houses
★ one of the finest restaurants in this region. Owners Joachim and Victoria Koerper preside over a small dining room and terrace. Their cooking is outstanding and imaginative, with the emphasis on French dishes. Highlights on the menu include *ensalada de salmonetes a la vinagretta de naranja* (red mullet salad with orange vinegar). ⊠ *Carretera Moraira a Calpe,* ☎ *96/574–4373. AE, DC, MC, V. Closed Jan. 15–Mar. 1 and Mon. Sept.–June. No lunch Mon.–Sat. July and Aug.*

$$$ ✕▣ **Hotel Swiss Moraira.** With a secluded location in a pine forest above Moraira (off the road to Calpe) and well-decorated rooms around an artistically conceived swimming pool, this low-rise, lux-

ury hotel is ideal for peace and comfort. During the day, guests leave for the beach and marina, 3.2 km/2 mi away. ⊠ *Club Moraira, 03724 Alicante,* ☎ *96/574–7104,* FAX *96/574–7074. 26 rooms with bath. Restaurant, bar, pool, tennis court. AE, DC, MC, V. Closed mid-Jan.–Feb. 5.*

Calpe★

8 *15 km (9 mi) southwest of Jávea, 8 km (5 mi) north of Altea.*

South of Moraira is Calpe and the dramatic outcrop, the **Peñón de Ifach.** The town was deserted for nearly 100 years after Barbary pirates killed or carried off as slaves the entire population in the 17th century. The 1,000-foot monolith of the Peñón rises from the sea; the summit is accessible by tunnel. Goatlike spirits are reputed to hurl to their deaths those who scale these heights at full moon.

Dining and Lodging

$$$ ✕🏨 **Venta la Chata.** This pretty hotel represents good value. The
★ downstairs is rustic, as are the wood furnishings and azulejo-tiled floors in the rooms. The premises include terraced gardens with views to the sea and a good restaurant serving fresh fish and vegetables. ⊠ *Carretera de Valencia (N332, Km 150), 03710 Alicante,* ☎ *96/583–0308. Restaurant, bar, tennis courts, Ping-Pong. AE, DC, MC, V.*

Altea

9 *10 km (6 mi) south of Calpe, 11 km (7 mi) north of Benidorm.*

Altea is an old fishing village with white houses and blue, ceramic-tiled domes. One of the best conserved villages on this coast, Altea is a foil to the skyscraping tourist towers of Benidorm.

Dining

$$$ ✕ **La Costera.** This restaurant offers bizarre decor, as well as a nightly show. The excellent cooking, with Swiss specialties, includes the delicious *rostit con carne troceada y champiñon* (chopped meat with mushrooms and potatoes). It is extremely popular and often booked long ahead. ⊠ *Costera del Mestre la Música 8,* ☎ *96/584–0230. DC, MC, V. Closed Wed. and Aug.*

Polop

10 *10 km (6 mi) northwest of Altea.*

In the center of Polop is a collection of taps, each donated by a different town or province, that serve the villagers with mountain water.

En Route Follow C3318 south to Benidorm.

Benidorm

11 *42 km (26 mi) northeast of Alicante, 11 km (7 mi) south of Altea.*

Benidorm is a hugely overdeveloped resort whose current capacity is said to be in the region of 300,000 beds! Its **twin, white, crescent-shape beaches** are enhanced by a continual topping-up of sand from other local beaches. Hidden among the concrete blocks, the original old village still survives. For a fantastic view, climb up to the **Rincón de Loix;** follow signs to Club Sierra Dorada at the far east end of town.

Dining and Lodging

$$$ ✕ **Tiffany's.** The red and white tones of Tiffany's are where Benidorm's jet set comes for intimacy and fine, international cuisine. Delicacies like *salmón con langostinos* (salmon with shrimp) and entrecote *al roque-*

fort are brought to you to the accompaniment of piano music. ⊠ *Avda. Mediterráneo, Edifício Coblanca 3,* ☎ *96/585–4468. AE, DC, MC, V. Closed Jan. 6–Feb. 6. No lunch.*

$ ✕ **I Fratelli.** The cooking here is Italian, with nouvelle French and international touches. Neapolitan music complements the stylish *modernista* decor: sleek, black chairs, white tablecloths, and exotic, potted plants. Try the *pescados a la sal* (fish baked in salt) or a pasta dish. ⊠ *Dr. Orts Llorca,* ☎ *96/585–3979. AE, DC, MC, V. Closed Nov.*

$$$ ✕🏨 **Gran Delfín.** Of the umpteen-thousands of hotel beds in Benidorm, those in the Gran Delfín are the most quietly situated. The salon downstairs is filled with a motley collection of furniture. The bedrooms are furnished Castilian-style with a smattering of bric-a-brac on the walls. Ask for a room at the front overlooking the beach. ⊠ *Playa de Poniente, Benidorm, 03500 Alicante,* ☎ *96/585–3400,* 𝔽𝔸𝕏 *96/585–2100. 87 rooms with bath. Restaurant, bar, pool, tennis courts. AE, DC, MC, V. Closed Oct.–Apr. 5.*

Nightlife and the Arts

For cabaret, try the **Benidorm Palace** (⊠ Diputación, ☎ 965/851661). Alternatively, visit the **Nuevo Gran Castillo Conde de Alfaz** (⊠ Camino Viejo del Albir, ☎ 96/588–8592), don a crown, and dine in front of jousting medieval knights. If it sounds touristy, that's because it is. Price per person is 3,500 ptas., including dinner, drinks, and the show.

Countless bars and discos, with names like Jockey's and Harrods, line Avenida de Europa and the Ensanche de la Playa de Levante.

INLAND: JÁTIVA AND ALCOY

For a break from sea and sand, cut inland and into some of the towns and landscapes that serve as deep background to the lighter atmosphere that seems to typify the Mediterranean coast. Játiva, Alcoy, Villena, and Bocairent have some of the most authentic and unchanged people and places in the Southeast.

Játiva

⑫ *42 km (26 mi) southwest of Cullera, 50 km (31 mi) north of Alcoy.*

Játiva rests on the dry, vine- and cypress-covered slopes of the Sierra de Alcoy, 43 km/26 mi from Cullera, and retains a pink **Old Quarter** dotted with fountains. Under the Moors, it was famous for paper production, and centuries later it became the birthplace of two of the Borgia popes—Calixtus III and his nephew Alexander VI. The latter issued the famous 1493 Papal Bull granting the Indies to Ferdinand and Isabella, though he's more often remembered for his scandalous private life and as the father of Caesar and Lucrezia.

To reach the **Castillo** set on the slopes of Mount Bernisa, follow signs up a steep path from the Plaza del Españoleto. Halfway up, the 13th-century **Ermita de San Felíu** (Hermitage of St. Felix) has a beautiful group of Valencian Primitive paintings. Felipe V did a fairly thorough job of destroying the fortress as part of his retribution for Játiva's opposition during the War of the Spanish Succession, but a partial restoration of the castle and a panoramic view reward your efforts. (Apply to the caretaker).

On the Plaza del Seo stands the monumental **Collegiata** church, remarkable for its size and housing some Borgia Renaissance marbles.

Opposite the Collegiata church is the ornate, 16th-century, Plateresque facade of the **hospital.** Down Calle Corretgeria, the **Museo Municipal** (Municipal Museum) has a small collection of archaeological finds and paintings by Játiva's other famous son, José de Ribera.

Alcoy★

🔞 *55 km (34 mi) north of Alicante, 50 km (31 mi) south of Játiva.*

Alcoy is at the confluence of three rivers and is famous for its **bridges** spanning their deep gorges. It owes its size (population, 67,000) to textile, paper, and fruit-canning industries. The annual **Moros y Cristianos** (Moors and Christians festival) around Sant Jordi (St. George's Day), April 23, is the most spectacular fiesta of its kind in Spain. Colorful processions and mock battles commemorate the battle of Alcoy in 1275, when St. George's intervention helped liberate the city from the besieging forces of Al Azraq, ensuring victory for the Christians.

If you miss this week, go down Calle Sant Miquel, which leads off Plaza de España, to **Casal de Sant Jordi,** which houses paraphernalia from the event, including costumes worn by the combatants. ⊠ *Sant Miquel 62.* 🖃 *350 ptas.* ☉ *Tues.–Fri. 11–1 and 5:30–8.*

NEED A BREAK? | Through arches from the Plaza de España is the enclosed Plaza de Dins, whose sidewalk cafés are ideal for a drink and local olives.

Dining and Lodging

$$–$$$ ★ ✗ **Venta del Pilar.** Two-and-a-half km/1½ mi out on the Valencia road, this 18th-century inn serves superb food. Downstairs the decor is more in keeping with the building. The cooking includes both local and international dishes; try the *salmón al vinagre de cava* (fresh baked salmon with champagne sauce). ⊠ *Carretera Valencia 118,* 🕾 *96/559–2325. AE, DC, MC, V. Closed Sun., Holy Week, and Aug.*

$$ ★ ✗🏨 **Reconquista.** There is nothing at all memorable about the modern highrise Reconquista, but it is the most comfortable option for miles around. You can compensate for the plain, dated decor in the bedrooms by requesting a view over the river gorge to old Alcoy. The public rooms have an institutional air, with their spotty, gray-tiled floors and functional, plastic furniture. ⊠ *Puente San Jorge 1, 03803 Alicante,* 🕾 *96/533–0900,* 🆁🆇 *96/533–0955, 77 rooms with bath. Restaurant, bar, dance club. AE, DC, MC, V.*

Villena

🔞 *40 km (25 mi) west of Alcoy.*

In Villena a collection of priceless, Bronze Age rings, bracelets, coronets, and bowls of gold was discovered on a dry riverbed in 1963. It is displayed in the archaeology section of the ayuntamiento.

Bocairent

🔞 *27 km (17 mi) northeast of Villena.*

On the way back to the N340 from Villena, find time to stop in Bocairent, where the **Museo Parroqial** displays paintings by Juan de Juanes, who died here in 1579, along with works by Francisco Ribalta and Joaquín Sorolla.

Guadalest

⑯ *36 km (22 mi) east of Alcoy.*

Guadalest is an old town within walls of a ruined castle, perched atop a crag, with tiny, stepped streets to overcome the steep terrain. Continue as far as Callosa, turn left to Tarbena, and brave a dip at the foot of the **El Algar falls,** icy whatever the time of year. Nearby **Tarbena,** a village famed for its sausages, introduces you to spectacular scenery.

ALICANTE, ELCHE, AND ORIHUELA

Luminous Alicante seems to shimmer with the kind of light the Mediterranean is famous for while inland Elche's palm forest shades its ancient treasures from the heat of the summer. Orihuela's twisting back streets tunnel through the town's long history under Moorish rule.

Alicante

⑰ *82 km (51 mi) northeast of Murcia, 183 km (113 mi) south of Valencia by the coast road, 42 km (26 mi) south of Benidorm, 55 km (34 mi) south of Alcoy.*

Alicante, at the convergence of inland and coastal roads, has always been known for its luminous skies. The Greeks called it Akra Leuka (White Summit) and the Romans, Lucentum (City of Light). The city is dominated by the **castle of Santa Bárbara,** set on a rocky peak. The pride of the city is its date-palm-lined avenue, the **Explanada.**

Begin your tour in the arcaded Plaza de Ayuntamiento at the tourist office. Look inside the Baroque ayuntamiento; ask gate officials for permission to explore the ornate halls and Rococo chapel on the first floor. Walk through to Plaza Santísima Faz behind the ayuntamiento, a trafficless square crowded with sidewalk cafés and restaurants.

From the Plaza Santísima Faz continue down the busy, pedestrianized Calle Mayor and turn right to the **cathedral of San Nicolás de Bari** (open for services), set on the site of a former mosque. It has both an austere 17th-century Renaissance facade in the style of Herrera (architect of the Escorial) and a lavish, Baroque side chapel.

Retrace your steps to the **Museo de Arte Siglo XX** (Museum of 20th-Century Art), at the other end of Calle Mayor. The collection of abstract art includes works by Picasso, Miró, Braque, Tàpies, Hockney, and Rauschenberg. 🖼 *Free.* ☉ *Oct.–Apr., Tues.–Sat. 10–1 and 5–8; May–Sept., Tues.–Sat. 10:30–1:30 and 6–9.*

Across the small plaza from the Museum of 20th-Century Art stands the **Church of Santa María,** with a rich, Baroque facade. From here, it's a short walk down steps, then left along the back of Playa Postiguet to the foot of Mt. Benacantil (700 feet) and the elevator up to the castle.

★ Originally built as a Carthaginian fortress around 3 BC, the **Castillo de Santa Bárbara** was extensively modified for numerous wars. From it you have a spectacular bird's-eye view of the city. Within the castle walls, a small museum displays objects associated with the San Juan bonfires, burned on midsummer night's eve each year. 🖼 *Castle 250 ptas., museum 100 ptas.* ☉ *Castle and elevator Sun.–Fri. 9–9; museum spring–fall, Sun.–Fri. 10–1 and 5–8, Sat. 10–1.*

NEED A BREAK?   The cafés along the Explanada offer a picturesque, if noisy, place for a drink. The bar below the Delfín restaurant has a wide selection of tapas.

Dining and Lodging

$$$ ✕ **Delfin.** Don't let the fantastic view over the palm-lined Explanada and Alicante's yacht culture distract you from the imaginative food offered here. Opened in 1961, Delfin remains in the gastronomic front line and wholly modern in its bright, first-floor decor and breezy terrace. The cooking is divided equally between seafood and meat dishes. Try the *tosta de* salmon (toasted salmon). ✉ *Explanada de España 14,* ☎ *96/521–4911. AE, DC, MC, V.*

$$ ✕ **Quo Vadis.** Recently redecorated, there is a cozy, village-like atmo-
★ sphere in this most "Spanish" of Alicante's restaurants, just behind the ayuntamiento. Friendly and fast service brings to you, indoors or out, dishes ranging from local seafood like dorada *a la sal* (baked in salt) to Castilian favorites like the various *carnes flambés* (barbecued meats). Come here at any time of day to sample the tapas that line the bar. ✉ *Plaza Santísima Faz 3,* ☎ *96/521–6660. AE, DC, MC, V. Closed Mon. in winter. No dinner Sun. in winter.*

$$$–$$$$ ✕🖿 **Meliá Alicante.** For proximity to the sea and good comfort, try the Meliá. This huge hotel stands on a reclaimed peninsula jutting out into the Mediterranean, close to the city center. The bedrooms have bright, modern decor and command sweeping views of the beaches and marina. Downstairs is a shrine to postmodernism, with cool, marble floors and low, black tables. ✉ *Playa del Postiguet, 03001 Alicante,* ☎ *96/520–5000,* ℻ *96/520–5746. 545 rooms with bath. 2 restaurants, piano bar, 2 pools, exercise room. AE, DC, MC, V.*

$$ ✕🖿 **Eurhotel Hesperia.** This modern and recently renovated hotel 300
★ yards from Alicante's port will satisfy all your practical necessities. Though uninspirational, the hotel's proximity to the train and bus stations makes it a handy place. The hotel restaurant, the Dona Blanca, does a thriving business. ✉ *Calle Pintor Lorenzo Casanova 33,* ☎ *96/513–0440,* ℻ *96/592–8323. 116 rooms with bath. Restaurant, bar, cafeteria, parking. AE, DC, MC, V.*

$$ ✕🖿 **Palas.** This is Alicante's oldest hotel, and it has a certain chaotic
★ charm. The rooms, with Regency furniture, lack carpets, but these shouldn't be necessary in any but the coldest months. Ask for a front room if you value a sea view more than tranquility. The restaurant, with its summer terrace, is popular for its rice dishes. ✉ *Plaza del Mar 5, 03002 Alicante,* ☎ *96/520–9310,* ℻ *96/514–0120. 49 rooms with bath. Restaurant, bar. AE, DC, MC, V.*

Nightlife and the Arts

Roughish, lively bars are found through the streets behind the ayuntamiento. Among the slicker pubs and discotheques are **Pachá** (✉ Avda. Aguilera 22) and the **Doña Pepa** (✉ Jorge Juan 18). In summer, the liveliest place is the beach at San Juan; **O'Ku** (✉ Avda. Costa Blanca), a discotheque, and **Caligula** (✉ Playa de San Juan), a pub, are popular.

Shopping

Local **crafts** include basketwork, embroidery, leatherwork, and weaving, each peculiar to a single town or village in the Southeast. You will find all these crafts for sale in major tourist resorts, although the prices may be inflated. Often the most satisfying places to shop are local markets, so be sure to check whether it is market day while you are in town.

For **ceramics,** go to Agost, 20 km/12 mi inland from Alicante, where they make good jugs and pitchers from the local white clay, whose porosity is ideal for keeping liquids cool.

Elche

18 *24 km (15 mi) southwest of Alicante, 34 km (21 mi) northeast of Ori-*
huela, 58 km (36 mi) northeast of Murcia.

If Alicante is torrid in summer, Elche is even hotter. Escape from the
worst of the heat is made possible in the largest palm forest in Europe,
which surrounds the city. The Moors first planted the palms for dates,
and the palms still produce Europe's most reliable crop, as well as providing yellow, Palm Sunday fronds, which, once blessed, are hung on
balconies to ward off evil during the coming year. This town, colonized
by ancient Rome, was later ruled by the Moors for 500 years. The remarkable stone bust known as *La Dama de Elche,* discovered here in
1897 (now in Madrid's Archaeological Museum) is one of the earliest
examples of Iberian sculpture. The *Misteri* (Mystery Play), performed
in the Basilica de Santa María on the Feast of the Assumption, draws
many visitors. The performances on August 14 and 15 are spectacular, involving the winching of a platform bearing the Virgin Mary and
guitar-playing angels 150 feet up into the dome of the church.

Be sure to visit the **Palm Grove,** with more than 200,000 trees, and
the beautiful **Huerto del Cura,** where flowers of vibrant colors grow
beneath magnificent palms. 🎟 *300 ptas.* ☉ *Apr.–Sept., daily 9–8;*
Oct.–Mar., daily 9–6.

Dining and Lodging

$$$ ✕🖬 **Huerto del Cura.** A subtropical location and a large, private gar-
★ den in Elche's palm grove render this perfect for rest and relaxation.
The main building of the modern semi-parador houses the excellent
Els Capellans restaurant, which serves regional rice and fish dishes. Bun-
galow huts contain the bedrooms, gloomy due to the shady location,
but with tasteful decor. The palm-ringed swimming pool resembles some-
thing you might hope for on a trip to the Seychelles. ✉ *Porta de la*
Morera, Elche, 03200 Alicante, ☏ *96/5458040,* 📠 *96/5421910. 70*
rooms with bath. Restaurant, bar, cafeteria, 2 pools, sauna, tennis courts.
AE, DC, MC, V.

Orihuela

19 *24 km (15 mi) northeast of Murcia, 34 km (21 mi) southwest of Elche,*
29 km (18 mi) inland from the Mediterranean coast at Guardamar del
Segura.

Palm and orange groves are scattered through market gardens as far
as Orihuela, on the banks of the Segura—another excuse to linger on
the N340 south. The town's air of fading grandeur stems from its for-
mer status as capital of Murcia until the Reconquest. Stroll through
Orihuela's winding streets and visit the Gothic **El Salvador Cathedral**
to see the rare, spiral vaulting. The adjoining museum has paintings
by Velázquez and Ribera.

APPROACHING MURCIA
VIA ALBACETE AND LA MANCHA

To get the feel of Don Quixote country, the drive from Madrid through
Albacete and the flat and arid La Mancha region to Murcia will suf-
fice. The Parador Nacional Marqués Villena at Alarcón, the Parador
de la Mancha at Albacete, the village promontory of Chinchilla de Monte
Aragón, and the Roman town of Cieza punctuate this three to four
drive with lunch, dinner, or overnight options.

Albacete

20 *172 km (107 mi) northwest of Alicante, 146 km (91 mi) northwest of Murcia, 183 km (114 mi) southwest of Valencia.*

Albacete is an agricultural town famous for **wines** and **saffron.** Lying 3,000 feet above sea level, it has a 15th- and 16th-century quarter on the crest of a hill, known as **Alto de la Villa,** and the **Ermita de San Antonio** (Hermitage of St. Anthony) is a good example of 17th-century, Castellano architecture.

Visit the **Museo Arqueológico** (Archaeological Museum) in the Parque Abelardo Sánchez, with Roman mosaics, ivory dolls, and objects dating from the Paleolithic era. ⌨ *300 ptas.* ⊘ *Tues.–Sat. 10–2 and 4–7, Sun. 10–2.*

Dining and Lodging

$$ ✕⊡ **Parador de la Mancha.** Set back from the highway, this low-rise, ★ whitewashed, *manchego*-style parador has a rustic, wood-beamed interior and comfortable, cozy bedrooms. The restaurant serves local cuisine; try the *chuletas de cordero* (lamb chops grilled with garlic). ✉ *Apdo. 384, Carretera N301, 02000 Albacete,* ☎ *967/509343,* ℻ *967/226092. 70 rooms with bath. Restaurant, bar, pool, tennis courts. AE, DC, MC, V.*

Chinchilla de Monte Aragón

21 *12 km (7 mi) east of Albacete.*

If you detour slightly along the freeway toward Alicante, you'll soon see the imposing 15th-century fortress-prison-castle of Chinchilla de Monte Aragón away on your left, and, if the day is clear, the distant Sierra de Alcaraz rising to nearly 6,000 feet to the south. Chinchilla is a fine old pottery town.

En Route Back on the N301, most of the 146 km/91 mi to Murcia run adjacent to the uplands of La Mancha, where Don Quixote adventured in Cervantes's famous novel. Across the border into Murcia and through the Roman town of Cieza, dominated by its feudal castle, the road drops some 2,700 feet to farmland before reaching the provincial capital.

MURCIA TO ALMERÍA

Soon after Orihuela, you enter the province of Murcia, where the N340 follows the course of the Segura, though the foothills of the Sierra de Carrascoy often intervene. This is the driest part of Spain, and the least visited. The tawny hills are punctuated by stretches of fertile huerta, moistened by life-giving rivers whose waters irrigate three crops in succession a year. Rich metal deposits supply a busy mining industry. As you cross into Murcia, the Valenciano language gives way to the Castilian dialect.

Murcia

22 *82 km (51 mi) southwest of Alicante, 146 km (91 mi) southeast of Albacete, 219 km (136 mi) northeast of Almería.*

Murcia, capital of the province, was first settled by Romans. The conquering Moors later used Roman bricks to build the 8th-century Murcia. The city was liberated and annexed to the crown of Castile in 1243; the Murcian dialect contains many Arabic words, and many of its inhabitants clearly reveal their Moorish ancestry. Modern Murcia is a university city with a population of more than 300,000.

★ The **cathedral** is a masterpiece of eclectic architecture. Begun in the 14th century, it received its magnificent **facade**—described by the 19th-century English traveler Richard Ford as "rising in compartments, like a drawnout telescope" as late as 1737. This facade is considered the fullest expression of the Churrigueresque style. From the 15th century are the **Gothic Door of the Apostles** and the splendid **Isabelline Vélez Chapel,** with beautiful, star vaulting and carvings by the 18th-century Murcian sculptor Francisco Salzillo. Look in the **museum,** off the north transept, to see Salzillo's polychrome-wood sculpture of the penitent St. Jerome. Ask the keeper for the keys to climb the monumental bell tower, built between 1521 and 1792, 312 feet high. 🕮 *Museum and bell tower 250 ptas.* ☉ *Daily 10–noon and 5–7:30.*

Go down Calle Trapería, the pedestrian shopping street. You soon reach the 19th-century **Casino,** worth a peep for its style and aura of a British gentlemen's club. The intricate Mudéjar decor was modeled on the Alhambra in Granada. Gambling hasn't taken place here for years; Murcians (men only!) come to read newspapers and play billiards.

<table>
<tr><td>NEED A
BREAK?</td><td>At the end of Trapería is a cluster of sidewalk cafés serving a wide variety of Murcian tapas. Look for the Hungaria in Plaza de Santo Domingo.</td></tr>
</table>

The **Salzillo Museum,** some way out by the bus station, has the main collection of Francisco Salzillo's disturbingly realistic, polychrome *pasos* (carvings), carried every Easter in the processions. 🕮 *250 ptas.* ☉ *Tues.–Sat. 9:30–1 and 4–7 (winter, 3–6), Sun. 11–1.*

Dining and Lodging

$$$ ✕ **Rincón de Pepe.** A rambling series of casually decorated dining
★ rooms greets locals and visitors. Chef Raimundo Frutos doubles as an organic farmer and sticks closely to these ingredients, with only the freshest supplements, such as the fish from Mar Menor. Highlights on the extensive menu include *ensalada de mariscos y trufas* (shellfish and truffle salad). ⊠ *Apóstoles 34,* ☎ *968/212239. AE, DC, MC, V. Closed Sun. in summer. No dinner Sun. in winter.*

$$ ✕ **Hispano.** For a typically Spanish brand of rusticity, look no further than the Hispano. A well-known Murcian family of restaurateurs/hoteliers created this restaurant some 20 years ago, and it is still extremely popular for Murcian, traditional, and nouvelle cuisine. ⊠ *Lucas 7,* ☎ *968/216152. AE, DC, MC, V. Closed Sat. in summer.*

$$$ 🏨 **Rincón de Pepe.** The name of this modern hotel is more famous for the restaurant next door. The location could not be better, in the center of the old town, 50 yards from the cathedral's apse. It offers good comfort and hospitality. The bedrooms all have modern, bright, and restrained decor. The lobby and reception rooms have cool, marble floors. ⊠ *Apóstoles 34, 30001 Murcia,* ☎ *968/212239,* 🗏 *968/221744. 115 rooms with bath. Bar, parking. AE, DC, MC, V.*

$ 🏨 **Hispano 1.** The bedrooms at this budget hotel are bright and airy; ask for an exterior one. The first-floor sitting room is large and tasteful. The location is central, and the street outside is pedestrianized. ⊠ *Trapería 8 y 10, 30001 Murcia,* ☎ *968/216152,* 🗏 *968/216859. 46 rooms with bath. Breakfast room, parking. AE, DC, MC, V.*

Nightlife and the Arts

Look for the pubs **Latino** and **B12** in the university district.

Cartagena

㉓ *48 km (29 mi) south of Murcia.*

Cartagena, founded in the 3rd century BC by the Carthaginians, is Spain's principal naval base. From here there is easy access to the resort of **La Manga del Mar Menor** and a twisty, scenic 100 km/62 mi along the N332 to the start of the Costa de Almería.

La Manga del Mar Menor

㉔ *45 km (28 mi) southeast of Murcia.*

La Manga del Mar Menor, Europe's largest salt water lake (170 sq. km/105 sq. mi) is warmer, saltier and higher in iodine content than the Mediterranean and is, as a result, well known as a therapeutic health resort for rheumatism patients. The Manga itself is a 21 km/13 mi spit of sand averaging some 990 feet in width enclosing the *Mar Menor* (smaller sea), a notoriously flat calm expanse of shallow water about 20 feet deep. Four canals, called *golas,* connect the Mar Menor with the Mediterranean. The Manga has 42 km/26 mi of immense, sandy beaches on both the Mediterranean and the Mar Menor sides, allowing bathers to choose more or less exposed locations and warmer or colder water according to season and weather. San Javier and Cartagena are the principal towns on or near the Mar Menor. La Manga Club-Hotel (☞ *below*) claims to be Europe's most complete sports hotel.

Dining and Lodging

$$$$ ✕🖾 **La Manga Club-Hotel.** Golf pervades this superbly situated, luxury club house-hotel, just above Mar Menor. Most of its patrons come here to wallow in the golfy ambience of what has become all but home course for Sevy Ballesteros. There is also a cricket pitch, which probably accounts for the surfeit of British-registered Range Rovers in the parking lot. You can also rent apartments or villas. ⊠ *La Manga Club, Los Belones, 30385 Murcia,* ☎ *968/564511,* 🖷 *968/564750. 47 rooms with bath. Restaurant, bar, 2 pools, 2 golf courses, hot tub, sauna, 17 tennis courts, squash, equestrian outings. AE, DC, MC, V.*

Outdoor Activities and Sports

SAILING

The Mar Menor, notable for the absence of waves of any kind, is a featured venue for sailing. Windsurfing, water skiing, catamaran sailing and other specialties are offered by various schools.

Lorca★

㉕ *62 km (39 mi) southwest of Murcia, 158 km (98 mi) northeast of Almería, 37 km (23 mi) inland from the Mediterranean at Águilas.*

Leave the main highway for a glimpse of Lorca, an old market town and scene of some of Spain's most colorful Holy Week celebrations. Your first stop should be the **tourist office** on Lope Gisbert, housed in the beautiful, dilapidated Casa de los Guevara. Head down Alamo to the elegant **Plaza de España,** ringed by a string of rich Baroque buildings, particularly the **ayuntamiento, law courts,** and **Colegiata Church.** Follow signs from this plaza up to the **castle.**

Dining

$$–$$$ ✕ **Cándido.** On the road into town, this rustic, old-fashioned restau-
★ rant has been going strong on its home cooking for more than half a century. The ambience is relaxed, and the clientele a happy mix of Lorcans and travelers. The inspiration in the kitchen comes from the region; try the *trigo con conejo y caracoles* (wheat with rabbit and

snails), a typical Lorca offering. ⊠ *Santo Domingo 13,* ☎ *968/466907. No credit cards. Closed Sun. in summer.*

Guadix

㉖ *146 km (88 mi) from Puerto Lumbreras.*

Turn at Puerto Lumbreras for the town of Guadix, which is on the road to Granada. Guadix is famous for its **cave dwellings** in the Barrio Santiago. Have a look inside one or two of the caves: They are warm in winter, cool in summer, and have electricity to power all the modern conveniences.

Dining and Lodging

$ ✕⊞ **Parador de Puerto Lumbreras.** South of Lorca, where the road divides to Granada or Almería, stands this modern parador with a garden and swimming pool. The tranquil setting and smart, modern decor provide a good base where you can pause before deciding which route south to take. ⊠ *Carretera N340, Avda. Juan Carlos I 77, 30890 Murcia,* ☎ *968/402025,* ℻ *968/402836. 60 rooms with bath. Restaurant, bar, pool. AE, DC, MC, V.*

Mojácar

㉗ *93 km (58 mi) northeast of Almería, 73 km (45 mi) southeast of Puerto Lumbreras, 135 km (83 mi) southwest of Murcia.*

A couple of miles inland on a hillside overlooking the sea, Mojácar is a cluster of white, Cubist houses attesting to the town's Moorish past. The North African feel and aesthetic has been carefully preserved. During the 60's, painters and writers gravitated to Mojácar's cliff-dwelling simplicity in search of inspiration, creating a movement that became known as the *Movimiento Indaliano,* named for the *Indalo,* an anthropomorphic protective deity associated with Almerí and, especially, with Mojácar since prehistoric times. Mojácar's beaches and reflective charm make it a top destination on this refreshingly undeveloped part of Spain's southeast corner. The most attractive part of the Almerían coast lies to the south of this whitewashed village.

Dining and Lodging

$$ ✕ **El Palacio de Mojácar.** Installed in an old, white Mojácar house with exposed beams and fireplace, this restaurant specializes in good food. The friendly owner-chef doesn't have a large menu, but what there is tends to be highly original and inventive. Ask for local specialties such as *ajo colorao* (red garlic) or *caldo de pescado* (fish broth). ⊠ *Plaza del Cano,* ☎ *950/478279. AE, MC, V. Closed Thurs. and Nov.–Feb.*

$$$ ✕⊞ **Parador Reyes Católicos.** If you prefer to be by the sea rather than **★** up in the old town, this rambling, white, modern parador is the best option in Mojácar. The public rooms are some of the most spacious and tasteful you'll find anywhere. Large, open-plan fireplaces contribute the rustic ingredient. Bedrooms are bright, with parador-style, Castellano furniture. ⊠ *Carretera de Carboneras, 04638 Almería,* ☎ *950/478250,* ℻ *950/478183. 98 rooms with bath. Restaurant, bar, pool, tennis courts. AE, DC, MC, V.*

$$ ✕⊞ **El Moresco.** Up in the village itself, this hotel has a stunning position and tasteful, country decor, but it tends to be descended upon by large tour groups. ⊠ *Avda. D'encamp 15, 04638 Almería,* ☎ *950/478025,* ℻ *950/478262. 147 rooms with bath. Restaurant, pool. AE, DC, MC, V.*

San José and the Cabo de Gata Nature Reserve

28 *40 km (25 mi) east of Almería, 86 km (53 mi) south of Mojácar.*

San José is a small, relaxed village, as yet out of developers' clutches, and well placed to take advantage of the nearly deserted beaches nearby. It has one tiny hotel, a handful of *hostales* (hostels), and a campsite. Just to the south is the **Cabo de Gata Nature Reserve.** Follow signs south to the beaches of **Genovese** and **Monsul;** a dirt track follows the coast around the spectacular cape, eventually linking up with the N332 to Almería.

Dining and Lodging

$$ ✕▦ **San José.** For access to the beautifully rugged coast toward Cabo
★ Gata, you couldn't choose a happier spot than this tiny hotel in the laidback village of San José. The medium-size villa, superbly positioned above San José's bay, has just 8 very large bedrooms, all tastefully decorated and with great sea views, around a central large sitting room with an open fire. Its size means that it is crucial to book well ahead of your visit. ⊠ *Carretera a Monsul y Genoveses, 04118 Almería,* ☎ *950/380116,* 𝔽𝔸𝕏 *950/380002. 8 rooms with bath. Restaurant, parking. MC, V. Closed mid-Jan.–mid-Mar.*

Almería

29 *219 km (136 mi) southwest of Murcia, 183 km (114 mi) east of Málaga.*

Almería has tree-lined boulevards and gardened squares. Its dazzling, white houses give it a Moroccan flavor. A mild climate makes this capital of the grape industry pleasant in spring and autumn. Its core still consists of distinctly Mudéjar, flat-roofed houses in a maze of narrow, winding alleys, though now framed by modern apartment blocks.

Dominating the city is its main sight, the **Alcazaba fortress,** built by the Caliph Abdu'r Rahman and provided with a bell tower by Carlos III. The fortifications command sweeping views of the port and city. Among the ruins of the fortress, damaged by earthquakes in 1522 and 1560, are landscaped gardens of rock flowers and cacti. ▦ *300 ptas.* ⊙ *Apr.–Oct., daily 10–2 and 5–8; Nov.–Mar., daily 9–1 and 3–6.*

Below the Alcazaba stands the **cathedral,** whose buttressed towers give it the look of a castle. The reason for these defenses was the frequency of raids by Barbary pirates in the 16th century. The overall design is Gothic, with some classical touches around the doors. ⊙ *10:30–noon and for services.*

NEED A | The liveliest cafés line the Paseo de Almería and nearby streets. Head
BREAK? | down Calle Tenor Iribarne, near the top on the left, for seafood bars.

If you are a film devotee intent on seeing where spaghetti westerns were and still are shot, head to **Mini Hollywood,** 24 km/15 mi north on the N340, a film set open to the public when there's no filming taking place. ☎ *950/365236.* ▦ *650 ptas.* ⊙ *Daily 10–6 (later in summer).*

Dining and Lodging

$$ ✕ **Valentin.** This centrally located spot serves fine regional specialties. *Cazuela de rape* (anglerfish baked in a sauce of almonds and pine nuts) is a typical entrée. The decor is Andalusian: white walls, wood, and glass. This is a popular spot, so be on the early side to get a table. ✉ *Tenor Iribarne 7,* ☎ *950/264475. AE, DC, MC, V. Closed Sun.*

$$ ✕ **Veracruz.** In Alicante's beach barrio of El Zapillo, this excellent seafood restaurant equipped with its own storage tank for keeping oysters, clams, prawns, and lobsters, is a local favorite. Its specialty is the *parillada de pescado* (a mixed grill of everything that swims in the Mediterranean). ✉ *Avda. Cabo de Gata 119, El Zapillo,* ☎ *950/251220. AE, DC, MC, V. Closed June 1–15.*

$ ✕ **Imperial.** White walls and orange tablecloths set the Andalusian scene for the local seafood and meat recipes cooked here. Outstanding dishes include the *zarzuela de marisco* (mixed seafood), *solomillo a la pimienta verde* (filet mignon with green peppers), and gazpacho andaluz. It is popular with Spanish families at lunchtime and has old-fashioned, semi-formal service. You can also dine outside on the canopied terrace. ✉ *Puerta Purchena 13,* ☎ *950/231740. MC, V. Closed Wed. in winter.*

$$$ ⌂ **Gran Hotel Almería.** The rooms here now have brightly painted walls and chintz coverings to complement their fine views over Almería's harbor. The huge, marbled reception rooms evoke the hotel's golden era, when it played host to the film directors who came to make spaghetti westerns in the desert interior. ✉ *Avda. Reina Regente 8, 04001 Almería,* ☎ *950/238011,* FAX *950/270691. 117 rooms with bath. Bar, breakfast room, pool. AE, DC, MC, V.*

$–$$ ⌂ **Torreluz II.** Value for money is the overriding attraction of this comfortable, elegant, and modern hotel. The bedrooms are slick and bright, with the kind of installations you'd expect to have to pay more for. ✉ *Plaza Flores 1, 04001 Almería,* ☎ *and* FAX *950/234799. 73 rooms with bath. Bar. AE, DC, MC, V.*

$ ⌂ **Hostal Andalucía.** If you stay in only one hostal during your time in Spain, make it this one. A scruffy facade leads through to a large, ornate lobby, off which open an azulejo-tiled restaurant and the bedrooms. Ask for a room with a view and then bask in the old-fashioned atmosphere and fantastic value. The non-air-conditioned sea air can make beds slightly damp, so air them on arrival. ✉ *Granada 9, 04003 Almería,* ☎ *950/237733. 76 rooms, 37 with bath. No credit cards.*

Nightlife and the Arts

There is no shortage of discotheques and flamenco *tablaos* (floor shows) along the Costa Blanca, and most towns are lively after dark if you find the right places.

Outdoor Activities and Sports

TENNIS

Most of the coastal hotels have tennis courts, although few will let you use them if you're not a guest. Some exceptions are **Hotel Eurotennis** (✉ Villajoyosa, ☎ 96/589–1250), **La Manga Club** (✉ Los Belones, ☎ 968/564511, Ext. 1666), and **Club de Tenis V. Alegre** (✉ Paraje El Olive, Huercal de Almería, ☎ 950/300390).

Shopping

Among the best buys in **antiques,** if you can find them at about 1,000 ptas. each, are antique azulejos. Look, too, for copper and brass, especially old Art Deco oil lamps. For quality, pricey antiques, visit **Domínguez Cazorla** in Almería (✉ Miguel Segura 3).

Biar, Chinchilla, and Níjar (north of Almería) are known for ceramics.

THE SOUTHEAST A TO Z

Arriving and Departing

By Boat

From Denia, Flebasa Lines (✉ Puerto de Denia, ☎ 96/578–4200) sails to Ibiza and Palma de Mallorca, 9 PM daily. From Almería, Trasmediterránea (☎ 950/236155) sails to Melilla, a Spanish outpost on the Moroccan coast, and to Tangier, Morocco.

By Bus

Private companies run buses down the coast, and from Madrid to Valencia/Benidorm/Alicante/Murcia/Mar Menor/Almería (☞ Getting Around, *below*).

By Car

The autopista A7 from Barcelona now runs through Valencia and Alicante as far as Murcia. Tolls, though quite high, are often worth it for the time saved, as well as for the safe driving conditions. The other main links with the region are the N III from Madrid to Valencia and the N301 from Madrid to Murcia via Albacete.

By Plane

The Southeast has four major airports: **Valencia** (☞ Chapter 8), **Alicante** (✉ El Altet, 12 km/7 mi south, ☎ 96/528–5011); **San Javier** (☎ 968/570073), for Mar Menor and Murcia; and **Almería** (6 km/3½ mi east, ☎ 951/220646). Iberia has the most flights (☎ 96/520–6000, 968/240050, or 950/230933).

By Train

For RENFE information, contact its offices in Valencia (☎ 96/352–9362), Alicante (☎ 96/522–3642), Murcia (☎ 968/252154), or Almería (☎ 950/251122).

Getting Around

By Boat

In summer there are crossings from both Alicante (☎ 96/521–6396) and Santa Pola (☎ 96/541–1113) to the island of Tabarca. From Benidorm, there are hourly crossings to the island of Plumbaria (⊙ 750 ptas. round-trip).

By Bus

Regular bus service connects the towns and cities of the region. Main bus depots are as follows: Alicante (✉ Avda. Portugal, ☎ 96/513–0700); Murcia, west of town (✉ Plaza San Andres, ☎ 968/292211); and Almería (✉ Plaza Barcelona, ☎ 950/221011).

By Car

Except for short distances, avoid coastal roads in summer. (The road that hugs the Almerian coast should be an exception to this rule.) Cars can be rented in the provincial capitals and all major resorts, though it is less expensive to rent ahead of time from the United States.

By Train

Frequent and comfortable RENFE trains connect the chief cities of the region. In addition there's an independent FGV line running along the Costa Blanca from Denia to Alicante.

Alicante has a RENFE station (✉ Avda. Salamanca, ☎ 96/522–6840) and a RENFE office (✉ Explanada de España 1, ☎ 96/521–1303); the FGV station is at the far end of Playa Postiguet (✉ Avda. Villajoyosa, ☎ 96/526–2731), reached by buses C1 and C2 from downtown. Murcia's RENFE station is some way out (⊠ Industria, ☎ 968/252154), but there is an office in town (⊠ Barrionuevo, ☎ 968/212842). Almería's station is off Carretera de Ronda (☎ 950/251135).

Guided Tours

Orientation Tours

The *ayuntamiento* or town hall (Plaza del Ayuntamiento), and travel agencies in Alicante organize tours of the city and bus and train tours to Guadalest, the Algar waterfalls, Benidorm, the Peñón de Ifach (Calpe), and Elche. From Benidorm, similar excursions are arranged by large hotels. The ayuntamiento in Elche (⊠ Plaça de Baix, ☎ 96/545–1240) organizes tours of the city and environs. From Mojácar, **Horizon** (⊠ Pueblo Indalo, ☎ 950/478376) tours the local countryside. In Murcia, contact **Alquibla** (⊠ González Adalid 13, ☎ 968/221219) for tours of the city and region, and in Almería, **Viajes Cemo** (⊠ Avda. Las Gaviotas, Urbanización Roquetas de Mar, ☎ 950/333502).

Special-Interest Tours

The ayuntamiento in Alicante also runs tours to Jijona, where you can visit one of the famous turrón nougat factories before seeing the amazing stalactites and stalagmites at the Cuevas de Canalobre (Canalobre Caves). This sometimes includes a concert in the cave.

Contacts and Resources

Consulates

United Kingdom: Alicante (⊠ Plaza Calvo Sotelo, ☎ 96/521–6022). **United States:** Valencia ⊠ C. La Paz 6, 3º, ☎ 96/351–6973. ☺ Weekdays 10–1.

Emergencies

Police: 091. **Ambulance:** Alicante (☎ 96/510–0822), Murcia (☎ 968/256900). **General medical assistance:** Alicante, Hospital del SVS (☎ 96/525–0060); Almería, Torrecárdenas (☎ 950/252211), Emergencies (☎ 950/235693).

Golf

Club de Golf Don Cayo (⊠ Conde de Altea 49, Altea, ☎ 96/584–0716), 9 holes; Campo de Golf Villa Martín (⊠ Apartado 35, Torrevieja, ☎ 96/676–5154), 18 holes; La Manga Club de Golf (⊠ Los Belones, ☎ 968/564511), two 18-hole courses; and Golf Almerimar (☎ 950/480950), 18 holes. Be sure to reserve tee times in advance, and expect to pay around 8,000 ptas. for 18 holes, 4,000 ptas. for nine.

Late-Night Pharmacies

Pharmacies in each town take turns staying open 24 hours. All pharmacies display the address of the *farmacia de guardia,* the one on duty that night.

Travel Agencies

Alicante: Viajes Barceló (⊠ San Telmo 9, ☎ 96/521–0011). **Benidorm:** Viajes Barceló (⊠ Gerona, Edif. Pinos, ☎ 96/585–4733). **La Manga del Mar Menor:** Viajes Hispania (⊠ Urbanización Las Sirenas 3, ☎ 968/564161). **Murcia:** Viajes Internacional Expreso 9 (⊠ Jaime I El Conquistador, ☎ 968/231662).

Visitor Information

Tourist offices offering information on the whole region are in **Valencia** (☞ Chapter 8); **Alicante** (⊠ Explanada de España 2, ☎ 96/520–0000); **Almería** (⊠ Parque Nicolas Salmeron, ☎ 950/274355); and **Murcia** (⊠ Alejandro Seiquer 4, ☎ 968/213716). Local tourist information of-

All the best trips start with **Fodors**.

EXPLORING GUIDES
Like the best of all possible travel magazines

"As stylish and attractive as any guide published." —*The New York Times*

"Worth reading before, during, and after a trip." —*The Philadelphia Inquirer*

More than 30 destinations available worldwide.
$19.95 - $21.00 ($27.95 - 28.95 Canada)

BERKELEY GUIDES

The hippest, freshest and most exciting budget-minded travel books on the market.
"Berkeley's scribes put the funk back in travel."
—*Time*

"Fresh, funny, and funky as well as useful."
—*The Boston Globe*

"Well-organized, clear and very easy to read."
—*America Online*

14 destinations worldwide. Priced between $13.00 - $19.50. ($17.95 - $27.00 Canada)

AFFORDABLES

"All the maps and itinerary ideas of Fodor's established Gold Guides with a bonus—shortcuts to savings." —*USA Today*

"Travelers with champagne tastes and beer budgets will welcome this series from Fodor's." —*Hartford Courant*

"It's obvious these Fodor's folks have secrets we civilians don't." —*New York Daily News*

Also available: Florida, Europe, France, London, Paris. Priced between $11.00 - $18.00 ($14.50 - $24.00 Canada)

At bookstores, or call **1-800-533-6478**

Fodors
The name that means smart travel.™

fices are at **Albacete** (✉ Virrey Morcillo 1, ☎ 967/215611); **Alicante** (✉ Avda. Portugal 17, ☎ 96/592–9802); **Benidorm** (✉ Avda. Martínez Alejos 166, ☎ 96/585–3224); **Calpe** (✉ Avda. Ejércitos Españoles s/n, ☎ 96/583–1350); **Cartagena** (✉ Plaza Castellini 5, ☎ 968/507549; ✉ Ayuntamiento, ☎ 968/506463); **Cullera** (✉ Calle del Riu 56, ☎ 96/152–0974); **Denia** (✉ Plaza Oculista Builges 9, ☎ 96/578–0724); **Elche** (✉ Parque Municipal, ☎ 96/545–3831); **Gandía** (✉ Marqués de Campo s/n, ☎ 96/287–7788); **Játiva** (✉ Moncada, ☎ 96/288–2561); **Jávea** (✉ Plaza Almirante Basterreche 24, ☎ 96/579–0736); **Lorca** (✉ López Gisbert, ☎ 968/466157); **Orihuela** (✉ Francisco Díez 25, ☎ 96/560–2747); **Santa Pola** (✉ Plaza Diputación, ☎ 96/541–1100); and **Torrevieja** (✉ Costera del Mar s/n, ☎ 96/685–1371).

10 The Balearic Islands

The strategic position of the Balearic Islands of Majorca, Menorca, Ibiza, and Formentera—off Spain's coast, halfway between France and Africa—has historically placed the archipelago in the middle of successive Mediterranean territorial disputes. While Menorca and Formentera remain largely unspoiled, great stretches of the coasts of Majorca and Ibiza have been marred by developments catering to tourists on package vacations. Still, Majorca's northern coast remains nearly as rough and irresistible as it was when George Sand and Frédéric Chopin spent a winter there a century and a half ago.

THE BALEARIC ISLANDS of Majorca, Menorca, Ibiza, and Formentera lie between 80 and 242 km (50 and 150 mi) from Spain's Mediterranean coast, halfway between France and Africa. Their strategic position made the islands an important maritime staging post, and they became, in turn, dominions of the Phoenician, the Roman, and the Byzantine empires before being occupied by the Moors in 902.

By Sean
Hignett

Updated by
George Semler

The Moors remained until ousted by Jaume I of the House of Aragón in the 13th century. For a brief period, the islands were an independent kingdom. In 1343, they became part of the Crown of Aragón under Pedro IV, and on the marriage of Isabella of Castile to Ferdinand of Aragón in 1469, the Balearics became part of a united Spain. During the War of the Spanish Succession, however, Britain occupied Menorca in 1704 to secure the superb natural harbor of Mahón as a naval base. The British remained for almost a century, interrupted only by an invasion in 1756 that gave the French control for 12 years and a shorter reoccupation by the Spanish 20 years later. Under the Treaty of Amiens, Great Britain finally returned Menorca to Spain in 1802.

Menorca diverged once more during the Spanish Civil War, declaring staunchly for the Republican cause while Majorca and Ibiza supported the Fascists. To this day, the topic is still one to be broached delicately within the islands, which, in many ways, remain fiercely independent of one another. Even Mahón and Ciutadella, at opposite ends of Menorca, all of 44 kilometers apart, remain locked in bitter opposition over historical differences and disputes never resolved.

The tourist boom, which started during the regime of General Franco, turned great stretches of the coastlines of Majorca and Ibiza into unplanned strips of high-rise hotels, fast-food restaurants, and discos. Recently, ecology-minded inhabitants have made some headway in lobbying for laws to restrict shoreline development.

In 1983 the Balearics became an autonomous province, and one effect has been the partial replacement of Castilian Spanish by the Catalan language (banned for official use by Franco) in its Mallorquín, Menorquín, and Ibizencan dialects. This is likely to confuse the visitor because outside the islands the Spanish names are still used. Within the islands the problem is compounded by the fact that where road signs have not been officially altered, they are sometimes obliterated by spray paints. In the sections that follow, Catalan or Spanish is used according to whichever seems to be used locally. *Carrer* (street) and *Plaça* (square) are Catalan; *calle* and *plaza* are Spanish.

Place names that may cause confusion are (Spanish version first):

Majorca: La Puebla/Sa Pobla; Santa Margarita/Santa Margalida; Colonia San Pedro/Colonia Sant Per; San Juan/Sant Joan. Road signs are sometimes sprayed with the word "Ciutat," meaning "the city," for example, Palma.

Menorca: Mahón/Maó; Ciudadela/Ciutadella.

Ibiza: Santa Inés/Santa Agnes; San Miguel/Sant Miquel; San Jorge/Sant Jordi; San Antonio Abad/Sant Antoni de Portmany; San José/Sant Josep; San Juan/Sant Joan; Ibiza/Eivissa (Ibiza town is also "Ciutat").

Formentera: San Francisco/Sant Francesc; San Fernando/Sant Ferran.

Pleasures and Pastimes

Beaches

Beaches are a major attraction in the Balearic Islands, although some of them are anything but peaceful and relaxing. Below is a listing of the major beaches on each of the islands:

MAJORCA

The closer it is to Palma, the more crowded a beach is likely to be. Going west from the city, Palma Nova/Magaluf, with a good, narrow beach, is backed by one of the noisiest resorts on the Mediterranean; Paguera, with several, small beaches, is the only sizable resort in this area not overshadowed by high-rises. Camp de Mar, a little farther along, with a good beach of fine, white sand, is small and relatively undeveloped but can be overrun with daytrippers arriving by bus and boat from other resorts. At the end of this coast, Sant Telm has a pretty little bay, with a tree-shaded parking lot.

East of Palma, a 5 km/3 mi stretch of sand runs beside the main coast road from C'an Pastilla to Arenals, the overbuilt package-tour mecca also known collectively as Playa de Palma. There's nothing wrong with the beach, but it's crowded.

The only real beach on the northwest coast is at Port de Sóller, an attractive bay nearly enclosed by its headlands. Cala St. Vicenç, at the top end of this coast, has fine, soft sand in an a narrow bay and is not overdeveloped. A little farther, on the north coast at Port de Pollença, sand has been imported, but it's an attractive resort, with good water sports. From Port de Pollença, there is a frequent watertaxi service to Formentor, one of the most attractive beaches on the island.

The north coast has the longest sand beach on the island. Shelving gently and backed in part by pines, it stretches 8 km/5 mi east from Port de Alcúdia to C'an Picafort and beyond.

On the map, the east coast may seem to be peppered with beaches and coves, but few are large. Canyamel, close to the Caves of Artà, is not over-commercialized.

A little farther south, Costa d'es Pins is an extensive, expensive urbanization, but it has a good, sandy stretch of public beach, backed by a thin line of pines. Tourist buses, disguised and decorated to look like train engines, run from here to Cala Millor, which has a long, narrow, sloping beach of soft sand. Much of the resort has pedestrian access only to the beach, so Cala Millor is ideal for children.

Moving south, Cala d'Or is a pleasant resort, and Cala Gran, a short walk away, is even more attractive. Cala Mondrajó, a tiny, sandy bay with little development and most easily reached by boat from Portopetre or Cala Figuera, is also a good bet.

On the south coast, the dune-backed beach at Es Trenc, near Colònia de Sant Jordi, is one of the few undeveloped Majorcan beaches.

MENORCA

North of Mahón, Mesquida is popular with the Mahonese, and you'll see few tourists. Beyond a watchtower on a headland is a second beach, free of development.

As you continue west, Es Grau, a sandy stretch with dunes behind it, is sometimes a bit littered. Behind Es Grau is the nature reserve of S'Albufera. Before the lighthouse at the end of Cap Favàritx are Cala Presili and Playa Tortuga, both nudist beaches. Arenal d'en Castell, a circular bay, sheltered and almost completely enclosed, and Arenal de Son

Saura, now known as Son Parc, are the biggest sandy beaches in the north of the island.

At the junction of the Mahón–Fornells and the Mercadal–Fornells roads, take the small lane leading west and follow signs to Binimellá, an excellent, sandy beach. It's often deserted, and the tiny coves to the west have small caves that give welcome shade in the summer months.

The only reasonable and generally accessible beach to the north of Ciutadella is Cala Morell. Menorcans claim that the coves of Cala Algaiarens are the nicest on the island, but a permanent guard with a radio telephone will allow only Menorcans onto the beach.

Son Saura, Cala en Turqueta, and Macarella, the beaches at the west end of the south coast, are all reached by driving southeast from Ciutadella toward Son Saura. You'll be halted by a gate and a sign prohibiting entry, but no one will bother you, provided you close the gate behind you. All are classical Menorcan beaches with trees to the water's edge, a horseshoe bay, and white sand. To the east, Cala Mitjana, Cala Trebaluger, Cala Fustam, and Cala Escorxada are accessible by land only on foot, but boats with outboard engines can be rented to reach them, as well as the Son Saura calas to the west. The long, straight, sandy stretches of Binigaus, Sant Adeodato, and Santo Tomas are reached from Mercadal, and Son Bou is reached from Alayor.

Cala 'n Porter is a British enclave. The rectangular cove has a sandy beach that is sheltered by cliffs and not too overrun.

IBIZA

Proceeding clockwise from Eivissa, immediately southwest is one of Ibiza's longest stretches of sandy beach at Playa d'En Bossa, now almost entirely developed. Farther on, a left turn at Sant Jordi on the way to the airport leads across the salt pans to the beaches of Cavallet and Mitjorn, two of the best on the island, with little development until recently. All beaches on Ibiza are topless, but Es Cavallet is the official nudist beach. The remaining beaches in this part of the island are all reached from the Eivissa–Sant Josep–Sant Antoni highway, down side roads that often end in rough tracks.

From Sant Antoni north, there are no easily accessible beaches until you reach Puerto San Miguel, an almost rectangular cove with relatively restrained development. Next along the north coast, reached via San Juan, is Portinaitx, a series of small coves with sandy beaches, of which the first and last, Cala Xarraca and Caló d'Es Porcs, are the best.

The beaches on the east coast have been developed, but Santa Eulàlia remains attractive. The resort has a narrow, sloping beach in front of a pedestrian promenade that, despite being entirely lined by hotels and apartment blocks, is not frenetic, like Sant Antoni.

FORMENTERA

Best for beaches is Formentera. Playa de Mitjorn is undeveloped and stretches for 7 km/4 mi along the south of the island. Trucadors, a long, thin spit at the north, has a mile of sand on each side, and in summer it is possible to wade to Es Palmador, where there are more sandy beaches. On Formentera, nudity is common.

Dining

MAJORCA

Seafood forms the basis of many local specialties, such as *espinigada* (a pie topped with tiny eels and spinach) and *panades de peix* (fish pies). Pork and its derivatives are also traditional. *Sobrasada* (the bright-red, Majorcan sausage paste) is basically pork and red pepper. Even the light and fluffy-looking *ensaimada* (the spiral pastry that ranges in size from a breakfast snack to a gift-boxed, party special a foot or more across) has *saim* (pork fat) as its essential ingredient. Other specialties are *butifarra* and *llonganissa* sausages and *cocas* (pastries filled with meat or a mixture of vegetables). *Frits* (fried sheep's intestines) may be offered as tapas or included in a main course, along with *seisos* (brains), and accompanied by *tumbet* (a ratatouille with potatoes). *Sopa Mallorquina* is fried vegetables in meat stock, usually served over pieces of thinly sliced bread; *escaldum* is a chicken broth thickened with potatoes and ground almonds.

MENORCA

Until recently Menorcan restaurant cuisine consisted almost entirely of seafood, offered by establishments lining the harbors in Mahón, Ciutadella, and the fishing village of Fornells. The last is famous for its very expensive *llagosta* (lobster), sold by weight and grilled or served as *caldereta* (soup). Lately, a country cuisine has developed, based on the slow-baked dishes traditionally served in the home.

Mayonnaise, which was invented in Menorca during the French occupation and named after Mahón, is usually freshly prepared. Local tapas include *tornellas* (sheep's intestines stuffed with bread crumbs, garlic, and meat, and braided and cooked).

IBIZA AND FORMENTERA

Because most produce comes to Ibiza and Formentera from the mainland via Palma, the cost of dining is often high. Sa Penya, the old fisherman's quarter that became famous as a hippie haven in the 1960s, is lined with restaurants of all styles.

CATEGORY	COST*
$$$$	over 7,500 ptas.
$$$	5,500–7,500 ptas.
$$	2,000–5,500 ptas.
$	under 2,000 ptas.

per person for a three-course meal, excluding drinks, service, and tax

Fiestas

MENORCA

Menorca's traditional fiestas are still essentially celebrations for the townsfolk and villagers and have changed not at all in deference to tourism. The summer round begins with the Feast of Sant Joan, in Ciutadella, on June 23, when *caixeres* (townspeople representing all classes) take part in a *jaleo,* dancing their horses to the sound of a band while the youths of the town attempt to make the animals rear up on their hind legs and to prove their virility by standing beneath. From July onward, fiestas follow one after another, ending with Mahón's Senyora de Gràcia (Nostra) in early September.

FORMENTERA

Sant Josep is known for its folk dancing; the Tourist Office in Eivissa will advise on dates and times. You can also see folk dancing at Sant Joan each Thursday evening and on June 24, the Feast of St. John the Baptist. July 15 and 16 are celebrated in honor of the Virgen del Carmen, the patron saint of sailors, with boat processions in the bay at Sant Antoni. Sant Francesc, on Formentera, has a fiesta with dancing on July 25, the Feast of St. James, the patron saint of Spain.

Lodging

MAJORCA

Majorca has more than 1,200 hotels, mostly serving the package-tour industry in the newer coastal resorts. Because they are often fully booked by tour operators, hotels in these resorts are not included in the selection below.

MENORCA

Apart from a few hotels and hostels in Mahón and Ciutadella, almost all the tourist accommodations are in newly developed beach resorts. As with the other Balearic islands, many of the hotels are fully reserved by travel operators in the high season, and it is more economical to book a package, including airfare and accommodations.

IBIZA AND FORMENTERA

The greatest concentration of hotels is in the coastal resorts of Sant Antoni and Playa d'En Bossa. Many of them are excellent, but unless you are anxious to be part of a mob, Sant Antoni has little to recommend it. Playa d'En Bossa, newer and close to Eivissa, is less brash, but it lies under the flight path of the airport.

CATEGORY	COST*
$$$$	over 20,000 ptas.
$$$	10,000–20,000 ptas.
$$	4,000–10,000 ptas.
$	under 4,000 ptas.

per standard double room, including tax

Exploring the Balearic Islands

Of the four main islands, Majorca and Ibiza are generally understood to be the most overdeveloped, while Menorca and Formentera remain less populated and wilder. The north coast of Majorca and parts of Ibiza still provide as much rocky coastline and diaphanous water as anyone can use at once, but—on balance—go to Formentera for solitude and intimacy, Ibiza for wilderness with heavy concentrations of humanity, Majorca for Palma's urban cosmopolitanism contrasted with the wild, north coast and parts of the interior, and Menorca for what may be the best blend of all of the above.

Great Itineraries

Visiting an archipelago or an island generally suggests going to a single destination and primarily staying there rather than exploring or touring a series of objectives. There are, however, inter-island flights and ferries for day excursions to neighboring isles, and over a stay of a week or 10 days, it would not be impossible to try to get a taste of each of the Balearic Islands.

A three-day visit to the Balearics requires making a choice and visiting just one island. Our choice would be Majorca for Palma's thick concentration of art and architecture with excursions to villages of the mountainous north coast and the interior. Five days would still suggest a one-island visit, with time to enjoy peace and quiet in one spot, as well as to explore the island. Ten days might just allow an ambitious and perhaps even hyper-curious traveller to see it all, and although we include an itinerary for this approach, we suggest a maximum of two islands, with maybe a day trip to Formentera or Ibiza. The most attractive 10-day suggestion, however, is to go someplace remote and quiet and collapse for the duration.

Numbers in the text below correspond to numbers in the margin and on the maps.

IF YOU HAVE 3 DAYS

Fly to ✈ **Palma de Mallorca** ① and spend your arrival day and the next morning exploring the historic center of this thick concentration of architectural and human treasure. On your second day, head for the hills, namely the Sierra de Tramuntana on the island's north coast and see the **Jardins d'Alfàbia** ②, **Sóller** ③, **Deya** ④, **Son Marroig** ⑤, and Sa Foradada before spending the night in 🖭 **Valldemossa** ⑥, where Frédéric Chopin and George Sand spent their best winter together. Your third day should be spent completing your exploration of the Tramuntana mountains. See Sa Granja and hike down into the Torrent de Pareis ravine and beach if you have time. See the monastery at Lluc before visiting the village and the port of **Pollença** ⑦. Alcúdia is the last stop before a 40-minute drive back to Palma de Mallorca for your last night.

IF YOU HAVE 5 DAYS

You can either do the Majorca loop from Palma, along the north coast and back through the center with more time to settle in and explore, or you can go to Menorca, a good fit for a five-day visit. Start from 🖭 **Mahón** ⑨ and spend a day exploring the city. On the second day, settle into some secluded beach hotel along the the southern coast. From there, combine sand and sun time with visits to the megalithic ruins and remains at Torre d'en Gaumés, Torralba, and Monte Toro on days three and four. Your fifth day can be dedicated to the remains at Naveta des Tudons, Cala Morell, and 🖭 **Ciutadella** ⑩.

When to Tour the Balearics

Summer is too hot and crowded. May and October are probably ideal, with June and September just behind. The winter, from November through March, is quiet and, while not always beach weather, good for walking, golfing, hunting, or hiking.

MAJORCA

Majorca, more than five times the size of either Menorca or Ibiza, is roughly saddle shaped. A tough mountain range, the Sierra de Tramuntana, soaring to nearly 5,000 feet, runs the length of the northwest coast; a ridge of hills borders the southeast shores; in between lies a great, flat plain that in early spring is a sea of almond blossoms, the "snow of Majorca." Though the island, with more than 5 million visitors per year, has the reputation of a cheap getaway, especially among British, the package-tour industry is confined to a narrow, coastal strip. Elsewhere, Majorca has relatively undiscovered charm, particularly in the mountains of the northwest and in the interior. It offers natural and historic sightseeing opportunities in caves, bird sanctuaries, abandoned monasteries, tiny museums, and village markets.

Numbers in the margin correspond with points of interest on the Majorca map.

Palma de Mallorca

① *A 40-minute flight from Barcelona.*

If you look at a map of the city of Palma, you will see, north of the cathedral—or La Seu, as it is known to Majorcans—the jumble of tiny streets around the Plaça de Cort that made up the early town. Farther out, a circle of wide boulevards, known as "the Avenues," zigzags around. These follow the path of the walls built by the Moors to defend the larger city that had grown up by the 12th century. The zigzags mark the bastions that jutted out at regular intervals. By the end of the last century the walls had largely been torn down, and the only place where the massive defenses can still be seen is along the seafront.

Through the middle of the old city ran a stream bed (*torrent*), dry for most of the year but, in the rainy season, often a raging flood that an-

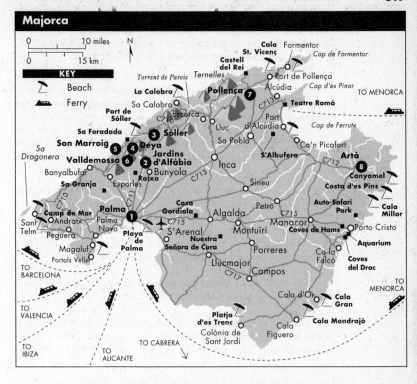

Majorca map

Majorca

nually caused destruction and drowning. In the 17th century this was diverted to the east, along the moat that ran outside the city walls. What was its natural course is now La Rambla and the Passeig d'Es Born, two of the principal shopping streets of Palma. The Born is also the place for the traditional evening *paseo* (promenade).

If you come by car, use the garage beneath the **Parc de la Mar.** On exiting, stroll along the park. Beside it run the huge bastions guarding the Almudaina Palace and the cathedral, golden and pinnacled. In the park are examples of **modern sculpture,** and **ceramic murals** by the late Catalan artist and Majorca resident Joan Miró.

From the Parc de la Mer, follow Avinguda Antoni Maura past the steps to the palace. At Plaça de la Reina, the **Born** begins—an avenue with a pedestrian promenade down its center and fashionable shops.

At the top of the Born, turn right on Carrer de la Unió, a little way along Plaça Santa Catalina Tomás. On the far side of the square the ornate facade of the building on the corner of Carrer Santacilia, now a **bank,** was designed by Antoni Gaudí.

Past the Palace of Justice—on the right—you'll find tucked in just before the steps leading up alongside the Teatro Principal, the **Forn Teatro** (Theater Bakery). You'll see pictures of it as a "typical Majorcan shop" in all the tourist literature, but in fact it's the only shop like this, with a facade that looks as though it came from a fairground organ. Forn Teatro is famous for its ensaimadas and its cocas. From the Forn Teatro, climb the steps to the Plaça Marqués Palmer. On the left an archway leads to the greater expanse of the **Plaça Major.** A good craft market is held here on Monday, Friday, and Saturday mornings 10–2.

From the Plaça Majors, make your way down Carrer Colon to Plaça Cort, where, on the south side of the square, is the 17th-century **Ajun-**

tament (Town Hall). The olive tree in the center of the square is reputed to be 500 years old. To the west of the Ajuntament, the Caja de Baleares Sa Nostra, on the corner of Carrer Jaume II and Plaça Cort, occupies a superb building designed in the style of Gaudí.

East of the Ajuntament, follow Carrer Cadena across Plaça Santa Eulàlia to Carrer Arquitecto Reynes and Plaça Sant Francesc. On the north of the plaza is the beautiful, **13th-century monastery church of Sant Francesc** founded by Jaume II when his eldest son took monastic orders and gave up rights to the throne. Later, Fray Junípero Serra, the missionary who founded San Francisco, was educated here. The entrance to the church and cloisters is through the collegiate buildings on the east side. 🖅 *350 ptas.* ⊘ *Mon.–Sat. 9:30–1 and 3:30–7.*

From the church of Sant Francesc, return to Plaça Santa Eulàlia. Ramón Llull, the 13th-century scholar, is said to have ridden his horse into the church of **Santa Eulàlia** in pursuit of a married lady of whom he was enamored in his wild, young days. It was in this church also that, in 1435, 200 Jews were converted to Christianity when their rabbis were threatened with being burned at the stake.

| NEED A BREAK? | For a light lunch on the plaza, **Café Moderno** has good *bocadillos* (sandwiches), while **Bar Santa Eulàlia** has tapas indoors. |

Just south of the plaza of Santa Eulàlia, off Carrer Morey, is Carrer Almudaina. The **archway** crossing the narrow street was one of the gates to the early Moorish citadel and, with the Arab Baths, is one of the few relics of Moorish occupation remaining on the island.

From the plaza of Santa Eulàlia continue down Carrer Morey and take the left fork down Carrer Portella. On the left at No. 5 is the **Museu de Majorca** (Museum of Majorca) with paintings and pottery ranging back to Moorish times. ⊘ *Tues.–Sat. 10–2 and 4–7, Sun. 10–2.*

At the bottom of Carrer Portella, turn left onto Carrer Formiguera, a short street that tunnels through the adjoining buildings, then turn left again—it's the only way you can go. A few yards up Carrer de la Serra, in a small garden, are the 10th-century **Banys Arabs** (Arab Baths). 🖅 *450 ptas.* ⊘ *Daily 10–1:30 and 4–6.*

The **Cathedral,** also known as La Seu, can be approached from the top of Carrer de la Serra, where you go left and follow the meandering streets west to Plaça Almoina, with its antiques shops and restorers, to the north of the cathedral. The visitor's entrance to the cathedral is here, through the **museum,** which displays ancient manuscripts, religious paintings, and precious jeweled crucifixes and reliquaries.

The cathedral proper is an architectural wonder. It took more than 300 years to build, from 1230 to 1601, and the open expanse of the nave is supported on 14 extraordinarily slender, 70-foot columns, which fan out like palm trees at the top. Look up the nave; suspended above the Chapel Royal is the curious, **asymmetrical canopy** constructed by Gaudí, who remodeled much of the interior at the beginning of this century. The lights, shining from within the canopy, come on at regular intervals, permitting photographs.

Be sure to take note of the **bell tower** above the cathedral's Plaça Almoina door. It holds nine bells, the largest of which is known as N'Eloi. N'Eloi was cast in 1389, weighs 4 tons, needs 12 men to ring it, and has been known to shatter the stained-glass windows with its sound. Continuing around the cathedral, you will come to the impressive **west facade.** The blocked windows are the result of alterations following earthquake damage in 1851. ▦ *450 ptas.* ◷ *Weekdays 10–12:30 and 4–6:30, Sat. 10–1:30.*

Opposite the Cathedral is the **Palau de l'Almudaina** (Almudaina Palace), originally an Arab citadel, which was the residence of the royal house of Majorca in the Middle Ages. It is now a military headquarters and can be visited only on guided tours (every half hour). If you go on Wednesdays and have an EU passport, you will get in free. ▦ *450 ptas.* ◷ *Weekdays 9:30–1:30 and 4–6:30, Sat. 9:30–1:30.*

Other key sights in Palma:

The **Llotja** (Exchange) on the seafront, a little west of the Born, was built in the 15th century as a commodities exchange. ◷ *Tues.–Sat. 11–2 and 5–9, Sun. 11–2, during exhibits only.*

The **Poble Espanyol** (Spanish Village) in the western suburbs of the city, is a kind of Disneyland of reproductions of Spanish buildings and styles with shops and crafts studios. ✉ *Carrer Capitán Mesquida Veny 39.* ▦ *450 ptas.* ◷ *Village daily 9–8, crafts shops, daily 10–6.*

Castell de Bellver (Bellver Castle) overlooks the city and the bay from a hillside above the Terreno nightlife area. Built on a circular design in the 14th century, there is a terrific view of Palma and the bay from its ramparts. ▦ *450 ptas.* ◷ *Oct.–Mar., Mon.–Sat. 8–6; Apr.–Sept., Mon.–Sat. 8–8.*

Dining and Lodging

$$$ ✕ **Koldo Royo.** The eponymous owner conjures up Basque specialties,
★ such as lamprey, salt cod, baked hake, tripe, and stuffed quail. The chic, yellow dining room, crowded with modern art, overlooks the marina. Try the *pechuquitas de codorniz rellenas de pétalos de rosas* (quail breasts stuffed with rose petals). ✉ *Passeig Marítim 3,* ☎ *971/457021. AE, MC, V. Closed Sun. No lunch Sat.*

$$$ ✕ **Porto Pi.** Dining in this old Majorcan villa in the Terreno area, 1 km/⅗ mi west of Plaza Gomila, is like eating in a private home. Several, high-ceilinged dining rooms, with round tables and oil paintings, lead off the elegant, central hall-cum-drawing room, and there's a terrace for the summer. The fine cooking is international. Try the *escalopines de foie gras a la parrilla* (barbecued escallops of foie gras). The once-excellent views over the bay have been almost totally obliterated by ugly, modern-apartment blocks. ✉ *Avda. Joan Miró 174,* ☎ *971/400087. AE, MC, V. Closed Sun. No lunch Sat.*

$$ ✕ **El Pilón.** In an old, vaulted building tucked between the top of the Born and Avinguda Jaume III, El Pilón has the widest range of tapas in town, from cheaper clams to more expensive eels. More substantial fish dishes can be chosen fresh from the tank. ✉ *Carrer Cifre 1,* ☎ *971/726034. AE, DC, MC, V. Closed Sun. and Feb.*

$ ✕ **Bon Lloc.** Just off the Born, decorated with New Age advertisements for massage and meditation; modern, square tables, and a tiled floor, this is the place for vegetarian food. There's a very good menú del día at lunch. ✉ *Carrer Sant Feliu 7,* ☎ *971/718617. No credit cards. Closed Sun. and Mon. No lunch Sat.–Thurs.*

$$$$ ✕▥ **Son Vida.** This Sheraton envelops a 13th-century castle on a hillside outside Palma. Antique furniture contrasts with the futuristic bronze-mirror interior of the El Jardín restaurant. Most rooms have panoramic views of Palma Bay to the south; a few standard rooms overlook the service area and hillside but are double size to compensate. ✉ *Castillo Son Vida, 07015,* ☎ *971/790000,* FAX *971/790017. 166 rooms with bath. 2 restaurants, 2 bars, indoor pool, 2 outdoor pools, beauty* *salon, 4 tennis courts, golf course, health club, library, playground, airport shuttle. AE, DC, MC, V.*

$$$$ ✕⊞ **Valparaiso Palace.** This hotel stands in landscaped gardens with
★   spectacular fountains and a small lake in a quiet district west of the
Poble Espanyol and Bellver Castle. After fire destroyed nearly the entire interior of the hotel in early 1995, the rooms were redesigned and
reconstructed completely. ⊠ *Carrer Fr. Vidal s/n, La Bonanova, 07015,*
☎ *971/400411,* FAX *971/405904. 138 rooms with bath. Restaurant, grill,
4 bars, outdoor and indoor pools, beauty salon, 2 tennis courts, miniature golf, health club, nightclub. AE, DC, MC, V.*

$$ ⊞ **Hotel Borne.** Right in the middle of Palma in a pedestrian street, the
★   building is a former mansion of one of Majorca's noble families. The
bedrooms are totally refurbished, but prices remain very reasonable.
Romanesque arches surround the central courtyard and reception
area. ⊠ *Carrer Sant Jaume 3, 07012,* ☎ *971/712942,* FAX *971/718618.
29 rooms with bath. AE, DC, MC, V.*

Nightlife and the Arts

The City of Palma Symphony Orchestra performs about twice a month
throughout the winter at the **Auditorium** (⊠ Passeig Marítim 18, ☎
971/234735), which also has ballet and theatrical performances
throughout the year, as does the **Teatre Principal** (⊠ adjacent to Plaça
Major, ☎ 971/784735).

With some 200 discos and music bars scattered throughout the city
and all over the island, Majorca's nightlife is never difficult to find. In
Palma itself, the **Plaça de la Lonja** is the place to go for "copas" (drinks,
tapas-sampling, and general carousing).

The most incandescent hot spots, however, are concentrated 6 km/3½
mi west of Palma at **Punta Portals** in Portals Nous, where King Juan
Carlos I moors his yacht along with those of many of Europe's most
beautiful people. **Tristan, Flannigan's,** and **Diablito** are the places to dine,
ranging in price and category from Tristan, the best and most expensive, to Diablito, which is a pizza emporium.

In the center of Palma, on the west side of the Born, **Carrer Apuntadores** is always lively at night. Passeig Marítim is another nucleus of
taverns and pubs, with **Tito's** and **Ib's** now the top places.

B.C.M. in Magaluf is the top disco.

Majorca's **Casino** is at Calvià, west of the city, and has a beach and
tennis club, as well as gambling; take your passport with you. ☎
971/454012. ☉ *Sun.–Thurs. 7 PM–4 AM, Fri. and Sat. 7 PM–5 AM.*

Outdoor Activities and Sports

GOLF

The island is well stocked with courses at **Canyamel** (⊠ Ctra. de las
Cuevas, 60 km/37 mi from Palma, ☎ 971/564457), with 18 holes; **Son
Vida** (⊠ adjacent to Sheraton Son Vida Hotel, 5 km/3 mi from Palma,
☎ 971/791210), with 18 holes; **Poniente** (Magalluf) (⊠ Ctra. Cala
Figuera, Calvia, ☎ 971/130148), with 18 holes; **Santa Ponça I** and **II**
(⊠ Calvia, ☎ 971/690211), with 18 holes on each course; **Real Golf
de Bendinat** (⊠ Ctra. Palma–Portals Nous, 5 km/3 mi from Palma, ☎
971/405200), with 9 holes; **Pollença** (⊠ Ctra. Palma–Pollença, Km 49.3,
☎ 971/533216), with 9 holes; **Vall d'Or** (⊠ Ctra. Porto Colom–Cala
d'Or, Km 7.7, ☎ 971/837001), with 9 holes; **Son Servera** (⊠ Bahía
de Los Pinos, ☎ 971/567802), with 9 holes; **Capdepera Golf Club** (⊠
Ctra. Palma a Cala Ratjada, Km 71, ☎ 971/56–58–75), with 18
holes; and **Son Antem** (⊠ Ctra. Lluchmayor-Palma, 3½ km/2 mi from

Lluchmayor [call Balearic Golf Federation, ⊠ Avda. Jaime III 17, Palma, ☎ 971/722753]), with 18 holes.

HORSEBACK RIDING

The Riding School of Majorca is at Km 12 on the Palma–Sóller road (☎ 971/613157).

SAILING

Balearic Sailing Federation (⊠ Avda. Joan Miró s/n, Palma, ☎ 971/40–25–12). The **Club de Mar in Palma** (☎ 971/403611), with its own hotel, bar, disco, and restaurant, is famous among yacht sailors and can provide details of other clubs on the island.

SCUBA DIVING

Check with **Escuba Palma** (⊠ C. Jaume I s/n, ☎ 971/694968).

TENNIS

Tennis is widely practiced, available at many hotels and at private clubs and tennis schools—or call the **Tennis Center** (⊠ Plaça de Santa Ponçay, ☎ 971/690414).

WALKING

Majorca is a walker's paradise, particularly in the mountains of the northwest, the Serra de Tramuntana. It's worth asking the Tourist Office for the excellent free booklet *20 Hiking Excursions on the Island of Majorca,* which has detailed maps and itineraries, although, sadly, it's now out of print. *12 Classic Hikes Through Majorca,* by the German author Herbert Heinrich, has excellent drawings and maps.

WATER SPORTS

Water sports of all varieties are, not surprisingly, practiced everywhere around Majorca. Windsurfers and dinghies are available for rental at most beach resorts. Yacht-berthing facilities are available all around the island. Skin and scuba diving are excellent.

Shopping

Specialties of Majorca are leather shoes and clothing, porcelain, souvenirs carved from olive wood, and artificial pearls.

In Palma big-name fashion stores line the Avinguda Jaume III; less expensive shopping areas are Carrer Sindicat and Carrer Sant Miquel, both pedestrian streets running north from Plaça Major, and the jumble of small streets south of Plaça Major. The square itself has an excellent crafts market.

Here's a selection, all central in Palma. **Leather:** Loewe (⊠ Borne 2), Pink (⊠ Plaça Pio XII), Piza (⊠ Carrer Sant Nicolau 20). **Pearls:** Perlas Majorica (⊠ Avinguda Jaume III 11). **Antiques:** Persepolis (⊠ Avinguda Jaume III 22), Casa Belmonte (⊠ La Rambla 8), and shops on Plaça Almoina. **Pottery:** Las Columnas (⊠ opposite tourist office, Carrer Sant Domingo 24). **Gift-wrapped ensaimadas** (fluffy, sweet Majorcan pastry) of all sizes: Forn Teatro (⊠ Plaça de Weyler, at foot of steps leading to Plaça Major).

Raixa

13 km (8 mi) north of Palma.

After about 13 km/8 mi out of Palma, look to the left to see Raixa, an 18th-century palace in the midst of landscaped gardens, at the top of a great flight of steps with statues and fountains on each side.

Jardins d'Alfàbia

2 *4 km (2½ mi) from Raixa on the right.*

Enter the gates to the Jardins d'Alfàbia (Alfàbia Gardens). At the top of the steps is a huge, vaulted cistern, built by a Moorish overlord to irrigate the gardens. A path leads around to a café and then winds through a small, thick wood. The chief attraction of the gardens is that they are there at all in a climate where water is not abundant. The house itself is furnished with antiques and lined with painted paneling. ✉ *450 ptas.* ⊙ *Nov.–Mar., Mon.–Sat. 9:30–5; Apr.–Oct., Mon.–Sat. 9:30–6:30; closed holidays.*

Sóller

3 *17 km (11 mi) north of Raixa; 30 km (19 mi) north of Palma.*

Sóller is an attractive, gray-stone town with a hardy, outdoorsy feel. Find your way to the main Plaça Constitució, dominated by the cathedral; arm yourself with a map from the Tourist Office in the Ajuntament; then hop on a tram down to the harbor (☞ *Getting Around by Train in* The Balearic Islands A to Z, *below*).

NEED A BREAK?
> Opposite the town hall on the Plaça Constitució, with characteristic Majorcan decor—white walls and little else—is the earthy **Sa Cova d'En Jordi** (☎ 971/633222), a great restaurant for typical Majorcan fare; try the *sopa Mallorquina,* a local vegetable stew.

Dining and Lodging

$–$$ ✕🏠 **Es Port.** The 15th-century manor house, built around a central courtyard, is the ancestral home of the Montis family, who have added a modern extension and run it as a hotel. The heavily beamed restaurant is in an old mill, where the olive press makes a striking centerpiece. Rooms in the old part have more character. The hotel's only drawback is its size, which attracts tour groups. ✉ *Carrer Antoni Montis s/n, Port de Sóller 07108,* ☎ *971/631650,* FAX *971/631662. 156 rooms with bath (plus 10 cottage accommodations). Restaurant, bar, pool, 3 tennis courts, playground. AE, MC, V.*

$ ✕🏠 **El Guía.** An elegant, old house typical of those built by the mer-
★ chants of this town on the rich rewards of the citrus trade, El Guía is furnished in keeping with its fin de siècle style. The excellent restaurant serves Majorcan specialties. ✉ *Carrer Castanyer 3, 07100,* ☎ *971/630227,* FAX *971/632634. 20 rooms with bath. Restaurant. AE, MC, V. Closed Nov.–Apr.*

Deya

4 *About 9 km (5 mi) from Sóller.*

Deya was made famous by the writer Robert Graves, who lived in the village. The local bar—up some steps on the left as you enter the village—is still the haunt of writers and artists. On warm afternoons, you'll find them congregated in the beach bar in the rocky cove, a 2 km/1 mi walk down from the village. Park here and walk up the narrow street, lined with titled Stations of the Cross, to the village church. From the small cemetery behind it, there are marvelous views of mountains terraced with olive trees, and of the coves below.

Dining and Lodging

$$$$ ✕🏠 **La Residencia.** A former 16th-century manor house, set in olive
★ and citrus groves above the village, the hotel is superbly furnished with antiques, modern canvases, and four-poster beds. The arched dining

room was formed from an old olive mill. ✉ *Son Moragues, 07179,* ☎ *971/639011,* FAX *971/639370. 65 rooms with bath. Restaurant, bar, pool, tennis courts. AE, DC, MC, V.*

$ ✕🏨 **Costa d'Or.** This attractive villa, a little way north of Deya, is set on the terraced cliffside with a footpath down to the cove. ✉ *Llucalcari, 07179,* ☎ *971/639025. 42 rooms with bath. Restaurant, pool. Closed Nov.–Apr.*

Son Marroig

❺ *4 km (2 mi) west of Deya.*

A little way beyond Deya is Son Marroig, one of the estates of Austrian archduke Luis Salvador (1847–1915), who arrived in Majorca as a young man and fell in love with the island. The archduke, who spoke 14 languages and wrote innumerable books on every aspect of Majorca, its history, its wildlife, and its folklore, acquired estates and built great houses, mostly along the northwest coast, which he adorned with miradors at each spectacular viewpoint. Son Marroig, now a museum but much as it was in the time of the archduke, contains his collection of Mediterranean pottery and ceramics, old Majorcan furniture, and paintings. ▦ *350 ptas.* ⊙ *Apr.–Oct., Mon.–Sat. 9:30–2:30 and 4:30–8; Nov.–Mar., Mon.–Sat. 9:30–2:30 and 4:30–6.*

From the mirador you can see, nearly 1,000 feet below, **Sa Foradada** ("perforated"), a spectacular rock peninsula, pierced by a huge archway under which the archduke moored his yacht. A pathway, adjacent to the café in the parking area, leads down to Sa Foradada (1 hour down, 1½ hours up). Four km/2½ mi farther, behind a restaurant on the right, is another of the archduke's miradors, **Ses Pites.**

En Route Now the road moves slightly inland and, in 2 km/1 mi, a left turn will take you into Valldemossa.

Valldemossa

❻ *18 km (11 mi) north of Palma.*

The tourist office, in the plaza next to the church, sells a ticket that gives admission to the monastery's various attractions. The **Reial Cartuja** (Royal Carthusian Monastery) was founded in 1339 but, on the expulsion of the monks in 1835, was privatized, and the cells became lodgings for travelers. Later they were leased as summer apartments, which they largely remain today. The most famous lodgers were Frederic Chopin and his mistress, the French novelist George Sand, who spent three tempestuous months here in the winter of 1839.

The guided tour of the monastery begins in the **church.** Note the frescoes above the nave—the monk who painted them was Goya's brother-in-law. The next stop, in the cloisters, is perhaps the most interesting: a **pharmacy,** equipped by the monks in 1723 and still almost exactly as it was. Up a long, wide corridor are the apartments occupied by Chopin and George Sand, furnished in period style. Only the piano is original—the effort required to transport it here from France and up the mountains was monumental. Nearby, another set of apartments houses the local **museum,** with mementos of archduke Luis Salvador and a collection of old printing blocks. From here, you return to view the ornately furnished rooms of what was originally **King Sancho's Palace,** where you may find a performance of local folk dancing. ▦ *850 ptas.* ⊙ *Nov.–Mar., Mon.–Sat. 9:30–1 and 3–5:30; Apr.–Oct., Mon.–Sat. 9:30–1 and 3–6:30.*

Dining and Lodging

$$$–$$$$ ✕⊡ **Vistamar.** An old *finca* set in 250 acres of olive groves overlooking the sea provides the setting for this charming, small hotel. The building has been faithfully restored; the sitting rooms and bedrooms have exposed beams, heavy furniture, and modern art. The Vistamar won popularity for its excellent Mediterranean cooking. ⊠ *Ctra. Valldemossa–Andratx, Km 2, 07170,* ☎ *971/612300,* ⅀ *971/612583. 18 rooms with bath. Restaurant, bar, pool. AE, MC, V. Closed Nov.–Feb.*

Sa Granja

21 km (13 mi) northwest of Palma.

Sa Granja (the Farm) was built by a noble family in the 17th century on what had been a farm. The family created pools and landscaped gardens. The house is now a historical museum of the Majorcan countryside, including an olive mill and free samples of country produce and pies made on the premises. If you are there at the right time, you may be able to see an exhibition of folk dancing. The admission fee also entitles you to a sampling of local wines and pastries. ☎ *971/610032.* ⅀ *850 ptas., folk dancing 400 ptas.* ☉ *House daily 10–6 (until 7 in June), folk dancing Wed. and Fri. 3:30–5.*

Inca

28 km (17 mi) east of Palma.

Drive east along the Passeig Marítim from Palma and take the bypass north. Follow it for about 3 km/2 mi to the Inca turnoff, a fast autopista for the first 8 km/5 mi until it rejoins the old Inca road, C713. Inca is known for its leather factories and Thursday market.

Shopping

Along the Inca road you'll find **siurells** (brightly colored, ceramic whistles) at Cabaneta, **pottery** at Marratxi, and **ilengos** (a traditional peasant fabric) at Santa María, where the amusingly named Mas Vieja que mi Abuela ("older than my grandmother") sells **antiques.** Inca has, in addition to **leather** factories, **galletas** (traditional local biscuits).

Alcúdia

54 km (34 mi) northeast of Palma.

Circle around the restored remains of Alcudia's **Moorish city walls** outside which, on Sundays and Tuesdays, you'll find a market. Inside, in the maze of narrow streets, are some fine, **17th-century houses** and the excellent **Museu Argueològic Municipal** with Roman and prehistoric items. ⊠ *Carrer Sant Jaume 2.* ☉ *Tues.–Sat. 10:30–1:30 and 3:30–6:30, Sun. 10:30–1:30.*

Just past Alcúdia on the right, a sign-posted road leads to the small **Teatre Romá** (Roman Amphitheater), which is carved directly from the rock. This was excavated in the 1950s and is permanently open.

From the Teatre Romá return toward town and, at the Inca junction, keep right for Port de Pollença. **Port de Pollença** is less hectic than many of Majorca's coastal resorts, and there are cafés and bars along the seafront where you can relax.

Outdoor Activities and Sports

BICYCLING

Bicycling is excellent in the flatlands around Port de Pollença; Alcúdia and C'an Picafort on the north coast are ideal for cycling. The roads have special bike lanes; rental outlets are on every block.

Pollença

❼ *5 km (3 mi) inland of the port.*

Climb the **Calvari,** a stone staircase of 365 steps. From the top there is a good view of the bays, Alcúdia and Pollença, and Capes Formentor and Pinar. Almost opposite the turnoff to Ternelles is Pollença's **Roman Bridge,** the only one on the island.

OFF THE
BEATEN PATH
CAP DE FORMENTOR – If you enjoy twisty, scenic roads to nowhere, pack a picnic and drive to Cap de Formentor, north of Puerto de Pollença. The road threads its way among huge teeth of rock before reaching a lighthouse at the extreme tip, where there is a spectacular view.

Dining and Lodging

$$$$ ✕🔝 **Formentor.** This famous hotel, founded in 1929, is beautifully situated at the northern tip of the island, with terraced gardens descending to an attractive, private beach where there is a barbecue at lunchtime. The building is long and white, the bedrooms comfortable but no more than par for hotels of this price; despite the remote site, it lacks intimacy. Former guests include the Duke of Windsor, Winston Churchill, Charlie Chaplin, Aristotle Onassis, and the Spanish royal family. ✉ 07460, ☎ 971/899100, 🖷 971/865155. *127 rooms with bath. Restaurant, grill, 3 bars, beauty salon, miniature golf, 5 tennis courts, horseback riding, boating, windsurfing, waterskiing, playground, airport shuttle. AE, DC, MC, V. Closed Jan. 15–Mar. 8.*

Lluc

20 km (12 mi) west of Port de Pollença.

The monastery of Lluc has a **17th-century church** and a **museum** with an eclectic collection of ceramics, paintings, clothing, folk costumes, and religious items. A boys' choir performs in the chapel at 11:15 AM and 8 PM (except June–mid-September). 🔝 *Museum 500 ptas.* ☉ *Museum Nov.–Mar., daily 10–5:30; Apr.–Oct., daily 10–6:30.*

Dining and Lodging

$
★
✕🔝 **Santuari de Lluc.** This is one of several monasteries on Majorca that offer accommodations. Some of the simply furnished monastic cells have kitchens; not all have baths. All have tiled floors and rather meager beds. The setting is terrific, high in the mountains between Sóller and Pollença. ✉ *Santuari de Lluc, 07315,* ☎ *971/517025. 113 rooms, 97 with bath. 3 restaurants, 2 cafeterias. MC, V.*

Torrent de Pareis

2 km (1¼ mi) east of Sa Calobra.

From Sant Pere Church in Escorca you can hike down the Torrent de Pareis, a ravine that drops dramatically to the sea. (Use proper footwear and don't go alone.)

En Route The turn to Sa Calobra is worth taking if you want to see the bottom of the Torrent without climbing down. The road descends in a series of sharp loops to the Mediterranean, but the touristy town and beach at its end is a letdown. Beyond the Sa Calobra junction, C710 passes through tunnels and beside reservoirs, with terrific views. If you have time, a short detour left through Fornalutz and Biniaraix is worthwhile before you reach Sóller.

Fornalutx/Biniaraix

East of Soller.

Both Fornalutz and Biniraix have been spruced up in recent years by tourist money, but their honey-colored, cobbled plazas and stepped streets are still undeniably charming. Each has its resident artist colony.

Banyalbufar

23 km (14 mi) northwest of Palma.

Make a quick stop at this tiny town perched high on a cliff overlooking its tiny harbor.

Dining and Lodging

$$ ✕⌷ **Mar y Vent.** The small, modern, family-run hotel is at the north
★ end of this very quiet village where the land was terraced by the Romans. Paths lead down to two, small, rocky coves for sea bathing. All the rooms, furnished in traditional style, have good sea views. ✉ *Carrer Major 49, 07191,* ☎ *971/610025. 19 rooms with bath. Restaurant, bar, pool, tennis courts. No credit cards. Closed Dec. and Jan.*

Andratx

25 km (16 mi) southwest of Banyalbufar.

Andratx is a pleasantly laidback town overlooked by the 3,300-foot Mt. Galatzo. There is an enjoyable route, on foot or by car, from here through S'Arracó to the **Castell Sant Telmo,** and on to the rocky shore opposite the **Isla Dragonera.**

Santa Ponsa

15 km (9 mi) west of Palma.

Santa Ponsa is a fishing and gin palace town that you can make a quick stop in before returning by way of the C719 and the autopista to Palma.

Excursions Around Majorca

Artà

❽ *78 km (48 mi) from Palma.*

The hills of the northeast, beyond Artà, are almost without roads, and Artà is less frequented by tourists. The north side of the town is dominated by its **castle** and the **church of San Salvador.** Just below the church, a sign points (somewhat ambiguously; confirm the direction) to the **Ermita de Betlem,** some 9 km/5 mi farther on. The road soon degenerates into a rocky track that twists hair-raisingly up between dwarf palms and sea holly and then circles down to the isolated hermitage, the home of a small number of hermit monks. Behind it, a path leads up the hillside to a mirador with fine views.

Randa
26 km (16 mi) from Palma.

For a jaunt close to Palma, take C715 east from the city to PM501, turn right, and follow signs to Llucmajor until, after about 3 km/2 mi, a left turn leads to Randa. At the center of this tiny village, turn right and follow a twisting road up the Puig de Randa, on which are three separate hermitages. From the terrace of the Franciscan monastery of **Nuestra Señora de Cura** on the summit, you will find the best views. The monastery was founded in the 13th century by philosopher Ramón Llull (☞ Palma, *above*), and its library contains many valuable books that, during quiet times, you may be able to see. Adjacent to the terrace are a bar and restaurant, and the monastery has rooms and apartments to rent. ✆ Moastery 350 ptas. ☉ Monastery Tues.–Thurs. 10–1 and 4–6, Fri. 10–1.

MENORCA

Menorca, northernmost island of the archipelago, is a cliffbound, rather knobbly plateau with a single central hill, Monte Toro, from whose 1,100-foot summit the whole island can be seen. Prehistoric monuments—*taulas* (huge stone T shapes), *talayots* (spiral cones made of stone), and *navetes* (stone structures shaped like upturned boats)—left by the first Neolithic settlers are thickly scattered over the countryside. Menorca shows the influence of its century of British rule in its Georgian-style architecture (especially in Mahón); its landscape of small and tidy fields bounded by hedgerows and drystone walls, and grazed by Holsteins; and in its language, which is sprinkled with English words. Tourism came late to Menorca, partly because it was traditionally more prosperous and, thus, less eager than its neighbors to encourage visitors, but also because Franco deliberately punished the Republican island by restricting tourist development there. Starting late, Menorca has managed to avoid many of the teething troubles of the other islands. There are no high-rise hotels, and its herringbone road system, with a single central highway, has meant that each resort is small and separate.

Numbers in the margin correspond to points of interest on the Menorca map.

Mahón

❾ *44 km (27 mi) east of Ciutadella.*

In Mahón, start from the northwest corner of the Plaça de s'Explanada and turn right onto Carrer Comte de Cifuentes. At No. 25 is the **Ateneo,** a cultural and literary society where visitors are welcome to view the collection of wildlife, seashells, seaweed, minerals, and stuffed birds. On the staircase are ceramics and old tiles and, in side rooms, paintings, prints, maps, and mementos of Menorcan writers, poets, and musicians. ✆ *Free.* ☉ *Daily 10–2 and 3–10.*

From the Ateneo: At the end of Carrer Comte de Cifuentes, turn left onto Carrer Dr. Orfila, a principal shopping street; then take the second right onto Carrer Bastió (Costa d'en Ga). Where the street curves left is the **Teatre Principal,** built in 1824 as an opera house and now a cinema and theater. You can usually manage to peep inside at the semicircular auditorium, whose columns support tiers of boxes and a gilded ceiling. Continue down Costa d'en Ga into Plaça Reial.

NEED A BREAK? | The **American Bar** on Plaça Reial is the place to watch the passing parade. Don't be in a hurry; they're not. Try the **Andalucía** next door.

S'Arravaleta, a pedestrian street with more smart shops, leads from Plaça Reial to Plaça del Carme. Up to the right is the **Verge del Carme Church,** which houses a fine painted and gilded retablo. Adjoining the church, you'll find the cloisters, now surprisingly a **public market.** As you pick your way between the colorful piles of fruit and vegetables, notice the carvings on the west and north walls.

From the Verge del Carme Church, return up S'Arravaleta and turn right onto Carrer Nou. At the end is Plaça de la Constitució, domi-

Menorca

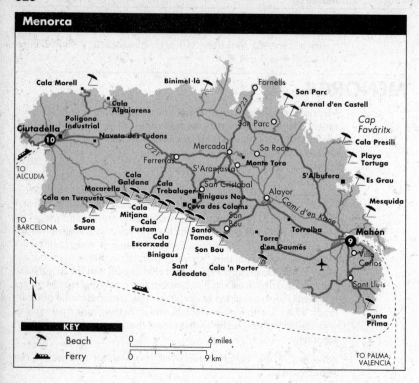

nated by the **Church of Santa María,** originally 13th-century but rebuilt in the 18th century during the British occupation. It was restored after being sacked during the Spanish civil war. The pride of the church is the 3,200-pipe Baroque organ, imported from Austria in 1810.

Behind the Santa María church is **Plaça de la Conquesta,** with a statue of Alfons III of Aragón. At the end of the tiny Carrer Alfons III that leads off the square is the best view of Mahón harbor.

Returning to the Plaça de la Constitució, you will find the **Ajuntament** on the right. Stroll up Carrer Isabel II, a pleasant street of fine houses. Notice the statue of the Virgin up on the wall on the corner of Carrer de Rosari and the **Governor's Palace** and courtyard on the right.

From the Carrer de Rosari return to the Ajuntament, and follow Carrer Port de Sant Roc immediately opposite. Ahead you'll see the 16th-century **San Roque Gate,** the only remnant of the city walls, which were built to protect Mahón from the pirate Barbarossa (Redbeard).

Dining and Lodging

$$$ ✕ **Jágaro.** Here you find an open-air feel with lots of greenery in the recently enlarged garden and huge windows overlooking the harbor. The conservatory is understandably very popular in summer. The seafood dishes are more inventive than elsewhere; try the carpaccio *de mero* (halibut). ⊠ *Moll de Llevant 334,* ☎ *971/362390. AE, MC, V. Closed Oct.–Apr. No dinner Sun. or Mon.*

$$$ ✕ **Rocamar.** At the extreme end of the twisting, quayside road in the direction of Villa Carlos, this restaurant is an established favorite that serves simply prepared, fresh seafood. You dine 4 floors up overlooking the creek, surrounded by dark wood paneling and maritime lights. The *pimientos rellenos de langostinos* (peppers stuffed with prawns)

are superb. ⊠ *Cala Fonduco 32, Port,* ☎ *971/365601. AE, DC, MC, V. Closed Mon. No dinner Sun. in winter.*

$ ⊠ ✕ **Bar Europa.** An ordinary town bar just behind the Esplanade, Eu-
★ ropa serves the best tapas in Menorca. The long list includes *pescado escabeche* (pickled fish), *caracoles* (snails), *cranca* (crab), *lomo con col* (meat in cabbage leaves), *marejas* (lamb tripe), *frito* (chitterling), *pulpo* (octopus), and *callos* (tripe). Red Damm beer crates and Formica ta-bles make up the decor. ⊠ *Carrer Cifuentes 68,* ☎ *971/361379. No credit cards. Closed Wed.*

$$–$$$ 🏨 **Port Mahón.** The only high-quality hotel actually in Mahón is mag-nificently situated overlooking the estuary in extensive, terraced gar-dens in a quiet, residential district. Steps lead directly down to the fashionable bars and restaurants that line the harbor. ⊠ *Avda. Fort de L'Eau s/n, 07700,* ☎ *971/362600,* FAX *971/364595. 74 rooms with bath. Restaurant, bar, piano bar, pool, beauty salon. AE, DC, MC, V.*

$$ 🏨 **Almirante (Collingwood House).** The 18th-century residence of Ad-miral Lord Collingwood is located between Mahón and Villa Carlos, with spectacular views over the creek. The Georgian house became a hotel in 1964 but retains its original character. Cottage accommoda-tions around a swimming pool were added later. ⊠ *Ctra. Villacarlos s/n, 07720,* ☎ *971/362700. 38 rooms with bath. Restaurant, bar, pool, 1 tennis court, game room. MC, V. Closed Nov.–Apr.*

Nightlife and the Arts

The bars opposite the ferry terminal in Mahón harbor are the late-night spots for locals. Discos include **Factory** in a cave at the edge of Mahón, just past the traffic circle on the Villa Carlos road (⊠ Sá Sinia de's Muret, ☎ 971/366368); **Pachá,** a branch of Ibiza's famous nightspot, on the left at the entrance to San Luis; and **Cova d'en Xoroi,** in a pirate's cave in the cliff high above the sea at Cala 'n Porter.

Outdoor Activites and Sports

BIRD-WATCHING

S'Albufera, a wetland nature reserve north of Mahón, attracts many species of migratory birds.

DIVING

Equipment and lessons are available at Cala En Bosc, Son Parc, and Cala Tirant. Compressed air is available at Club Marítimo, Mahón and Club Náutico, Ciutadella. The only decompression chamber on the is-land is at S'Algar.

GOLF

Urbanización Son Parc (☎ 971/368806), 9 holes, with 9 more under construction) has the only course.

HORSEBACK RIDING

There are stables on the left of the main road between Alayor and Mer-cadal, just after the turn to the new *urbanización* of Torre Son Bou, as well as between Sant Climent and Cala 'n Porter. Elsewhere on the is-land, look for the sign *picadero* (riding school). **Es Fornás** (⊠ Box 842, ☎ 971/364422) in Mahón organizes equestrian tours of the island by day or night for beginner and advanced riders, and tours by carriage.

WALKING

In the south, each cove has a barranca (ravine or gully) leading down to it, often from several miles inland, which makes a pleasant, untax-ing excursion. The head of **Barranca Algendar** is down a small, un-marked road immediately on the right of the Ferreries–Cala Galdana road. The barranca ends in the beach resort of Cala Galdana.

WINDSURFING AND SAILING

Knowledgeable windsurfers and dinghy sailors head for Fornells Bay. Several miles long and a mile wide, but with a narrow entrance to the sea, it gives the beginner a feeling of security and the expert plenty of excitement. **Windsurfing Fornells** (☎ 971/376636) rents boards and offers excellent lessons in English and Spanish.

A little south of Fornells, at Ses Salines on the same bay, **Minorca Sailing Holidays** (✉ 256 Green La., London N134XE, ☎ 0181/8867193) offers a package that includes airfare and accommodations with opportunities to enjoy the rest of the island.

Shopping

Menorca is known for **shoemaking** and **gin,** both introduced by the British. The Xoriguer distillery on Mahón quayside, close to the ferry terminal, offers a guided tour, free samples, and bottles for sale. **Fashionable footwear** can be found along Carrer Dr. Orfila. In Mahón, there's **leatherwear** at Marks (✉ S'Arravaleta 18 and Hanover 38), Patricia (✉ 31/33 Carrer Dr. Orfila), and Musupta (✉ S'Arravaleta 26) and **costume jewelry,** also a local specialty, at Bali (✉ corner of Carrer de Lluna). Up on the Esplanade, there's an open-air market with cheap clothing and souvenirs.

Ciutadella

🔟 *44 km (27 mi) west of Mahón.*

Before the British came and set up their capital in Mahón, Ciutadella was capital of Menorca, and its history and architecture are much richer than Mahón's. As you arrive from Mahón by way of the main road across the island, turn left at the traffic lights and circle the old part of the city to the north end of the coniferous **Plaça de s'Explanada.** Turn left here, down Camí de Sant Nicolau. At the end, near an old watchtower and two rather rusty cannons, is a **monument to David Glasgow Farragut,** the first admiral of the U.S. Navy, whose father emigrated from Ciutadella to the United States. From here you also get a good view of the distant jagged peaks of Majorca.

From the Farragut monument, return up Sant Nicolau and park near the Plaça d'es Born. Next to the Ajuntament, on the west side of the Born, steps lead up to the **Mirador d'es Port,** from which you can survey the whole length of Ciutadella Creek. The **Ajuntament** houses the local museum, a repository of anything to do with the city—old street signs, keys, shoes, even a record of land grants made by Alfons III after defeating the Moors. ☉ *Daily 10–1 and 4–6.*

Circle the Born to the north, with more views of the narrow harbor. The monument in the center of the plaza commemorates the resistance of the citizens to an invasion by the Moors in 1588. Continue south along the east side of the Born. The whole of this first block is the **palace of the Torresaura family.** It's worth going into one of the tiny shops here to look at the complex pattern of archways and stairwells.

Turn left into Carrer Major to enter the old city, where you'll find many interesting brass and bronze door fixtures. On the left, at No. 8 (even palaces have street numbers!), over the doorway of the Palau Torresaura, is a strange carving of a veiled female face. On the right is the **Palau Salort,** its door knockers carved to resemble entwined serpents. The latter is the only noble's house regularly open to the public. The coats of arms on the ceiling are those of the families Salort (a salt pit and a garden: *sal* and *ort,* or *huerta*) and Martorell (a marten). ☉ *Mon.–Sat. 10–2.*

From the Palau Salort, continue up Carrer Major to Plaça de la Catedral (Plaça Píus XII). Inside the Gothic **cathedral** you'll find beautifully carved woodwork and choir stalls. The side chapel has round Moorish arches with intricate carving, remnants of the mosque that was originally on this site.

From the cathedral, turn south from the Plaça de la Catedral onto Carrer Roser. Turn left onto Carrer Santíssims, where, on the right, there is another **noble home,** one of the Saura palaces. Its ground floor is occupied by one of the best antiques shops in the Balearic Islands. Don't miss the coat of arms dated 1718, some primitive naval paintings at the end of the entrance hall, and the carved, domed ceiling.

Turn left onto Carrer del Seminari (Carrer Obispo Vila). On the right is the **Seminari,** the setting for Ciutadella's annual music festival.

Return, keeping north of the cathedral, along Carrer Sant Sebastià. Twisting left and right, you'll reach the steps leading down into the **port.** The waterfront here is lined with seafood restaurants, some of which burrow into caverns far under the Born. Between the restaurants, Carrer Costa del Moll leads left up to the Born again.

Many of the archaeological curiosities for which Menorca is famous are close to Ciutadella. Returning around the Avenues, continue straight at the traffic lights, take the next right (Carrer de Pere Martorell), and follow the signs for **Cala Morell.** Soon you'll be in open countryside, where numerous talayots, or prehistoric stone towers, dot the fields.

Returning to Ciutadella from Cala Morell, take a shortcut through the Polígono Industrial on the left to the CiutadellaMahón road. Turn left toward Mahón, and in a mile or so on the right are a parking lot and a path leading to the **Naveta des Tudons,** one of the best preserved of Menorca's mysterious prehistoric remains. The name derives from its shape, that of an upturned boat.

Dining and Lodging

$$ ✕ **Casa Manolo.** This well-established paella and seafood restaurant is at the seaward end of the many eating places that rub shoulders along the east side of the narrow harbor. The maritime dining rooms with white walls and exposed beams extend back into the rock face. ⊠ *Marina 117,* ☎ *971/380003. AE, DC, MC, V. Closed Dec.–Mar.*

$$$ ✕▥ **Patricia.** On a quiet boulevard just south of the main plaza, it is close to Ciutadella creek. The hall is marble, light, and modern. Bedrooms have pale carpets, pastel wallpaper, and watercolors. ⊠ *Camí Sant Nicolau 9092, 07760,* ☎ *971/385511,* 𝖥𝖠𝖷 *971/481120. 44 rooms with bath. Restaurant, bar. AE, DC, MC, V.*

$ ▥ **Hostal Ciutadella.** In the center of town, a block southwest of Plaça Alfonso III, is a pleasant, modern bar with bedrooms upstairs. The latter have white walls, shutters, shiny, tiled floors, and comfortable beds. ⊠ *Carrer Sant Eloi 10, 07760,* ☎ *971/383462. 17 rooms with bath. Cafeteria, bar. MC, V.*

Shopping

The industrial estate (*polígono*) on the right as you enter Ciutadella has a number of shoe factories, each with shops. Prices may be no lower, but the range on view is greater. The Rubrica shoe factory in Ferreries is where locals head. In Ciutadella, Carrer del Seminari 36 has designer leatherwear. Sa Celeria (⊠ 33 Carrer de Santa Clara), a saddler and harness maker, stocks elegant riding boots, and No. 48 has interesting pottery. One of the few antiques shops on the island is on the ground floor of the Saura Palace (✉ Carrer de Santíssim).

Excursions Around Menorca

En route between Mahón and Ciutadella, or on the way to the beach, three other pieces of the Menorcan countryside may be fit in.

Monte Toro
Northwest of Mahón.

Follow the signs in Mercadal to the peak of Monte Toro, Menorca's highest point. From the monastery on top, you can see the whole island and, on a clear day, across the sea to Majorca.

DINING

$$ ✕ **Ca'n Olga.** Difficult to find but worth it, off the Camino de Tra-
★ muntana, Olga's is under an archway to the left (or ask for directions). Make for the small patio and try the inventive country cuisine, such as local snails or quail in sherry. ✉ *Pont Na Macarrana s/n,* ☎ *971/375459. AE, MC, V. Closed Mon. and Tues. Jan. and Feb.*

$ ✕ **Bar Sa Plaça.** This local bar serves substantial helpings of good, local food. Try *pan amb oli con jamón serrano* (bread and oil with cured ham) for starters and *guisantes con cerdo* (pork with peas) to follow. ✉ *Plaça Constitució 2,* ☎ *971/375048. MC, V.*

Torralba
West of Mahón.

Coming from Mahón, turn south immediately upon entering Alayor toward Cala 'n Porter. Torralba, a megalithic site with a number of stone constructions, is 2 km/1¼ mi ahead at a bend in the road, marked by an information kiosk on the left that, as is so often the case in Menorca, you will be lucky to find open. The massive, T-shape taula is through an opening to the right. Behind it, from the top of a stone wall, you can see, in a nearby field, the monolith Fus de Sa Geganta.

Torre d'en Gaumés
West of Mahón.

Turn south toward Son Bou on the west side of Alayor. In about a mile, the first fork left will lead you to Torre d'en Gaumés, a much more complex set of prehistoric ruins, with fortifications, monuments and deep pits of ruined dwellings, huge vertical slabs, and taulas. How much longer it will last is difficult to say. Motorists already drive right through on a tiny path, and sightseers clamber all over it, pulling stones from top to bottom. See it while you can.

Cova des Coloms
West of Mahón.

The Cave of Pigeons is the most spectacular cave on the island. To reach it, take the Ferreries road at San Cristobal and turn up to the primary school. Beyond the school the paved road continues for about 3 km/2 mi toward Binigaus Nou. At an easily recognized parking place you'll see wheel marks and possibly cars as well; leave the car. Climb a stile and take a path that follows the righthand side of the barranca (ravine) toward the sea. You'll come to a well-trodden path bearing down into the bottom of the barranca and up the other side. The entrance to the cave is around an elbow, well camouflaged by a tree. Remember to bring a flashlight.

IBIZA AND FORMENTERA

Settled by the Carthaginians in the 5th century BC, Ibiza (Eivissa in Mallorquín and Catalan) in the 20th century was transformed by tourism. From a peasant economy, it became a wild, "anything goes," gathering place for the international jet set and for the hippies of the 1960s, only to enter the 1990s with its principal resort, Sant Antoni, regarded as one of the most boorish, noisy, and brash on the Mediterranean. And yet, of the islands, only on Ibiza and on tiny Formentera, just off Ibiza's southern tip, will you still see women in the fields dressed in the simple, country costume of long, black skirt and wide-brimmed straw hat, gathering almonds in their aprons or herding errant goats.

Numbers in the margin correspond to points of interest on the Ibiza and Formentera map.

Eivissa

⓫ *A 40-minute flight from Barcelona.*

Running along the quayside in the town of Eivissa is the area known as **Sa Penya** (the crag or cliff). Once a quiet, fisherman's quarter, since the 1960s it has been a tourist mecca, springing into life each evening with lively bars and restaurants and flea markets.

Enter Sa Penya via Carrer Rimbau, which you'll find at the end of Passeig Vara de Rey, opposite Hotel Montesol, whose fashionable pavement café is a favorite place for people-watching. Carrer Rimbau has some of the more exotic, fashion boutiques for which Ibiza is renowned, and off it are alleys crammed with stalls, boutiques, and restaurants.

Continue on Carrer Major, just east of San Telmo Church. In this part of Sa Penya none of the streets is quite straight, and the miniature houses appear to have been randomly dumped along tiny passageways.

From Carrer Major, return to Plaça de la Constitució, just north of San Telmo, where a pretty, little building that looks something like a miniature Parthenon houses the local market. Beyond it a ramp leads up to Las Tablas, the main gate of **Dalt Vila,** the walled, upper town. On each side stands a statue, Roman in origin, both now headless, Juno on the right, an armless male on the left.

Inside, the ramp continues to the right between the outer and inner walls and opens into a long, narrow plaza lined with stalls and pavement cafés. Don't worry about losing your way in the Dalt Vila. Aim uphill and you will arrive at the cathedral. Aim downhill and you will return to the gate. A little way up Sa Carroza, a sign on the left points back toward the **Museu d'Art Contemporani** (Museum of Contemporary Art, housed in the gateway arch. ⊠ *Ronda Pintor Narcis Putget s/n,* ☎ *971/302723.* 🎫 *350 ptas.* ☉ *Daily 10:30–1 and 6–8:30.*

Farther uphill from the Museum of Contemporary Art is a sculpture of a priest sitting on one of the stone seats in the gardens. On the left the wide **Bastion of Santa Lucia** offers a panoramic view.

Wind your way up past the 16th-century church of **Sant Domingo,** its roof an irregular landscape of tiled domes, and turn right in front of the **Ajuntament,** housed in the church's former monastery, then follow any of the streets or steps leading uphill to Carrer Obispo Torres (Carrer Major).

NEED A
BREAK?

Take a break at **Café Torre Canónigo** on the ground floor of an ancient mansion, halfway up the street. Opposite is a small art gallery.

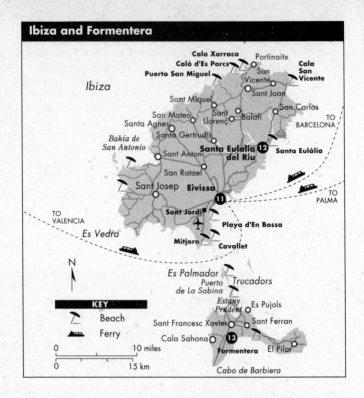

Ibiza and Formentera

At the top of Carrer Major is the **cathedral** on the site of religious structures from each of the cultures that have ruled Eivissa since the Phoenicians. Built in the 13th and 14th centuries and renovated in the 18th century, the cathedral has a Gothic tower and a Baroque nave. The painted panels above the small vault adjoining the sacristy depict souls in purgatory being consumed by flames and tortured by devils while angels ascend to heaven. A visit to its museum reached through the nave, is well worthwhile. Inside the sacristy is a collection of religious art, relics, and ecclesiastical treasures. ⊠ *Museum 250 ptas.* ☉ *Cathedral Sun.–Fri. 10–1 and 4–6:30, Sat. 10–1.*

Across the plaza from the cathedral, the **Museu Dalt Vila** (Museum of Archaeology) has Phoenician, Punic, and Roman finds. ⊠ *Plaça Catedral 3,* ☎ *971/301231.* ⊡ *450 ptas.* ☉ *Mon.–Sat. 10–1.*

A passageway leads between the cathedral and the castle, which has recently been restored, to the **Bastion of Sant Bernardo.** From here there is a panoramic view of the wide bay from Playa d'En Bossa to Figueretas, and of the chain of islands that stretches across the sea to Formentera. Steps lead down to a small gate in the bastion from which it is not too difficult to pick your way along the clifftop to Figueretas, where you can also continue along the top of the wall, the Route of St. John the Baptist, by way of the bastions of Sant Joan and Santiago, until you reach the steps to the **Portal Nou** (New Gate).

Go down the dark, curving tunnel of Portal Nou and up the Vía Romana to reach, on the left, the **Puig des Molins,** so called because it was once covered in windmills. A major Punic necropolis, with more than 3,000 tombs, has been excavated here, and many of the finds can be seen in the new **Museu Puig d'Es Molins** (Punic Archaeological Museum) adjacent to it. ⊠ *Vía Romana 31,* ☎ *971/301771.* 🎫 *450 ptas.* 🕓 *Mon.–Sat. 10–1.*

Dining and Lodging

$$$ ✕ **Ca Na Joana** (formerly Can Pujolet). A small, 200-year-old coun-
★ try house on a hillside in Sant Josep (10 km/6mi from Eivissa) gives the feeling of dining in a private home. Joana Biarnés, in a former life a well-known journalist, has put together one of the finest restaurants in the Balearics, complete with an acclimatized wine cellar. The *esto-fado de buey* (ragout of beef) is excellent. ⊠ *Ctra. Eivissa-Sant Josep Km 10,* ☎ *971/800158. AE, MC, V. Closed Mon. Dec. 30–May. No dinner Sun.*

$$–$$$ ✕ **El Porralón.** Just inside and left of the main gate into Dalt Vila, a front terrace announces this intimate French restaurant. One dining room is medieval, with exposed, heavy beams, antiques, oils, and coats of arms; and another, modern, blending dark, orange walls with sleek, black furniture. *Pato con salsa de frambuesa* (duck with raspberry sauce) is worth trying if you can't decide. ⊠ *Plaza Desamparados 12,* ☎ *971/303901 or 971/300852. AE, DC, MC, V.*

$$–$$$ ✕ **S'Oficina.** The entrance from Avinguda d'Espanya is uninviting but leads to an attractive restaurant with a small patio and some of the best Basque cuisine on the island. Marine prints hang on white walls and ships' lanterns from the ceiling. *Lomo de merluza con almejas* (hake with clams) and *kokotxas* (cod cheeks) are house specialties. ⊠ *Avda. d'Espanya 6,* ☎ *971/300016. AE, MC, V. Closed Sun.*

$$ ✕ **Rias Baixas.** One of the best fish restaurants on the island, serving Galician cuisine, provides possibly the only reason for visiting Sant An-toni (15 km/9 mi from Eivissa). Leave your car on the seafront—the one-way street system is impossible to divine. ⊠ *Carrer Ignacio Ri-quer 4,* ☎ *971/340480. AE, DC, MC, V. Closed Dec. 15–Feb. 15.*

$ ✕ **Comidas San Juan.** This small café at the beginning of Sa Penya has marble-top tables, reminiscent of a Paris bistro. The gloss-painted decor is sterile, but the owners are cheerful, the fish dishes usually good, and the value unbeatable; try the grilled sole. ⊠ *Carrer Montgri 8,* ☎ *971/310766. No credit cards. Closed Sun. and holidays.*

$$$–$$$$ ✕🏨 **Hacienda Na Xamena.** Ibiza's most exclusive hotel is also the most
★ isolated, on a rocky headland in Sant Miquel in the north of the is-land. Access to the sea is difficult and involves a long hike down steep steps, but the rooms are elegant, around a pretty, little, central patio with a fountain and trees. Reserve well in advance. ⊠ *Apdo. 423, Sant Miquel, 07815,* ☎ *971/333046,* 🖷 *971/333175. 63 rooms with bath, 33 with hot tubs. Restaurant, bar, 3 pools, 1 tennis court, health club. AE, DC, MC, V. Closed Nov.–Mar.*

$$–$$$ ✕🏨 **Los Molinos.** Technically in Figueretas but a five-minute walk
★ from the center of Eivissa, Los Molinos is the best hotel in town, at the end of a relatively quiet street. The bedrooms are standard mod-ern; the more expensive ones have balconies that look out to the bay. ⊠ *Carrer Ramón Muntaner 60, Apdo. 504, 07800 Figueretas,* ☎ *971/302250/54,* 🖷 *971/302504. 147 rooms with bath. Restaurant, bar, pool, beauty salon, beach, waterskiing. AE, DC, MC, V.*

$–$$ 🏨 **La Torre Canónigo.** These modern apartments, built into a 16th-century tower at the top of the Dalt Vila, 55 yards from the cathedral, have open fireplaces and the flavor of their ancient surroundings. ⊠ *Carrer Major 8 Calle Obispo Torres 8, Dalt Vila, 07800,* ☎ *971/303884. 7 apartments with bath. Snack bar. No credit cards. Closed Nov.–Mar.*

$ 🏨 **La Peña.** This small, very simple guest house is in an ancient fish-erman's cottage right at the end of Sa Penya and close to the lively nighttime scene. ⊠ *Carrer Verge 76, Sa Penya, 07800. 13 rooms, 2 with shower. No credit cards. Closed Nov.–Mar.*

Nightlife

If the arts are relatively neglected, nightlife certainly is not, and the discos of Ibiza are famous throughout Europe. In Eivissa, the trendy place to begin the evening is **Keeper** (⊠ Passeig Marítim), where you can sip your drink perched atop a carousel horse. There is also a lively, very young scene at **Divino,** another of the music bars on the Passeig Marítim. The in place for older nighthawks is the foyer of the former **Teatre Pereira** (⊠ Carrer Comte Roselló).

Favorites are **Pachá** (⊠ Passeig Marítim s/n), **Amnesia** San Rafael (⊠ Sant Antoni road, opposite Km 5 marker), and **Ku** (farther along the same road). Hardened discomanes end the night at **Space** (⊠ far end of Playa d'En Bossa), which doesn't even open until 5 AM.

Ibiza's **casino** is in a Cubist building whose architectural style resembles that of an Ibizan church, with a pizzeria and piano bar in the side chapels. ⊠ *Passeig Marítim s/n,* ☎ *971/313312.* ☉ *Weekdays 10 PM–4 AM, weekends 10 PM–5 AM.*

Outdoor Activities and Sports

HORSEBACK RIDING

In Sant Antoni **Club Hípico** (⊠ Ctra. de Circunvalación) has horses and equipment.

SPORTS AND FITNESS COMPLEX

Ahmara (⊠ Centro Deportivo, Ctra. Sant Josep Km 2.7, ☎ 971/307762 or 971/307950), on the road to Sant Josep, has tennis courts (lessons available), four squash courts, badminton, indoor football, a gymnasium, an exotic Turkish bath, massage, sauna, hot tub, a pool, a grill-restaurant, and a bar.

TENNIS

Ibiza Club de Campo (⊠ Ctra. Sant Josep Km 2, ☎ 971/300088); **Aqualandia** (⊠ Urbanización Punta Martinet, Playa Talamanca, ☎ 971/314060); **Port Sant Miquel** (☎ 971/333019), with 5 public courts; **Formentera** (⊠ Avda. Port Saler, Sant Francesc).

WALKING

Landscapes of Ibiza (Sunflower Press) is about walking in Ibiza, with itineraries for 22 different walks, none very strenuous, and six bicycle tours of Formentera.

Shopping

During the late 1960s and '70s, Ibiza built a reputation for extremes of fashion, of which not much survives, though the softer designs of Smilja Mihailovich, under the **Ad Lib** label, still prosper. While Sa Penya still has a few designer boutiques, much of that famous area is now a so-called hippie market of over-priced tourist ephemera. You'll still find designer leather clothing at **Azara 5** (☎ 971/310671) in front of the Teatro Pereira. **Pink Fly** (⊠ Rimbau 4, ☎ 971/310655) and **The End** (⊠ Carrer de la Creu 26) are well-known boutiques.

In the newer part of town, **Krystal** (⊠ Carrers Canarius and Aragón) specializes in designer glassware. **Casa del Café** (⊠ Carrers Bisbe Carrasco and Médico Rapuchin) has an amazing range of coffees, teas, and preserves. **Front Line** (⊠ Bartolomé Rosello 1) stocks fashions for adults and children.

Excursions Around Ibiza

Head out from Eivissa and explore Santa Eulàlia del Riu with its Moorish-influenced church and the fortified village of Balafi.

Santa Eulàlia del Riu

⑫ *15 km (9 mi) from Eivissa.*

Visit the church at Santa Eulàlia del Riu. At the edge of the town, to the right just below the road, a Roman bridge crosses what is claimed to be the only permanent river in the Balearics (hence, "del Riu"), although it is usually only damp. Ahead, on the hilltop, are the cubes and domes of the church. Look for a narrow lane to the left, signed Puig de Missa, and follow it to the church. A stoutly arched, crypt-like covered area, clearly of Moorish influence, guards the entrance. Inside are a fine gold reredos and blue-tiled Stations of the Cross.

DINING AND LODGING

$$–$$$ ✕ **Doña Margarita.** This elegant restaurant on the waterfront has won several awards for its Ibizan seafood cuisine. You eat at pine tables, overlooked by Ibizan landscapes that hang on the white walls. The outside terrace, next to the crescent beach, is especially pleasant in the evenings. ✉ *Passeig Marítim s/n,* ☎ *971/330655. AE, DC, MC, V. Closed Mon. and Dec.*

$$ ✕ **C'as Pagès.** This old farmhouse with bare stone walls, wood beams,
★ and columns made of olive-press "screws," is for meat-eaters only. Try the leg of lamb with baked potato or roast peppers or *sofrit pagès* (lamb and chicken stew), followed by *graixonera* (a mixture of sugar, milk, eggs, and cinnamon). ✉ *Ctra. de San Carlos Km 10 (Pont de S'Argentara), no phone. No credit cards. Closed Tues. and Feb. and Mar.*

$$ ✕🏨 **Sol Los Loros.** Striking architecture in extensive gardens and well-designed interiors are the appeal here, but it is a bit isolated at the end of a half-finished development and nearly a half mile from the town center. ✉ *Urbanizacion S'Argamassa, 07840,* ☎ *971/330761,* 🅕🅐🅧 *971/339542. 262 rooms with bath. Restaurant, bar, beauty salon, tennis courts, dance club, playground. AE, DC, MC, V. Closed Nov.–Mar.*

SHOPPING

In Santa Eulàlia, **Broch** on Plaça de Espanya has leatherwear.

Balafi

Northwest of Santa Eulàlia.

To reach the fortified village of Balafi, take the Sant Joan road from Eivissa and, passing the left turn to Sant Llorenç, look for a bar on the right next to a ceramics workshop, and turn right onto Sant Carles. Almost opposite on the left, a rough, narrow track leads to Balafi. In the distance you can make out some towers. These have no entrance on the ground floor, and, in times of peril, local inhabitants climbed a ladder to the first floor and pulled the ladder up after them.

Formentera

⑬ *Ferries leave from Eivissa for the port of La Sabina on Formentera.*

You can begin this tour from Eivissa, Sant Antoni, or Santa Eulàlia, all of which have ferries to Formentera. Because Formentera is essentially an island of beach and countryside, you may wish to picnic; buy supplies in Ibiza. During the short passage it's well worth standing on deck. You'll have excellent views of the Dalt Vila and of the smaller islands en route; look for Trucadors, the long stretch of sand almost linking Formentera to Es Palmador.

From the port of La Sabina it's only 3 km/2 mi to the island's tiny capital, **Sant Francesc Xavier,** which is a few yards off the main road. In the small plaza before the church, there's an active, hippie market. The interior of the whitewashed church is quite simple, its rough, old wooden door encased in iron and studded with nails. Down a short street directly opposite the church, there's a good antiques and junk shop on the left, with a small art gallery displaying paintings and olive-wood carvings.

<table>
<tr><td>NEED A
BREAK?</td><td>At **Estrella Dorada,** a few yards down Carrer Jaume I, you can sit outside and enjoy good coffee and a selection of tapas. In an alleyway to the right of Estrella Dorada is a chocolate house, **Café Matinal,** white and tiled and very stylish.</td></tr>
</table>

At the main road, turn right toward **Sant Ferran,** 2 km/1 mi away. Beyond Sant Ferran the road travels for 7 km/4 mi along a narrow isthmus, keeping slightly closer to the rougher northern side where, if a wind is blowing, the waves come crashing over the rocks. Just beyond El Pilar you'll see, on the right, a windmill, still in good order, with all its sails flying.

The plateau that forms the east end of the island ends at the lighthouse, **Faro de la Mola.** Nearby is a **monument to Jules Verne,** who used Formentera as a setting in his novel *Journey Through the Solar System.* Around the lighthouse, in autumn and spring, the bare rock, despite the feet of thousands of tourists, is carpeted with flowers and purple thyme and sea holly, while below hundreds of swallows soar. At the edge of the cliff you may see turquoise–viridian lizards.

On the main road, turn right at Sant Ferran toward Es Pujols. Its few hotels are the nearest Formentera comes to having a beach resort, although the beach is not the best. Beyond Es Pujols the road skirts **Estany Pudent,** one of two lagoons that almost enclose La Sabina. Salt was once extracted from Pudenthence its name, which means "stinking," although it no longer does so. The other lagoon, **Estany de Peix** (Fish Pond), was once a fish farm.

At the northern tip of Pudent, a road to the right leads to a footpath that runs the length of **Trucadors,** the narrow sand spit that reaches the island of Es Palmador. The beaches here are excellent.

Dining and Lodging

$$$ ✕ **Le Cyrano.** This family-run restaurant on the water at Es Pujols is the best on Formentera. French cuisine, especially foie gras, snails, and pastries, are the prime movers here. ⊠ *Paseo Maritimo, Es Pujols,* ☎ *971/328386. MC, V.*

$$$ ✕▥ **Hotel Club La Mola.** This whitewashed spa right on the water at Playa de Migjorn has a certain Aztec, cliff-dwelling look, and as many comforts as you can possibly consume. The Playa de Migjorn, while not as wild as it once was, is still one of the least spoiled beaches in the Mediterranean. ⊠ *Apdo. de Correos 23, Playa de Migjorn,* ☎ *971/328051,* ▨ *971/328069. 326 rooms with bath. Restaurant, bar, miniature golf, tennis court, convention center, car rental.*

$ ✕▥ **Fonda Can Rafalet.** This simple inn and restaurant, 12 km/7½ mi from Formentera's La Savina port, is known for its fresh seafood and rustic setting. Just yards from the water on the tiny fishing port of Es Caló, the sound of inboard engines is the most distressing noise you will hear. The thought that they will be back with the raw materials for your lunch more than makes up for any lost sleep. ⊠ *Apdo. de*

Correos 225, Es Caló, ☎ FAX *971/327016. 15 rooms with bath. Restaurant, bar. MC, V.*

Outdoor Activities and Sports

BICYCLING

Cycling is very popular, with numerous rental outlets in La Sabina, the port of arrival.

THE BALEARIC ISLANDS A TO Z

Arriving and Departing

By Ferry

BETWEEN THE BALEARICS AND THE MAINLAND

Majorca: Trasmediterránea (✉ Est. Marítima 2, Muelle Pelaires 07012, ☎ 971/405014, FAX 971/405964) sails at least once a day between Palma and Barcelona and Valencia; once a week (Sunday) between Palma and Mahón (Menorca) and Palma and Ibiza. Fares are, oddly enough, higher than the airline fares. From May to October there is also a daily hydrofoil (**Hidrojet**) service between Palma and Ibiza: **Naviera Mallorquina** (☎ 971/710153). From France a service operates between Sète and Palma twice a week, June to September. The short sea crossing between **Ciutadella,** at the western tip of Menorca, and **Alcúdia,** in the north of Majorca, has been reopened; details are available at the ticket offices in Ciutadella and Alcúdia harbors.

Menorca: Trasmediterránea (☎ 971/366050) sails from Mahón three times a week to Barcelona Easter and summer (June 15–September 15), daily except Fridays, once a week to Palma and Valencia. Journey times: Barcelona, 9 hours; Valencia, via Palma, 16 hours overall.

Ibiza: Trasmediterránea (☎ 971/315011) sails at least twice a week to and from Barcelona, Palma, and Valencia. From May until October there is also daily hydrofoil (**Hidrojet**) service from Palma and Denia, as well as less frequent services from Valencia and Barcelona. A service operates between Sète (France) and Ibiza twice a week, June to September, calling at Palma on the way.

Between San Antonio in the west of Ibiza and Denia on the mainland, **Flebasa** (✉ Estació Marítim, Eivissa, ☎ 971/310927; ✉ Edificio Faro, San Antonio, ☎ 971/342871; ✉ Madrid, ☎ 91/473–2055; ✉ Denia, ☎ 96/784011) operates both a car ferry and a fast hydrofoil with coach connections to Madrid and Valencia.

INTER-ISLAND SERVICE

Flebasa (☞ *above*) can ferry you and your car from Alcudia, Majorca to Ciutadella, Menorca in 2½ hours. Finally, a Hovercraft covers the journey between San Antonio and Benidorm on the mainland in 2½ hours, daily in the summer months; for information and reservations, contact **Coral Travel** (✉ Carrer Mar 11, Sant Antoni, ☎ 971/343711 or 971/343752, FAX 971/344266; ✉ Carrer Isadora Macabich 14, Santa Eulàlia, ☎ 971/330512 or 971/330561).

Frequent services to **Formentera** from Ibiza by car ferry, catamaran, and hydrofoil are operated by **Transmapi** (☎ 971/314513 or 971/310711; ✉ Formentera, ☎ 971/320703), **Marítima de Formentera** (☎ 971/320157), and **Flebasa** (☎ 971/310927).

By Plane

MAJORCA

Iberia and Aviaco and new carriers Spanair and Air Europa have direct flights daily between Palma (☎ 971/264624) and Barcelona,

Madrid, Alicante, Valencia, Menorca, and Ibiza, as well as direct flights two or three times a week to Bilbao and Vitoria. The inter-island flights (Ibiza and Menorca) in the summer months should be booked well in advance. Iberia and a large number of charter operators also have flights between Palma and major European cities. Bus 17 runs between Palma Airport and the out-of-town bus station on Plaça d'Espanya, next to the Inca railway terminus. On both outward and inward journeys, it travels first to Terminal B, then to Terminal A, every 30 minutes until 9 PM, then once an hour. The last bus from town is at 11 PM; the last bus from the airport is at midnight. The fare is 400 ptas. (evenings and holidays 450 ptas.), and the journey takes 30 minutes. Taxi fare from Palma Airport to downtown is about 2,500 ptas.

MENORCA

Iberia-Aviaco flies direct to Mahón from Barcelona, from Palma three or four times daily. Air Europe and Spanair also fly to Mahón. Direct charter flights go to Menorca from many European cities in the summer. A metered taxi to Mahón costs about 1,100 ptas.

IBIZA

Iberia-Aviaco (☎ 971/395377) has several direct, scheduled flights daily to Ibiza from Barcelona, Madrid, Valencia, and Palma. These are supplemented in season by charter flights from many European cities. For airport information, call 971/157000. An hourly bus service runs between Ibiza Airport and Eivissa (Ibiza Town) from 7 AM to 10:30 PM (on the hour from town, on the half hour from the airport; fare: 450 ptas.; journey time: 15 minutes). A taxi costs about 2,500 ptas.

Getting Around

By Boat

MAJORCA

Boats from Palma, Majorca, to neighboring beach resorts leave from the jetty opposite the Auditorium on the Passeig Marítim. The Tourist Office has a detailed timetable.

MENORCA

Despite the fact that many of Menorca's beaches are difficult to reach by road, the only bays to which boat trips are organized are Macarella, Cala Mitjana, and Cala Trebaluger, all reached from Cala Galdana.

By Bus

MAJORCA

A good network of bus services fans out from Palma to towns and villages throughout Majorca. Most leave from the out-of-town bus station (✉ Estació Central, ☎ 971/752224) adjacent to the Inca railway terminus on Plaça d'Espanya; a few terminate at other points within the city. Details and timetables are available from the Tourist Office.

MENORCA

Several buses a day run the length of Menorca, between Mahón and Ciutadella, calling at the island's other principal towns (Alayor, Mercadal, and Ferreries) en route. From the smaller villages there are buses each day to Mahón and some to Ciutadella. A regular bus service from the west end of the Plaça Explanada in Ciutadella ferries visitors between the town and the tourist resorts to the south and west.

IBIZA

In Ibiza buses run every half hour from Eivissa (✉ bus terminal, Avinguda Isadora Macabich) to Sant Antoni and to Playa d'En Bossa and about once an hour to Santa Eulàlia. Buses from Eivissa to other parts

Your passport around the world.

- Worldwide access
- Operators who speak your language
- Monthly itemized billing

MCI ★   Calling Card

415 555 1234 2244
J.D. SMITH

Use your MCI Card® and these access numbers for an easy way to call when traveling worldwide.

Austria (CC) ♦†	022-903-012
Belarus	
From Gomel and Mogilev regions	8-10-800-103
From all other localities	8-800-103
Belgium (CC) ♦†	0800-10012
Bulgaria	00800-0001
Croatia (CC) ★	99-385-0112
Czech Republic (CC) ♦	00-42-000112
Denmark (CC) ♦†	8001-0022
Finland (CC) ♦†	9800-102-80
France (CC) ♦†	0800-99-0019
Germany (CC)†	0130-0012
Greece (CC) ♦†	00-800-1211
Hungary (CC) ♦	00▼800-01411
Iceland (CC) ♦†	800-9002
Ireland (CC)†	1-800-55-1001
Italy (CC) ♦†	172-1022
Kazakhstan (CC)	1-800-131-4321
Liechtenstein (CC) ♦	155-0222
Luxembourg†	0800-0112
Monaco (CC) ♦	800-90-19

Netherlands (CC) ♦†	06-022-91-22
Norway (CC) ♦†	800-19912
Poland (CC) ÷†	00-800-111-21-22
Portugal (CC) ÷†	05-017-1234
Romania (CC) ÷	01-800-1800
Russia (CC) ÷♦	747-3322
For a Russian-speaking operator	747-3320
San Marino (CC) ♦	172-1022
Slovak Republic (CC)	00-42-000112
Slovenia	080-8808
Spain (CC)†	900-99-0014
Sweden (CC) ♦†	020-795-922
Switzerland (CC) ♦†	155-0222
Turkey (CC) ♦†	00-8001-1177
Ukraine (CC) ÷	8▼10-013
United Kingdom (CC)†	
To call to the U.S. using BT ■	0800-89-0222
To call to the U.S. using Mercury ■	0500-89-0222
Vatican City (CC)†	172-1022

To sign up for the MCI Card, dial the access number of the country you are in and ask to speak with a customer service representative.

MCI

http://www.mci.com

(CC) Country-to-country calling available. May not be available to/from all international locations. (Canada, Puerto Rico, and U.S. Virgin Islands are considered Domestic Access locations.) ♦ Public phones may require deposit of coin or phone card for dial tone. † Automation available from most locations. ★ Not available from public pay phones. ▼ Wait for second dial tone. ÷ Limited availability. ■ International communications carrier.

It helps to be pushy in airports.

Introducing the revolutionary new TransPorter™ from American Tourister. It's the first suitcase you can push around without a fight. TransPorter's™ exclusive four-wheel design lets you push it in front of you with almost no effort—the wheels take the weight. Or pull it on two wheels if you choose. You can even stack on other bags and use it like a luggage cart.

TransPorter™ is designed like a dresser, with built-in shelves to organize your belongings. Or collapse the shelves and pack it like a traditional suitcase. Inside, there's a suiter feature to help keep suits and dresses from wrinkling. When push comes to shove, you can't beat a TransPorter™. For more information on how you can be this pushy, call 1-800-542-1300.

Stable 4-wheel design.

Shelves collapse on command.

American Tourister®

Making travel less primitive.®

©1996 American Tourister®

of the island are less frequent, as is the cross-island bus between Sant Antoni and Santa Eulàlia. The timetable is published in newspapers.

FORMENTERA

A very limited bus service operates between the villages of **Formentera,** shrinking to one bus each way between San Francisco and Pilar on Saturdays and disappearing altogether on Sundays and holidays. Details are in Ibizan newspapers.

By Car
MAJORCA

In Majorca main highways are well surfaced, and traveling times can be reasonably fast on the flat plain that comprises most of the island. Driving in the mountains that run the length of the northwest coast and descend to a cliffside corniche is a different matter. Not only will the winding roads slow you down; so will the tremendous views and the cars of other tourists.

MENORCA

If you want to go beach hopping in Menorca, a car is essential; few of the island's beaches and *calas* (coves) are served by public transport. However, most of the sights are in Mahón or Ciutadella, both of which have a reasonable bus service from other parts of the island, and once you are in town, everything is within walking distance. The island's archaeological remains can easily be seen in a day's drive, so a reasonable compromise might be to rent a car for just a part of your visit. The main roads are good; others may be narrow.

IBIZA

A car or motor scooter is the best means of exploring Ibiza, because many of the beaches lie at the end of rough, unpaved roads. The main highways are well surfaced and relatively straight, making for fast driving. Several new roads, crossing the island in the north, have recently been constructed, replacing twisting country lanes.

By Carriage
MAJORCA

In Majorca horse-drawn carriages, accommodating four to five passengers, can be found in Palma at the bottom of the Born, on Avinguda Antonio Maura, in the Cathedral Square nearby, and on Plaça d'Espanya, at the side farthest from the railway station. A city tour costs about 4,000 ptas.

By Taxi

Taxis in Palma, **Majorca,** have meters. For trips beyond the city, there are standard charges, displayed at the taxi ranks. In **Menorca** taxis can be found at the airport and in Mahón (✉ Explanada; radio taxi, ☎ 971/367111) and Ciutadella (✉ Carrer Josep Antoni; radio taxi, ☎ 971/381896). In **Ibiza,** taxis are available at the airport (☎ 971/305230) and in Eivissa (✉ Passeig Vara de Rey, ☎ 971/301794; radio taxi, ☎ 971/307000 or 971/306602), Figueretas (☎ 971/301676), Santa Eulalia (☎ 971/333033), and San Antonio (☎ 971/340074 or 971/341721). In **Formentera** taxis are in La Sabina (☎ 971/322002 or 971/323016) and Es Pujols (☎ 971/328016).

By Train
MAJORCA

Majorca has two separate railway systems. The Palma-Inca line travels to Inca, with stops at Santa María and Consell, from the Palma terminus (✉ Ferrocarriles de Majorca, Plaça d'Espanya, ☎ 971/752245). A journey on the privately owned Palma-Sóller railway is a must. Built by the citrus-fruit farmers of Sóller at the beginning of the century, it still uses the carriages of that era. The line trundles across the plain to Bunyola, then winds through tremendous mountain scenery to emerge high above Sóller. An ancient tram connects the Sóller terminus to Port de Sóller, leaving every hour on the hour, 9–7. The Palma terminal (☎ 971/752051) is near the corner of Plaça d'Espanya, on Calle Eusebio Estada, just north of the Inca railway station.

Guided Tours

Most hotels in **Majorca** offer a variety of guided tours; ask the hotel porter for information. Typical itineraries are to the Caves of Artà or Drac on the east coast, taking in the Auto Safari Park nearby and stopping off at an artificial pearl factory in Manacor on the way; to the Chopin museum in the former monastery at Valldemossa, returning through the writers' and artists' village of Deya; the port of Sóller and the Arab gardens at Alfabia; the Thursday market and leather factories at Inca; Port de Pollença; Cape Formentor; and northern beaches.

Boat Tours

MAJORCA

Around Majorca, almost every resort has excursions to neighboring beaches and coves, many of them inaccessible by road, and to the offshore islands of Cabrera and Dragonera. There are also morning shopping trips by boat from Magaluf and Palma Nova to Palma. A detailed timetable is available from the Tourist Office.

MENORCA

In Menorca there are various types of sightseeing trips around Mahón harbor, all originating at the quayside near the Xoriguer gin factory. Tickets for the day trips on the *Don Pancho,* which run between 10 AM and 5 PM, can be bought at the Aquarium (☎ 971/350537). The cost is around 4,000 ptas., including lunch; special prices for groups can be negotiated. Tickets for one-hour trips are available at the Xoriguer ginnery and cost about 1,000 ptas. Outings can be organized directly with the captain of the *Menorquin,* Olegario Preto (☎ 971/353152). Excursions from Es Grau to the Illa d'en Colom can be reserved at the Bar Can Bernat (✉ Es Grau, ☎ 971/369936).

IBIZA

Trips from Ibiza to Formentera include an escorted coach tour, and every resort offers trips to neighboring beaches and to islands off the coast. At San Antonio, which has little to offer in the way of a beach itself, a whole flotilla advertises trips.

Contacts and Resources

Car Rental

Cars are available through **Avis** and **Betacar** (Palma, Mahón, and Ibiza airports); **Hertz** (Palma and Ibiza airports); **Hiper RentaCar** (✉ Majorca, Son Garcias, Apartado de Correos 50, Ca'n Pastilla, ☎ 971/269911 or 971/262223, FAX 971/492000); and **Pitiusas** (Ibiza Airport). Local firms rent motorbikes, scooters, mopeds, and bicycles as well (ask for a crash helmet).

Emergencies

Police, ☎ 091 or 092 (except Ciutadella, ☎ 971/381095; and Formentera, ☎ 971/320210). **Medical emergencies,** Clínica Juaneda (✉ Son Espanyolet, ☎ 971/722222).

Consulates: United States (✉ Avinguda Jaume III 26, Palma, Majorca, ☎ 971/722660). **United Kingdom** (✉ Plaça Major 3D, Palma, Majorca,

☎ 971/712447; ✉ Torret 28, Sant Lluis, Mahón, Menorca, ☎ 971/366439).

Pharmacies

Pharmacies are open late by rotation. Schedules are posted on the door of each pharmacy and in local newspapers.

Travel Agencies

Viajes Barcelos (Palma, Majorca, ✉ Avda. Jaume III 2, ☎ 971/5590874; Mahón, Menorca, ✉ Avda. Josep María Cuadrado 1, ☎ 971/360250; Ciutadella, Menorca, ✉ Cami de Maó 5, ☎ 971/380487; Eivissa, Ibiza, ✉ Avda. d'Espanya s/n, ☎ 971/303250); **Viajes WagonsLits Cook** (Mahón, Menorca, ✉ Plaça Constitució 9, ☎ 971/364162; Eivissa, Ibiza, ✉ Passeig Vara de Rey 3, ☎ 971/301503).

Visitor Information

The regional tourist office for the Balearic Islands is the **Consellaria de Turismo de Balear** (✉ Avda. Jaume III 10, Palma, ☎ 971/712216).

MAJORCA

The **Majorcan Tourist Board** (Palma Airport, ☎ 971/260803) is supplemented in **Majorca** by municipal tourist offices in **Alcúdia** (✉ Ctra. Port d'AlcúdiaArta s/n, ☎ 971/548615); **Palma** (✉ Carrer Sant Domingo 11, ☎ 971/724090; kiosk on northeast side of Plaça d'Espanya, facing railway station, ☎ 971/711527); **Pollença** (✉ Carrer Miquel Capllonch, Port de Pollença, ☎ 971/534666); **Sóller** (✉ Plaça de Sa Constitució 1, ☎ 971/630200; ✉ y Carrer Canónigo Oliver, Port de Sóller, ☎ 971/630101); and **Valldemossa** (✉ ticket office adjacent to monastery, Cartuja de Valldemossa, ☎ 971/612106).

MENORCA

Local tourist information for **Menorca** can be obtained in **Mahón** (✉ Oficina de Información Turística de Menorca, Plaça Explanada 40, ☎ 971/363790) and in **Ciutadella** (mobile office, open irregularly April–September, and at the police station in the Ajuntament, Plaça d'Es Born); the best map for all purposes is the *Mapa Arqueológico de Menorca,* available in bookshops and some hotels.

IBIZA

Local tourist offices in **Ibiza: Eivissa** (✉ Oficina de Información Turística de Ibiza, Passeig Vara de Rey 13, ☎ 971/301900). **Santa Eulalia** (✉ Carrer Mariano Riquer Wallis s/n, ☎ 971/330728). **Sant Antoni** (✉ Passeig de Ses Fonts s/n, ☎ 971/343363). **Formentera** (✉ Port de a Savina, ☎ 971/322057).

11 The Costa del Sol

Most of the stretch of the Andalucían coast known as the Costa del Sol is an overdeveloped, package-tour mecca for northern European sun-seekers and a retirement haven for Britons and Americans. With its luxury hotels, Marbella attracts a more glamorous crowd. In the mountains, however, there are remote villages that belong to a world light-years away from the hedonistic carnival raging down on the coast. The tiny British colony of Gibraltar provides yet another, English, atmosphere. Morocco is just a short boat trip across the straits of Gibraltar, a logical and memorable step back into the history of al-Andalus, *the* 700-year Moorish reign on the Iberian Peninsula.

THE STRETCH OF ANDALUCÍAN SHORE known as the Costa del Sol runs officially from Cabo de Gata, beyond Almería in the east, all the way to the tip of Tarifa, past Gibraltar in the west. For most of the European vacationers who have flocked here during the 35 years of its popularity, though, the Sun Coast has been largely restricted to 70 km/43 mi of concrete playground between Torremolinos, just west of Málaga, and Estepona, 50 km/31 mi short of Gibraltar. Since the late 1950s this area has mushroomed from impoverished fishing villages afflicted with malaria and near starvation into an overdeveloped, package-tour mecca of sunseekers and a retirement haven for Britons and Americans.

By Hilary
Bunce

Updated by
George Semler

In the '60s and early '70s, hundreds of concrete highrises shot up to scar the skylines of Torremolinos and Fuengirola, and luxury hotels and leafy villas erupted on the shoreline of Marbella, pushing this former fishing village to the forefront of Europe's upscale resorts. The late 1980s witnessed a second boom, generating new golf courses, luxury marinas, villa developments, and yet more world-class hotels.

The Costa averages some 320 days of sunshine a year, and balmy days are not unknown even in January or February. It's also a good place to unwind. You can bask or stroll on mile upon mile of beaches and enjoy a full range of land and water sports.

Sunseekers from bleaker climes seem crammed into every corner of the Costa. Choose your resort carefully. Málaga and Ronda, though not strictly resorts, are the most authentically Spanish cities—especially Ronda. Torremolinos caters almost exclusively to the mass market; it's a budget destination that appeals very much to singles and to those who come to soak up the sun and disco the night away. Fuengirola is quieter and much more geared to family vacations, whereas farther west, the Marbella-San Pedro de Alcántara area is more exclusive and, of course, more expensive.

In places, mountains roll down to the sea; in others, unfolding hillsides of olive groves, cork oaks, and terraced vineyards provide vistas of the Mediterranean glinting in the distance. The developed coastal strip contrasts vividly with its hinterland. Just a few miles up in the mountains, you'll find remote villages where black-shawled women go about their daily routine much as they did a quarter century or so ago, and donkeys and mules are still used for farm work. Steeped in medieval lore and the scene of many turbulent battles of the Reconquest, the perched, white villages (*pueblos blancos*) belong to a world light-years away from the hedonistic carnival of the coast. Gibraltar provides yet another atmosphere, with its British policemen, pubs, and regal guardsmen.

Pleasures and Pastimes

Beaches

The beaches of the Costa del Sol run from shingle and pebbles at worst (Almuñécar, Nerja, Málaga) to a fine, gray, gritty sand (Torremolinos westward). Swimming in the sea is not always pleasant because of pebbles underfoot and pollution. Look for a beach flying the blue EU flag, which indicates that the water conforms to European Union standards. All the beaches are very crowded in July and August, when Spanish families take their annual vacation, and on Sundays from May to October, when they become picnic sites.

All Spanish beaches are free; changing facilities are usually not available, although you'll find free, cold showers on the major beaches. It's quite acceptable for women to go topless on beaches. If you want to take it all off, you'll have to drive to the more deserted beaches, and beware the odd, awkward civil guard who can, and often does, make arrests for total nudity. Costa Natura, 3 km/2 mi west of Estepona, is the coast's official nudist colony.

The best, though the most crowded, beaches are El Bajondillo and La Carihuela in Torremolinos; the long stretch between Carvajal, Los Boliches, and Fuengirola; and those on both sides of Marbella. You may find the odd secluded beach to the west of Estepona.

Dining
The Costa del Sol is known for fresh seafood exquisitely fried in especially fine flour. Fish roasted on skewers at beachside shack-restaurants, are another typical and unforgettable treat. Gazpacho comes in the Andalucían culinary canon, both as complement and antidote. Málaga is best for traditional Spanish cooking, with a wealth of bars and seafood restaurants serving *fritura malagueña* (Málaga's famous fried fish). Torremolinos's Carihuela district is also a paradise for lovers of Spanish seafood. In the resorts you will also find every conceivable variety of foreign cuisine, from Scandinavian *smörgåsbord* to the delicacies of Thailand. Marbella has internationally renowned restaurants such as Paul Schiff's La Hacienda. At the other end of the scale, perhaps even more enjoyable, are the Costa's traditional *chiringuitos* or *merenderos*. Strung out along the beaches, and open in summer only, these rough-and-ready restaurants serve seafood fresh off the boats.

Reservations are advisable for all Marbella restaurants listed as $$$–$$$$ and for the Café de Paris and parador dining room in Málaga. Elsewhere, reservations are rarely essential. Expect beach restaurants, such as Málaga's Casa Pedro and all those on Torremolinos's Carihuela seafront, to be packed on Sundays after 3 PM.

CATEGORY	COST*
$$$$	over 6,500 ptas.
$$$	4,000 ptas.–6,500 ptas.
$$	2,500 ptas.–4,000 ptas.
$	under 2,500 ptas.

per person for a three-course meal, including house wine and coffee, and excluding tax

Golf
Certain hotels cater almost exclusively to golfers, offering guests reduced greens fees: Parador de Golf, near San Pedro de Alcántara, the Hotel Atalaya Park in Estepona, and the El Paraíso, between San Pedro and Estepona. Other hotels, such as Los Monteros near Marbella, also have their own golf courses.

Indispensable for anyone trying to make his or her own golfing arrangements is a copy of *Costa Golf,* a monthly magazine available from all newsstands. The *Andalucía Golf Guide,* published by the tourist department of the Regional Government of Andalucía, lists details of all courses on the Costa del Sol; it is available free from the Tourist Office of Spain.

Lodging
The most highly developed stretch of the Costa del Sol lies between Torremolinos and Fuengirola, where the concrete highrises of the '60s and early '70s are now showing their age; poorly built in the first place, they're often in need of total refurbishment and improvement in standards of service. They do offer large, functional rooms close to the sea at competitive rates. The never-waning popularity of this area as a low-

budget vacation destination means that most such hotels are booked in high season by foreign package-tour operators. Finding a room at Easter, in July and August, or around the October 12 holiday weekend can be difficult if you haven't prebooked.

Málaga is poorly endowed with hotels for a city of its size. It has an excellent but small parador that can be hard to book, and few other hotels of note. Marbella, conversely, boasts more than its fair share of grand hotels, with five five-star hotels, three of which are classed as "grand deluxe" and rank among Spain's most expensive lodgings.

CATEGORY	COST*
$$$$	over 23,000 ptas.
$$$	11,000 ptas.–23,000 ptas.
$$	7,000 ptas.–11,000 ptas.
$	under 7,000 ptas.

per standard double room, excluding breakfast, tax, and service charge.

Exploring the Costa del Sol

While the coast is generally understood as the prime resource along the Costa del Sol, much of it is lined with skyscrapers and crowded with tourists, which may not be what you had in mind when you came to Spain. Inland are some of Andalucía's most charming secrets.

Great Itineraries

The Costa del Sol may be approached from east to west along the coastal highway N340. This famous route starts in the province of Granada, then heads west along the entire coastline of Málaga province, to enter Cádiz province briefly at Sotogrande and San Roque, before terminating at the Rock of Gibraltar. The main centers along this route are Nerja, Málaga (the region's capital and only major city), Torremolinos, Fuengirola, Marbella, and Estepona. You'll also find suggestions for detours inland to mountain villages and the dramatic scenery of El Chorro gorge. A major detour from the coastal highway not to be missed, is to Ronda, high in the mountains, 54 km/34 mi inland.

A week to 10 days would give you time to see nearly all of the major beaches and cities, venture inland, and maybe even hop across to Morocco. Five days is really the lower limit for seeing the Costa del Sol and doing anything other than drive. Three days is time for a taste of the major sights and a look at the coast.

Numbers in the text below correspond to numbers in the margin and on the maps.

IF YOU HAVE 3 DAYS

Start with the Costa Tropical, formerly the Costa del Sol Oriental, this coast's eastern end. See the villages of **Salobreña** ① and **Almuñecar** ② and the town of **Nerja** ③ and its Balcón de Europa over the sea. Have lunch at one of the perched restaurants near the square with sea views. Visit the village of **Frigiliana** ④ before proceeding to 🖫 **Málaga** ⑦ for the night. Your second morning explore Málaga before moving up into the hills for lunch at the Parador de **Antequera** ⑧. From Antequera, make the 100 km/62 mi drive over to 🖫 **Ronda** ⑰ for your second night. See Ronda in the early morning and drive to **Marbella** ⑯ on the coast for lunch at the beach. From Marbella you can either move west to Sotogrande, **San Roque** ㉖, and **Gibraltar** ㉗–㊴ or back east to tumultuous 🖫 **Torremolinos** ⑫ for a night on the town.

IF YOU HAVE 5 DAYS

Explore Granada's Costa Tropical, seeing the villages of **Salobreña** ① and **Almuñecar** ② before the town of **Nerja** ③ and its Balcón de Europa over the sea. Have lunch at one of the restaurants near the square with balconies and sea views. Visit the village of **Frigiliana** ④ before proceeding to ⊞ **Málaga** ⑦ for the night. Your second day can be dedicated to exploring Málaga before moving up into the hills for the sunset and a night in the Parador de ⊞ **Antequera** ⑧. On the third day, drive from Antequera up to the village of Archidona before working your way back through the Parque Natural de Antequera, **Alora** ⑨, the Garganta (gorge) del Chorro (stream) to the coast at ⊞ **Torremolinos** ⑫ for a radical change of scenery in the lively Carihuela beach district. On your fourth day, drive to **Mijas** ⑮ and explore this picturesque village before moving on to ⊞ **Marbella** ⑯ for an afternoon among the glitterati. If everything is too manicured for your taste, hop up to the village of Ojen for a complete change of pace. Spend the early evening getting to ⊞ **Ronda** ⑰ for a look at one of Andalucía's most stunning mountain enclaves. Day five is a chance to see more of Ronda before touring through **Olvera** ⑱ and the mountain towns of **Setenil de las Bodegas** ⑲, **El Gastor** ⑳, Ronda la Vieja, and the Roman settlement of Acinipo and the village of **Zahara de la Sierra** ㉑. Finish this ambitious day with a look at Sotogrande and **San Roque** ㉖ on your way into ⊞ **Gibraltar** ㉗–㉟ for the night.

When to Tour the Costa del Sol

Winter is a good time to be on the Costa del Sol. The temperatures are more moderate and there are fewer vacationers. Fall and spring are also prime opportunities. Avoid the summer: it's too hot and crowded. The longest days with the fewest tourists are in May and June. Many ceremonies and processions of Holy Week are memorable.

THE COSTA TROPICAL

East of Málaga and west of Almería, the so-called Costa Tropical has escaped the worst excesses of the property developers. Housing developments inspired by Andalucían village architecture, rather than faceless, concrete tower blocks, are the norm and the tourist onslaught has been milder. You may find packed beaches and traffic-choked roads at the height of the season, but for most of the year, it's relatively free from tourists, if not from foreign expatriate residents.

Numbers in the margin correspond to points of interest on the Costa del Sol map.

Salobreña

❶ *102 km (63 mi) east of Málaga.*

Salobreña is reached either by descending through the mountains from Granada or continuing west from Almería on the N340 coast road. A short detour to the left from the highway brings you to this unspoiled village whose near-perpendicular streets and old, white houses perch on a steep hill beneath a Moorish fortress. Salobreña provides a sample of the Andalucían pueblo atmosphere.

Almuñecar

❷ *85 km (53 mi) east of Málaga.*

Almuñécar has been a fishing village since Phoenician times, 3,000 years ago, when it was called Sexi. The Moors built a castle here, where the kings of Granada once kept their treasures. Today, Almuñécar is a small-time resort with a shingle beach, popular with Spanish and Belgian vacationers. To get there, the road from Motril to Málaga passes through

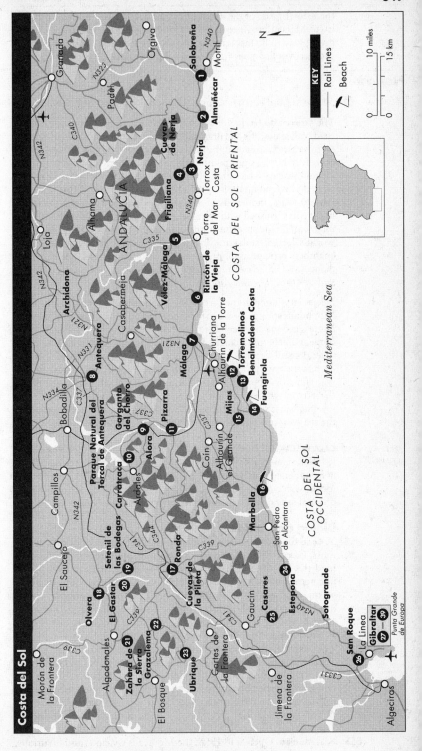

Costa del Sol

the former heart of the empire of sugar barons who brought prosperity to Málaga province in the 19th century. Today, the cane fields are giving way to litchis, limes, mangoes, papaws, and olive groves. Avocado groves line your route on the descent into the village.

Nerja ★

❸ *52 km (32 mi) east of Málaga; 22 km (14 mi) west of Almuñecar.*

The **Cuevas de Nerja** are between Almuñecar and Nerja, a stretch of road with giant cliffs and dramatic seascapes that provide the best scenery on this eastern stretch of the Costa. Above the village of Maro, 4 km/2½ mi before Nerja, signs point to the entrance to the caves. These huge, Paleolithic caves, thought to be between 12,000 and 20,000 years old, were discovered in 1959 by children playing on the hillside. Over the past 30 years, thousands of tourists have tramped through the flood-lit caverns furnished with spires and turrets created by centuries of dripping water. One suspended pinnacle, 200 feet long, claims the title of world's largest stalactite. In summer these awesome, subterranean chambers provide an impressive setting for concert and ballet performances. ☎ *95/252–9520.* ☞ *450 ptas.* ☾ *Sept.–June, daily 10:30–2 and 3:30–6; July and Aug., daily 10:30–6.*

Nerja—its name comes from the Moorish word *narixa,* meaning "abundant springs"—is a rapidly developing resort. Happily, much of Nerja's growth has been confined to *urbanizaciones* ("village" developments). The old village of Nerja is clustered on a headland above several small beaches and rocky coves that offer reasonable bathing despite the gray, gritty sand. In high season Nerja's beaches are packed with sun-worshipping northern Europeans, but at other times wandering the narrow, whitewashed streets and courtyards of the old town is enjoyable. Nerja's highlight is the **Balcón de Europa,** a lookout high above the sea on a promontory just off the central square.

NEED A BREAK?
> **CALA BELLA** – (⊠ Puerta del Mar 10, ☎ 95/252–0700) and **Portofino** (⊠ Puerta del Mar 4, ☎ 95/252–0150) are medium-priced restaurants in neighboring Andalucían houses close to the main square. Their dining rooms, with outdoor balconies offering dramatic cliff-top sea views, are an ideal setting for lunch, or dinner on a summer evening.

Dining and Lodging

$$ ✕ **Casa Luque.** One of the most authentically Spanish of Nerja's restau-
★ rants, Casa Luque is located in a charming, old Andalucían house behind the Balcón de Europa Church. The menu features dishes from northern Spain, often of Basque or Navarrese origin, with an emphasis on meat and game, although good, fresh fish is available, too. A lovely patio makes a perfect setting for summer dining. ⊠ *Plaza Cavana 2,* ☎ *95/252–1004. AE, DC, MC, V. Closed Mon. and Feb.*

$$ ✕ **Udo Heimer.** Your host is a genial German who will give you a warm welcome at his Art Deco villa in a new development to the east of town. The menu is a combination of traditional German dishes and local products. Ham-stuffed pumpkin, giant prawns wrapped in bacon and served in a curried banana sauce, and pork knuckle and sauerkraut are just some of the concoctions you might try. ⊠ *Pueblo Andaluz 27,* ☎ *95/252–0032. AE, DC, MC, V. Closed Wed. and Jan. No lunch.*

$$$ ✕▦ **Mónica.** Opened in 1986, the Mónica is spacious and luxurious, with cool, Moorish-style architecture and lots of marble. Popular with package tours, it's also within easy walking distance of the center of town. ⊠ *Playa Torrecilla, 29780,* ☎ *95/252–1100.* 𝔽𝔸𝕏 *95/252–*

*1162. 234 rooms. 2 restaurants, bar, 2 pools, tennis court, nightclub.
AE, DC, MC, V.*

$$$ ✕⏁ **Parador de Nerja.** This modern (as opposed to a castle) parador
is located east of Nerja's center and stands in a pleasant, leafy garden
on the cliff edge. Rooms in the original, two-story building have bal-
conies overlooking the garden and, obliquely, the sea, and those in the
newer, single-story wing, open onto their own patios. An elevator will
take you down to the rocky beach. The restaurant concentrates on local
cuisine and is known for its fish dishes; try the *pez espada a la naranja*
(swordfish in orange sauce) or the giant langostino shrimp. ✉ *Almuñecar
8, 29780,* ☎ *95/252–0050,* ⊞ *95/252–1997. 73 rooms. Restaurant,
pool. AE, DC, MC, V.*

Nightlife and the Arts

El Colono (✉ Granada 6, Nerja, ☎ 95/252–1826) is a flamenco club
and restaurant in a typical Andalucían house in the town center. Din-
ner shows begin at 9 PM on Wednesdays in winter, and at 9:30 or 10
PM Wednesdays through Fridays in summer. There's a choice of three
set-price menus.

Frigiliana

④ *58 km (36 mi) east of Málaga.*

The village of Frigiliana perches on a mountain ridge overlooking the
ocean. In 1567, one of the last battles between the Moors and Chris-
tians was fought here. Spectacular views and an old quarter with cob-
bled streets and ancient houses reward this short drive off the main
road. Frigiliana can also be reached by bus from Nerja.

Vélez-Málaga

⑤ *36 km (22 mi) east of Málaga.*

Vélez-Málaga is the capital of the Ajarquía region. A pleasant, agri-
cultural town of white houses, Vélez-Málaga is a center for strawberry
growing and vineyards producing the sweet muscatel grapes for which
Málaga is famous. A **Thursday market, ruins of a Moorish castle,** and
the **church of Santa María la Mayor,** built in Mudéjar (Spanish Mus-
lim) style on the site of a mosque destroyed when the town fell to the
Christians in 1487, all merit a quick visit.

Rincón de la Vieja

⑥ *1 km (⅔ mi) outside Rincón de la Victoria.*

Visit the Cueva del Tesoro (Treasure Cave), where Moorish kings re-
putedly hid their treasure as they fled Christian attackers. The caves
were inhabited in prehistoric times, and early domestic utensils are on
display. ☎ *95/240–2907.* ◷ *Apr.–Sept., daily 10–2 and 4–7; Oct.–Mar.,
Tues.–Sun. 10–2 and 4–7.*

MÁLAGA AND INLAND

The city of Málaga and the towns and villages of the upland hills and
valleys to the north provide the kind of sharp contrasts that make trav-
elling in Spain exciting. From the tiny streets honeycombing the steamy
depths of Málaga to the rocky cliffs and gorges between Alora and Archi-
dona, the Moorish legacy is the most unifying theme throughout.

Málaga

❼ *175 mi (109 mi) southeast of Córdoba.*

The city of Málaga, with about 670,000 inhabitants, claims the title of Capital of the Costa del Sol, though in reality most tourists simply use its airport and bypass the city itself. Approaching the city from the airport, you'll be greeted by urban sprawl, where the huge highrises flung up in the 1970s march determinedly toward Torremolinos. But don't despair, for in its center and eastern suburbs, Málaga is a pleasant port city, with ancient streets and lovely villas set amid exotic foliage. It enjoys a subtropical climate, is blessed with lush vegetation, and averages some 324 days of sunshine a year.

Arriving from Nerja, you'll come into Málaga through the suburbs of El Palo and Pedregalejos, once traditional fishing villages in their own right. Here you can eat wonderfully fresh fish in the numerous rough-and-ready *chiringuitos* (fishermen's restaurants) on the beach and enjoy a stroll on Pedregalejos's seafront promenade or on the tree-lined streets of El Limonar. At sunset take a walk along the **Paseo Marítimo,** and watch the lighthouse start its nightly vigil.

Once you reach the center, the **Plaza de la Marina,** with its outdoor cafés and illuminated fountain overlooking the port, is a pleasant place for a drink. From here stroll through the shady, palm-lined gardens of the **Paseo del Parque,** scene of Málaga's August fair, or browse on Calle Marqués de Larios, the main shopping street.

The narrow streets and alleyways on each side of **Calle Marqués de Larios** have a charm of their own. Wander the warren of passageways around Pasaje Chinitas, off Plaza de la Constitución; peep into the dark, vaulted bodegas where old men down glasses of *seco añejo* or *Málaga Virgen,* local wines made from Málaga's muscatel grapes. Silversmiths and vendors of religious books and statues ply their trade in shops that have changed little since the turn of the century. Across Larios, in the streets leading through to Calle Nueva, you'll find shoe-shine boys, lottery ticket vendors, carnation-sporting Gypsies, beggars, and a wealth of tapas bars dispensing wine from huge barrels.

A word of warning: Málaga has one of the highest unemployment rates in Spain; poverty and crime are rife (although drug peddling, once fairly common in the streets, has declined). There have been numerous reports of muggings, and you're better off not carrying purses or valuables in the streets or on the way up to Gibralfaro (☞ *below*).

NEED A
BREAK?

EL BOQUERÓN DE LA PLATA – (✉ Alarcón Luján 6) is one of Málaga's most famous tapas bars. The counter is piled high with fresh seafood, and the floor is ankle deep in discarded shells.

After exploring the alleyways of the old town, visit the **cathedral,** built between 1528 and 1782 on the site of the former mosque. Mainly Renaissance in style, Málaga Cathedral is not one of the great cathedrals of Spain and is unfinished, the funds having run out. One story has it that the allocated money was donated instead to the American War of Independence. The lovely, enclosed choir, which miraculously survived the burnings of the civil war, is the work of the great 17th-century artist Pedro de Mena, who in places has carved the wood wafer-thin to express the fold of a robe or shape of a finger. ✉ *Calle de Molina Lario,* ☎ *95/221–5916.* 🎫 *Cathedral free, choir 300 ptas.* ⏱ *Daily 10–12:30 and 4–5:30.*

Near the cathedral, the **Museo de Bellas Artes** (Fine Arts Museum) is set in the old Palace of the Counts of Buenavista, reached across a courtyard off Calle San Agustín. Inside, you'll find Roman mosaics and minor canvases by Luis de Morales, Alonso Cano, Murillo, Zurbarán, and Ribera, as well as 19th- and 20th-century paintings. Its most interesting treasure is a gallery of early childhood drawings by Málaga's most famous native son, Pablo Picasso, who was born only a few hundred yards away in a house on Plaza de la Merced (Number 15). ⊠ *San Agustín 6,* ☎ *95/22–18387.* ☜ *300 ptas.* ☉ *Apr.–Oct., Tues.–Sat. 10–1:30 and 5–8, Sun. 10–1:30; Nov.–Mar., Tues.–Fri. 10–1:30 and 4–7, weekends 10–1:30.*

The **Alcazaba,** undoubtedly the city's best sight, is a fortress begun in the 8th century, when Málaga was the principal port of the Moorish kingdom. The ruins of the Roman amphitheater at its entrance were uncovered when the fort was restored. The inner palace was built between 1057 and 1063, when the Moorish emirs took up residence here. Ferdinand and Isabella lived here, too, for a while, after their conquest of Málaga in 1487. Orange trees and bougainvillea have been planted among the ruins, whose heights offer great views of the park and port. Inside the enclosure you'll find the **Museo Arqueológico** (Archaeological Museum), with displays from Málaga's Roman and Moorish periods. ⊠ *Entrance on Alcazabilla.* ☎ *95/222–0043.* ☜ *300 ptas.* ☉ *Apr.–Sept., Mon.–Sat. 11–2 and 5–8, Sun. 10–2; Oct.–Mar., Mon.–Sat. 10–1 and 4–7, Sun. 10–2.*

★ Magnificent views will reward a climb up through the Alcazaba gardens to the summit of **Gibralfaro.** (There have been reports of thieves here, so don't go alone, and don't carry valuables.) Alternatively, you can drive to Gibralfaro by way of Calle Victoria or take a minibus that leaves roughly every 1½ hours from near the cathedral on Calle Molina Larios for the parador at the top of Gibralfaro. The Gibralfaro fortifications were built for Yusuf I in the 14th century. The Moors called them Jebelfaro, meaning "rock of the lighthouse," after a beacon that stood here to guide ships into the harbor and warn of invasions by pirates. Today the beacon is gone, succeeded by the small parador, a delightful place for a meal or a drink.

On the far side of the city center, beside the river, you'll find the **Museo de Artes Populares** (Arts and Crafts Museum), housed in the old Mesón de la Victoria, a 17th-century inn. On display are horse carriages and carts, old agricultural implements, folk costumes, a forge, a bakery, an ancient grape press, and Málaga ceramics and sculptures. ⊠ *Pasillo de Santa Isabel 10,* ☎ *95/221–7137.* ☜ *200 ptas.* ☉ *Apr.–Oct., Tues.–Sat. 10–1:30 and 5–8, Sun. 10–1:30; Nov.–Mar., Tues.–Sat. 10–1:30 and 4–7, Sun. 10–1:30.*

Dining and Lodging

$$$ ★ ✕ **Café de París.** The owner of this elegantly intimate restaurant with warm, pink decor, in the Paseo Marítimo area, is a former chef of Horcher, in Madrid, and La Hacienda, in Marbella. Sophisticated Spanish diners come from far afield for such specialties as *rodaballo sobre espinacas* (turbot on a bed of spinach) and *hojaldre de langostinos* (giant shrimp en croûte). The *menú de degustación* allows you to try a little of everything. ⊠ *Vélez Málaga 10,* ☎ *95/222–5043. Reservations essential. AE, DC, MC, V. Closed Sun.*

$$$ ✕ **Casa Pedro.** It's crowded and noisy, but Malagueños have been flocking to this no-frills fish restaurant for more than 50 years. Out in El Palo, the restaurant has a huge, bare dining room that overlooks the ocean. If you know a little Spanish, are adventurous and patient, and like local color, try joining families who come for lunch on Sundays.

It's quieter at other times. ⊠ *Quitapenas 121, El Palo beach (Bus 11)*, ☎ *95/229–0003. AE, DC, MC, V. No dinner Mon.*

$–$$ ✕ **Rincon de Mata.** This is one of the best of the many restaurants in the pedestrian shopping area between Calle Larios and Calle Nueva. The menu is more interesting than most, with house specialties such as *tunedor* (calf in sauce). In summer there are tables on the sidewalk. ⊠ *Esparteros 8,* ☎ *95/222–3135. AE, DC, MC, V.*

$ ✕ **La Cancela.** Located in an alley off Calle Granada at the top of Molina Lario, this pretty bistro serving standard Spanish fare is ideal for lunch after a morning's shopping in the town center. The two dining rooms (one upstairs, one down) are crowded with curious objects: iron grilles, bird cages, potted plants, and plastic flowers. In summer, tables are placed on the sidewalk for outdoor lunching on what amounts to a sheltered patio. ⊠ *Denís Belgrano 5,* ☎ *95/222–3125. AE, DC, MC, V.*

$$–$$$ ✕⌸ **Parador de Málaga-Gibralfaro.** Surrounded by pine trees on top
★ of Gibralfaro mountain (3½ km/2 mi) above the city, this cozy parador, built of gray stone and smothered in ivy, offers spectacular views of the city and bay. Recent renovations have added a swimming pool and doubled the number of rooms. Its typical parador accommodations (twin beds, matching curtains and bedspreads, and woven rugs on a bare floor) are the best in Málaga. Reservations are *required long in advance.* ⊠ *Apd. de Correos 274, Gibralfaro, 29016,* ☎ *95/222–1903,* FAX *95/222–1904. 38 rooms. Restaurant, bar, pool, conference rooms. AE, DC, MC, V.*

$$ ✕⌸ **Las Vegas.** In a pleasant, though somewhat tumultuous, part of
★ town, just east of the center, this conveniently located hotel has a dining room overlooking the Paseo Marítimo, a pool, and a large, leafy garden. This option remains the best choice if you can't get into the parador. The rooms at the back enjoy a good view of the ocean, as does the spacious, panoramic dining room. ⊠ *Paseo de Sancha 22, 29016,* ☎ *95/221–7712,* FAX *95/222–4889. 107 rooms. Restaurant, bar, pool. AE, DC, MC, V.*

$$$ ⌸ **Los Naranjos.** This compact hotel is on a pleasant but busy avenue in a residential district one kilometer east of the city center. There's a small garden with *naranjos* (orange trees) in front, but rooms overlooking the street can be noisy with the windows open. ⊠ *Paseo de Sancha 35, 29016,* ☎ *95/222–4317 or 95/222–4319,* FAX *95/222–5975. 41 rooms. Breakfast room, bar. AE, DC, MC, V.*

$ ⌸ **Victoria.** This small, renovated hostel offers excellent budget accommodations in a very central location. Situated in a 19th-century, stone row house whose facade has been painted gleaming white, it is on a side street just off Calle Larios. ⊠ *Sancha Lara 3, 29015,* ☎ *95/ 222–4223. 13 rooms. AE, DC, MC, V.*

Nightlife and the Arts

The region's main theater is the **Teatro Cervantes** (⊠ Ramos Marín, Málaga, ☎ 95/222–4100). It puts on plays (in Spanish), concerts, and flamenco performances.

The Málaga Symphony Orchestra gives a winter season of orchestral concerts and chamber music, and most performances are held at the **Teatro Cervantes** in Málaga (⊠ Ramos Marín, ☎ 95/222–4100 or 95/222–4109). Evening concerts (chamber music, organ, and choral recitals) are held in the beautiful setting of the **Hotel la Bobadilla** (☎ 958/321861), in the heart of the countryside about 60 km/37 mi north of Málaga on the Málaga-Granada provincial border (☞ Chapter 12).

Famous flamenco stars perform at the **Teatro Cervantes** (✉ Ramos Marín, ☎ 95/222–4100), drawing enthusiastic audiences.

The main nightlife districts are along the Paseo Marítimo and out in the eastern suburbs on Avenida Juan Sebastián Elcano and the beachfront at Pedregalejos.

Shopping

In Málaga, the **Corte Inglés** department store, the only store open during siesta, provides English interpreters, mailing, tax-refund, and money-changing facilities. ✉ *Avda. de Andalucía 46,* ☎ *95/230–0000.* ☉ *Mon.–Sat. 10–9.*

Antequera

❽ *64 km (40 mi) from Málaga, 43 km (27 mi) from Pizarra, 108 km (67 mi) from Ronda (via Pizarra).*

Antequera became one of the great strongholds of the Moors following their defeat at Córdoba and Seville in the 13th century. Its fall to the Christians in 1410 opened the gateway to Granada. The Moors retreated, leaving behind a **fortress** on the town heights in whose midst the parador now stands. Of the town's many churches, the collegiate church of **Santa María la Mayor,** a 16th-century sandstone building with a fine ribbed vault, used today as a concert hall and crafts training center, is one of the best. Another landmark is the **church of San Sebastián,** with a brick Baroque-Mudéjar tower.

Antequera's pride and joy is **Efebo,** a beautiful bronze statue of a boy that stands almost 5 feet high and dates back to Roman times. It's on display in the **Museo Municipal** (Municipal Museum). ✉ *Palacio de Nájera, Coso Viejo.* ☉ *Tues.–Sat. 10–1:30, Sun. 11–1.*

From Antequera several options are open to you. To the east of town along N342 the dramatic silhouette of the **Peña de los Enamorados** (Lovers' Rock) is an Andalucían landmark. Legend recounts how a Moorish princess and a Christian shepherd boy eloped here one night and next morning cast themselves to their deaths from its famous peak. Its outline is often likened to the profile of the Cordoban bullfighter Manolete. Eight km/5 mi beyond the Peña, the village of Archidona winds its way up a steep mountain slope beneath the ruins of a Moorish castle. This picturesque white cluster is worth a detour for the sake of its contrasting **Plaza Ochavada,** a magnificent 17th-century square resplendent in red and ocher stone.

Ten km/6 mi to the south of Antequera on C3310, the **Parque Natural del Torcal de Antequera** has well-marked walking trails (for which you'll need sturdy shoes) that guide you among eerie pillars of pink sandstone sculpted by millennia of wind and rain.

Dining and Lodging

$–$$ ✗ **Las Pedrizas.** This restaurant, serving regional Andalucían cooking, is owned by a local fraternal organization but is open to the public. Local favorites include *choto* (roast kid) and *jamon ibérico* (Iberian ham), but their quality has declined recently. ✉ *Km 527 on Carretera Malaga–Madrid,* ☎ *95/275–1250. MC, V.*

$$ ✗▥ **Parador de Antequera.** This white parador is set among the ruins of a Moorish fortress on the heights overlooking Antequera. The public rooms are sparsely decorated, with Alpujarran rugs on tile floors and paintings on the walls. The comfortable rooms have twin beds, covered with woven rugs, and spacious, tile bathrooms. ⊠ *García del Olmo, 29200,* ☎ *95/284–0261,* 𝐅𝐀𝐗 *95/284–1312. 55 rooms. Restaurant, pool. AE, DC, MC, V.*

Alora★

❾ *37 km (23 mi) from Antequera, 6 km (4 mi) from Pizarra.*

C337 to the southwest of Antequera will bring you to the turnoff for Alora. From Alora follow a small road north to the awe-inspiring **Garganta (gorge) del Chorro.** Here, in a deep chasm in the limestone cliff, the Guadalhorce River churns and snakes its way some 600 feet below the road. The railroad track that worms in and out of tunnels in the cleft is, amazingly, the main line out of Málaga heading north for Bobadilla junction and, eventually, Madrid.

Carratraca

❿ *17 km (11 mi) northwest of Alora, 54 km (34 mi) northeast of Ronda.*

The old spa town of Carratraca has a Moorish-style **Ayuntamiento** (City Hall) and unusual **polygonal bullring.** It was formerly a favorite watering hole of the Spanish and foreign aristocracy. Its hotel, the Hostal del Príncipe, once sheltered Empress Eugénie, wife of Napoleon III. Lord Byron, too, came to partake of the cure. Today, you can still relax in the sulfur baths of Carratraca's splendid **marble and tile bathhouse.**

En Route   From Carratraca return to Alora, from which C337 takes you back to the coast through groves of citrus and olives.

Pizarra

⓫ *6 km (4 mi) south of Alora, 65 km (40 mi) east of Ronda.*

At Pizarra, you will be able to visit the **Museo Municipal de Pizarra,** formerly known as the Hollander Museum. Gino and Barbara Hollander, originally from the United States, founded the museum in their converted, 18th-century farmhouse home, with an exceptional collection of paintings and objets d'art, furniture and archeological finds. ⊠ *Cortijo Casablanca 29, 29560, 1 km/½ mi south of Pizarra,* ☎ *95/248–3257.* ▣ *250 ptas.* ☉ *Daily 10–2 and 4–8.*

THE COSTA DEL SOL OCCIDENTAL

After rejoining N340, the coastal highway, 12 km/7 mi to the west of Málaga, the sprawling outskirts of Torremolinos mark the beginning of the "real Costa del Sol." This overdeveloped stretch of beaches, high-rise hotels and tourist activity may be what you want, but if you're not looking for cities on the sand, pass on quickly to the next section.

Torremolinos

⓬ *12 km (7 mi) west of Málaga, 16 km (10 mi) northeast of Fuengirola, 43 km (27 mi) east of Marbella.*

Fun in the sun is what Torremolinos is all about. Swarms of northern European vacationers, the young and not so young, throng its streets in season. Scantily attired and pink-fleshed, they shop for bargains on the Calle San Miguel, down sangría in the bars of La Nogalera, and dance the night away in discotheques. By day the sunseekers flock to the El Bajondillo and La Carihuela beaches, whose sand is the usual fine, gray grit, and in high summer it's hard to find a patch to call your own.

Torremolinos has two distinct sections. The first, **Central T-town,** is built around the Plaza Costa del Sol; Calle San Miguel, the main shopping street; and the brash Nogalera Plaza, full of overpriced bars and "foreign" restaurants. The Pueblo Blanco area off Calle Casablanca is pleasant, and the Cuesta del Tajo, at the far end of San Miguel, winds down a steep slope to the Bajondillo Beach. Here, crumbling walls, bougainvillea-clad patios, and old cottages give a hint of the fishing village this once was.

The second section of Torremolinos is the much nicer district of **La Carihuela.** To reach it, head west out of town on Avenida Carlota Alessandri, and turn left by the Hotel La Paloma. Far more authentically Spanish, the Carihuela retains many of its old fishermen's cottages and several excellent fish restaurants. Its traffic-free esplanade makes for an enjoyable stroll, especially on a summer evening or at Sunday lunchtime, when it's packed with Spanish families.

NEED A BREAK? **La Casita** (⊠ Calle Bulto 42) is a small bar in an old fisherman's cottage. Look in here any night after dinner (10 PM onward) and you'll find a nucleus of the faithful unravelling the mysteries of the universe.

The **Atlantis Mundo Aquatico** off the bypass, near the Palacio de Congresos Convention Center, has water chutes, artificial waves, water mountains, and pools. ☎ 95/238–8888. ⊡ 1,595 ptas. ☉ May–Sept., daily 10–7.

Two km/1 mi inland, at Arroyo de la Miel, you can visit **Tivoli World,** the Costa del Sol's leading amusement park. Don't expect the sleek perfection of Disneyland, but there's a 4,000-seat, open-air auditorium that often features international stars alongside the cancan, flamenco, or Spanish ballet. You'll also find roller coasters, a Ferris wheel, illuminated fountains, a Chinese pagoda, Wild West shows, and some 40 or so restaurants. ☎ 95/244–2848. ⊡ Sept.–Apr. 450 ptas., May –Aug. 600 ptas. ☉ Winter, weekends and holidays; summer, daily.

Dining and Lodging

$$$ ✕ **Juan.** This Carihuela hotspot is a good place for seafood in summer, with a sunny, outdoor patio facing the sea. The specialties include the great Costa del Sol standbys–*sopa de mariscos* (shellfish soup), *dorada al horno* (oven-roasted giltheads), and fritura malagueña. ⊠ *Paseo Marítimo 29, La Carihuela,* ☎ 95/238–5656. AE, DC, MC, V.

$$ ✕ **Casa Guaquin.** On a seaside patio in La Carihuela, this is widely known as the best seafood restaurant in the region. Ever-changing daily catches are served alongside such menu stalwarts as *coquillas al ajillo* (sea cockles in garlic sauce). ⊠ *Paseo Marítimo 63,* ☎ 95/238–4530. AE, MC, V. Closed Thurs. and mid-Dec.–mid-Jan.

$$ ✕ **El Atrio.** In Torremolinos-center, there is a definite French feel–with white walls, pink tablecloths, dark, wood tables and chairs in the small dining room–to this restaurant. Snails, onion soup, and quiche lorraine are often on the menu; the entrées are predominantly meat (a welcome change in this mecca of seafood); and for dessert, you'll find it hard to resist the mouth-watering profiteroles. On summer evenings you can dine outside in the square. ⊠ *Casablanca 9, Plaza Pueblo Blanco,* ☎ 95/238–8850. AE, MC, V. Closed Sun. and Dec. No lunch.

$$ ✕ **Europa.** A short walk from the Carihuela, this villa in a large garden is a very Spanish institution (rare for Torremolinos). You can dine in leafy surroundings, and it's best on Sundays, when local families come here for a leisurely lunch. ⊠ *Via Imperial 32,* ☎ 95/238–8022. AE, DC, MC, V.

$–$$ ✕ **El Roqueo.** Owned by a former fisherman, this is one of the locals' favorite Carihuela fish restaurants. Ingredients are always fresh and prices are very reasonable. ⊠ *Carmen 35,* ☎ *95/238–4946. AE, DC, MC, V. Closed Tues. and Nov.*

$$$ ⌂ **Cervantes.** This busy, cosmopolitan hotel, one of Torremolinos's consistently good places to stay in the heart of town, is ideal for those who want to be in the center of things. It's not by the beach, but there's a pool, and the rooms are well furnished and comfortable. The service is good, and the panoramic dining room on the top floor is a favorite with locals. ⊠ *Las Mercedes, 29620,* ☎ *95/238–4033,* 𝐅𝐀𝐗 *95/238–4857. 396 rooms with bath. Dining room, 2 pools, sauna, hairdresser, shops, nightclub. AE, DC, MC, V.*

$$$ ⌂ **Lago Rojo.** In the heart of the old Carihuela district, this three-story, modern, white apartment building stands just two blocks back from the seafront. The well-maintained rooms all have balconies that overlook the the pool and small, tree-filled garden. There's no great view, but advantages are the modest prices and location close to the best bars and restaurants in town. ⊠ *Miami 1, 29620,* ☎ *95/238–7666,* 𝐅𝐀𝐗 *95/238–0891. 144 rooms. Pool. AE, DC, MC, V.*

$$$ ⌂ **Tropicana.** On the beach at the far end of the Carihuela in one of the most pleasant parts of Torremolinos, this is a relaxing resort hotel with its own beach club. A range of good restaurants are within five minutes' walk. ⊠ *Trópico 6, 29620,* ☎ *95/238–6600,* 𝐅𝐀𝐗 *95/238–0568. 86 rooms. Pool, beach. AE, DC, MC, V.*

$ ⌂ **Miami.** Set in an old, Andalucían villa in a shady garden west of the Carihuela, this is something of a find amid the ocean of concrete highrises. Staying here is like visiting a private Spanish home; the rooms are individually furnished, and there's a sitting room with a cozy fireplace. It's very popular, so book ahead. ⊠ *Aladiño 14, at Miami, 29620,* ☎ *95/238–5255. 26 rooms. Pool. No credit cards.*

Nightlife and the Arts

Taberna Flamenca Pepe López (⊠ Plaza de la Gamba Alegre, ☎ 95/238–1284) is the best bet for flamenco in Torremolinos. **Molino de la Bóveda** (⊠ Cuesta del Tajo 8, Torremolinos, ☎ 95/238–1185) is a lively club with South American guitar music and flamenco singing and dancing. Also try **La Carreta** (☎ 95/238–2649) in the Eurosol building and **Cal Viva** (☎ 95/237–2345) on the Paseo Marítimo in Playamar, Edificio Copacabana.

The theater of the amusement park **Tivoli World** (☎ 95/244–2848) often puts on cabarets with international stars and flamenco dancing.

Benalmádena Costa

⑬ *9 km (6 mi) west of Torremolinos, 9 km (6 mi) east of Mijas.*

West of Torremolinos come the similar but more staid resorts of Benalmádena Costa and Fuengirola. Benalmádena Costa is run almost exclusively by package-tour operators and offers little to draw the independent traveler, though there's a pleasant-enough marina.

Dining and Lodging

$$$ ✕ **Ventorillo de la Perra.** If you've been searching the coast for somewhere typical, then this old inn, which dates to 1785, could well be the place. Outside there's a leafy patio, and inside a cozy, rustic atmosphere prevails in the dining room and in the bar, with its ham-hung ceiling. Choose between local Malagueño cooking, regular Spanish fare, and international favorites. The *ajo blanco* (a cold garlic soup) makes a particularly good appetizer. ✉ *Avda. Constitución, in Arroyo de la Miel,* ☎ *95/244–1966. AE, DC, MC, V. Closed Mon.*

$$ ✗ **Casa Fidel.** Rustic touches like heavy beams and a large fireplace adorn this restaurant in Benalmádena Pueblo. The menu is based on expertly cooked international dishes. For appetizers, you could try *entremeses Casa Fidel* (a tasty selection of hors d'oeuvres); main courses include old favorites such as grilled sole, or you could go for something more exotic, like *perdiz en salsa de vino de Málaga* (partridge in Málaga wine). ✉ *Maestra Ayala 1,* ☎ *95/244–8221. AE, DC, MC, V. Closed Tues.*

Nightlife and the Arts

The **Fortuna Nightclub** of the **Casino Torrequebrada** (✉ Km 226 on N340, Benalmádena Costa, ☎ 95/244–2545) has flamenco and an international show with dancing to an orchestra, beginning at 9:30.

Fuengirola

⓵ *16 km (10 mi) west of Torremolinos, 27 km (17 mi) east of Marbella.*

Fuengirola is the poor stepsister of Torremolinos. It is duller and cheaper; many of the concrete pyramids along its promenade are holiday apartments catering to budget-minded vacationers from northern Europe. Fuengirola is a British and American retirement haven.

Dining and Lodging

$$ ✗ **La Cazuela.** An old fisherman's cottage, with low ceilings and white walls decorated with ceramic plates, houses this small Andalucían restaurant. The menu offers inexpensive daily specials as well as regular à la carte selections. Old favorites include chicken Kiev, pork chop and applesauce, and pepper steak. ✉ *Miguel Márquez 8,* ☎ *95/ 247–4634. AE, MC, V. Closed Oct.–Easter.*

$$ ✗▥ **Florida.** A simple hotel with basic accommodations, almost opposite the water chute, is set back from the seafront behind a shady, semi-tropical garden where you can sunbathe and enjoy a drink at the poolside bar. One of Fuengirola's original hotels, it dates back to the years before the land boom and is actually run by its owners. ✉ *Paseo Marítimo s/n, 29640,* ☎ *95/247–6100. 116 rooms. Restaurant, bar, pool. AE, DC, MC, V.*

$ ▥ **Sedeño.** This small, family-run hostel, renovated in 1992, makes an ideal base for anyone seeking simple, budget accommodations. It's in the center of town, one block back from the harbor, just off Jacinto Benavente, the café-lined street running down to the seafront. The rooms have balconies overlooking a tree-filled garden. ✉ *Don Jacinto 1, 29640,* ☎ *95/247–4788. 34 rooms. No credit cards.*

Nightlife and the Arts

For plays in English, try the **Salón de Variétés Theater** (✉ Emancipación 30, ☎ 95/247–4542).

Mijas★

⓵ *8 km (5 mi) north of Fuengirola, 18 km (11 mi) west of Torremolinos.*

The picturesque village of Mijas is in the foothills of the sierra just north of the coast. Every half hour buses leave Fuengirola bus station for the 8 km/5 mi drive through pine-clad hills. If you have a car and don't mind a mildly hair-raising drive, there's a far prettier approach from Benalmádena Pueblo by way of a winding, mountain road (currently being widened and straightened) that affords some great views. Though

Mijas was discovered long ago by the foreign-retiree community, and the large, touristy square where you arrive may well seem like an extension of the Costa, beyond this are hillside streets of whitewashed houses and a somewhat authentic village atmosphere.

Park in the Plaza Virgen de la Peña, where you can hire a "burro taxi" to explore the village, take a quick look at the Chapel of Mijas's patroness, the Virgen de la Peña, or, if such things appeal, visit the **Carromato de Max** with its collection of miniature curiosities from all over the world. ☜ *500 ptas.* ☉ *Weekdays 11–8, weekends 10–3.*

Wander over to the Plaza Constitución, the real village square, then walk up the slope beside the Mirlo Blanco restaurant to Mijas's tiny **bullring**. It's one of the few square bullrings in Spain. ☎ 95/248–5248. ☜ *Ring and museum 500 ptas.* ☉ *Weekdays 10–6.*

Visit the delightful **church** just up the hill from the bullring. It is impeccably decorated, especially at Easter, and its terrace and gardens afford a splendid panorama.

Wander at will through any of the **white streets** of Mijas; be sure to head up the hill behind the village; the higher you go, the more authentic the atmosphere. Take a peep inside the tiny church at the bottom of Calle San Sebastián; it's filled with flowers, and Rococo decorations on gleaming white walls.

NEED A
BREAK?
At No. 4 Calle Sa Sebastián, the **Bar Menguine** (or **Casa de los Jamones**) has row after row of hams strung from its ceiling and a couple of tables set aside for inexpensive meals.

Dining and Lodging

$$$ ╳ **El Padrastro.** Perched on a clifftop above the Plaza Virgen de la Peña, this restaurant is reached via an elevator from the square or by steps if you're energetic. The views over Fuengirola and the coast are its main drawing card. The menu features international and Spanish dishes such *lubina flameada al hinojo* (sea-bass flambéed in fennel). There is also a pool and outdoor terrace. ⊠ *Paseo del Compás,* ☎ *95/248–5000,* ℻ *95/248–5197. AE, DC, MC, V.*

$$$ ╳ **Valparaíso.** The setting is the attraction of this restaurant on the road leading up from Fuengirola to Mijas. The villa stands in its own garden with a swimming pool; you can dine on the outdoor terrace in summer, and afterward dance the night away to live music. In winter logs burn in a cozy fireplace. Try the *pato a la naranja* (duck in orange sauce). ⊠ *Carretera de Mijas, Km 4,* ☎ *95/248–5996. AE, MC, V. Closed Sun. Nov.–May. No lunch.*

$ ╳ **Mirlo Blanco.** Here sample Basque specialties such as *txangurro* (crab) and *merluza a las vasca* (hake with asparagus, eggs, and clam sauce). ⊠ *Plaza de la Constitución 13,* ☎ *95/248–5700. AE, MC, V.*

$$$$ ╳▣ **Byblos Andaluz.** In this luxury hotel (the coast's most expensive)
★ set in a huge garden of palms, cypresses, and fountains, you'll find every comfort for a pampered vacation. It is first and foremost a spa hotel, French owned, and famed for its thalasso-therapy, a treatment that uses seawater and seaweed and is applied in a Roman temple of cool, white marble and blue tiles. There are two outstanding restaurants: El Andaluz, which offers lunchtime buffets and low-calorie menus, and the superb Le Nailhac, with elegant decor and superb French cusine. ⊠ *Urbanización Mijas-Golf, 29640,* ☎ *95/247–3050,* ℻ *95/247–6783. 144 rooms. 2 restaurants, indoor and outdoor pools, spa, beauty salon, health club, 18-hole golf course, tennis courts, shops. AE, DC, MC, V.*

$$$ ✕⊞ **Mijas.** This beautifully situated hotel at the entrance to Mijas village offers a poolside restaurant and bar, gardens with views of the hillsides stretching down to Fuengirola and the Mediterranean, marble floors, wrought-iron window grilles, and Moorish shutters. The reception area is large and airy, and there's a delightful glass-roofed terrace. ⊠ *Urbanización Tamisa, 29650,* ☎ *95/248–5800,* ℻ *95/248–5825. 97 rooms with bath. Restaurant, indoor and outdoor pools, spa, tennis, health club. AE, DC, MC, V.*

Nightlife and the Arts

Between Benalmádena Costa and Carvajal, the **Casino Torrequebrada** (⊠ Km 226 on N340, Benalmádena Costa, ☎ 95/244–2545) is a huge, well-lit salon in the Hotel Torrequebrada. It's open 8 PM–4 AM, requires passport and jacket and tie, and offers roulette and blackjack.

The Hotel Mijas in Mijas Pueblo often has small art exhibitions in its lobby.

Marbella

⑯ *27 km (17 mi) west of Fuengirola, 28 km (17 mi) east of Estepona, 50 km (31 mi) southeast of Ronda.*

Marbella, the playground of the rich and home of movie stars, rock musicians, and dispossessed royal families of Europe, has attained the top rung on the ladder of social chic. Dip into any Spanish gossip magazine, and the glittering parties that fill its pages are doubtless taking place in Marbella.

Much of the action takes place on the fringes, for grand hotels and luxury restaurants line the waterfront for 20 km/12 mi on each side of the center. In the town itself, you may well wonder just why Marbella became so famous. The main thoroughfare, Avenida Ricardo Soriano, is singularly lacking in charm, and the Paseo Marítimo, though pleasant enough, with its array of seafood restaurants and pizza houses overlooking an ordinary beach, is far from spectacular.

The real charm of Marbella is to be found in the heart of the **old village,** which remains miraculously intact, a block or two back from the main highway. Here, narrow alleyways of whitewashed houses cluster round the central Plaza de los Naranjos, where colorful restaurants vie for space under the orange trees. Climb up on what remains of the old fortifications and stroll along the quaint Calle Virgen de los Dolores to the Plaza de Santo Cristo. Wander the maze of lanes and enjoy the geranium-bedecked windows and splashing fountains.

NEED A BREAK? | Virgen de Dolores is lined with inviting restaurants with prices more manageable than in nearby Plaza de los Naranjos. **Casa Eladio** (⊠ No. 6, ☎ 95/277–0083) has a charming indoor patio.

For a contrast to the glamour of the coast, drive up to **Ojén,** in the hills above Marbella. When you reach this ancient village, you enter another world. Don't miss the pretty pottery sold here or the Andalucían cemetery, with its rows of chambers for burial urns.

The road to Puerto Banús has been dubbed the Golden Mile. Here, a mosque, Arab banks, and the one-time residence of King Fahd of Saudi Arabia proclaim the influence of petro-dollars in this enclave of the rich. Seven km/4 mi west of central Marbella (between Km 175 and Km 174), a sign indicates the turnoff that leads down to **Puerto Banús.** Marbella's plush marina, with its 915 berths, is a gem of ostentatious wealth, a kind of Spanish answer to Saint Tropez. Huge, flashy yachts, beautiful people, and countless expensive shops and restaurants make up the glittering parade that continues long into the night. The set is an Andalucían pueblo of the 1980s built to emulate the typical fishing villages that once lined this coast.

Dining and Lodging

$$$$ ✕ **La Hacienda.** La Hacienda is one of the highest-rated restaurants in
★ Spain. The menu reflects the influence of both the late chef-proprietor Paul Schiff's native Belgium and his adopted Andalucía. The menú de degustación (about 7,500 ptas.) will enable you to sample creations such as *tortilla fría de trufas y foie gras* (cold truffle and foie gras omelette) and *solomillo de pato relleno de aceitunas* (duck breast stuffed with olives). The setting is an elegant villa on a hillside overlooking the ocean. ⊠ *Urbanización Las Chapas, Km 193 on N340, 12 km/7½ mi east of Marbella,* ☎ *95/283–1116. AE, DC, MC, V. Closed Mon., Tues., and mid-Nov.–mid-Dec.*

$$$$ ✕ **La Meridiana.** Another of Marbella's outstanding restaurants, and a favorite with the local jet set, La Meridiana is located west of town, behind the mosque. Moorish influence is apparent in its striking, modern architecture, and an enclosed terrace makes "outdoor" dining possible year-round. The cuisine is famous for its quality and the freshness of the ingredients, and here, too, there's a menú degustación. This is a good place to sample *ajo blanco* (a garlicky local version of gazpacho). ⊠ *Camino de la Cruz,* ☎ *95/277–6190. AE, DC, MC, V. Closed Nov. and Dec. No lunch June–Aug., or Mon. or Tues. Sept.–May.*

$$$ ✕ **La Fonda.** This is an 18th-century house filled with antique furni-
★ ture in one of the loveliest squares in Marbella's old town. La Fonda is owned by Horcher, one of Madrid's leading restaurateurs, and its cuisine combines the best of Spanish, French, and Austrian influences. A garden-patio filled with potted plants allows summer dining alfresco. ⊠ *Plaza del Santo Cristo 9,* ☎ *95/277–2512. AE, DC, MC, V. Closed Sun. No lunch.*

$$ ✕ **Cenicienta.** A friendly welcome, superb cuisine and professional service await you at "Cinderella's." The modern, white-stucco villa surrounded by a leafy garden and pine grove is on the ring road about a mile from the center of town. ⊠ *Cánovas del Castillo,* ☎ *95/277–4318. AE, MC, V. Closed Sun. and mid-Jan.–mid-Feb.*

$$ ✕ **La Tricicleta.** Located in an old house on a narrow alley in the center of town, English-owned La Tricicleta has become something of an institution among Marbella restaurants. You can have a pre-dinner drink in the downstairs bar, which is furnished like a private sitting room and heated with a log fire, and then dine upstairs or outside on the covered, rooftop patio. A longstanding favorite is the duck in beer sauce. ⊠ *Buitrago 14,* ☎ *95/277–7800. AE, MC, V. Closed Sun.*

$ ✕ **Mesón del Pollo.** This small, charming, and delicious "house of chicken" illustrates how Marbella, despite its tourism, can remain truly Spanish. Porcelain lampshades, azulejo tiles, and the scents of roasting chicken fill this popular lunch spot. Try the *pollo a la sevillana* dinner (roast chicken with squid, fried potatoes, salad, and cider), fritura malagueña, or tapas of octopus or meatballs. ⊠ *Antonio Martín across from El Fuerte Hotel, no phone. No credit cards.*

$$$$ ✕🏠 **Marbella Club.** This grande dame of Marbella hotels was the cre-
★ ation of Prince Alfonso von Hohenlohe, the man who "founded" Marbella. The club attracts a long-established clientele, as well as local patricians. The bungalow-style rooms range from cramped to spacious, and the decor varies from regional to modern. The grounds are exquisite, and breakfast is served on a patio where songbirds flit through the lush, subtropical vegetation. ⊠ *Blvd. Príncipe Alfonso von Hohenlohe s/n*

(1¼ mi west of Marbella), 29600, ☎ 95/282–2211, ℻ 95/282–9884. 129 rooms, including suites and bungalows, some of which have private pools. Restaurant, 2 pools, beauty salon, sauna, exercise room, nightclub. AE, DC, MC, V.

$$$$ ✕⛨ **Puente Romano.** The spectacular, super-deluxe, modern hotel and
★ apartment complex of low, white-stucco buildings is located west of Marbella between the Marbella Club and Puerto Banús. The "village" has a genuine Roman bridge in its beautifully landscaped grounds, which run right down to the beach. A disco (Olivia Valere) and two outstanding restaurants, El Puente and La Plaza, complete the picture. ⊠ *Carretera Cádiz at Km 177, 29600, ☎ 95/277–0100, ℻ 95/277–5766. 219 rooms. 2 restaurants, indoor pool, outdoor pool, tennis courts, shops, nightclub. AE, DC, MC, V.*

$$$ ✕⛨ **El Fuerte.** The hotel was built in the 1950s, and the decor is in keeping with that era. The rooms are simply but adequately furnished and have balconies overlooking the sea. A five-minute walk from the town center, El Fuerte stands at the end of the Paseo Marítimo, separated from the beach by a pleasant, palm-filled garden with an outdoor pool. ⊠ *Avda. El Fuerte, 29600, ☎ 95/286–1500. 263 rooms. Restaurant, outdoor and indoor pools, tennis courts, health club, squash. AE, DC, MC, V.*

$$$ ✕⛨ **Los Monteros.** Situated 5 km/3 mi east of Marbella, on the road to Málaga, this exclusive hotel stands surrounded by pine woods and luxurious gardens on the sea side of the highway. It offers a wide range of facilities, including gourmet dining in its famous El Corzo Grill restaurant. The rooms are formally decorated, and the service is impeccable. British visitors make up some 80% of the guests. ⊠ *Urbanización Los Monteros, Carretera N340 at Km 187, 29600, ☎ 95/ 277–1700, ℻ 95/282–5846. 165 rooms. 2 restaurants, 1 indoor and 2 outdoor pools, beauty salon, sauna, 18-hole golf course, 10 tennis courts, exercise room, squash, horseback riding, shops, nightclub. AE, DC, MC, V.*

$ ⛨ **Pilar.** This may be the best find in Marbella: a cheerful and charming hotel in a central location–and very fairly priced to boot. It was taken over in 1992 by Scotsman Michael Wright, a former butler and master of guest houses in Edinburgh. It's clean and intimate and includes such delightful surprises as a log fire in winter. ⊠ *Mesoncillo 4, ☎ 95/282–9936. 17 rooms. Bar. No credit cards.*

Nightlife and the Arts

Olivia Valere at the supersleek Puente Romano hotel is the Costa del Sol's most exclusive disco; call ahead and take your passport. ⊠ *Km 184 on N340, ☎ 95/277–0100. ☉ Tues.–Sun.*

Willy Salsa (⊠ Km 186 on N340, ☎ 95/277–0279) is one of Marbella's best-known discos and is usually thronged with young people.

The **Casino Nueva Andalucía** (⊠ Bajos Hotel Andalucía Plaza, N340, Nuevo Andalucía, Marbella, ☎ 95/281–4000) is a chic gambling spot in the Hotel Andalucía Plaza, just east of Puerto Banús on the road to Marbella. It's open 8 PM–4 AM, and men are required to wear a jacket and tie; passports also are required.

Art exhibitions are held in private galleries (see *Lookout* Magazine for details) and in several of Marbella's leading hotels, especially the Puente Romano.

Bar Ana María is a crowded tapas bar packed with locals who come here to enjoy regular flamenco *tablaos* and the spontaneous singing and dancing of the owner and her cronies. ⊠ *Plaza Santo Cristo 45,* ☎ *95/277–5646 or 95/286–0704.* ⊙ *Dec.–Oct., Tues.–Sun.*

Casino Nueva Andalucía (⊠ Bajas Hotel Andalucía Plaza, Nuevo Andalucía, about 8 km/5 mi west of Marbella, ☎ 95/281–4000) has *sevillanas* (a Sevillian dance) and flamenco dancing in **La Caseta del Casino** from midnight onward in summer.

RONDA AND THE PUEBLOS BLANCOS

Ronda and the whitewashed villages of the mountains behind the Costa del Sol are among Spain's most moving and emblematic routes. The contrast with Torremolinos could not be more complete. Leave time for this section, because it will be among the most indelible memories you take away from this, or any, trip.

Ronda

❼ *61 km (38 mi) northwest of Marbella, 108 km (67 mi) southwest of Antequera (via Pizarra).*

Ronda, one of the oldest towns in Spain, is also one of the most moving and picturesque. To get there take the well-maintained road, C339 from San Pedro de Alcántara, up through the mountains of the Serranía de Ronda to the town of Ronda, 49 km/30 ⅓ mi inland. Secure in its mountain fastness perched atop a rock high over the River Guadalevín, Ronda, once a stronghold for the legendary Andalucían bandits, is famed for its spectacular position and views. The town's most dramatic feature is its ravine, 360 feet deep and 210 feet across,
★ known as **El Tajo** which divides La Ciudad, the old Moorish town, from El Mercadillo, the "new town," which grew up after the Christian Reconquest of 1485. Tour buses roll in daily with sightseers from the coast, and on weekends affluent sevillanos flock to their second homes here; stay overnight midweek and you'll see this noble town revert to its true identity.

Begin in El Mercadillo, in the Plaza de España, where it's a good idea to drop into the Tourist Office for a map and to double-check opening times of sights. Immediately to the south is the most famous of Ronda's bridges, the **Puente Nuevo,** an amazing architectural feat built between 1755 and 1793, whose lantern-lit parapet offers dizzying views of the river far below. Just how many people have met their deaths in this gorge nobody knows, but the architect of the Puente Nuevo fell to his death here while inspecting work on the bridge. During the civil war hundreds of victims of both sides were hurled from it.

Cross the bridge into **La Ciudad,** the old Moorish town, where you can wander through twisting streets of white houses with bird-cage balconies, punctuated by stately Renaissance mansions. Turn left down Santo Domingo until you come to the **Casa del Rey Moro.** This so-called House of the Moorish King was, in fact, built in 1709 on the site of an earlier Moorish residence. Despite its name and the azulejo plaque of a Moor on its facade, it's unlikely that Moorish rulers ever lived here. Its garden offers a great view of the gorge, and from here a stairway of some 365 steps, known as La Mina, descends to the river.

Just down the street from the Casa del Rey Moro is the **Palacio del Marqués de Salvatierra,** a Renaissance mansion with wrought-iron balconies and an impressive portal. Note the strange figures carved on its facade. Though the house is still occupied by descendants of the orig-

inal family, you can visit the interior with a guide. ☎ 95/287–1206.
🖃 200 ptas. ۞ Sept. 16–July, Fri.–Mon. 11–2 and 4–6.

Below the Salvatierra palace, a road leads down into the ravine, where
two more bridges span the river: the Puente Viejo (Old Bridge), built
in 1616 on Roman foundations, and the Puente Arabe, a much-restored
Moorish bridge. Beside the river are the excavated remains of the
Baños Arabes (Arab Baths), from Ronda's time as capital of a Moorish *taifa* (kingdom). (Gangs of youths have been known to threaten
tourists for money here, so be careful.) The star-shaped vents in the
roof are an inferior version of the ceiling of the beautiful bathhouse in
Granada's Alhambra. 🖃 Free. ۞ Tues.–Sun. 9–2 and 4–6.

Climb back up the hill from the river and make your way to the Plaza
de la Ciudad. At the end of Marqués de Salvatierra you'll pass the restored **Minarete Árabe** (Minaret of San Sebastián). The minaret is all
that remains of a mosque destroyed after the Reconquest of 1485. The
collegiate church of **Santa María la Mayor,** which serves as Ronda's
cathedral, has roots in Moorish times. Originally the Great Mosque
of Moorish Ronda, it was rebuilt as a Christian church and dedicated
to the Virgen de la Encarnación following the Reconquest. Today, its
flamboyant mixture of styles reflects Ronda's heterogeneous past.
While the naves are late Gothic and the main altar is heavy with
Baroque gold leaf, the Renaissance belfry incorporates part of the
original minaret.

Below the cathedral stands the ruined **Alcazaba,** blown up by the
French in 1809, and beyond it, the Moorish **Puerta de Almocobar,**
through which a triumphant Ferdinand led his troops in 1485.

From the west front of Santa María, the Ronda de Gameros leads to
a stone palace with twin Mudéjar towers, known as the **Casa de Mondragón** (Plaza de Mondragón). Appropriated by Ferdinand and Isabella
following their victory in 1485, it was probably the residence of
Ronda's Moorish kings. Today it is used as an exhibition center where
you can wander around the patios, with their brick arches and delicate, Mudéjar, stucco tracery, and admire the mosaics and *artesonado*
(coffered) ceiling. ☎ 95/287–0818. 🖃 200 ptas. ۞ Daily 9–6.

The Plaza Campillo offers good views of the gorge and terraced hillsides. From here, Calle Tenorio leads back up to the Puente Nuevo and
into **El Mercadillo,** the commercial heart of town, where you'll find the
hotels, restaurants, bars, banks, and stores. Most of the activity takes
place around the Plaza del Socorro and along the Carrera de Espinel,
the main shopping street.

NEED A
BREAK?

The **Mesón Santiago** (✉ Marina 3, ☎ 95/287–1559), a colorful Andalucían tavern with a pretty, vine-covered patio, is a good place to
break for a moderately priced lunch.

The main sight here is the **Plaza de Toros,** one of the oldest—it was
completed in 1784—and most picturesque bullrings in Spain. Here, Pedro
Romero (1754–1839), father of modern bullfighting and Ronda's
most famous native son, is said to have killed 5,600 bulls during his
long career, and in the **Museo Taurino** beneath the plaza, you can see
posters for the very first fights, held in the ring in 1785. The plaza,
rarely used for fights now except during Ronda's May and September
fairs, is owned by the famous, now-retired bullfighter, Antonio Ordóñez,
on whose nearby ranch Orson Welles had his ashes scattered. The ring
has become a firm favorite with moviemakers. Each year, in September, the bullring is the scene of Ronda's *corridas goyescas,* named after

the artist Goya, whose bullfight sketches, known as the *tauromaquías,* were inspired by the skill and art of Pedro Romero. Seats for these fights cost a small fortune and are booked long in advance; both the participants and the dignitaries in the audience don the costumes of Goya's day for the event. ☎ *95/287–4132.* ☞ *Ring and museum 200 ptas.* ☉ *Daily 10–6:30 (until 7 in summer).*

Beyond the bullring you can relax in the shady **Alameda del Tajo** gardens, one of the loveliest spots in Ronda. Stroll on along the clifftop walk to the Old World Reina Victoria hotel (☞ Dining and Lodging, *below*), built by the British from Gibraltar at the turn of the century as a fashionable resting place on their Algeciras-Bobadilla railroad line.

About 30 km/18 mi west of Ronda are the prehistoric **Cuevas de la Pileta** (Pileta Caves). Head out along C339 toward Algodonales and turn left after a few miles where you see the sign to the caves. The road winds up through the villages of **Montejaque** (worth a stop) and **Benaoján** to peter out at the entrance to the caves. A guardian from the farm in the valley below will show you around, but you will probably have to ask a local where to find him. Armed with lamps, you'll set off on a visit of about 1½ hours that will reveal prehistoric wall paintings of bison, deer, and horses outlined in black, red, and ocher. One of the highlights is the Cámara del Pescado (Chamber of the Fish), where the drawing of a huge fish, thought to be 15,000 years old, is outlined on the chamber wall.

Clinging to the mountainsides of the vast, impressive landscape that surrounds Ronda are villages of white houses with honey-colored, tile roofs. These are the remote **pueblos blancos** of Cádiz province, on the one-time frontier between Moors and Christians, all within a day's drive of Ronda. If you've time for only one, then make it Grazalema.

Dining and Lodging

$$–$$$ ✕ **Don Miguel.** The restaurant stands at the end of the bridge over the Tajo gorge, and its two terraces offer breathtaking views of the ravine. *Pierna de cordero lechal* (baby lamb, reared on the owner's farm) is the house specialty. The bar, set inside the bridge in what was once Ronda's prison, is a good place for a drink and tapas. ⊠ *Villanueva 4,* ☎ *95/287–7410. AE, DC, MC, V. Closed mid-Jan.–mid-Feb.; Sun., and Wed. in summer.*

$$ ✕ **Pedro Romero.** This restaurant is opposite the bullring and, named after the father of modern bullfighting, it's packed with colorful, taurine decor. Melancholy-eyed bulls peer down at you from the walls as you tuck into *sopa del mesón* (the house soup) or enjoy a *tocino del cielo al coco* (a sweet caramel custard flavored with coconut). ⊠ *Virgen de la Paz 18,* ☎ *95/287–1110 and 95/287–1618. AE, DC, MC, V.*

$$$ ✕🖼 **Polo.** A cozy, old-fashioned, homey hotel in the center of town, the Polo offers comfortably furnished rooms and a good, reasonably priced restaurant. ⊠ *Mariano Soubirón 8, 29400,* ☎ *95/287–2447,* FAX *95/287–2449. 33 rooms. Restaurant. AE, DC, MC, V.*

$$$ ✕🖼 **Reina Victoria.** This grande dame of Spanish hotels was built in ★ 1906 by the British in Gibraltar as a weekend retreat for passengers traveling the newly constructed rail line between Algeciras and Bobadilla. In 1912 it became famous when the ailing German poet Rainer Maria Rilke came here to convalesce. His room has been preserved as a museum. Today, the Reina Victoria maintains its air of faded English gentility. Its spacious rooms and suites are furnished with comfortable sofas and armchairs, and most have balconies. Perched on a clifftop, amid luxuriant gardens, this hotel commands one of the most striking locations in Andalucía. It is popular with tour groups. ⊠ *Jerez 25,*

29400, ☎ 95/287–1240, ꜰᴀx 95/287–1075. 89 rooms. Restaurant, pool. AE, DC, MC, V.

Olvera

⑱ *59 km (37 mi) north of Ronda (via Agodonales), 68 km (42 mi) from Antequera.*

Two imposing silhouettes dominate the crest of the hill on which the town stands: the **11th-century castle of Vallehermoso,** legacy of the Moors, and the neoclassical **church of La Encarnación,** reconstructed in the 19th century on foundations of the old Arab mosque.

Setenil de las Bodegas

⑲ *13 km (8 mi) southeast of Olvera.*

Setenil de las Bodegas lies south of the N342 just southeast of Olvera, on a small mountain road. The village nestles in a cleft in the rock cut by the River Guadalporcín. Its houses seem to be sculpted from the rock itself; streets resemble long, narrow caves; and on many houses the roof is formed by a projecting ledge of heavy rock.

El Gastor

⑳ *18 km (11 mi) from Setenil, 14 km (9 mi) from Olvera, 30 km (19 mi) from Ronda.*

To the west of Setenil is El Gastor, south of which lie the twin ravines of Alagarines. Nearby are the remains of an ancient dolmen known as **La Sepultura del Gigante** (Giant's Tomb). **Ronda la Vieja,** site of the Roman settlement of Acinipo, is found down a track off the Setenil–El Gastor road. (Another track off C339 also leads to it.) A reconstructed theater is the only vestige of the Roman town.

Zahara de la Sierra

㉑ *35 km (22 mi) northwest of Ronda, 32 km (20 mi) southwest of Olvera.*

West of the C339, a little south of Algodonales, a solitary **watchtower** dominates a crag above the village of Zahara de la Sierra, its outline visible for miles around. The tower is all that remains of a Moorish castle where Alfonso X once fought the emir of Morocco. It remained an important Moorish stronghold until its fall to the Christians in 1470. Along the streets of Zahara you can see door knockers fashioned like the hand of Fatima. The fingers represent the five laws of the Koran and serve to ward off evil.

En Route The winding mountain road between Zahara and Grazalema, via the Puerto de las Palomas (4,300 feet), is for adventurous drivers. The views from its heights are breathtaking, but unless you have nerves of steel and a head for heights, take a more conventional approach.

Grazalema

㉒ *28 km (17 mi) northwest of Ronda, 23 km (14 mi) northeast of Ubrique.*

Nestled in the Sierra del Endrinal, the town is the prettiest of the pueblos blancos. Because it's on a west-facing slope where rain clouds roll in from the Atlantic, Grazalema is also the wettest spot in Spain. Cobbled streets of houses with pink and ocher roofs wind up the hillside;

red geraniums splash white walls, and black, wrought-iron lanterns and grilles cling to the house fronts.

Ubrique

㉓ *48 km (30 mi) west of Ronda, 89 km (55 mi) north of San Roque.*

Ubrique, spread on the slopes of the Saltadero Mountains southwest of Ronda and Grazalema on C3331, is known for its leather tanning and embossing industry. Look for the **Convento de los Capuchinos** and the **churches of San Pedro and Nuestra Señora de la O.**

ESTEPONA TO GIBRALTAR

Estepona's fishing village and Moorish old quarter can still be found amid the booming coastal development while just inland Casares piles whitewashed houses over the bright blue Mediterranean below. Sotogrande, with its golf courses and long stretch of beach and the old part of San Roque, are the last stops before the British enclave at Gibraltar, a bizarre anomaly of Moorish, Spanish, and British history.

Estepona

㉔ *17 km (11 mi) west of San Pedro de Alcántara.*

Until recently, Estepona marked the end of the urban sprawl of the Costa del Sol, but today, thanks largely to the increasingly important role of Gibraltar Airport, it's fast becoming the biggest boomtown on the coast. Nevertheless, the old fishing village can still be detected. Its beach, more than 1 km/⅔ mi long, is lined with fishing boats, and along the promenade are well-kept gardens with aromatic flowers. Back from the main Avenida de España, the old Moorish village is surprisingly unspoiled.

Dining and Lodging

$$$ ✕ **El Molino.** In an old windmill, 12 km/8 mi out on the road to Málaga, this restaurant has professional service and classic French cuisine. Try the *lubina al hinojo* (sea bass in fennel), *perdiz al champán* (partridge in champagne), or the delicious Chateaubriand steak. ⊠ *Carretera N340 at Km 166,* ☎ *95/288–2135. AE, DC, MC, V. Closed Tues., Sun., and Jan. No lunch.*

$$–$$$ ✕ **Alcaría de Ramos.** José Ramos, winner of the National Gastronomy Prize, opened this restaurant in a restored building outside town in 1990, and it has quickly garnered a large and enthusiastic following. Try the *ensalada de lentejas con salmón ahumado* (lentil salad with smoked salmon), followed by *cordero asado* (roast lamb) and the chef's justly famous fried ice cream. ⊠ *Carretera N340 at Km 167,* ☎ *95/288–6178. MC, V. Closed Sun. No lunch.*

$ ✕ **Costa del Sol.** This friendly French bistro offers French and Spanish dishes in an informal setting. It's located on a side street beside the Portillo bus station. French favorites include bouillabaisse and duck in orange sauce. ⊠ *San Roque s/n,* ☎ *95/280–1101. AE, DC, MC, V. Closed Sun. No lunch Mon.*

$$$ ✕▥ **Atalaya Park.** Closer to San Pedro de Alcántara than to Estepona itself, this very comfortable resort hotel is set in subtropical gardens beside the sea and offers extensive sporting facilities. Rooms overlooking the sea are more expensive than those at the back facing the mountains. ⊠ *Carretera N340 at Km 169, 29680,* ☎ *95/288–4801,* Ⅲ *95/288–5735. 448 rooms. 2 restaurants, 2 bars, indoor pool, 4 outdoor pools, beauty salon, sauna, massage, golf, tennis courts. AE, DC, MC, V.*

$$ ✕🖾 **Santa Marta.** This is a small, quiet hotel with rooms in chalet bungalows arranged in a large, peaceful tropical garden. Some of the rooms are a little faded after 30-odd years, but the tranquil setting is a definite plus. In summer, good lunches are served by the pool. 🖂 *Carretera N340 at Km 173, between Estepona and San Pedro, 29680,* 🕾 *95/288–8180. 37 rooms. Pool. AE, DC, MC, V. Closed Oct.–Mar.*

Casares

㉕ *20 km (12 mi) northwest of Estepona.*

The mountain village of Casares lies high in the Sierra Bermeja above Estepona. Streets of ancient, white houses, piled one on top of the other, perch on the slopes beneath a ruined but impressive Moorish castle. Its heights afford stunning views over orchards, olive groves, and cork woods to the Mediterranean sparkling in the distance.

San Roque

㉖ *92 km (57 mi) southwest of Ronda, 64 km (40 mi) west of Marbella.*

San Roque is the point at which you leave the coastal highway and drive the final 8 km/5 mi to La Línea and Gibraltar along the peninsula that forms the east side of Algeciras Bay. The town of San Roque was founded within sight of Gibraltar by Spaniards who fled the Rock when the British captured it in 1704. Almost 300 years have done little to diminish the chauvinism of San Roque's inhabitants, who have protested their displeasure at the prominence Gibraltar is now assuming at this end of the Costa del Sol by declaring a ban on the use of English on all billboards and other advertising.

Dining

$$$$ ✕ **Los Remos.** The dining room inside this gracious, colonial villa has peach-colored walls adorned with gilt, rococo mirrors, swirling cherubs, friezes of grapes, and crystal lamps. It overlooks a formal, leafy garden full of palms, cedars, and trailing ivy. Among the main courses offered is *urta del estrecho en salsa de erizos marinos* (perch from the Straits of Gibraltar in sea urchin sauce). All the fish and seafood are from the Bay of Algeciras area, and the wine cellar boasts some 20,000 bottles. 🖂 *Villa Victoria, Campo de Gibraltar between San Roque and Campamento,* 🕾 *956/106812. AE, DC, MC, V. Closed Sun. Sept.–July.*

Gibraltar

㉗ *20 km (12 mi) east of Algeciras, 77 km (48 mi) west of Marbella.*

The tiny British colony of Gibraltar, nicknamed Gib, whose impressive silhouette dominates the straits between Spain and Morocco, is a rock just 5 ⅘ km/3 mi long, ⅘ km/½ mi wide, and 1,369 feet high. In ancient times it was one of the two Pillars of Hercules, which marked the western limits of the known world. Its position commanding the narrow entrance to the Mediterranean led to its seizure by the Moors in 711 as a preliminary to the conquest of Spain. They held it longer than either the Spaniards or the British ever have—a fact to which tribute is paid unconsciously whenever anyone pronounces its name—for Gibraltar is a corruption of Jebel Tariq (Tariq's Rock), Tariq being the Moorish commander who built the first fort of Gibraltar.

After 750 years of Moorish rule, the Spaniards recaptured Tariq's Rock in 1462, on the feast day of St. Bernard, now co-patron of the colony along with Our Lady of Europe, whose shrine you will see at the Rock's southernmost tip. The English, heading an Anglo-Dutch fleet in the War of the Spanish Succession, seized the Rock in 1704, after three days of fighting. Following several years of skirmishing in the vicinity, Gibraltar was finally ceded to Great Britain by the Treaty of Utrecht, in 1713. With the exception of the Great Siege, when a Franco-Spanish force battled at its ramparts for three years (1779–82), Gibraltar has lived a relatively peaceful existence ever since. During the two world wars, it served the Allies well as an important naval and air base.

Today, much of Gibraltar creates the impression of a somewhat faded, garrison town. The number of British troops stationed here is being cut back, and millions of dollars are currently being invested in developing the Rock's tourist potential. A further, big boost has been given to the economy of this tiny colony by the 100,000-plus expatriate Britons living on the Costa del Sol, many of who take advantage of Gibraltar's reasonable prices, freeport status, and British consumer goods.

There can be few places in the world that one enters by walking or driving across an airport runway. But that's what you'll have to do in Gibraltar. First show your passport, then make your way out onto the narrow strip of land linking Spain's La Linea with the Rock. Here, you have a choice: Either plunge straight into exploring Gibraltar town or opt first for a tour of the Rock's circumference. If you don't have your own transport, several minibus tours of the latter route are readily available at the point of entry.

Numbers in the margin correspond to points of interest on the Gibraltar map.

To begin on the Rock's eastern side, turn left down Devil's Tower Road as you enter Gibraltar. Here, on the eastern shores, you'll find **Catalan Bay,** a fishing village founded by Genoese settlers and now a picturesque resort. On the eastern side you'll see the massive water catchments that supply the colony's drinking water; Sandy Bay, another resort; and the Dudley Ward tunnel, which brings you out at the Rock's southern tip, **Punta Grande de Europa** (Europa Point). Stop here for the view across the straits to Morocco, 23 km/14 mi away. You are standing on one of the two Pillars of Hercules; across the water, in Morocco, a mountain between the cities of Ceuta and Tangiers formed the second pillar. In front of you, the Europa Point lighthouse has dominated the meeting place of the Atlantic and the Mediterranean since 1841. Sailors can see its light from a distance of 27 km/17 mi. Near the Europa Point lighthouse, on **Europa Flats,** you can see an ancient Moorish cistern, known as the **Nun's Well,** and the **Shrine of Our Lady of Europe,** venerated by seafarers since 1462.

From Europa Flats, follow Europa Road along the western slopes of the Rock, high above **Rosia Bay,** to which Nelson's flagship, HMS *Victory,* was towed after the Battle of Trafalgar in 1805. Aboard were the dead of the battle, who were buried in Trafalgar Cemetery on the southern edge of town—except, that is, for Admiral Nelson, whose body went home to England preserved in a barrel of rum.

From Rosia Bay, continue on Europa Road as far as the Casino, above the Alameda Gardens. Make a sharp right here up Engineer Road to **Jews Gate,** an unbeatable lookout point over the docks and Bay of Gibraltar to Algeciras, in Spain. Here you can gain access to the **Upper Nature Preserve,** which includes St. Michael's Cave, the Apes' Den, the Great Siege Tunnel, and the Moorish Castle. ▨ *£4.50 includes all attractions, plus £1.50 per vehicle.* ☉ *Daily 10–6.*

Alternatively, you can take the cable car from Gibraltar town. ▨ *£4 includes cable-car ride, St. Michael's Cave, and Apes' Den.*

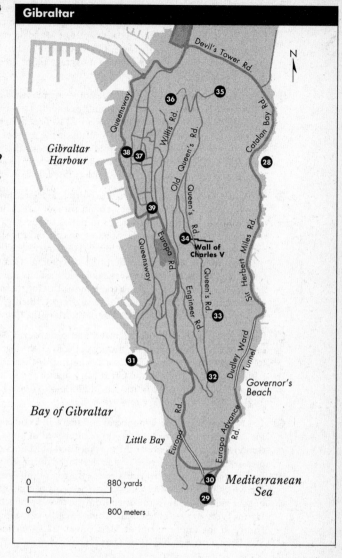

33 Queens Road leads to **St. Michael's Cave,** a series of underground chambers adorned with stalactites and stalagmites, which provides an admirable setting for concerts, ballet, and drama. Sound-and-light shows are held here most days (at 11 and 4). The skull of a Neanderthal woman (now in the British Museum in London) was found nearby at Forbes Quarry some eight years *before* the world-famous discovery in Germany's Neander Valley in 1856.

34 Drive down Old Queens Road from St. Michael's Cave to the **Apes' Den,** near the Wall of Charles V. The famous Barbary Apes are a breed of cinnamon-colored, tail-less monkey, native of the Atlas Mountains in Morocco. Legend holds that as long as the apes remain, the British will keep the Rock. Winston Churchill himself issued orders for their preservation when the ape colony's numbers began to dwindle during World War II. Today, they are fed twice daily, at 8 and 4. The apes are mischievous, as well as expert purse and camera snatchers.

㉟ At the northern end of the Rock, the **Great Siege Tunnel,** formerly known as the Upper Galleries, was carved out during the Great Siege of 1779–82. Here, in 1878, Governor Lord Napier of Magdala entertained ex United States president Ulysses S. Grant at a banquet in St. George's Hall. The Holyland Tunnel leads to a vantage point on the east side of the Rock high above Catalan Bay.

㊱ The **Moorish Castle** on Willis Road, restored and reopened in 1993 after being closed for many years, was built originally by the descendants of Tariq, who conquered the Rock in 711. The present Tower of Homage dates from 1333, and its walls bear the scars of sieges when stones from medieval catapults, and later cannonballs, were hurled against it. Admiral Rooke hoisted the British flag from its summit when he captured the Rock in 1704, and it has flown here ever since.

㊲ Willis Road leads steeply down to the colorful, congested **town of Gibraltar,** where the dignified Regency architecture of Great Britain blends well with the shutters, balconies, and patios of southern Spain. Visit the tourist office on Cathedral Square. Apart from the shops, restaurants, and pubs that beckon on busy Main Street, you'll want to see the **Governor's Residence,** where the ceremonial Changing of the Guard and Ceremony of the Keys take place, usually about five times a year; the **Law Courts,** where the famous case of the *Mary Celeste* sailing ship was heard in 1872; the Anglican **Cathedral of the Holy Trinity;** and the Catholic **Cathedral of St. Mary the Crowned.**

㊳ Don't miss the recently reorganized and refurbished **Gibraltar Museum,** whose exhibits recall the history of the Rock throughout the ages. Its well-presented displays include a beautiful, 14th-century Moorish bathhouse, evocations of the Great Siege and of the Battle of Trafalgar, and an 1865 model of the Rock. ⊠ *Bomb House La.,* ☎ *9567/74289.* ⊡ *£1.50.* ⊙ *Weekdays 10–6, Sat. 10–2.*

㊴ The **Nefusot Yehudada Synagogue** on Line Wall Road is worth a look for its inspired architecture. If you're interested in guns, the **Koehler Gun** in Casemates Square at the northern end of Main Street is an impressive example of the type of gun developed during the Great Siege.

★ Finally, take a ride on the **cable car** to the top of the Rock. The cable car, which resembles a ski gondola, isn't especially high off the ground, but the views of Spain and Africa from the rock's pinnacle are superb. It runs every day except Sunday from the cable-car station on Grand Parade at the southern end of Main Street. ⊡ *£4 includes cable car, St. Michael's Cave, and Apes' Den.*

Dining and Lodging

$$$ ✗ **La Bayuca.** One of the Rock's oldest restaurants, La Bayuca is renowned for its onion soup and Mediterranean dishes. Prince Charles and Prince Andrew both dined here while on naval service. ⊠ *21 Turnbull's La.,* ☎ *9567/75119. AE, DC, MC, V. Closed Tues. No lunch Sun.*

$$–$$$ ✗ **Country Cottage.** Set back from Main Street, this is the place to go for a taste of Old England. You can dine by candlelight on white linen tablecloths with pink napkins and enjoy old favorites, such as steak and kidney pie, roast beef and Yorkshire pudding, and Angus steak. ⊠ *13 Giro's Passage,* ☎ *9567/70084. AE, MC, V. Closed Sun.*

$–$$ ✗ **Strings.** This small, popular bistro is one of the few places open in Gibraltar on Sunday nights. Prints, nautical paraphernalia, ensigns, and badges cover every inch of the walls, and there are just six, dark, wooden booths clustered around a small bar. Red and orange lamps complete the cozy, cave-like decor. The menu is English bistro-style, and daily specials are chalked up on a blackboard. ⊠ *44 Cornwall La.,* ☎ *9567/78800. AE, DC, MC, V. Closed Sun. No lunch Mon.*

$$$ **╳▣ The Rock.** The Rock has undergone a massive refurbishment pro-
★ gram. The predominance of muted pink, peach, and beige in the decor
of the rooms and restaurant, the deep, fitted carpets, glowing table lamps,
and cane furniture evoke the atmosphere of good "international" ho-
tels everywhere, yet the establishment manages to preserve something
of the old, English colonial style with ceiling fans and a fine bar-ter-
race. Located on Gibraltar's western slopes, the hotel overlooks the town
and harbor. ⊠ *3 Europa Rd.,* ☎ *9567/73000,* ⅿ *9567/73513. 143
rooms, 5 suites. Restaurant, bar, pool, beauty salon. AE, DC, MC, V.*

$$ **▣ Bristol.** This colonial-style hotel is in the heart of town, overlooking the cathedral. Rooms are spacious but in need of renovation. The
tropical garden is a real haven. The wood-paneled lounge has two pool
tables. ⊠ *10 Cathedral Sq.,* ☎ *9567/76800. 60 rooms. Breakfast
room, bar, pool. AE, DC, MC, V.*

Nightlife and the Arts
The **Casino** (⊠ Europa Rd., ☎ 9567/76666) is open 9 PM–4 AM; jacket
and tie are advised but not required for the gaming rooms.

THE COSTA DEL SOL A TO Z

Arriving and Departing

By Bus
Long-distance buses serve Málaga from Madrid, Cartagena, Almería,
Granada, Ubeda, Córdoba, Seville, and Badajoz. Málaga's main bus
station is on Paseo de los Tilos (☎ 95/235–0061). Marbella and Algeciras can be reached direct from Madrid or Seville; other services are
between Fuengirola and Seville, and Cádiz and Algeciras. Marbella's
bus station is at Avenida Ricardo Soriano 21 (☎ 95/277–2192).

By Car
Málaga is 580 km/360 mi from Madrid by way of N IV to Córdoba,
then N331 to Antequera and N321; 182 km/114 mi from Córdoba
via Antequera; 214 km/134 mi from Seville; and 129 km/81 mi from
Granada by the shortest route of N342 to Loja, then N321 to Málaga.
Numerous highway projects completed in connection with the 1992
International Exposition in Seville improved highways and traveling
time between Seville and Granada and the Costa del Sol.

By Plane
Gibraltar Airport (☎ 9567/73026) is worth considering if you're arriving from Great Britain, especially if you're visiting the coast west
of Marbella. It is next to the frontier, and once you've crossed into Spain,
you can make bus connections at La Linea for all coastal resorts.

Málaga Airport (☎ 95/224–0000; Iberia information, 95/213–6166/67)
lies 16 km/10 mi west of Málaga. If you fly from the United States,
you'll have to make connections in Madrid. Iberia and British Airways
operate several scheduled flights a day from London; Dan Air operates from London Gatwick, as do other charter flights. Most major
European cities have direct flights to Málaga on either Iberia or their
own national airlines. Iberia and its subsidiary, Aviaco, have up to eight
flights a day from Madrid (journey time 1 hour), three flights a day
from Barcelona (1½ hours), and regular flights from other Spanish cities.

Iberia has offices in Málaga (⊠ Molina Lario 13, ☎ 95/213–
6146/47/48) and at the airport (☎ 95/213–6166).

BETWEEN THE AIRPORT AND DOWNTOWN

From Málaga Airport, a train service runs regularly to nearby cities (☞ Getting Around, *below*), and an Iberia bus leaves every 20 minutes for downtown Málaga (6:30 AM–midnight, fare 115 ptas.). Taxis are plentiful, and official fares to Málaga, Torremolinos, and other resorts are posted inside the terminal buildings. The trip from the airport to Torremolinos will cost about 1,800 ptas. The airport was recently modernized, and now consists of one large terminal.

By Train

Málaga is the main rail terminus, with five through trains a day from Madrid and one from Barcelona and Valencia. Most Málaga trains leave from Madrid Chamartín, though most of those also stop at Atocha. Travel time varies between 7 and 10 hours; the best trains are the daytime Pendular (7 hours) and the overnight Talgo (9½ hours), both from Chamartín. All Madrid-Málaga trains stop at Córdoba; there are also local trains direct from Córdoba to Málaga. From both Seville (4 hours) and Granada (3–3½ hours), you will have to change at Bobadilla for Málaga, making buses a better bet for those traveling from these cities. In fact, other than the direct Madrid-Córdoba-Málaga line, trains in Andalucía can be slow because of the terrain, and you may find buses quicker and more convenient.

Málaga Station (✉ Explanada de la Estación, ☎ 95/236–0202) is 15 minutes' walk from the center, across the river. For tickets and information, the central RENFE office is much more convenient. ✉ *Strachan 2, off Larios,* ☎ *95/221–4127.* ☉ *Weekdays 9–1:30 and 4:30–7:30.*

Getting Around

By Bus

Buses are the best way of getting around the Costa del Sol (as well as reaching it from Seville or Granada). Málaga's bus station is on the Paseo de los Tilos (☎ 95/235–0061). The **Portillo** bus company, with offices at the Málaga Station (☎ 95/236–0191), serves most of the Costa del Sol. Another company with offices at the station, **Alsina Gräells** (☎ 95/231–8295), has service to Granada, Córdoba, Seville, and Nerja. Málaga Tourist Office has details on other bus lines.

By Car

A car will enable you to explore some of the mountain villages for which Andalucía is famous. Mountain driving can be an adventure because hair-raising curves, precipices, and mediocre road services are often the norm. But this is changing as highways throughout the region are resurfaced and widened; in some cases completely new roadbeds have been built. Though the busy coastal N340 is good by Spanish standards and is currently being widened in parts, it is a death trap known locally as the Carretera de la Muerte (the Highway of Death). A useful tip: When you want to turn left from N340, you do so in most cases by exiting right and looping in a circle, often controlled by traffic lights. To take a car into Gibraltar, drivers, in theory, need an international driver's permit, an insurance certificate, and a logbook; in practice, all you need show is your passport. Be prepared for parking problems—space is scarce—but beware of phony offers of help from "parking/insurance agents" on the frontier approach.

By Train

A useful suburban train service runs between Málaga, Torremolinos, and Fuengirola, calling at the airport and all resorts along the way. It leaves Málaga every half hour between 6 AM and 10:30 PM and from

Fuengirola every half hour from 6:35 AM to 11:35 PM. Its terminus in Málaga is the **Guadalmedina** Station, more or less opposite the Corte Inglés; it also calls at Málaga RENFE Station. Its Fuengirola terminus is just across from the bus station, where you can make connections for Mijas, Marbella, Estepona, and Algeciras.

Two trains a day run between Málaga and Ronda through dramatic El Chorro gorge. Journey time is around three hours, and you change at Bobadilla. Between Ronda and Algeciras three direct trains a day (two hours) travel a spectacular mountain track.

Contacts and Resources

Consulates
United Kingdom (⊠ Duquesa de Parcent 8, Málaga, ☎ 95/221–7571). **Canada** (⊠ Plaza de la Malagueta 3, Málaga, ☎ 95/222–3346). **United States** (⊠ Centro Comercial Las Rampas, Fuengirola, ☎ 95/247–4891).

Cultural Events
The best place to look for news of what's on along the coast is in *Lookout*, an English-language, glossy monthly available on newsstands. Its "Costa del Sol Events" section lists art exhibitions, concerts, theater, local fiestas, and films in English. Try also Málaga's daily newspaper, *El Sur*, or its weekly English–language version, *Sur in English*.

Guided Tours
Numerous one- and two-day excursions from Costa del Sol resorts are run by **Julia Tours** (⊠ Emilio Esteban 1, Torremolinos, ☎ 95/238–7222), **Pullmantur** (⊠ Avda. Imperial, Torremolinos, ☎ 95/238–4400), and various smaller companies. Leaflets are available in most hotels, and tours can be booked through your hotel desk or any travel agent. Excursions operate from Málaga, Torremolinos, Fuengirola, Marbella, and Estepona; prices vary slightly, according to your departure point; in most cases, you can be picked up from your hotel.

Local Tours
Most of the following local tours are half day: Málaga, Cuevas de Nerja, Mijas, Marbella, and Puerto Banús; Burro safari in Coín; countryside tour to villages of Alhaurín de la Torre, Alhaurín el Grande, Coín, Ojén, and Ronda. Night tours include a barbecue evening, a bull-fighting evening with dinner, and a night at the Casino Torrequebrada.

Travel Agencies
The chief international agencies are **American Express** (⊠ Avda. Arias Maldonado 2, Marbella, ☎ 95/282–1494 or 95/282–2820) and **Wagons Lits Viajes** (⊠ Strachan 10, Málaga, ☎ 95/221–7695).

Visitor Information
The Costa del Sol's main information office is in **Málaga** (⊠ Pasaje de Chinitas 4, ☎ 95/221–3445 or 95/222–8948). Local tourist offices can be found in **Algeciras** (⊠ Juan de la Cierva, ☎ 956/572636), **Antequera** (⊠ Palacio de Najera, Coso Viejo, ☎ 95/284–1827), **Benalmádena Costa** (⊠ Avda. Antonio Machado 14, ☎ 95/244–2494), **Estepona** (⊠ Paseo Marítimo, ☎ 95/280–0913), **Fuengirola** (⊠ Avda. Jesús Santos Rein 6, ☎ 95/246–7457), **Gibraltar** (⊠ 6 Kent House, Cathedral Sq., ☎ 9567/74950), **La Línea** (⊠ Avda. 20 de Abril, ☎ 956/769950), **Málaga Airport** (☎ 95/224–0000), **Marbella** (⊠ Glorieta de la Fontanilla, ☎ 95/277–1442 or 95/277–4693), **Nerja** (⊠ Puerta del Mar 2, ☎ 95/252–1531), **Ronda** (⊠ Plaza de España 1, ☎ 95/287–1272), **Torremolinos** (⊠ Guetaria 517, ☎ 95/238–1578).

EXCURSION TO MOROCCO

By George
Semler

The crossing to Morocco, just 14 km/9 mi across the Straits of Gibraltar, may be the longest short trip on the globe. A 90-minute cruise from Algeciras to Tangier replaces late-20th-century Europe with timeless and tumultuous North Africa.

Islam is the state religion, and Arabic is the official language, but French, Berber, Spanish, and English are also spoken. Berbers, Romans, Vandals, and Arabs inhabited Morocco in the country's early history: Incessant conflict between Arabs and Berbers left Morocco ripe for invasion. Spain and Portugal, after expelling the Moors from the Iberian Peninsula, attacked the Moroccan coast. European countries, including Germany, France, and Spain, fought over the country's aegis until 1956, when all foreign rights were relinquished, except for those to the Western Sahara, which is still disputed territory.

Great Itineraries

IF YOU HAVE 1 DAY

Even if you can only manage a single day's browse through Tangier, you will, in the Fondouk Market, encounter a flavor and color nearly as exciting and astounding as any in Morocco. The boat back across the Straits of Gibraltar in the sunset will provide one of those geographic and strategic thrills that are what travelling is all about. Then again, in a country where travelling by air makes a lot of sense to save time, general hassle, and possibly your life, one day in Morocco would probably best be spent at Djemâa el Fna square in Marrakesh.

IF YOU HAVE 3 DAYS

Find a way to see Marrakesh and Fez, spending a day and a half in each, either by plane (to save time) or train (to save money). The Grand Mosquée Hassan II in Casablanca is perhaps the third most essential sight in Morocco.

IF YOU HAVE 5 DAYS

Explore Marrakesh and Fez in greater detail and less haste. See the Grand Mosquée Hassan II in Casablanca. Visit Tangier on your way in and out of Morocco.

In addition to the following seven-day itinerary, which affords the most complete Moroccan experience on a time budget, try to visit the elegant beach town of Asilah, south of Tangier; the capital at Rabat; the beach at Essouaira on the Atlantic coast, south of Casablanca; and the imperial city of Meknes, next to Fez. Also, the trip over the High Atlas range to Ouarzazate is spectacular, as is the southern desert.

Day 1: Algeciras–Tangier–Casablanca. Take the boat to Tangier for the day, and the train to Casablanca for the first night.

Day 2: Casablanca–Marrakesh. After a morning tour of Casablanca's spectacular Mosquée Hassan II and the spice market, take the afternoon express to Marrakesh.

Days 3 and 4: Marrakesh. Savor Djemâa el Fna square and visit the Koutoubia minaret, the Majorelle and Menara Gardens, the souks, the Saadian Tombs, the Palais el Bahia, and the El Badi Palace.

Day 5: Marrakesh–Fez. Flying from Marrakesh to Fez is safest and fastest; otherwise, rent a car or take an eight-hour bus ride.

Day 6: Fez. See Fez el Bali, the water clock, the Kairaouine Mosque and Kairaouine University, the souks and fondouks.

Day 7: Fez–Tangier–Algeciras. Take the 7 AM train back to Tangier and an evening ferry across the strait.

The 5 PM or 7 PM return ferry from Tangier to Algeciras sails as the sun sets, spotlighting the Spanish coast. North Africa behind you seems almost peaceful at this safe remove.

Tangier

40 *14 km (9 mi) across the Straits of Gibraltar, 350 km (220 mi) northeast of Casablanca.*

In Tangier, walk up the Rue Portugal, just right of the port entrance, skirting the left-hand edge of the medina. Continue up the hill through a small gate in the medina wall to the **Fondouk (caravanserai) Market,** where you will be surrounded by the color and vitality—men and women with bright *djellabas* (full-length robes with pointed hoods) that inspired Delacroix, Regnault, Fortuny, and so many others to make Morocco a leit-motif. A left on Rue de la Liberté leads up to Place de France and the sumptuous French consulate. Another left on Boulevard Pasteur takes you down past a belvedere to the Tourist Office.

Walk down the Grand Socco (large market) through the pointed archway to the Petit Socco (small market) into the heart of Tangier's old city and artisan district. Uphill to the left is the **Place de la Kasbah,** where there is another belvedere with views over the port.

Dining and Lodging

$$$$ ✕🏨 **El Minzah Hotel.** Ask anyone where the best place in town is, for ★ both dining and lodging, and the immediate answer will be the El Minzah. Lovely, studded, wooden doors; hotel staff in Ottoman costumes, and fine, fine views over the Straits of Gibraltar to Spain prove them right. ⊠ *85 Rue de la Liberté,* ☎ *2129/935885,* FAX *2129/934546. 100 rooms with bath. Restaurant, bar, pool. AE, MC, DC, V.*

$$ 🏨 **Hotel Continental.** Overlooking the port from the edge of the medina, this wonderful, old-world palace built in 1888 is the best buy in town for aesthetes and romantics (who else goes to Morocco anyway?). Bertolucci stayed in room 108 while shooting *The Sheltering Sky.* Monsieur Abdessalam is a gracious host. ⊠ *36 rue Dar el Baroud,* ☎ *212–9–931024,* FAX *2129/931143. 15 rooms with bath, 30 rooms share 10 baths. Bar. AE, DC, MC, V.*

$ 🏨 **Hotel Muniria.** William Burroughs wrote *Naked Lunch* in room 9, now the home of Madame Rabia, the lovely owner. The Tangerinn underneath is *the* expatriate late-night haunt, once habitat for Kerouacs and Ginsbergs. Room 8 overlooks the Bay of Tangier. Rue Magellan can be tricky to find. ⊠ *2 Rue Magellan,* ☎ *2129/935337. 6 rooms with bath, 2 rooms share bath. Bar. No credit cards.*

Casablanca

41 *289 km (180 mi) southwest of Fez, 238 km (148 mi) north of Marrakesh.*

Casablanca, a booming metropolis of 3.5 million, is bound to disappoint cineasts and romantics expecting to bump into Ingrid Bergman and Humphrey Bogart at the counterfeit Rick's Bar in the Hyatt Regency (where waiters take orders in trench coats and fedoras). The **Grand Mosquée Hassan II,** however, will not disappoint. Opened in 1994, the mosque has room for 20,000 worshipers inside, where the glass floor reveals the ocean below, and 80,000 in the courtyard. The 200-meter minaret is Morocco's tallest structure; the mosque is second only in

Morocco

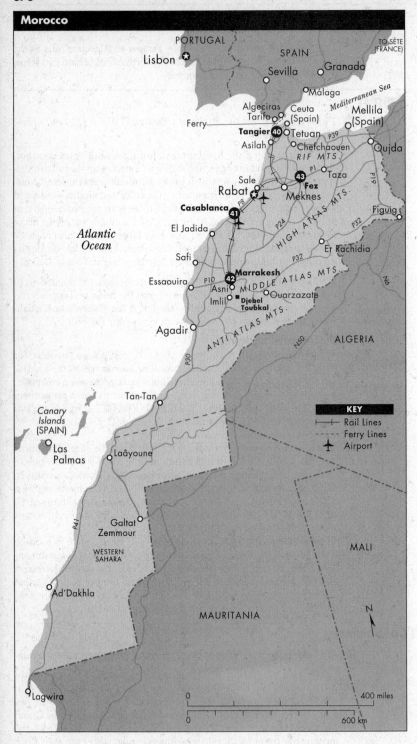

PORTUGAL

SPAIN

Lisbon

Sevilla

Granada

TO SÈTE
(FRANCE)

Málaga

Mediterranean Sea

Algeciras

Tarifa

Ceuta
(Spain)

Mellila
(Spain)

Ferry

Tangier 40

Tetuan

Oujda

Asilah

Chefchaouen

RIF MTS

P39

Taza

P1

43

Sale

Fez

P19

Rabat

Meknes

Figuig

P8

*Atlantic
Ocean*

Casablanca 41

P24

HIGH ATLAS MTS.

El Jadida

P32

Safi

P32

Er Rachidia

Essaouira

Marrakesh

MIDDLE ATLAS MTS.

42

Asni

Ouarzazate

N6

Imlil

■ **Djebel
Toubkal**

Agadir

ANTI ATLAS MTS.

N50

ALGERIA

Tan-Tan

P30

KEY

+ Rail Lines

-- Ferry Lines

✈ Airport

*Canary
Islands*
(SPAIN)

Las
Palmas

Laâyoune

Galtat
Zemmour

P41

MALI

WESTERN
SAHARA

Ad'Dakhla

MAURITANIA

N

Lagwira

0   400 miles

0   600 km

size to the one in Mecca. Casablanca's **Corniche** is a pleasant promenade, and the **spice market** in the medina is another attraction.

Dining and Lodging

$$ ✗ **Al Mounia.** The best spot in Casablanca for authenticity and value, Al Mounia serves the classic Moroccan specialties: *pastilla* (pigeon pie), *harira* (lentil, chickpea, and meat soup), *tajines* (meat or fish stewed in almonds, plums, and/or vegetables), *mechoui* (roast lamb), and couscous. ⊠ *95 Rue du Prince Moulay Abdallah,* ☎ *2122/22669. AE, DC, MC, V. Closed Sun.*

$$$$ ✗🔳 **Royal Mansour.** One of Morocco's top hotels, the Royal Mansour's
★ extras are a treat: fabulous food served in a lush, garden courtyard accompanied by live, Cole Porter tunes, and a rooftop *hammam* (Turkish bath). ⊠ *27 Ave. des F.A.R.,* ☎ *2122/313011,* FAX *2122/312583. 159 rooms with bath, 23 suites. 3 restaurants, piano bar, sauna, Turkish bath, meeting rooms. AE, DC, MC, V.*

$$ 🔳 **Hotel Moussafir.** New, impeccably clean, and well located near the Casa-Voyageurs train station, the Moussafir is about one-tenth as expensive as the Royal Mansour and not nearly as far removed in quality. ⊠ *Blvd. Bahmir,* ☎ *2122/401984,* FAX *2122/400799. 99 rooms with bath. Restaurant, bar. AE, DC, MC, V.*

Marrakesh

㊷ *238 km (148 mi) south of Casablanca, 483 km (300 mi) southwest of Fez.*

The tumultuous and panoramic **Djemâa el Fna** (Assembly of the Dead) square, the highlight of a visit to Marrakesh, is a sensorial feast. Great clouds of aromatic smoke from the outdoor kitchens in the center of the square combine with the sounds of Berber musicians and storytellers, the eerie call to prayer of the muezzin, the flutes of snake charmers, and water vendors' bells; scribes and clients are tucked intimately in the shade of umbrellas, tooth-pullers are surrounded by even rows of molars; the snow-capped Atlas peaks rise behind the Kotoubia minaret; and the warmth of the fires meets the cool evening breeze from the mountains. (Marrakesh is equidistant from the Atlantic and the Sahara.)

Dining and Lodging

$$$ ✗ **Dar Marjana.** Diners feel like they've walked into a Delacroix paint-
★ ing with excellent cuisine, beautiful surroundings, Nubian waiters uniformed in rich greens, belly dancing, and folk music. ⊠ *15 Derb Sidi Ali Tair, Bab Doukkala,* ☎ *2124/445773. MC, V. Closed Tues.*

$$$$ ✗🔳 **La Mamounia.** Everyone from Winston Churchill to Bryan Ferry
★ has loved this unique oasis within an oasis. One of the most famous hotels in the world, La Mamounia is worth every one of the many nickels it costs. The hotel is walking distance from Djemâa el Fna square; its grounds, facilities, service, and taste are sensational. ⊠ *Ave. Bab Jdid,* ☎ *2124/448981,* FAX *2124/444940. 171 rooms with bath, 64 suites, 3 villas. 5 restaurants, 5 bars, pool, beauty salon, massage, sauna, Turkish bath, tennis, squash, billiards, shops, meeting rooms. AE, DC, MC, V.*

$$ ✗🔳 **Le Tikida.** This is an ideal family spot a few minutes' taxi ride (free shuttle bus during the day) from Djemâa el Fna square. ⊠ *Palmeraie de Marrakesh, Rte. de Fez–Route Principale 24, BP, 1585 Daoudiate,* ☎ *2124/309099,* FAX *2124/309343. Restaurant, piano bar, pool. AE, DC, MC, V.*

Fez

❹❸ *483 km (300 mi) northeast of Marrakesh, 60 km (37 mi) east of Meknes, 303 km (188 mi) southeast of Tangier.*

Traditionally considered Morocco's intellectual and spiritual capital, Fez can at first seem almost too quiet after tumultuous Marrakesh. Fez is more refined, Andalucían, Mediterranean, and Islamic. The 9th-century medina of **Fez el Bali** (Old Fez) is a labyrinth of mosques (360 of them) and *medersas* (medieval residential colleges), shops, and artisans. Nowhere in Morocco is a good guide more indispensable.

The architectural treasures here are many: carving and tilework, the **water clock,** the **Kairaouine Mosque,** and **Kairaouine University,** which, founded in the 9th century, predates Bologna's university by 200 years and Oxford's by 300. The souks and fondouks are all hauntingly ancient and aesthetically perfect.

Dining and Lodging

$$ ✕ **Al Andalus.** This excellent spot on the airport road in the modern
★ part of town is a local secret. Owner Hilali Fouad's collection of curios and antiques is as enticing as the food. ⊠ *34 Rte. d'Immouzzer,* ☎ *2125/603162,* ℻ *2125/600548. AE, DC, MC, V.*

$$$$ ✕🖬 **Hotel Merinides.** This spectacular hotel is usually booked well in advance. The views over Fez el Bali from the pool, nicely raised above the fray, are unique. ⊠ *Borj Nord,* ☎ *2125/646040,* ℻ *2125/645225. 90 rooms with bath. 2 restaurants, 2 bars, pool. AE, DC, MC, V.*

$$–$$$$ ✕🖬 **Palais Jamai.** This elegant palace, built 120 years ago, was once the residence of the Vizir Jamai. There are views over the medina, and it is close to the old part of Fez. ⊠ *Bab Guissa,* ☎ *2125/634331,* ℻ *2125/635096. 145 rooms with bath. 2 restaurants, pool, tennis. AE, DC, MC, V.*

MOROCCO A TO Z

You will not need a visa; the water is potable, and the time is usually one hour behind Spain. Women traveling alone or without men will have difficulty: Hire a reputable guide, wear conservative clothing, and be on guard at all times.

Getting Around

By Boat

From Algeciras to Tangier, **Transmediterranea** (⊠ Recinto del Puerto s/n, Algeciras, ☎ 956/663850; ⊠ Calle Pedro Muñoz Seca 2, Madrid, ☎ 91/431–0700; ⊠ 31 Ave. de la Resistance, Tangier, ☎ 2129/941101) has a 90-minute hydrofoil and a two-hour car ferry. The slow boat is bigger, more stable, and offers better views than the somewhat claustrophobic hydrofoil. Having your passport stamped and getting your yellow exit card before you leave the boat can save you an hour or more.

By Bus

Bus stations: **Casablanca** (⊠ 303 Blvd. Brahim, ☎ 2122/252901), **Fez** (⊠ Ave. Mohammed V, ☎ 2125/622041), **Marrakesh** (⊠ Bab Doukkala, ☎ 2124/434518), **Tangier** (⊠ Place d'Espagne, ☎ 2129/946682).

By Car

Moroccan roads are free-for-alls: In addition to the poor surfaces, there is a bumper-car, helter-skelter confusion from which, miraculously, most people emerge unscathed. If you choose to brave the roads in search of freedom from set schedules, international car-rental agencies are well represented. Agencies in **Casablanca:** Budget (✉ Torres de los Habous, Ave. des F.A.R., ☎ 2122/314027) and Hertz (✉ 25 Rue Foucault, ☎ 2122/312223); **Fez:** Avis (✉ 50 Blvd. Chefchaouen, ☎ 2125/626746), Budget (✉ Bureau Grand Hotel, Ave. Chefchaouen, ☎ 2125/620919), and Hertz (✉ Hotel de Fez, Ave. des F.A.R., ☎ 2125/622812); **Marrakesh:** Budget (✉ 213 Ave. Mohammed V, ☎ 2124/434604) and Hertz (✉ 154 Ave. Mohammed V, ☎ 2124/434680); **Tangier:** Budget (✉ 79 Ave. du Prince, Moulay Abdallah, ☎ 2129/937994) and Hertz (✉ 36 Ave. Mohammed V, ☎ 2129/933322).

By Plane

Royal Air Maroc (☎ 91/541–1288; in the U.S. outside NY, ☎ 800/344–6726; in NY, 212/750–6071) and **Iberia Airlines** (☎ 91//261–9100; in the U.S., ☎ 800/772–4642) fly to Casablanca from Madrid in 90 minutes. The former has comprehensive domestic service.

By Train

The overnight Madrid-to-Algeciras train leaves Chamartin station at 10 PM and arrives at 8:30 AM. You can buy a boat ticket and change money at the train station before walking to the ferry terminal. Trains from Tangier to Casablanca leave at 4 PM and arrive six hours later. There are two stations in **Casablanca,** the Gare du Port (also called Casa–Port, ☎ 2122/223011) and the Gare des Voyageurs (also called Casa–Voyageurs, ☎ 2122/243818). The latter serves Marrakesh and the south. The stations in **Fez** (☎ 2125/625001), **Marrakesh** (☎ 2124/434518), and **Tangier** (☎ 2129/931201) do not have proper names that are used locally.

Guided Tours

Most Moroccan cities have a swarm of very insistent, unofficial "guides." The best way to get rid of these volunteers, who may falsely assure you that all hotels are full and take you to shops where they get commissions on purchases, is to ignore them and seem to know exactly where you are going. If you do want a guide, hire a cheaper and better one at the local tourist office.

An American tour operator that specializes in Morocco is G.W.T. Inc. (✉ 190 Moore St., Suite 470, Hackensack, NJ 07601, ☎ 201/343–3929 or 800/868–7498, FAX 201/343–7591). Globus (✉ 5301 S. Federal Circle, Littleton, CO 80123, ☎ 303/797–6000, FAX 303/795–0962) has packages that include the Iberian Peninsula as well as Morocco.

If you decide to join a group while you're in Spain, try A Taste of Morocco (✉ Apdo. 349, 29680 Estepona, Málaga, ☎ 95/288–6590), which only runs tours in autumn and winter, or Ambassador Tours (in Barcelona, ☎ 93/482–7100; in Madrid, ☎ 91/359–5005; in Valencia, ☎ 96/374–7855), which is high-end.

Visitor Information

United States (✉ 20 E. 46th St., Suite 1201, New York, NY 10017, ☎ 212/557–2520), **United Kingdom** (✉ 205 Regent St., DEW 1R7, London, ☎ 44171/437–0073), **Madrid** (✉ Calle Quintana 2, 28008, ☎ 91/541–2995), **Casablanca** (✉ 55 Rue Omar Slaoui, ☎ 2122/221177), **Fez** (✉ Place de la Resistance, ☎ 2125/623460), **Marrakesh** (✉ 176 Blvd. Mohammed V, ☎ 2124/432097; ✉ Pl. Abdel-Moumen ben Ali, ☎ 2124/448906), **Tangier** (✉ 29 Blvd. Pasteur, ☎ 2129/948661).

12 Granada, Córdoba, and Eastern Andalucía

Eastern Andalucía is a region of colorful contrasts: lively cities with a deep sense of history, glorious beaches and mountainous landscapes, and white-washed villages clinging to parched hillsides. Here you'll find two of Spain's most famous monuments, the magical palace of the Alhambra in Granada and the great mosque of Córdoba; the Sierra Nevada mountain range; and the mighty Guadalquivir River.

FROM THE DARK MOUNTAINS of the Sierra Morena in the north to the mighty, snowcapped peaks of the Sierra Nevada in the south, Andalucía (Andalusia) rings with echoes of the Moors. These Muslim invaders from North Africa dwelled here for almost 800 years, from their first conquest of Spanish soil (Gibraltar) in AD 711 to their expulsion from Granada in 1492. The name Andalucía itself comes from the Moors' name Al-Andalus for the land they conquered from the Vandals. Two of Spain's most famous monuments, Córdoba's great mosque and Granada's Alhambra, were the inspired creations of Moorish architects and craftsmen working for the Arab emirs. The brilliant, white villages with narrow, shady streets; the sturdy-walled houses clustered around cool inner patios; and the whitewashed facades with modestly grilled windows all stem from centuries of Moorish occupation. The Guadalquivir, the "great river" of the Arabs, traverses the whole region; town names like Úbeda and Jaén are derivations of old Arabic names; ruined *alcazares* (fortresses) dot the landscape; and *azahar* (orange blossom) perfumes its patios. It's hard to find a church in Andalucía that wasn't built on the site of an Arab mosque, and high on the southern slopes of the Sierra Nevada, the villages of the Alpujarras, with their cube-shaped houses, flat roofs, and chimney stacks, could be North African.

In the 13th century King Ferdinand III, one of the Reconquest's greatest soldiers, captured Baeza, Úbeda, Córdoba, and Jaén from the Moors. From their defeats, the Moors fled south to Granada, where they tarried for another 250 years. The next two centuries (14th and 15th) were punctuated by constant battles and skirmishes between Moors and Christians, until Ferdinand of Aragón and Isabella of Castile, known jointly as the Catholic Monarchs, scored the ultimate victory of the Reconquest in 1492. They entered Granada and accepted the Moors' final surrender. In honor of this victory, the Catholic Monarchs chose to be buried in Granada.

The Moors left a legacy, but so did the Christian conquerors and their descendants. There are Gothic chapels, Renaissance cathedrals, and fanciful Baroque monasteries and churches. The sturdy, golden-stone mansions of Úbeda and Baeza contrast intriguingly with the humble, whitewashed villages of much of Andalucía.

The landscape is varied and powerful, too. To the south, the fertile plain of Granada, known as *la vega*, with its tobacco and poplar groves and lush orchards, stretches to meet the mountains of the majestic Sierra Nevada. In this range, snowclad for most of the year, you'll find Spain's highest peaks—the 11,407-foot Mulhacén and the 11,215-foot Veleta. The Guadalquivir River rises in the east in the heights of the Sierra de Cazorla. Flowing westward toward Córdoba, it is bounded on the north by the rugged, shrub-covered Sierra Morena, and in the south by the rolling olive groves of Jaén. Next come the orchards of Córdoba, where fruit and almond trees line the river's banks. Vineyards cover the Córdoban *campiña* (fertile plain south of the Guadalquivir), and white villages cling to hillsides below ruined castles.

Pleasures and Pastimes

Dining

Córdoba's restaurants are a gourmet's paradise, whereas Granada's are respectable if undistinguished. Córdoba's specialties are *salmorejo* (a thick, very garlicky version of gazpacho) and *rabo de toro* (bull's tail or oxtail stew). Many of the city's restaurants are now coming up with creative dishes based on old Arab recipes from Córdoba's Moorish past. Here, *finos* (a dry sherry) or *montillas* (a sherrylike wine) from the province's Montilla-Moriles district, make good aperitifs or bar drinks. Granada's typical dishes are tortilla *al Sacromonte* (omelet made of calf's brains, sweetbreads, diced ham, potatoes, and peas), *habas con jamón* (ham stewed with broad beans), and *sopa sevillana* (tasty fish and seafood soup made with mayonnaise).

Lunch is the main meal here. Restaurants start serving around 2, but most tables don't fill up until at least 3. Most people are still at the table at 5 or later. After such a long, late lunch, few locals dine out in the evening. Instead, they do the rounds of the bars, dipping into tapas and plates of ham or cheese. Ham from the Alpujarran village of Trevélez is famous throughout Spain; ask for it in Granada. Reservations are rarely needed (except where specified) if you go for lunch around 2; wait until 3 and you may have trouble finding a table. In the evening, if you dine early, say 9–10, you shouldn't have problems.

Neat, casual dress is acceptable in all restaurants in this region. Shorts and cut-off jeans are best avoided in all but inexpensive restaurants. Spanish diners are more casually dressed in summer than in winter.

CATEGORY	COST*
$$$$	over 12,000 ptas
$$$	8,500–12,000 ptas
$$	5,000–8,500 ptas
$	under 5,000 ptas

per person for a three-course meal, including house wine and coffee, and excluding tax and service

Fiestas

Jan. Celebrate Granada's 1492 surrender to the Catholic Monarchs on January 2 and on January 6, the Día de los Reyes, there is a procession of the three Wise Men.

Feb. Granada holds a Pilgrimage to the Monastery of San Cecilio on Sacromonte, February 1 and parties hard at Carnival, February 28.

Apr. Holy Week takes place in Granada April 9–15.

May In Córdoba the Las Cruces de Mayo, Fiesta de los Patios, and Feria de Nuestra Señora de la Salud all take place during this month. In Granada there's the Day of the Cross on May 3, San Isidro on May 15, and Mariana Pineda on May 26.

June In Granada there are two fiestas: Corpus Christi, June 15, and San Pedro, June 29.

Sept. Córdoba celebrates Nuestra Señora de Fuensanta, and Granada observes Nuestra Señora de las Angustias the last Sunday in September and the Romería de San Miguel on September 29.

In Córdoba other fiestas include the Carnival celebrations before Lent and Holy Week processions at Easter. Check with local tourist offices for details of fiestas in the Alpujarras—there are many during the summer months.

Hiking and Walking

Thanks to a number of well-run outdoor clubs, and local interest in preserving natural lands, parks for recreation and camping in Andalucía are easily accessible. In addition, hikes in nearby Granada and Córdoba can be had in between visiting the city's main attractions. The Andalucían village of Cazorla in Jaén province leads to the pine-clad slopes of the Parque Natural de Cazorla. South of Granada in the Sierra

Nevada and the Alpujarras, visitors can find some of the most impressive vistas in all of Spain, terrific skiing in the winter time, and the full breadth of outdoor activities in the summer.

Lodging

Andalucía has accommodations for all budgets, from low-key bed-and-breakfasts to luxurious paradores. The Parador de San Francisco, for example, nestled beside Granada's Alhambra is a magnificent way to enjoy the city and southern Spain's storied past. Bed-and-breakfast accommodations, which can be found in many villages, give visitors access to the countryside and the rich ways of folk life.

Córdoba has seen a recent spate of building and is now home to some very pleasant hotels set in houses in the old town close to the mosque. It's rarely hard to find accommodations in Córdoba if you haven't booked, though watch out for Holy Week and the May Patio Festival. Granada, on the other hand, can be very difficult—it contains the Alhambra, which is Spain's most-visited monument. Hotels on the Alhambra hill need to be booked long in advance; those in the city center around the Puerto Real and Acera del Darro are unbelievably noisy—ask for rooms at the back. Granada has plenty of hotels, but the busy season runs from Easter until late October. Beware Holy Week and the International Festival of Music and Dance (mid-June–mid-July) when rooms are particularly hard to come by.

CATEGORY	COST*
$$$$	over 20,000 ptas.
$$$	11,500–20,000 ptas.
$$	8,000–11,500 ptas.
$	under 8,000 ptas.

per standard double room, excluding tax

Exploring Andalucía

Great Itineraries

Our itineraries explore three of Andalucía's eight provinces: Granada, Jaén, and Córdoba. If you have limited time, begin in Granada then make excursions to the neighboring towns of Santa Fe and Fuente Vaqueros and the Sierra Nevada mountains. Continue on to Baena before winding up your "quickie" tour in Córdoba. The five-day itinerary begins in Córdoba and takes you to Jaén with its historic towns and Cazorla Nature Park. Explore Granada before heading out to the Sierra Nevada and the quaint towns of the Alpujarras region. If you have seven days, begin your tour in Córdoba before continuing on to Baeza and Granada; end your journey in the Alpujarras.

Numbers in the text below correspond to numbers in the margin and on the maps.

IF YOU HAVE 3 DAYS

Begin your tour in ⊡ **Granada** ①–⑬, where you should plan to spend your first night. On day one visit the mystical Alhambra and walk in the Albaicín where you can immerse yourself in the city's rich Moorish quarter. Have lunch and tea along the Cuesta de Elvira. Spend the afternoon in the alleyways in the Alcaicería visiting the Cathedral and the Capilla Real; then take an evening tour of the Alhambra. On the morning of the second day, head for the village of Baena in the **Subbetica** ㊶ area. Take in the scenery before spending the night in ⊡ **Córdoba** ㉓–㊴. On the third day, spend the morning touring the magical Mezquita before walking about the Judería, the city's old Jewish Quarter. Head out to the River Guadalquivir to view the city and walk across the Puente Romano to the Torre de la Calahorra, which houses a fine museum detailing the region's history.

IF YOU HAVE 5 DAYS

🖼 **Córdoba** ㉓–㊴ makes a good starting point for this more in-depth tour of the region. Take in the city's sites giving the Mezquita and the Judería a good, long look. Next morning, head out towards Granada and, along your way, tour the towns of Baena, Rute, and Priego de Córdoba in the **Subbetica** ㊶ region. Overnight it in 🖼 **Granada** ①–⑬. On the third day, tour Granada's Alhambra, the Albaicín, and the alleyways in the Alcaicería. On the fourth day rise early to get on mountain roads to visit the **Sierra Nevada** ⑰. Spend the night in the 🖼 **Alpujarras** ⑱; next day, take a morning walk and eventually make your return to Granada.

When to Tour Andalucía

The spring and summer are the best times to visit Andalucía. Temperatures can drop to the 30s in the winter, and the wind off the Guadalquivir in Córdoba can be as stiff as any in New England. Most monuments don't open before 9:30 and are closed for the lunch hour, anywhere between 1:30 and 4:00.

GRANADA AND ENVIRONS, THE SIERRA NEVADA, AND THE ALPUJARRAS

The city of Granada, the last stronghold of the Moors, is home to the splendid Alhambra with its many fountains, lush gardens, and once-luxurious baths. Visit the tomb of Isabel and Ferdinand, weave your way through the Albaicín neighborhood, and relax in the fragrant gardens of the Generalife. Outside of the city you'll find the craggy peaks of the Sierra Nevada mountains, seventh heaven for skiers, and the craft-rich and picturesque Alpujarras region.

Granada

Numbers in the margin correspond to points of interest on the Granada map.

❶ *430 km (265 mi) south of Madrid, 261 km (162 mi) east of Córdoba.*

The city of Granada rises majestically from a fertile plain onto three hills, dwarfed—on a clear day—by the mighty snowcapped peaks of the Sierra Nevada. Atop one of these hills perches the pink-gold palace of the Alhambra, at once splendidly imposing and infinitely delicate. From it can be seen the roofs of the old Moorish quarter, the Albaicín; the caves of the Sacromonte; and, in the distance, the fertile vega, rich in orchards, tobacco fields, and poplar groves.

Granada's Moorish Nasrid dynasty, split by internal squabbles, presented Ferdinand of Aragón with the chance he needed in 1491. Spurred by Isabella's religious fanaticism, he laid siege to the city for seven months. On January 2, 1492, the Rey Chico (Boy King), Boabdil, was forced to surrender the keys of the city to the triumphant Catholic Monarchs. As Boabdil fled the Alhambra by the Puerta de los Siete Suelos (Gate of the Seven Sighs), he asked that this gate be sealed forever.

The Plaza Nueva is the crossroads for the city's main boulevards. The Cuesta de Gomérez leads up a steep grade from here to the cool vale ★ ❷ of the **Alhambra** precincts, and the narrow, charming passageways of the Albaicín. Climb the slopes of green elms planted by the Duke of

Wellington to reach the **Puerta de las Granadas**, a Renaissance gateway built by Charles V (note that it is topped by three pomegranates—a symbol of Granada) that leads to the the **Puerta de la Justicia** and the Alhambra. Yusuf I built this Gate of Justice in 1348. On its two arches are carved a hand and a key, the five fingers representing the five laws of the Koran.

The Alhambra was founded in the 1240s by Ibn el-Ahmar, or Alhamar, the first king of the Nasrids. The great citadel once comprised an entire complex of houses, schools, baths, barracks, and gardens surrounded by defense towers and seemingly impregnable walls. Today, only the Alcazaba fortress and the Royal Palace, built chiefly by Yusuf I (1334–54) and his son Mohammed V (1354–91), remain. The palace is an intricate fantasy of endless patios, arches, and cupolas fashioned from wood, plaster, and tiles; lavishly colored and adorned by geometric patterns of marquetry and ceramics; and surmounted by delicate, frothy profusions of lacelike stucco and *mocárabes* (ornamental stalactites). Built of perishable materials, it was never intended to last but to be forever replaced and replenished by succeeding generations.

By the early 17th century, ruin and decay had set in, and it was abandoned by all but tramps and stray dogs. Napoleon's troops commandeered it in 1812, but their attempts to blow it up were happily foiled. In 1814, the Alhambra's fortunes rose with the arrival of the duke of Wellington, who came to it to escape the pressures of the Peninsular War. Soon afterward (1829), Washington Irving came to live in it and did much to promote a revival of interest in the crumbling palace. His 1832 book, *Tales of the Alhambra,* played an important role in this. In 1862, Granada finally embarked upon a complete restoration program that has been carried on ever since.

Purchase your entrance ticket and wander over to your left, to the original fortress of the **Alcazaba**. Its ruins are dominated by a tower, the **Torre de la Vela**, whose summit offers superlative views of the city, to the north, the Albaicín; to the northeast, the Sacromonte; and to the west, the cathedral. The tower's great bell was used as an alarm signal by the Moors, and later by the Christians, to control the opening and closing of the gates of the Granada vega's irrigation system.

The Renaissance **Palacio de Carlos V** (Palace of Charles V), with a perfectly square exterior but a circular interior courtyard, stands imposing but totally incongruous on the site where the sultans' private apartments once stood. Begun in 1526 and designed by Pedro Machuca, a pupil of Michelangelo, the palace was once used for bullfights and mock tournaments. Today, its perfect acoustics make it a fine setting for symphony concerts during Granada's International Festival of Music and Dance, held annually in June and July.

A wisteria-covered walkway leads into the heart of the Alhambra, the **Casa Real** (Royal Palace). Delicate apartments, lazy fountains, and tranquil pools form a vivid contrast to the sturdy, surrounding defense walls. The Royal Palace is divided into three sections. The first is the *mexuar,* where the business, government, and administration of the Alhambra were conducted. Here are the Oratory and the Cuarto Dorado (Golden Room); make sure you don't miss the views of the Albaicín and Sacromonte from their windows.

The *serrallo* is a series of state rooms where the sultans held court and entertained their ambassadors. In the heart of the serrallo, you'll find the **Patio de los Arrayanes** (Court of the Myrtles), with a long goldfish pool surrounded by fragrant shrubs. At its northern end, in the **Salón de Embajadores** (Hall of the Ambassadors)—which has a mag-

Andalucía: Granada to Córdoba

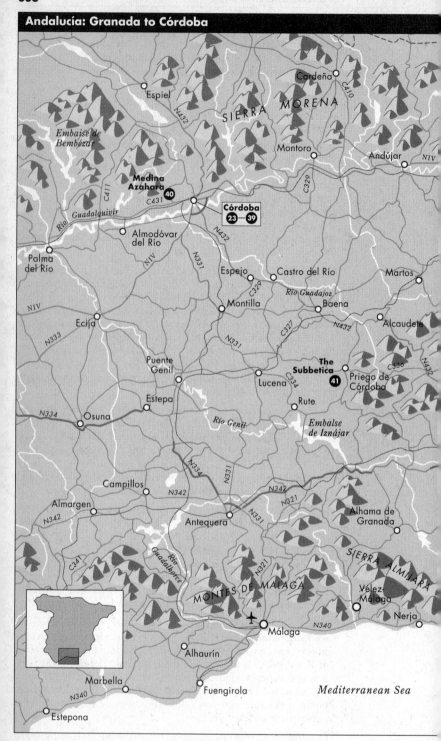

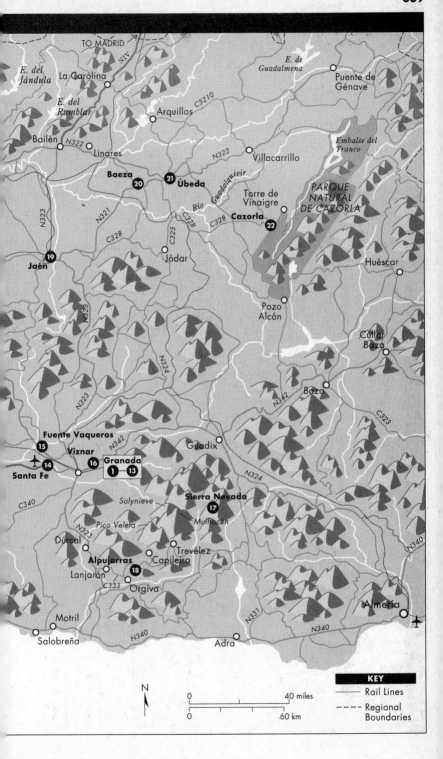

Granada

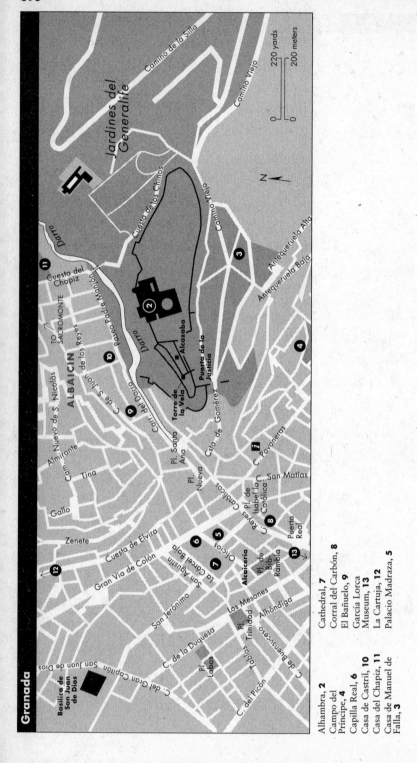

Alhambra, **2**
Campo del Príncipe, **4**
Capilla Real, **6**
Casa de Castril, **10**
Casa del Chapiz, **11**
Casa de Manuel de Falla, **3**

Cathedral, **7**
Corral del Carbón, **8**
El Bañuelo, **9**
García Lorca Museum, **13**
La Cartuja, **12**
Palacio Madraza, **5**

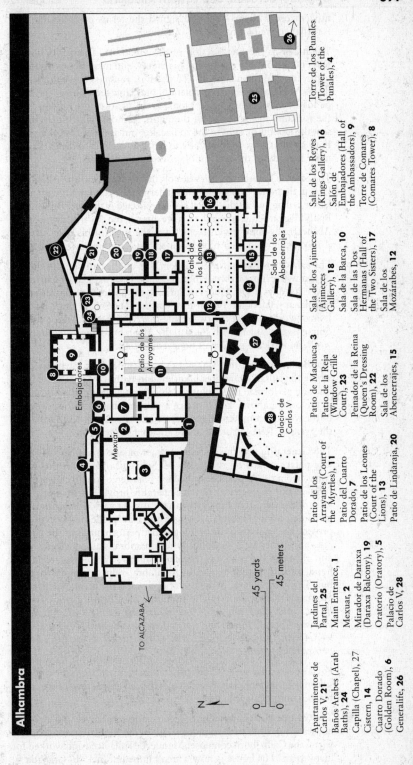

Alhambra

Apartamientos de Carlos V, **21**
Baños Arabes (Arab Baths), **24**
Capilla (Chapel), **27**
Cistern, **14**
Cuarto Dorado (Golden Room), **6**
Generalife, **26**

Jardines del Partal, **25**
Main Entrance, **1**
Mexuar, **2**
Mirador de Daraxa (Daraxa Balcony), **19**
Oratorio (Oratory), **5**
Palacio de Carlos V, **28**

Patio de los Arrayanes (Court of the Myrtles), **11**
Patio del Cuarto Dorado, **7**
Patio de los Leones (Court of the Lions), **13**
Patio de Lindaraja, **20**

Patio de Machuca, **3**
Patio de la Reja (Window Grille Court), **23**
Peinador de la Reina (Queen's Dressing Room), **22**
Sala de los Abencerrajes, **15**

Sala de los Ajimeces (Ajimeces Gallery), **18**
Sala de la Barca, **10**
Sala de las Dos Hermanas (Hall of the Two Sisters), **17**
Sala de los Mozárabes, **12**

Sala de los Reyes (Kings Gallery), **16**
Salón de Embajadores (Hall of the Ambassadors), **9**
Torre de Comares (Comares Tower), **8**

Torre de los Punales (Tower of the Punales), **4**

Patio de los Leones

Sala de los Abencerrajes

Embajadores

Patio de los Arrayanes

Mexuar

Palacio de Carlos V

TO ALCAZABA

N

45 yards

45 meters

0

0

nificent cedar dome—Boabdil signed the terms of surrender, and Isabella received Christopher Columbus.

The **harem** is the final section of the Alhambra. During its time, it was entered only by the sultan, his family, and their most trusted servants, most of them eunuchs. To reach it, you pass through the **Sala de los Mozárabes**—note its splendid but damaged ceiling. The **Patio de los Leones** (Court of the Lions) is the heart of the harem. From the fountain in the center of the patio, 12 lions, which may represent the months or signs of the zodiac, leer out at the hordes of tourists. Four streams flow symbolically to the four corners of the earth, and more literally to the surrounding state apartments.

The **Sala de los Abencerrajes** lies on the south side of the Alhambra. It is, perhaps, the most beautiful gallery in the Alhambra, with a stalactite ceiling and a star-shaped cupola reflected in the pool below. Here Boabdil's father is alleged to have massacred 16 members of the Abencerrajes family, whose chief was the lover of his own favorite, Zoraya, and piled their blood-stained heads in this now-serene font.

The **Sala de los Reyes** (Kings' Gallery) lies on the patio's east side decorated with ceiling frescoes that may have been painted by Christians in the last days of the Moors' tenure. To the north, the **Sala de las Dos Hermanas** (Hall of the Two Sisters) was the abode of the king's favorite. Its name comes from the two white-marble slabs in its floor, and its ceiling is resplendent with some of the Alhambra's most superb stucco work, an intricate pattern of honeycomb cells.

The **Baños Arabes,** the Alhambra's semi-subterranean bathhouse, is where the sultan's favorites luxuriated in baths of brightly tiled mosaic and performed their ablutions lit by star-shaped pinpoints of light in the ceiling above. You'll notice a balcony that looks out over one of the rooms; from here, the sultan would choose his bed partner for the evening. Relax or stroll in the adjacent gardens.

The **Generalife** was the ancient summer palace of the Nasrid kings. The palace stands on the Cerro del Sol (Hill of the Sun); its name comes from the Arabic Gennat Alarif (Garden of the Architect). The terraces and promenades of the Generalife provide an incomparable view of the city, stretching away to the distant vega. During the summer International Festival of Music and Dance, the stately cypresses provide the backdrop for evening ballet performances in the Generalife amphitheater. The walk to the Alhambra is along a steep road, and although the road has many nice shops in a colorful neighborhood, some may want to take the Alhambra Train, a comfortable minibus. The Plaza Nueva, in the center of town, is the point of departure. 50 ptas. Trains leave every 15 minutes. ✉ *Alhambra and Generalife 625 ptas., free Sun. after 3. ☉ Mar.–Oct., daily 9–8, and floodlit visits Tues., Thurs., and Sat. 10 PM–midnight; Nov.–Feb., daily 9–5:45, and floodlit visits Sat. 8 PM–10 PM; ticket office closes 1 hour before closing time.*

For a spectacular view of the city, return to town from the opposite side of the Alhambra hill. Pass through the elm groves toward the ocher-red Alhambra Palace hotel.

❸ The **Casa de Manuel de Falla,** lodged next to some lovely old Granada houses along a hill with stunning views of the Alpujarra mountains, is where the Cádiz-born composer Manuel de Falla lived and worked for many years. His house is now a small museum. In 1986 Granada finally paid tribute to him by dedicating its new concert hall in his memory, naming it the Manuel de Falla Auditorium. ✉ *C. Antequeruela Alta*

11, ☎ 958/229421. ⚏ 250 ptas. ⊘ Apr.–Sept., daily 9–3; Oct.–Mar., daily 10–4.

❹ The **Campo del Príncipe** is a handsome square surrounded by many lively tapas bars and shops. In the middle, next to an ornate fountain, lies a much-venerated crucifix with Cristo de los Faroles (Christ of the Lanterns). Women often come here to pray and offer flowers. Príncipe is a good place to come at lunchtime or early in the evening to sample plates of seafood or *jamón serrano* (mountain-cured ham prized throughout the peninsula).

The **Casa de los Tiros** (✉ Cementerio de Santa Escolástica 3, ☎ 958/ 221072), a 16th-century mansion, has been converted into a private museum and research institution. Group tours of the mansion and its classic patios are welcome with advance arrangement.

The **Plaza de Isabel la Católica,** with its statue of Columbus presenting Queen Isabella with his maps of the New World, is one of the main crossroads of the city. Ahead of you lies one of Granada's main thoroughfares, the Gran Vía de Colón, named for Columbus. This thoroughfare was built in the late 19th century in an effort to modernize cross-town transportation; unfortunately, several wonderful old palaces were destroyed in the process. To your left, Calle de los Reyes Católicos leads down to Puerta Real, the commercial hub of the city; and up to your right is the café-filled Plaza Nueva.

The **Alcaicería,** once the Arabs' silk market, is now home to a series of alleys chock full of tourist shops and good restaurants. This was the hub of the Moorish city, and though the Alcaicería is not authentic—the old one burned down in the 1840s and was rebuilt as arcades of souvenir shops—it is particularly beautiful at night, when its arches and courtyards are lit by rows of white lanterns. Take time to wander over to the Plaza de la Pasiegas to admire the cathedral and some of the quarter's more authentic shops.

❺ The **Palacio Madraza** on Gran Vía de Colón conceals the old Moorish university, built in 1349 by Yusuf I. Take note of the Baroque facade. Inside you'll find an octagonal room crowned by a dome of Moorish inspiration. The building is now an exhibition and cultural center, open only during exhibitions. ⚏ *Free.*

★ ❻ The **Capilla Real (Royal Chapel)** is a shrine of Granadan history second only to the Alhambra. This is the burial place of the Catholic Monarchs, Isabella of Castile and Ferdinand of Aragón. They had originally planned to be buried in San Juan de los Reyes, in Toledo, but following their conquest of Granada in 1492, Isabella decreed that their final resting place would be here. When Isabella died in 1504, her body was at first laid to rest in the Convent of San Francisco (now the parador) on the Alhambra hill. In 1506 the architect Enrique Egas began work on the Royal Chapel and completed it 15 years later. It is a masterpiece of the ornate Gothic style known in Spain as Isabelline. In 1521 Isabella's body was brought to a simple lead coffin in the Royal Chapel crypt, where it was joined by that of her husband, Ferdinand, and later her unfortunate daughter, Juana la Loca, and son-in-law, Felipe el Hermoso. Felipe died young and Juana la Loca (Joan the Mad) had his casket borne about the peninsula with her for years, opening the lid each night to kiss her embalmed spouse good night. The elaborate marble tombs in which Ferdinand and Isabella now lie side by side were commissioned by their grandson, Charles V, and fashioned by the sculptor Domenico Fancelli. The altarpiece by Felipe Vigarini (1522) shows Boabdil surrendering the keys of the city to its conquerors. In the sacristy you'll find Ferdinand's sword, Isabella's crown and scepter, and a fine collection of Flemish paintings once owned by Isabella. ✉ *Oficios.* ☎ *958/229239,* ✇ *200 ptas.* ☉ *Mar.–Sept., daily 10:30–1 and 4–7; Oct.–Feb., daily 10:30–1 and 3:30–6:30.*

NEED A BREAK? From the Cathedral follow Libreros street south one block to the relaxed **Plaza de Bib-Rambla**—a perfect place to grab an ice-cream at the colorful Cafe Bib-Rambla. Also, the **Plaza del a Universidad,** a lovely square in the heart of the University of Granada, is bordered by bookstores, cafes, gardens and lots of young people.

❼ The huge **cathedral** was commissioned in 1521 by Charles V who considered the Royal Chapel "too small for so much glory" and determined to house his illustrious grandparents somewhere more worthy. Charles undoubtedly had great designs; Granada cathedral is the creation of some of the greatest architects of its time: Enrique Egas, Diego de Siloé, Alonso Cano, and sculptor Juan de Mena. But his ambitions came to little, for the cathedral is a grandiose and gloomy monument, not completed until 1714, and never used as the crypt of his parents and grandparents. ☎ *958/222959.* ✇ *200 ptas.* ☉ *Mar.–Sept., Mon.–Sat. 10:30–1 and 4–7, Sun. 4–7; Oct.–Feb., Mon.–Sat. 10:30–1:30 and 3:30–6:30, Sun. 3:30–6.*

❽ The **Corral del Carbón** means Coal House or Coal Store, and this is what it was used for in the 19th century, but its origins are much earlier. One of the oldest Moorish buildings in the city, it dates back to the 14th century, when Moorish merchants used it as a lodging house and stored their goods on the upper floor. This old Arab inn, the only one of its kind in Spain, was later used by Christians as a theater. It's been expertly restored and now displays Spanish furniture and handicrafts. ✉ *Plaza Mariana Pineda 10, 1 block from Puerta Real,* ☎ *958/226688.* ✇ *Free.* ☉ *Weekdays 9–8, Sat. 10–2.*

The **Albaicín** is a very special part of Granada. Standing on a hill of its own, across the ravine of the Darro from the Alhambra, this old Moorish quarter is a fascinating mix of dilapidated, white houses and immaculate *carmenes* (private villas in gardens enclosed by high walls). This hillside quarter, with its cobbled alleyways and secret corners, was founded in 1228 by Moors who were expelled from Baeza after its capture by the Saint King Ferdinand. The Albaicín guards its old Moorish atmosphere jealously, though its 30 mosques have long been converted into Baroque churches. A stretch of the original Moorish city wall runs beside the Cuesta de la Alhacaba.

If you're on foot, you can enter the Albaicín from either the Cuesta de Elvira or the Plaza Nueva. On Cuesta de Elvira be sure to try one of the delightful tea shops; because of its Moorish history, Granada offers some of the best spots for drinking tea in all of Spain. On foot or by car—take a taxi rather than your own car; parking is impossible—begin in Plaza Santa Ana and follow the Carrera del Darro, Paseo Padre Manjón, and the Cuesta del Chapiz.

❾ **El Bañuelo** (Little Baths) are the 11th-century Arab steam baths which may be a little dark and dank now, but try to imagine how it would have been some 900 years ago when it was filled with Moorish beauties, and bright ceramic tiles and hangings adorned the dull, brick walls. From the ceiling, light comes in through star-shaped vents, just as it does in the Alhambra bathhouse. ✉ *Carrera del Darro 31,* ☎ *958/222339.* ✇ *100 ptas.* ☉ *Tues.–Fri. 9:30–2, weekends 10–2.*

❿ The **Casa de Castril** is a richly decorated 16th-century palace that once belonged to Bernardo Zafra, secretary to Queen Isabella. Before you enter the Castril, notice the exquisite portal and the facade carved with a phoenix and scallop shells. The house is the home of the **Museo Archeológico** (Museum of Archaeology); here you'll find a beautiful Moorish room, Egyptian burial urns from near Almuñécar, and artifacts from the caves of Granada province. ⊠ *Carrera del Darro 41,* ☎ *958/225640.* 🎫 *250 ptas.* ☾ *Tues.–Sun. 10–2.*

NEED A
BREAK?

The **park at Paseo Padre Manjón** along the Darro River is a terrific place for a coffee break. Among the fountains and stone walkways, the park affords a stunning view of the backside of the Alhambra.

The **Palacio de los Córdoba** at the end of the Paseo Padre Manjón is a noble house of the 17th century. Today, it's used for art exhibitions and municipal functions.

⓫ The **Casa del Chapiz** on the Cuesta del Chapiz at its junction with Camino del Sacromonte is a fine 16th-century Morisco house with a delightful garden. It's the home of the School of Arabic Studies and is not generally open to the public. But if you knock, the caretaker may well show you around.

★ The **balcony** in front of **San Nicolás Church** gives one of the finest views in all Granada. On the hill opposite, the turrets and towers of the ocher-colored Alhambra are dramatically silhouetted against the snowcapped peaks of the Sierra Nevada. This view is at its most magical at dawn, dusk, and when the Alhambra is floodlit.

Rising behind the Albaicín, the third of Granada's three hills, the **Sacromonte,** is dotted with prickly-pear cacti and riddled with caverns. The name Granada, by the way, comes from the Arabic word *garnathah* (mountain cave). These caves may possibly have sheltered early Christians, for 15th-century treasure-hunters found instead a collection of bones there. Some of these they assumed belonged to San Cecilio, the city's patron saint, and so the hill was sanctified—*sacro monte* (holy mountain)—and a monastery built on its summit.

The Sacromonte is the domain of Granada's Gypsies. Though fewer and fewer of them actually live in the district today, a good number still earn a healthy living there fleecing the city's tourists. The flamenco shows they stage are generally abysmal, the drinks watered down, and the prices vastly inflated for performances that are not so very *auténtico*. But on another level, these shows are certainly colorful, and they do provide a chance to go inside the famous *cuevas* (caves). Richly colored rugs and gleaming copper utensils adorn their caves—as do such modern conveniences as refrigerators and dishwashers. On summer evenings enterprising Granadinos run minibus tours to the Gypsy caves—your hotel can often put you in touch. The price of the trip usually includes a drink in the Albaicín first, and though not cheap, it may well be the safest way to visit the Sacromonte. Only the most adventurous should attempt the trip on their own. Don't bring valuables up here or more cash than you can afford to lose.

⓬ **La Cartuja,** a Carthusian monastery in the north of the city (2 km/1 mi from the center) was begun in 1506 and moved to its present site in 1516, although construction continued for the following 300 years. In time, La Cartuja became one of the most outstanding examples of lavish Baroque style in Andalucía. When you enter the church and gaze at its twisted, multicolored marble columns; the profusion of gold and silver, tortoise-shell, and ivory; the intricate stucco; and the extravagant Churrigueresque sacristy, you'll see why the Cartuja has often been called the Christian answer to the Moors' Alhambra. ⊠ *Camino de*

Alfacar, ☎ *958/201932.* 🖃 *200 ptas.* 🕙 *May–Sept., daily 10–1 and 4–7; Oct.–Apr., daily 10–1 and 3:30–6.*

⑬ The **García Lorca Museum** pays tribute to Granada's most famous native son, the poet Federico García Lorca. Located on the western fringes of the city, the poet's one-time summer home, **La Huerta de San Vicente,** was turned into a full-time museum in 1995. 🖃 *C. de la Virgen Blanca,* ☎ *958/258466.* 🕙 *Oct.–Apr., Tues.–Sun. 10–1:00 and 4–7; summer, Tues.–Sun. 10–1 and 6–9.*

Dining and Lodging

$$$$ ✕ **Diego Morales.** Locals consider this restaurant, one block above the
★ Camino de Ronda, Granada's best. The menu favors international cuisine; desserts are especially good. Service is professional and the ambience agreeable. 🖃 *Pedro Antonio de Alarcón 34,* ☎ *958/521904. AE, DC, MC, V. Closed Sun. and Aug.*

$$$ ✕ **Carmen de San Miguel.** Set on the Alhambra hill in a villa with a glass-enclosed dining room, an Andalucían patio and fountain, and a terrace, this restaurant offers magnificent views over Granada. The food is less spectacular. Entrées may include the delicious *paletilla de cordero con piñones* (shoulder of lamb with pine nuts). 🖃 *Paseo Torres Bermejas 3,* ☎ *958/226723. AE, DC, MC, V. No dinner Sun.*

$$$ ✕ **Cunini.** Just below the cathedral, Cunini is Granada's best fish
★ restaurant. Fresh seafood is heaped on the long tapas bar, and the menu offers fish dishes from all over Spain, including some Basque specialties. Both the *pescaditos fritos* (fried) and the *parrillada* (grilled) fish are good choices, or you may prefer *zarzuela* (fish stew). 🖃 *Pescadería 9,* ☎ *958/250777. AE, DC, MC, V. Closed 4 PM–8 PM and Mon.*

$$$ ✕ **El Molino.** The setting is an 18th-century mill house on a wooded
★ hillside some 20 km (12 mi) outside the city of Granada in the town of Durcal. Besides a restaurant, you'll find a gastronomy museum with a working mill, a wine museum-cum-bodega, a center for research into the ancient cuisine of Andalucía, and a cooking and restaurant-management school. The center, partly sponsored by the Andalucían Regional Government and the European Union, is staffed by 60 students. Its owner-director, Manuel Carrillo, runs regular, open, cooking courses on such themes as Sephardic Jewish cuisine, tapas cookery, and Moorish breads and pastries. Instruction is available in English by arrangement. The elegant but rustic dining room overlooks an aromatic herb garden. The seasonal menu makes good use of local almonds and olive oil and offers only ancient Andalucían, Jewish, and Moorish dishes. Your best bet is to try the *menú de degustación* (tasting menu)—seven small courses that won't leave you feeling overfed and sleepy. Hors d'oeuvres may include *remojón* (a salad of oranges and codfish); a main course might be *pastel de pichón* (a flaky pigeon pie dusted with cinnamon). Desserts are of Arab origin: you might try the figs in caramel-almond sauce. For details and enrollment in cookery courses, write to the Center for Andalucían Culinary Research at the address below. 🖃 *Camino de las Fuentes, Paraje de la Isla, 18650 Durcal (Granada),* ☎ *958/780247. AE, DC, MC, V. Closed Mon.*

$$–$$$ ✕ **Ruta del Veleta.** Just over 5 km (3 mi) out in Cenes de la Vega, this
★ typically decorated restaurant offers some of Granada's best cuisine. Its specialties are *carnes a la brasa* (succulent grilled meats) and fish dishes from Cantabria and the Levante cooked in rock salt. Dessert might be pudding *de manzanas en salsa de moras* (apple pudding in blackberry sauce). 🖃 *Carretera Sierra Nevada, Km 5.4,* ☎ *958/436134. AE, DC, MC, V. No dinner Sun.*

$$ ✕ **Sevilla.** García Lorca and Manuel de Falla used to dine in this col-
★ orful restaurant, which has been going strong since 1930. There's a superb tapas bar and four picturesque dining rooms; you can also eat

on the outdoor terrace overlooking the Royal Chapel. The menu features such Granadino favorites as sopa sevillana and tortilla *Sacromonte* (omelet with kid's brains, ham, and vegetables). ⊠ *Oficios 12,* ☎ *958/ 221223. AE, DC, MC, V. Closed Sun.*

$ ✗ **Los Manueles.** The food isn't that special, but the decor, atmosphere, and friendly waiters at this traditional inn off Reyes Católicos make it popular with Granadinos and visitors. Alpujarran rugs, copper plates, and other knickknacks cover the walls, and gigantic hams adorn the bar; this ancient tavern is usually packed. ⊠ *Zaragoza 2,* ☎ *958/223415. AE, DC, MC, V. Closed 5 PM–7:30 PM.*

$$$$ ✗🏨 **Alhambra Palace.** This flamboyant, ocher-red Moorish palace was
★ built in 1910 and commands a superb position, in leafy grounds on the back of the Alhambra hill. The interior is exotic and Asian, with green-and-blue-tile walls and Moorish arches and pillars. Even the bar is incongruously decorated as a mosque. The rooms overlooking the town have the most magnificent views; so, too, does the terrace, a perfect place to watch the sun set on the Sierra Nevada. ⊠ *Peña Partida 2, 18009,* ☎ *958/221468, FAX 958/226404. 123 rooms with baths, 9 suites. Restaurant, 2 bars. AE, DC, MC, V.*

$$$$ ✗🏨 **La Bobadilla.** Found halfway between Granada and Málaga, this
★ luxurious complex, with its white walls, tile roofs, patios, fountains, and artificial lake, resembles a Moorish village or a rambling Andalucían *cortijo* (ranch). The buildings cluster around a 16th-century-style chapel whose 1,595-pipe organ is used for weekend concerts. Each bedroom is individually designed and decorated, with its own terrace, patio, or garden. The elegant haute-cuisine restaurant, La Finca, features fresh, organically grown produce from the hotel garden and meat reared on the hotel farm. ⊠ *Finca La Bobadilla north of Granada-Seville highway between Salinas and Rute, 18300,* ☎ *958/321861, FAX 958/321810. 60 rooms with baths. 2 restaurants, pools, hot tub, saunas, tennis courts, exercise room, horseback riding, convention center. AE, DC, MC, V.*

$$$$ ✗🏨 **Parador de San Francisco.** Magnificently located within the Alhambra precincts, Spain's most popular parador stands in an old Franciscan convent built by the Catholic Monarchs after their capture of Granada. The rooms in the old section are furnished with antiques, woven curtains, and bedspreads; those in the new wing are simpler and less expensive. Reservations should be made four to six months in advance. ⊠ *Alhambra, 18009,* ☎ *958/221440, FAX 958/222264. 36 rooms with baths. Restaurant, bar. AE, DC, MC, V.*

$$$–$$$$ ✗🏨 **Triunfo.** Opened in 1988, this comfortable hotel is at the far end of the Gran Vía de Colón. Public rooms have gleaming marble floors, deep sofas, and a generous number of paintings on the walls. Rooms are furnished in traditional style, with dark wood fittings and apricot curtains and bedspreads. The handsome Puerta Elvira Restaurant serves typical Andalucían dishes. ⊠ *Plaza Triunfo 19, 18010,* ☎ *958/ 207444 or 958/207673, FAX 958/279017. 37 rooms with baths. Restaurant, cafeteria, AE, DC, MC, V.*

$$$ ✗🏨 **Inglaterra.** Set in a period house just two blocks above the Gran Vía de Colón in the heart of town, this is a hotel that will appeal to those who prefer Old World charm to creature comforts, though the accommodations are perfectly adequate for the reasonable rates. *Cetti Meriem 6,* ☎ *958/221559, FAX 958/227100. 36 rooms with baths. AE, DC, MC, V.*

$$ ✗🏨 **América.** This simple but charming hotel, located within the Alhambra precincts, is very popular; you should book months ahead. It feels like a private home, with simple bedrooms, a sitting room decorated with local handicrafts, and a shady patio where home-cooked

meals are served in the summer months. Some readers, however, have written complaining about the service. ⊠ *Real de la Alhambra 53, 18009,* ☎ *958/227471,* FAX *958/227470. 14 rooms with baths. Restaurant. No credit cards. Closed Nov.–Feb.*

$$ ✗⊡ **Reina Cristina.** In an old house near the lively Plaza de la Trinidad in the heart of the city, this hotel has been thoroughly modernized. Plants trail from the windowsills of the patio-reception area, where a small marble fountain splashes beneath a Moorish lamp. There is a lively cafeteria for afternoon conversation. A marble stairway leads to the bedrooms, which are simply but cheerfully furnished with red curtains and red-and-white-checked bedspreads. ⊠ *Tablas 4, 18002,* ☎ *958/253211,* FAX *958/255728. 43 rooms with baths. Restaurant, bar-cafeteria. AE, DC, MC, V.*

$$ ✗⊡ **Victoria.** An Old World hotel, overlooking the Puerta Real, the Victoria is something of a gem—but a bit of a chipped and faded one. There's an impressive entrance lobby, with a glittering chandelier and coral-colored marble decor, and the carpeted bedrooms are furnished with old-fashioned headboards and dark, polished furniture. However, some readers have complained of less-than-satisfactory rooms. ⊠ *Puerta Real 3, 18005,* ☎ *958/257700,* FAX *958/263108. 68 rooms with baths, 2 suites. 2 restaurants, 2 bars. AE, DC, MC, V.*

$ ✗⊡ **Britz.** This hotel is at the base of the Alhambra hill and close to downtown attractions. Rooms are small but comfortable, with modern, characterless decor. It's a good budget option. ⊠ *Plaza Nueva y Gomerez 1, 18009,* ☎ *958/223652, 22 rooms with baths. MC, V.*

$ ✗⊡ **Montecarlo.** This old-fashioned hotel overlooks the Fuente de las Batallas, in the city center. The entrance lobby and stairways have some nice, old touches—ornate tables and Moorish lamps. Most rooms have been refurbished, but avoid front rooms, which are horrendously noisy. ⊠ *Acera del Darro 44, 18005,* ☎ *958/257900,* FAX *958/255596. 73 rooms with baths. Bar, cafeteria. AE, MC, V.*

Nightlife and the Arts

Information on what's going on arts-wise is available through the **Area de Bienestar Social Cultura y Juventud** located at the Palacio de los Condes de Gabia (⊠ Plaza de los Girones 1, ☎ 958/247383); information about art events for young people can also be found here. Theatre performances take place at the **Teatro Alhambra** (⊠ Molines 56, ☎ 958/220447). Information on art exhibitions is available through the **Centro Cultural Manuel de Falla** (☎ 958/229421). Frequent performances of the **Granada City Orchestra** are held in the Manuel de Falla Auditorium (⊠ Paseo de los Martires, ☎ 958/220022). French-oriented events and gatherings can be had through the Alliance Francaise (☎ 957/287251).

The **Granada International Theater Festival,** organized by the Granada Ayuntamiento (⊠ City Hall, ☎ 958/274000), is held for 10 days annually in May. The **Granada International Festival of Music and Dance** (⊠ Paseo de los Martires 64, ☎ 958/229681) is held annually from mid-June to mid-July. Tickets are also available at the Corral del Carbón on ⊠ Mariana Pineda, 1 block from Reyes Católicos. For information about the **November Jazz Festival,** contact the Granada City Hall (☎ 958/263791 or 958/222111) or the tourist office.

The flamenco show at **Jardines Neptuno** (⊠ C. Neptuno, ☎ 958/522533 or 958/251112), though tourist-oriented, can be colorful and often includes a mixture of ballet and folk music. There's a similar nightly show in a somewhat smaller venue at **Reina Mora** (⊠ Mirador de San Cristobal, ☎ 958/272228). Tickets are available from many hotels. Flamenco is performed at **El Corral del Príncipe** (⊠ Campo del Príncipe, ☎

958/226159) and at the **Corral del Carbón** (✉ Plaza Mariana Pineda, ☎ 958/226688). Never go before 11 PM; the best time is around 1 AM. For *zambra* (singing and dancing) performances by Gypsies in the Sacromonte caves, join one of the tours organized for tourists through a travel agent or your hotel. If you want to go on your own (call ahead for times of performances and be prepared to part with lots of money), these are some of the caves: **Cueva los Tarantos** (✉ Camino del Sacromonte 9, ☎ 958/206035), and **Zambra María la Canastera** (☎ 958/121183).

Outdoor Activities and Sports

BICYCLING

Bicycles can be rented from **Taller Manolo** (✉ Manuel de Falla 12, 1 block off Recogidas).

HIKING AND CAMPING

Good information on mountain trails, overnight camping and other treks is available through the **Federación Montaña** (✉ Camino de Ronda 101, ☎ 958/291340).

HORSEBACK RIDING

Contact **Cabalgar** (☎ 958/763135) in Bubeon.

SOCCER

Granada's second division soccer team can be viewed from their brand new stadium. Ticket information at ☎ 958/132652.

Shopping

Granada's handicrafts are very much a legacy of the Moors and include **brass** and **copperware, ceramics, marquetry** (objects made of inlaid wood), and **woven goods.** The main shopping streets, centering on the Puerta Real, are Reyes Católicos, Zacatín, Ángel Ganivet, and the Gran Vía de Colón. Most of the antiques stores are on Cuesta de Elvira.

Tapas Bars

For the most colorful bars, look around the Albaicín, Campo del Príncipe, Plaza del Carmen-Calle Navas, and Pedro de Alarcón-Martínez de la Rosa. **Bar El Ladrillo** (✉ Plaza de Fátima, ☎ 958/295405) is a tiny but popular tapas bar in the Albaicín with outside tables in summer. If you're in the mood for a splendid array of regional wines with your tapas, try **La Puerta del Vino** (✉ Paseo Padre Manjón 5, ☎ 958/210026), a 10-table bar hung with old paintings. **Chikito** (✉ Plaza del Campillo 9, ☎ 958/223364) is best known for the superb food its restaurant serves, but the bar is an excellent spot to sample tapas. The place is usually packed, even in summer when an additional 25 tables are set up in the plaza. **Bodegas Castañeda** (✉ Elvira 6, ☎ 958/227554) is a popular bar that attracts many locals.

Santa Fe

Numbers in the margin correspond to points of interest on the Andalucía: Granada to Córdoba map.

⑭ *8 km (5 mi) west of Granada just south of the N342.*

The village of Santa Fe was founded in the winter of 1491 as a campground for the 150,000 troops of Ferdinand and Isabella as they prepared for the Siege of Granada. It was in Santa Fe, in April, 1492, that Isabella and Columbus signed the agreements that were to finance his historic voyage. Often known as the "Cradle of America," Santa Fe is full of historic monuments.

Fuente Vaqueros

⑮ *10 km (6 mi) west of Santa Fe.*

The village of Fuente Vaqueros just beyond Santa Fe is where, on June 5, 1898, Federico García Lorca was born. His birthplace was opened as a museum in 1986, when Spain was commemorating the 50th anniversary of Lorca's assassination and celebrating his reinstatement as a national figure after 40 years of nonrecognition during the Franco dictatorship. ⊠ *Poeta García Lorca 4,* ☎ *958/516453.* ⊡ *200 ptas.* ☉ *July–Sept., Tues.–Sun. 10–1 and 6–8; Oct.–Mar., Tues.–Sun. 10–1 and 4–6; Apr.–June, 10–1 and 5–7.*

The village of Valderrubio, not far from Fuente Vaqueros, inspired Lorca's *Libro de Poemas* and one of his best-loved plays, *La Casa de Bernarda Alba.*

Viznar

⑯ *9 km (6 mi) northeast of Granada (the easiest route is to head northeast on the N342, then turn left, and left again, when you see signs for Viznar).*

If you're a devotee of Lorca, make the short trip to Viznar. The **Federico García Lorca Memorial Park,** between the villages of Viznar and Alfacar, marks the spot where Lorca was shot without trial by Nationalists at the beginning of the civil war in August, 1936 and where he is probably buried. Lorca, who today is venerated by most Spaniards, was hated by Fascists for his liberal ideas and his homosexuality.

The Sierra Nevada

⑰ *The drive from Granada to Pradollano along C420 by way of Cenes de la Vega takes about 45 minutes—you'd be wise to carry snow chains even as late as April or May.*

Even if you do not have a car, the mountains of the Sierra Nevada make for an easy, worthwhile excursion. From December to May, the **Solynieve ski resort** at Pradollano draws crowds of winter-sports enthusiasts, but it is quiet in the summer. Buses leave Granada daily at 9, returning at 5 (⊠ Autocar Bonal, ☎ 958/273100). Buses depart year-round from the Bar El Ventorillo (where you also buy tickets, for 640 pesetas), next to the Palacio de Congresos. In July and August you can drive right up to the summit of the Veleta on one of Europe's highest roads. It's cold up here, so be sure to bring a warm jacket, scarf, and sunglasses, even when the weather in Granada is sizzling hot. The **Veleta,** Spain's third-highest mountain, stands at 11,125 feet, and the view from its summit across the Alpujarra range to the sea at distant Motril is stunning. On a very clear day you can even see the coast of North Africa. Away to your left, the mighty Mulhacén, continental Spain's highest peak, soars to 11,407 feet.

NEED A BREAK? Splashing about at the **Aquaola water park** (⊠ 4 km/2½ mi, from Granada in Cenes de la Vega on the road to the Sierra Nevada) will refresh even the most parched sightseer.

Skiing

The **Solynieve** ski resort, at Pradollano, has 21 lifts, 29 runs, and around 50 km (31 mi) of marked trails. Solynieve also has a **children's ski school.** Contact the Sierra Nevada Information Center (⊠ Plaza de Pradollano, Edificio Telecabina, Pradollano Granada, ☎ 958/249100). You can also call for snow, weather, and road conditions

(☎ 958/489119). To reserve hotels or apartments around the area, call ☎ 958/249111.

The Alpujarras

⑱ *The village of Lanjarón is 46 km (29 mi) south of Granada.*

A trip to the villages of the Alpujarras region, on the southern slopes of the Sierra Nevada, will take you to one of the highest, most remote, and most picturesque regions of Andalucía. There are many beautiful villages with handsome artisan shops where you can find handwoven textiles and handmade basketware, pottery and other goods. If you're driving, the road as far as Lanjarón and Orgiva is plain sailing; after that you should be prepared for twisting, steep mountain roads and few gas stations.

The region—known for its poverty—was populated originally by Moors fleeing the Reconquest, first from Seville after its fall in 1248 and later, after 1492, from Granada. It was also the last fiefdom of the unfortunate Boabdil, conceded to him by the Catholic Monarchs after his surrender of Granada. From the arras in 1568, the Moors made their final stand against Spain's Christians. Their revolt was ruthlessly suppressed by Philip II and followed by the forced conversion of all Moors to Christianity.

The villages of the Alpujarras were then repopulated with Christians from Galicia in northern Spain. To this day the Galicians and their descendants have continued the Moorish custom of weaving rugs and blankets in traditional arran colors of red, green, black, and white, and you'll find such craft items on sale in many of the villages. The houses of the arran villages are squat and square; one on top of another, they spill down the mountainside, bearing a strong resemblance to the Berber homes in the Rif Mountains across the sea in Morocco.

En Route A few kilometers east of Granada on N323, the road reaches a spot known as the **Suspiro del Moro (Moor's Sigh).** Pause here a moment and look back at the city, just as the boy king Boabdil, last ruler of the Moors of Granada, did 500 years ago. As he wept over the city he'd surrendered to the Catholic Monarchs, his scornful mother bestowed upon him the now famous rebuke: "You weep like a boy for the city you could not defend as a man."

Lanjarón, some 46 km/29 mi from Granada, is a faded spa town famous for its mineral water gathered from the melting snows of the Sierra Nevada and drunk throughout Spain. **Orgiva** is the main town of the western Alpujarra, where you leave C333 and follow the signs for Pampaneira and Capileira in the arra Alta (High Alpujarra).

The villages of the **Poqueira Ravine**—Pampaneira, Bubión, and Capileira—are probably the best known in the Alpujarra region. The looms of **Pampaneira's** workshops produce many of the woven goods you'll see on sale in the surrounding villages. **Capileira,** at the end of the road, is one of the prettiest villages; in the Plaza Mayor, the Museo Alpujarreño has a colorful display of local crafts. From Capileira, a winding track leads over the mountain peaks to join the road to the Veleta summit. It's passable only in July or August, and then only in a four-wheel-drive vehicle.

If you make it as far as **Trevélez,** which lies on the slopes of the Mulhacén at 4,840 feet above sea level, you will have driven on one of the highest roads in Europe. Reward yourself with a plate of the locally produced jamón serrano.

Dining and Lodging

$$ ✕🏨 **Villa Turística del Poqueira.** This apartment-hotel offers individ-
★ ual, whitewashed houses, each with its own sitting room, kitchen,
bathroom, and bedrooms that sleep two, four, or six people. The hotel
nestles beneath the Veleta and overlooks splendid mountain scenery.
✉ *Barrio Alto, 18412,* ☎ *958/763111,* 🆑 *958/763136. 43 rooms with
baths. Restaurant, bar, AE, DC, MC, V.*

JAÉN, BAEZA, ÚBEDA, AND CAZORLA

North of Granada, Jaén has a rich Moorish legacy—Arab baths and
a former alcázar—as well as an ornately decorated cathedral. From Jaén,
head northeast along the N321 to the olive-produing towns of Baeza
and Úbeda. The typical Andalucían town of Cazorla is the gateway to
the Parque Nacional de Cazorla where you might spot wild boar.

Jaén

🟤 *93 km (58 mi) north of Granada.*

The city of Jaén nestles in the foothills of the Sierra de Jabalcuz, sur-
rounded by towering peaks and rolling, olive-clad hillsides. The Arabs
called it Geen (Route of the Caravans) because it formed a crossroad
between Castile and Andalucía. Captured from the Moors by the Saint
King Ferdinand in 1246, Jaén became a frontier province and, for the
next 200 years, witnessed many battles and skirmishes between the
Moors of Granada and Christians from the north and west. Today, the
province of Jaén has lead and silver mines and endless olive groves.

★ The **Castillo de Santa Catalina,** perched on a rocky crag 5 km (3 mi)
from the center of Jaén, is the city's starring monument. The origins
of the castle may have been a tower erected by Hannibal, and the site
was fortified continuously over the centuries. The Nasrid king, Alhamar,
builder of Granada's Alhambra, constructed an alcázar, but King Fer-
dinand III captured it from him in 1246 on the feast day of Santa
Catalina. Santa Catalina consequently became Jaén's patron saint,
and when the Christians built a new castle and a chapel on this site,
they dedicated them to her. The castle ruins make a dramatic setting
for the parador that has been built in their midst.

The Jaén **cathedral** is an imposing hulk that looms above the modest
buildings around it. It was begun in 1500 on the site of a former
mosque and not finished until the end of the 18th century. Its chief ar-
chitect was the brilliant Andrés de Vandelvira (1509–75), many more
of whose buildings can be seen in Úbeda and Baeza. The ornate facade
was sculpted by Pedro Roldán, and if you look up at the figures on
top of the columns, you can see San Fernando (King Ferdinand III) sur-
rounded by the four evangelists. In the Cathedral Museum look for
the *Immaculate Conception* by Alonso Cano, *San Lorenzo* by Martínez
Montañés, and a Calvary scene by Jácobo Florentino. ✉ *Plaza Santa
María.* 🎟 *Cathedral free, museum 100 ptas.* ☉ *Cathedral daily 8:30–
1 and 4:30–7, museum weekends 11–1.*

Explore the narrow alleyways of the old part of town as you walk from
the cathedral to the **Baños Árabes** (Arab Baths), which once belonged
to Ali, a Moorish king of Jaén, and probably from the 11th century.
Four hundred years later, a viceroy of Peru chose to build himself a
mansion, the Palacio de Villardompardo, right over them; it has taken
years of painstaking excavation to restore the baths to their original
form. ✉ *Palacio de Villardompardo, Plaza Luisa de Marillac,* ☎
953/223392. 🎟 *Free.* ☉ *Tues.–Sat. 10–2 and 5–8, Sun. 10:30–2.*

The **Museo Provincial** is a delightful small museum housed in a 1547 mansion. In its patio stands the facade of the Church of San Miguel, another work of Andrés de Vandelvira. One of the highlights of the fine arts section is a room of Goya lithographs. ⊠ *Paseo de la Estación 29,* ☎ *953/250320.* 🎫 *Free.* ◷ *Tues.–Fri. 10–2 and 4–7:30, weekends 10–2; closed summer afternoons.*

Dining and Lodging

$–$$ ✕ **Casa Vicente.** Hidden away on a narrow pedestrian street near the cathedral square, this popular restaurant is usually packed with locals. Enter through a colorful mesón-bar, where you can have pre-lunch drinks and tapas; then move on to a cozy dining room. Traditional Jaén dishes, such as game casseroles, are especially good. ⊠ *Arco del Maestra 8,* ☎ *953/274542. AE, MC, V. Closed Sun.*

$$$ ✕🖭 **Parador de Santa Catalina.** Built on a rocky crag amid the towers
★ of a medieval Moorish castle, Jaén's parador is one of the showpieces of the parador chain, and one of the main reasons for visiting Jaén. Lofty ceilings, tapestry-hung walls, baronial shields, and suits of armor add to the medieval-castle atmosphere. The comfortable bedrooms with canopied beds all have balconies overlooking the mountains. ⊠ *Castillo de Santa Catalina, 23001,* ☎ *953/230000,* 🖷 *953/230930. 45 rooms with baths. Restaurant, pool. AE, DC, MC, V.*

Shopping

Jaén province is known for its **pottery** and **ceramics,** and wares woven from **esparto grass**—baskets, mats, and ornaments.

Baeza

★ ❷ *48 km (30 mi) northeast of Jaén on the N321.*

The delightful town of Baeza is set among rolling hills and olive groves. Baeza dates back to the Romans; the Visigoths lived here, too, and under the Moors Baeza became the head of a *taifa* (Moorish kingdom). Saint King Ferdinand captured it in 1227, and for the next two centuries, Baeza stood on the frontier with the Moorish kingdom of Granada. In the 16th and 17th centuries Baeza's noble families endowed the city with a wealth of splendid Renaissance palaces.

The **Casa del Pópulo** in the village's central paeso, where the Plaza del Pópulo (or Plaza de los Leones) and Plaza del Mercado Viejo merge to form a delightful cobbled square, is a beautiful Plateresque structure built around 1530. The casa now houses the town's Tourist Office. On its curved balcony the first Mass of the Reconquest is reputed to have been celebrated.

In the center of the village square is an ancient Iberian-Roman statue, thought to be of Imilce, wife of Hannibal. The hapless figure is now headless, having been decapitated by an anticlerical crowd who apparently mistook her for the Virgin in the 1930s. At the foot of her column is the **Fuente de los Leones (Fountain of the Lions).**

The old **university** can be found by following a series of steps on the south side of the plaza. When the college opened in 1542 it was one of 32 universities in Spain. It closed in 1824 and later became a high school where, from 1912 to 1919, the poet Antonio Machado (author of *Tierras de Castilla*) taught French.

The golden-stoned **Palacio de Jabalquinto** on the Cuesta de San Felipe was built by Juan Alonso Benavides, second cousin of Ferdinand of Aragón. Its facade is a true gem of late-15th-century Isabelline Gothic.

Opposite the cathedral, at the end of Cuesta San Felipe, the **Seminary of San Felipe Neri** dates from 1660. The ancient student custom of inscribing names and graduation dates in bull's blood is still evident on the walls.

Baeza's **cathedral** was begun originally by Ferdinand III on the site of a former mosque, but it has undergone many transformations since his day. It was largely rebuilt by Vandelvira, architect of Jaén's cathedral, between 1570 and 1593, though the west front has architectural traits of an earlier period. A fine, 14th-century rose window crowns the 13th-century Puerta de la Luna (Door of the Moon). Don't miss the decorative Baroque silver monstrance, which is carried in Baeza's Corpus Christi processions. It's kept in a concealed niche behind a painting, and if you want to see it in all its flamboyant splendor, you'll have to put a coin in a slot to reveal its hiding place and light it up—it's money well spent. In the cathedral's Gothic cloisters, you can see the remains of the original mosque. ⊙ *Daily 10:30–1 and 5–7.*

| NEED A BREAK? | Wander around the **Old Quarter** between the cathedral and the Paseo de las Murallas to see noble, old mansions with emblazoned facades. From the balcony of Paseo de las Murallas, there's a view over the wheat fields and olive groves. |

The **Ayuntamiento (City Hall)** on Plaza Cardenal Benavides, just north of Plaza del Pópulo, features an ornate Plateresque facade. Its architect was Vandelvira. Look up at its facade between the balconies and you'll see the coats of arms of Felipe II, the city of Baeza, and the Magistrate Juan de Borja.

Dining and Lodging

$–$$ ✕🏨 **Juanito.** Located on the edge of town on the way to Úbeda, this small, unpretentious hotel provides simple accommodations—the best you'll find in Baeza. Its rooms are clean and comfortable. Juanito's real drawing card is its well-known restaurant. The chef has done much to revive the art of cooking regional specialties of Jaén province, such as *ensalada de perdiz* (partridge salad), and *cordero con habas* (lamb and broad beans). Desserts are based on old Moorish recipes. ⊠ *Paseo Arca de Agua, 23440,* ☎ *953/740040,* 🅵🅰🆇 *953/742324. 36 rooms, 1 suite. Restaurant.*

Úbeda

㉑ *9 km (6 mi) northeast of Baeza on the N321.*

Úbeda stands in the heart of the olive groves of Jaén province. Olive oil production is the main concern of the region, and although this modern town of 30,000 is fairly dull and uninteresting, seek out the **Casco Antiguo** (Old Town), a superb example of a pure Renaissance town, and one of the most outstanding enclaves of 16th-century architecture in Spain. Follow the signs to the **Zona Monumental,** where you're bound to pass countless Renaissance palaces and stately mansions, each with its own distinctive features—an unusual balcony or a fine sculptured facade. Though many of Úbeda's churches are open to visitors, most of its palaces can be viewed from the outside only.

The **Hospital de Santiago,** on Avenida Cristo Rey, in the modern section of town, is only a short walk from the bus depot and the main street, Ramón y Cajal. This huge, quadrangular building, often jokingly known as the Escorial of Andalucía, is the masterpiece of Andrés de Vandelvira, who was responsible for most of Úbeda's monuments.

Its generally plain facade is decorated with ceramic medallions and a relief of St. James as a warrior on horseback over the main entrance. Inside are a fine, arcaded patio and a grand staircase.

The **Plaza del Ayuntamiento** in the Old Town is where you'll pass the **Palacio de Vela de los Cobos,** built in the mid-16th century by Vandelvira for the magistrate of Úbeda, Francisco de Vela de los Cobos. Its special feature is the corner balcony, with its central column of white marble, which you can see echoed in the gallery above.

The **Palacio de las Cadenas (House of Chains),** another work of Vandelvira's, is so called because iron chains were once fixed to the columns of its main doorway. It currently houses the city's government.

The **Plaza Vásquez de Molina,** in the heart of the Old Town, is home
★ to the **Sacra Capilla del Salvador,** the most elaborate and ornate of Úbeda's churches. Not surprisingly, it is photographed so often that it has become the city's unofficial symbol. The Sacra Capilla was built by Vandelvira, though he based his design on some 1536 plans by Diego de Siloé, architect of Granada cathedral. It was sacked in the frenzy of church burning at the outbreak of the civil war but retains its ornate west front and an altarpiece with a rare Berruguete sculpture.

The **Plaza del Mercado,** by way of the Calle Horno Cantador, leads you to the **Ayuntamiento Antiguo** (Old City Hall), begun in the early 16th century but restored as a beautiful arcaded Baroque palace in 1680. From its upper balcony the Town Council watched celebrations and *autos da fe* ("acts of faith"—executions of heretics sentenced by the Inquisition) in the square below. On the north side is the 13th-century church of San Pablo, with its Isabelline south portal.

Dining and Lodging

$$$–$$$$ ✕⌂ **Parador Condestable Dávalos.** The *only* place to stay or dine in
★ Úbeda is at this splendid parador, located in a 16th-century ducal palace. A grand stairway leads up to the bedrooms, which have tile floors, lofty wood ceilings, antiques, and deliciously large baths. In the dining room the condestable's portrait hangs above the fireplace, the menu features regional dishes, and waitresses wear local costumes. Try one of the *perdiz* (partridge) specialties. Desserts have intriguing names like *suspiros de monja* (nun's sighs). ✉ *Plaza Vázquez de Molina 1, 23400,* ☎ *953/750345,* ℻ *953/751259. 31 rooms with baths. AE, DC, MC, V.*

$ ⌂ **La Paz.** This modern, homey hostel offers simply furnished rooms, all with private bathroom and telephone. Breakfast is served, but not dinner. ✉ *Andalucía 1, 23400,* ☎ ℻ *953/750848. 40 rooms with baths. AE, DC, MC, V.*

Shopping

Calle Valencia is Úbeda's crafts center. **Antonio Almazara** (✉ Valencia 34, ☎ 953/751200) is a small ceramics shop specializing in Úbeda's green-glazed pottery. **Paco Tito** (✉ Valencia 22, ☎ 953/751496) is a large pottery workshop run by two generations of the same family; a showroom is above the studio area. All kinds of ceramics are sold at **Alfarería Góngora** (✉ Merced 32, ☎ 953/754605). For handmade esparto grass wares like rugs, mats, and baskets, the best bet is the sprawling **Ana Ubalde Plaza** (✉ Real 47, ☎ 953/750456), which is supplied by its own factory in Úbeda. Finally, Úbeda has its own brand of olive oil, Oro de la Loma; ask for Extra Virgin.

Cazorla

22 *48 km (35 mi) southeast of Úbeda.*

The remote and unspoiled Andalucían village of Cazorla in the far east of Jaén province, is a treat for young and old. The pine-clad slopes and towering peaks of the Sierras of Cazorla and Segura rise above the village, and below it stretch endless miles of olive groves. In spring, purple Judas trees blossom in picturesque squares.

Cazorla Nature Park is administered by the environmental agency Agencia de Medio Ambiente (AMA). For information on hiking, camping, canoeing, Jeep excursions with park guides, or horseback-riding tours, contact its offices at Cazorla village, Jaén, or the Park Visitor Center: **AMA, Cazorla** (⊠ Tejares Altos, Cazorla [Jaén], ☎ 953/720125), **AMA, Jaén** (⊠ Avda. de Andalucía 79, ☎ 953/215000), or **AMA, Sierra** (⊠ Centro de Visitantes, Torre del Vinaigre, Parque Natural de Cazorla [Jaén], ☎ 953/713001). For fishing and hunting permits, apply well in advance to **IARA** (Jefatura de Jaén, (⊠ Avda. de Madrid 25, Jaén, ☎ 953/221150).

The park, an area of remote mountain scenery 80 km/50 mi long and 30 km/19 mi wide, is where deer, wild boar, and mountain goats roam the slopes, and hawks, eagles, and vultures soar over 6,000-foot peaks. This carefully protected wilderness is the source, at Canada de las Fuentes, of Andalucía's great river, the Guadalquivir. The road through the park follows the course of the river to the shores of the **Tranco de Beas lake.** The park's alpine meadows, pine forests, springs, and waterfalls make it a perfect place for hiking.

At the visitor center at **Torre de Vinaigre** (☎ 953/713001), a short film will introduce you to the park's main sights, and you can get information on camping, fishing, and hiking trails. There are also displays on the park's plants and geology. Nearby is a **botanical garden** and a **game reserve.** The park has four, well-equipped campsites (open June–October).

Dining and Lodging

$$ ✕🏨 **Parador El Adelantado.** This modern, whitewashed parador with a red-tile roof stands isolated on a pine-covered mountain slope on the edge of Cazorla Nature Park, 26 km (16 mi) above Cazorla village—a quiet spot popular with hunters and fishermen. The restaurant specializes in regional cooking, such as *ajo blanco* (almond soup with garlic) and game dishes in season. ⊠ 23470, ☎ 953/727075, FAX 953/727077. 33 *rooms with baths. Restaurant, pool. AF, DC, MC, V.*

$ ✕🏨 **Sierra de Cazorla II.** A low, white, two-story hotel nestles in a bend of the road leading up into the mountains 2 km/1¼ mi above Cazorla village at La Iruela. Rooms in the modern section, opened in 1987, are functional but comfortable. ⊠ *Carretera Sierra de Cazorla, Km 2, 23476, La Iruela (Jaén),* ☎ *953/720015,* FAX *953/720017. 59 rooms with baths. Restaurant, pool. AE, DC, MC, V.*

CÓRDOBA AND ENVIRONS

The city of Córdoba is home to one of Spain's most spectacular monuments, the Mezquita (mosque), which dates from the 8th through 10th centuries. Wander along the narrow alleys past tiled patios, visit the old Jewish Quarter, and explore the only synagogue in Andalucía to survive the expulsion of the Jews in 1492. If you tire of Córdoba, head west to the ruins of Medina Azahara, the site of a once-magnificent palace complex. Or if you have more time and are feeling adventurous, visit the Subbetica region south of Córdoba, a cluster of small towns virtually unknown to tourists.

Córdoba

㉓ *166 km (103 mi) northwest of Granada, 407 km (250 mi) southwest of Madrid.*

Numbers in the margin correspond to points of interest on the Córdoba map.

On the right bank of the Guadalquivir stands one of Spain's oldest cities. Córdoba is chilly and small, but nevertheless it contains some of the most interesting cultural monuments on the peninsula. The city was both the Roman and the Moorish capital of Spain, and its Old Quarter, clustered around its famous mosque (Mezquita), remains one of the best examples of Moorish heritage in Andalucía. From the 8th to the 11th century, the Moorish emirs and caliphs of the West held court here. During these 300 years, Córdoba's magnificence and opulence were legendary. Its population grew to around a million, making it the largest city in Europe (today, just 285,000 residents remain). Under the Moors it became one of the Western world's greatest centers of art, culture, and learning; one of its libraries boasted more than 400,000 volumes. Moors, Christians, and Jews lived together in harmony within its walls.

Córdoba remained in Moorish hands until it was conquered by the Saint King Ferdinand in 1236. The Catholic Monarchs held court here and used the city as a base from which to plan the conquest of Granada. It was in Córdoba that Queen Isabella granted Columbus the commission for his first voyage to the New World. In Columbus's time the Guadalquivir was navigable as far upstream as Córdoba, and great galleons sailed its waters. Today, the muddy water and unkempt banks of Andalucía's great river evoke little of the city's glorious past, but the impressive bridge of Roman origin—though much restored by the Arabs and successive generations—and the old Arab waterwheel are vestiges of a far grander era.

㉔ Before you head out to explore the city, visit the **Córdoba Tourist Office** which is located in the Palacio de Congresos y Exposiciones (✉ C. Torrijos 10, west side of mosque).

★ **㉕** The **Mezquita** (mosque), built between the 8th and 10th centuries, is one of the earliest and most breathtakingly beautiful examples of Spanish Muslim architecture. The shabby, crenellated walls of the outside do little to prepare you for the beauty of the interior. As you enter through the **Puerta de las Palmas** (Door of the Palms), some 850 columns rise before you in a forest of onyx, jasper, marble, and granite. The pillars are topped by ornate capitals taken from the Visigoth church that was razed to make way for the mosque. Crowning these, an endless array of red-and-white-striped arches curves away into the dim interior. These horseshoe arches in alternating colors are one of the characteristic features of Moorish architecture. The ceiling is of carved of delicately tinted cedar.

The Mezquita has served as a Christian cathedral since 1236, but its origins as a mosque are clear. Built in four stages, it was founded in 785 by Abd ar-Rahman I (756–788) on a site he bought from the Visigoth Christians. He pulled down their church and replaced it with a mosque, one-third the size of the present one, into which he incorporated marble pillars from earlier Roman and Visigothic shrines. Under Abd ar-Rahman II (822–852) the Mezquita, which boasted possession

Córdoba

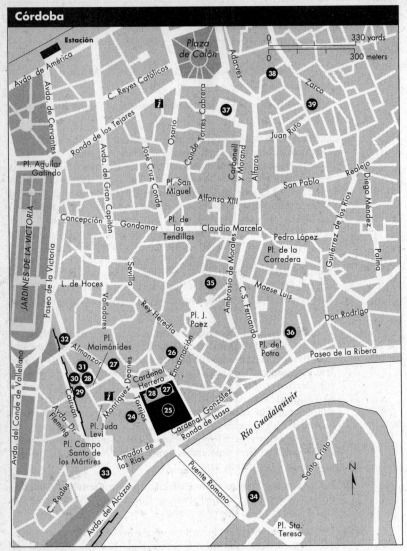

Alcázar de los Reyes
Cristianos, **33**

Callejón de las
Flores, **26**

Córdoba Tourist
Office, **24**

Judería, **27**

Mezquita, **25**

Museo
Arqueológico, **35**

Museo de Bellas
Artes, **36**

Museo Taurino, **28**

Palacio de los
Marqueses de
Viana, **39**

Plaza de los
Dolores, **37**

Plaza Santa Marina
de las Aguas, **38**

Puerta de
Almodóvar, **32**

Statue of
Maimónides, **29**

Synagogue, **30**

Torre de la
Calahorra, **34**

Zoco, **31**

of an original copy of the Koran and a bone from the arm of the prophet Mohammed, became a place of Muslim pilgrimage second only to Mecca.

Al Hakam II (961–976) built the beautiful **Mihrab,** the Mezquita's greatest jewel. Make your way over to the **Qiblah,** the south-facing wall in which this sacred prayer niche was hollowed out. (Muslim law decrees that the Mihrab face east, toward Mecca, as it is the point in the mosque toward which worshipers turn to pray. Here, in Córdoba, because of an error in calculation, the Mihrab faces more south than east. Al Hakam II spent hours agonizing over a means of correcting such a serious mistake but was persuaded by wise architects to let it be.) Before the Mihrab, you'll find the **Maksoureh,** a kind of anteroom reserved for the caliph and his court. Its delicate mosaic and plasterwork make it a masterpiece of Asian art. The final stage of the mosque was completed around 987 by Al Mansur, who more than doubled its size.

After the Reconquest, the Christians, for the most part, left the Mezquita undisturbed. They simply dedicated it to the Virgin Mary and set about using it as a place of Christian worship. The Christian clerics did erect a wall closing off the mosque from its courtyard, dimming the interior. In the 13th century Christians had the **Villaviciosa Chapel** built by Moorish craftsmen, its Mudéjar architecture blending harmoniously with the lines of the mosque. Not so the heavy, incongruous Baroque structure of the **cathedral** sanctioned in the very heart of the mosque by Charles V in the 1520s. To the emperor's credit— though it didn't stop him from tampering with the Alhambra (the Palacio Carlos V) and with Seville's Alcázar—it must be said that he later regretted this action and accused the clergy of having destroyed something unique to build something commonplace. ⊠ *Torrijos and Cardenal Herrero,* ☎ *957/470512.* ☐ *750 ptas.* ⊙ *May–Sept., daily 10–7; Oct.–Apr., daily 10–6.*

The **Patio de los Naranjos,** perfumed in springtime by orange blossoms, is a good place to take a break and admire the Mezquita. The **Puerta del Perdón** (Gate of Forgiveness) along the north wall, serves as the formal entranceway to the mosque. The **Virgen de los Faroles** (Virgin of the Lanterns), a small statue in a niche along the north wall, on Cardenal Herrero, of the Mezquito, stands demurely behind a lantern-hung grille, rather like a lovely lady awaiting a serenade. The painting of the Virgin is by Julio Romero de Torres, an early 20th-century Cordoban artist. The **campanario** (bell tower), used in times past to summon the faithful to prayer, is well worth climbing for the view of the Guadalquivir and tiled rooftops of the old city. The tower was closed for nearly five years for repairs but is scheduled to open in the spring of 1996. A Baroque belfry now adorns the minaret. ⊙ *May–Sept., daily 10–7; Oct.–Apr., daily 10–6.*

26 Outside the Mezquita along Calle Velázquez Bosco, a narrow alleyway known as **Callejón de las Flores** (Alley of the Flowers) is famous for its plethora of ebullient, hanging flower baskets. You'd be hard put to find prettier patios than these, with their abundant foliage, ceramics, and wrought-iron grilles. Patios are very much the key to Córdoba's architecture, at least in the old town, where life is lived behind sturdy, outer walls—a legacy of the Moors, who believed in the sanctity of the home just as much as they did in shutting out the fierce summer sun. In early May Córdoba celebrates its Patio Festival, when private patios are filled with flowers and opened to the public.

NEED A BREAK? The **Plaza de Juda Levi** is a lively, tree-lined patio great for a snack or ice cream at the Helados Juda Levi.

㉗ The **Judería,** the old Jewish Quarter, is packed with houses, museums and monuments that best typify Córdoba's storied past. Enter the Judería from Cardenal Herrero through the labyrinth of narrow streets lined with ancient, white houses. Unfortunately, the streets around the Mezquita leading up to the Judería have a few too many tourist shops selling the same souvenirs.

㉘ The **Museo Taurino** (Museum of Bullfighting), on the Plaza Maimónides (or Plaza de las Bulas), is housed in two adjoining Córdoban mansions. Whatever your thoughts on bullfighting, this museum is worth visiting, as much for the chance to see a restored mansion as for the well-displayed collection of posters, Art Nouveau paintings, and memorabilia of famous bullfighters who were native sons of Córdoba. ⌧ *Plaza Maimónides,* ☎ *957/472000, Ext. 211.* 🎫 *400 ptas.* ⊙ *May–Sept., Tues.–Sat. 9:30–1:30 and 5–8, Sun. 9:30–1; Oct.–Apr., Tues.–Sat. 9:30–1 and 4–6:30, Sun. 9:30–1.*

㉙ The **statue of Maimónides,** the famous Jewish philosopher who was born nearby in the Judería in 1135, stands in the Plaza Tiberiades just
㉚ around the corner from the Plaza Maimónides. The well preserved **synagogue** along Judíos, the main street of the Jewish Quarter, is the only Jewish temple in Andalucía to have survived the expulsion and inquisition of the Jews in 1492. Though it is no longer in use as a place of worship, it has become a treasured symbol for the Jewish communities of Spain. It is one of only three remaining ancient synagogues in the entire country—the other two are in Toledo. The outside is plain, but inside you'll find some exquisite Mudéjar stucco tracery—look for the fine plant motifs and the Hebrew inscription stating that the synagogue was built in 1315. The women's gallery still stands, and in the east wall you can see the arch where the sacred scrolls of the law were kept. ⌧ *C. Judíos,* ☎ *957/202928.* 🎫 *50 ptas.* ⊙ *Tues.–Sat. 10–2 and 3:30–5:30, Sun. 10–1:30.*

Across the way from the synagogue and through an arch, you'll enter
㉛ an inner courtyard called the **Zoco.** This former Arab souk hosts flamenco performances on summer evenings, and through much of the year displays local handicrafts for sale. Enter the Zoco's courtyard from Calle Judíos.

㉜ The **Puerta de Almodóvar** marks the western limit of the Judería. Outside this old Moorish gate is a **statue of Seneca,** the Córdoban-born philosopher who rose to prominence in Nero's court in Rome and who, on his emperor's command, committed suicide.

★ ㉝ The **Alcázar de los Reyes Cristianos,** on the Plaza Campo Santo de los Mártires, is a Mudéjar-style palace with splendid gardens. The original Moorish Alcázar stood beside the Mezquita on the site of the present Bishop's Palace. This one was built by Alfonso XI in 1328. In the 14th century the Catholic Monarchs often held court here, using it as a base from which to launch their conquest of Granada. Boabdil was imprisoned here for a time in 1483, and for nearly 300 years the Alcázar served as a base for the Inquisition. ⌧ *Plaza Campo Santo de los Mártires.* 🎫 *400 ptas. (Tues. free).* ⊙ *May–Sept., Tues.–Sat. 9:30–1:30 and 5–8, Sun. 9:30–1:30; Oct.–Apr., Tues.–Sat. 9:30–1 and 4–7, Sun. 9:30–1.*

From **Plaza Campo Santo,** three choices are possible: Hire a *coche caballo* (horse and buggy) for a tour of the city—but haggle over the price first (around 4,000 ptas an hour is enough); wander back to the shops on Deanes and Cardenal Herrero by way of Manríquez and Plaza Judá Leví; or walk back along Amador de los Ríos to the bottom of Torrijos, turn down past the Puerta del Puente (Gate of the Bridge), and cross the **Puente Romano** (Roman Bridge), whose 16 arches span the Guadalquivir. From the bridge you'll get a good view of **La Albolafia,** the huge wheel used to carry water to the gardens of the Alcázar.

㉞ The **Torre de la Calahorra,** on the far side of the Puente Romano bridge, was built in 1369 to guard the entrance to Córdoba. It now houses the **Museo Histórico** (Córdoba City Museum), where multiscreen shows and audiovisual guides in English will help you learn more of Córdoba's history. The museum focuses on Córdoba's tricultural past. ☎ 957/293929. ▣ *Tower 350 ptas., multiscreen show 500 ptas.* ☉ *May–Sept., Mon.–Sat. 10–2 and 5:30–8:30, Sun. 10–2; Oct.–Apr., Mon.–Sat. 10–6, Sun. 10–2.*

㉟ The **Museo Arqueológico** on the Plaza Jerónimo Paez, in the heart of the the old town to the north and east of the mosque, houses finds from Córdoba's varied cultural past, including Mudéjar and Renaissance displays. Warning: It's best to avoid exploring this area in the deserted siesta hours; the narrow streets are a prime spot for muggers. Otherwise, the alleyways and steps along Altos de Santa Ana make for great wandering. ▢ *Plaza Jerónimo Paez,* ☎ *957/474011.* ▣ *250 ptas.* ☉ *June 15–Sept. 15, Tues.–Sat. 10–2 and 6–8, Sun. 10–1:30; Sept. 16– June 14, Tues.–Sat. 10–2 and 5–7, Sun. 10–1:30.*

Wind your way southeast from the Museo Arqueológico to the **Plaza del Potro (Colt Square)** through the maze of narrow alleys. The plaza, named after the Fountain of the Colt in its center, was mentioned by Cervantes in *Don Quixote.* Cervantes himself reputedly stayed at the nearby inn, the beautifully restored **Posada del Potro,** now used for shows of local craftwork and painting.

| NEED A BREAK? | The relaxed cafés around the **Plaza del Potro** and its fountain are good places for a drink. |

㊱ The **Museo de Bellas Artes** (Fine Arts Museum) is located in a courtyard just off the Plaza del Potro. Its deep pink facade belongs to a former Hospital de la Caridad (Charity Hospice) founded by Ferdinand and Isabella, who twice received Columbus here. Its art collection includes paintings by Murillo, Valdés Leal, Zurbarán, Goya, and Sorolla. ▢ *Off Plaza del Potro,* ☎ *957/471314.* ▣ *250 ptas.* ☉ *June 15–Sept. 15, Tues.–Sat. 10–2 and 6–8, Sun. 10–1:30; Sept. 16–June 14, Tues.–Sat. 10–2 and 5–7, Sun. 10–1:30.*

The **Plaza de la Corredera** (some maps call it Plaza Constitución), is an intriguing, if sadly dilapidated, arcaded square that dates from around 1690. Major rehabilitation effort is attempting to restore the plaza to its original splendor. A market is held here most mornings.

| NEED A BREAK? | Head for the **Plaza de las Tendillas,** the central square of modern Córdoba. Here, the outdoor terraces (open during warm weather) of the **Café Boston** and **Café Siena** are good places to relax over a coffee. |

Wine lovers should check out the huge wooden wine vats of **Bodegas San Rafael,** where you can get a tour of the wine making itself, or buy a bottle right off the company shelf (▢ R. Sanchez and Jesús María near Plaza Tendillas). Follow the Calle Diego Leon from the north side of the Plaza de las Tendillas to the small **Plaza San Miguel,** whose 13th-century, Gothic-Mudéjar church dates to the time of Córdoba's **㊲** conquest by Saint King Ferdinand. The charming **Plaza de los Dolores** (Square of Sorrows) can be found after wandering through twisting streets north of the Plaza San Miguel. This small square, surrounded by the 17th-century Convento de Capuchinos, is a secret place, one where you can sense most deeply the city's languid pace. In its center a statue of **Cristo de los Faroles** stands amid eight lanterns that hang from twisted, wrought-iron brackets. Around the corner from the Plaza de los Dolores you'll find the **Casa de los Fernández de Córdoba,** which boasts a Plateresque facade.

❸❽ In the **Plaza Santa Marina de las Aguas,** a statue of the legendary bullfighter Manolete stands on the edge of the **Barrio de los Toreros,** the quarter where many of Córdoba's famous bullfighters were born and lived. Not far from the Plaza Santa Marina de las Aguas, on the **Plaza de la Lagunilla,** you'll find a bust of Manolete.

❸❾ The 17th-century **Palacio de los Marqueses de Viana** is one of Córdoba's most splendid aristocratic palaces. It is known as the Museum of Patios for its 14 patios, each different. Inside are a carriage museum, a library, embossed leather wall hangings, filigree silver, and grand galleries and staircases. The patios and gardens are planted with cypresses, orange trees, and myrtles. ⊠ *Plaza Don Gomé,* ☎ *957/480134.* ⊡ *400 ptas., Thurs. free.* ☉ *June–Sept., Thurs.–Tues, 9–2; Oct.–May, Mon., Tues., and Thurs.–Sat. 10–1 and 4–6, Sun. 10–2.*

The **Iglesia San Nicolás de Villa,** a classically dark Spanish church featuring the Mudéjar style of Islamic decoration and Islamic art forms, lies at the top of the narrow and colorful Calle San Felipe. The well-kept city park, the **Jardín Victoria,** with tiled benches and manicured bushes, lies just a block west of the Iglesia San Nicolás.

NEED A BREAK?   The **Plaza R. y Cabal** at the backside of San Nicolás is a tiny square good for watching Córdoba's well-dressed going to work or taking a break at one of the many tapas bars nearby. Check out the **Bar San Felipe** or **El Borracho del Oro.** Be mindful of speeding motorbikes.

Dining and Lodging

$$$ ✕ **Casa Pepe de la Judería.** This three-floor labyrinth of neat rooms is just around the corner from the Mezquita toward the Judería. Flamenco shows are given here nightly, and during the summer, the rooftop opens for barbecue serving a full selection of tapas, and house specialties such as the *Rabas de Toro* (oxtails). ⊠ *Romero 1, off Deanes,* ☎ *957/200744 and 957/200766, AE, DC, MC, V.*

$$$ ✕ **El Blasón.** Owned by El Caballo Rojo (☞ *below*), this restaurant has rapidly gained a name for fine food and unbeatable ambience. It's tucked away in an old inn one block west of Avenida Gran Capitán. A Moorish-style entrance bar leads onto a patio enclosed by ivy-covered walls. Upstairs are two elegant dining rooms; blue walls, aquamarine silk curtains and candelabras create the atmosphere of early 19th-century luxury. The innovative menu includes *salmón con naranjas de la mezquita* (salmon in oranges from the mosque) and *musclo de oca al vino afrutado* (leg of goose in fruited wine). ⊠ *José Zorrilla 11,* ☎ *957/480625. AE, DC, MC, V.*

$$$ ✕ **El Caballo Rojo.** The Red Horse, on the north side of the mosque, ★ is Córdoba's best restaurant, winner of the National Gastronomy Prize. The decor resembles a cool, leafy, Andalucían patio, and the menu features traditional specialties such as rabo de toro and salmorejo, as well as exotic creations inspired by Córdoba's Moorish and Jewish heritage. ⊠ *Cardenal Herrero 28,* ☎ *957/478001. AE, DC, MC, V.*

$$ ✕ **El Churrasco.** A long-standing Córdoban institution that ranks sec-★ ond only to El Caballo Rojo (☞ *above*), El Churrasco is in the heart of the Judería, just two minutes' walk from the mosque. Its colorful bar is an ideal place for pre-lunch tapas. There's a wine museum and bodega specializing in the restaurant's own Montilla-Morilés wine. It

is known for its succulent grilled meats, such as *churrasco* (pork in pepper sauce), and an excellent salmorejo. ⊠ *Romero 16,* ☎ *957/290817. AE, DC, MC, V. Closed Aug.*

$$ ✕ **La Almudaina.** This attractive restaurant is located in a 15th-century house across the square from the Alcázar gardens, at the entrance to the Judería. There's an Andalucían patio and a mesón bodega in the cellar. The menu concentrates on fresh market produce and local recipes. You might try pudding *de calabacines* (pumpkin mousse) or *lubina al hinojo* (sea bass in fennel). ⊠ *Campo Santo de los Mártires 1,* ☎ *957/474342. AE, DC, MC, V. No dinner Sun.*

$ ✕ **Federación de Peñas Cordobesa.** You'll find this popular budget restaurant on one of the main thoroughfares of the old town, halfway between the mosque and the Plaza Tendillas. You can eat inside or at one of several tables around the fountain in the spacious courtyard surrounded by horseshoe arches. The food is traditional Spanish fare. ⊠ *Conde y Luque 8,* ☎ *957/475427. MC, V. Closed Wed.*

$ ✕ **Mesón El Burladero.** This one's located off a small patio at the end of an alley near the back entrance to El Caballo Rojo (☞ *above*). There are a few tables outside on the patio; indoors, you'll be seated among bullfight posters and the eclectic array that adorns the whitewashed walls: stags' heads, stuffed birds, and a boar's head. The menú *Manolete* offers *revuelto de la casa* (scrambled eggs) and *solomillo de cerdo* (pork steak), with bread, wine, and dessert included. ⊠ *Calleja la Hoguera 5, off Deanes,* ☎ *957/472719. AE, DC, MC, V.*

$$$–$$$$ 🏨 **Conquistador.** On the east side of the mosque, this contemporary hotel is built in Andalucían Moorish style, making good use of ceramic tiles and inlaid marquetry in the bar and public rooms. The reception area overlooks a colonnaded patio, fountain, and small, enclosed garden. The rooms are comfortably and elegantly furnished. Those at the front have small balconies overlooking the walls of the mosque, floodlit at night. ⊠ *Magistral González Francés 17, 14003,* ☎ *957/481102 or 957/481411,* 🅵🅰🆇 *957/475079. 100 rooms with baths, 3 suites. Bar, sauna. AE, DC, MC, V.*

$$$ 🏨 **Parador La Arruzafa.** Five kilometers (3 miles) north of town, this modern parador is set in a peaceful, leafy garden on the slopes of the Sierra de Córdoba. Rooms are traditional, with dark wood fittings, and many have balconies overlooking the garden or with good views toward Córdoba. Rates are determined by the view. ⊠ *Avda. de la Arruzafa, 14012,* ☎ *957/275900,* 🅵🅰🆇 *957/280409. 94 rooms with baths. Pool, tennis courts. AE, DC, MC, V.*

$$–$$$ 🏨 **El Califa.** This modern hotel in the old town is convenient to both the mosque and the shopping area around Plaza Tendillas. The rooms are fairly spacious, with tile floors. The patio has red and white flagstones and Moorish-style arches. In summer snacks are served outdoors among the geraniums. ⊠ *Lope de Hoces 14, 14003,* ☎ *957/299400. 66 rooms with baths. Bar, cafeteria. AE, MC, V.*

$$ 🏨 **Albucasis.** Tucked away in the heart of the old town is this friendly, family-run hotel. Its air-conditioned rooms are spotlessly clean, with marble-tile floors, white and green decor, and green-tile bathrooms. Doubles overlook the pretty, ivy-covered patio and have a limited view of the mosque tower. Breakfast and drinks are served in the attractive reception-bar area. ⊠ *Buen Pastor 11, 14003,* ☎ 🅵🅰🆇 *957/478625. 15 rooms with baths. Bar. MC, V.*

$$ 🏨 **Amistad Córdoba.** This hotel was built around two former 18th-century mansions which looked out upon the Plaza de Maimónides in the heart of the Judería. It features a Mudéjar (a combination of Islamic and Christian style) courtyard, wood-carved ceilings, and a plush lounge area. The rooms are large and comfortable. ⊠ *Plaza de Maimónides 3,* ☎ *957/420335,* FAX *957/420365. AE, DC, MC, V.*

$$ 🏨 **González.** This hotel is in a restored 16th-century palace in the heart of the Judería, near the mosque. The entrance hall, with a white-marble floor and a massive 18th-century brass lamp, opens off the Plaza Judá Levi. Rooms are simply but comfortably furnished: tile floors, white walls, twin beds, and air-conditioning. The quietest rooms have black, wrought-iron balconies heaped with flowerpots and overlook the fountain in the central patio. Some readers have noted security problems; think twice about leaving valuables in the hotel safe. ⊠ *Manríquez 3, 14003,* ☎ *957/479819,* FAX *957/486187. 17 rooms with baths. Restaurant. MC, V.*

$–$$ 🏨 **Marisa.** The Marisa's facade is an old Andalucían house that overlooks the north side of the mosque and the Patio de los Naranjos. Inside, the hotel has been modernized, and the rooms are simple and sparsely furnished. Those on the front face the mosque walls, magnificent when floodlit. (Ask for an inside room to avoid street noise.) Breakfast and drinks are served in the bar area. The staff is friendly and helpful. ⊠ *Cardenal Herrero 6, 14003,* ☎ *957/473142,* FAX *957/474144. 28 rooms with baths. AE, DC, MC, V.*

Nightlife and the Arts

Orchestral concerts are given in the Alcázar garden on Sundays in summer; **Orchestra, ballet and theatre performances** are also held in the Gran Teatro (⊠ Avda. del Gran Capitan 3, ☎ 957/489237 or 958/480644). **Flamenco performances** take place in the Zoco, off Calle Judíos, summer evenings. One of Córdoba's favorite flamenco clubs is **Mesón la Bulería** (⊠ Pedro López 3, ☎ 957/483839); the club is closed in summer.

Outdoor Activities and Sports

BICYCLING

Bicycle rentals by the hour or day are available at **Quicksilver** (⊠ C. Céspedes 12, near Mezquita).

HORSEBACK RIDING

The **Club Hípico (Riding Club)** is at Km 3 on the Carretera de Trassierra.

Shopping

The main shopping district is around Avenida Gran Capitán, Ronda de los Tejares, and Plaza de Colón. **Artesanía Andaluza** (⊠ Tomás Conde 3, no phone), near the Museum of Bullfighting, sells a wide range of Córdoban handicrafts, including fine embossed leather (a legacy of the Moors) and filigree silver (from the mines of the Sierra Morena) jewelry. The **Association of Córdoban Artisans** (⊠ C. Judíos opposite synagogue, no phone) sells craft wares in the Zoco (many stalls are open May–September only). **Meryan** (⊠ Callejón de las Flores 2, ☎ 957/475902) is one of Córdoba's best embossed-leather workshops.

Medina Azahara

Numbers in the margin correspond to points of interest on the Andalucía: Granada to Córdoba map.

❹⓪ *8 km (5 mi) west of Córdoba on the C431.*

The ruins and partial reconstruction of the fabulous Muslim palace of Medina Azahara are well worth a visit. Begun in 936, Medina Azahara was built by Abd ar-Rahman III for his favorite, az-Zahra. According to contemporary chroniclers, it took 10,000 men, 2,600 mules, and 400 camels 25 years to erect this fantasy of 4,300 columns in dazzling pink, green, and white marble and jasper brought from Carthage. Here, on three terraces, stood a palace, a mosque, luxurious baths, fragrant gardens, fish ponds, and even an aviary and a zoo. In 1013 this Moorish paradise was sacked and destroyed by Berber mercenaries. In 1944 the Royal Apartments were rediscovered and there followed a careful reconstruction of the Throne Room. The outline of the mosque has also been excavated. ⊠ *Off C431, follow signs on way to Almodóvar del Río*, ☎ *957/329130.* 🎫 *250 ptas.* ☉ *May–Sept., Tues.–Sat. 10–2 and 6–8:30, Sun. 10–2; Oct.–Apr., Tues.–Sat. 10–2 and 4–6:30, Sun. 10–2.*

| OFF THE BEATEN PATH | **ALMODÓVAR DEL RÍO** – If you're driving, continue to Almodóvar del Río, a further 18 km (11 mi) along C431, where just beyond the town a restored castle towers dramatically over the surrounding countryside. |

The Subbetica

㊶ *Priego de Córdoba is 103 km (64 mi) southeast of Córdoba.*

In the southeastern corner of Córdoba province lies a relatively undiscovered cluster of villages and small towns known to locals as the Subbetica. For hiking or general information, contact the **Asociación para el Fomento del Turismo Rural** (☎ 957/553177) or **Iniciativas Subbéticas** (☎ 957/694545). You'll need a car to explore this area, and in places you'll find the roads bumpy and rather rough going.

Just inside the southern tip of Córdoba province, southeast of Lucena, C334 crosses the **Embalse de Iznájar** (reservoir of Iznájar) amid spectacular scenery. Midway between Lucena and the reservoir on the C334, in **Rute**, you can sample the potent *anís* liqueur for which this small, white town is famous. In **Lucena** you can see the Torre del Moral, where Boabdil was imprisoned in 1483 after he launched an unsuccessful attack on the Christians. Today, the town makes furniture and brass and copper pots.

The jewel of this area is **Priego de Córdoba,** a town of 14,000 people lying at the foot of Mt. Tinosa (from Lucena, head north 9 km/6 mi on the C327 to Cabra, where you'll turn right, or east, on the C336; after 32 km/20 mi, you'll reach Priego). Wander down Calle del Río opposite the Ayuntamiento to see fine 18th-century mansions, once the homes of silk merchants. At the end of the street is the Fuente del Rey, with some 130 jets of water, built in 1803. Don't miss the lavish Baroque churches of La Asunción and La Aurora or the Barrio de la Villa, an old Moorish quarter.

Baena, surrounded by chalk fields producing top-quality olive oil, is an old town of narrow, white streets, ancient mansions, and churches clustered beneath Moorish battlements. **Castro del Río** has an old Roman bridge; here in 1592 the unfortunate Cervantes was jailed in the City Hall. At **Espejo,** a majestic castle towers over the countryside. You're now in the Montilla-Morilés vineyards of the Córdoban campiña. Each autumn 47,000 acres' worth of Pedro Ximénez grapes are crushed here to produce the rich Montillas of the region, a fortified wine not unlike sherry. You can visit the bodegas.

ANDALUCÍA A TO Z

Arriving and Departing

By Bus

If you're not driving, buses are the best method of transportation in this region. They run to most of the outlying towns and villages, and bus connections between major cities are generally faster and more frequent than by train (☞ Arriving and Departing, *above*). If you're using public transportation to reach the villages of the arras, check details of bus schedules and accommodations carefully with the Granada Tourist Office and the Alsina Gräells bus company before you set off.

Buses connect several Spanish cities and **Córdoba.** For bus information, go either to the main tourist office (✉ Torrijos 10) or to the following bus companies: **Alsina Gräells** (✉ Avda. Medina Azahara 29, ☎ 957/236474) for services to Badajoz, Cádiz, Granada, Seville, and Málaga; **Ureña** (✉ Avda. Cervantes 22, ☎ 957/472352) for Seville and Jaén; **Priego** (✉ Paseo de la Victoria 29, ☎ 957/290158 or 957/290769) for Madrid (via N IV), Barcelona, and Valencia; **Secorbus** (✉ Camino de los Sastres 1, Avda. República Argentina across from Hotel Meliá) for Madrid and Andújar ☎ 957/468040. **López** (✉ Paseo de la Victoria 15, ☎ 957/477551 or 957/474592) for Ciudad Real and Madrid (via Ciudad Real). **Ramírez** (✉ Avda. de la República Argentina 26, ☎ 957/410100 or 957/410901) serves small towns in Córdoba province.

Granada's main bus station is **Alsina Gräells** (✉ Camino de Ronda 97, ☎ 958/251358), with services to and from Madrid, Algeciras, Málaga, Córdoba, Seville, Jaén, Motril, and Almería. The other main bus company is **Bacoma** (✉ Avda. Andaluces 10, ☎ 958/284251), which runs services from Granada to Murcia, Alicante, Valencia, and Barcelona. Both can be reached on the circular Bus 11 from Puerta Real or Gran Vía Colón.

By Car

In the cities of Granada and Córdoba, be prepared for parking problems and, particularly in Granada, the ever-present threat of break-ins. Most of Córdoba's hotels are located in a labyrinth of narrow streets that can be a nightmare to negotiate, even with a small car. In Córdoba, all sights are within easy walking distance of one another; in Granada, it's simpler to take a taxi up to the Alhambra or the Albaicín Quarter than to negotiate the extremely complicated one-way system and narrow Moorish streets in a rented car.

If you do decide to go by car, the route from Granada to Jaén, Baeza, Úbeda, and Cazorla is not one of Andalucía's most tourist-packed, though between Granada and Jaén you'll no doubt encounter the odd tour bus. Still, the roads are smooth, and driving through the region is one of the more pleasant ways to see the countryside.

By Plane

Granada Airport (☎ 958/446411 or 958/447081) is 18 km/11 mi west of Granada. **Aviaco** has daily flights to and from Madrid and Barcelona and three flights weekly to Valencia.

BETWEEN THE AIRPORT AND DOWNTOWN

J. González buses (☎ 958/131309) run between the airport and city center, leaving Plaza Isabel la Católica approximately 1¼ hours, less often in winter, before flight departures. Times are listed at the bus stop.

By Train

Services from Córdoba to Granada are poor. There is no train service between Granada and Jaén or between Jaén and Córdoba. Both Córdoba and Jaén have trains to Linares-Baeza Station, but from there you must take a bus into Baeza or Úbeda.

Contacts and Resources

Car Rentals

In Granada: **Autos Fortuna**, Camino de Purchil 2, at Camino Ronda. ☎ 958/260254 and 958/271987.

Emergencies

Police, emergency telephones: Policía Nacional (☎ 091); Policía Municipal (☎ 092).

Guided Tours

Pullmantur and **Julia Tours** (☞ Getting Around by Bus *in* the Gold Guide) run numerous tours to this region, which can be booked through most travel agents, many hotels, or with their Madrid (☞ Chapter 2) or Costa del Sol (☞ Chapter 11) offices. **Córdoba Vision** offers day and night-time tours which can include trips to the monument of Medina Azahara (✉ Escritor Conde Zamora ☎ 957/299577 or 957/299777, FAX 957/299968).

SPECIAL-INTEREST TOURS

The Andalusian Express is a luxury vintage train with cars from the '20s that makes a weekly trip in season from Madrid to Aranjuez, Úbeda, Córdoba, Seville, Jerez, Málaga, and Granada. For reservations and information contact **Abercrombie & Kent** or **DER** (☞ Tour Operators *in* the Gold Guide).

Horseback riding tours—some with English guides—are offered in the villages of the Alpujarras and the Sierra Nevada and sometimes elsewhere. Contact tourist offices for information; one agency in the arras is **Cabalgar** (✉ Bubeon, Granada, ☎ 958/763135, FAX 958/763136).

In the **Cazorla Nature Park,** four-wheel-drive or horseback excursions and more specific nature tours, such as bird-watching, can be arranged through the Torre de Vinaigre Visitor Center (☎ 953/713001).

WALKING TOURS

In **Córdoba,** English-speaking guides for the Mezquita and Synagogue can be contacted through the **Asociación Profesional de Informadores Turísticos** (✉ Torrijos 2, Córdoba, ☎ 957/293133). In **Granada,** multilingual guides can be contacted through the **Asociación Provincial de Guías** (✉ Puerta del Vino, La Alhambra, Granada, ☎ 958/229936). In **Jaén** and **Úbeda,** ask at the Tourist Office.

Travel Agency

American Express, Viajes Bonal (✉ Avda. de la Constitución 19, Granada, ☎ 958/276312 or 958/276316).

Visitor Information

The main tourist office for the region is in **Granada** (✉ Plaza Mariana Pineda 10, ☎ 958/226688), with information on both the province and the city. A much smaller regional office is found in **Córdoba** (✉ Plaza de Judá Leví, ☎ 957/200522 or 957/200277).

13 Seville and Western Andalucía

The flat landscape of fertile pastures, muddy marshlands, chalky vineyards, and sandy beaches in western Andalucía contrasts vividly with the mountainous provinces to the east. Enjoy the history and romance of Seville; trace the career of Christopher Columbus; sample the famous sherries of Jerez; and visit the region's famous tapas bars.

THROUGH A TRIANGLE formed by the cities of Huelva, Seville, and Cádiz flows the estuary of Andalucía's great river, the Guadalquivir. This flat landscape of fertile pastures, muddy marshlands, chalky vineyards, and sandy beaches contrasts vividly with the mountainous provinces of eastern Andalucía. Here the banks of the Guadalquivir are lined with fields of cotton and rice, orange groves, stud farms, and bull ranches.

By Hilary Bunce

Updated by Nancy Hennessey

This is a land with a proud seafaring history. The career of Christopher Columbus can be traced here, from the monastery at La Rábida, whose friars pleaded his cause with Queen Isabella, to Palos, where he set sail on his epic voyage of 1492; and to Seville. Its shores and rivers echo with the names of other maritime adventurers: Ferdinand Magellan, Juan Sebastián de Elcano, Sir Francis Drake, and Pierre de Villeneuve, to name just a few. For more than two centuries Spain's trade with the New World centered on Seville and treasures from the Americas flowed into her coffers. Later, when this maritime and trading role passed to Cádiz, its lucrativeness funded the notable buildings of that city.

Many towns of this region are called "de la frontera," such as Arcos, Jerez, and Palos, because for 250 years they stood on the battlefront between Christian Spain and Infidel Granada.

Pleasures and Pastimes

Bullfighting
Seville is home to one of Spain's leading bullrings—few *toreros* (bullfighters) gain nationwide recognition until they have fought in the Maestranza ring. The season runs from Easter until late October, reaching its pinnacle early on when Spain's leading toreros fight each day during Seville's April Fair.

Dining
The western corner of Andalucía is well-known in Spain as a gourmet's paradise. Many Spaniards drive for miles to sample the giant shrimp and succulent seafood of Puerto de Santa María or Sanlúcar de Barrameda and to enjoy the *finos* (a dry and light sherry) and *manzanillas* (a dry and delicate sherry with a hint of saltiness) from the vineyards of Jerez. Others come to enjoy the tapas of Seville.

The restaurants listed for Seville are those within easy walking distance of the center of town. Many restaurants are closed on Sunday evenings, and several in Seville close for a month's vacation in August.

Restaurants in the $$$ and $$$$ categories tend to be more formal in winter than in summer. In these places jacket and tie are advisable but rarely essential, especially in hot weather. Formal dress is usually required only in restaurants of five-star hotels.

CATEGORY	COST*
$$$$	over 5,000 ptas.
$$$	3,500–5,000 ptas.
$$	2,500–3,500 ptas.
$	under 2,500 ptas.

per person for a three-course meal, excluding tax and service

Fiestas
The fame of the region's fiestas has spread far beyond the borders of Spain. Visitors come from far and wide to witness the pageant of Seville's Holy Week processions and to join in the fun of its April Fair.

Cádiz's carnival is one of the best in the land. Crowds also flock to the revelries of Jerez's May Horse Fair and September Vintage Festival.

Feb. Weeklong Carnival celebrations are held in Cádiz.

Mar. or Apr. Seville's Holy Week processions are the most famous in Spain. Jerez and Cádiz also have Semana Santa processions.

Apr. The Feria de Abril, Seville's annual Horse Fair, is celebrated with top bullfights; horse parades; flamenco costumes; and singing, dancing, and fireworks nightly in the fairground across the river.

May. The Andalucían horses of Jerez de la Frontera are the showpiece of this city's Feria del Caballo (May Horse Fair).

May or June. A famous Whitsuntide pilgrimage is made to the shrine of the Virgen del Rocío (Virgin of the Dew) in the village of El Rocío (Huelva). Corpus Christi (second Thursday after Whitsun) is celebrated with processions in Cádiz, Jerez, and Seville.

Aug. International flamenco courses are held in Jerez de la Frontera. The Assumption of the Virgin Mary is celebrated everywhere on the 15th, but especially in Seville, where it's the day of the city's patroness, the Virgen de los Reyes.

Sept. The Fiesta de la Vendimia (Grape Harvest Festival) is celebrated in all the wine-producing towns of Cádiz province. Jerez's Harvest Festival is particularly spectacular.

Oct. Celebrations for Cádiz's patroness, the Virgen del Rosario, are held.

Dec. National Contest of Flamenco Guitar at the Fundación Andaluza de Flamenco in Jerez de la Frontera.

If you prefer touring without the extra tourists brought by the fiestas, be sure to avoid the biggest of the celebrations: Seville in April, Cádiz during its Carnival in February, and the May Horse Fair in Jerez.

Flamenco

Seville and Jerez are widely acknowledged as the home of flamenco, and Jerez now has an institute dedicated to the history and performance of this very Andalucían art form. In Seville, you can experience the emotion and excitement of flamenco first-hand at some of the finest clubs in Spain (☞ Nightlife and the Arts *in* Seville, *below*).

Horses

Jerez's pure-bred Carthusian horses are shown off in the annual Feria del Caballo (☞ *above*) at the end of April. These handsome animals also perform every Thursday throughout the year at the Royal Andalusian School of Equestrian Art (☞ Jerez de la Frontera, *below*).

Lodging

This region has several fine hotels. You'll find four paradors; those at Carmona and Arcos de la Frontera are ancient palaces with great views and both are worth a special visit. Those at Mazagón (Huelva) and the Atlántico in Cádiz are modern, comfortable hotels. In addition, you can stay at converted monasteries in Puerto de Santa María and Sanlúcar de Barrameda or on a private luxury ranch near Arcos de la Frontera. Seville has grand old hotels like the famous Alfonso XIII and the Colón, both newly renovated. Thanks to Expo '92, it also has a total of 22 new hotels—nine of them four-star establishments. Another fantastic hotel, one of the best in Spain, is the Casa de Carmona in tiny Carmona outside of Seville.

If you plan to visit during famous festivals, such as Seville's Holy Week or April Fair or Jerez's May Horse Fair or September Vintage

Festival, it is essential to book early—four to eight months in advance in Seville. If you intend to visit Cádiz during its February Carnival celebrations, it would be wise to book at least a month or so in advance.

Seville's hotel prices skyrocketed to absurd levels during Expo '92, but a post-party reality check convinced officials to lower rates. It's also still possible to find genuinely inexpensive lodging, but the rooms will be tiny, and you'll have to scour areas far from the city center. Prices fluctuate dramatically with the seasons—much more so than in most other parts of Spain—so you'd be wise to check ahead.

During Holy Week and the April Fair, all hotel rates in Seville rise steeply by at least half as much.

CATEGORY	COST*
$$$$	over 20,000 ptas.
$$$	11,500–20,000 ptas.
$$	8,000–11,500 ptas.
$	under 8,000 ptas.

per standard double room, excluding tax

Exploring Seville and Western Andalucía

This region covers the provinces of Seville and Cádiz and part of Huelva in western Andalucía. For touring purposes it can be divided into three parts, starting with the busy city of Seville. From there, you can go on to visit the Doñana National Park, Matalascañas or Mazagón, and the villages that played important roles in the voyage of Christopher Columbus. Finally, head for Jerez de la Frontera to taste the sherry, relax in the whitewashed village of Arcos de la Frontera, and feast on seafood in Cádiz.

Great Itineraries

A week in this region is ideal and allows time to explore the diverse landscapes. If time is short, however, just a few days will be enough time for sunny Seville to capture your heart and make a lasting impression. Depending on your interests, from there you may choose to head south and trace the history of the ancient city of Cádiz, where you can savor the famous sherry from the bodegas in Jerez. Or, venture further west to the province of Huelva where you can take a tour of one of Europe's finest wildlife reserves, the Doñana National Park. Your mode of transportation will also help to determine your itinerary; although the major cities and towns are available by train or bus, touring by car will give you the freedom to explore some smaller, charming "pueblos" that charaterize much of the region.

Numbers in the text below correspond to numbers in the margin and on the maps.

IF YOU HAVE 3 DAYS

Stay in 🎫 **Seville** ①–㉚, thought by many to be the most beautiful city in Spain. On your first day, visit the Cathedral and the Giralda, along with the neighboring Moorish Alcázar. Later, wander the orange-scented streets of the Barrio Santa Cruz. On the second day, enjoy the Parque de María Luisa and the colorful Plaza de América. Before leaving the area, stop at the monumental Plaza de España. Head over to the Torre de Oro, before enjoying the lively Calle Betis, with its many tapas bars. On your final day, visit the ancient city of **Carmona** ㉛ with its Roman Necropolis; then head to the Roman ruins at **Itálica** ㉜ before returning to Seville.

IF YOU HAVE 5 DAYS

Follow this tour if you have more time to venture out beyond ⌘ **Seville** ①–㉚. Still, it is best to begin in this city. Start with the Cathedral and Giralda, and spend some time in the Moorish Alcázar. Then relax and enjoy a lively walk through the narrow byways of the Barrio Santa Cruz. On the next day, take in the impressive collection of art in the Museo de Bellas Artes. Then head toward the river and walk the Paseo de Colón, where you can see the Maestranza bullring and visit the Torre de Oro. On your third day, take a walk in the Parque de María Luisa and stop at the Plaza de América and the monumental Plaza de Espana. On your way back to the center of town, watch for Seville University, the old tabacco factory of Carmen fame. Next, head for ⌘ **Jerez de la Frontera** ㊵, famous for its sherry production. If your fourth day falls on a Thursday, you can see the spectacular horse show at The Royal Andalusian School of Equestrian Art. Also in Jerez, take in a tour at one of the local bodegas and sample some of the world's finest sherry. Spend your final night in the small port town of ⌘ **Puerto de Santa María** ㊸. On your last day, visit the ancient city of **Cádiz** ㊹, before returning to Seville.

When to Tour Seville and Western Andalucía

If you want to experience the excitement of Spanish fiestas, this is the place to come. Book accommodations long in advance. Aside from fiestas, spring and late fall are partcularly nice, when the weather is warm but not unbearable. Winters are also mild if you prefer uncrowded touring. If you plan to visit Jerez de la Frontera, arrange to be there on a Thursday so you can watch the impressive horse exhibition at the Royal Andalusian School of Equestrian Art. Lastly, keep in mind that many museums and monuments are closed on Monday.

SEVILLE AND ENVIRONS

Lying on the banks of the Guadalquivir, Seville is Spain's fourth-largest city and the capital of Andalucía. Its whitewashed houses bright with bougainvillea, its ocher-colored palaces, and its Baroque facades have long enchanted visitors. In addition to the charms that have drawn visitors for centuries, the city offers many new attractions that are the legacy of the Expo '92 including an opera house, a new riverfront esplanade, a completely renovated Fine Arts Museum and several dozen other buildings. Seville also benefits from much-needed transportation improvements including new train and bus stations, an enlarged and modernized airport, new highways in and around the city, seven new bridges, and high-speed rail and four-lane highway links with Madrid.

Of course, this bustling city of almost 800,000 also has a negative side: traffic-choked streets, high unemployment, a notorious petty crime rate, and, at times, the kind of impersonal treatment you won't find in smaller cities like Granada or Córdoba. But Seville's artistic heritage and its citizens' zest for life more than compensate for the city's disadvantages. Be warned, however, that schedules for the city's monuments and other institutions have a habit of changing almost monthly.

If you want to venture out of Seville on a quick day trip, head to Carmona with its stunning Roman Necropolis and terrific hotels (either the Casa de Carmona or the parador are the perfect places for a leisurely lunch), the ancient town of Itálica, or Aracena with its stalactite- and stalagmite-rich caverns.

Numbers in the margin correspond to points of interest on the Western Andalucía: Seville and the Guadalquivir Delta map.

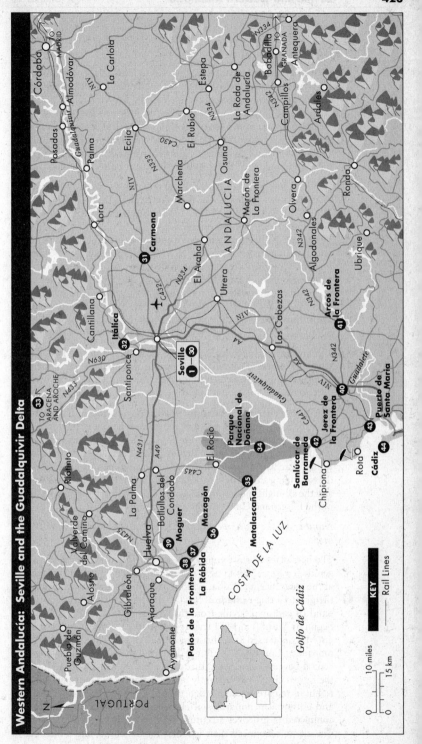

Western Andalucía: Seville and the Guadalquivir Delta

Seville

❶ *550 km (340 mi) southwest of Madrid, 220 km (140 mi) northwest of Málaga.*

Seville has a long and noble history. Conquered by the Romans in 205 BC, it gave the world two great emperors, Trajan and Hadrian (you can see the latter's birthplace at nearby Itálica). The Moors held Seville for more than 500 years and bequeathed to it one of the greatest examples of their art in the form of the well-loved Giralda tower. Saint King Ferdinand (Ferdinand III) lies enshrined in glory in the cathedral, one of Seville's greatest monuments. His rather less saintly descendant, Pedro the Cruel, builder of the splendid Alcázar, is buried here, too.

Seville is justly proud of its literary and artistic associations. The painters Diego Rodríguez de Silva Velázquez (1599–1660) and Bartolomé Esteban Murillo (1617–82) were natives of Seville, as were the poets Gustavo Adolfo Bécquer (1836–70), Antonio Machado (1875–1939), and Nobel Prize winner Vicente Aleixandre (1898–1984). The tale of that ingenious knight of La Mancha was begun in a Seville jail, for Don Quixote's creator, Miguel de Cervantes, twice languished in a debtors' prison here. Tirso de Molina's character Don Juan carried on his amorous pursuits in the mansions of Seville, later scheming as Don Giovanni in the Barrio de Santa Cruz. The barrio also provided the setting for the nuptials of Rossini's barber, Figaro. Nearby, at the old tobacco factory, Bizet's sultry Carmen first met Don José.

The vivacity and color of Seville are most intense during Holy Week, when the lacerated Christs and bejeweled, weeping Virgins of the city's 24 parishes are paraded through the streets on floats borne by barefoot penitents.

Two weeks later, the *sevillanos* (Sevillians), this time in flamenco costume, celebrate the Feria de Abril, the greatest parade of the year. Begun as a horse-trading fair in 1847, today it recalls its equine origins in the midday horse parades, with men in broad-brim hats and Andalucían riding gear astride prancing steeds, their women in long, flounced dresses riding side-saddle behind them. Bullfights, fireworks displays, and the all-night singing and dancing of sevillanos in the *casetas* (tents) of the fairground complete the spectacle.

Numbers in the margin correspond to points of interest on the Seville map.

The best place to start your exploration of Seville is in the Plaza Virgen de los Reyes. From next to the central fountain you can gaze up at the magnificent Giralda, symbol of Seville, and at the east facade of
★ ❷ the great Gothic **cathedral,** Seville's leading monument. After Ferdinand III captured Seville from the Moors in 1248, the great mosque begun by Yusuf II in 1171 was at first simply reconsecrated to the Virgin Mary and used as a Christian cathedral, in much the same way the mosque at Córdoba was. But in 1401 the citizens of Seville saw fit to erect a new and glorious cathedral, one more worthy of the status of their great city. They promptly pulled down the old mosque—all, that is, but its minaret and outer court—and set about their task with a zeal and enthusiasm unparalleled elsewhere. This mighty building was completed in just over a century—a remarkable record for the time. The clergy renounced their incomes for the cause, and a member of the chapter is said to have proclaimed: "Let us build a church so big that we shall be held to be insane." And this they proceeded to do, for today Seville's cathedral can be described only in superlatives: It is the biggest and highest cathedral in Spain, the largest Gothic building in

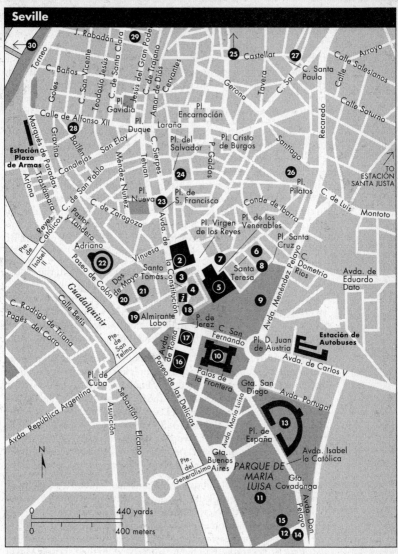

Seville

the world, and the world's third-largest church after St. Peter's in Rome and St. Paul's in London.

The exterior of the cathedral, with its rose windows and magnificent flying buttresses, is a monument to pure Gothic beauty. The badly lit interior can be disappointing, with its five naves and numerous side chapels shrouded in gloom. Gothic purity has been submerged in ornate, Baroque decoration lit only by flickering candles. Still, there is much worth seeing inside, even if you do have to strain your eyes.

Just south of the visiting entrance, the **Capilla Real** (Royal Chapel), is one area of the cathedral that shines brightly today. At the sides of this chapel stand the tombs of Ferdinand's wife, Beatrix of Swabia, and his son, Alfonso X, called the Wise (died 1284). In a silver urn before the high altar rest the precious relics of Ferdinand III, Seville's liberator (canonized 1671), who was said to have died from excessive fasting. In the vault below (rarely open) lie the tombs of Ferdinand's descendant, Pedro the Cruel, and his mistress, María de Padilla. Don't forget to look above the entrance grille, where you can see Ferdinand III, on horseback, receiving the keys of Seville.

Spend some time in the **Capilla Mayor** (Main Chapel), in the central nave, and study the intricately carved altarpiece begun by a Flemish carver in 1482. This magnificent retablo, the largest in Christendom (65 feet high by 43 feet wide), depicts some 36 scenes from the life of Christ; its pillars are carved with more than 200 figures; and the whole work is lavishly adorned with immeasurable quantities of gold leaf.

At the south transept, you can't miss the flamboyant **monument to Christopher Columbus.** The great explorer knew triumph and disgrace and found no repose—he died at Valladolid, bitterly disillusioned. Columbus's coffin is borne aloft by the four kings representing the medieval kingdoms of Spain: Castile, León, Aragón, and Navarra. Columbus's son, Hernando Colón (1488–1539), is also buried here. His tombstone, inscribed with the words A CASTILLA Y A LEÓN, MUNDO NUEVO DIÓ COLÓN (TO CASTILE AND LEÓN, COLUMBUS GAVE A NEW WORLD), lies between the great west door, the Puerta Mayor, and the central choir.

Between the elder Columbus's tomb and the Capilla Real, the **main treasure houses** of the cathedral display a wealth of gold and silver (much of it brought from the New World), relics, and many rather neglected works of art. In the dome of the **Sala Capitular** (Chapter House), in the cathedral's southeast corner, you'll see one of Murillo's finest *Immaculate Conceptions,* painted in 1668. Next, in the **Sacristía Mayor** (Main Sacristy) are the keys of the city, which the Moors and Jews of Seville presented to its conqueror, Ferdinand. Finally, in the **Sacristía de los Cálices,** look for Martínez Montañés's crucifixion, *Cristo de la Clemencia*; Valdés Leal's *St. Peter Freed by an Angel*; Zurbarán's *Virgin and Child*; and Goya's *St. Justa* and *St. Rufina.*

★ The **Giralda,** undisputed symbol of Seville, dominates the skyline and can be glimpsed from almost every corner of the city. Built originally as the minaret of Seville's great mosque, from which the faithful were summoned to prayer, it was constructed between 1184 and 1196, just 50 years before the Reconquest of Seville. When the Christians tore down the mosque, they could not bring themselves to destroy this tower and so incorporated it into their new cathedral. In 1565–68 they added a lantern and belfry to the old minaret, installing 24 bells, one for each of Seville's 24 parishes and the 24 Christian knights who fought with Ferdinand III in the Reconquest. They also added the bronze statue of Faith, which turns as a weather vane (*el giraldillo,* or "something that turns"), providing the name Giralda.

With its Baroque additions, the slender Giralda now rises 322 feet. In its center, in place of steps, 35 sloping ramps, wide enough for two horsemen to pass abreast, climb to a viewing platform 230 feet up. It is said that Ferdinand III rode his horse to the top to admire the view of the city he had conquered. If you follow in his footsteps, your efforts will be rewarded by a glorious view of pan-tile roofs and the Guadalquivir shimmering beneath palm-lined banks. ⊠ *Plaza Virgen de los Reyes; Cathedral,* ☎ *95/421–4971; Giralda,* ☎ *95/456–3321.* ◼ *Cathedral and Giralda 600 ptas.* ☉ *Cathedral Mon.–Sat. 11–5, Sun. 2–4, also open for mass; Giralda Mon.–Sat. 11–5, Sun. 10–4.*

Before you leave the cathedral precincts, take a look inside the **Patio de los Naranjos** (Courtyard of Orange Trees). The old fountain in the center was used for ritual ablutions before entering the mosque. See if you can find the alligator by the Puerta del Largato in the corner near the Giralda—thought to have been a gift from the emir of Egypt in 1260 as he sought the hand of Alfonso the Wise's daughter—and the ivory elephant tusk found in the ruins of Itálica. Across the patio, the Sacristy houses the Columbus Library, a collection of 3,000 volumes bequeathed by his son Hernando.

❸ The **Archivo de Indias** (Archives of the Indies) opened in 1785 in the former Lonja, the Merchants' Exchange, designed by the architect of the Escorial, Juan de Herrera, in 1572. This dignified Renaissance building houses an impressive collection of documents relating to the discovery of the New World. Its collection of maps includes Juan de la Cosa's *Mappamundi,* and among the logbooks you'll find one kept by Columbus. There are drawings, trade documents, plans of South American towns, and even the autographs of Columbus, Magellan, and Cortés. Many of the 38,000 documents have yet to be sorted and properly catalogued, and the exhibits on display are constantly being shifted. ⊠ *Avda. de la Constitución,* ☎ *95/421–1234.* ◼ *Free.* ☉ *Weekdays 10–1 (8–3 for researchers).*

❹ Beside the Archives of the Indies, you'll find the **Museo de Arte Contemporáneo** (Museum of Contemporary Art), housed in a fine old mansion. Its 20th-century Spanish paintings and sculpture includes works by Romero de Torres, Carlos Saura, Antoni Tàpies, Fernando Zobel, and the sculptor Eduardo Chillida. Temporary exhibitions by contemporary Andalucían artists are also held here. ⊠ *Santo Tomás 5,* ☎ *95/421–5830.* ◼ *250 ptas.* ☉ *fall–spring, Tues.–Fri. 10–8, weekends 10–2; summer, Tues.–Sun. 10–2; closed weekends in Aug.*

★ ❺ On the Plaza Triunfo you'll find the entrance to the **Alcázar** (Reales Alcázares), the Mudéjar palace built by Pedro I (1350–69), on the site of the former Moorish alcázar (fortress). Don't mistake the Alcázar for a genuine Moorish palace, like the Alhambra in Granada. It may look like one, and was indeed designed and built by Moorish workers brought in from Granada, but it was commissioned and paid for by a Christian king, more than 100 years after the Reconquest of Seville. Into its construction, Pedro the Cruel incorporated stones and capitals he pillaged from elsewhere—from Valencia, from Córdoba's Medina Azahara, and from Seville itself. The Alcázar is the finest example of Mudéjar architecture in Spain today, though its purity of style has been much diluted by the alterations and additions of successive Spanish rulers. Today, the Alcázar is the official residence in Seville of the king and queen of Spain.

You enter the Alcázar through high, fortified walls of genuine Moorish origin that belie the exquisite delicacy of its interior. Cross the **Patio de la Montería** to Pedro's Mudéjar palace, arranged around the beautiful **Patio de las Doncellas** (Court of the Damsels). Its name most likely pays tribute to the annual gift of 100 virgins to the Moorish sultans. Resplendent with the most delicate of lacelike stucco, its Granada craftsmanship is instantly reminiscent of the Alhambra, though the upper galleries were added by Carlos V. Opening off this patio, the **Salón de Embajadores** (Hall of the Ambassadors), with its cedarwood cupola of green, red, and gold, is the most sumptuous hall in the palace. It was here in 1526 that Carlos V married Isabel of Portugal—for which occasion he added the wooden balconies.

Other royal rooms include Felipe II's dining hall and the three apartments of Pedro's wily mistress, María de Padilla. María's hold over her royal lover, and seemingly over his courtiers, too, was so great that they apparently lined up to drink her bathwater. The **Patio de las Muñecas** (Court of the Dolls) takes its name from two tiny faces carved on the inside of one of its arches, no doubt as a joke on the part of its Moorish creators. Here, in 1358, Pedro reputedly had his half brother Don Fadrique slain. And here, too, he murdered his guest Abu Said of Granada for his jewels. One of these, a huge, uncut ruby, Pedro presented to the Black Prince (Edward Prince of Wales [1330–76], eldest son of England's Edward III) in 1367. It now sits among other priceless gems in the Crown of England.

Next, you'll come to the **Apartments of Carlos V,** built by the emperor at the time of his marriage. The walls carry a rich collection of Flemish tapestries depicting Carlos's victories at Tunis. Look at the tapestry of the map of Spain—it shows the Iberian Peninsula upside down, as was the custom in Arab mapmaking.

The end of your visit will bring you out into the **Alcázar Gardens,** where you can enjoy the fragrance of jasmine and myrtle, the beautiful terraces and ornamental baths, and the well-stocked goldfish pond covered with water lilies. In the midst of this oasis of green is an orange tree said to have been planted in the time of Pedro the Cruel. From the gardens, a passageway leads to the **Patio de las Banderas,** which offers a classic view of the Giralda. ⊠ *Plaza del Triunfo,* ☎ *95/422–7163.* ▣ *600 ptas.* ☉ *Tues.–Sat. 10:30–5, Sun. 10–1.*

★ ❻ The twisting alleyways, cobbled squares, and whitewashed houses of the **Barrio de Santa Cruz,** the old Jewish Quarter, were much favored by Seville's nobles in the 17th century. Today its houses are beautifully preserved, and the barrio boasts some of Seville's most expensive properties. Wrought-iron lanterns cast shadows on whitewashed walls and ocher-framed windows hide behind potbellied grilles. In some places bars nestle side by side with antiques shops and souvenir stores, but most of the quarter is made up of quiet, residential streets. The Callejón del Agua, beside the wall of the Alcázar Gardens, boasts some of the quarter's finest mansions and patios.

Pause awhile to enjoy the antiques shops and the outdoor café in the **Plaza Alianza.** A starkly simple crucifix hangs on the dazzling, white wall shrouded in bougainvillea, and blue-and-white tiles bear the square's name. In the **Plaza de Doña Elvira,** with its fountain and azulejo benches, the youth of Seville gather to play guitars. The heart of the Barrio Santa Cruz is the colorful **Plaza de los Venerables.**

NEED A
BREAK?

Enjoy a drink or a plate of ham here in the fine old bar known as **Casa Román,** or stop for lunch in either of the two outdoor restaurants (**Hostería del Laurel** or **Restaurante Santa Cruz**).

❼ The **Hospital de los Venerables,** once a retirement home for priests, has opened after extensive renovation; don't miss its splendid azulejo patio and small museum of floats from the Cruces de Mayo processions. ⊠ *Plaza de los Venerables,* ☎ *95/456–2696.* ⊡ *500 ptas.* ☉ *Daily 10–2 and 4–8.*

Just around the corner from the Hospital de los Venerables at Callejón del Agua and Jope de Rueda, you'll find the **Plaza Alfaro,** where Rossini's Figaro serenaded Rosina on her famous balcony. In the **Plaza Santa Cruz** a 17th-century, filigree iron cross marks the site of the Santa Cruz church destroyed by Napoleon's General Soult. Here, the painter **❽** Murillo was buried in 1682. On Calle Santa Teresa 8 see the **Casa de Murillo,** which houses frequent exhibits of all types. Call for current events (☎ 95/421–7535) or check with the tourist office. The street itself is named for Santa Teresa de Ávila (1515–82), who stayed here once on a visit to Seville and was so enchanted by the city that she decreed that anyone who stayed free from sin in Seville was indeed on the path to God.

❾ From the Plaza Santa Cruz, you can stroll through the **Jardines de Murillo** (Murillo Gardens), where you'll find a statue of Christopher Columbus. At the far end of the gardens opposite Calle San Fernando stands what used to be the *Fábrica de Tabacos* (tobacco factory) that has been **❿** home to **Seville University** since the 1950s. Built between 1750 and 1766, some 10,000 *cigarreras* (female cigar makers) were employed here less than a century later, including, of course, the heroine of Bizet's opera *Carmen,* who rolled her cigars on her thigh. Today, the new factory is located across the river.

⓫ For a visit to one of the loveliest parks in Spain, head to the **Parque de María Luisa** (María Luisa Park)—the main entrance is at the Glorieta San Diego. Here, you'll also find a **statue of El Cid** (Rodrigo Díaz de Vivar, 1043–99, who fought for and against the Muslim rulers during the Reconquest); and the old **Casino** building of the 1929 Exhibition, now the Teatro Lope de Vega. The park itself, formerly the garden of the Palacio de San Telmo, is a blend of formal design and wild vegetation. In the burst of development that gripped Seville in the 1920s, it was redesigned for the 1929 Hispanic-American Exhibition, and the impressive villas you'll see here today are the fair's remaining pavilions, many of them now consulates or schools.

On the south end of the Parque de María Luisa, past the Isla de los **⓬** Patos (Island of Ducks), you'll reach the **Plaza de América.** This plaza, designed by Aníbal González, is a blaze of color with deep, orange sand, flowers, shrubs, ornamental stairways, and fountains of yellow, blue, and ocher tiles. The three impressive buildings in neo-Mudéjar, Gothic, and Renaissance style that surround the square were built by González for the 1929 fair. Today, two of them serve as museums.

⓭ Just east of the Parque de María Luisa, the monumental **Plaza de España** should not be missed. This grandiose structure, also designed by architect Aníbal González, was Spain's centerpiece pavilion at the 1929 fair. The brightly colored azulejo pictures in its arches represent the 50 provinces of Spain, and the four bridges over the ornamental lake, the medieval kingdoms of the Iberian Peninsula.

⓮ The **Museo Arqueológico** (Archaeology Museum), in the Renaissance building, houses finds from Phoenician, Greek, Carthaginian, Iberian, Roman, and medieval times. Its best exhibits include marble statues and mosaics from the Roman excavations at Itálica and the fabulous Carambolo treasure found on a hillside outside Seville in 1958. It consists of 21 pieces of jewelry, all of 24-karat gold, that date from the

7th and 6th centuries BC. ⊠ *Plaza de América*, ☎ *95/423–2401.* ▦ *250 ptas.* ☉ *Tues.–Sun. 9–2:30.*

⑮ The Mudéjar pavilion opposite the Museo Arqueológico is the home of the **Museo de Artes y Costumbres Populares** (Museum of Folklore). Here, on the first floor, you'll find re-creations of a forge, a bakery, a winepress, a tanner's shop, and a pottery studio. Upstairs, the exhibits include 18th- and 19th-century court dress, regional folk costumes, carriages, and musical instruments. ⊠ *Plaza de América*, ☎ *95/423–2576.* ▦ *250 ptas.* ☉ *Tues.–Sun. 9–2:30.*

⑯ On Avenida de Roma stands a splendid Baroque palace, the **Palacio de San Telmo.** Chiefly the work of architect Leonardo de Figueroa, the palace which was built between 1682 and 1796, today holds the seat of the Presidencia de Junta de Andalucía, the regional government's executive. Look for the exotic main portal. It dates from 1734 and is a superb example of the fanciful Churrigueresque style. The grand Mudéjar-style building behind San Telmo is Seville's leading hotel, the **⑰ Alfonso XIII,** built—and named—for the king's visit to the 1929 fair. You can explore its inner courtyard or sip a cool martini in the bar and enjoy its ornate Moorish decor. On the north side of Puerta de Jerez **⑱** is the **Palacio de Yanduri,** where the Nobel Prize–winning poet Vicente Aleixandre was born.

⑲ On the riverside just a short walk from the Puerta de Jerez, the **Torre de Oro** (Tower of Gold) marks another of Seville's great landmarks. A 12-sided tower built by the Moors in 1220 to complete the city's ramparts, it served to close off the harbor by attaching a chain across the river from the base of the Tower of Gold to another tower on the opposite bank. In 1248 Admiral Ramón de Bonifaz succeeded in breaking through this barrier, thus enabling Ferdinand III to capture the city. Today, the tower houses a small but well-displayed Naval Museum. ☎ *95/422–2419.* ▦ *100 ptas.* ☉ *Tues.–Fri. 10–2, weekends 11–2.*

NEED A BREAK?   Cross the San Telmo Bridge and stroll along the **Calle Betis** to the Isabel II Bridge. You can take in the river as well as the street famed for nightlife and tapas bars.

⑳ Opposite the Torre de Oro is Seville's new opera house, the **Maestranza Theatre** (⊠ Nuñez de Balboa 5, ☎ 95/422–6573), which opened in 1991. Now one of Europe's leading venues, the theatre offers opera, classical music, zarzuela (comic opera), and even jazz.

㉑ Behind the Maestranza Theatre, the **Hospital de la Caridad,** today an almshouse for the sick and elderly, displays six paintings by Murillo (1617–82) and two gruesome works by Valdés Leal (1622–90) depicting the Triumph of Death. The Baroque hospital was founded in 1674 by Seville's original Don Juan. Miguel de Mañara (1626–79), a nobleman of licentious character, was returning one night from a riotous orgy when he had a vision of a funeral procession in which the partly decomposed corpse in the coffin was his own. Accepting the apparition as a sign from God, Miguel de Mañara renounced his worldly goods and joined the Brotherhood of Charity, whose unsavory task it was to collect the bodies of executed criminals and bury them. He devoted his fortune to building this hospital and is buried before the high altar in the chapel. Artist Murillo was a personal friend of Mañara's, thus the reason for La Caridad's chief attractions. ⊠ *C. Temprado 3,* ☎ *95/422–3232.* ▦ *200 ptas.* ☉ *Mon.–Sat. 10–1 and 3:30–6.*

㉒ Sevillanos have spent many thrilling Sunday afternoons in **La Maestranza Bullring.** Built between 1760 and 1763, this deep ocher-painted bullring is the oldest and most beautiful plaza de toros in Spain. ⊠ *Paseo de Colón,* ☎ *95/422–4577,* ▨ *Plaza and bullfighting museum 250 ptas.* ⊘ *Mon.–Sat. 10–1:30.*

㉓ The **Ayuntamiento** (City Hall), designed by Diego de Riaño and built between 1527 and 1564, is located in the heart of Seville's commercial center, the Plaza Nueva. The facade, which overlooks the plaza, dates from the 19th century, but walk around to the opposite side on the Plaza de San Francisco, and you'll find Riaño's original building.

At the beginning of **Calle Sierpes,** Seville's main shopping artery, a plaque and a small bronze bust of Cervantes mark the spot where the Cárcel Real (Royal Prison) once stood. In one of its cells Cervantes began work **㉔** on *Don Quixote.* On the Plaza del Salvador, the **Iglesia del Salvador** (Church of El Salvador, 1671–1712) stands on the site of Seville's first great mosque. Inside, look especially for the image of *Jesus de la Pasión,* carved by Martínez Montañés. This statue is borne through the streets on Holy Thursday in one of Semana Santa's most moving processions. ⊠ *Plaza San Salvador,* ☎ *95/438–5454.* ▨ *Free.* ⊘ *Daily 8–1:45 and 6–9.*

Calle Gallegos will lead you back to Sierpes. A small **alleyway** on your right is named Monardes, after the apothecary who opened the first herbalist store in Seville with samples of New World flora.

NEED A
BREAK?
At the far end of Sierpes you can relax over a coffee at one of the sidewalk tables of the old-fashioned **Café Campaña**.

If you've time to spare, Seville has several other interesting sights located somewhat away from the center. With the possible exception of the Macarena, they are all still within walking distance.

㉕ At the **Basílica de la Macarena** you'll find Seville's most revered image, the Virgin of Hope, more familiarly known as the *Macarena,* because her church adjoins the *Puerta de la Macarena* (Macarena Gate), a remnant of the old Roman wall. Bedecked with candles and carnations, her cheeks streaming with glass tears, La Macarena is the focus of the procession on Holy Thursday that is the highlight of Seville's Holy Week pageant. She is the patroness of Gypsies and the matador's protector. Few matadors would dream of entering the ring without addressing a prayer to her. So great are her charms that the Sevillian bullfighter Joselito spent half his personal fortune buying her four emeralds. When, in 1920, he was killed in the ring at the tender age of 25, the Macarena was dressed in widow's weeds for a full month. ⊠ *Puerta de la Macarena,* ☎ *95/437–0195.* ▨ *Basílica free, treasury 250 ptas.* ⊘ *Basílica daily 9–1 and 5–9, treasury daily 9–1 and 5–8.*

㉖ The **Casa de Pilatos** was built at the turn of the 16th century by the dukes of Tarifa, ancestors of the present owner, the duke of Medinaceli. It's known as Pilate's House because of a popular belief that Don Fadrique, first marquis of Tarifa, modeled it on Pilate's house in Jerusalem, where he went on a pilgrimage in 1519. This palace, with its fine patio and superb azulejo decorations, is, in fact, a beautiful blend of Spanish Mudéjar and Renaissance architecture. ⊠ *Plaza Pilatos,* ☎ *95/422–5298.* ▨ *1,000 ptas.* ⊘ *Daily 9–7.*

㉗ The 15th-century Gothic **Convento de Santa Paula** boasts a fine facade and portico with ceramic decoration by Nicolaso Pisano. The chapel has some beautiful azulejos and sculptures by Martínez Montañés. ⊠ *C. Santa Paula,* ☎ *95/442–1307.* ▨ *Free; donations accepted.* ⊘ *Tues.–Sun. 9–1 and 4:30–6:30.*

㉘ The **Museo de Bellas Artes** (Fine Arts Museum), which recently underwent extensive renovations, contains a fine collection of Murillo, Zurbarán, Velázquez, Valdés Leal, and El Greco, said by locals to be second only to the Prado's. ⊠ *Plaza del Museo*, ☎ *95/422–0790.* ⊠ *250 ptas.* ☉ *Tues.–Sun. 9–3.*

㉙ The church of **San Lorenzo y Jesús del Gran Poder** has many fine works by such artists as Montañés and Pacheco, but its most outstanding piece is Juan de Mesa's *Jesús del Gran Poder* (Christ Omnipotent). The *paso* (float) for the procession of El Gran Poder that takes place on Good Friday morning is the work of Ruíz Gijón (1690). ⊠ *C. Jesús del Gran Poder*, ☎ *95/438–5454.* ⊠ *Free.* ☉ *Daily 8–1:45 and 6–9.*

The year 1992 brought the universal exhibition, Expo '92, to Seville's island of La Cartuja, on the Guadalquivir. Seven new bridges across the river were constructed, as well as numerous pavilions and other facilities. Although some pavilions were dismantled in late 1992, most **㉚** of the **Expo site** remains as a permanent public area. Concerts, audiovisual shows, and other events are regularly held here; inquire at the tourist office. Some areas are to be used for a technological business center and a campus extension to the University of Seville.

Bars and Cafés

Because most of the locals eat their main meal at lunchtime, Seville's bars are packed in the evenings with people making a supper of tapas. Popular **La Alicantina** (⊠ Plaza del Salvador 2, ☎ 95/422–6122) has a tapas bar with pastoral scenes of wine- and beer-making decorating its azulejo-tile walls. **Casa Román** (⊠ Plaza de los Venerables, ☎ 95/421–6408), open since 1934, is a classic tapas bar, with wood-paneled walls and ceilings and hanging hams. The **Cervecería Giralda** (⊠ Mateos Gago 9, ☎ 95/421–3170) is a lovely corner bar, set with Moorish-style marble columns and azulejo-tile walls, and usually thronged with a hip, young crowd. **Rincón San Eloy** (⊠ San Eloy 24, ☎ 95/421–8079) is a popular spot for tapas among sevillanos.

Boating

The Guadalquivir has a variety of choices for boating enthusiasts: paddleboats or canoes (☞ Boating *in* Seville and Western Andalucía A to Z, *below*).

Bullfighting

The season runs from Easter until late October. Most corridas are held on Sundays, with the exception of special fiestas. In Seville, bullfights take place at the **Maestranza bullring,** on the Paseo de Colón (☎ 95/422–4577). The best season is during the April Fair, when fights take place each day with Spain's leading toreros. Tickets for these fights are expensive, and you should buy them in advance from the official *despacho de entradas* (ticket office) on Calle Adriano, beside the Maestranza ring. Other genuine, but unofficial, despachos on Calle Sierpes sell tickets, too, but they charge a 20% commission.

Dining and Lodging

$$$–$$$$ ✕ **Egaña-Oriza.** One of Seville's newest and most acclaimed restaurants, ★ the Egaña-Oriza is beautifully situated on the edge of the Murillo Gardens. The decor is modern, with walls painted in deep peach and air-force blue. José Mari Egaña, the owner, is Basque, and the menu reflects the influence of his homeland's cuisine. For an entrée you might try the *estofado de jabalí con ciruelas y pasas* (casserole of wild boar with plums and raisins). ⊠ *San Fernando 41*, ☎ *95/422–7271. AE, DC, MC, V. No lunch Sat. Closed Sun. and Aug.*

$$$–$$$$ ✕ **La Albahaca.** One of Seville's prettiest restaurants is located in the heart of the Barrio de Santa Cruz. This typical Andalucían house was

built by the celebrated architect Juan Talavera as a home for his own family. Inside, three dining rooms are colorfully decorated with ceramic tiles and leafy, potted plants. The service is friendly and professional; entrées include *suprema de lubina con almejas negras* (sea bass supreme with venus clams). ⊠ *Plaza Santa Cruz 12*, ☎ *95/422–0714. AE, DC, MC, V. Closed Sun.*

$$$–$$$$ ✕ **La Isla.** At this restaurant in the Arenal district, fresh fish is brought in daily from the Cádiz and Huelva coasts. The two attractive dining rooms have cream stucco walls above blue-and-white tile decor. *Parrillada de mariscos y pescados* (a fish and seafood grill for two people), is one of the best bets. Simply cooked meat dishes are also available. ⊠ *Arfe 25*, ☎ *95/421–5376. AE, DC, MC, V.*

$$$–$$$$ ✕ **San Marco.** This is an Italian restaurant in an old neoclassical-style house in Seville's shopping district. It has a leafy patio and is furnished with antiques. The menu is a happy combination of Italian, French, and Andalucían cuisines. You'll find good pasta dishes, such as ravioli stuffed with sea bass in clam sauce. ⊠ *Cuna 6*, ☎ *95/421–2440. Reservations essential. AE, DC, MC, V. Closed Mon. and Aug.*

$$–$$$ ✕ **La Judería.** This bright, modern restaurant is fast gaining recogni-
★ tion for the quality of its Andalucían and international cuisine and reasonable prices. Fish dishes from the north of Spain and meat from Ávila are specialties. Try *cordero lechal* (roast lamb) or *urta a la roteña* (a fish dish unique to Rota). ⊠ *Cano y Cueto 13*, ☎ *95/441–2052. Reservations essential. AE, DC, MC, V. Closed Sun. Aug.*

$$ ✕ **Enrique Becerra.** This small, cozy restaurant, a short walk from the
★ cathedral, is in a whitewashed house with wrought-iron window grilles. Inside, a lively, crowded bar, decorated with Sevillian ceramic tiles, is a meeting place for locals who enjoy its excellent selection of tapas. The menu concentrates on traditional Andalucían home-cooked dishes, such as *jarrete de ternera a la cazuela* (veal stew). ⊠ *Gamazo 2*, ☎ *95/421–3049. AE, DC, MC, V. Closed Sun.*

$$ ✕ **Mesón Don Raimundo.** Tucked into an alleyway off Calle Sierpes,
★ this small restaurant is prettily decorated with blue-and-white tile walls and stained-glass windows. The house specialties are meat dishes from the north, such as *solomillo a la castellana* (steak Castilian style), though you'll find fish dishes, too. ⊠ *Argote de Molina 26*, ☎ *95/422–3355. AE, DC, MC, V. No dinner Sun.*

$–$$ ✕ **El Bacalao.** Its specialty is, of course, *bacalao* (salt cod), which you'll find prepared in 101 different ways. The decor is modern mesón: rough, white walls, wooden tables and chairs, and just a touch of Sevillian ceramics. The bar is popular for tapas and sherry or white wine. ⊠ *Plaza Ponce de León 15*, ☎ *95/421–6670. AE, DC, V. Closed Sun.*

$–$$ ✕ **Hostería del Laurel.** This restaurant is geared to tourists, but its big advantage is its location in the Barrio de Santa Cruz. In summer you can dine on the outdoor terrace in the square, surrounded by beautiful, white-and-ocher-painted houses. It has two indoor dining rooms decorated in traditional Castilian style: wood paneling, white walls, and heavy, wooden tables and chairs. There's a menu in English offering a wide choice of traditional Spanish fare. ⊠ *Plaza de los Venerables 5*, ☎ *95/422–0295. AE, DC, MC, V.*

$–$$ ✕ **La Cueva.** The Cave is a colorful, tourist-oriented mesón just off Plaza Doña Elvira. The restaurant has two white-walled dining rooms, located across from one another on both sides of the street. The service is friendly and helpful, and an English menu offers a good choice of traditional Spanish meat and fish dishes. ⊠ *Rodrigo Caro 18*, ☎ *95/421–3143. AE, DC, MC, V.*

$–$$ ✕ **Modesto.** This restaurant, on the edge of the Barrio de Santa Cruz, is popular among sevillanos, who come here for the excellent value. Downstairs is a lively, crowded tapas bar, and upstairs is a restaurant where the stucco walls are decorated with blue-and-white tiles. Try the *Tío Diego* (ham, mushrooms, and shrimp). ✉ *Cano y Cueto 5,* ☎ *95/441–1816. AE, DC, MC, V.*

$ ✕ **Girarda.** You'll find this kitschy but charming tourist restaurant (which doubles as a small hostel) in the heart of the Barrio de Santa Cruz. Half a dozen tables are set in the patio of a private house. Colorful tiles add to the already lively atmosphere. The fare is traditional Spanish. ✉ *Justin de Neve 8,* ☎ *95/421–5113. AE, MC, V.*

$ ✕ **Mesón Castellano.** This recently refurbished old house opposite the church of San José is an ideal place for lunch after a morning's shopping on Calle Sierpes. Specialties are Castilian meat dishes. ✉ *Jovellanos 6,* ☎ *95/421–4028. AE, DC, MC, V. No dinner. Closed Sun.*

$$$$ ✕▥ **Alfonso XIII.** Inaugurated by King Alfonso XIII on April 28, 1929, ★ this splendid Mudéjar Revival palace is in many ways one of the great hotels of Europe. Its public rooms are resplendent with marble floors, wood-paneled ceilings, heavy Moorish lamps, stained glass, and ceramic tile decor in the typical blue, green, and yellow of Seville. The hotel is built around a huge, central patio surrounded by ornate, brick arches and filled with potted plants and a central fountain. The restaurant, with its painted, wood-paneled ceiling; heavy drapes; huge, central table; and ornate, wrought-iron gate, is imposing. Much of the hotel, both inside and out, was renovated for Expo '92. ✉ *San Fernando 2, 41004,* ☎ *95/422–2850,* FAX *95/421–6033. 146 rooms and suites. Restaurant, bar, pool, shops, meeting rooms. AE, DC, MC, V.*

$$$$ ✕▥ **Colón.** A grand old hotel, the Colón was built for the 1929 Ex- ★ hibition. A white-marble staircase leads up to the central lobby, which has a magnificent stained-glass dome and crystal candelabra. The reception area, La Fuente restaurant, and the Bar Majestic open off this circular lobby. Downstairs is the renowned El Burladero restaurant, with a bullfight ambience, and La Tasca tavern. The stylish, old-fashioned rooms are elegantly furnished in pink and green, with silk drapes and bedspreads and dark wood fittings. ✉ *Canalejas 1, 41001,* ☎ *95/422–2900,* FAX *95/422–0938. 204 rooms, 14 suites. 2 restaurants, 2 bars, beauty salon, meeting rooms. AE, DC, MC, V.*

$$$ ✕▥ **Inglaterra.** This modern hotel overlooking the central Plaza Nueva ★ has long had a reputation for individual attention and excellent service. No tour groups stay here, and the staff make an effort to call their guests by name. The best rooms are on the fifth floor; they are furnished with comfortable settees, armchairs, and flowered curtains, and have big balconies. The wood-paneled, first-floor dining room overlooks orange trees and the Plaza Nueva. ✉ *Plaza Nueva 7, 41001,* ☎ *95/422–4970,* FAX *95/456–1336. 113 rooms, 1 suite. Restaurant, bar. AE, DC, MC, V.*

$–$$ ✕▥ **Giralda.** This modern hotel, in a cul-de-sac off Recaredo, caters largely to tour-bus groups, but the service is friendly and professional. Paintings of Spanish scenes, an enormous cage, and Moorish grilles decorate the lobby. The adjoining restaurant has glazed, half-tile walls ornamented with ceramic plates and urns. The spacious, light rooms are furnished in typical Castilian style. ✉ *Sierra Nevada 3, 41003,* ☎ *95/441–6661,* FAX *95/441–9352. 96 rooms, 5 suites. Restaurant, bar, meeting rooms. AE, DC, MC, V.*

$$$ ▥ **Doña María.** Close to the cathedral, this is one of Seville's most charming hotels. Some rooms are small and plain; others are tastefully furnished with antiques. Room 310 has a four-poster double bed, and 305 has two single four-posters—both have spacious bathrooms. There's no restaurant, but a breakfast buffet is served. There's also a rooftop pool with a good view of the Giralda, just a stone's throw away. ✉

Don Remondo 19, 41004, ☎ *95/422–4990,* FAX *95/421–9546. 70 rooms. Pool. AE, DC, MC, V.*

$$$ 🏨 **Meliá Sevilla.** This vast, modern, airy hotel behind the Plaza de España resembles the best American business hotels. Ask for a room at the front facing the pool and Plaza de España, which is illuminated Friday to Sunday; those at the back have poor views. The best rooms and suites are on the ninth floor. ✉ *Dr. Pedro de Castro 1, 41004,* ☎ *95/442–2611,* FAX *95/442–1608. 366 rooms, 5 suites. Restaurant, coffee shop, bar, pool, meeting rooms. AE, DC, MC, V.*

$$$ 🏨 **Pasarela.** Close to the Meliá (see *above*), behind the Plaza de España, the Pasarela is smaller and cozier than its giant neighbor. On the ground floor you'll find several small sitting rooms; oil paintings and table lamps give it a homey atmosphere. The rooms are large and fully carpeted, with predominantly brown-and-beige modern decor and white bedspreads. ✉ *Avda. de la Borbolla 11, 41004,* ☎ *95/441–5511,* FAX *95/442–0727. 82 rooms. Bar, breakfast room, sauna, exercise room. AE, DC, MC, V.*

$$ 🏨 **Bécquer.** Well-maintained and located near the main shopping districts, this hotel is one of the best mid-range picks. Marble floors, dark wood and leather furniture dominate the public areas; while the rooms, with white walls, carved wood headboards, and woven bedspreads are traditionally Spanish. There is also a small sitting room dedicated to the poet Gustavo Adolfo Bécquer. ✉ *Reyes Católicos 4, 41001,* ☎ *95/422–8900,* FAX *95/421–4400. 120 rooms. Bar, breakfast room. AE, DC, MC, V.*

$$ 🏨 **La Rábida.** A charming, old Andalucían house in the Arenal district has been converted into a comfortable, modestly priced hotel that retains its Old World atmosphere. Many rooms overlook a leafy patio with oblique views of the Giralda. The hotel is popular with tour groups and individuals. ✉ *Castelar 24, 41001,* ☎ *95/422–0960,* FAX *95/422–4375. 87 rooms. Restaurant, bar. AE, DC, MC, V.*

$$ 🏨 **Murillo.** In the very heart of the Barrio de Santa Cruz, the Murillo can be reached only on foot; take a taxi to the Plaza de Santa Cruz and a porter will collect your luggage. The rooms are simple, with bare floors, white walls, and bright red bedspreads. But the location, friendly atmosphere, and wonderfully ornate public rooms are splendid. ✉ *Lope de Rueda 7, 41004,* ☎ *95/421–6095,* FAX *95/421–9616. 57 rooms. Bar, breakfast room. AE, DC, MC, V.*

$ 🏨 **Girarda.** One of several very basic, family-run hostels in the Barrio Santa Cruz, the Girarda is in an old, Moorish-style building with a colorful interior patio. ✉ *Justino de Neve 8, 41004,* ☎ *95/421–5113, no phone. 5 rooms. Restaurant. AE, MC, V.*

$ 🏨 **Internacional.** If you are looking for an inexpensive alternative and won't miss the comforts of home, this old Andalucían house near the Casa de Pilatos is for you. The friendly, family-run hotel has a heavy, wrought-iron gate that opens into the central patio-reception area. A white-marble staircase leads to the upstairs bedrooms, which are plain and very simply furnished with twin beds. ✉ *Águilas 17, 41003,* ☎ FAX *95/421–3207. 26 rooms. AE, DC, MC, V.*

Nightlife and the Arts

To find out what's on in Seville, look in the local press, in the *ABC, Correo de Andalucía, Sudoeste,* or *Nueva Andalucía,* or pick up a copy of the free monthly leaflet *El Giraldillo.* It lists classical music and jazz venues, movies (for original version films in English, look for V.O.), theater performances, art exhibitions, and dance events in Seville and all major Andalucían cities. A quarterly leaflet of events at municipal theaters (*Programación Teatros Municipales*) is published by Seville City Hall and is available from the tourist office. You can also call a city information line (☎ 010) for up-to-the-minute information on art shows and cultural events; most operators speak English.

FLAMENCO

Seville has three regular flamenco clubs, patronized more by tourists than by locals. Tickets are sold in most hotels; otherwise, make your own reservations (essential for groups, advisable for everyone in high season) by calling the club during the evening.

El Arenal is in the back room of the picturesque Mesón Dos de Mayo. Here, you have your own table rather than having to sit in rows. ⊠ *Rodo 7,* ☎ *95/421–6492.* ➣ *3,500 ptas., excluding dinner.* ☉ *Daily 9:30 and 11:30.*

El Patio Sevillano caters mainly to tour groups; the show is a mixture of regional Spanish dances (often performed to taped music) and pure flamenco by some outstanding guitarists, singers, and dancers. ⊠ *Paseo de Colón,* ☎ *95/421–4120.* ➣ *3,200 ptas.* ☉ *Daily 10.*

Los Gallos is a small, intimate club in the heart of the Barrio de Santa Cruz that has good, fairly pure flamenco. ⊠ *Plaza Santa Cruz 11,* ☎ *95/421–6981.* ➣ *3,000 ptas.* ☉ *Daily 9 and 11:30.*

MUSIC

A city that has long figured prominently in the opera world, Seville opened its new opera house, **Teatro de la Maestranza** (⊠ Paseo de Colón at Nuñez de Balboa, ☎ 95/422–6573), in late 1991. Be sure to check out what's on here—it's usually the best show in town. Classical concerts and ballet performances are held at the **Teatro Lope de Vega** (⊠ Avda. María Luisa, ☎ 95/459–0855). Classical concerts are also sometimes held at the **Conservatorio Superior de Música** (⊠ Jesús del Gran Poder), in the **cathedral,** and in the church of **San Salvador.** The **Teatro Alameda** (⊠ C. Calatrava 13, ☎ 95/490–0164) puts on a variety of productions, including some children's plays.

Shopping

Seville is the region's main shopping center, and here you'll find all the souvenirs associated with Andalucía. You'll find most of these souvenirs in the Barrio de Santa Cruz and on the streets around the cathedral and Giralda, especially Calle Alemanes.

The main shopping area—for sevillanos, as opposed to tourists—is the Calle Sierpes, and its neighboring streets of Tetuan, Velázquez, Plaza Magdalena, and Plaza Duque. The **Corte Inglés** (⊠ Plaza Duque 10, ☎ 95/422–0931; ⊠ Marques de Nervion, ☎ 95/457–7700) is a well-run department store that stays open during siesta hours.

ANTIQUES

Look along Mateos Gago opposite the Giralda; on Jamerdana in the Barrio de Santa Cruz; and Rodrigo Caro, between Plazas Alianza and Doña Elvira in the Barrio Santa Cruz.

BOOKS

A large assortment of books in English, Spanish, French, and Italian can be found at the American-owned **Librería Vértice** (⊠ San Fernando 30, ☎ 95/421–1654), just by the gates of the university. The **English Bookshop** (⊠ Marqués de Nervion 70, ☎ 95/465–5754) also sells English-language books.

CERAMICS

Martian Ceramics (⊠ Sierpes 74, ☎ 95/421–3413) has a good range of high-quality plates and dishes, especially the flowers-on-white patterns native to Seville. It's a bit touristy, but fairly priced. Try also along Mateos Gago; Romero Murube, between Plaza Triunfo and Plaza

Alianza, on the edge of the barrio; and between Plaza Doña Elvira and Plaza de los Venerables Sacerdotes, also in the barrio.

FANS

Casa Rubio (⊠ Sierpes 56, ☎ 95/422–6872) is Seville's premier fan store, no mean distinction. It has everything from traditional to very modern-looking fans.

FLAMENCO DRESSES

Beware, these are prohibitively expensive. You'll find the cheapest ones in the **Corte Inglés,** or surprisingly, in the souvenir shops on Calle Alemanes. For those interested in serious, and seriously expensive, flamenco dresses and other costumery, **Pardales** (⊠ Cuna 23, ☎ 95/421–3709) is the place to go. Esperanza Pardales Acosta makes most of its clothing to order, but also sells some off-the-rack pieces.

PORCELAIN

El Corte Inglés (☞ *above*) is your best bet.

STREET MARKETS

The **Plaza del Duque** has a daily crafts market; the **El Jueves** flea market is on Calle Feria on Thursday mornings; the **Alameda de Hercules** crafts market takes place on Sunday mornings; and there is a coin and stamp market on the **Plaza del Cabildo** on Sunday mornings.

WOVEN GOODS

You'll find all kinds of handwoven blankets, shawls and embroidered tablecloths at **Artesanía Textil** (⊠ Sierpes 70, ☎ 95/456–2840), a modern shop on a busy shopping street that's supplied by local artisans. **Juan Foronda** (⊠ Plaza Virgen de los Reyes, ☎ 95/421–1856) sells handwoven goods as well as Lladro porcelain and tourist souvenirs.

Carmona

Numbers in the margin correspond to points of interest on the Western Andalucía: Seville and the Guadalquivir Delta map.

31 *32 km (20 mi) east of Seville off NIV.*

Claiming to be one of the oldest inhabited places in Spain where the Phoenicians and the Carthaginians once had settlements, Carmona later became an important town under both the Romans and the Moors. It is the site of the Roman Necropolis where there are approximately 900 tombs dating from the 2nd century BC. Today, Carmona is a quiet Andalucían town occupying a dramatic position on a steep, fortified hill.

As you wander Carmona's ancient, narrow streets, you'll come upon a wealth of Mudéjar and Renaissance churches, medieval gateways, and simple, whitewashed houses of clear Moorish influence, punctuated here and there by an occasional Baroque palace. Pick up a street plan in the parador then set out on a tour of the town.

Stroll down to the **Puerta de Córdoba (Córdoba Gate)** on the eastern edge of town. This old gateway was first built by the Romans around AD 175, then altered by Moorish and Renaissance additions. One of Carmona's chief attractions is in what in Moorish times was the **Alcázar de Arriba (Upper Fortress),** built by the Moors on Roman foundations and later converted by King Pedro the Cruel into a fine Mudéjar palace. Pedro's summer residence was destroyed in 1504 by an earthquake, but the parador (☞ Dining and Lodging, *below*) that now stands amid its ruins commands a breathtaking view.

The Gothic **church of Santa María,** built between 1424 and 1518 stands on the site of the former Great Mosque. Santa María is a contemporary of the Seville cathedral, and it, too, retains its Moorish court-yard, once used for ritual ablutions. The heart of the old town is the **Plaza San Fernando,** whose 17th-century houses show clear Moorish inspiration.

At the **Puerta de Sevilla** (Seville Gate), the imposing **Alcázar de Abajo (Lower Fortress),** another Moorish fortification built on Roman foundations, marks the limits of the old town.

On the edge of the "new town," across the road from the Alcázar de Abajo stands the **church of San Pedro,** which was begun in 1466. Its extraordinary interior is an unbroken mass of sculptures and gilded surfaces, and the church's **Baroque tower,** erected in 1704, is an unabashed imitation of Seville's famous Giralda.

At the far end of town lies Carmona's most outstanding monument, its splendid **Roman Necropolis.** Here, in huge underground chambers, some 900 family tombs dating from the 2nd century BC to the 4th century AD have been chiseled out of the rock. The necropolis's walls, decorated with leaf and bird motifs, are punctuated with niches for burial urns. The most spectacular tombs are the **Elephant Vault** and the **Servilia Tomb,** with colonnaded arches and vaulted side galleries. A museum houses the chambers' archaeological finds. ⊠ *C. Enmedio,* ☎ *95/414–0811.* ⌸ *250 ptas.* ⊙ *Summer, Tues.–Sat. 9–2; winter, Tues.–Fri. 10–2 and 4–6, weekends 10–2.*

Dining and Lodging

$$$$ ✕⊞ **Casa de Carmona.** Located in the historic Lasso de la Vega Palace,
★ the Casa de Carmona is one of the most unique and elegant hotels in Spain. The public rooms are beautifully decorated with antiques, rich fabrics, and museum-quality rugs. Relax in the Arabian-style garden with its fountain and orange trees, or swim in the tiled pool. The rooms are large and luxuriously furnished. The only reminder that you haven't traveled back in time is the digital key card that lets you into your room. ⊠ *Plaza de Lasso, 41410,* ☎ *95/414–3300,* ⅏ *95/414–3752, 30 rooms. Restaurant, bar, pool, sauna, health club, library, laundry service, concierge. AE, DC, MC, V.*

$$$ ✕⊞ **Parador Alcázar del Rey Don Pedro.** This delightful parador com-
★ mands superb views from its hilltop position among the ruins of Pedro the Cruel's summer palace. The public rooms open off a central, Moorish-style patio; the vaulted dining hall and adjacent bar open onto an outdoor terrace that overlooks the sloping garden, where even the pool is tiled in Moorish patterns. The rooms are spacious, with polished tile floors, dark wood furniture, and green and blue woven rugs and bedspreads. Rooms on the top floor have south-facing balconies. ⊠ *Alcázar, 41410,* ☎ *95/414–1010,* ⅏ *95/414–1712, 63 rooms. Restaurant, bar, pool. AE, DC, MC, V.*

Itálica

㉜ *12 km (7 mi) north of Seville, 1 km (⅔ mi) beyond Santiponce.*

This ancient city was founded by Scipio Africanus in 206 BC as a home for veteran soldiers. By the 2nd century AD, it had grown into one of Roman Iberia's most important cities and had given the Roman world two great emperors, Trajan (52–117) and Hadrian (76–138). Itálica once had 10,000 inhabitants who lived in 1,000 dwellings. About 25% of the site has been excavated, and work is still in progress.

The most important monument is the huge, elliptical **amphitheater** that once held 40,000 spectators. You'll find traces of city streets, cisterns, and the floor plans of several villas, some with mosaic floors, though all the best mosaics and statues have been removed to Seville's Archaeological Museum. A small **museum** contains relics found on the site of a fully excavated Roman theater in Santiponce. Itálica was abandoned and plundered as a quarry by the Visigoths, who preferred Seville. It fell into decay around AD 700. *Excavation information,* ☎ *95/599–7376.* 🖾 *250 ptas.* ☉ *Tues.–Sat. 9–5:30, Sun. 9–3.*

Aracena

③③ *90 km (56 mi) northwest of Seville along N630, then N433.*

If you've a day to spare in Seville and want to go somewhere that not too many tourists know about, then drive out to Aracena in the Sierra Morena mountains in the north of Huelva province. The main attraction is the spectacular cave known as the **Gruta de las Maravillas** (Cave of Marvels). There are 12 caverns with stalactites and stalagmites arranged in wonderful patterns, long corridors, and beautiful lakes. ⊠ *Plaza Pozo de Nieves, Pozo de Nieves,* ☎ *959/128355.* 🖾 *800 ptas.* ☉ *Guided tours daily 10:30, 11:30, 12:30, 1:30, 3, 4, 5, and 6.*

Aracena has many fine old mansions that were once the summer homes of wealthy Sevillian families. Be sure to sample a plate of the local serrano ham from nearby Jabugo, famous for its acorn-fed, gray pigs.

OFF THE BEATEN PATH
AROCHE – For something really off the beaten path, continue 40 km (25 mi) west of Aracena on N433 to Aroche, a village of 4,000 people with a 12th-century Arab castle and ancient Gothic and Baroque houses. Here you'll find the **Museo del Santo Rosario (Rosary Museum),** with a collection of more than 1,100 rosaries donated by famous Catholics. ⊠ *Alferez Lobo 7.* 🖾 *100 ptas.* ☉ *Daily 10–1.*

HUELVA PROVINCE

Doñana National Park, Matalascañas, Mazagón, La Rábida, Palos de la Frontera, and Moguer

If you are ready to bid farewell to the hustle and bustle of Seville, nature awaits you in the province of Huelva. One of the largest and richest wildlife refuges in Europe—the Doñana National Park—and pristine beaches along the Costa de la Luz can be found just about an hour's drive from Seville. This is also a land rich in history—you can trace the beginnings of the discovery of the New World here at the monastery of La Rábida and in Palos de la Frontera. From Seville, turn off the Seville-Huelva highway, drive through Almonte and El Rocío, scene of the famous Whitsuntide pilgrimage to the Virgin of the Dew, and you'll come to the Information Center of La Rocina.

Parque Nacional de Doñana (Doñana National Park)

③④ *100 km (62 mi) southwest of Seville.*

One of Europe's last corners of wilderness, these wetlands which lie beside the Guadalquivir estuary constitute one of Spain's largest national parks. They cover an area of 188,000 acres, 64 km/40 mi by 14½ km/9 mi, and are a paradise for nature lovers, especially birdwatchers. The park sits on the migratory route from Africa to Europe and is the winter home and breeding ground for as many as 150 species of rare birds. Their habitats range from beaches and shifting sand dunes to marshes, dense brushwood, and sandy hillsides of pine and cork oak.

Two of Europe's most endangered species, the imperial eagle and the lynx, make their homes here. Kestrels, kites and buzzards, egrets, storks, and spoonbills breed among the cork oaks. The marshlands are also home to one of Europe's last remaining colonies of flamingos. More than 14,000 come here to nest each February.

At **La Rocina Information Center** (☎ 959/442340), less than a mile from El Rocío, you can enjoy the many species of birds along a 2-km (1¼-mi) footpath. This center also offers four observatories and is open daily 8–7. A short distance away, an exhibition at the **Acebrón Palace** explains the park's ecosystems; the exhibition is open daily 8–7 (last entrance is one hour before closing). Two kilometers (1¼ miles) before Matalascañas, you'll find the park's main **Reception and Interpretation Center** at Acebuche (☎ 959/448711), which is open daily 8–7. Jeep tours of the park, which must be reserved in advance, start from here. Tours last four hours, cost 2,500 ptas., and take you on a 70-km/43-mi route across beaches, sand dunes, marshes, and scrub. Off-season (November–February), you can usually book a tour with just a day's notice; at other times, book as long in advance as possible (☞ Guided Tours *in* Seville and Western Andalucía A to Z, *below*).

Matalascañas

㉟ *3 km (2 mi) south of Acebuche, main reception center at Doñana; 85 km (53 mi) southwest of Seville.*

This town's close proximity to the main reception center (Acebuche) at Doñana makes it a convenient spot for park visitors to spend the night. There are also some nice beaches for those wishing to relax in the sun; for those looking for more excitement, the ocean waters here are a haven for windsurfers and other watersport enthusiasts.

Dining and Lodging

$$ ✕🏨 **El Cortijo.** With two floors centered around a fountain courtyard, this typical Andalucían hotel attracts a lot of organized tour groups visiting the park. The restaurant here is also quite good, serving a variety of native dishes. ⊠ *Sector E, Parcelas 15,* ☎ *959/448570,* FAX *959/430258. 53 rooms. Restaurant, bar, pool, tennis courts. AE, MC, V.*

$$ 🏨 **Tierra Mar.** If you want to stay longer to explore the Doñana park, you can find lodging nearby at the Tierra Mar. ⊠ *Matalascañas Parc. 120 Sector M,* ☎ *959/440300,* FAX *959/440720. 253 rooms. Café, pool, sauna, tennis courts. AE, DC, MC, V. Closed Nov.–Feb.*

Mazagón

㊱ *22 km (14 mi) northwest of Matalascañas.*

Although there is not much to see or do in this coastal town, the parador here makes a nice base from which to tour the surrounding areas of La Rábida, Palos de la Frontera, and Moguer. Or you can enjoy the beautiful beach, among the nicest in the region.

Dining and Lodging

$$$ ✕🏨 **Parador Cristóbal Colón.** This peaceful, modern parador, 3 km/2 mi southeast of Mazagón, stands on a cliff surrounded by pine groves and overlooks a sandy beach. The rooms are all well-equipped; most have balconies overlooking the garden. Traditional Andalucían dishes and local seafood specialties, like stuffed baby squid, are served in the restaurant. ⊠ *Carretera Huelva-Matalascañas Km. 24, 21130,* ☎

959/536300, FAX *959/536228. 43 rooms. Restaurant, bar, pool, tennis courts, beach. AE, DC, MC, V.*

La Rábida★

㊲ *30 km (19 mi) northwest of Doñana, 8 km (5 mi) northwest of Mazagón.*

You may want to extend your Doñana tour to include a visit to the **monastery** of La Rábida, "birthplace of America." This place was inundated with tourists in 1992, the 500th anniversary of Columbus's first trip to the New World. In 1485 Columbus came from Portugal with his son Diego to stay in this Gothic Mudéjar monastery. Here, he discussed his theories with friars Antonio de Marchena and Juan Pérez, who interceded on his behalf with Queen Isabella. In its church, which dates from the early 1400s, you'll find a much-venerated **14th-century statue of the Virgen de los Milagros** (Virgin of Miracles). The **frescoes** in the gatehouse were painted by Daniel Vázquez Díaz in 1930. ☎ *959/350411.* ✉ *Free; donations accepted.* ☉ *Tues.–Sun. 10–1 and 4–6:15 (until 7 in summer).*

Palos de la Frontera

㊳ *4 km (2½ mi) northeast of La Rábida, 12 km (7 mi) northeast of Mazagón.*

On August 2, 1492, Columbus's three caravels, the *Pinta*, the *Niña*, and the *Santa María*, set sail from here. Most of his crew were men of Palos and neighboring Moguer. Here, you can see the **church of San Jorge** (1473), at whose door the royal letter ordering the levy of the crew and equipment of the caravels was read aloud; and the Fontanilla, the well from which the caravels took their water supplies.

Moguer

㊴ *12 km (7 mi) northeast of Palos de la Frontera.*

The inhabitants of this old port town now spend more time growing strawberries than they do in seafaring, as you'll see from the surrounding fields. Visit the **Monastery of Santa Clara,** which dates from 1337. ✉ *250 ptas.* ☉ *Tues.–Sat. 11–1 and 4:30–6:30, Sun. 11–1.*

Also head for the **home of Nobel Prize–winning poet Juan Ramón Jiménez,** author of the much-loved *Platero y Yo.* ✉ *C. Nueva.* ✉ *250 ptas.* ☉ *Mon.–Sat. 10–2 and 4–8.*

PROVINCE OF CÁDIZ

Jerez de la Frontera, Arcos de la Frontera, Sanlúcar de Barrameda, Puerto de Santa María, and Cádiz

Through winding roads and varying landscapes, ranging from flat and barren to seemingly endless manzanilla vineyards, this area will take you for a different kind of trip—one which goes back in time. Throughout the province, *los pueblos blancos* (white villages) provide stiking contrasts against the terrain, especially at Arcos de la Frontera, where the village sits dramatically on a crag overlooking the gorge of the Guadalete River. In Jerez, you can savor the internationally famous sherry, or delight in the skill of the pure-bred Carthusian horses. Finally, in

Cádiz, take in about 3000 years of history, as this is one of the oldest, continuously inhabited cities of the western world.

Jerez de la Frontera

40 *97 km (60 mi) south of Seville.*

Jerez, the home of sherry, is surrounded by immense vineyards of chalky soil, whose Palomino grapes have funded a host of churches and noble mansions. An hour's stroll around the center is all you'll need to get a feel for this small, unprepossessing town. May and September are the most exciting times to visit Jerez, when spectacular fiestas transform this otherwise modest town. In early May Jerez's *Feria del Caballo* (Horse Fair) fills the streets with carriages and riders, and pure-breds from the School of Equestrian Art are entered in races and dressage displays. September sees the celebration of the Vintage Festival, when the grapes are blessed on the steps of the cathedral.

The 12th-century **Alcázar** was once the residence of the caliph of Seville. The Moorish mosque inside was later transformed into a catholic church by Alfonso the Wise. The terrace of the Alcázar provides views down on the cathedral ⊠ *Alameda Vieja.* ☉ *Mon.– Fri. 10–2 and 4–6, Sat. 10–1:30.*

Visit the **cathedral,** with its octagonal cupola and separate bell tower. ⊠ *Plaza del Arroyo.* ☉ *Weekdays 6–8, Sat. 6–9, Sun. 11–2 and 6:30–8:30.*

On the **Plaza de la Asunción,** one of Jerez's most intimate squares, you'll find the Mudéjar **church of San Dionisio** and the ornate **Cabildo Municipal** (City Hall), with a lovely Plateresque facade (1575).

Jerez also has an interesting and unusual museum devoted to clocks: the **Museo de los Relojes (Clock Museum).** ⊠ *C. Cervantes,* ☎ *956/182100.* 🔳 *300 ptas.* ☉ *Fri., Sat., and Mon.–Wed. 10–2; Thurs. 9:30–3.*

The **Centro Andaluz de Flamenco (Flamenco Center)** has frequent showings of Spanish-language movies on flamenco. ⊠ *Palacio Pemartín, on Plaza San Juan* ☎ *956/349265.* 🔳 *Free.* ☉ *Weekdays 10–2, plus Tues. 5–7.*

Names such as González Byass, Domecq, Harvey, Sandeman, and Williams are inextricably linked with Jerez, and the word *sherry,* first used in Great Britain in 1608, is an English corruption of the town's old Moorish name of Xeres. Both sherry and horses are very much the domain of Jerez's Anglo-Spanish aristocracy, whose Catholic ancestors came here from England two or three centuries ago.

★ At any one time there are more than a million barrels of sherry maturing in Jerez's vast aboveground wine cellars. If you visit a **bodega,** the guide will explain the *solera* method of blending old wine with new and the importance of the *flor* (a sort of yeast) in determining the kind of sherry. Afterward you'll be able to sample generous amounts of pale, dry fino; nutty amontillado; or rich, deep oloroso. Domecq is Jerez's oldest bodega, founded in 1730; but if you only have time for one, tour the prestigious González Byass, home of the famous Tío Pepe.

★ ☾ The **Real Escuela Andaluza del Arte Ecuestre** (Royal Andalusian School of Equestrian Art) stands on the grounds of the Recreo de las Cadenas, a splendid 19th-century palace. The establishment of this prestigious school was masterminded by Alvaro Domecq in the 1970s. Every Thursday the Cartujana horses, a breed created from a cross between the native Andalucían workhorse and the Arabian, and skilled riders in 18th-century riding costume demonstrate intricate dressage techniques and jumping in the spectacular show, *Como Bailan los Caballos Andaluces.* ⊠ *Avda. Duque de Abrantes,* ☎ *956/311111.* ☑ *Numbered seats 1,750 ptas., unnumbered seats 1,425 ptas.* ⊙ *Thurs. noon–1:30, box office opens 11 (go early).*

Throughout the rest of the week you can visit the stables and tack room and watch the horses being schooled along with rehearsals for the show. ☑ *425 ptas.* ⊙ *Mon.–Wed. and Fri. 11–1.*

Bullfighting

Jerez's bullring is situated on Calle Circo, northeast of the city center. Tickets are sold at the official ticket office on Calle Porvera (☎ 956/343764), although there are now only about five bullfights held each year, during May and October.

Dining and Lodging

$$$ ✕ **Gaitán.** This restaurant, within walking distance of the riding school, has white walls and brick arches decorated with colorful, ceramic plates and photos of famous diners. It's crowded with businesspeople at lunchtime. The menu is Andalucían with a few Basque dishes. When in season, *setas* (wild mushrooms) make a delicious starter. ⊠ *Gaitán 3,* ☎ *956/345859. AE, DC, MC, V. No dinner Sun.*

$$–$$$ ✕ **Venta Antonio.** Crowds come from far and wide to dine in this humble inn on the outskirts of Jerez. The decor is functional, but what counts is the superb, fresh seafood cooked in top-quality olive oil. Here you can try the specialties of the Bay of Cádiz, such as *sopa de mariscos* (shellfish soup) for starters and *bogavantes de Sanlúcar* (succulent local lobster) for your entrée. ⊠ *Carretera de Sanlúcar, Km 5,* ☎ *956/140535. AE, DC, MC, V.*

$$ ✕ **Tendido 6.** This restaurant is near the bullring, opposite Gate 6— hence its name. The tables, set in an enclosed patio decorated with bullfight posters, are draped with bright red tablecloths. The menu lists all the Spanish standbys: *jamón serrano* (cured ham), *gambas al ajillo* (garlic shrimp), and *tarta de almendra* (almond tart). ⊠ *Circo 10,* ☎ *956/344835. AE, DC, MC, V. Closed Sun.*

$–$$ ✕ **La Posada.** The tiny, white-walled dining room, decorated with iron grillwork, has only half a dozen tables. It is tucked away behind a bar in the side streets of central Jerez, just a three-minute walk from the Hotel Ávila. The menu is small, but both the meat and the fish dishes are well prepared. Let the chef advise you on the daily specials. ⊠ *Arboledilla 2,* ☎ *956/337474. AE, MC, V. No dinner Sat. Closed Sun.*

$$$ ✕🏠 **Jerez.** This luxury hotel is set in a low, white, three-story building in the residential neighborhood north of town. The bar and elegant El Cartujano restaurant overlook the sun terrace, the large, outdoor pool and a big, leafy garden. Public rooms are light and airy. The best rooms overlook the pool and garden; back rooms face the tennis courts and parking lot. ⊠ *Avda. Alvaro Domecq 35, 11405,* ☎ *956/300600,* ℻ *956/305001. 121 rooms, 4 suites. Restaurant, bar, pool, tennis courts. AE, DC, MC, V.*

$$$ ✕🏠 **Royal Sherry Park.** This gleaming, modern hotel is set back from
★ the road in an unusually large, tree-filled garden. It is designed around several patios filled with exotic foliage, and modern paintings decorate its light, sunny hallways. The rooms are bright and airy, and most have balconies overlooking the garden. ⊠ *Avda. Alvaro Domecq 11, 11405,* ☎ *956/303011,* ℻ *956/311300. 173 rooms. Restaurant, coffee shop, bar, pool, meeting rooms. AE, DC, MC, V.*

$$ ✕🏠 **Avenida Jerez.** Opposite the Royal Sherry Park, this modern hotel has light, airy, and sunny rooms with hard-wood floors and a rich blue

decor. All rooms also have VCRs. Ask for a room at the back; those at the front are close to the road and can be noisy despite double glazing. ✉ *Avda. Alvaro Domecq 10, 11405,* ☎ *956/347411,* FAX *956/337296. 95 rooms. Coffee shop, bar. AE, DC, MC, V.*

$–$$ ⊡ **Ávila.** This friendly hotel in a side street off Calle Arcos offers good-value, central accommodations. A television lounge and a small bar and breakfast room open off the lobby. The rooms have basic furnishings and tile floors. ✉ *Ávila 3, 11401,* ☎ *956/334808,* FAX *956/336807. 32 rooms. Bar, breakfast room. AE, DC, MC, V.*

Racing
Formula One Grand Prix car and motorcycle races are held at the race circuit at Jerez de la Frontera. Late September and early October see the Formula One Tío Pepe Grand Prix. For information, call the Circuit Office (☎ 956/308016) or check with the tourist office.

Shopping
In this town famous for its horses, **Duarte** (✉ Larga 15, ☎ 956/342751) is the most famous saddle shop, sending beautifully wrought leather all over the world, including to the British royal family. It's worth a visit even for tourists, who can choose from all kinds of other smaller, but beautifully worked, leather items. You can also find some nice wicker and ceramic pieces along Calle Corredera and Calle Bodegas.

Arcos de la Frontera★

④ *31 km (19 mi) east of Jerez.*

Perched dramatically on a wild crag crowned by a castle, this white village overlooks the gorge of the Guadalete River. On the main square, the Plaza de España, the **Church of Santa María** is a fascinating blend of architectural styles: Romanesque, Gothic, and Mudéjar, with a Platersque doorway, a Renaissance retablo, and a 17th-century Baroque choir.

Dining and Lodging

$$$ ✕⊡ **Parador Casa del Corregidor.** From the semicircular terrace of this
★ parador on Arcos's main square, you can see both Arcos castle and the rolling valley of the Guadalete River. Charles de Gaulle wrote part of his memoirs while staying here. Among the public rooms are a bar decorated with ceramic tiles and bullfight pictures, a panoramic restaurant that opens onto the terrace, and an enclosed patio. Rooms are furnished in traditional parador style. Local dishes in the restaurant include *berenjenas arcenses* (spicy eggplant with ham and chorizo). ✉ *Plaza del Cabildo, 11630,* ☎ *956/700500,* FAX *956/701116. 24 rooms. Restaurant, bar. AE, DC, MC, V.*

$$–$$$ ✕⊡ **Cortijo Faín.** This resort hotel is set in a 17th-century farmhouse on a ranch 3 km (2 mi) southeast of Arcos. The old *cortijo* (farm-estate) is surrounded by olive groves and enclosed in high, white walls covered in bougainvillea. The atmosphere is personal and intimate. Stay in one of the two suites which have their own fireplace. Kick back and hit the books—the ranch has an outstanding 10,000-volume library. Advance reservations are essential. ✉ *Carretera de Algar, Km 3, 11630,* ☎ FAX *956/701167. 7 suites, 1 double room. Restaurant, pool, horseback riding, library, meeting rooms. AE, MC, V.*

$ ✕⊡ **El Convento.** An inexpensive alternative, this tiny hotel is in part of an old convent. Perched on top of the cliff right behind the parador, it shares the same splendid view. There are just eight rooms and a four-table restaurant with a large, sunny patio. Dishes in the restaurant are lovingly prepared and often include local game specialties, such as *perdiz* *estofado* (partridge stew). Save room for dessert—pastries are made from old convent recipes. ☒ *Maldonado 2, 11630,* ☎ 🖷 *956/702333. 8 rooms. Restaurant. AE, DC, MC, V.*

Sanlúcar de Barrameda

㊷ *24 km (15 mi) west of Jerez.*

In 1498, Columbus sailed from here on his third voyage to the Americas. Twenty years later, Magellan steered his ships out of the same harbor on the start of his world-circling exploit. Today this unspoiled fishing town is primarily known for its *langostinos* (giant shrimp) and manzanilla. From its *puerto pesquero* (fishing port), 4 km/2½ mi north of the town center, there's a fine view of fishing boats and the pine trees of the Doñana on the opposite bank of the Guadalquivir. Sandy beaches extend along Sanlúcar's southern promontory to Chipiona, where the Roman general Scipio Africanus built a beacon tower.

Dining

$$$ ✕ **Bigote.** On the Bajo de Guía beach, this fish restaurant is colorful and informal. ☒ *Bajo de Guía,* ☎ *956/362696 or 956/363242. AE, DC, MC, V. Closed Sun.*

Puerto de Santa María ★

㊸ *12 km (7 mi) southwest of Jerez, 17 km (11 mi) north of Cádiz.*

On the northern shores of the Bay of Cádiz, this attractive, if somewhat dilapidated, small fishing port displays an array of white houses with peeling facades and floor-length, green grilles covering their doors and windows. The town is dominated by the sherry and brandy bodegas of Terry and Osborne. Columbus once lived in a house on the square that bears his name (Cristóbal Colón) and at Calle Palacios 57, Washington Irving spent the autumn of 1828.

NEED A BREAK? On NIV, just north of Puerto de Santa María, the **AquaSherry aquapark** provides opportunities for splashers.

Bars

The *marisco* (seafood) bars along the *Ribera del Marisco* (Seafood Way) constitute Puerto Santa María's current claim to fame. **Casa Paco** and neighboring **Bar Salva** are two of the most popular.

Dining and Lodging

$$$ ✕ **El Faro.** This name may sound familiar if you've already been to Cádiz. This branch is run by Gonzalo's son. ☒ *Carretera de Rota, Km 0.5,* ☎ *956/858003 or 956/870952. AE, DC, MC, V. No dinner Sun. Sept.–July.*

$$ ✕ **María Regina.** The new owners of this restaurant have given it an Italian flavor that is once again drawing enthusiastic crowds of locals. In winter, a fireplace warms the dining room; in summer, you can eat on an outdoor terrace. ☒ *Cáceres (Playa de Valdelagrana),* ☎ *956/561296. AE, MC, V.*

$–$$ ✕ **El Patio.** Tucked away one block behind the Ribera del Marisco, this pretty restaurant is built around an 18th-century patio. Colorful ceramic plates and potted plants decorate the dining room. The menu combines local seafood from the Bay of Cádiz with Andalucían dishes like *rabo de toro* (oxtail). The homemade desserts are especially good. ☒ *Plaza de la Herrería,* ☎ *956/540506. AE, DC, MC, V.*

$$$ ✕🖪 **Monasterio de San Miguel.** This monastery, which dates to 1733, ★ is in the heart of town, a few blocks from the harbor. There's nothing

spartan about the former cells, now air-conditioned rooms with all the modern conveniences. The Baroque church is a concert auditorium, and the cloister gardens provide a peaceful refuge for visitors. Beamed ceilings, polished marble floors, and huge, brass lamps help retain the 18th-century atmosphere. ✉ *Monasterio de San Miguel, 11500,* ☎ *956/540440,* FAX *956/542604. 177 rooms. Restaurant, bar, pool, squash. AE, DC, MC, V.*

Nightlife and the Arts

The **Casino Bahía de Cádiz,** on the road between Jerez and Puerto de Santa María, is the only casino in this part of Andalucía. You can play the usual range of games, and there's a restaurant and discotheque. You must present your passport to enter. ✉ *NIV, Km 650,* ☎ *956/871042.* 🎫 *250 ptas.* ☉ *Daily 7 PM–4 AM (until 6 AM weekends).*

Sailing

There are yacht clubs and marinas in most towns on and around the Bay of Cádiz. About 50 regattas are held each year for all kinds of boats. For information on sailing, inquire at the local tourist office. The region's newest marina is **Puerto Sherry** (☎ 956/870203), on the Bay of Cádiz, near Puerto de Santa María.

Cádiz ★

④ *32 km (20 mi) southwest of Jerez, 149 km (93 mi) southwest of Seville.*

Spaniards flock here in February to revel in its famous Carnival celebrations, but as yet, few foreigners have discovered the real charm of this city. Founded as Gadir by Phoenician traders in 1100 BC, Cádiz, surrounded on three sides by the Atlantic Ocean, claims to be the oldest, continuously inhabited city in the Western world. Here Hannibal lived and Julius Caesar first held public office.

After centuries of decline during the Middle Ages and under Moorish rule, Cádiz regained its commercial importance following the discovery of America. Columbus set out from here on his second voyage, and Cádiz later became the home base of the Spanish fleet. Its merchants competed fiercely with those of Seville. In the 18th century, when the river to Seville silted up, Cádiz took over the monopoly of New World trade and became the wealthiest port in Western Europe. Most of its buildings date from this period, and the cathedral was begun then, built with gold and silver brought from the New World.

The old city is African in appearance and immensely intriguing—a cluster of narrow streets opening onto charming, small squares. The golden cupola of the cathedral looms above low, white houses, and the whole place has a slightly dilapidated air. In an hour's walk around the headlands, you'll visit the entire old town and pass through some enchanting parks with fine views of the bay.

You might begin your explorations in the Plaza de Mina, a large, leafy square with palm trees and plenty of benches for relaxation. On the square's western flank, the ornamental facade of the College of Architects is especially beautiful. On the east side, you'll find the **Museo de Bellas Artes y Arqueología (Fine Arts and Archaeology Museum),** well worth visiting for its works by Murillo and Alonso Cano and the *Four Evangelists* and set of saints by Zurbarán, which have much in common with his masterpieces at Guadalupe in Extremadura. ✉ *Plaza de Mina,* ☎ *956/212281.* 🎫 *250 ptas.* ☉ *Tues.–Sun. 9:30–2.*

A few blocks west of the Plaza de Mina is the **Oratorio de la Santa Cueva,** an oval 18th-century chapel that contains three frescoes by Goya. ✉ *C. Rosario,* ☎ *956/222262.* 🎫 *50 ptas.* ☉ *Weekdays 10–1.*

Don't forget to look up while walking the steets around here—the facades are quite splendid. Near another impressive square, the Plaza de San Antonio, you'll find the **Oratorio de San Felipe Neri.** This church was the scene of the declaration of Spain's first liberal constitution in 1812, and here the Cortes of Cádiz met when the rest of Spain was subjected to the rule of Napoleon's brother, Joseph Bonaparte—more popularly known as Pepe Botella for his love of the bottle. On the main altar is an Immaculate Conception by Murillo, the great Sevillian artist who in 1682 fell to his death from a scaffolding while working on his Mystic Marriage of St. Catherine in the Chapel of Santa Catalina in Cádiz. ☒ *Santa Inés,* ☎ *956/211612.* ☞ *Free.* ☉ *Daily 8:30–10 and 7:30–10.*

Next door to the Oratorio de San Felipe Neri, the small but pleasant **Museo Histórico Municipal (Municipal Museum)** has a 19th-century mural depicting the establishment of the Constitution of 1812. Its real showpiece is a fascinating ivory and mahogany model of the city made in 1779, which depicts in minute detail all the streets and buildings much as they are now. ☒ *Santa Inés,* ☎ *956/221788.* ☞ *Free.* ☉ *Tues.–Fri. 9–1 and 5–8 (4–7 in winter), weekends 9–1.*

Four blocks to the west of Santa Inés is the Plaza Manuel de Falla, overlooked by an amazing neo-Mudéjar red-brick building, the **Gran Teatro Manuel de Falla.** The interior is impressive as well, if you have time to catch a show while you're in town. Check with the tourist office to find out about events. There's a model of this unusual theater in the nearby parador, the Atlántico (☞ Dining and Lodging, *below*).

The **cathedral,** with its gold dome and Baroque facade, was begun in 1722, when Cádiz was at the height of its power. The Cádiz-born composer Manuel de Falla, who died in 1946 at the age of 70, is buried in the crypt. The cathedral museum, on Calle Acero, overflows with gold, silver, and precious jewels brought from the New World. One of its most priceless possessions in Enrique de Arfe's processional cross, which is carried in the Corpus Christi parades. ☒ *Plaza Cathedral, museum* ☎ *956/286154.* ☞ *Cathedral free, museum 250 ptas.* ☉ *Service Sat. 6:30, Sun. noon and 6; museum Tues.–Sat. 10–12:30.*

The impressive **Ayuntamiento (City Hall)** overlooks the Plaza San Juan de Diós, one of the city's liveliest hubs. Built in two parts, in 1799 and 1861, the building is attractively illuminated at night.

The **Plaza San Francisco,** near the Ayuntamiento and surrounded by houses painted white and yellow, is a pretty square filled with orange trees and beautiful street lamps. It's especially lively during paseos.

Dining and Lodging

$$$ ✕ **El Faro.** Gonzalo Córdoba's restaurant, located in a fishing quarter, ★ justly deserves its fame as the best restaurant in the province. On the outside it's one of many low, white houses decorated with bright blue flowerpots. Inside the decor is warm and inviting, with half-tile walls, glass lanterns, oil paintings, and photos of old Cádiz. Hams hang from the ceiling of the bar, and the counter is piled high with oranges. Fish and seafood dominate the menu, but there are plenty of alternatives, such as *cebón al queso de cabrales* (venison in blue cheese sauce). ☒ *San Felix 15,* ☎ *956/211068. AE, DC, MC, V.*

$$$ ✕▦ **Atlántico.** This parador stands in a privileged position on the headland overlooking the bay. Its spacious public rooms have gleaming marble floors, and, in a small outdoor patio, chairs and tables are set around a fountain. The cheerful, bright-green bar, decorated with ceramic tiles and bullfight posters, is a popular meeting place for Cádiz

society. Most of the rooms have small balconies facing the sea. ⊠ *Parque Genovés 9, 11002,* ☎ *956/226905,* ⅢX *956/214582. 149 rooms. Restaurant, bar, pool. AE, DC, MC, V.*

$$ 🕮 **Francia y Paris.** The advantage of this hotel is its central location on a pretty pedestrian square in the heart of the old town. The house has a rather boring, modern interior that includes a vast lobby, a big sitting room, and a small bar and breakfast room (no other meals). The rooms are simple, and some have small balconies facing the square. ⊠ *Plaza San Francisco 2, 11004,* ☎ *956/222348,* ⅢX *956/222431. 57 rooms. Bar, breakfast room. AE, DC, MC, V.*

Nightlife and the Arts
The major venue for all cultural events in **Cádiz** is the **Gran Teatro Manuel de Falla** (⊠ Plaza de Falla, ☎ 956/220828).

Shopping
In Cádiz, you'll find all the usual Andalucían handicrafts, especially ceramics and wicker, but no specialized local crafts. **Belle Epoque** (⊠ Antonio Lopez 2, ☎ 956/226810) is one of Cádiz's better—and more reasonably priced—antiques stores, specializing in furniture. **Casa Rodríguez** (⊠ Enrique de las Marinas 1, ☎ 956/213104) displays an extensive selection of all kinds of antiques in a large showroom in one of Cádiz's older houses.

SEVILLE AND WESTERN ANDALUCÍA A TO Z

Arriving and Departing

By Bus
Long-distance bus services connect Seville with Madrid and with Cáceres, Mérida, and Badajoz in Extremadura and Córdoba, Granada, Málaga, Ronda, and Huelva in Andalucía. Through buses take the coastal route from Granada, Málaga, and Marbella to Cádiz. Buses from Ronda run to Arcos, Jerez, and Cádiz. Bus services throughout Andalucía, and between Extremadura and Seville, tend to be more frequent and convenient than trains.

By Car
The main road into the region from Madrid is the NIV highway through Córdoba. It has recently been made into a four-lane *autovía,* but it's one of Spain's busiest roads, and trucks can cause delays. From Granada or Málaga, head for Antequera; then take N334 by way of Osuna to Seville. Several highways in and around Seville were improved and rebuilt in connection with 1992's International Exposition; road trips from Córdoba, Granada, and the Costa del Sol by way of Ronda have all become far quicker and more pleasant as a result. From the Costa del Sol, the coastal N340 highway is well paved and rarely very busy beyond Algeciras.

By Plane
The region's main airport is Seville's **San Pablo Airport** (☎ 95/444–9000), 12 km/7½ mi east of the city on NIV to Córdoba. It has international flights from Amsterdam, Brussels, Frankfurt, London, and Paris; and domestic flights from Madrid, Barcelona, Valencia, and other major cities. Seville's **Iberia** office is on Almirante Lobo 2 (☎ 95/422–8901 or 901/333111). There is no bus or train service to the airport; you'll have to take a taxi.

The region's other airport is Jerez de la Frontera's **Aeropuerto de la Parra** (☏ 956/150000), 7 km/4½ mi from Jerez on the road to Seville. It has domestic flights only, on **Aviaco,** which is owned by Iberia Airlines (✉ airport, ☏ 956/150010). Aviaco has flights to Madrid, Barcelona, Valencia-Palma de Mallorca, and Zaragoza.

By Train

Seville, Jerez, and Cádiz all lie on the main rail line between Madrid and the southwest corner of Spain. From Madrid there are approximately six trains a day, via Córdoba, to Seville; three of these continue on to Jerez and Cádiz. RENFE also operates the high-speed AVE train between Madrid and Seville; it costs more than regular trains but it makes the journey in about 2 hours, and has become the most popular mode of transportation between the two cities. From Granada, Málaga, Ronda, and Algeciras, trains run to Seville by way of Bobadilla junction, where, more often than not, you have to change.

Crime

WARNING: With chronic high unemployment, Seville and Cádiz have developed a bad reputation for petty crime, such as purse snatching and thefts from parked cars, even the occasional robbery. Drive with your car doors locked; lock all your luggage out of sight in the trunk; never leave *anything* in a parked car; and keep a wary eye on scooter riders, who have been known to snatch purses or even smash the windows of moving cars. Take only a small amount of cash and just one credit card out with you. Leave your passport, traveler's checks, and other credit cards in the hotel safe, and avoid carrying purses and expensive cameras or wearing valuable jewelry.

Getting Around

By Bus

There are services connecting all the towns and villages in the region. **Cádiz** has two bus depots: **Comes** (✉ Plaza Hispanidad, ☏ 956/211763 or 956/224271) runs buses to most destinations in Andalucía; **Los Amarillos** (✉ Avda. Ramón de Carranza 31, ☏ 956/285852) runs services to Jerez, Seville, and Córdoba and to Puerto de Santa María, Sanlúcar de Barrameda, and Chipiona. **Jerez** bus station is on the Plaza Madre de Dios, and is served by two companies: La Valenciana (☏ 956/341063) and Los Amarillos (☏ 956/347844). In **Seville,** there are now two bus stations. The older one is the **Estación del Prado de San Sebastián** (✉ Prado de San Sebastián, ☏ 95/441–7111), just off the Plaza de San Sebastián between Manuel Vázquez Sagastizabal and José María Osborne; buses from here serve points to the west and northwest. The second, a glittering, modern terminal on the banks of the Guadalquivir River downtown, is the **Estación Plaza de Armas** (✉ Arjona next to east end of Cachorro Bridge, ☏ 95/490–8040). This station serves central and eastern Spain. Check with the tourist office to make sure which station you need.

By Car

Driving in the region is easy—the terrain is mostly flat or gently rolling hills, and the roads are straight. From Seville to Jerez de la Frontera and Cádiz, you can choose between NIV and the slightly faster A4 toll road. The only access by road to the Coto Doñana is to take the A49 Seville-Huelva highway, exit for Almonte/Bollullos del Condado, and then follow the signs for El Rocío and Matalascañas. Getting into and out of Seville, long a nightmarishly confusing ordeal, has become far easier as a result of a new ring road and several altered accesses, although getting around the city by car is still trying. Try to avoid the

7:15–8:30 PM rush hour in Seville and Cádiz; the lunchtime rush hour around 2–3 PM can be another problem. Don't try taking a car to Cádiz at Carnival time (pre-Lent) or to Seville during Holy Week or the April Fair—processions close most of the streets to traffic. *See* Crime, *above,* for a safety warning about driving and parking in Seville).

By Train

A dozen or more local trains each day connect Cádiz with Puerto de Santa María, Jerez de la Frontera, and Seville. Journey time from Cádiz to Seville is 1½ to 2 hours. There are no trains to the Coto Doñana, Sanlúcar de Barrameda, or Arcos de la Frontera or between Cádiz and the Costa del Sol.

Cádiz station is on Plaza de Sevilla near the docks; **Jerez** station is on Plaza de la Estación, off Diego Fernández Herrera, in the east of town. For information regarding train schedules for the entire province of **Cádiz,** call RENFE in **Cádiz** (☎ 956/254301). In **Seville,** the sprawling new Santa Justa station, built in conjuction with Expo '92, is on Avenida Kansas City. For information and reservations, contact the downtown RENFE Office (✉ Zaragoza 29, ☎ 95/454–0202).

Contacts and Resources

Boating

The Guadalquivir has many options for boating aficionados: paddleboats or canoes (ask at the tourist office or on the riverbank near the Torre del Oro); or **Cruceros Turísticos Torre del Oro** (✉ Paseo Marqués de Contadero beside Torre del Oro, ☎ 95/421–1396 or 95/456–1692), which has hourly river cruises. The cost is 1,000 pesetas.

Consulates

Canada (✉ Avda. Constitución 302–4, Seville, ☎ 95/422–9413). **United Kingdom** (✉ Plaza Nueva 8, Seville, ☎ 95/422–8874/75). **United States** (✉ Paseo de las Delicias 7, Seville, ☎ 95/423–1883, 95/423–1884, or 95/423–1885).

Emergencies

Police: Cádiz (✉ Avda. de Andalucía 28, ☎ 956/286111), **Jerez de la Frontera** (✉ Plaza de Silos, ☎ 091), **Seville** (✉ Plaza de la Concordia 1, ☎ 95/422–8840 or 95/422–8849). **Ambulance: Seville** (☎ 061).

Guided Tours

In Seville, any of the following organizations can put you in touch with qualified English-speaking guides: **Asociación Provincial de Informadores Turísticos** (✉ Glorieta de Palacio de Congresos, Sevilla, ☎ 95/425–5957), **Guidetour** (✉ Lope de Rueda 13, ☎ 95/422–2374/2375), and **ITA** (✉ Santa Teresa 1, ☎ 95/422–4641). For English-speaking local guides in Cádiz or Jerez, contact the tourist office.

DOÑANA NATIONAL PARK

Jeep tours of the reserve depart twice daily (Tuesday–Sun. 8:30 and 3) from the park's reception center, 2 km/1 mi from Matalascañas. Tours (maximum 125 people) should be booked well in advance. Passengers can often be collected from hotels in Matalascañas. Write or call Parque Nacional de Doñana (✉ Cooperativa Marisma del Rocío, Centro de Recepción, 21760 Matalascañas, Huelva, ☎ 959/430211).

SHERRY BODEGAS

Tours can be arranged from Seville and Cádiz. In **Jerez,** bodegas are open to visitors, except during Aug. and some of Sept. for harvest. Tours, which include a tasting of brandy and sherry, should be booked in advance; English-speaking guides are usually available. Call the bodega and ask for Public Relations: Domecq (☎ 956/151500), with free admission; González Byass (☎ 956/340000), which charges 350 pesetas on weekdays, 450 pesetas on weekends; and Williams (☎ 956/346539), which charges 300 pesetas; reservations are essential for all three. Harvey (☎ 956/151030), which charges 200 pesetas, and Wisdom (☎ 956/184306), which charges 250 pesetas, have differing schedules; call first or check with the Jerez tourist office.

To visit bodegas in **Puerto de Santa María,** contact Osborne (✉ Fernán Caballero 3, ☎ 956/855211) or Terry (✉ Santa Trinidad, ☎ 956/483000). Ask locally for other bodegas in **Sanlúcar de Barrameda** and **Lebrija.** Tours should be booked one day in advance if possible; otherwise call before noon.

Travel Agency
American Express (✉ Viajes Alhambra, Teniente Coronel Seguí 6, Seville, ☎ 95/421–2923 or 95/421–8321).

Visitor Information
Local tourist offices in major towns covered in this chapter are **Arcos de la Frontera** (✉ Cuesta de Belén, ☎ 956/702264), **Cádiz** (✉ Calderón de la Barca 1, ☎ 956/211313), **Jerez de la Frontera** (✉ Alameda Cristina 7, ☎ 956/331150 or 956/331162), **Puerto de Santa María** (✉ Guadalete 1, ☎ 956/542475 or 956/542413), **Sanlúcar de Barrameda** (✉ Calzada del Ejército, ☎ 956/366110), and **Seville** (✉ Avda. de la Constitución 21, ☎ 95/422–1404 or 95/421–8157, FAX 95/422–9753); and the less useful offices at Costurero de la Reina, (✉ Paseo de las Delicias 9, ☎ 95/423–4465); and at the airport, (☎ 95/425–5046).

14 Extremadura

The very name Extremadura—"the land beyond the Duero"—suggests the wild, remote, and isolated character of this haunting region. The area, which has poor soil and is scarcely industrialized, has experienced extreme poverty. Once, however, it was a hub of activity: No other place in Spain has as many Roman monuments as Mérida, and magnificent palaces constitute the glory of such towns as Cáceres and Trujillo. Hervás and Cáceres have two of the best preserved Sephardic Juderías (Jewish quarters) in the country.

By Michael
Jacobs

Updated by
Mary Ellen
Schultz

THE VERY NAME EXTREMADURA—the "land beyond the Duero"—suggests the wild, remote, and isolated character of this haunting region. The area, which has poor soil and is scarcely industrialized, has experienced extreme poverty. The film director Luis Buñuel established his reputation in the late 1920s with a powerful documentary *Un Chien Andalou* about the mountainous district of Las Hurdes, in northern Extremadura, then desperately poor, virtually unchanged since the Middle Ages, and still accessible only on foot or donkey. The Nobel Prize–winning novelist Camilo José Cela made his own debut with *The Family of Pascual Duarte*, a bleakly realistic study set in the southern half of Extremadura, in a village "crouched over a road as long and as flat as a day without bread."

In 1601, at Fuente de Cantos between Andalucía and Extremadura, the great artist Francisco de Zurbarán was born. A visit to the town is essential for an understanding of Zurbarán's art. The simplified forms, unmodulated colors, and powerful austerity of his works are mirrored in the tree-less, undulating ocher expanses that surround his birthplace; it is one of the most abstract landscapes imaginable. In the 19th century, after a long period of neglect, Zurbarán's art was hailed as representing all that was most profound in the Spanish temperament. Similarly, today the region of Extremadura has been recognized as the pure, unsullied essence of Spain. It is a region that has resisted more than any other the onslaught of the 20th century, a place where travel remains an adventure.

Though a strong backward character pervades the whole of Extremadura, the diverse lands that surround it have had their influence also. Officially, Extremadura comprises two provinces: Badajoz to the south, and Cáceres to the north. The dazzlingly white villages and sun-baked landscape of the former have much in common with neighboring Andalucía; Cáceres, meanwhile, with its wooded mountain valleys and half-timbered, gray-stone houses, is reminiscent of both Castile and northern Spain. Yet another influence is that of Portugal, which borders on both Badajoz and Cáceres.

Extremadura has not always been such an isolated and impoverished region. No other place in Spain has so many Roman monuments as the Extremaduran town of Mérida, which, in fact, was the capital of the vast Roman province of Lusitania. Economic and artistic decline set in after the Romans, but in the 16th century the region revived as the survivors among the famous and ruthless men who conquered and explored the New World—from Francisco Pizarro and Hernán Cortés to Nuñez de Balboa and Francisco de Orellana, first navigator of the Amazon—returned to their birthplace. They were responsible for the magnificent palaces that today constitute the glory of towns such as Cáceres and Trujillo. They, too, turned the remote monastery of Guadalupe—the miraculous Virgin of which had inspired their exploits overseas—into one of the great artistic repositories of Spain.

Pleasures and Pastimes

Boating
All sorts of water sports are practiced in Extremadura, thanks to the presence of numerous artificial lakes, most notably Borbollón and Gabriel y Galán in northern Cáceres and Cíjara and García Sola in northwestern Badajoz.

Dining

The food of Extremadura reflects the austerity of the landscape. It is true peasant cuisine, conditioned by poverty, but with a strong character and a reliance on fresh produce. Its basis is the pig, of which no part is spared, including the *criadillas* (testicles), not to be confused with the *criadillas de la tierra* (earth testicles), which are truffles. The charcuterie products are outstanding, most notably the sweetish cured hams from Montánchez, the chorizo (spiced sausage), and *morcilla* (blood pudding), which is often made here with potatoes.

Caldereta (a particularly tasty lamb stew) should be tried if found on a restaurant's menu. Game is also common, a famous specialty being *perdiz al modo de Alcántara* (partridge cooked with truffles). Certain Extremaduran dishes appall many foreigners, as well as many other Spaniards—in particular, those involving *ranas* (frogs) and *lagartos* (lizards), the latter usually eaten with an almond sauce. In the south, numerous Andalucían specialties are to be found, such as gazpacho and *ajo blanco* (cold almond and garlic soup). A common accompaniment throughout the region is *migas* (bread crumbs soaked in water and fried in olive oil with garlic and specks of bacon). The excellent local cheeses generally have a crumbly texture and strong flavor; be sure to savor *tortas*, the typical round, semi-soft cheeses of Cáceres. Desserts include the extremeño favorite, *técula mécula,* an almondy marzipan tart combining the flavors of Spain and its border-sharing neighbor, Portugal. The little-known wines of the area are equally full of character: Try Lar de Lares. Almendralejo is the wine-growing center.

There is little tradition in Extremadura for going to restaurants, and some of the best food is to be found in modest bars. Reservations are usually unnecessary.

CATEGORY	COST*
$$$$	over 6,500 ptas
$$$	4,000–6,500 ptas
$$	2,300–4,000 ptas
$	under 2,300 ptas

per person for a three-course meal, excluding tax

Fiestas

The province of Cáceres has its share of colorful *fiestas* commemorating and celebrating saints and sinners long gone. If your travel plans take you to Extremadura during the **Fiesta de San Estéban** (Feast of St. Stephen), on January 20th, you'll have the opportunity to witness several interesting displays of local folklore in several of the smaller towns in the region. In **Arcehúche** (near Garovillas), *carantonas* ("ugly mugs," men costumed in animal skins and frightening masks) bow before the statue of St. Stephen during his procession through town. In **Navaconcejo** (near Jarandilla), a *taraballos* (bogeyman) dressed in white and brandishing a rope whip, chases the young men during the procession. In **Piornal** (near Plasencia), the *jaramplas* (a grotesquely costumed, masked jester) is pursued through the town and pelted with turnips.

February 3rd is the day to toast **San Blas** (St. Blaise), the patron saint of sore throats, with hot cakes bearing his name and numerous feasts. In **Montehermoso** (near Plasencia) you may be lucky enough to catch the *Baile de los Negros* (Black Men's Dance), performed by six men with dyed faces.

During Carnival, **Villanueva de la Vera** (near Jarandilla) is where you can witness the *Pero Palo,* a large, rag-doll figure with a deadpan expression, carried in a procession throughout the town.

The province of Badajoz doesn't have as crowded a fiesta calendar as its neighboring Extremeño province to the north, but Carnival is celebrated with processions in most towns and villages.

If your travel plan dates take you to **Badajoz** in time to say *adios* to winter and *hola* to spring, you'll be lucky to enjoy the *Fiestas de la Primavera* and *Las Mayos* (Spring Festival or Maydays), usually held during the end of April and beginning of May. The most important date of these celebrations is May 3rd; the exaltation of the holy cross. A local family is selected a month in advance to prepare a cross in their own home for the procession. Some of these crosses are magnificent works of art and patience, lovingly created and tended by the host family, many times using up hard-earned savings. Songs are sung as statues of the Virgin Mary and the cross are paraded through various neighborhoods. These colorful festivals can be seen in Badajoz as well as in the neighboring towns of Corte de Peleas and Feria.

Fishing
Trout fishing is popular in the Vera and Jerte districts, while tench, carp, royal carp, barbel, and pike abound in the Tajo and Guadiana Rivers.

Lodging
No other region of Spain can boast such a remarkable group of state-run paradors as can Extremadura. They cover all the main tourist areas of the region, and all are in buildings of great historical and architectural interest; early reservations are usually needed on weekends. The other luxury hotels of the region are generally in modern buildings of little character. If you prefer character to luxury, you might try your luck with the region's modest *fondas* (inns). If you want to establish a base for a series of day trips, consider Cáceres; from there easy, day-long jaunts can be made to Trujillo, Mérida, and Plasencia.

CATEGORY	COST*
$$$$	over 14,000 ptas
$$$	11,000–14,000 ptas
$$	7,000–11,000 ptas
$	under 7,000 ptas

*per standard double room, excluding tax and service.

Exploring Extremadura

Extremadura is one of the most beautiful, and perhaps least known of the interior regions of Spain. The province is divided into two sections: upper Extremadura, called Cáceres, and lower Extremadura, named Badajoz. It is a dry, brown-colored land which is, at the same time, an area full of water. The best way to see Extremadura is by car, since bus and train connections are not particularly suited to a leisurely exploration of what some refer to as "essential Spain." We describe highlights of both regions their own sections, below.

Great Itineraries
If you are seeking outdoor activities and beautiful landscapes, include Plasencia, which will also appeal to anyone interested in the life of the emperor Carlos V. If Roman ruins attract you, go to Mérida, while Cáceres and Trujillo are a must if you love good food and are fascinated with the Spain of the conquistadors. A singularly outstanding attraction of the region is Guadalupe: It combines a spectacular setting, an appealing village and one of the most richly endowed and historically important monasteries in Spain.

Numbers in the text below correspond to numbers in the margin and on the Extremadura map.

IF YOU HAVE 1 DAY

You can get a lightning impression of the region in the course of a day's drive between Madrid and Seville. First, head toward **Mérida** ⑩, ancient capital of Roman Spain, and one of the country's most popular historic attractions, with its beautiful ruins. Stop off on the way for sightseeing and an excellent lunch at the city of the conquistadors, **Trujillo** ⑧, with its unusually shaped Plaza Mayor. This is a good way to get to the south of Spain, and infinitely preferable to the usual route through the monotonous plains of La Mancha.

Another one-day Extremadura exploration might include the drive from Madrid to one of the most revered sites in Spain, the monastery of **Guadalupe** ⑨, nestled in the heart of conquistador country and symbolizing the link between Spain and Spanish America. Christopher Columbus had his two Indian servants baptized in the fountain standing at the main entrance of the monastery. The sacristy here contains eight paintings by the Spanish master Zurburán. You could return to Madrid the same afternoon, or decide to spend the night here, surrounded by the mountains.

IF YOU HAVE 3 DAYS

If you have three days to tour from Madrid, take the slow, winding, but very beautiful C501 to **Plasencia** ①, the most important town in the far north of Extremadura. You could wander through the *casco viejo* (old town) and then drive to the **Monasterio de Yuste** ⑤ (where Roman Emperor Carlos V spend his final days) and perhaps stay the night in nearby 🔛 **Jarandilla de la Vera** ④. Next day, go south through the provincial capital of **Cáceres** ⑦ to 🔛 **Mérida** ⑩, with its evocative Roman ruins, and on day three head back north by way of **Trujillo** ⑧ and **Guadalupe** ⑨, where you could either return to Madrid the same evening on the well-paved N5 highway, or spend the night.

IF YOU HAVE 5 DAYS

Start by heading up to **Plasencia** ① and enjoy the scenery of the lovely Jerte Valley. Time permitting, make a slight detour and wander through the ancient *Judería* (Jewish Quarter) of **Hervás** ②, one of the country's National Heritage Sites. Visit the well-preserved village of **Cabezuela del Valle** ③ with its half-timbered houses and curious doorways built to admit visitors on horseback. Continue on to the the town of 🔛 **Jarandilla de la Vera** ④ and spend the night in the parador, located in the fortified palace where Carlos V lived for awhile, before moving to his final domicile, the nearby **Monasterio de Yuste** ⑤. On day two, start heading south and pass by the **Parque Natural del Monfragüe** ⑥ on C 524, connecting Plasencia and 🔛 **Trujillo** ⑧, a national wildlife preserve and ecological paradise. Spend the night in Trujillo and look for stork nests on top of the higher buildings. Day three could be spent exploring Trujillo in the morning, then on to **Cáceres** ⑦, so picturesque that it's served as background for several period films. Enjoy your midday meal there, then continue on to 🔛 **Mérida** ⑩ and its splendid Roman monuments. On day four, you can spend your time exploring the city and then head on the capital of the region's other province, **Badajoz** ⑪, and then on to Andalucía and points south. A second option is to head back north on the road to Trujillo and Madrid, and turn off to be astounded by the monastery of **Guadalupe** ⑨.

When to Tour Extremadura

Throughout Spain, the most popular revered festivals take place during the pre-Lenten Carnival (dates vary, but generally fall between late February and early March) and Easter's *Semana Santa* (holy week). This is not the most lively region for fiestas, though, and not the place to visit if you're looking for bulls running in the streets and wild carryings-on. The churches, monasteries, villages, and cities personify the almost fiercely old-fashioned Spain.

Summer is a good time to come if you plan to hike in the nature parks or spend time in the mountains; however, you may find the lower areas brutally hot. Spring and fall are considered by many to be the ideal time to explore, since winters can be cold and rainy.

This is still a relatively unknown part of the country for many travelers, indeed, almost the last "wild" region of Spain, so you will not be running into too many fellow explorers while sightseeing.

UPPER EXTREMADURA

Extremadura stretches from the La Vera valley to the Sierra de Tentudía, and from Toledo to Ciudad Real. As mentioned above, the province is divided into two provinces or sections: upper Extremadura, called Cáceres, and lower Extremadura, named Badajoz.

It is a dry, brown-colored land which is, at the same time, crossed from east to west by two important rivers: the Tagus and the Guadiana. The Alcántara reservoir (fed by the Tagus River) is the largest in western Europe. The resulting rugged and fertile landscape has been a source of food for much of Europe for many centuries.

Plasencia

1 *200 km (124 mi) west of Madrid, 79 km (49 mi) north of Cáceres, 126 km (78 mi) northwest of Trujillo.*

The most important town in the far north of Extremadura, Plasencia is on the banks of the narrow Jerte River, and has good views of the Sierra de Gredos. It was founded by Alfonso VIII in 1180, just after he had captured the whole area from the Moors. The town's motto of *placeat Deo et hominibus* ("it pleases both God and men") might well have been a ploy on Alfonso's part to attract settlers to this wild and isolated place on the southern borders of the former kingdom of León. Badly damaged during the Peninsular War of 1808, Plasencia has today preserved far less of its medieval quarter than have other Extremaduran towns. Nonetheless, it still retains extensive fragments of its medieval walls and boasts a scattering of fine old buildings.

The **cathedral,** rising above the town's western fortifications, was founded in 1189 and rebuilt after 1320 in an austere Gothic style. Then, in 1498, the great Enrique de Egas designed a new structure, which was to be only partially completed. The entrance to this curious and not wholly satisfactory complex is through the portal on the new cathedral's ornate but somber north facade. The dark interior of the new cathedral is notable for the beauty of its pilasters, which sprout tree-like into the ribs of the vaulting. You enter the old cathedral through the Gothic cloister, off which also stands the oldest surviving part of the building, the 13th-century chapter house (now the chapel of San Pablo)—a late-Romanesque structure with an idiosyncratic, Moorish-inspired dome. The **museum** installed within the truncated nave of the old cathedral contains a miscellaneous collection of ecclesiastical and archaeological display. ☏ *927/414852.* ⌦ *Old cathedral 150 ptas.* ☉ *Daily 9–1 and 4–6.*

Surrounding the old and new cathedrals are several austerely elegant structures of the Renaissance, most notably the **Palacio Episcopal** (Bishop's Palace, closed to the public), the **Hospital de Santa María**

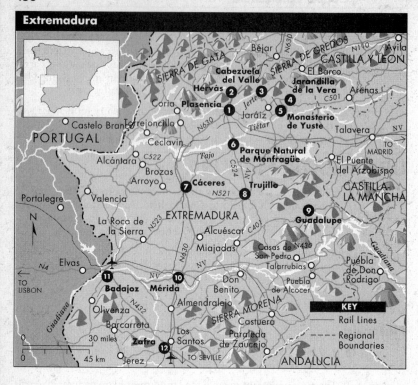

Extremadura

(now a cultural center), and the **Casa del Deán** (Dean's House; now a rather run-down police station).

In the center of town you'll find the narrow **Plaza de San Vicente.** This carefully preserved square, lined with orange trees, is dominated on its northern side by the Renaissance **Palacio de Mirabel** (Palace of the Marquis of Mirabel); go through the arch in its middle and you will come to an alley affording a back view of the palace. ☎ *Tip caretaker.* ⊙ *Usually daily 10–2 and 4–6.*

East from the Plaza de San Vicente, at the other end of the Rua Zapatería, is the **Plaza Mayor,** a cheerful, arcaded square, with a market that has been held here every Tuesday morning since the 12th century. Farther east, you come to a large section of the town's medieval wall, on the other side of which is a heavily restored Roman aqueduct.

NEED A BREAK?

At the tapas bars lining the Plaza Mayor, you can people-watch while you fill your stomach. **El Español** has a good selection of ham and cheese tapas; **Casa Pepe** takes pride in its *pinchos* (tidbits given free with your drink) of squid and octopus; the specialty at **Bar Gabi** is *caracoles picantes* (snails served in a spicy paprika sauce).

Dining and Lodging

$$–$$$ ✕▥ **Alfonso VIII.** The sturdy, gray exterior of this centrally located hotel shields an interior attempting a French rococo elegance, with gilt plaster and red upholstery. Grand, but slightly past its prime, this curious survival of the Franco era is strangely agreeable. The hotel restaurant has long been renowned for its food, which has a strong Extremaduran accent; the Parisian-style dining room seems the least likely setting for *lagarto en salsa verde* (lizard in a green sauce). The menu changes seasonally; the lizards are available only in the spring. ⊠ *Alfonso VIII*

32, 34, 10600, ☎ *927/410250,* FAX *927/418042. 59 rooms with bath. Restaurant. AE, DC, MC, V.*

Shopping

If you happen to be in Plasencia on a Tuesday, visit the **Plaza Mayor** and do what Extremeños have been doing since the 12th century: scouting out bargains in the weekly market.

Hervás

❷ *63 km (39 mi) northeast of Plasencia, 142 km (88 mi) northeast of Cáceres, 25 km (16 mi) west of Cabezuela del Valle.*

This picturesque village surrounded by pine and chestnut groves makes for an interesting detour. It is believed that the town became a predominantly Jewish settlement during the Middle Ages, populated by Jews escaping Christian and Muslim persecution in the larger cities. In 1492, however, when the Jews were expelled from Spain, their neighborhood was left intact, and their possessions ceded to the local nobility. Stipped of its wealth, the town lost its commercial reputation and faded into the background.

Now, thanks to the recent efforts of the mayors of seven Spanish cities pledged to creating a network (known as *El Camino de Sefarad,* The Journey Through Sepharad) of several of the country's most important Jewish settlements, Hervá is recognized for what it is: the best preserved *Judería* (Jewish Quarter) in Spain. Many of the residents here claim to be descendants of *conversos,* Jews who converted to Christianity.

Cabezuela del Valle

❸ *34 km (21 mi) northeast of Plasencia. For a scenic route, follow N110 towards Ávila.*

The route north from Plasencia north to Ávila (150 km/90 mi) follows the narrow, fast-flowing Jerte River almost to its source, then climbs above it to enter the bleak plateau of Castile. To the Greeks, the **Jerte Valley** was supposedly "the Valley of Pleasure." Its lower slopes are covered with a dense mantle of ash, chestnut, and cherry trees, their richness contrasting with the granite cliffs of the Sierra de Gredos. One of the best preserved of the area's many attractive villages is Cabezuela del Valle, full of half-timbered, stone houses. Like other settlements in this area, it once had a significant Jewish population.

En Route   Tornavacas is a rough track (passable only on foot or in a strong car) leading over the Sierra de Gredos and down toward the village of Jarandilla de la Vera, in the valley of the Tiétar River. (You'll have to turn right off the N110, following signs for the village, to pick up the track.) The track, with extensive views in its upper stages, descends into a narrow gorge with the dramatic name of La Garganta de los Infiernos (the Gorge of Hell). The Holy Roman Emperor Carlos V took this very path in 1556; the litter he was carried in is on display at the monastery of Yuste, near Jarandilla.

Jarandilla de la Vera

❹ *55 km (33 mi) northeast of Plasencia, 17 km (11 mi) southeast of Cabezuela del Valle. For an easier drive than you will have on N110, take C501, which runs from Plasencia in a northeasterly direction almost to Madrid.*

The village of Jarandilla de la Vera has a fortified palace of the 15th and 16th centuries (this is now the **Parador Nacional Carlos V;** ☞ Dining and Lodging, *below*); Carlos V stayed here for a year while waiting for his quarters to be ready at Yuste.

Dining and Lodging

$$$ ✕🏨 **Parador Nacional Carlos V.** Historically, this is one of the most important buildings in the parador chain, the emperor Carlos V having stayed here for a year. Built in the early 16th century as a fortified palace, it has an arcaded patio with flattened arches. The stylish hotel is filled with pseudo-medieval furnishings and suits of armor, and its regal dining room provides a fitting setting in which to play "royalty for a night." Try the *sopa de gañan* (hearty chicken and vegetable soup) to start, then savor *zancarrón braseado con higos de la Vera* (roast loin of pork with braised figs) as your main dish. ✉ *Carretera Plasencia s/n, 10450,* ☎ *927/560117,* ℻ *927/560088. 53 rooms with bath. Restaurant, bar, pool, tennis court. AE, DC, MC, V.*

Shopping

If you like to cook, pick up a tin or two of *pimentón de la Vera* (paprika), made from the region's famed red peppers. You'll find it in Jarandilla and other towns in the La Vera area.

Monasterio de Yuste

❺ *2 km (1 mi) northwest of Cuacos, 17 km (11 mi) southeast of Jarandilla de la Vera, 45 km (28 mi) from Plasencia. Turn left off C501 at Curacos. The way is well marked with signs for the monastery.*

The Monasterio de Yuste (Monastery of Yuste) was founded by Hieronymite monks in the early 15th century. It was badly damaged in the Peninsular War and left to decay after the suppression of Spain's monasteries in 1835, but has been restored and taken over again by the Hieronymites. You can visit the Royal Chambers where Carlos stayed; the bedroom where he died has a view into the church, which enabled Carlos to hear mass from his bed. A ramp, originally intended to be climbed on horseback, leads up to a terrace overlooking a fish pond. ☎ *927/172130.* 🎫 *200 ptas.* ☉ *Oct.–May, daily 9:30–12:30 and 3–6; June–Sept., daily 9–12:30 and 3:30–6:30.*

OFF THE   **GARGANTA LA OLLA –** Another town worth finding in the Vera valley is
BEATEN PATH   Garganta La Olla, about 10 km/6 mi east of Yuste. The road dips into the village's narrow, twisting streets. Visit the Museo de la Inquisición, where you'll find kitchen utensils from Yuste displayed alongside instruments of torture used by the Inquisitors. You can also visit the Casa de Putas (a brothel used by soldiers of Carlos V's army), now a butcher shop, but still painted the traditional "brothel" blue.

Parque Natural de Monfragüe

❻ *20 km (12 mi) south of Plasencia, off of C524, which connects Plasencia with Trujillo.*

The Parque Natural de Monfragüe (Monfragüe Nature Park) is at the confluence of the Rivers Tiétar and Tajo. This beautiful, wild area was turned into a national park in 1979 and is known for its wide range of plant and animal life, including lynx, boar, deer, fox, black storks, imperial eagles and the world's largest colony of black vultures. Bring binoculars to better enjoy these graceful birds.

Cáceres

★ **❼** *307 km (190 mi) west of Madrid.*

Originally a Roman colony and later heavily disputed between the Moors and Christians, Cáceres is today a provincial capital and prosperous agricultural town. The bus and railway stations are next to each other, a good half-hour walk from the old center, along the characterless Avenida de España. Once you are on the Calle San Anton, the look of the town improves considerably, particularly as you reach the intimate Plaza de San Juan, where you will find one of Extremadura's greatest restaurants, El Figón de Eustaquio (☞ Dining and Lodging, *below*). Beyond this square is the long, inclined, and arcaded **Plaza Mayor**; in the middle of the arcade is the entrance to the lively Calle General Ezponda, lined with tapas bars and busy as a hive in the evening.

On high ground on the eastern side of the Plaza Mayor are the town's fortifications—intact though heavily restored—which contain one of the best-preserved old quarters in Spain. The **old town** of Cáceres is small but without a single distracting modern building—a cold, stony, and dreamlike place that is one of the high points of a visit to Extremadura. Almost empty of shops, restaurants, and even bars, virtually deserted outside the tourist season, and crammed with medieval and Renaissance palaces somberly constructed out of heavy, gray blocks of stone, it looks like the stage set for a tragedy—and in fact has served as a background in numerous movies.

Enter the old town by the gate next to the Torre de la Hierba from the Plaza Mayor. Immediately inside, turn right along the Adarves de San Juan, and you will soon pass the **upper Palace of the Golfines,** which is dominated by a soaring tower dating from 1515.

Skirt the town walls until you reach the Mérida Gate, on the southern side of the old town. Leading from here to the old town center is the Calle Ancha, at the beginning of which is the **Casa de Sanchez de Paredes,** a 16th-century palace that has been converted into a parador (☞ Dining and Lodging, *below*).

NEED A BREAK? Adjoining the Casa de Sanchez de Paredes parador, at No. 4 Calle Ancha, is **El Palacio de los Vinos,** a stylish snack bar and liquor store. Sample a creation of the bar's Mexican owner—acorn liqueur, called *El Beso Extremeño* (Extremaduran Kiss).

On the Plaza San Mateo, at the northern end of the Calle Ancha, stands one of the town's most important churches, **San Mateo.** Built mainly in the 14th century, but with a 16th-century choir, it has an impressively austere interior, the main decorative notes being the Baroque high altar and some heraldic crests. On the square facing the southern side of the building is the battlemented tower of **Las Cigüeñas** (Palace of the Storks), so called because of the stork's nest attached to it.

Farther down the Plaza San Mateo is the **Casa de las Veletas** (House of the Weathervanes). This now contains a small museum, the **Museo Arqueológico,** devoted to archaeology and folklore. ☎ 924/247234. 🖭 *250 ptas.* ☉ *Tues.–Sat. 9:30–2:30, Sun. 10:15–2:30; closed holidays.*

The narrow street that descends from the eastern end of San Mateo to the town's other main church, Santa María, passes first the Jesuit church of **San Francisco Xavier** and then the lower **Palacio de los Golfines.** The latter has he finest exterior of any Cáceres palace, the austerity of the stone relieved by Mudéjar (Spanish Muslim) and Renaissance decorative motifs.

The Gothic church of **Santa María,** which can be visited during mass and is now serving as the town's cathedral, was built mainly in the 16th century and has an elegantly carved high altar of 1551, just about visible in the surrounding gloom. Nearby is the **Palacio de Caruajal** (Plaza de Santa María), the only old palace apart from the Casa de las Veletas that can be toured. Ask at the tourist office to arrange a visit.

A 110-yard walk from Santa María down Calle Tiendas will take you to the northern walls of the town. Don't miss the 16th-century **Casa de los Toledo-Moctezumas** (now a bank), which was built by Juan Cano de Saavedra with the dowry provided by his wife—none other than the princess daughter of the Aztec ruler Montezuma.

The chief building of interest outside the town walls is the church of **Santiago** (go through the Socorro Gate, and continue north along the Calle de Villalobos). It was rebuilt in the 16th century by Rodrigo Gil de Hontañón, the last great Gothic architect of Spain.

OFF THE
BEATEN PATH

GAROVILLAS – A possible excursion from Cáceres is to Garrovillas, 10 km/6 mi off the main road between Cáceres and Plasencia (turn left, or northwest, onto C522, 25 km/15 mi north of Cáceres). Now partially deserted, it is a perfectly preserved village of the late 15th century. The walls and pillars appear to be tilting at dangerously uneven angles, but this was done to offset the natural slope of the land.

Dining and Lodging

$$$ ✕ **Atrio.** Slickly elegant in an unprepossessing modern setting, this restaurant offers adventurous and ultra-refined modern cooking. Truffles appear in many of the dishes—for instance, in the tastefully presented version of perdiz al modo de Alcántara, a traditional Extremaduran delicacy. ✉ *Avda. España 30, Bloque 4, 10003,* ☎ *927/242928. DC, MC, V.*

$$$ ✕ **El Figón de Eustaquio.** On the quiet and pleasant Plaza San Juan,
★ this is a justly famed Extremaduran gastronomic institution. Comprising a jumble of small, old-fashioned, intimate dining rooms, it is always busy, especially at lunchtime. Excellent cured ham from Montánchez, *angulas en ensalada* (eel salad, resembling small pieces of grey spaghetti mounded on greens and drizzled with a viagrette dressing), and *truchas del Jerte a la Extremeña* (trout from the Jerte Valley) are among its specialties. ✉ *Plaza San Juan 12, 10003,* ☎ *927/244372. Reservations essential. AE, MC, V.*

$$$ ✕🏠 **Parador Nacional de Cáceres.** This state-run parador is in a 16th-century palace, right in the heart of the old town. Soft cream tones and wooden beams warm up the plain architecture, and the rooms are cozily comfortable. The noble dining room serves tasty, local game specialties, such as *lomo de venado al queso del Casar* (venison with Casar cheese sauce) and *jabalía al cacereña* (wild boar marinated in red wine and herbs). ✉ *Ancha 6, 10003,* ☎ *927/211759,* 🆇 *927/211729. 27 rooms with bath. Restaurant. AE, DC, MC, V.*

$$$$ 🏠 **Meliá Cáceres.** Equally historic and somewhat more comfortable than
★ the Parador Nacional de Cáceres, the Meliá Cáceres occupies a renovated, 16th-century palace just outside the walls of the old town. It gracefully blends exposed stone, indirect spot lighting, and designer furnishings. Rooms have huge double beds, wall-to-wall carpeting, and ample baths. The street-level bar, with charming wine-bottle lighting, is the town's most popular meeting spot. ✉ *Plaza San Juan 11, 10003,*

☎ 927/215800, 🗚 927/214070. *88 rooms with bath. Restaurant, bar. AE, DC, MC, V.*

$$$$ 🖵 **Quinto Centenario.** Opened in 1992 just outside Cáceres on the road to Plasencia, the Quinto Centenario offers remarkable warmth for a modern, high-rise hotel. Rooms are large and carpeted, with oversize beds and luxurious baths. The swimming pool and outdoor terrace dining make it a good choice for hot summer days. ⊠ *Manuel Pacheco s/n, 10003,* ☎ *927/232200,* 🗚 *232202. 138 rooms with bath. Restaurant, bar, pool, tennis court. AE, DC, MC, V.*

Nightlife and the Arts

The region is not renowned for its nightlife, although bars in Cáceres are lively until the wee hours. The Plaza Mayor is practically ringed with places to slake your thirst and quell hunger pangs. Or, try the Calle de Pizarro, on the west side of town, for more serious bar-hopping; the **Taberna la Marocantana** serves interesting Moroccan style-tapas.

Trujillo

★ ❽   *48 km (30 mi) east of Cáceres, 250 km (155 mi) southwest of Madrid; at the junction of N521 and NV.*

Anyone who comes to Cáceres province should not fail to visit Trujillo. It is an extreme example of the Extremaduran look—a lonely, nearly deserted place built of cold and imposing stone that is nonetheless thrilling to both eye and soul. The stork nests that top several towers in and around the center of the old town—and that have become something of a symbol of the town—only add to this strange effect. Unlike Cáceres, Trujillo has none of the hustle and bustle of the new Spain; indeed, it seems almost stuck in the time when Extremadura was a symbol of Spanish poverty. Dating to at least Roman times, when its castle was first constructed, Trujillo was captured from the Moors in 1232 and colonized by a number of leading military families. However, it was only after the discovery of America in 1492 that the town's fame spread. Known today as "the Cradle of the Conquistadors," Trujillo gave birth to some of the leading explorers and conquerors of the New World, men who were later to bring great wealth to their native town and build here, in the course of the 16th and 17th centuries, a splendid series of palaces—radically changing what had been a poverty-stricken provincial town into a showcase of 16th- and 17th-century conspicuous consumption. The most famous of these conquistadors was Francisco Pizarro, conqueror of Peru, born in Trujillo in 1475. His educated half brother Hernando, also an adventurer in Peru, built perhaps the most magnificent palace in Trujillo.

Trujillo's economic boom during the Golden Age of Spain led the town to expand well beyond its medieval walls. Then, from the mid-17th century onward, building ceased almost completely, and the town went into a long decline. Today, it is possible to wander endlessly and at random around its maze of streets and still uncover at every turn poignant memorials of its glorious past. A word of warning, however: It is only practical to see Trujillo on foot, as the streets are mainly cobbled or crudely paved with stone and rarely flat. The two main roads through Trujillo leave you at the singularly unattractive and unspectacular bottom of the town. The town becomes progressively older the farther you climb, but even on the lower slopes—where most of the shops are concentrated—you need walk only a few yards to step into what seems like the Middle Ages.

The large **Plaza Mayor,** one of the finest in Spain, is a superb 16th- and early 17th-century creation, one of the few contemporary features being, ironically, the modern tourist office in its center. At the foot of the stepped platform that rises on the north side of the Plaza Mayor, stands a large, bronze equestrian statue of the great conqueror of Peru, Francisco Pizarro.

The church behind the Pizarro statue, **San Martín,** is a Gothic structure of the early 16th century, with some fine Renaissance tombs and an old organ. If you visit at dusk, you may lucky enough to hear the men's parish's choir group rehearsing, a magical note to eventide.

In the northeastern corner of the Plaza Mayor is the **Palacio de los Duques de San Carlos** (Palace of the Dukes of San Carlos), which has a majestically decorated facade from around 1600; the building is now a convent of Hieronymite nuns, one of whom will show you around the austere, arcaded inner courtyard. ☎ 927/320058. ✉ *Offering to nuns.* ⊙ *Daily 9–1 and 4–6.*

NEED A BREAK?	The Clarisse nuns now live in a modern building between the palace and the Trujillo parador. They make some of the best sweets and pastries in town.

The most interesting part of Trujillo extends to the west of the Plaza Mayor. Your tour proper of the town could begin near the southwestern corner of the square, outside the **Palacio de la Conquista** (Palace of the Conquest), the most dramatic building on the plaza. This was built by Francisco Pizarro's brother Hernando and is immediately recognizable by its rich covering of exquisite Renaissance ornamentation. Flanking its corner balcony, around which most of this ornamentation is concentrated, are lively, imaginative busts of the Pizarro family. Prominent in the coat of arms above, and an interesting reflection of the conquest's spirit of brutal subjugation, are representations of chained Indians. The magnificent interior of the palace has now been partially opened to the public and features a grandiose staircase, a courtyard, and some 16th-century stables. The palace was closed for renovations at press time; check with the tourist office.

Adjacent to the Palacio de la Conquista is the arcaded, former town hall (now a law court). The alley that runs through this building's central arch will take you to the **Palacio de Pizarro de Orellana** (now a school), where you will find the most elegant Renaissance courtyard in town. ✉ *Free.*

The oldest part of Trujillo, known as **La Villa,** is entirely surrounded by its original, if much restored, walls. The Calle Almenas, which runs west from the Palace of Pizarro de Orellana, skirts these walls up to the **Puerta de San Andrés,** one of the four surviving gates of the Villa (there were originally seven). Once inside, you enter a world inhabited by storks, which, in the spring and early summer months, adorn the many crumbling chimneys and towers of old palaces and churches.

The cobbled, climbing Calle Palomas (Dove Street) leads you into the Plaza de Santa María, on which stands the town's major monument of artistic interest, the church of **Santa María.** This Gothic structure attached to a Romanesque bell tower is occasionally used for services, but the interior has been virtually untouched since the 16th century and has an upper choir with an exquisitely carved balustrade. The coats of arms at each end of this balustrade indicate the seats that were used by Ferdinand and Isabella when they attended mass here. The chief attraction in the church is the high altar of circa 1480, adorned with one of the greatest Spanish paintings of the 15th century, Fernando Gallego. (To see this properly illuminated, you must place a 100-ptas. coin

in the box adjacent to the church entrance.) ☜ *100 ptas. plus tip.* ☉
Daily 9–2 and 4–6:30 (until 7:30 in summer).

Climbing north from the Santa María church, you will come almost
immediately to the Pizarro family home. The small house has been restored and turned into a museum, the **Casa Museo de Pizarro,** dedicated to the links between Spain and Latin America. ☜ *300 ptas.* ☉
*June–Oct., Tues.–Sun. 11–2 and 6–8; Nov.–May, Tues.–Sun. 11–2 and
4:30–6:30.*

Standing in isolation beyond The Casa Museo de Pizarro are the
perimeter walls of the large **castle,** built by the Moors on Roman foundations. ☜ *Free.* ☉ *Daily 8–dusk.*

Dining and Lodging

$ ✕ **Mesón La Troya.** Although the food here is not up to the standard
of the neighboring Pizarro, there can be few more entertaining places
to eat a meal. Occupying the vaulted, ground-floor room of a beautiful old building, this lively and raucous restaurant is often filled with
carousing soldiers. The elderly woman who runs the place is a known
eccentric, who scolds you if you are unable to finish the remarkably
copious helpings. At the beginning of the meal you are served a *tortilla de patatas* (potato omelet), whether you want it or not. ☒ *Plaza
Mayor 10,* ☎ *927/321364. MC, V.*

$ ✕ **Pizarro.** Occupying a small but quietly elegant upstairs room, this
★ is a celebrated establishment with a warm and friendly atmosphere. It
is run by two sisters who have lovingly maintained traditional Extremaduran home cooking. A specialty of the house is *gallina truffada*
(an elaborately prepared chicken pâté with truffles), which was once
a common Christmas dish but which few today know how to make.
☒ *Plaza Mayor 13,* ☎ *927/320255. MC, V.*

$$$ ✕▥ **Parador Nacional de Trujillo.** This unusually friendly parador
★ was originally the convent of St. Clare, and its bedrooms surround a
harmonious, Renaissance courtyard. The decoration aims for the
mock-medieval chic common to most of the paradors, but the atmo-
sphere is endearingly homey. An unusual, and welcome touch is the
heated bathroom floor. A blue-and-white-tile panel adds a dramatic
note to the dining room, where you can sup on local specialties such
as *criadillas de la tierra en caldereta* (white truffle and meat stew) or
chuleta de novillo retinto con patatas (braised young bull filet with pota-
toes). ☒ *Santa Clara s/n, 10200,* ☎ *927/321350,* ☒ *927/321366. 46
rooms with bath. Restaurant, pool, meeting room. AE, DC, MC, V.*

$$ ✕▥ **Finca Santa Marta.** This is an interesting alternative to being in
town. Located 14 km (9 mi) outside of Trujillo on the road to Guadalupe,
this ancient oil and wine farm owned by a retired Dutch diplomat and
his Spanish wife has been converted into an oh-so-comfortable country refuge. The restored living quarters have stone floors (rugs keep
your feet warm), wood-beamed ceilings, and lots of fresh flowers
everywhere. Meals are available if requested in advance. ☒ *Finca
Santa Marta, Pago de San Clemente, Trujillo,* ☎ *927/319203;* ☒ *Juan
Ramón Giménez 12, 8A, 28036 Madrid,* ☎ ☒ *91/3502217. 12 rooms
with bath, 2 suites. Restaurant, bar, pool, meeting room. MC, V.*

$ ✕▥ **Mesón La Cadena.** In a rambling, 16th-century palace on the
★ Plaza Mayor, this bar and restaurant has some simple but very comfortable upstairs rooms, with wonderful views. Savor the gazpacho *de
fiesta extremeña* (made with brilliantly yellow-orange tomatoes). ☒
Plaza Mayor 8, 10200, ☎ *927/321463. 7 rooms with shower. Restaurant, bar. AE, MC, V.*

Nightlife and the Arts

Should you want to go to a discotheque in Cáceres, the street to find is Dr. Fleming.

Shopping

The town of Trujillo has a wider range of crafts products on sale than almost any other place in the region. Near the tourist office on the Plaza Mayor are several shops with enticing selections of regional folk arts and crafts.

Among the most attractive of Extremadura's crafts products are its multicolored rugs, blankets, and embroideries—you'll find the very best embroidered and woven products at **Maribel Vallar** (✉ Domingo de Ramos 28, no phone) where a centuries-old loom is still in use.

If your passion is woodworking products, **Domingo Pablos Barquillo** (✉ Plazuela de San Judas 3, ☎ 927/321066), just 100 yards from Trujillo's parador, specializes in locally produced wood carvings, basketwork, and furniture.

Guadalupe

★ ❾   *200 km (125 mi) southwest of Madrid, 143 km (88 mi) east of Cáceres, 96 km (60 mi) east of Trujillo, 200 km (125 mi) northeast of Mérida.*

One of the most inspiring sites in Extremadura is the monastery of Guadalupe. The journey is in itself worthwhile. Whether you are coming from Madrid, Trujillo, or Cáceres, the last stage of your trip will take you through wild, breathtakingly beautiful mountain scenery. The monastery itself clings to the slopes, forming a magical profile echoing that of the gaunt wall of mountains behind. Pilgrims have been coming here since the 14th century, but only in recent years have they been joined by a growing number of tourists. Even so, the monastery's very isolation—it is a good two- to three-hour drive to the nearest town—has saved it from the worst excesses of tourism.

The story of Guadalupe goes back to around 1300, when a shepherd uncovered a miraculous statue of the Virgin, supposedly carved by St. Luke. Its fame might have been only local had it not come to the attention of King Alfonso XI, who frequently hunted here. Alfonso had a church built to house the statue and later vowed to found a monastery, should he defeat the Moors at the battle of Salado of 1340. After his victory, he kept his promise. The greatest period in the monastery's history was between the 15th and 18th centuries, when, under the rule of the Hieronymites, it was turned into a pilgrimage center rivaling even Santiago de Compostela in importance. Documents authorizing Columbus's first voyage to America were signed here and the first American Indians to be converted to Christianity were brought here to be baptized. The Virgin of Guadalupe became the patroness of Latin America, testimony to which is found in the thousands of churches and towns dedicated to her in the New World. The decline of the monastery coincided with Spain's loss of overseas territories in the 19th century. Abandoned for 70 years and left to decay, it was taken over after the civil war of 1936–39 by Franciscan brothers, who slowly restored it.

The bus station lies just below the village of Guadalupe, leaving you with a steep climb up to the **monastery.** On sale everywhere is the copperware that has been made here since the 16th century. In the middle of the tiny, irregularly shaped main square (transformed during festivals into a bullring) is a 15th-century **fountain** where Columbus's two Indian servants were baptized in 1496. Looming in the background is the late-Gothic south facade of the **monastery church,** covered in swirling decorative motifs and flanked by battlemented towers.

The entrance to the building is to the left of the church. From the large Mudéjar cloister you progress to the chapter house, with its collection of choir books, illustrated manuscripts, and paintings, including a series of small panels by Zurbarán. The ornate, 17th-century sacristy contains the monastery's most important works of art—a series of eight paintings of 1638–47 by Zurbarán. These powerfully austere works representing monks of the Hieronymite order and scenes from the life of St. Jerome are the only important paintings by this artist still in the setting for which they were originally intended. The tour concludes with the garish, late-Baroque Camarín—the chapel where the miraculous Virgin is housed. Outside, the monastery's gardens have been renovated in the original geometric Arab style. However, the focal point is the Virgin of Guadalupe, a dark and shriveled wood object hiding under a great veil and mantle. ☎ 927/367000. ☞ *350 ptas.* ☉ *Daily 9:30– 1 and 3:30–6:30.*

Dining and Lodging

$$–$$$ ✕🏨 **Parador Nacional Zurbarán.** Occupying a former hospital and pil-
★ grim's hostel dating to the 15th century, this parador has a particularly luxuriant character, owing to its Mudéjar architecture, Moorish-style rooms with blue tile bathrooms, and exotic vegetation. The restaurant, in keeping with the spirit of the locale, serves simple local dishes, such as *bacalao monocal* (cod with spinach and potatoes) and migas. ⊠ *Marqués de la Romana 10, 10140,* ☎ *927/367075,* FAX *927/367076. 40 rooms with bath. Restaurant, pool, tennis court. AE, DC, MC, V.*

$–$$ ✕🏨 **Hospedería del Real Monasterio.** An excellent alternative if the Parador Nacional Zurbarán is full is this inn situated around the 16th-century, Gothic cloister of Guadalupe's monastery. The simple, traditionally furnished rooms with dark, wood-beam ceilings are exceptionally quiet. Despite its grand, unforgettable setting in the cloister, the restaurant is a place of unpretentious charm, specializing in modest local dishes such as *sopa de tomate* (tomato soup). ⊠ *Plaza Juan Carlos I s/n, 10140,* ☎ *927/367000,* FAX *927/367177. 47 rooms with bath. Restaurant, bar. MC, V. Closed Jan. 15–Feb. 15.*

Shopping

Guadalupe is the place to go for copper and tinware. The industry has been established here for more than four centuries.

LOWER EXTREMADURA
Mérida, Badajoz, and Zafra

This is the southern part of Extremadura, with an ocassionally more pronounced Andalucían or even Portuguese flavor. Both southern and northern provinces do share the dubious honor of having been jewels in the crown of the ancient Roman empire—the modern city of Mérida was established in 26 BC as a settlement for Roman soldiers. Named *Agusta Emerita,* it was capital of the Roman province of Lusitania.

Badajoz, historically considered a gateway to Portugal (only 7 km/4 mi from the border), has been a settlement since prehistoric times; paleolithic remains have been found in the area.

Mérida

★ ❿ *70 km (43 mi) south of Cáeres, 66 km (40 mi) east of Badajoz, 250 km (155 mi) north of Seville.*

Founded by the Romans in 25 BC on the banks of the River Guadiana and strategically situated at the junction of major Roman roads between Salamanca and Seville and Lisbon and Toledo, Mérida today is a rather unattractive, lifeless town—with the exception of its dramatic Roman complex. After its founding, the city soon became capital of the vast Roman province of Lusitania. A bishopric in Visigothic times, Mérida never regained the importance that it had had under the Romans; however, today the town boasts a series of Roman monuments finer than those in any other town in Spain.

The new, glass-and-steel bus station stands in a modern district on the other side of the River Guadiana from the center of Mérida. It commands a good view of the exceptionally long **Roman Bridge,** which spans two forks of this sluggish river.

As you cross the bridge leading into Mérida, you see in front of you the sturdy square **alcazaba** (fortress), built originally by the Romans and later strengthened by the Visigoths and Moors. To go inside, follow the fortress walls around to the side farthest from the river. Climb up to the battlements for the sweeping views of the river. ☎ 924/317309. ⌨ 350 ptas., including admission to Roman theater and amphitheater. ☉ Mon.–Sat. 9–1:45 and 5–7:15 (4–6:15 in winter), Sun. 9–1:45.

Mérida's main square, the **Plaza de España,** adjoins the northwestern corner of the fortress and is extremely animated both day and night. Its oldest building is the 16th-century palace that served for many years as the Hotel Emperatriz. Between this hotel and the town's stylish parador (☞ Dining and Lodging, *below*) stretches the most charming and best-preserved area of Mérida, comprising Andalucían-style, white houses shaded by palms.

Off the tiny Plaza de Santa Clara, at the heart of the well-preserved casco viejo, is an abandoned 18th-century church that has been turned into a dusty, old-fashioned **Museo Visigótico** (Visigothic Museum), filled with fragments of Visigothic stonework. ☎ 924/311690. ⌨ Free. ☉ June–Sept., Tues.–Sat. 10–2 and 5–7, Sun. 10–2; Oct.–May, Tues.–Sat. 10–2 and 4–6, Sun. 10–2.

NEED A
BREAK?
The Plaza de España and nearby Plaza de Santa Clara are the best places in town to linger at bars and enjoy good snacks. **Bar Lusi** (⌂ Plaza de Santa Clara s/n) serves regional delicacies.

From the Plaza de España, head for the Calle Santa Eulalia, a lively pedestrian shopping street, and continue along the **Rambla Mártir Santa Eulalia** until you reach the church of that name, which was originally a Visigoth structure marking both the site of a Roman temple and the supposed place where the child martyr Eulalia was roasted alive in AD 304 for spitting in the face of a Roman magistrate.

Try not to miss a visit to Mérida's superb, modern **Museo Nacional de Arte Romano** (Museum of Roman Art), housed in a monumentally large, brick building and containing outstanding mosaics, jewelry, statues, and other Roman works. ⌂ José Ramón Mélida 2, ☎ 924/311690. ⌨ 400 ptas. ☉ June–Sept., Tues.–Sat. 10–2 and 5–7, Sun. 10–2; Oct.–May, Tues.–Sat. 10–2 and 4–6, Sun. 10–2.

Just past the museum are the town's best-preserved Roman monuments, the **teatro** (theater) and **anfiteatro Romano** (amphitheater), arranged in a verdant park. The former, dating from 24 BC, is notable for the elegant colonnade (in front of which plays are put on during the summer months) on its stage.

OFF THE
BEATEN PATH

EXTREMADURAN SIBERIA – If you want a taste of a virtually unchanged Spain, visit the "Extremaduran Siberia," which lies between Mérida and the La Mancha town of Ciudad Real (leave N430, which links the two towns, by following signs for Casas de Don Pedro, and continue south toward Talarrubias). This poor area of wild, rolling scrubland owes its exotic name to the 12th duke of Osuna, who came here after 10 years as Spanish ambassador in Russia and was reminded of the Siberian steppes. The rickety old bus that until a few years ago served this area was even known as "the Trans-Siberian." Of the handful of villages here, the oldest is **Puebla de Alcocer,** which has an arcaded square. More unusual is the nearby village of **Peloche,** to the north of Talarrubias, where you can still see women embroidering in the streets; this same place also continues to have its ferryman, "Tío Vito," an old man in traditional costume who, for many years, has ferried people and cattle over the River Guadiana.

Dining and Lodging

$$$$
★

✕⊟ **Parador Nacional Vía de la Plata.** Built over the remains of what was first a Roman temple, then a Baroque convent, and for a while even a prison, this spacious, whitewashed building exudes an Andalucían cheerfulness, tinged with hints of its Roman and Mudejar past. The rooms are bright, with traditional, dark-wood furniture. The brilliant, white interior of the former church has been turned into a particularly restful lounge. In the dining room, be brave and try the *revuelto de criadillas* (scrambled eggs with pigs testicles) or *ranas con aroma de pimentón* (frogs legs in paprika sauce). Other traditional offerings include *cabrito al ajillo* (fried kid with garlic). ⊠ *Plaza Constitución 3, 06800,* ☎ *924/313800,* FAX *924/319208. 82 rooms with bath. Restaurant. AE, DC, MC, V.*

Nightlife and the Arts

Calle John Lennon has a number of bars and discos.

The cultural event of note on the region's artistic calendar is the **Theater Festival** at Mérida, which is held in the town's Roman theater every summer from late June to early August; for tickets and information, contact the tourist office.

Shopping

In Mérida, **Antonio Zambrano** (⊠ José Ramon Mélida 40, ☎ 924/312818) has a large selection of pottery from southern Extremadura, which is reddish brown, with delicate designs incised into the wet clay with a stone.

Badajoz

⑪ *66 km (40 mi) west of Mérida, 90 km (59 mi) southwest of Cáceres, 85 km (53 mi) northwest of Zafra.*

Badajoz is the capital of the province and is also on the main road to Portugal. It is not a particularly picturesque town; its reputation is mainly as a suitable resting point on your way though Extremadura. Be sure to admire the **Puerta de Palmas,** the 16th-century gateway into the city. The symbol of Badajoz, the gate consists of two circular, crenellated towers surrounded by decorative cordons (or guardposts) with different motifs on each façade. The other site of note in Badajoz is the **Torre Espantaperros** (Espantaperros Tower) defense watchtower of the city's *alcazaba* (Arab fortress); the practice of building such towers served as a model for the Golden Tower in Seville.

If you are in the mood for something deliciously local, simple, filling, and easy on the pesetas, stop in at **Mesón el Tronco** (⊠ Muñoz Torrero 16, ☎ 924/222076) and feast on a Badajoz-style breakfast of fried eggs with migas or hand-sieved (not blender-created) gazpacho.

Dining and Lodging

$$$ ✕ **La Toja.** This intimate, family-run restaurant specializes in Galician food, and at the entrance is one of the more familiar sights of the Galician countryside: a *horreo* (small barn raised on stilts). The emphasis is on fish, including such delicacies as *merluza a la Gallega* (hake stewed in onions, potatoes, parsley, and paprika). ⊠ *Sanchez de la Rocha 22,* ☎ *924/273477. AE, DC, MC, V. Closed Sun.*

$$$$ 🏨 **Gran Hotel Zurbarán.** This large, modern building has a beautiful position near the River Guadiana and overlooking the Castelar park. The look of the place is brash and slightly dated, but the service is nonetheless impeccable, and there are few hotels in Extremadura that offer such a range of luxury features. ⊠ *Paseo Castelar s/n, 06001,* ☎ *924/223741,* FAX *924/220142. 214 rooms with bath. Pool, tennis court, dance club, meeting rooms. AE, DC, MC, V.*

Nightlife and the Arts

The more or less swinging center of Badajoz after dark is Avenida República Argentina with its many bars and restaurants.

Zafra

⑫   *62 km (38 mi) south of Mérida, 85 km (53 mi) southeast of Badajoz, 135 km (84 mi) north of Seville.*

Worth a stop on your way up north from Andalucía or south to Seville, Zafra is unusual for its Plaza Mayor, which is actually two contiguous squares, the **Plaza Chica** (at one time a marketplace) and the 18th-century **Plaza Grande** (ringed by mansions flaunting their coats-of-arms), connected by a graceful archway. Both plazas are fun for "doing" tapas.

There are several churches here, the most noteworthy being **Nuestra Señora de Candelaria**, near the Parador Nacional Hernán Cortés; it has nine extraordinary panels by Zurburán in the *retablo* (altarpiece).

Dining and Lodging

$$$–$$$$ ✕🏨 **Parador Nacional Hernán Cortés.** The parador, which is the dom-
★   inant building in this attractive and lively town, occupies the 15th-century castle where Cortés stayed before going to Mexico. The building's military exterior conceals an elegant, 16th-century courtyard attributed to Juan de Herrera. The rooms are white and cheerful, some with wood-beam ceilings, others with windows overlooking the marble courtyard. There is a suite with a superbly elaborate *artesonado* (coffered) ceiling and the magnificent chapel now serves as the conference room. The dining room staff will make you feel like an honored explorer home from a daring journey, and will suggest you restore yourself with *caldereta de cordero* (lamb stew). For dessert, try the poached figs with vanilla ice cream or *leche frita* (fried milk custard). ⊠ *Plaza Corazón de María 7, 06300,* ☎ *924/554540,* FAX *924/551018. 45 rooms with bath. Restaurant, pool. AE, DC, MC, V.*

EXTREMADURA A TO Z

Arriving and Departing

By Bus

The bus links between Extremadura and the other Spanish provinces are far more frequent, extensive, and reliable than are the links by plane or train; the journeys also tend to be shorter. There are regular bus services to the main centers of the province from Madrid, Seville, Lisbon, Valladolid, Salamanca, and Barcelona. All the buses from Madrid go past Trujillo. The main company serving the province is **Auto Res** (⊠ Plaza Conde de Casal 6, ☎ 91/551–7200).

By Car

It is best to rent a car outside the region, either in Madrid or Seville, or before leaving for Spain. The main highway from Madrid to Extremadura, the N V, was upgraded to four lanes in 1993, greatly reducing travel time from the capital. The N630, or Via de la Plata, which crosses Extremadura from north to south, is currently being improved, with construction expected to finish in late 1996. The fastest approach from Portugal is along N4 from Lisbon to Badajoz.

By Plane

The international airports nearest to Extremadura are at Madrid and Seville; Iberia (☎ 91/329–4353) runs daily flights from both cities to Badajoz. (For airlines serving Madrid and Seville, *see* Madrid A to Z *in* Chapter 2 and Seville A to Z *in* Chapter 13.)

By Train

The principal train link with Extremadura is the line running from Madrid to Seville, passing through Plasencia, Cáceres, Mérida, and Zafra. The journey from Madrid to Plasencia takes three hours; from Seville to Zafra, 3½ hours. There is also a direct train from Lisbon, in Portugal, to Badajoz (five hours). Unfortunately, the trains run infrequently, making this a less convenient means of travel. Contact the RENFE office in Madrid for more information (91/328–9020).

Getting Around

By Bus

As with most of the traditionally poor parts of Europe, nearly every village in Extremadura is accessible by bus. However, on the lesser routes, buses tend to set off at an extremely early hour of the morning and may leave you stranded at your destination for many hours, if not overnight.

By Car

This is the most feasible way of exploring Extremadura if you are in a hurry. Off the autoroute, the main roads through the province are well surfaced and not too congested; the side roads, particularly those that traverse the wilder mountainous districts, such as the Sierra de Guadalupe, can be poorly paved and badly marked.

By Train

Only the main towns in the province can be reached by train, and the services are very infrequent: For instance, the line connecting Plasencia, Cáceres, Mérida, and Zafra has just two trains a day, one of which runs at night. The stations also tend to be some distance from the town centers.

Contacts and Resources

Bus Tours

For specialized art tours, accompanied by an expert, contact the English-based firm **Prospect Art Tours Ltd.** (✉ 454–458 Chiswick High Rd., London W4 5TT, ☎ 0181/995–2163).

Emergencies

Police: ☎ 091.

Fishing Permits

A fishing permit can be obtained from Agencia de Media Ambiente offices (✉ Enrique X Canedo, Mérida, ☎ 924/384111) and ICONA offices (✉ Avda. General Primo de Rivera 2–7, Cáceres, ☎ 927/224666).

Visitor Information

The most helpful and well equipped of Extremadura's tourist offices is at the entrance to **Mérida**'s Roman Theater (✉ Pedro María Plano s/n, ☎ 924/315353). The other tourist offices in the region are in **Alcántara** (✉ Avda. de Mérida 21, ☎ 927/390863), **Badajoz** (✉ Plaza de la Libertad 3, ☎ 924/222763), **Cáceres** (✉ Plaza Mayor 37, ☎ 927/246347), **Plasencia** (✉ C. del Rey 8, ☎ 927/422159), **Trujillo** (✉ Plaza Mayor, ☎ 927/320653), and **Zafra** (✉ Plaza de España, ☎ 924/551036). In places without tourist offices, information and maps can generally be found at the town hall (*ayuntamiento*) or the local *casa de cultura* (town cultural events center).

15 The Canary Islands

The Canary Islands are Europe's winter place in the sun. The volcanic archipelago, much closer to Morocco than to Spain, is comprised of seven major islands, each with its own personality. Visitors can explore caves, mountains, banana plantations, and pine forests, or bask on beaches and dance till dawn at glittering discos.

By Deborah
Luhrman

THE CANARY ISLANDS, a volcanic archipelago 1,280 km/800 mi southwest of mainland Spain and 112 km/70 mi off the coast of southern Morocco, lie at about the same latitude as central Florida. There are seven major islands in the chain, each with its own personality. Some are fertile and overgrown with exotic tropical vegetation; others are as dry as a bone, with lava caves and desert sand dunes. There is also Spain's highest peak, Mt. Teide, which is snowcapped for much of the year.

The best thing about the Canaries is their climate, warm in winter and tempered by cool Atlantic breezes in summer. Swimming is possible year-round. The first modern-day tourists arrived at the turn of the century from England to spend the winter months at Puerto de la Cruz in Tenerife. Today huge charter flights from Düsseldorf, Stockholm, Zürich, Manchester, and dozens of other northern European cities unload 6 million pasty-faced visitors a year.

The Canary Islands fell one at a time to Spanish conquistadors during Spain's Golden Age, at the end of the 1400s, and for centuries they lay on the edge of navigators' maps. Columbus resupplied his ships in the Canaries in 1492 before heading west to the New World; he is sometimes called the islands' first tour operator, because he helped establish the archipelago as an important trading port.

Before the arrival of the Spanish, the islands were populated by cave-dwelling people called Guanches. Their ranks were decimated by slave traders by the end of the 16th century; their most significant remains are the Cenobio de Valerón ruins on Gran Canaria.

Pleasures and Pastimes

Beaches
Most visitors come to the Canaries for the sun, and each island offers different types of beaches on which to enjoy it. The most pristine and longest beaches are the white sand strands of Fuerteventura. Lanzarote and Gran Canaria offer golden sand beaches, which come with plenty of tourist amenites like lounge chairs and para-sailing. Tenerife, despite its fame as a resort, has few natural beaches. The crowded ones that exist are man-made with imported yellow sand.

The islands of La Palma, La Gomera, and El Hierro have black sand beaches, usually in rock-flanked coves. Remember the Atlantic Ocean can be rough and chilly in the winter months.

Dining
Canarian cuisine is based on the delicious rockfish that abound near the coast and features some distinctive specialties that are worth searching out. Prices are lower than in mainland Spain.

A typical meal begins with a hearty stew, such as *potaje canario* (vegetables, potatoes, and garbanzo beans), *rancho canario* (vegetables and meat), or *potaje de berros* (a watercress soup). Although it is hard to find in restaurants, Canarian residents eat *gofio* (similar to mashed potatoes, but made by toasting wheat, corn, or barley flour and then adding milk or broth) with their first course.

The next course is fresh native fish, the best of which are *vieja, cherne,* and *sama,* all firm-fleshed, white rockfish. Accompanying the fish are *papas arrugadas* (literally, wrinkled potatoes), tiny new potatoes boiled in seawater so that salt crystals form on them as they dry. Other specialties include *cabrito* (roast baby goat) and *conejo* (rabbit), both served in *salmorejo,* a slightly spicy paprika sauce.

Another island specialty is goat's-milk cheese; the best variety comes from La Palma. Canarian malmsey wines from Lanzarote, a favorite with Falstaff in Shakespeare's *Henry IV,* are still produced today.

Meals are generally informal on the islands, although dressy clothing is appropriate when you dine in luxury hotels.

CATEGORY	COST*
$$$$	over 4,000 ptas.
$$$	3,000–4,000 ptas.
$$	1,500–3,000 ptas.
$	under 1,500 ptas.

*per person for a three-course meal, including tax but excluding drinks and service

Lodging
There are hundreds of hotels in the Canary Islands, but they tend to fray rapidly with the masses of tourists who use them. With a few exceptions noted in the hotel descriptions, it is best to stay in the newest facilities.

Through package tours, most visitors pay reasonable prices for hotel rooms, but rates for independent travelers are often exorbitant and out of line with the quality offered. For economy-minded individual travelers, the solution is to stay in newly constructed apartment complexes. Although simply furnished, they have reception desks and swimming pools, and many have restaurants. There is also the added advantage of a kitchenette in each unit.

Since it was opened in 1994, the Gran Hotel Bahía del Duque in Tenerife has consistently been voted Spain's best vacation hotel and is worth a trip in itself. The Canaries also boast two of the most romantic paradors in the national chain. The colonial Parador Conde de la Gomera on the island of La Gomera and the seafront Parador El Hierro are both unbeatable retreats. Don't go alone.

CATEGORY	COST*
$$$$	over 19,000 ptas.
$$$	12,000–19,000 ptas.
$$	6,500–12,000 ptas.
$	under 6,500 ptas.

*per standard double room, including tax

Shopping
The Canary Islands are free ports, meaning no value-added tax is charged on luxury goods such as jewelry, alcohol, and cigarettes. The streets are packed with shops, but the prices do not represent a significant saving for Americans. The islands are also famous for lacy, hand-embroidered tablecloths and place mats.

Water Sports
The Canaries have steady winds and perfect waves that attract windsurfers and surfers from all over the world. International windsurfing competitions are held here each year on Tenerife. Surfers claim the best waves in Europe break along the west coast of Lanzarote.

Exploring the Canary Islands

Tenerife has suffered most at the hands of developers, but it also has the largest number of attractions to tempt visitors, who can ride a cable car up the slopes of Mt. Teide, swim in a huge artificial lake, explore

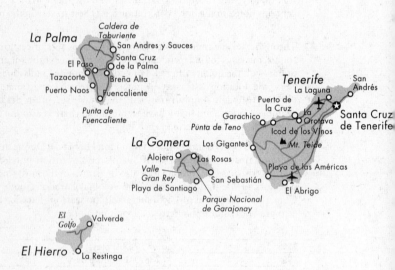

ATLANTIC

La Palma

Caldera de Taburiente
San Andres y Sauces
Santa Cruz de la Palma
El Paso
Tazacorte   Breña Alta
Puerto Naos   Fuencaliente
Punta de Fuencaliente

Tenerife   San Andrés
La Laguna
Puerto de la Cruz
Garachico   La Orotava   Santa Cruz de Tenerife
Punta de Teno   Icod de los Vinos
Los Gigantes   ▲ Mt. Teide

La Gomera
Alojera   Las Rosas
Valle Gran Rey   Playa de las Américas
Playa de Santiago   San Sebastián
El Abrigo
Parque Nacional de Garajonay

El Golfo   Valverde
El Hierro   La Restinga

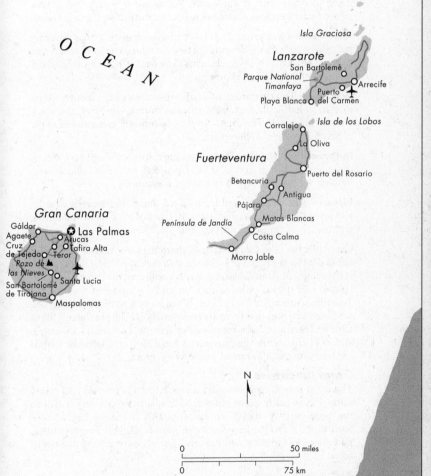

O C E A N

Isla Graciosa

Lanzarote

San Bartolomé

Parque National Timanfaya

Puerto del Carmen

Playa Blanca

Arrecife

Isla de los Lobos

Corralejo

La Oliva

Fuerteventura

Puerto del Rosario

Betancuria

Antigua

Pájara

Matas Blancas

Península de Jandía

Costa Calma

Morro Jable

Gran Canaria

Gáldar

Agaete

Cruz de Tejeda

Pozo de las Nieves

San Bartolomé de Tirajana

Maspalomas

Arucas

☆ Las Palmas

Tafira Alta

Teror

Santa Lucía

N

0   50 miles

0   75 km

AFRICA

botanical gardens, or dance at glittering discos. The beaches are small, with black sand. The verdant (read rainy) north coast retains unspoiled villages, while the southern Playa de las Américas is built chock-a-block with hotels.

Gran Canaria was the hot spot of the '60s and has an image of being passé, but its Maspalomas beach is one of the most beautiful, and an area of sand dunes behind the beach is being turned into a nature reserve. The island's capital, Las Palmas, is a vibrant Spanish city with a sparkling sandy beach right downtown.

Lanzarote is a desert isle made beautiful through thoughtful development. It has golden-sand beaches, white villages, caves to explore, and a volcanic national park where heat from an eruption in 1730 is still rising through vents in the earth. Vegetation is scarce, but grapes grown by farmers in volcanic ash produce a distinctive Canarian wine.

Fuerteventura was ignored until recently, but construction is now racing to keep up with the demands of tourists who come to windsurf and enjoy its endless, white-sand beaches. The barren interior of the island is largely the domain of goatherds.

La Palma, called the garden isle, has only recently been discovered by tourists. It has luxuriant foliage, tropical storms, rainbows, and black crescents of beach. The capital city is a beautifully preserved example of Spanish colonial architecture.

La Gomera is a paradise for backpackers. Ruggedly mountainous, it offers good hiking, and UNESCO protects its forests. Black-sand beaches are usually fringed by banana plantations.

El Hierro is the smallest and least-visited island. For tourists who really want to be alone, it offers a few beaches of black sand and a cool, highland, pine forest for walking and picnicking.

Many places in the Canary Islands share the same names. Be careful not to confuse the island of La Palma with the city of Las Palmas, which is the capital of Gran Canaria. Equally confusing, the capital of the island of La Palma is called Santa Cruz and the capital of the island of Tenerife is also called Santa Cruz. When writing to an address on one of the islands, note that there are two provinces: The province of Santa Cruz de Tenerife includes the islands of Tenerife, La Palma, La Gomera, and El Hierro, while the province of Las Palmas includes the islands of Gran Canaria, Lanzarote, and Fuerteventura.

Great Itineraries

The main reason to go to the Canary Islands is for rest and relaxation, but to really get to know the islands, try to combine a visit to the more touristy islands—Tenerife, Gran Canaria, or Lanzarote—with side trips to the less-developed islands, such as Fuerteventura, La Palma, La Gomera, or El Hierro. Each has something distinct to offer.

IF YOU HAVE 3 DAYS

A long weekend in the Canary Islands is a pricey, but effective, antidote to the stress of city living or fast-paced sightseeing. If you are flying in from mainland Spain, pick one resort, go directly there and unwind. Tenerife is a good option for first time visitors—Playa de las Américas in the winter or **Puerto de la Cruz** ② in the summer. The second day rent a car and drive up to **Mount Teide** ⑤ with a stop at the historic town of Orotava and the Casa de Vino near Los Rodeos Airport. Spend the third day working on your tan.

A ritzy alternative is to fly into Reina Sofía Airport and go to **Playa Los Cristianos** ⑥, where a 35-minute hydrofoil ride will whisk you to tiny La Gomera for three days of swimming and hiking.

IF YOU HAVE 7 DAYS

A one week visit to the Canary Islands allows enough time for a combination trip to two islands. Those who enjoy lots of touring should visit Tenerife and Lanzarote, two islands that offer an interesting contrast between lush green and volcanic desert landscapes. Begin your stay in Tenerife with an afternoon at the beach or your hotel swimming pool. The second day, rent a car to explore the center of the island, visiting **Mt. Teide** ⑤ and the town of Orotava. On the third day, spend the morning visiting **Santa Cruz** ① and perhaps the nearby town of La Laguna. Stop for lunch or wine-tasting at the Casa de Vino and in the afternoon explore the north coast villages of **Icod de los Vinos** ③ and **Garachico** ④. A 30-minute flight will get you to Lanzarote; the fifth day should be spent exploring the northern part of the island, with stops at the Jameos del Agua and the Cuevas Verdes and perhaps a visit to the César Manrique house. On the sixth day, head for Timanfaya National Park for a tour of the volcanic zone. In the afternoon detour to **Playa Blanca** and Playa Papagayo at the southern tip of the island. Save the last day for sunning and swimming before heading home.

IF YOU HAVE 14 DAYS

Two weeks is the normal length of time that European tourists spend in the Canary Islands. This would allow you to complete the above itinerary with a few extra days to relax and add an excursion to a third island. From Tenerife, La Gomera is a one-hour ferry ride away, or from Lanzarote a 45-minute ferry ride to Fuerteventura. Either option allows you to keep the same rental car and take advantage of weekly rates. If you choose La Gomera, spend one day making an excursion to Parque Nacional de Garajonay and the northern coast of the island. A second day will be needed for exploring the southern coast, with a drive out to **Valle Gran Rey.** Fuerteventura is a better choice for beachcombers or windsurfers. One day here should be sufficient for exploring the island, leaving the rest of the time for loafing or sports.

When to Tour the Canary Islands

As the tourist office loves to point out, the Canary Islands enjoy warm weather in the winter and cool breezes in summer. Christmas and Easter are peak periods for northern European tourists, while Spaniards and Italians tend to go during their August holidays. Reservations are essential at those times. The profusion of wildflowers in spring, makes it the most beautiful time to visit the islands.

Since it is a year-round destination, prices tend to be about the same no matter when you go. However, you may have some luck negotiating discounts during the slower months of May and November.

TENERIFE

Tenerife is the largest of the Canary Islands and roughly triangular in shape. It is towered over by the volcanic peak of Mt. Teide, which at 12,198 feet is Spain's highest mountain. The slopes leading up to it are forested with pines in the north, or barren lava fields in the south.

Tenerife's capital, Santa Cruz de Tenerife, is an important shipping port and the site of Spain's wildest fiesta, the pre-Lenten Carnival. (Hotels hand out awards to regular visitors, some of whom have spent 30 consecutive winters here.) In the rainy north, mixed in among the tourist attractions, are banana plantations and vineyards.

In the dry south, the resort of Playa de las Américas has sprung up at the edge of the desert over the past 15 years. It is especially popular with young couples and singles, who appreciate the world-class hotels and swinging nightlife.

Santa Cruz

Numbers in the margin correspond to points of interest on the Tenerife map.

❶ *10 km (6 mi) southwest of Los Rodeos Airport, 75 km (45 mi) northeast of Playa de las Américas.*

The port city of Santa Cruz is the capital of Tenerife. Begin with a visit to the city's heart, the **Plaza de España.** The cross is a monument to those who died in the Spanish Civil War, actually launched from Tenerife by General Franco, who had been exiled to the island. For two weeks before Lent each year, during Carnival, Santa Cruz throbs to a Latin beat emanating from the plaza.

Primitive ceramics and mummies are on display at the **Museo Arqueológico Provincial** (Archaeology Museum). The ancient Guanches mummified their dead by rubbing the bodies with pine resin and salt and leaving them in the sun to dry for two weeks. The **tourist office** is just around the corner in the same building. ⊠ *Bravo Murillo 5, 3rd floor,* ☎ *922/242090).* ▨ *400 ptas.* ☉ *Tues.–Sun. 10–8.*

The **Iglesia de la Concepción** or Church of the Conception (⊠ Plaza de la Iglesia, s/n), noted for its six-story, Moorish bell tower, is expected to remain closed for restoration until the year 2000, as part of a massive urban-renewal project that has already razed blocks of slums in this area.

The colorful city market **Mercado de Nuestra Señora de Africa** or Market of Our Lady of Africa (⊠ Avda. de San Sebastián) is part bazaar and part food emporium. Stalls outside sell household goods; inside, stands, selling everything from flowers to canaries, are arranged around a sunny patio. Downstairs, a stroll through the seafood section will acquaint you with the local fish. The market opens at 5 AM and is busy from about 6 AM to noon, Monday–Saturday.

Old Masters and modern works are housed in the two-story **Museo de Bellas Artes** (Museum of Fine Arts), including canvases by Breughel and Rivera. Many works depict local events. The museum is on the Plaza Príncipe de Asturias. ⊠ *José Murphy 12,* ☎ *922/244358.* ▨ *Free.* ☉ *Tues.–Fri. 10–7:30.*

NEED A
BREAK?

The **Bar Avenida,** an old-style sidewalk café in front of the taxi stand on the Plaza de España, is a favorite local meeting place.

A plaza on the northern outskirts of town preserves 18th-century cannons on the site of what was the **Paso Alto Fortress.** In 1794 these weapons held off an attack led by Britain's Admiral Nelson; the cannon on the right fired the shot that cost Nelson his right arm.

Santa Cruz's beach, **Las Teresitas,** is about 7 km/4 mi northeast of the city, near the town of San Andrés, and is especially popular with local families. It was constructed using white sand imported from the Sahara Desert, and planted with palms.

Tenerife

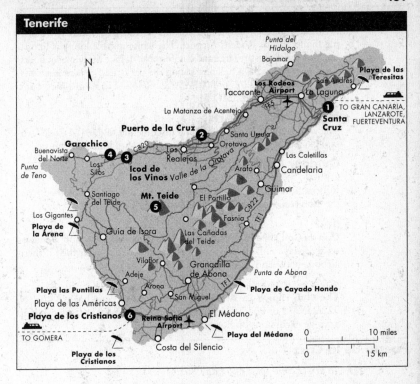

OFF THE
BEATEN PATH

LA LAGUNA – The university town of La Laguna was the first capital of the island and retains many colonial buildings along Calle San Agustin. One of these buildings, the 400-year-old colonial home of a former slave trader, was reopened as the **Tenerife History Museum.** Here you can see antique navigational maps and learn about the evolution of the island's economy. It's just 5 km/3 mi northwest of Santa Cruz. ⊠ *C. San Agustin 22,* ☎ *922/630103.* 🎫 *400 ptas.* ⏱ *Tues.–Sat. 10–5, Sun. 10–2.*

Dining and Lodging

$$$ ✕ **Mesón El Drago.** Located in the village of El Socorro, 6 km/3 mi north
★ of Los Rodeos Airport, this green-and-white, 18th-century farmhouse with brick floors and a flower-filled patio has been converted into a showcase of typical Canarian cookery. Among the best dishes on the menu are fish casserole, and *puchero canario* (a tangy stew of vegetables and meats). ⊠ *Urbanizacion San Gonzalo,* ☎ *922/543001. AE, MC, V. Closed Mon. No dinner Sun.–Thurs.*

$$ ✕ **Los Troncos.** In a middle-class neighborhood near the bullring is one of the few restaurants in Santa Cruz serving Canarian cuisine. A white, Andalucían entryway greets diners; steak and spare ribs are grilled to perfection. ⊠ *C. de General Goded 15,* ☎ *922/284152. AE, V.*

$$$$ 🏨 **Hotel Mencey.** "Mencey" was the name for the ancient Guanche kings, and you'll probably feel like one if you stay at this grandiose, beige, stucco-and-marble hotel. Crystal chandeliers and gold-leaf columns ornament the lobby. The rooms feature French Louis XIV–style furnishings. ⊠ *José Naveiras 38, 38001,* ☎ *922/276700,* 🄵🄰🄷 *922/280017. 298 rooms with bath. Restaurant, bar, pool, beauty salon, tennis court. AE, DC, V.*

$$ ▣ **Hotel Taburiente.** Across the street from the city park, this hotel is favored by businesspeople and visitors who need to catch early morning flights at Los Rodeos Airport. The white-marble lobby is luxurious, and the rooms are large and comfortable, despite the linoleum floors. Try to get one with a balcony facing the park. ⊠ *Dr. José Naveiras, 24A, 38001,* ☎ *922/276000,* ℻ *922/270562. 116 rooms with bath. Restaurant, pool. AE, MC, V.*

Nightlife and the Arts

The wood and brass-laden bar and discotheque **Andén** (⊠ C. de General Goded 41) attracts a hip young crowd with loud rock music.

Outdoor Activities and Sports

DIVING

Information on diving and underwater fishing can be obtained from the **Club Nautico** (☎ 922/273700) in Santa Cruz.

GOLF

Club de Golf El Peñon (☎ 922/636487) can be used by non-members on weekdays only. Reservations essential. Located near the northern airport, between La Laguna and Tacorante at Guamasa.

HORSEBACK RIDING

The **Club Hípica La Atalaya** (⊠ Camino de San Lazaro s/n, ☎ 922/255739 or 922/251410) on the outskirts of Santa Cruz can help arrange excursions on horseback.

Puerto de la Cruz

❷ *36 km (22 mi) west of Santa Cruz.*

Puerto de la Cruz is the oldest resort in the Canary Islands. Despite mass tourism, it remains a town with character. The old sections of town have colonial plazas and paseos for an evening stroll.

Because Puerto de la Cruz has uninviting, black-sand beaches, the town in 1965 commissioned Lanzarote artist Cesar Manrique to build **Lago Martianez,** a forerunner of today's water parks. It is an immense, public swimming pool at the seafront with landscaped islands and bridges, and fountains that spray sky-high. The complex also includes a restaurant-nightclub and several smaller pools.

Stroll from Lago Martianez along the coastal walkway until you reach the **Plaza de la Iglesia,** beautifully landscaped with flowering plants. Here you can stop at the **tourist office** for a copy of a walking tour that details all the architecturally important buildings.

NEED A
BREAK?   The **Hannen Tab**—a beer bar of burlap and rough-hewn wood, between the Plaza de Charco and the fishing port—is a great place to stop for dark German beer or a light meal.

☙ **Loro Parque** is a subtropical garden that is home to 1,300 parrots, many of which are trained to ride bicycles and perform other tricks. There's also a dolphin show, one of Europe's largest aquariums with an underwater tunnel, and a replica of a village in Thailand. ⊠ *Puerto de la Cruz,* ☎ *922/373841.* ☜ *2,300 ptas.* ☉ *Daily 8:30–5.*

Filled with thousands of varieties of exotic tropical plants, the **Jardín Botánico** (Botanical Gardens) were founded on the orders of King Carlos III in 1788 to propagate warm-climate species brought back to Spain from the Americas. ⊠ *Carreterra del Botánico* ☎ *922/383572.* ☜ *100 ptas.* ☉ *Oct.–Mar., daily 9–6; Apr.–Sept., daily 9–7.*

Wine lovers should make a point of visiting the **Casa de Vino La Baranda,** located about halfway between Puerto de la Cruz and Los Rodeos airport at the El Sauzal exit on the main highway. Opened by the Canary Islands' government in 1996 to promote local vintners, it includes a wine museum, shop, and tasting room, where for a small fee you can sample and learn about some of the best Tenerife wines. The complex also houses a tapas bar and a gourmet restaurant specializing in nouvelle Canarian cuisine. ⊠ *Km 21, Autopista General del Norte,* ☎ *922/572535.* ⊘ *Tues.–Sat. 11–8, Sun. 11–6.*

Dining and Lodging

$$$ ✕ **La Magnolia.** Perched near the botanical gardens, La Magnolia offers dining in the garden or in the main dining room, where the decor is stalled in the '60s with a purple ceiling and gold tablecloths. The open kitchen serves huge platters of seafood in garlicky sauces. ⊠ *Carretera Botánico 5,* ☎ *922/385614. AE, MC, V.*

$$$ ✕ **Palatino.** Despite its large, neon sign and a dining room that lacks atmosphere, Palatino is where local residents go when they want to eat the best fresh seafood in town. The menu is extensive, but you won't go wrong if you stick with the mixed fish or shellfish grills. ⊠ *C. El Lomo 28,* ☎ *922/382374. AE, MC, V.*

$$ ✕ **Casa de Miranda.** Just off the central square, this restored house traces its history back to 1730. On the ground floor is an inviting tapas bar, strung with gourds and garlands of red peppers, that spills onto a plant-filled patio. The high-ceilinged dining room upstairs offers favorites, such as filet mignon in pepper sauce and turbot in shrimp sauce. ⊠ *Santo Domingo 13,* ☎ *922/373871. AE, DC, MC, V.*

$$ ✕ **El Pescador.** This restaurant claims to be located in the oldest house in town, and you'll believe it when you feel the wood floor shake as the waiters walk by. Slatted green shutters, high ceilings, and rhythmic salsa music create a tropical air. Specialties include avocado stuffed with shrimp. Ask for papas arrugadas or you'll get french fries. ⊠ *Puerto Viejo 8,* ☎ *922/384088. AE, DC, MC, V.*

$$$$ ✕🏨 **Hotel Botánico.** Recently purchased by the owner of Loro Parque, this luxury, hilltop hotel was remodeled in 1996; its famous sub-tropical gardens remain untouched but the lobby now displays a collection of art from Thailand. Rooms have been spruced up with elegant, new furnishings and marble baths. Owner Wolfgang Kiessling, who is also an honorary consul of Thailand, has opened Tenerife's first Thai restaurant, **The Oriental,** on the ground floor. The first-floor restaurant, **La Parilla,** specializes in Spanish cuisine and seafood. ⊠ *Avda. Richard J. Yeoward 1, Urbanización Botánico, 38400,* ☎ *922/381400,* FAX *922/381504. 282 rooms with bath. 3 restaurants, bar, 2 pools, sauna, tennis court, gymnasium, health spa. AE, MC, V.*

$$$ ✕🏨 **Meliá San Felipe.** This 19-story hotel has the best location in Puerto de la Cruz, with million-dollar views of the coast and Mt. Teide. It has been a landmark for decades, but the large, carpeted rooms are well cared for. They feature balconies and large baths. An elegant, champagne-breakfast buffet is included in the room rate. ⊠ *Avda. de Colón 22, 38400,* ☎ *922/383311,* FAX *922/373718. 260 rooms with bath. Restaurant, bar, pool, sauna, tennis court. AE, MC, V.*

$$ 🏨 **Hotel Monopol.** One of the town's first inns, the Monopol has been lodging tourists for 103 years. Before that it was a private home, built in 1742. The small, carpeted rooms are arranged on four stories of wooden balconies around a central courtyard. Most overlook the sea or the town's main plaza. ⊠ *Quintana 15, 38400,* ☎ *922/384611,* FAX *922/370310. 100 rooms with bath. Restaurant, 2 bars, pool. AE, MC, V.*

Nightlife and the Arts

For gambling, Puerto de la Cruz has the **Casino Taoro** (⊠ Carretera del Taoro s/n, ☎ 922/380550), in a stately former hotel.

Almost all hotels have live music at night. For dancing try **Victoria** at the Hotel Tenerife Playa (⊠ Avda. de Colón s/n), a favorite with all age groups, or **El Coto** (⊠ Avda. Litoral 24, next door to the Meliá San Felipe Hotel), which is usually jammed with a young, fast crowd.

Shopping

The largest selection of hand-embroidered tablecloths and place mats is available here at **Casa Iriarte** (⊠ San Juan 17), located in the patio of a ramshackle Canarian house.

Icod de los Vinos

❸ *26 km (16 mi) west of Puerto de la Cruz.*

The quiet town of Icod de los Vinos boasts attractive plazas of unspoiled colonial architecture and Canarian pine balconies in the heart of Tenerife's most historic wine district.

A 3,000-year-old **dragon tree** towers 57 feet above the coastal highway, C820. These trees were worshiped as a symbol of fertility and knowledge by the Guanches; the sap, which turns red on contact with air, was used in healing rituals.

The **Casa Museo del Vino,** (⊠ Plaza de la Pila 4) is a tasting room where you can sample the sweet local malmsey and other Canary Island wines and cheeses.

Garachico

❹ *5 km (3 mi) west of Icod de los Vinos.*

Garachico is one of the most idyllic and best-preserved towns in the islands. It was the main port of Tenerife until May 5, 1706, when Mt. Teide blew its top, sending twin rivers of lava downhill. One filled in Garachico's harbor, and the other destroyed most of the town. Legend has it that the eruption was unleashed by an evil monk.

One of the buildings that withstood the eruption was the **Castillo San Miguel,** the tiny, 16th-century fortress on the waterfront. Island crafts, such as embroidery and basketmaking, are demonstrated inside. From the roof you can see the two rivers of lava, which are now solidified on the mountainside. The **Convento de San Francisco,** also untouched, can be visited, as can the 18th-century parish **church of Santa Ana.**

Mount Teide

❺ *60 km (36 mi) southwest of Puerto de la Cruz, 63 km (39 mi) north of Playa de las Américas.*

Four roads lead to Mt. Teide from various parts of the island, but the most beautiful approach is the road from Orotava. As you head out of town to the higher altitudes, the banana plantations give way to fruit and almond orchards that bloom in January. Higher up is a fragrant pine forest.

Orotava boasts a row of stately mansions on Calle San Francisco, just north of the Baroque church Nuestra Señora de la Concepción. At the Casa de los Balcones (⊠ C. San Francisco 3) and just across the street at the Casa del Turista (⊠ C. San Francisco 2), you can see a variety of island craftspeople at work: basketmakers, cigar rollers, and sand painters. ▦ *Free.* ⊘ *Daily 8:30–6:30.*

★ You enter the Parque Nacional del Teide at El Portillo. There is a visitors' center here where you can see exhibits explaining the region's natural history. The center also offers trail maps, guided hikes, and bus tours. ☎ 922/290129. ☉ Daily 9–4.

The park includes the volcano itself and a 6-km-/4-mi-long sunken crater at the foot of the mountain called the **Cañadas del Teide.** The cañadas area is a violent jumble of rocks and minerals, a stark landscape that looks as if it belongs to another planet. About 10 km/6 mi farther on, in the middle of the sunken crater, the cable car to Mount Tiede carries you close to the top; the final 534 feet require at least a half-hour's climb. On the way you will notice sulfur steam vents. Cable car, ☎ 922/383711. ☜ 1,000 ptas. ☉ Daily 9–5, last trip up at 4.

The trail to the rim is closed to cable-car riders when it is snowy, usually about four months a year. In that case you can still get a good view of southern Tenerife and Gran Canaria from the top of the cable-car line, but you will be confined to the tiny terrace of the bar.

Across from the Parador Nacional Cañadas del Teide are the **Roques de Garcia**—rocks that have eroded into fantastic shapes and provide a good foreground for a photo of Mt. Teide.

Dining and Lodging

$$ ✕🏨 **Parador Nacional Cañadas del Teide.** Built of stucco in the style of a ski chalet, with green shutters and balconies, the parador offers basic accommodations amid fantastic rock formations in the center of the Las Cañadas plateau at the foot of Mt. Teide. The large rooms have heavy, dark furniture and tile floors. ✉ 38300 La Orotava, ☎ 922/386415. 23 rooms with bath. Restaurant, bar, pool, tennis court. AE, DC, MC, V.

Shopping

Contemporary island crafts and traditional musical instruments can be found at the government-sponsored shop **Casa Torrehermosa** (✉ Tomás Zerolo 27) in Orotava.

Playa de Los Cristianos

❻ 74 km (44 mi) southwest of Santa Cruz, 10 km (6 mi) west of Reina Sofía Airport.

This is the newest, largest and sunniest tourist area on the island with modern, highrise hotels built chock-a-block overlooking the beaches. The attractions here are sun and nightlife. Playa de Las Américas and Los Christianos are located on the southwest island, about 1 km/⅗ mi from each other.

Los Cristianos Beach is a small crescent of gray sand surrounded by apartment houses, while Playa de las Américas is a man-made, yellow-sand beach protected by an artificial reef.

Los Gigantes, about 7 km/12 mi north of Playa de las Américas, is a smallish, gray-sand cove surrounded by rocks and towering cliffs.

☾ The **Yellow Submarine** cruises beneath the coastal waters, allowing glimpses of the rich undersea life of Tenerife's south coast. ✉ Las Galletas, ☎ 922/730013. ☜ 3,950 ptas. ☉ Daily 10–5 in good weather.

☾ **Octopus Aguapark,** a huge water park, has tall slides, meandering streams for innertubes and swimming pools. ✉ San Eugenio, Playa de las Américas, ☎ 922/792266. ☜ 1,500 ptas. ☉ Daily 10–6.

Dining and Lodging

$$$ ✕ **El Patio.** On the grounds of the Jardín Tropical Hotel, this ocean-side restaurant is spectacularly located. The famous patio ranks as the south coast's top gourmet dining spot, serving up such dishes as cold mussel soup with saffron and duck breast in mandarin orange sauce. ⊠ *Hotel Jardín Tropical,* ☎ *922/794111,* 𝖥𝖠𝖷 *922/750100. AE, DC, MC, V. Closed Mon. and June.*

$$ ✕ **Masia del Mar.** There's no menu here; you simply point to what you ★ want from the vast display of fresh fish and shellfish. Add a salad and a bottle of white wine to the order and then find a seat on a wide ter-race. ⊠ *Caleta de Adeje, 5 km/3 mi west of Playa de las Américas,* ☎ *922/710241. MC, V.*

$$$$ ✕🏨 **Jardín Tropical.** Spread on many levels over several hills, the Jardín Tropical has white turrets and archways, Moorish tile floors, and bright, flowering plants cascading everywhere. The rooms are decorated with carved-pine and wicker furniture and pastel, paisley prints; all have balconies. Baths are decorated with colorful Spanish tile. ⊠ *38660 San Eugenio, Adeje,* ☎ *922/750100,* 𝖥𝖠𝖷 *922/752844. 376 rooms with bath. Restaurant, bar, 2 pools, beauty salon, sauna, exercise room. AE, MC, V.*

$$$$ ✕🏨 **Mediterranean Palace.** Replicas of Greek statues line the entrance and the vast swimming pool, while the six-story lobby is a high-tech synthesis of marble, neon, and chrome. Glass elevators glide up to the rooms, filled with black leather and brass furniture. Beds are extra large; Baths are black marble, and each room has a terrace. ⊠ *Avda. del Litoral s/n, 38660 Arona,* ☎ *922/794400,* 𝖥𝖠𝖷 *922/793622. 532 rooms with bath. Restaurant, piano bar, pool, beauty salon, sauna, tennis court, health club, squash. AE, DC, MC, V.*

$$$ ✕🏨 **Gran Hotel Bahía del Duque.** A cross between a Canarian village ★ and an Italian hill town, this sprawling hotel is a striking jumble of pastel-colored houses and palaces, all presided over by a clock tower copied from the Torre de la Concepción in Santa Cruz. The five-story lobby is a marvel in itself, with tropical birds, palm-filled bars, and two glass elevators. All employees are dressed in traditional Canarian costumes. Guest rooms feature oversize beds, summery wicker and pine furnishings. The hotel provides opportunities for sailing and diving and runs boat trips to see a colony of whales that cavort just off the coast. ⊠ *Adeje 38660,* ☎ *922/713000,* 𝖥𝖠𝖷 *922/712369. 362 rooms. 5 restau-rants, bars, 4 pools, beauty salon, sauna, tennis court, exercise room, squash, sailing, dive shop. AE, MC, V.*

$$ ✕🏨 **Hotel Atlantic Playa.** This beachfront hotel near the Reina Sofía Airport is a favorite with windsurfers. The lobby is arranged around a fountain while the rooms have separate sleeping and sitting areas, modern, black furniture and terraces. A breakfast buffet is included, and children under 12 stay free. ⊠ *Avda. Europa, 2, 38612 El Mé-dano,* ☎ *922/176234,* 𝖥𝖠𝖷 *922/176114. 155 rooms with bath. Restau-rant, piano bar, pool, hot tub, sauna, exercise room, squash, windsurfing, playground. AE, MC, V.*

Nightlife and the Arts

For gambling in the south island, there is the **Casino Playa de las Améri-cas** (⊠ Avda. Marítima s/n, ☎ 922/793758), located in the Hotel Gran Tenerife.

In Playa de las Américas most bars are within a three-building com-plex called **Veronica's.** There you'll find places like the **Kangaroo Pub, Busby's,** and **Sgt. Pepper's,** all with young, rowdy crowds. **The Banana Garden** (☎ 928/790365) attracts an older but no less sedate crowd with live salsa music, and the disco **Prismas** (in the Hotel Tenerife Sol) remains on top after nearly a decade.

Outdoor Activities and Sports

DIVING

Information on diving and underwater fishing can be obtained from the school in Playa de las Américas at **Las Palmeras Hotel** (✉ Avda. Marítima, ☏ 922/790991).

GOLF

In the south, **Campo Golf de Sur** (☏ 922/738170) has 27 holes near Reina Sofía Airport, and not far away there are two 18-hole links at the **Amarilla Golf Club** (☏ 922/730319) in San Miguel.

WINDSURFING

Windsurfing rentals and lessons can be arranged at the **SunWind Windsurf School** (☏ 922/176174) in Playa del Médano.

GRAN CANARIA

The circular island of Gran Canaria has three distinct identities. Its capital, Las Palmas, with 370,000 people, is a thriving business center and shipping port, while the white-sand beaches of the south coast are a tourist mecca. The interior remains rural.

Las Palmas, the largest city in the Canary Islands, is very Spanish, with traffic jams, diesel-spewing buses, and hordes of shoppers. One side of the city is lined with docks for huge container ships, while the other harbors the 7-km/4-mi-long Canteras Beach.

The south coast, a boxy '60s development along wide avenues, is a family resort. At the southern tip of the island the popular Playa del Ingles gives way to the empty dunes of Maspalomas.

The interior of Gran Canaria is steep highlands that reach an elevation of 6,435 feet at Pozo de las Nieves. Although it is green in winter, Gran Canaria does not have the luxurious tropical foliage of the western islands of the archipelago.

Las Palmas

Numbers in the margin correspond to points of interest on the Gran Canaria map.

❼ *35 km (21 mi) north of Gran Canaria Airport, 60 km (36 mi) north of Maspalomas.*

Las Palmas is strung out for 10 km/6 mi along the waterfront. Begin in the old quarter, called La Vegueta, at the **Plaza Santa Ana,** with its bronze dog statues. You may be surprised to learn that the Canary Islands were not named after the yellow songbirds, but for a breed of dog (canum in Latin) found here by ancient explorers. The birds were named after the island.

The smog-stained **Catedral Santa Ana** faces the Plaza Santa Ana. The cathedral took four centuries to complete, so the 19th-century exterior with its neoclassical Roman columns contrasts sharply with the Gothic ceiling vaulting of the interior.

Baroque statues carved in the Andalusian style are on display in the cathedral's **Museo de Arte Sacro** (Museum of Religious Art), which is arranged around a peaceful cloister. Ask the curator to open the *sala capitular* so you can see the 16th-century Valencian tile floor. The trea-

Gran Canaria

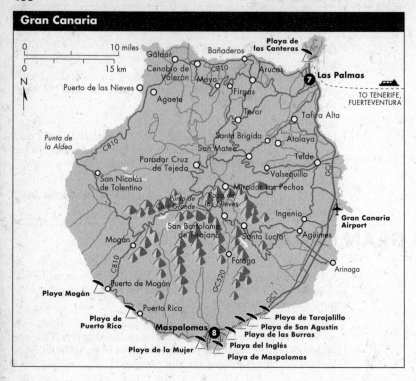

sury is closed to the public. ☎ 928/314989. 🎟 300 ptas. ⊙ Weekdays 10–4:30, Sat. 9–1:30.

The **Casa Museo Colón** (Columbus Museum) is housed in a palace where Christopher Columbus may have stayed when he stopped to repair the rudder on the *Pinta*. Models of Columbus's three ships, nautical instruments, and copies of early navigational maps are on display. Two rooms showcase pre-Columbian artifacts. ⊠ *C. Colón 1*, ☎ 928/317652. 🎟 *Free*. ⊙ *Sept.–July, weekdays 9–6, weekends 9–3.*

It's worth stopping in to see what temporary exhibits are showing at the **Centro Atlántico de Arte Moderno** (Atlantic Center for Modern Art). Although it has only been open since 1991, the center has already earned a reputation for putting together some of the best avant-garde shows in Spain. ⊠ *Los Balcones 11*, ☎ 928/311824. 🎟 *Free*. ⊙ *Tues.–Sat. 10–9, Sun. 10–2.*

A stop at the **Parque Doramas** will let you peek at the elegant Santa Catalina Hotel and Casino. Inside the park you will also find the **Pueblo Canario**, a model village designed with typical Canarian architecture. Regional folk dancing takes place in the village on Thursdays (5:30–7) and Sundays (11:30–1).

The **Castillo de la Luz**, a fortress in the port district that dates to 1494, is currently closed to the public. Nearby the sparkling, white sands of **Las Canteras Beach** are perfect for a swim or a stroll along the paseo.

Beaches

The beaches along Gran Canaria's eastern and southern coasts are the island's major tourist attraction. **Las Canteras** beach in Las Palmas is made safe for swimming by an artificial reef. It can be extremely crowded in the summer, but the sand is swept clean every night.

Dining and Lodging

$$ ✕ **Hamburg Restaurant.** Tops for atmosphere, the Hamburg specializes in filet mignon cooked a dozen different ways. The walls of the tiny restaurant are crammed with crockery, photos, and silver pitchers. For dessert, try the homemade German cakes. ⊠ *Mary Sanchez 54,* ☎ *928/222745. AE, V. No dinner Sun.*

$$ ✕ **Julio.** In this small dining room decorated with ropes, portholes, and
★ polished wood, you can tuck into 12 different types of shellfish or local fish, such as *cherne* and *vieja* served in a white-wine clam sauce. A typical Canarian soup or stew is prepared each day. ⊠ *La Naval 132,* ☎ *928/460139. AE, V.*

$$ ✕ **Mesón de la Paella.** Green-latticework window trim and lace curtains give the white-stucco mesón a homey feel. The kitchen serves up rice dishes from Spain's Mediterranean coast, such as *arroz negro* (black rice) and seafood paella. Look for the big, paella-pan sign one block from the Plaza España. ⊠ *Jose María Duran 47,* ☎ *928/271640. AE, V. Closed Sun. No dinner Sat.*

$$$ ✕⌂ **Meliá Las Palmas.** Aimed at businesspeople, the Meliá has a superb location and offers large, comfortable rooms with orange-striped carpet and orange vinyl headboards. There is a pool on a terrace overlooking the sea. A breakfast buffet is included in the room rate. ⊠ *Gomera 6, 35008,* ☎ *928/268050,* ⅛ *928/268411. 316 rooms with bath. Restaurant, coffee shop, piano bar, pool, dance club, business services. AE, DC, MC, V.*

$$ ✕⌂ **Hotel Imperial Playa.** Renovated in 1991 with business travelers in mind, the hotel sits right on Las Canteras beach and provides bright rooms with Scandinavian furniture and marble baths. The small terraces have good beach views. ⊠ *Ferreras 1, 35008,* ☎ *928/468854,* ⅛ *928/469442. 142 rooms with bath. Restaurant, snack bar, sauna, exercise room, beach. AE, MC, V.*

$ ⌂ **Apartments Brisamar Canteras.** The best-maintained of all the beach apartments, the Brisamar's are a favorite with tourists from Finland. The rooms are only functional but freshly painted and cheerful. ⊠ *Paseo de las Canteras 49, 35010,* ☎ ⅛ *928/269400. 52 studio apartments. No credit cards.*

Nightlife and the Arts

The **Las Palmas Philarmonic Orchestra** (⊠ Bravo Murillo 2123, ☎ 928/320513), one of Spain's oldest, offers an ample program of concerts between October and May. Its classical music festival in January brings in leading musicians from around the world. Information on tickets is available at the box office of the Teatro Pérez Galdós (⊠ Plaza Mercado, ☎ 928/361509).

Gamblers choose the **Gran Casino de Las Palmas** in the Santa Catalina Hotel (⊠ León y Castillo 227, Parque Doramus, ☎ 928/243040).

Las Palmas has a lively nightlife, with disco at **Ecu** and **Utopia,** both on Calle Tómas Miller, and a salsa beat emanating from **Yuca** (⊠ C. Nicolás Estebanez). The discotheque on the eighth floor of the **Hotel Reina Isabel** (⊠ Alfred L. Jones 40, ☎ 928/260100) is tops with a middle-age, international crowd and offers great views of the city.

Outdoor Activities and Sports

GOLF

The **Las Palmas Golf Club** (☎ 928/767343), on the rim of the Bandama crater about 15 minutes outside the capital, was founded in 1891 and is Spain's oldest course.

HORSEBACK RIDING

To rent horses, contact the Las Palmas Golf Club (☎ 928/351050).

Shopping

Gran Canaria has the best duty-free shops in the islands; it also boasts a department store, **El Corte Inglés** on Avenida Mesa y Lopez in central Las Palmas. For more unusual gift items, try **Antigüedades Linares** or **La Fataga** in the Pueblo Canario. The shops have a good selection of crafts from all over Spain.

Maspalomas

❽ *60 km (36 mi) southwest of Las Palmas and 25 km (15 mi) southwest of Gran Canaria Airport.*

Maspalomas is a heavily built beach resort area with all the trappings. However, it retains an appealing stretch of sand dunes and a bird sanctuary backs its popular strand. German tour operators, who bring in masses of visitors, have been instrumental in recent years in putting a new emphasis on protecting the environment.

🅒 **AquaSur** water park has chutes and tubes for splashing the day away. ⊠ *Carretera Palmitos Park, Km 3,* ☎ *928/769918.* 🎫 *1,500 ptas.* ☉ *Daily 10–6.*

🅒 **Holiday World** amusement park has roller coasters and a Ferris wheel that children can see from miles away. ⊠ *Carretera General,Campo Internacional Lote 18, Maspalomas* ☎ *928/767099.* 🎫 *Admission to park free; unlimited rides 1,550 ptas.* ☉ *Daily 5 PM–1 AM.*

🅒 **Palmitos Park** is part botanical garden and part zoo, with tropical birds and an open-air butterfly house. Trained parrots also perform. ⊠ *Carretera Palmitos, about 6 km/4 mi inland from Maspalomas,* ☎ *928/760458.* 🎫 *1,000 ptas.* ☉ *Daily 9–6.*

Beaches

Playa de Tarajalillo, with alternating areas of black sand and gravel, is the first beach of the southern resort area and a popular choice of local families. **Playa de San Agustín** is a half-mile strip of black sand fringed with a palm garden. It has rental areas for sailboards, pedal boats, and lounge chairs. **Playa de las Burras** is a gray-sand beach surrounding a crescent-shape harbor sometimes used by local fishermen.

★ **Playa del Inglés** is the most famous of Gran Canaria's beaches. Its white sands, which extend over 3 km/2 mi, swarm with beach-chair rentals, ice cream vendors, and fast-food restaurants. West of here is an area of sand dunes and a signposted nude beach.

Maspalomas Beach comes next. Its 1-km/⅔-mi-stretch of golden sand is bordered by endless dunes that provide a sense of isolation and refuge from the hustle of other Canarian resorts. Dozens of varieties of native birds and plants also find refuge in a lagoon alongside the dunes. The western edge of Maspalomas is marked by a lighthouse. **Playa de la Mujer** is a rocky beach around the point from Maspalomas and a good place to watch the sunset.

Dining and Lodging

$$ ✕ **Loopy's Tavern.** An island tradition that few visitors can resist, Loopy's is modeled after a U.S.-style western steakhouse. It features friendly waiters, imaginative cocktails, and great meat. Try the shish kebabs, which are served dangling from a metal contraption over your table. ⊠ *Las Retamas, San Agustín,* ☎ *928/762892. V.*

$$ ✕ **Tenderete II.** Canarian cuisine is cherished at Tenderete, one of the
★ few restaurants in the islands where you can order gofio, made here
with roasted corn flour and fish broth. Typical soups and stews are
served for the first course, and the main course is always fish, grilled
or baked in rock salt. Pick it out from the display hooks in the front
window. Wines from Lanzarote, El Hierro, and Tenerife are available.
⊠ *Avda. de Tirajan, Edificio Aloe,* ☎ *928/761460. AE, DC, MC, V.*

$$$$ ✕⊞ **Hotel Palm Beach.** The most sophisticated and luxurious hotel in
★ the Canary Islands, the Palm Beach is located on the edge of Maspalomas
beach in the middle of a 1,000-year-old palm oasis. The lobby is ele-
gantly striped with black-and-white marble. Spacious rooms are dec-
orated with dark, bamboo furniture and are equipped with huge closets
and large, marble baths. The terraces overlook the sea or the palms.
⊠ *Avda. del Oasis s/n, 35106,* ☎ *928/141808,* FAX *928/145108. 358
rooms with bath. Restaurant, bar, pool, beauty salon, hot tub, sauna,
tennis court, exercise room, beach, shops. AE, DC, V.*

$$$ ✕⊞ **Hotel Don Gregory.** Located on the crescent-shape Las Burras beach
is this modern, eight-story, brown-brick hotel with a relaxed atmosphere.
The large, carpeted rooms have blond-wood furniture, marble baths,
and large terraces; all overlook the beach. ⊠ *Las Tabaibas 11, 35100,*
☎ *928/773877,* FAX *928/769996. 241 rooms with bath. Restaurant, bar,
pool, tennis court, beach, dance club. AE, MC, V.*

$$ ✕⊞ **Hotel Bahía Feliz.** A sports-oriented, high-rise hotel, the Bahía Feliz
is decorated in an eclectic style that mixes Moorish tiles with Polyne-
sian batiks. The bar is a romantic spot out of the *Arabian Nights,* and
the swimming pool is the largest on the island. Rooms are split-level
and the hotel sits on its own tiny, private beach. ⊠ *Playa del Tarajalillo,
Carretera del Sur, Km 44, 35479,* ☎ *928/774025,* FAX *928/774163. 255
rooms with bath. Restaurant, bar, pool, miniature golf, tennis court,
beach, windsurfing. AE, V.*

$ ✕⊞ **Duna Flor.** This new complex of two-story, blue-and-white apart-
ment buildings is located near the Maspalomas golf course on a free
bus line to the beach. The large pool area is landscaped with bright
bougainvillea. The units have twin beds and a small balcony upstairs,
with a sitting area and kitchen downstairs. ⊠ *Avda. de Neckerman
s/n, 35100,* ☎ *928/765704,* FAX *928/766228. 282 units with bath.
Restaurant, 2 bars, kitchens, pool, playground. AE, V.*

Nightlife

Gamblers go to the **Casino Gran Canaria** in the Hotel Tamarindos in
St. Agustín (⊠ La Retama 3, Playa de San Agustín, ☎ 928/762600).

"In" discos on the south coast currently include **Spider** (⊠ Avda. Italia
s/n, Playa del Inglés, ☎ 928/264132), the **St. Agustín Beach Club** (⊠
Playa Cocoteros s/n, ☎ 928/760370), and **La Bamba** (⊠ Avda. Tira-
jana s/n, Playa del Inglés).

Outdoor Activities and Sports

GOLF
The 18-hole **Maspalomas Golf Course** (☎ 928/762581) is near the dunes.

HORSEBACK RIDING
To rent horses, contact the Palmitos Park (⊠ Carretera Palmitos,
about 6 km/4 mi inland from Maspalomas, ☎ 928/760458).

SAILING
The famous **Escuela de Vela de Puerto Rico** sailing school (☎
928/560772), where Spain's gold medalists in the 1984 Olympics
trained and teach, is at Puerto Rico (about 13 km/8 mi west of
Maspalomas).

WINDSURFING

Windsurfing equipment can be rented from the Club Mistral at the Hotel Bahía Feliz (⊠ Playa del Tarajalillo, Carretera del Sur, Km 44, 35479, ☎ 928/764600, FAX 928/764612).

Central Highlands

From Maspalomas on the southern coast, take Route GC520 toward Fataga for a good drive through the center of the island. This is sagebrush country, with interesting rock formations and cactus. A **mirador** (lookout) about 7 km/4 mi uphill offers views of the coast and mountains.

San Bartolomé de Tirajana

23 km (14 mi) north of Maspalomas, 20 km (12 mi) east of Cruz de San Antonio.

The administrative center of the south coast, San Bartolomé de Tirajana is an attractive town planted with pink geraniums. Its Sunday morning market, in front of the church, is popular with tourists, who come for the tropical produce and island crafts.

Just to the east, the village of **Santa Lucía,** is filled with crafts shops and has a small museum devoted to Guanche artifacts.

En Route   Drive up to the Cruz Grande summit on the GC520 road. To the left you can see several of the island's reservoirs, known as the lakes of Gran Canaria. They are stocked with trout, and you can fish in them if you obtain a permit from the forest service, ICONA (☎ 928/248735).

Continue on GC520 in the direction of Tejeda, past rural mountain villages. On the right is the spike-shaped Roque Nublo, an eroded volcanic chimney worshiped by the Guanches.

Tejeda

Southwest of Las Palmas de Gran Canaria.

At the village of Tejeda, the road begins an ascent through a pine forest dotted with picnic spots to the Parador Cruz de Tejada.

NEED A
BREAK?
Inside the stone-and-stucco **Parador Cruz de Tejeda** you can feast on watercress soup and swordfish, lamb, or pork served with mojo sauces. Canarian cheeses and homemade fig ice cream are on the dessert menu.

From the parador continue uphill about 21 km/13 mi to the **Mirador Los Pechos,** the highest viewing point on the island.

OFF THE
BEATEN PATH
ARTEMARA – If you want to avoid the crowds of tourists stopping for lunch at the Parador Cruz de Tejeda on your mountain tour, follow the signs to the village of Artemara, about 13 km/8 mi west of the road leading to the parador. It is an unspoiled hamlet with many cave houses built right into the side of the mountain. The restaurant **Mirador de la Silla** is in one of these cave entrances, but the cavern opens up to the other side of the mountain, where you can sit in the sun and enjoy a spectacular view. Canarian specialties are served at bargain prices.

San Mateo

15 km (9 mi) northeast of the parador.

From Tejeda, the road winds down to San Mateo, which has the **Casa Cho Zacarias** museum of rural life and a winery. The museum is open Monday–Saturday 9–1. Pass **Santa Brígida** and turn right toward the golf club on the rim of the Bandama crater. Continue to the village of **Atalaya,** where there are cave houses and pottery workshops.

Tafira Alta

7 km (4 mi) west of Las Palmas.

Located along the main road leading into Las Palmas from San Mateo, is Tafira Alta, an exclusive enclave of the city's wealthy families.

The **Jardín Canario Viero y Clavijo** botanical gardens are here, with a respected collection of plants from all the Atlantic islands grouped in their natural habitats. ☉ *Daily 9–noon and 3–6.*

The North Coast

Leaving Las Palmas by the northern road, you pass grim shantytowns before reaching the banana plantations of the coastal route. This is the greenest part of the island and is worth the trip to enjoy a seaside lunch in the pleasant village of Agaete.

Arucas

13 km (7 mi) west of Las Palmas.

An agricultural center, Arucas is the island's third-largest town. Its great, gray-stone, Gothic church looks wildly out of place among the small, white houses.

Teror

10 km (6 mi) south of Arucas.

Amidst the most verdant vegetation on Gran Canaria is the village of Teror, an obligatory stop on all island tours.

In the 18th-century church, **Nuestra Señora del Pino** (Our Lady of the Pine Tree), Gran Canaria's patron saint is seated on a silver throne above the altar. The statue, said to have been found in a pine tree in the 15th century, is now taken out for special fiestas.

Heading west, the hillside villages of **Firgas** and **Moya** are filled with more tropical foliage.

SHOPPING

Parfumes Oceano, near the church parking lot in the village of Teror, offers perfumes made locally from tropical flowers.

Agaete

8 km (5 mi) southwest of Galdar.

The quiet, leafy town of Agaete is famous for the annual fiesta of the *rama* (branch). During the August 4 fiesta, pine branches from the island's upper slopes are carried by dancing throngs of people to the town. The ritual is a variation on a rain dance dating to pre-Christian days that was used by the Guanches in times of drought.

Just beyond Agaete is the port of **Puerto de las Nieves,** where painted boats bob in the tiny harbor. The short Avenida de las Poetas leads to an old windmill on the point. Look for the rocky point called the **Dedo de Dios** (Finger of God).

NEED A BREAK? The **Cápita** restaurant (☎ 928/898272) is a favorite with Gran Canaria residents. The simple plant-filled dining room has wide windows on the harbor and classical music.

Back towards Las Palmas it is worth stopping at **Cenobio de Valerón** (Monastery of Valerón), a group of caves cut out of the rockface of a cliff and one of the islands' few accessible, Guanche archaeological sites.

Some believe that the caves were used for food storage; others, that the site was a type of convent for training the young daughters of noble families from nearby **Gáldar**, capital of the Guanche kingdom.

LANZAROTE

The fourth largest of the Canary Islands, Lanzarote is mostly solidified lava. There are no springs or lakes, and it rarely rains, so all fresh water comes from desalination plants. Despite its inhospitable volcanic landscape, however, the island has turned itself into an inviting resort through good planning and conservation.

Lanzarote was named for the Italian explorer Lancelotto Malocello, who arrived in the 14th century. But the founder of modern-day Lanzarote was artist César Manrique, whose aesthetic hand is evident throughout the island.

César Manrique, an artist and architect who died in 1992, was the unofficial artistic guru of the Canary Islands. In Lanzarote he designed most of the tourist attractions and convinced authorities to require all new buildings to be painted white with green trim to suggest coolness and fertility. He also led the fight against overdevelopment.

Arrecife

6 km (4 mi) east of the airport.

The capital city of Arrecife, with its cinderblock houses, is the most unattractive part of the island. But stop at the well-organized **tourism office** in the municipal park.

The **Castillo San Gabriel** is a double-walled fortress once used to keep pirates at bay. An archaeology museum is housed within, and you can see copies of some of the Guanche cave drawings found on the island. ⌨ *250 ptas.* ☉ *Weekdays 8–3.*

On the waterfront, the old fortress **Castillo San José** was turned into the stunning **Museo de Arte Contemporaneo** (Museum of Contemporary Art) by Manrique, one of whose paintings is on exhibit, along with other modern Spanish works. Go down the space-tunnel staircase for a look at the glass-walled restaurant that faces the harbor. ⌨ *Avda. de Naos s/n,* ☎ *928/812321.* ⌨ *Free.* ☉ *Museum daily 11–9.*

Dining

$$$ ✕ **Castillo San Jose.** Black and white furniture, glass walls, and modern art give the remodeled fortress an elegant feel. At the equally sophisticated restaurant try the cold avocado soup with caviar, or salmon steak wrapped in cured ham. ⌨ *C. Puerta de Naos s/n,* ☎ *928/812321. AE, V.*

Costa Teguise

7 km (4 mi) northeast of Arrecife.

Costa Teguise is a tasteful, green-and-white development of apartments and a few large hotels. Notice how the chimneys on the bungalows all have different decorative shapes. King Juan Carlos owns a villa here near the Meliá Salinas hotel. Costa Teguise has several small beaches; the best is **Las Cucharas.**

The **Jardín de Cactus** (Cactus Garden), just north of Costa Teguise between Guatiza and Mala, was the last Manrique-designed addition to the island. The giant, green, metal cactus that marks the entrance comes perilously close to tacky, but the gardens artfully display nearly

10,000 cacti. There is also a restored windmill that grinds and sells gofio. ☎ 928/529397. ☒ 425 ptas. ☉ Daily 10–6.

Nearby, **Playa de la Garita** is a wide bay favored by surfers in winter, while snorkelers enjoy the crystal water in summer.

★ **Los Jameos del Agua** (water cavern), 15 km/9 mi north of the Costa Teguise, is a natural wonder created when molten lava streamed through an underground tunnel and hissed into the sea. Eerie music creates a mysterious atmosphere as you explore the cavern. Look for the tiny white crabs on the rocks in the underground lake. This species of blind, albino crab is found nowhere else in the world, and there is talk of closing the jameos to save the crabs from extinction. ☎ 928/835010. ☒ Days 800 ptas., nights 1,100 ptas. ☉ Daily 11–6:45, Tues. and Sat. also 7 PM–3 AM.

★ ♺ Across the highway from the Jameos del Agua, the **Cuevas Verdes** are for more adventurous cave explorers. There are guided walks through a 2-km/1-mi section of underground volcanic passageway. There is so little humidity that no stalactites have formed, but the walk is one of the best tours on the island. ☎ 928/173220. ☒ 700 ptas. ☉ Daily 10–6, last tour at 5.

The little fishing village of **Orzola,** is 9 km/5 mi north of Jameo del Agua. A small excursion boat leaves here each morning for the neighboring islet of **La Graciosa,** where there are only 500 people and plenty of solitary beaches.

NEED A BREAK?

In Orzola, stop at the sunny, harborside restaurant **Perla del Atlantico** (✉ Avda. Marítima, ☎ 928/835146) for a memorable lunch.

♺ **Guinate Tropical Park,** in the northern part of the island, has 1,300 species of exotic birds and animals. ☉ Daily 10–5.

Dining and Lodging

$$$ ✕ **La Jordana.** This unpretentious restaurant with a beamed ceiling and white walls is one of Lanzarote's most popular dining spots. The menu features international fare with French touches. Try the homemade pâté, veal with apples, or locally caught cherne in orange sauce. ✉ Los Geranios 10–11, ☎ 928/590328. AE, V. Closed Sun. and Sept.

$$ ✕ **Grill Casa Blanca.** Inside a tiny, octagonal house, this restaurant has the atmosphere of an English country cottage, with stained-wood floors and wreaths of dried flowers. There is an open kitchen in the main dining room where you can watch the chef. Try the avocado and shrimp salad, steak with green peppercorns, or local fish dishes. ✉ Las Olas 4, ☎ 928/590155. AE, MC, V. No lunch.

$$$$ ✕🏨 **Meliá Salinas.** A stunning hotel built around an interior tropical ★ garden with hanging vines, palms, waterfalls, and songbirds, the Meliá Salinas offers a chance to rub elbows with vacationing political leaders from Europe. The guest rooms have louvered closets and doors, and all have large, flower-filled terraces that face the sea. The hotel's gourmet restaurant, La Graciosa, is Lanzarote's swankiest dining spot; peruse such menu items as giant prawns, duck breast in plum sauce, and halibut wrapped in chard. ✉ Costa Teguise 35509, ☎ 928/590040, FAX 928/590390. 310 rooms with bath. 2 restaurants, 2 bars, pool, beauty salon, sauna, 5-hole golf course, tennis court, exercise room, squash, basketball, football, archery, beach, shops. AE, DC, MC, V.

$$$ ✕🏨 **Teguise Playa.** Don't be put off by the cold, glass exterior of this hotel; the six-story lobby is filled with plants, and the staff is friendly. The rooms have white-tile floors and bamboo furniture. Each has a

geranium-filled terrace with a sea view over the hotel's private beach. ✉ *35509 Urbanización Costa Teguise,* ☏ *928/590654,* FAX *928/590979. 325 rooms with bath. Restaurant, bar, 2 pools, beauty salon, sauna, tennis court, exercise room, squash, beach. AE, MC, V.*

$
★   ✕🖫 **Apartamentos Las Cucharas.** Housed in attractive, three-story buildings with decorative chimneys, these new apartments sit right on Las Cucharas beach. They have knotty-pine furniture and terraces, with one or two bedrooms. The pool area is beautifully landscaped. ✉ *35509 Urbanización Costa Teguise,* ☏ *928/590700. 66 units with bath. Restaurant, bar, pool, beach. AE, V.*

Outdoor Activities and Sports

DIVING

The island's only official diving center is at Las Cucharas. **Diving Lanzarote** (☏ 928/590407) is run by a German who speaks perfect English. He rents equipment, leads guided dives, and offers a certification course.

GOLF

Lanzarote's 18-hole **Campo de Golf Costa Teguise** (☏ 928/590512) is just outside the Costa Teguise development and features unusual sand traps filled with black-lava cinders.

WINDSURFING

Water-sports fanatics can arrange windsurfing lessons and rent equipment from the **Lanzarote Surf Company** (☏ 928/591974) at Las Cucharas beach.

Shopping

For a good selection of island crafts, spend your Sunday morning between 10 and 2 at the open market in the village of **Teguise.** Some vendors set up stalls in the plaza; others simply lay out a blanket in the street and sell embroidered tablecloths, leather goods, costume jewelry, African masks, and thousands of other items.

Puerto del Carmen

12 km (7 mi) southwest of Arrecife.

Lanzarote has good, sandy strands in the Puerto del Carmen area, and this is where most tourists head. **Playa Grande,** the main beach of Puerto del Carmen, is a long strip of yellow sand where you can rent sailboards, jet skis, skates, and lounge chairs. It is backed by a 3-km/2-mi stretch of souvenir shops and restaurants of every national persuasion. **Playa de los Pocillos** is slightly north of Puerto del Carmen, and the site of most of the area's development. Hotels and apartments are restricted, however, to the other side of the highway, leaving the 2-km (1¼-mi) beach of yellow sand surprisingly untamed. **Playa Matagorda,** the northern extension of Playa de los Pocillos, has alternating sections of gravel and gray sand. It is favored by surf fishermen.

Dining and Lodging

$$
✕ **El Varadero.** This converted fishermen's warehouse on the tiny harbor features a honky-tonk piano player and an informal atmosphere. The food is typically Canarian with fresh fish and papas arrugadas, and the tapas bar at the entrance is also popular. ✉ *Varadero 22,* ☏ *928/825711. AE, V.*

$$
✕ **Grill La Cascada.** Named for the gushing waterfall in the middle of the spacious dining room, La Cascada is a favorite with local families as well as tourists, all attracted by the ambitious food at moderate prices. Start with stuffed avocados, then the brochette of fish and prawns. ✉ *Roque Nublo 5,* ☏ *928/513162. AE, V.*

$$ ✕⊞ **La Geria.** You enter on the third floor, where a marble staircase leads to lower floors. The rooms are carpeted and decorated with a sophisticated color scheme of slate blue and gray. Each has a little terrace with views of the beach across the street. ⊠ *Playa de los Pocillos, Tias, 35510,* ☎ *928/511351,* FAX *928/510441. 244 rooms with bath. Restaurant, bar, pool, beauty salon, sauna, tennis court, exercise room, shops, playground. AE, DC, MC, V.*

$$ ✕⊞ **Los Farriones.** The granddaddy of Lanzarote's resorts has retained an exclusive, elegant atmosphere as its tropical gardens designed by César Manrique have matured. The rooms are smallish with rattan furniture and linoleum flooring, but each has a terrace with views of the gardens and sea. ⊠ *Roque del Oeste 1, 35510,* ☎ *928/510175,* FAX *928/510202. 237 rooms with bath. Restaurant, bar, pool, sauna, miniature golf, tennis court, exercise room. AE, V.*

Nightlife and the Arts

Most nightlife in Lanzarote centers on the hotel bars, all of which feature live music. The island's most popular bar and meeting place is the **Hawaiian Pub** (⊠ Avda. Marítima 74) in Puerto del Carmen. For dancing, try **Tiffany's** (⊠ Avda. de Suiza 2, Playa de los Pocillos, ☎ 928/511344), an upscale disco for all ages; or **Jokers** (⊠ Avda. de las Playas, ☎ 928/510242), a disco with a giant aquarium on the strip in Puerto del Carmen. The **Casino** (⊠ Avda. de las Playas, s/n) has moved to Puerto del Carmen at Playa de los Pocillos.

Outdoor Activities and Sports

Mountain biking has become very popular here in the last few years. It's actually a very practical way to tour the island: Lanzarote is not particularly hilly, so you don't have to be a veteran of bike marathons to enjoy the ride. Rentals are available at **Fire Mountain Biking** (☎ 928/512267) in Puerto del Carmen.

Tahíche

5 km (3 mi) south of Teguise.

In Tahíche, the unusual, former home of artist Manrique has been opened to visitors as the **Fundación César Manrique.** On display are a collection of his paintings and sculptures, as well as works by other 20th-century artists. But the real attraction is the house itself, designed by Manrique to blend in with the volcanic landscape. The lower level is built in a series of caves. ⊠ *Carretera Tahíche-San Bartolomé, 2 km/1¼ mi west of Tahíche,* ☎ *928/843078, 843038.* ⊡ *800 ptas.* ☉ *Mon.–Sat. 10–7, Sun. 10-3; closed holidays.*

Yaiza

14 km (8 mi) west of Puerto del Carmen.

Yaiza is a quiet, whitewashed village with good restaurants. It was mostly destroyed by a river of lava in the 1700s and is best known as the entryway to the volcanic national park.

★ The **Parque National Timanfaya,** popularly known as the fire mountains, takes up much of the volcanic southern part of the island. As you enter the park from Yaiza, the first thing you'll see is the staging area for the **camel rides.** Many of the Canary Islands offer camel rides, but these are the most famous and a big attraction for tourists. The brief rides are so bumpy you'll be glad they're not longer.

The volcanic landscape inside Timanfaya is a violent jumble of exploded craters, cinder cones, lava formations, and heat fissures. The park is strictly protected, and you can visit it only on a bus tour. Taped commentary in English explains how the parish priest of Yaiza took notes during the 1730 eruption that buried two villages. ☎ 928/840057. ✉ 900 ptas. ⊙ Daily 9–5.

NEED A BREAK?	Timanfaya is the site of one of the world's most unusual restaurants, **El Diablo,** where chicken, steaks, and spicy sausages are cooked over the crater of the volcano using the earth's natural heat. If you're not hungry, you can still watch, and there are additional heat vents below the restaurant if you want to have your own volcanic barbecue.

Dining

$–$$ ✕ **La Era.** One of the only three buildings that survived the eruption of the volcano of Yaiza in 1730, this farmhouse restaurant offers simple dining rooms with blue-and-white checkered tablecloths on tables arranged around a center patio. This is a great place to try regional dishes such as goat stew, cherne in cilantro sauce, or Canarian cheeses. ✉ Barranco 3, Yaiza ☎ 928/830016. AE, DC, MC, V.

Playa Blanca

15 km (9 mi) south of Yaiza.

Playa Blanca is Lanzarote's newest resort area. The ferry for Fuerteventura leaves from here, but there's not much more to the town. Tourists come for the exquisite, white-sand beaches, reached via hard-packed dirt roads on **Punta de Papagayo.** The most popular beach is **Playa Papagayo.** Bring your own picnic; there's just one bar.

Lanzarote's agricultural belt can be seen just north of here. Notice the way grapes in **La Geria** are grown in cinder pits surrounded by a ring of volcanic rock. The rocks provide protection from the wind, and the cinders allow dew to drip through to the roots.

Dining and Lodging

$$ ✕🏨 **Lanzarote Princess.** Located near the virgin beaches of Lanzarote's south shore, the Lanzarote Princess is a modern, white, three-story building with an airy, plant-filled lobby. The rooms are a bit small and have linoleum floors; bright flowered bedspreads compensate a little for the somewhat sterile effect. The grounds, on the other hand, are vast and have good sports facilities and a huge pool with a bar on an island in the middle. ✉ Playa Blanca, Yaiza 35570, ☎ 928/517108, 🖷 928/517011. 439 rooms with bath. Restaurant, bar, beauty salon, miniature golf, tennis court, squash, playground. AE, MC, V.

Outdoor Activities and Sports

CYCLING
Mountain bike rentals are available in Playa Blanca at **Zafari Cycle** (☎ 928/517691).

FUERTEVENTURA

The dry island of Fuerteventura is a beachcomber's dream come true. It's the second largest of the Canary Islands, but the least inhabited, with only 20,000 people.

The two main resort areas are Corralejo, known for its acres of sand dunes, and the Jandia peninsula, with dozens of beaches, including one that's 26 km/16 mi long. Tourism is relatively new to Fuerteventura, and both areas are in the midst of an uncontrolled building craze.

Puerto del Rosario

5 km (3 mi) north of the airport.

Fuerteventura's capital, Puerto del Rosario, has long suffered from an image problem. It used to be called Puerto de Cabra (Goat Port), but the improved name has not changed the fact that it is a poor city with little of interest.

Corralejo

38 km (23 mi) north of Puerto Rosario.

Towering sand dunes that dwarf the beachfront hotels are the most characteristic feature of Corralejo. These hills of sand have blown across the sea from the Sahara Desert, just 96 km/60 mi away, and it's not hard to imagine the island as a detached piece of Africa.

South 19 km/11 mi on the inland road, is the **Casa de los Coroneles,** the island's principal historic building. Military governors built the immense house in the 1700s and ruled the island from it until the turn of the century. It is not open to the public.

Beaches

Playa de Corralejo, about a mile south of the town, is fringed by mountains of sand dunes and faces Los Lobos Island across the channel. Nude sunbathing is the norm at the more remote spots.

Playa el Algibe de la Cueva, on the northwest side of the island, has a castle once used to repel pirates and is frequented by locals.

Dining and Lodging

$$$$ ✕🏨 **Tres Islas.** This luxury resort sits right on the empty, white beach near the Correlejo dunes. The hotel is built around a central swimming pool complex decorated with yellow-and-white-striped tents. The bedrooms are more formal, with soft green carpeting, dark wood furniture, and floral prints. All have terraces. ✉ *Grandes Playas, 35660 Corralejo,* ☎ *928/535700,* 𝗙𝗔𝗫 *928/535858. 365 rooms with bath. Restaurant, piano bar, 2 pools, beauty salon, sauna, tennis court, exercise room, beach, shops, playground. AE, V.*

$$ ✕🏨 **Oliva Beach.** The boxy, eight-story Oliva Beach is next door to Tres Islas and owned by the same company. The rooms are smallish with linoleum floors and orange drapes, but each has a furnished terrace with views of the endless beach. There is an Olympic-size swimming pool, and the friendly staff runs a miniclub to keep youngsters busy all day. ✉ *Grandes Playas, 35660,* ☎ *928/866100,* 𝗙𝗔𝗫 *928/866154. 410 rooms with bath. Restaurant, bar, pool, beauty salon, tennis court, dance club, playground. AE, V.*

Outdoor Activities and Sports

DIVING
The channel between Corralejo and the tiny Isla de Lobos is rich in undersea life and favored by divers as well as sport fishermen.

WINDSURFING
One of Fuerteventura's biggest tourist attractions is **windsurfing.** Boards are for rent at most hotels, and one of the main schools is **Ventura Surf** (☎ 928/866040) in Corralejo.

Betancuria

25 km (15 mi) southwest of Puerto Rosario.

Betancuria was once the capital of Fuerteventura but now is almost a ghost town, with only 150 residents.

Tourists come to visit the weather-worn colonial **church of Santa María de Betancuria**, originally intended to be the cathedral of the Canary Islands. The **Museo de la Iglesia** (church museum) contains a replica of the banner carried by the Norman conqueror Juan de Bethancourt when he seized Fuerteventura in the 15th century. Most of the artwork was salvaged from the convent now in ruins nearby. ✉ *Museum 100 ptas.* ☉ *Weekdays 9:30–5, Sat. 9:30–2.*

The **Museo Arqueológico** (Archaeology Museum) and a crafts workshop are on the other side of the ravine that cuts through the tiny hamlet.

In **Antigua,** 8 km/5 mi east, you can visit a restored, white, Don Quixote–style windmill that was once used for grinding gofio. The modern, metal windmills you see throughout the island have been imported from the United States and are used for pumping water.

Pájara

16 km (10 mi) south of Betancuria.

Pájara is the administrative center of the booming Jandia peninsula and sports a two-block strip of boulevard, pretty wrought-iron street lamps, and a brand-new city hall.

NEED A BREAK?   Typical Fuerteventura lunches are served at **El Brasero,** a patio-style grill along the highway in Tarajalejo, 34 km/20 mi south of Pájara. The island specialties are roast goat and goat cheese.

Fuerteventura was once divided into two kingdoms, and a wall was built across the Jandia peninsula to mark the border. Remnants of that wall are still visible today inland from **Matas Blancas,** 42 km/26 mi south of Pájara on highway GC640.

Costa Calma

7 km (4 mi) south of Matas Blancas.

As you continue south along the coast from Matas Blancas, the beaches become longer, the sand whiter, and the water bluer. The famous **Playas de Sotavento** (Sotavento Beaches) begin near the Costa Calma developments and extend gloriously for 26 km/16 mi. Nude sunning is favored here, except for directly in front of hotels.

Dining and Lodging

$ ✕ **La Taberna Costa Calma.** Usually packed with locals and tourists, La Taberna serves Mexican specialties such as guacamole, as well as typical Canarian dishes, in several small dining rooms with stone archways and checked tablecloths. Try the *pescado a la sal* (fish baked in a crust of rock salt that is chipped away before eating). Garlic soup and goat cheese with mojo sauce are other specialties. ✉ *Carretera Jandia s/n, no phone. No credit cards.*

$$$ ✕▥ **Fuerteventura Playa.** This sophisticated, low-slung hotel, built around a large, kidney-shape pool and thatch-roof bar, is located at the north end of the 26-km/16-mi Sotovento beach. The rooms have slate-blue carpet and modern, white furnishings with extra-large beds. Plant-filled terraces overlook the beach. ✉ *Urbanización Canal del Río Poligono C1, 35627,* ☎ *928/547344,* 🖷 *928/547097. 300 rooms*

with bath. *Restaurant, bar, pool, beauty salon, sauna, tennis court, exercise room, windsurfing. AE, V.*

$$–$$$ ✗ 🏨 **Sol Gorriones.** All by itself in the middle of the Sotavento coast, the Sol Gorriones, Jandia's first resort, is beginning to show its age. Most guests ignore the shag carpeting and '60s-style room decor, preferring to spend all their time outdoors. ✉ *Playa Barca, Gran Tarajal 35620,* ☎ *928/547025,* ℻ *928/547000. 309 rooms with bath. Restaurant, bar, 3 pools, beauty salon, miniature golf, tennis, windsurfing, playground. AE, MC, V.*

$$ ✗ 🏨 **Barlovento Club Hotel.** The Barlovento is a full-service, all-suite hotel and an excellent value. The three-story building with blue, metal railings looks a bit like a ship run aground on Sotovento beach. The suites include separate bedrooms, sitting areas, terraces, and kitchenettes. ✉ *Costa Calma, 35627,* ☎ *928/547002,* ℻ *547038. 226 suites. Restaurant, piano bar, kitchenettes, pool, sauna, miniature golf, tennis court, exercise room, squash. AE, V.*

Outdoor Activities and Sports

Windsurfing boards can be rented at most beach hotels. For lessons try **Windsurf Urlaub** (☎ 928/870825) at the Sol Gorriones hotel on Sotavento Beach.

Morro Jable

★ *At the southernmost tip of the island.*

At the southernmost point of the island is the old fishing port of Morro Jable, well on its way to becoming the next Tenerife. Many more miles of virgin coast exist beyond here—down a dirt road that eventually leads to the lighthouse—and beaches along the entire windward side of the peninsula remain untouched.

Beaches

Beyond the town of Morro Jable, a dirt road leads to the isolated beaches of Juan Gomez and **Playa de las Pillas.** Following the dirt tracks across the narrow strip of land, you can visit the equally empty **Playa de Cofete** and **Playa de Barlovento de Jandia.**

Dining

$$ ✗ **Casa Emilio.** The best of the restaurants blossoming along Morro Jable's harbor, Casa Emilio has a wood-burning grill in the dining room where fresh fish is cooked as you watch. The kitchen also turns out delicious crab cocktail, pepper steak, and paella. ✉ *1 block uphill from harbor (sign visible from harbor),* ☎ *928/540054. No credit cards.*

Outdoor Activities and Sports

For **scuba diving** and **snorkeling,** head for rocky outcroppings on the windward side of Jandia.

LA PALMA

La Palma is a green and prosperous island that managed to exist quite successfully in the past without tourism. But now that it has been "discovered," La Palma is handling the new visitors with good taste by emphasizing the island's natural beauty, traditional crafts, and cuisine. The local residents, called Palmeros, are especially friendly.

Santa Cruz de la Palma

★ *6 km (4 mi) north of the airport.*

Santa Cruz de la Palma is the capital of the island and was an important port and bustling shipbuilding center in the 16th century. Then in 1533 a band of buccaneers led by French pirate François le Clerc raided the city and burned it to the ground. With money from the Spanish king, La Palma was rebuilt, which is why the city today has such a unified colonial appearance.

Walk up the cobblestone main street, Calle O'Daly, which everyone calls Calle Real. Take a peek inside the elegant patio of the **Palacio Salazar,** where the tourist office is located.

The triangular **Plaza de España** in front of the **Iglesia El Salvador** is the focus of city social life and fills with people in the early evening. The church is the only building that survived the pirate fire; it has a handsome, Moorish, carved ceiling. Bring a flashlight if you want to see the religious art on the walls. Note the stone shields on the **city hall,** across the plaza. One is the coat of arms of Spain's Habsburg kings, and the other is the emblem of La Palma. Walk uphill one block to the corner of Calle de la Puente, then look back at one of the most charming streets in the Canaries.

NEED A BREAK?	The **Café La Placeta,** in a small plaza on Avenida Perez de Brito, is a good place for a break. You can sit under the striped umbrellas next to the splashing stone fountain.

Located in the restored cloisters of the church of San Francisco the **Museo Insular** houses exhibits tracing the navigational and trading history of La Palma, as well as Guanche artifacts. ⊠ *Avda. Perez de Brito,* ✉ *200 ptas.* ⊙ *Weekdays 9:30–1 and 4–7:30.*

The **Museo Bellas Artes** (Fine Arts Museum) next door to the Museo Insular has a good collection of Flemish and Spanish paintings. ✉ *Free.* ⊙ *Weekdays 9:30–1 and 4–7:30.*

You can't miss the life-size, cement replica of **Columbus's ship** *Santa María,* at the end of the Plaza Alameda. A tiny naval museum is below decks. ✉ *150 ptas.* ⊙ *Weekdays 9:30–2 and 4–6:30.*

The star-shape **Castillo Real** on Calle Mendez Cabezola, is a fortress that dates to the 16th century. Nearby, along **Avenida Marítima,** is a much-photographed row of Canarian houses with the typical green balconies. Stop in at **Tabacos Vargas** (⊠ Avda. Marítima 55) to see the famous palmero cigars being rolled by hand. The cigar industry is a result of constant migration between the Canary Islands and Cuba. Those with a taste for fine cigars claim hand-rolled palmeros are better than the cigars now being manufactured in Cuba.

The hilltop village of **Las Nieves,** 3 km/2 mi northwest of Santa Cruz, has a beautifully preserved colonial plaza and the opulent **church of Nuestra Señora de las Nieves** (Our Lady of the Snows), which houses La Palma's patron saint, the Virgin of the Snows. The Virgin, credited with saving many a ship from disaster, sits on a gold altar wearing vestments studded with pearls and emeralds.

Dining and Lodging

$$ ✕ **El Brasero.** Located along the seafront, this is where native Palmeros head for a special meal of grilled steaks or fish served by especially friendly waiters. ⊠ *Avda. Marítima 54,* ☏ *922/414360. MC, V.*

$$ ✕ **Mesón del Mar.** If you take an excursion to the north part of the island, follow the road down from San Andrés to the tiny fishing harbor at Puerto Pesquero Espindola, and you'll end up at this popular seafood house. Fish couldn't be any fresher than it is here. ⊠ *Puerto Pesquero Espindola,* ☏ *922/450305. No credit cards.*

$ ✕ **Chipi Chipi.** In the hills above Santa Cruz and 3 km/2 mi beyond the
★ church in Las Nieves is this restaurant, tucked away behind dense tropical gardens with chirping parrots. Each party of diners is seated in a
private stone hut. The food is strictly local, and portions are huge. You
can start with salad or garbanzo-bean soup, followed by grilled meats
washed down with local red wine. ⊠ *Carretera de las Nieves,* ☎
922/411024. MC, V. Closed Wed.

$ ✕⌂ **Castillete Aparthotel.** Right on the seafront but down the street
from the heavy traffic, this new hotel is the best choice if you want to
stay in the city. Most of the units are studios with divided sitting and
sleeping areas and small kitchens. White wood and natural-pine furniture give the rooms a clean, modern look. ⊠ *Avda. Marítima 75,
38700,* ☎ *922/420054,* FAX *922/420067. 42 apartments. Restaurant,
pool, hot tub. AE, MC, V.*

Shopping
The best crafts and food products La Palma has to offer can be found
at **La Graja Centro de Artesania,** near the Mirador de la Concepción
outside Santa Cruz. Listen to the folk music on the stereo and sample
the local wine. Embroidery, baskets, pottery, cookbooks, bottled mojo
sauce, cigars, and other locally produced items are available.

Playa de los Cancajos

5 km (2 mi) south of Santa Cruz de la Palma.

While La Palma is not known for its beaches, these black-sand coves
are popular with summertime swimmers. Los Cancajos, 5 km/2 mi south
of the capital, is a small town with a crescent-shape beach and crys-
talline water.

Dining and Lodging

$$ ✕ **Tres Chimineas.** An outgoing Palmero married to an Englishwoman
runs this attractive restaurant just outside Los Cancajos. Three deco-
rative chimneys mark the building; inside you'll find fresh flowers and
a sunny, yellow decor. Local fish are the specialty—vieja is the best. ⊠
Carretera de Los Llanos de Aridane, Km 8, ☎ *922/429470. AE, V.*

$$ ✕⌂ **Hacienda San Jorge.** Built to resemble a Canarian village, the San
★ Jorge offers apartment units grouped in pastel-colored bungalows.
The apartments have summerhouse furniture, separate bedrooms, living area, kitchenette, bath, and terrace. The complex is built on several different levels surrounding a lake-size swimming pool just a few
steps up from the black-sand beach. ⊠ *38700,* ☎ *922/181066,* FAX
*922/434528. 155 apartments. Restaurant, bar, kitchenettes, pool, hot
tub, sauna, exercise room, beach, playground. AE, V.*

$$ ✕⌂ **Taburiente Playa.** Opened in 1996, this crescent-shaped resort hotel
has fantastic sea-views from nearly every room. It is designed so the
guest never needs to leave the premises, with two swimming pools, a
gym, activities for children, and nightime entertainment for the adults.
⊠ *Playa de los Cancajos, 38712,* ☎ *922/181277,* FAX *922/181285. 293
rooms with bath. Restaurant, satellite TV, 2 pools, wading pool, sauna,
gym, nightclub, playground. AE, V, MC.*

Fuencaliente

28 km (17 mi) south of Santa Cruz de la Palma.

Near Fuencaliente, the scenery becomes dry as you reach the volcanic,
southern tip of the island. Visit the **San Antonio volcano** and the
Teneguía volcano, the site of the most recent eruption in the Canary

Islands. In 1971 Teneguía burst open, sending rivers of lava toward the sea and extending the length of the island by 3 km/2 mi. There are good beaches in the cinders below the volcano, reached over unpaved roads.

Fuencaliente is the heart of La Palma's wine region, and the modern **Teneguía cooperative winery** can be visited. Also notice the solar-powered streetlights.

NEED A BREAK?   A restaurant in a cave awaits you 16 km/10 mi north of Fuencaliente. Look for the door in the side of a mountain and a sign that says **Restaurant Tamanco.**

Tazacorte

28 km (17 mi) northwest of Fuencaliente.

Drive down through the banana plantations to Tazacorte, the old Guanche capital, or explore **Puerto Naos**, 5 km/3 mi south, where a sunny, black-sand bay, created by a volcanic eruption in 1947, has now been turned into a beach resort.

Beaches

The black-sand bay of **Puerto Naos** is the island's biggest beach and the most popular on the west coast of the island.

Dining and Lodging

$$ ✕ **Restaurant Playa Mont.** Looking like an upscale beach shack and
★ open on one side to the ocean breezes, the Playa Mont serves some of the best seafood in the islands. The secret is the sauces: traditional mojos and a delicious lemon-butter. ⊠ *Puerto de Tazacorte*, ☎ 922/480443. *AE, V. Closed Thurs.*

$$ ✕▥ **Sol La Palma.** Perched at the end of La Palma's best beach, the Sol hotel was the island's first real resort. It has a flashy, marble lobby with crystal chandeliers and fountains. The hotel rooms are huge, with understated, beige furnishings, gray-tile floors, sun terraces, and extra-large baths. The restaurant buffet is bountiful with expensive treats (such as fresh shrimp and papaya) not normally found at moderately priced resorts. ⊠ *Puerto Naos 38760*, ☎ 922/408000, 𝔽𝔸𝕏 922/408014. *308 rooms with bath, 163 apartments. Restaurant, 3 bars, 2 pools, tennis court, exercise room, dance club. AE, V.*

Parque Nacional de La Caldera de Taburiente

10 km (6 mi) east of Tazacorte.

Occupying most of the center of the island is the Parque Nacional de La Caldera de Taburiente. The visitor's center is 3 km/2 mi east of El Paso. The park is inside what looks like a huge crater in the middle of the island; modern geologists think that the crater was formed by a series of small eruptions that pulled the center of the mountain apart.

A narrow paved road leads through pine forests to the **Mirador Cumbrecita** at 6,014 feet on the crater's rim. It's often raining or snowing up here, and bright rainbows span the canyon. The white dome and tower on the opposite side are the **Observatono Roque de los Muchachos**, home of Europe's largest telescope. Astronomers say the Canary Island peaks have some of the cleanest air and darkest skies in the world.

Canarian pine trees are especially adapted to fire and volcanic eruptions, taking only four years to regenerate themselves. There are lots of interesting hiking trails in the park, and camping is allowed on the valley floor with a permit obtainable at the visitor center.

LA GOMERA

One of the least developed of the Canary Islands, tiny La Gomera attracts scores of denim-clad backpackers on shoestring budgets, as well as other travelers who care little for the disco beat of the more touristy islands. The mossy, fern-filled central peaks make up the Garajonay National Park and include a rare forest of fragrant laurel trees.

The mountains fan out into six, steep-sided valleys called *barrancos*. Villages in the barrancos are chiefly dedicated to small-scale banana growing, and you'll see three or four stalks of bananas outside each house in the morning awaiting pickup. The serpentine roads leading in and out of the valleys are so filled with switchbacks that traveling is slow and villages remain isolated.

Allow plenty of time for a drive around La Gomera, two days if possible. The distances are short, but travel takes a long time, and the island's roads are not for those who are afraid of heights.

San Sebastián

East of Valle Gran Rey.

La Gomera's scraggly capital makes the most of its historical links with Christopher Columbus, who made his last stop on charted territory at San Sebastián before setting out for the edge of the earth in 1492.

The **Torre del Conde** (Tower of the Count) was built by the Spanish in 1450 for protection from Guanche tribes. It came in handy in 1487 when the count's wife, Beatriz de Bobadillo, took refuge in the tower after island chieftains killed her husband. The beautiful, black-haired widow is better known for her love affair with Columbus.

The **Pozo de la Aduana** (Customs House Well) at the head of Calle del Medio, is the well that Columbus used to resupply his ships with water, which was also used to baptize the New World. 🖭 *Free.* ☉ *Mon.–Sat. 9–1:30 and 3:30–6, Sun. 9–1:30.*

Nuestra Señora de la Asunción (Our Lady of the Assumption) church was just a tiny chapel when Columbus prayed there. Since then it has been enlarged in a variety of styles. Farther up the street you can visit the **Casa Colón,** the simple Canarian house where the explorer supposedly stayed during his time on the island with Beatriz. It is now devoted to exhibits by local artists. 🖭 *Free.* ☉ *Tues.–Thurs. 4–6.*

The **Degollada de Peraza** 14 km/9 mi south of San Sebastián over a winding road, has a lookout with great views. Guanche chiefs pushed Beatriz's cruel husband, Fernan Peraza, to his death from this cliff.

Beaches
A strong current makes La Gomera's northern beaches dangerous for swimming. If you want sun, head for the volcanic sands of the island's southern shores. **San Sebastián**'s black-sand beach near the ferry dock is clean and popular with local families.

Dining and Lodging
$$ ✕ **Marqués de Oristano.** Acquired in 1996 by local owners, this is really three restaurants in one. The Canarian patio in the entryway is a tapas bar; in the back is an informal, open-air grill where you can select your fresh fish or a cut of beef or lamb from a bright butcher's case. An upstairs dining room serves more sophisticated cuisine, such

as pork tenderloin in prune sauce, at higher prices. ⊠ *C. del Medio 26,* ☎ *922/870930. AE, V. Closed May and Nov.*

$$$ ✕⌂ **Parador Conde de la Gomera.** Built in 1970 in the style of an old,
★ island manor-house, the parador has breezeways decorated with Spanish antiques. The large rooms combine bare-wood floors with French-provincial furniture and have louvered shutters that open onto interior patios. The dining room has a barnlike, Canarian ceiling and the kitchen specializes in such local dishes as rabbit in salmorejo with papas arrugadas. ⊠ *San Sebastián, 38800,* ☎ *922/871100,* ℻ *922/871116. 42 rooms with bath. Restaurant, bar, pool. AE, V.*

$ ✕⌂ **Hostal El Pajar.** This small hotel in the center of San Sebastián is aimed at local residents and offers basic rooms arranged around a typical Canarian patio. ⊠ *C. del Medio 23, 38800,* ☎ *922/870207. Restaurant, bar.*

Shopping

There is a refreshing lack of shops in La Gomera. If you are looking for typical souvenirs, buy a bottle of palm syrup or a bag of macaroons from the little market on the Plaza de América in San Sebastián. Typical ceramics, formed without the use of a potter's wheel, are still made and sold by village women in El Cercado.

Playa de Santiago

34 km (20 mi) southwest of San Sebastián.

Playa de Santiago, with its fishing port and banana plantations, is at the bottom of a steep canyon. Until very recently the people who lived on the almost vertical slopes of the island's canyons used a mysterious whistling language called silbo to communicate across the canyons. Although the language is dying out, most of the older generation in the rural areas still understand silbo, and the gardeners at the parador in San Sebastián sometimes give demonstrations.

Boat excursions leave several times a week from Playa de Santiago to view **Los Organos,** a cliff made up of hundreds of tall, basalt columns that resemble the pipes of an organ.

Beaches

Playa de Santiago is a rocky, black beach that surrounds a small fishing bay. It has the sunniest weather on the island and is destined to become La Gomera's major resort area.

Lodging

$$$ ⌂ **Hotel Jardines Tecina.** La Gomera's only real resort hotel, the Tecina sprawls luxuriously over a series of terraces high above the sea. There's an elevator down to the beach. The rooms, grouped in hillside bungalows, all have summery, green and pine furniture with big, wooden terraces for sunbathing. Baths are decorated with Spanish tile. ⊠ *Playa de Santiago, 38800,* ☎ *922/895050,* ℻ *922/895302. 326 rooms with bath. Restaurant, pool, bar, sauna, tennis court, exercise room, squash, dance club. AE, MC, V.*

$ ⌂ **Apartamentos Tapahuga.** This attractive building in Playa de Santiago sits right on the fishing harbor, and apartments have Canarian, carved-pine balconies overlooking it. Kitchens and country-style Spanish furnishings give the apartments a homey feel, and there's a swimming pool on the roof. ⊠ *Avda. Marítima, 38800,* ☎ *922/895159,* ℻ *922/895127. 20 apartments. Kitchens, pool. MC, V.*

Parque Nacional de Garajonay

20 km (12 mi) west of San Sebastián.

On the central highway you drive past fantastic geological formations as you enter Parque Nacional de Garajonay. The road heads into the forest; much of the year this area is in the clouds, and the mossy trees drip with mist. The highest point on the island, Garajonay peak (4,832 feet), is to the right.

To learn more about Garajonay National Park, take the turnoff at Las Rosas for the **Juego de Bolas Visitor's Center.** Exhibits explain the rare laurel forest, and a garden houses vegetation found in various parts of the island. In crafts shops alongside the visitor center, you can watch artisans at work. *Visitor's center,* ☎ *922/800993.* ☞ *Free.* ◷ *Tues.–Sun. 9:30–4:30.*

Outdoor Activities and Sports

HIKING

Garajonay National Park provides miles of interesting hikes. A trail map can be obtained at the visitor center or the San Sebastián tourist office.

Shopping

Handicrafts, including rag rugs, baskets, and Gomeran drums, are available in the workshops at the **Juego de Bolas Visitor's Center** in Garajonay National Park.

Valle Gran Rey

72 km (43 mi) west of San Sebastián.

The terraced farms of Valle Gran Rey, planted with bananas and palms, look like something out of a Gauguin painting. The valley boasts two black-sand beaches and is home to a number of young, German families who have followed the artist's example.

OFF THE BEATEN PATH

CASA EFIGENIA – Take your taste buds on a trip off the beaten path with a stop at the Casa Efigenia in the hamlet of Las Hayas, about 30 minutes uphill from Valle Gran Rey. The plain, whitewashed walls of this restaurant are decorated with a few cobs of dried corn and a dusty case of citations that Doña Efigenia has received for her efforts at keeping traditional Gomeran cookery alive. It's simple food, prepared and served by Doña Efigenia herself, definitely not gourmet but certainly authentic. The main course is a vegetable stew, and dessert is a heavy raisin-and-almond cake, to be smothered in palm tree syrup. The inexpensive restaurant is only open for lunch.

Beaches

In Valle Gran Rey, **Playa del Inglés** is a sandy, black crescent of a beach favored by young people in search of an inexpensive hideaway, while **Las Vueltas** beach is a favorite with local residents.

Dining and Lodging

$ ✕ **Charco del Conde.** This restaurant is named for the *Conde* (Count) of La Gomera, since this is where the Guanche chiefs hatched the plot to toss him off the cliff. There are good fish, steaks, and chicken with papas arrugadas and mojo sauces. ✉ *Carretera Puntilla Vueltas,* ☎ *922/805403. No credit cards. AE, V. Closed Wed.*

$$ ▥ **Apartamentos Charco del Conde.** These low-rise, flower-bedecked apartments across from Las Vueltas beach offer simple, pine furnish-

ings, a kitchen, and a private terrace. ✉ *Avda. Marítima s/n, 38870,* ☎ *922/805597,* FAX *922/805380. 24 apartments. Kitchens, pool. No credit cards.*

Alojero

43 km (26 mi) northwest of San Sebastián.

Crowning the northern rim of La Gomera is the town of Alojera, with its beautiful, little, black-sand beach. This area is known for its palm syrup. At night the syrup trees, which have a metal collar around them, produce up to 3 gallons of sap each, which is boiled down into syrup over wood fires the following day.

Alojero and other northern villages on the island are becoming popular centers of bed and breakfast tourism. Color brochures of the homes, most with only two to five rooms, can be obtained by contacting the tourism office in San Sebastián.

EL HIERRO

The smallest of the Canary Islands, El Hierro is strictly for those who enjoy nature and plenty of solitude. Most residents live in mountain villages that have little in common with the tropical beach towns of the other islands. The few visitors who do find their way to El Hierro usually come for the hiking, the scuba diving, or pure relaxation.

Valverde

10 km (6 mi) west of the airport.

The island's capital, Valverde, sits on a hillside at 2,000 feet. To protect it from pirate raids, the town was located inland in the clouds, where its cobblestone streets always seem to be wet with mist. The church, with its balconied bell tower, was once a lookout for pirates.

Heading north around El Hierro you'll pass terraced farms still plowed with mules. The **Mirador de la Peña,** 22 km/13 mi west of Valverde stands at 2,200 feet and offers a spectacular view of El Golfo on the back side of the island.

NEED A BREAK? The mirador's brand-new garden restaurant, **Mirador de la Peña,** designed by Cesar Manrique, is surely the island's most elegant eating spot. Glass walls allow a panoramic view of El Golfo below.

El Golfo (the Bay) is formed by what looks like a half-submerged, volcanic crater. The part above water is a fertile, steep-sided valley. At the far end is a health spa with salty, medicinal waters, called **Pozo de la Salud;** those who prefer tastier medicine can visit the island's **winery** in the big, beige building near Frontera. The rocky coast along El Golfo is safe for swimming only during the summer.

The **Hoya del Morcillo** picnic area is in the midst of the fragrant pine forest that covers the center of El Hierro. It is equipped with barbecue pits, rest rooms, and a playground. Camping is permitted, and this is a good starting point for forest hikes.

Dining and Lodging

$$ ✕🅃 **Parador Nacional El Hierro.** The road to the parador takes you around a point jutting into the sea and deposits you at the bottom of a 3,500-foot cliff. Guest rooms are large, with Castilian furniture and heavy, folk-art spreads. In the dining room, delicious tidbits of island specialties are set out for appetizers, but the rest of the gourmet menu

goes way beyond the chef's abilities; it's best to stick to grilled fish and steak. ⊠ *38915 Las Playas,* ☎ *922/558036,* FAX *922/558086. 47 rooms with bath. Restaurant, bar, pool. AE, V.*

$ ✗🏨 **Hotel Boomerang.** Owned by a local man who once worked in Australia, the Boomerang is in the middle of town and offers clean and comfortable rooms with country, pine furniture and tile baths. ⊠ *Dr. Gost 1, 38900,* ☎ *922/550200. 19 rooms with bath. Restaurant, bar. AE, DC, V.*

$ ✗🏨 **Hotel Puntagrande.** Built on an old dock that extends into the sea, the four-room Puntagrande boasts a certificate from the *Guinness Book of Records* naming it the world's smallest hotel. Rooms have exposed rock walls and nautical decor, with porthole windows turned into nightstands. An old diving suit and ship's lanterns hang in the dining room, which serves fresh fish and local wine. Don't worry about the tiny hotel being full; the owner also has apartments for rent up the road. ⊠ *38911 Las Puntas, Frontera,* ☎ FAX *922/559081. 4 rooms with bath. Restaurant, bar. AE, V.*

La Restinga

54 km (33 mi) south of Valverde.

At the southern tip of the island, La Restinga is a small, rather ugly fishing port surrounding by lava fields. The tourists who occasionally come here are generally scuba fanatics who say the diving is some of the best in the Canary Islands.

Dining and Lodging

$ ✗ **Casa Juan.** The two plain dining rooms have large tables to accommodate families who come from all over the island for the delicious seafood soup. Their mojo sauces, served with papas arrugadas, are also outstanding. ⊠ *Juan Gutierrez Monteverde 23,* ☎ *922/558002. No credit cards.*

$$ 🏨 **Club El Submarino.** Created by and for sports fans, this ultramodern, isolated hotel offers diving, hiking, cave-exploring, hang gliding, windsurfing, mountain biking, deep-sea fishing, and a few more mundane sports. ⊠ *Frontera, 38915,* ☎ FAX *922/559202. 10 rooms with bath. Snack bar, pool. AE, V.*

$ 🏨 **Apartamentos La Marina.** A brand-new, three-story building on the harbor houses these tourist apartments. The furnishings are basic but clean, and all units have kitchens and balconies that offer unbeatable sunset viewing. ⊠ *Avda. Marítima 10, 38915,* ☎ *922/559016. 12 apartments. Kitchens. No credit cards.*

THE CANARY ISLANDS A TO Z

Arriving and Departing

By Boat

Trasmediterranea (⊠ Pedro Muñoz Seca 2, Madrid, ☎ 91/431–0700, FAX 91/431–0804) operates a slow, comfortable ferry service between Cádiz and the Canary Islands (Tenerife, 42 hours; Gran Canaria, 54 hours; Lanzarote, 66 hours). The boat is equipped with cabins, a tiny swimming pool, restaurants, a game room, and a discotheque, but it is not a luxury cruise.

By Plane

Iberia and its sister carrier **Aviaco** offer several direct flights a day to Tenerife, Gran Canaria, La Palma and Lanzarote from most cities in mainland Spain (2½ hours from Madrid). **Air Europa** and **Spanair** have flights from Madrid and Barcelona at slightly lower prices. The other three islands are reached by connecting flights.

From the United States, **Air Europa** (⊠ 136 E. 57th St., Suite 1602, New York, NY 10022, ☎ 212/888–7010) flies once a week directly from New York to Tenerife (6 hours). Package information is available from **Spanish Heritage Tours** (⊠ 116–47 Queens Blvd., Forest Hills, NY 11375, ☎ 718/544–2752 or 800/221–2580). Seats can sometimes be purchased without the hotel package if space is available.

Getting Around

By Boat

Trasmediterranea operates inter-island **car ferries**. Trips often take all night, and the ferries are equipped with sleeping cabins. Schedules and reservations are available in Tenerife (⊠ Marina 59, Santa Cruz, ☎ 922/287850), Gran Canaria (⊠ Muelle Rivera Oeste s/n, Las Palmas, ☎ 928/267766), Lanzarote (⊠ Jose Antonio 90, Arrecife, ☎ 928/811188), La Palma (⊠ Avda. Perez de Brito 2, Santa Cruz de la Palma, ☎ 922/411121), La Gomera (⊠ C. del Medio 41, San Sebastián, ☎ 922/871324), Fuerteventura (⊠ León y Castillo 58, 928/850877), and El Hierro (⊠ Puerto de la Estaca, ☎ 922/550129).

Passenger-only **hydrofoil** service is also available through Trasmediterranea three times a day between Las Palmas and Tenerife (80 minutes). One hydrofoil a day links Morro Jable in southern Fuerteventura with Las Palmas (90 minutes) and Tenerife (3½ hours). La Gomera can be reached by hydrofoil (30 minutes) from Los Cristianos in southern Tenerife.

The **Ferry Gomera** takes cars and people between Tenerife (⊠ Muelle Los Cristianos, ☎ 922/790217) and La Gomera (⊠ Avda. Fred Olsen, San Sebastián, ☎ 922/871007) three times a day. At night, the same ferry plies between La Gomera and La Palma.

Southern Lanzarote and northern Fuerteventura are linked by two ferry companies. **Linea Fred Olson** (⊠ Avda. de Llegada s/n, Playa Blanca, ☎ 928/517301, FAX 928/517214) makes five round-trips a day, and so does **Lineas Armas** (⊠ Main Pier, Playa Blanca, ☎ 928/517266, FAX 928/517912).The voyage takes about one hour, and the ferries take cars.

By Bus

In Tenerife, buses meet all arriving Iberia flights at Reina Sofía Airport and transfer passengers to the bus terminal on the outskirts of Santa Cruz de Tenerife. From there you can get a taxi or another bus to the northern side of the island. Buses also meet the Gomera hydrofoil and ferry to take passengers on to Santa Cruz.

Each island has its own bus service geared for local residents. Generally buses leave the villages early in the morning for shopping in the capital and depart from its main plaza in the early afternoon. Tourist offices have details.

By Car

Most visitors rent a car or Jeep for at least part of their stay in the Canary Islands. It is by far the best way to explore the countryside. The roads are generally good, but not for those with vertigo, as they frequently curve over high mountain cliffs with nothing but the sea below. Car-rental companies abound on every island, sometimes doubling as bars. Good prices can be found with a little shopping around.

Reservations for car rental are necessary only during the Christmas and Easter holidays. **Hertz** and **Avis** have representatives on all the islands, although better rates can be obtained from the Spanish company **Cicar** (☎ 928/802790), located at all the airports except El Hierro. The only airport rental agency in El Hierro is **Cruz Alta** (☎ 922/550004).

By Plane

All the Canary Islands are served by air except La Gomera. **Tenerife** has two airports. **Reina Sofía** (TFS) is near Playa de las Américas in the south, and **Los Rodeos** (TFN) is in the north near Puerto de la Cruz. As a general rule, long-distance flights arrive at the southern terminal, and inter-island flights use the northern one, but there are exceptions. Try to book a flight that gets you to the part of the island where you are staying, and be sure to allow plenty of time to travel between airports for connecting flights. Driving time from one airport to the other is about 1½ hours; taxis charge up to 7,500 ptas., or you can rent a car for about 4,000 ptas.

Airport information can be obtained in Tenerife (Reina Sofía, ☎ 922/759200; Los Rodeos, ☎ 922/635800), Gran Canaria (☎ 928/ 579000), Lanzarote (☎ 928/811450), Fuerteventura (☎ 928/851250), La Palma (☎ 922/411540), and El Hierro (☎ 922/550725).

Inter-island flights are handled by **Iberia** and its regional subsidiary, **Binter Airlines,** using small turboprop planes that allow great, low-altitude views of the islands. Reservations can be made in Tenerife (⊠ Avda. de Anaga 23, Santa Cruz, ☎ 922/284951), Gran Canaria (⊠ Alcalde Ramirez de Bethancourt 8, Las Palmas, ☎ 928/370877), Lanzarote (⊠ Avda. Rafael Gonzalez 2, Arrecife, ☎ 928/810358), Fuerteventura (⊠ 23 de Mayo 11, Puerto de Rosario, ☎ 928/852310), La Palma (⊠ Apurón 1, ☎ 922/411345), and El Hierro (⊠ Dr. Quintero 6, ☎ 922/550854).

Contacts and Resources

Guided Tours

One-day tours of Tenerife and sightseeing excursions to other islands with English-speaking guides can be arranged through **Viajes Insular** (⊠ Avda. Generalisimo 20, Puerto de la Cruz, ☎ 922/380262), which has branches on every island except La Gomera and El Hierro. Tours generally last all day and include a lunch or folklore presentation.

Visitor Information

Each of the Canary Islands has its own tourist offices. They are in **Tenerife** ⊠ Plaza de España 1, Santa Cruz, ☎ 922/605592.◷ 8–5:45; Plaza de la Iglesia, Puerto de la Cruz, ☎ 922/386000. ◷ 9–8. **Gran Canaria** ⊠ Parque de Santa Catalina, Las Palmas, ☎ 928/264623. ◷ 8–2. **Lanzarote** ⊠ Parque Municipal, Arrecife, ☎ 928/81–37–92. ◷ 8–3. **Fuerteventura** ⊠ 1 de mayo 33, Puerto de Rosario, ☎ 928/851024. ◷ 9–2. **La Palma** ⊠ Palacio Salazar, C. Real, s/n, Santa Cruz de la Palma, ☎ 922/41210. ◷ 8–1 and 5–7). **La Gomera** ⊠ C. del Medio 20, San Sebastián, ☎ 922/140147. ◷ 9–2. **El Hierro** ⊠ Licinardo Bueno 1, Valverde, ☎ 922/550302. ◷ 8:30–2:30.

INDEX

NOTES

NOTES

NOTES

NOTES

Escape to ancient cities and

journey to  *exotic islands with*

CNN Travel Guide, a wealth of valuable advice. Host

Valerie Voss will take you to

all of your favorite destinations,

 *including those off the beaten*

path. Tune-in to your passport to the world.

CNN TRAVEL GUIDE
SATURDAY 12:30 PM ET   SUNDAY 4:30 PM ET

CNN✈
Airport Network

Your
Window
To The
World
While You're
On The
Road

Keep in touch when you're traveling. Before you take off, tune in to CNN Airport Network. Now available in major airports across America, CNN Airport Network provides nonstop news, sports, business, weather and lifestyle programming. Both domestic and international. All piloted by the top-flight global resources of CNN. All up-to-the minute reporting. And just for travelers, CNN Airport Network features two daily Fodor's specials. "Travel Fact" provides enlightening, useful travel trivia, while "What's Happening" covers upcoming events in major cities worldwide. So why be bored waiting to board? TIME FLIES WHEN YOU'RE WATCHING THE WORLD THROUGH THE WINDOW OF CNN AIRPORT NETWORK!

Fodor's Travel Publications

Available at bookstores everywhere, or call 1–800–533–6478, 24 hours a day.

Gold Guides
U.S.

Alaska

Arizona

Boston

California

Cape Cod, Martha's
Vineyard, Nantucket

The Carolinas & the
Georgia Coast

Chicago

Colorado

Florida

Hawai'i

Las Vegas, Reno,
Tahoe

Los Angeles

Maine, Vermont,
New Hampshire

Maui & Lāna'i

Miami & the Keys

New England

New Orleans

New York City

Pacific North Coast

Philadelphia & the
Pennsylvania Dutch
Country

The Rockies

San Diego

San Francisco

Santa Fe, Taos,
Albuquerque

Seattle & Vancouver

The South

U.S. & British Virgin
Islands

USA

Virginia & Maryland

Washington, D.C.

Foreign

Australia

Austria

The Bahamas

Belize & Guatemala

Bermuda

Canada

Cancún, Cozumel,
Yucatán Peninsula

Caribbean

China

Costa Rica

Cuba

The Czech Republic
& Slovakia

Eastern &
Central Europe

Europe

Florence, Tuscany
& Umbria

France

Germany

Great Britain

Greece

Hong Kong

India

Ireland

Israel

Italy

Japan

London

Madrid & Barcelona

Mexico

Montréal &
Québec City

Moscow, St.
Petersburg, Kiev

The Netherlands,
Belgium &
Luxembourg

New Zealand

Norway

Nova Scotia, New
Brunswick, Prince
Edward Island

Paris

Portugal

Provence &
the Riviera

Scandinavia

Scotland

Singapore

South Africa

South America

Southeast Asia

Spain

Sweden

Switzerland

Thailand

Tokyo

Toronto

Turkey

Vienna & the Danube

Fodor's Special-Interest Guides

Caribbean Ports
of Call

The Complete Guide
to America's
National Parks

Family Adventures

Gay Guide
to the USA

Halliday's New
England Food
Explorer

Halliday's New
Orleans Food
Explorer

Healthy Escapes

Kodak Guide to
Shooting Great
Travel Pictures

Net Travel

Nights to Imagine

Rock & Roll Traveler
USA

Sunday in New York

Sunday in
San Francisco

Walt Disney World,
Universal Studios
and Orlando

Walt Disney World
for Adults

Where Should We
Take the Kids?
California

Where Should We
Take the Kids?
Northeast

Worldwide Cruises
and Ports of Call

Special Series

Affordables

Caribbean

Europe

Florida

France

Germany

Great Britain

Italy

London

Paris

Fodor's Bed & Breakfasts and Country Inns

America

California

The Mid-Atlantic

New England

The Pacific Northwest

The South

The Southwest

The Upper Great Lakes

The Berkeley Guides

California

Central America

Eastern Europe

Europe

France

Germany & Austria

Great Britain & Ireland

Italy

London

Mexico

New York City

Pacific Northwest & Alaska

Paris

San Francisco

Compass American Guides

Arizona

Canada

Chicago

Colorado

Hawaii

Idaho

Hollywood

Las Vegas

Maine

Manhattan

Montana

New Mexico

New Orleans

Oregon

San Francisco

Santa Fe

South Carolina

South Dakota

Southwest

Texas

Utah

Virginia

Washington

Wine Country

Wisconsin

Wyoming

Fodor's Citypacks

Atlanta

Hong Kong

London

New York City

Paris

Rome

San Francisco

Washington, D.C.

Fodor's Español

California

Caribe Occidental

Caribe Oriental

Gran Bretaña

Londres

Mexico

Nueva York

Paris

Fodor's Exploring Guides

Australia

Boston & New England

Britain

California

Caribbean

China

Egypt

Florence & Tuscany

Florida

France

Germany

Ireland

Israel

Italy

Japan

London

Mexico

Moscow & St. Petersburg

New York City

Paris

Prague

Provence

Rome

San Francisco

Scotland

Singapore & Malaysia

Spain

Thailand

Turkey

Venice

Fodor's Flashmaps

Boston

New York

San Francisco

Washington, D.C.

Fodor's Pocket Guides

Acapulco

Atlanta

Barbados

Jamaica

London

New York City

Paris

Prague

Puerto Rico

Rome

San Francisco

Washington, D.C.

Mobil Travel Guides

America's Best Hotels & Restaurants

California & the West

Frequent Traveler's Guide to Major Cities

Great Lakes

Mid-Atlantic

Northeast

Northwest & Great Plains

Southeast

Southwest & South Central

Rivages Guides

Bed and Breakfasts of Character and Charm in France

Hotels and Country Inns of Character and Charm in France

Hotels and Country Inns of Character and Charm in Italy

Hotels and Country Inns of Character and Charm in Paris

Hotels and Country Inns of Character and Charm in Portugal

Hotels and Country Inns of Character and Charm in Spain

Short Escapes

Britain

France

New England

Near New York City

Fodor's Sports

Golf Digest's Best Places to Play

Skiing USA

USA Today The Complete Four Sport Stadium Guide

Fodor's Vacation Planners

Great American Learning Vacations

Great American Sports & Adventure Vacations

Great American Vacations

Great American Vacations for Travelers with Disabilities

National Parks and Seashores of the East

National Parks of the West

WHEREVER
YOU TRAVEL,
*H*ELP IS NEVER
FAR AWAY.

From planning your trip to providing travel assistance
along the way, American Express® Travel Service Offices
are always there to help.

> ## *Spain*

American Express Travel Service
Paseo De Gracia 101
Barcelona
3/415-2371

American Express Travel Service
Plaza De Las Cortes 2
Madrid
1/322-5418

American Express Travel Service
Duque De Ahumada
EDF Occidente - Local 3 Comercia
Marbella
5/282-1494

Travel
http://www.americanexpress.com/travel

**American Express Travel Service Offices
are found in central locations throughout Spain.**